FUNDAMENTAL TAX REFORM

United States Congress House of
Representatives Committee on Ways and Means

FUNDAMENTAL TAX REFORM

HEARING

BEFORE THE

COMMITTEE ON WAYS AND MEANS
HOUSE OF REPRESENTATIVES

ONE HUNDRED SIXTH CONGRESS

SECOND SESSION

APRIL 11, 12, and 13, 2000

Serial 106–115

Printed for the use of the Committee on Ways and Means

U.S. GOVERNMENT PRINTING OFFICE

71–879 DTP   WASHINGTON : 2001

For sale by the U.S. Government Printing Office
Superintendent of Documents, Congressional Sales Office, Washington, DC 20402

COMMITTEE ON WAYS AND MEANS

BILL ARCHER, Texas, *Chairman*

PHILIP M. CRANE, Illinois
BILL THOMAS, California
E. CLAY SHAW, JR., Florida
NANCY L. JOHNSON, Connecticut
AMO HOUGHTON, New York
WALLY HERGER, California
JIM McCRERY, Louisiana
DAVE CAMP, Michigan
JIM RAMSTAD, Minnesota
JIM NUSSLE, Iowa
SAM JOHNSON, Texas
JENNIFER DUNN, Washington
MAC COLLINS, Georgia
ROB PORTMAN, Ohio
PHILIP S. ENGLISH, Pennsylvania
WES WATKINS, Oklahoma
J.D. HAYWORTH, Arizona
JERRY WELLER, Illinois
KENNY HULSHOF, Missouri
SCOTT McINNIS, Colorado
RON LEWIS, Kentucky
MARK FOLEY, Florida

CHARLES B. RANGEL, New York
FORTNEY PETE STARK, California
ROBERT T. MATSUI, California
WILLIAM J. COYNE, Pennsylvania
SANDER M. LEVIN, Michigan
BENJAMIN L. CARDIN, Maryland
JIM McDERMOTT, Washington
GERALD D. KLECZKA, Wisconsin
JOHN LEWIS, Georgia
RICHARD E. NEAL, Massachusetts
MICHAEL R. McNULTY, New York
WILLIAM J. JEFFERSON, Louisiana
JOHN S. TANNER, Tennessee
XAVIER BECERRA, California
KAREN L. THURMAN, Florida
LLOYD DOGGETT, Texas

A.L. SINGLETON, *Chief of Staff*
JANICE MAYS, *Minority Chief Counsel*

Pursuant to clause 2(e)(4) of Rule XI of the Rules of the House, public hearing records of the Committee on Ways and Means are also published in electronic form. **The printed hearing record remains the official version.** Because electronic submissions are used to prepare both printed and electronic versions of the hearing record, the process of converting between various electronic formats may introduce unintentional errors or omissions. Such occurrences are inherent in the current publication process and should diminish as the process is further refined.

CONTENTS

SUBMISSIONS FOR THE RECORD

FUNDAMENTAL TAX REFORM

TUESDAY, APRIL 11, 2000

COMMITTEE ON WAYS AND MEANS,
HOUSE OF REPRESENTATIVES,
Washington, DC.

The Committee met, pursuant to notice, at 10:02 a.m., in room 1100, Longworth House Office Building, Hon. Bill Archer (Chairman of the Committee) presiding.

[The advisories announcing the hearing follow:]

ADVISORY

FROM THE COMMITTEE ON WAYS AND MEANS

FOR IMMEDIATE RELEASE
April 3, 2000
FC–20

CONTACT: (202) 225–1721

Archer Announces Hearing on
Fundamental Tax Reform

Congressman Bill Archer (R–TX), Chairman of the Committee on Ways and Means, today announced that the Committee will hold a hearing to consider fundamental tax reform proposals. **The hearing will begin on Tuesday, April 11, and be continued on Wednesday, April 12, and Thursday, April 13, 2000, in the main Committee hearing room, 1100 Longworth House Office Building, beginning at 10:00 a.m. each day.**

Oral testimony at this hearing will be from invited witnesses only. Witnesses will include Members of Congress, prominent tax reform experts, well-known economists, and other interested parties. However, any individual or organization not scheduled for an oral appearance may submit a written statement for consideration by the Committee and for inclusion in the printed record of the hearing.

BACKGROUND:

In the past several years a host of legislative proposals have been offered which would significantly change the kind of tax regime contained in the Internal Revenue Code. These include the flat tax, the national retail sales tax, and the USA and Simplified USA tax. Other ideas not yet in legislative form abound. In 1995, 1996, and 1997, the Committee on Ways and Means held extensive hearings on many of these specific proposals and more generally on the subject of fundamental tax reform. Leading advocates of specific legislation introduced as well as economists, business leaders, and Members of Congress testified. In particular, the Committee devoted considerable attention to both H.R. 1040, the flat tax proposal introduced by the Majority Leader Richard Armey (R–TX) and H.R. 1467 a retail sales tax proposal introduced by Rep. W.J. (Billy) Tauzin (R– LA).

Since those hearings, a number of new legislative proposals have been introduced. These include H.R. 134 by Rep. Phil English (R–PA) and H.R. 2525 by Rep. John Linder (R–GA) and Rep. Collin Peterson (D–MN) among others. This hearing will provide the opportunity for the Committee to consider these newer proposals as it has with prior proposals.

In announcing the hearing, Chairman Archer stated: "Over the past 5 years, I've made cutting taxes and simplifying the tax code a top priority. Still, the tax code is too complicated and confusing, and we need to get the IRS out of the lives of American taxpayers. That's why I'm proud to announce this three day hearing as part of the first ever Congressional summit on fundamental tax reform. We'll look at a host of new ideas which will eliminate our current tax code and replace it with something that is simpler and fairer. We need to rip the current tax code out by the roots so that it can never grow back."

FOCUS OF THE HEARING:

The focus of the hearing will be on which tax system is best for America in the new millennium, with a particular emphasis on tax reform proposals that have been introduced since the last set of hearings in 1997. In particular, the Committee will want to hear from witnesses as to the relevance of these proposals to the international marketplace in which our companies and individuals must live and compete and whether these proposals meet the established criteria of being fair, simple, enforceable, and compatible with the other parts of the tax regimes which exist in America, namely State taxes.

DETAILS FOR SUBMISSION OF WRITTEN COMMENTS:

Any person or organization wishing to submit a written statement for the printed record of the hearing should submit six (6) single-spaced copies of their statement, along with an IBM compatible 3.5-inch diskette in WordPerfect or MS Word format, with their name, address, and hearing date noted on a label, by the *close of business*, Tuesday, April 25, 2000, to A.L. Singleton, Chief of Staff, Committee on Ways and Means, U.S. House of Representatives, 1102 Longworth House Office Building, Washington, D.C. 20515. If those filing written statements wish to have their statements distributed to the press and interested public at the hearing, they may deliver 200 additional copies for this purpose to the Committee office, room 1102 Longworth House Office Building, by close of business the day before the hearing.

FORMATTING REQUIREMENTS:

Each statement presented for printing to the Committee by a witness, any written statement or exhibit submitted for the printed record or any written comments in response to a request for written comments must conform to the guidelines listed below. Any statement or exhibit not in compliance with these guidelines will not be printed, but will be maintained in the Committee files for review and use by the Committee.

1. All statements and any accompanying exhibits for printing must be submitted on an IBM compatible 3.5-inch diskette in WordPerfect or MS Word format, typed in single space and may not exceed a total of 10 pages including attachments. Witnesses are advised that the Committee will rely on electronic submissions for printing the official hearing record.

2. Copies of whole documents submitted as exhibit material will not be accepted for printing. Instead, exhibit material should be referenced and quoted or paraphrased. All exhibit material not meeting these specifications will be maintained in the Committee files for review and use by the Committee.

3. A witness appearing at a public hearing, or submitting a statement for the record of a public hearing, or submitting written comments in response to a published request for comments by the Committee, must include on his statement or submission a list of all clients, persons, or organizations on whose behalf the witness appears.

4. A supplemental sheet must accompany each statement listing the name, company, address, telephone and fax numbers where the witness or the designated representative may be reached. This supplemental sheet will not be included in the printed record.

The above restrictions and limitations apply only to material being submitted for printing. Statements and exhibits or supplementary material submitted solely for distribution to the Members, the press, and the public during the course of a public hearing may be submitted in other forms.

Note: All Committee advisors and news releases are available on the World Wide Web at "http://waysandmeans.house.gov".

The Committee seeks to make its facilities accessible to persons with disabilities. If you are in need of special accommodations, please call 202–225–1721 or 202–226–3411 TTD/TTY in advance of the event (four business days notice is requested). Questions with regard to special accommodation needs in general (including availability of Committee materials in alternative formats) may be directed to the Committee as noted above.

NOTICE-CHANGE IN TIME

ADVISORY

FROM THE COMMITTEE ON WAYS AND MEANS

FOR IMMEDIATE RELEASE   CONTACT: (202) 225–1721
April 10, 2000
FC–20–Revised

Time Change for Full Committee Hearing
on Thursday, April 13, 2000, on
Fundamental Tax Reform

Congressman Bill Archer (R–TX), Chairman of the Committee on Ways and Means, today announced that the full Committee hearing on Fundamental Tax Reform, previously scheduled for Thursday, April 13, 2000, at 10:00 a.m., in the main Committee hearing room, 1100 Longworth House Office Building, **will begin at 10:30 a.m.**

All other details for the hearing remain the same. (See full Committee press release No. FC–20, dated April 3, 2000.)

Chairman ARCHER. The committee will come to order.

Today, we begin our Congressional Summit on Fundamental Tax Reform, which will be a 3-day open discussion that will hopefully lead to an overhaul of the archaic and meddling income tax code that has outlived its useful life. Americans spend 6.1 billion hours each year filling out the IRS forms and $200 billion in compliance costs. And I am told that is a conservative estimate, and some national magazines say that it could go as high as $500 to $600 billion a year. All of that means that the tax code is too complicated and confusing, unnecessarily so.

In addition, Americans treasure their privacy and their individual freedom, and the income tax is the most intrusive part of the Federal Government in the lives of each American.

We had a witness not too long ago who sat right at the chair in front of me, and as I asked other witnesses what would you give not to have to deal with the IRS every year, she—a middle-income lady from Connecticut—responded, "I would give my first-born child." Obviously, she had an untoward experience with the IRS.

But the IRS is not really at fault most of the time. The fault is their responsibility to enforce a law that has grown from 16 pages in 1913 to 2,840 pages today. And when you include all of the regulations, I believe it is in excess of 14,000 pages.

It is true the IRS has had its problems, but I am glad that Congress took action in 1998 to help at least fix some of those problems. Yet unless we face the fact that the income tax cannot be fixed—and I believe that to be a fact, having participated in numerous efforts at reform in the 29-plus years that I have been here in the Congress—there will always be a need for the IRS as long as we have an income tax and a host of interpretation about what is income on which no two economists completely agree.

Because of our income tax, American workers are caught in a tax trap: The harder they work, the longer they work, the more they pay, and that is wrong.

What are we taxing when we tax income? We tax work. We tax savings. We tax upward mobility. We tax productivity. In sum, we tax success. And that is just not right.

Most economists believe that the more you tax of something, the less you are going to get of it. Do we really want less work, less savings, less upward mobility, less productivity, and less success? I don't think so, not in America. And yet that is what is driving our taxation program when we tax income as the base.

Last week, President Clinton celebrated our new economy, but our new economy is shackled by an ancient tax code, a code that gives us headaches, invades our privacy, and hurts our ability to compete and win the international marketplace competition. Our tax code simply can't keep up with the economy and the rest of the world in the 21st century.

We see that in the Internet tax debate. We see it in the WTO decision on FSC, Foreign Sales Corporations. We see it in the flight of U.S. corporations overseas to escape our tax code: Chrysler has become a German corporation, Amoco has become a British corporation, and Bankers Trust has become Deutschebank, a German corporation, because of our tax code.

We have heard a lot about corporate tax shelters recently, but the ultimate tax shelter for U.S. firms is just to pick up and leave. Do we really want that? I don't think so.

So this summit is to show Americans that our horse-and-buggy tax code won't work in our Internet economy. It is time to work together to replace it with a fairer, simpler, and better system.

I now recognize Mr. Rangel for any statement he would like to make.

Mr. RANGEL. I appreciate this opportunity, Mr. Chairman. For a long time, you have been very concerned about the complexity of the tax code and its unfairness to taxpayers. I would have thought, however, that since the Republicans have shown an equal concern about this very sensitive subject matter during all these years that you have enjoyed the Majority, that we wouldn't have had to wait 6 years just to have another hearing.

I would have hoped that, during this period of time that you have enjoyed the Majority, a piece of legislation would have been drafted, we would be holding hearings on specifics, and it would not be a Republican idea but it would be Republicans and Democrats working together in trying to improve the tax system.

But, consistently, there hasn't been just a lack of cooperation between our parties. There has been a lack of conversation between our parties.

Take this hearing, for example. Why, if you had discussed this with me or the Speaker had discussed this sensitive subject matter with our Democratic Minority Leader, we would have said that these hearings are far too important for the tax-writing committee to be holding at the same time that we are debating and voting on tax legislation on the House Floor. I don't see how you expect Members of this Committee to be in attendance at hearings, to listen to our Members and other witnesses, and at the same time expect us to be on the Floor supporting our legislation or at least protecting our jurisdiction on the House Floor.

But I really don't think that this hearing has anything to do with legislation. I think this has to do with lack of a political legislative agenda on which we can work together. And so, once again, we have got to talk about pulling up the income tax code by the roots—pulling it up by the roots and substituting it with what? Substituting with ideas that we will hear about today? Is there a bill? No. Have we had hearings? No.

We have a document here that is in front of the Members. It has a concept called Americans for a Fair Taxation. Very well prepared. What we don't have is something that we will go into later. We don't have a statement from the Joint Committee on Taxation.

Now, I know how much you depend on the private sector to provide for progressive legislation, but the Joint Committee is nonpartisan. They are supposed to give revenue estimates on these bills. One way or the other, we have got to get a document before this Committee so we can see how much these concepts really cost us.

Now, from time to time, Mr. Chairman, you will find some Members here, Republicans and Democrats. I hope our witnesses will understand that our absence from these hearings is no disrespect to the Chair, to our colleagues, or to the witnesses. It is because the very same 3 days that we have scheduled hearings on tax reform are the very same 3 days that we have scheduled tax legislation on the House Floor.

Why it was done this way I really don't know. But it is clear that these hearings are for public consumption and not legislation. We have no bill. We don't expect to have a bill. We don't expect to legislate in this area this year, or for the last 6 or 7 years. We never expected to.

So there are so many other questions I have, but out of respect to our two colleagues who have come here to testify. I would tell you that the Chair has no plans for any legislation on this subject matter, not this, not Social Security, not Medicare reform. But it is interesting because it really closes out the years of the Republican Majority. This is how they started it off—with hearings about pulling the tax code up by the roots. And, this is how we are going to end it with hearings about pulling it up by the roots.

Thank you, Mr. Chairman.

Chairman ARCHER. We have two of our colleagues who will lead off the testimony this morning. Are you gentlemen prepared to speak about phantom legislation for which there is no bill before the committee?

Mr. LINDER. No, sir, but we would be pleased to talk about H.R. 2525 that was introduced by a Republican and a Democrat on July 14th of last year.

Chairman ARCHER. So there is legislation before the committee on which we are holding these hearings today.

Mr. LINDER. That is correct.

Chairman ARCHER. Would the gentleman also venture a guess as to whether this is appropriate procedure to hold hearings on legislation before there might be any action on the legislation?

Mr. LINDER. It strikes me as the right thing to do.

Chairman ARCHER. Well, the Chair welcomes our two colleagues, Mr. Peterson and Mr. Linder, to present their bill, H.R. 2525, and, Congressman Linder, if you would lead off. First, welcome to the Committee.

Mr. LINDER. Thank you.

Chairman ARCHER. I compliment both of you on the work on this bill, and the committee is prepared to hear your testimony, and you may proceed, Mr. Linder.

STATEMENT OF HON. JOHN LINDER, A REPRESENTATIVE IN CONGRESS FROM THE STATE OF GEORGIA

Mr. LINDER. Thank you, Mr. Chairman. Mr. Chairman, I have a prepared statement that I have submitted for the committee, and I will summarize, if you don't mind, the aspects of H.R. 2525.

It strikes me that if Congress had sat down in 1912 and said how can we build a tax system that is destructive of capital formation, that is inefficient, is unproductive, and is punitive, they couldn't over 88 years have come up with a better solution than we have got today.

This is inefficient. We have seen studies from a variety of sources that for a small businessperson to collect, comply, and remit $1 in business income taxes, it costs them anywhere from $4 to $7 to do it.

It is unfair to young people. It is the single largest stumbling block and impediment to getting from the first rung of the economic ladder to the second because, as you said in your statement, the harder you work, the more you save, the more you invest, the more we take.

It is undecipherable. As you know, the IRS tells us if you call them asking for help in your tax return, 25 percent of the answers you get are going to be in error. They don't even understand it.

Our proposal is to abolish all taxes on income, to change the paradigm. Do not tax what we put into society but tax what we take out in terms of personal consumption. Abolish all taxes on income, the gift tax, the estate tax, capital gains tax, and the payroll tax, which supports Social Security and Medicare and which is the largest tax that three-fourths of America pays, larger than their income tax, and replace it with a one-time frank, transparent, at-the-checkout national sales tax. You spend $100, the first $23 goes to the tax man, the rest goes to the merchant.

Under today's system, if you earn $100 and you are in the average income withholding bracket of 28 percent, the Government is going to take the first 36 bucks whether you spend it or not. So everyone is going to have improved purchasing power.

We have learned from studies that there is no way for a corporation or a business to pay a tax. They don't have a mechanism. I have been built seven businesses, and there is simply not a secret drawer where money piles up behind you that you find your money for the corporate share of the payroll tax. There is not a secret drawer for the income tax. It comes out of price. It is passed down the line in price until somebody finally consumes the product, and that person not only consumes the product but all the taxes that have been embedded in it along the way.

What would happen to the system? Just imagine being the only nation in the world selling goods and services into a global economy with no tax component in our prices. Exports go up. You, Mr. Chairman, have said—you have quoted on this floor on several occasions that a research group interviewed 500 international corporations domiciled overseas, asked them what they would do if we abolished all taxes on income and went to a sales tax. Eighty percent said they would build their next plant in America; 20 percent said they would relocate to America. You referred to that actually in your statement about all the companies leaving this country. Exports increase.

What would happen——

Chairman ARCHER. Congressman Linder, I am informed by members of the committee they are having difficulty understanding your presentation—or hearing it, not understanding it.

Mr. LINDER. Okay.

Chairman ARCHER. Perhaps you are too close to the mike, or maybe it is that the sound system just isn't working well this morning.

Mr. LINDER. Well, I will try it again. Is this better? Can you hear it better? Collin says I talk too fast.

Mr. Chairman, for those who say that the sales tax is regressive on the poor, let me say the most regressive tax they have is the payroll tax that taxes, between what they and their corporation pay on their behalf, 15.3 percent of everything they earn up to $76,000. We not only get rid of that, we also get rid of the embedded cost of the IRS, and we believe at retail 22 percent of everything you pay is embedded business cost of the IRS. But we also give to every family a rebate at the beginning of every month that totally rebates the tax consequences of spending up to the poverty line. So everyone will have increased purchasing power, and everyone will have increased freedom.

Can you imagine the privilege in a free society where no one knows how much you make, how you make it, how you invest it, if your investment makes money or loses, or how you spend your money? You will have the privilege of anonymity again, which we think is important in a free society.

There are 100,000 people today at the IRS who know more about me than I am willing to tell my children, and I want them out of my life, and yours, too. And I agree that they are just doing their job, but nobody should know that detailed information about us.

In 1912, a Senator in the discussion of the 16th Amendment was ridiculed and laughed off the floor of the Senate for making this statement: "Mark my words, that before this is over, they will be taking 10 percent of what everybody earns." Oh, how I wish it were so, giving fresh meaning, I think, to that wonderful country western song, "If 10 Percent's Enough for Jesus, It Ought to Be Enough for Uncle Sam."

We want to get rid of the tax on incomes entirely and tax what people choose to spend.

[The prepared statement follows:]

9

Statement of the Hon. John Linder, a Representative in Congress from the State of Georgia

Thank you Mr. Chairman and members of the committee. I appreciate the opportunity to testify today about H.R. 2525, the FairTax Act of 1999, which I introduced along with Collin Peterson earlier in this Congress. Mr. Chairman, I ask that my written statement and a series of articles discussing the FairTax be made a part of the record.

The FairTax Act would repeal all individual income taxes, corporate income taxes, payroll taxes, self-employment taxes, capital gains taxes, and death and gift taxes. It would replace these with a 23 percent national retail sales tax on all new goods and services sold to consumers. All sales of new goods and services to consumers would be taxed once and only once, without any exceptions. Business inputs would not be taxed since those items will ultimately be taxed when they are sold to consumers, thus adhering to the principle that goods be taxed once and only once.

Because there are no exceptions to the FairTax, and because we realize that those Americans at the low end of the income scale spend a higher proportion of their income, the FairTax provides every household in America with a rebate of the sales tax paid on necessities. Thus the FairTax is progressive, and every family is protected from tax on essential goods and services. The rebate would be paid monthly in advance in an amount equal to the sales tax rate multiplied by the federal poverty level—that level of spending literally defined by the U.S. government as required to purchase necessities. For a family of four, the rebate level is $22,500—meaning that every family of four will receive a check at the first of each month for $431.25, the amount that family would pay in taxes on monthly poverty level spending. If you spend more than the poverty level, you pay the sales tax. If you spend less than the poverty level, you get to keep the rebate check anyway.

It would be a mistake to emulate the states' attempt to achieve sales tax progressivity by exempting various categories of goods or services from tax because that methodology doesn't achieve progressivity at all. For example, affluent people buy more expensive food, housing and clothing than do poor people, so when these categories of goods are exempted, affluent people benefit disproportionately. In addition, these exemptions add complexity and compliance costs to the system, and lead to outrageous results. In any New York bagel shop, for example, a plain bagel is tax-free but a bagel with cream cheese is taxable. Moreover, any one exception to the sales tax will inevitably lead to efforts to exempt other products. Not only would those efforts lead to a perversion of the sales tax just as lobbying today has perverted the income tax, but also when some goods or services are exempted, a higher tax rate must be charged on those things that remain taxable to maintain the same level of revenue. Such a preferential scheme is bad as a matter of economics and unfair to those companies and workers who make the goods that remain taxable.

The FairTax will end the complexity of compliance with our current system. Today, according to the Tax Foundation, we spend about $250 billion each year filling out forms, hiring tax lawyers and accountants and collecting information needed only for tax purposes. These unnecessary costs amount to about $850 for every man, woman and child in America. To the extent these costs are incurred by businesses, those businesses hide them in the cost of everything that we buy. The Tax Foundation has estimated that compliance costs would drop by about 90 percent under a national sales tax. Why? Because the present system requires that Americans must provide over one billion information returns to the IRS annually. Americans file a quarter billion tax returns annually. Under the FairTax, this would be an unpleasant memory.

The FairTax would be collected by states and retailers just as current state sales taxes are. The FairTax gives retailers a 25 basis point commission for collecting the tax and offers state sales tax authorities another 25 basis point commission to administer the tax. We believe that it makes the most sense for state civil servants that have years of experience administering a sales tax to take that job. The FairTax would then dismantle the IRS and create a sales tax bureau in the Treasury to administer the collection of sales tax from the states. The only tax collector that the consumer would ever see is the smiling face behind the register at the local grocery store.

Beyond simplicity, the FairTax holds the promise of ecomomic growth and a higher American standard of living. The FairTax would stop the punitive taxation of work inherent in the income and payroll tax and end the multiple taxation of savings and investment. The FairTax would end the bias against investment in education. Economists anticipate the FairTax, because it is neutral toward savings and investment, will lead to much higher levels of savings and investment which in turn will lead to greater productivity and output. Dr. Dale Jorgenson of Harvard and Dr.

Laurence Kotlikoff of Boston University estimate, in two separate studies, that the FairTax would increase GDP between 7 to 14 percent over the current system. While clearly not endorsing the FairTax specifically, even our current Treasury Secretary, Dr. Larry Summers, concluded in some of his academic writings that a complete shift to consumption taxation might raise steady-state output by double digits.

Why is such growth predicted? Because by giving Americans their entire paycheck, American consumption is increased. And, by untaxing our business and corporations, American businesses will become more competitive with foreign businesses. Consider the recent WTO ruling that found the Foreign Sales Corporation (FSC) export incentives to be a violation of WTO rules. Congress created FSCs with the knowledge that our current tax system was undermining our ability to compete abroad. The FairTax would solve this problem by removing the current tax burden on American production and allowing American goods to be sold overseas with no tax consequences embedded in the price. Further, the FairTax would apply to all imported goods sold in America. In contrast, today foreign goods enter the U.S. market free of any significant tax burden. This places U.S. produced goods at a big competitive disadvantage. This disadvantage is made worse because most of our major trading partners eliminate a big part of their tax burden on exports since their value added taxes are border adjusted. They impose a large VAT on U.S. goods imported into their country. This disadvantage is built into our tax system, and it exports high paying U.S. jobs to our foreign competitors.

Unlike our perversions of the income tax, the FairTax is in compliance with the WTO rules because it is an indirect tax, it. For the first time, American businesses and American workers will be competing on a level playing field with our foreign competitors.

The FairTax is simple, understandable and transparent. People understand the FairTax. They don't understand the present tax system. Even tax professionals and tax administrators don't understand the present system. Moreover, today a huge proportion of the overall tax burden is hidden from the ordinary taxpayer's view and passed on to those who can least afford it. Under the FairTax, people will for the first time actually understand their tax burden and have confidence that their fellow citizens are bearing their fair share.

Mr. Chairman and members of the Committee, the present system is broken beyond repair. It is costing the American people dearly in terms of opportunities lost and a lower standard of living. It is time to start over. I believe that the FairTax—as the only proposal today that ends the regressive payroll tax and allows American workers to compete fairly with our foreign competition—represents the best alternative to the present system. I think that after you study the plan you will agree. Thank you.

[Attachments are being retained in the Committee files.]

Chairman ARCHER. I thank the gentleman for his testimony, and because I assume this bill is a bipartisan bill, inasmuch as Congressman Peterson is with you there at the witness table as a cosponsor of this legislation, we will be happy to now hear your testimony, Congressman Peterson.

STATEMENT OF HON. COLLIN C. PETERSON, A REPRESENTATIVE IN CONGRESS FROM THE STATE OF MINNESOTA

Mr. PETERSON. Well, thank you, Mr. Chairman, and members of the committee, and it is bipartisan. We have four Republicans and four Democrats on the bill, and we are hoping to add some more. But we appreciate your calling this hearing and appreciate your leadership on this issue.

Mr. Chairman, I have some materials that I would like entered in the hearing record immediately following the testimony, if that is appropriate.

Chairman ARCHER. Without objection, so ordered.

Mr. PETERSON. Thank you.

Mr. Chairman, not too long ago, it was inconceivable that this committee would focus on a replacement as comprehensive as the national sales tax, which is embodied in H.R. 2525. We had a few lonesome voices like Democratic Member Sam Gibbons, who used to rage against the tax system and say that there was a better way to collect taxes. But it didn't seem like there was enough time to ever consider them, and each year we get into the tax policy game of musical chairs that began to see which of the tax extenders would remain standing. We saw a constant flow of new ideas for credits and deductions that vied for the ultimate award to be enshrined in the Internal Revenue Code.

So I think we have come far as Republicans and Democrats to be here today, and no group is more pleased, I think, that we are having this hearing than the American people.

Now, why as a CPA, and especially a Democratic CPA, do I believe in the Fair Tax and why do I think this is the best replacement for the current system? I have watched the making of tax laws as a practitioner on the outside. I have been here as a legislator now for 10 years under Democrats and Republicans. And every tax simplification Congress has passed has added more pages to the U.S. Tax Code and has made the system more complicated. And that was under both Democrats and Republicans.

I have been highly critical of my own party on this point. I think that the 1986 Tax Act was without a doubt the worst piece of legislation that has ever been passed in this Congress. It did lasting damage to many Americans for no good reason. And it complicated the code to the point where we can't understand it a lot of times, and it complicated our lives.

But, in all due respect, since the Republicans have taken over in 1994, you have added 547 pages of statute and 2,327 pages of regulations, just through 1999. So we have kind of got the same thing going on here, and I think that is why it is so positive that we are looking at legislation to replace the whole system here today.

When 49 practitioners last year were given the same information and asked to complete a Federal income tax return, they came back with 49 different answers. No matter what your intentions, you know, we haven't simplified the tax code, and it is time that I think we admit that this system cannot be fixed in spite of all of our best efforts.

I don't think this system can be salvaged even if we all wanted to do so. And I also don't think that taxing income is the best way for us to raise revenue in this country given the way the economy is changing.

Mr. Chairman, I think Americans want true tax reform. Poll after poll shows we are collectively disgusted with our system. Members are hearing from their constituents about this. We are now on the third edition of the Taxpayer Bill of Rights. Each taxpayer gripe hearing is like watching Halloween I, II, and III. Only the names and witnesses change, but the plot does not. The unofficial annual holiday honoring the height of our enmity for our income tax system is just around the corner, April 15th.

Congress has voted to scrap the tax code once and is likely going to do it again. But while something called tax reform just might happen, the real question is this: By what criteria will its success be judged? And what do we want to see in an ideal tax system?

I have come to the conclusion that the Fair Tax fits the bill for a number of reasons.

First of all, there are no exemptions, so we might actually be able to keep this simple and not give preference to one group or another and not give rise to a whole horde of lobbyists descending on your committee asking for special treatment.

It would help solve one of our biggest problems today, and that is this trade deficit, the balance of trade deficit that we have. As John said, the current tax system has an embedded cost that the economists tell us is around 20 or 22 percent. That means that we are exporting all of these taxes, American taxes, in the price of our exports. One of the biggest pluses of this system is it will take that out of the export stream, it will reduce the cost of what we are charging for goods and services sold around the world by an average of 20 or 22 percent, and it will be GATT legal.

In addition to that, when imports come into this country, they are going to be taxed the same as domestic goods and services if they are used for personal consumption, just like goods and services that are made here in the United States.

It also eliminates the most regressive tax, the payroll and self-employment taxes. These are, as I say, I think, the most regressive, and they are the toughest thing for many of our farmers and small businesses because in a lot of cases they pay more in those kinds of taxes than they do in income taxes.

It makes equity capital more available and affordable because we will no longer be taxing savings and investment.

It will be much easier to administer. We would only need to keep track of the approximately 1.6 million retail and service businesses in the U.S., as opposed to the more than 169 million individuals who file tax returns and pay taxes now under the current system.

The Fair Tax plan makes sense, and it will work for the 21st century. I would be willing to predict that most States, if we pass this, will get rid of their income tax because they won't have an income base to place it on, and piggyback on to our system for collecting sales taxes in their State. If they do that, we would have a mechanism to tax Internet businesses the same as we tax businesses on Main Street, which is something that we are going to have to do, and there is no reason why we ought to prefer an Internet business over one that has a store on Main Street.

So I think, understandably, the people so far don't have a lot of faith or confidence that Congress is going to come up with tax reform, and that is too bad. And when I explained this to my father, he said, "Well, you know, that is never going to happen. That makes too much sense."

I hear that from a lot of my constituents as well when I tell them about it, but the Fair Tax is well thought out, it is well researched, it is simple, and it is fair.

So let's show the American people that we can take bold steps and do what is right. Let's move this Fair Tax through the Congress. Doing so would make the American people keep every penny of their paychecks and have some say over how much tax they pay, and really, I think, be a tremendous boom for the economy because we would not tax—if you didn't spend your money and you saved it, you could keep it. And if you want to go out and buy a new Mercedes or a new airplane, you would pay tax and, you know, that just drives the whole decisionmaking process in the right way.

So this, I think, the right solution to tax reform. I hope that we can move this ahead in a bipartisan manner.

Thank you, Mr. Chairman.

[The prepared statement follows:]

Statement of the Hon. Collin C. Peterson, a Representative in Congress from the State of Minnesota

Thank you Mr. Chairman and Members of the Committee. Mr. Chairman, I have some materials I would like to have entered into the hearing record immediately following my testimony this morning.

Mr. Chairman, not too long ago, it was inconceivable this committee would focus on a replacement as comprehensive as a national sales tax. A few lonesome voices, like Democratic Member Sam Gibbons, raged that there could be a better way to collect taxes—but there was never enough time to consider them. Each year the tax policy game of musical chairs began to see which of the tax extenders would remain standing. The constant flow of new ideas for credits and deductions vied for the ultimate award, to be enshrined in the Internal Revenue Code. We have come far, both Republicans and Democrats to be here today. But no group is more pleased than the American people.

Why, as a C.P.A., and especially a Democrat C.P.A., do I believe the Fair Tax is the best replacement for our current system? I've watched the making of tax laws as a practitioner and as a legislator—under Democrats and Republicans—and every tax "simplification" Congress has passed has added more pages to the US Tax Code and made the system more complicated.

I have been highly critical of my own party on this point. I think the 1986 Act was the worst piece of legislation ever passed. It did lasting damage to many Americans for no good reason and it complicated the Code and our lives.

But since the Republicans took over, you've added some 547 pages of statute and 2,327 pages of regulation—through 1999. When 49 practitioners were given the same information and asked to complete a federal tax return they came back with 49 different answers. No matter what your intentions, you have not simplified the federal tax code.

I don't think we'll ever fix this system. I don't think this system can be salvaged even if we wanted to do so. I also don't think that taxing income is the best way to raise the revenue this country needs.

Mr. Chairman, Americans want true tax reform. Poll upon poll shows we are collectively disgusted with our system. Members are hearing from their constituents. We are now on the third edition of the taxpayer bill of rights. Each taxpayer gripe hearing is like watching Halloween I, II and III. Only the names and witnesses change. The plot does not. The unofficial annual Holiday honoring the height of our enmity for our income tax system is just around the corner. Congress has voted to scrap the Code once and likely will again. But while something called tax reform just might happen, the real question is this: By what criteria will its success be judged? What do we want to see in an ideal tax system?

I've come to the conclusion that the Fair Tax fits the bill because:

1) There are no exemptions, so we might actually be able to keep this simple and not give preference to one group or individual over another.

2) It would help solve one of our biggest problems, our balance of trade deficit. With our current federal tax system we are exporting the cost of the tax system in most goods and services. The economists who worked on developing the Fair Tax estimate that this cost averages about 20%. The Fair Tax would eliminate that cost, and it would be "GATT legal." In addition, imports coming into the U.S. would be taxed the same as domestic goods and services if they are used for personal consumption.

3) It eliminates payroll taxes and self-employment taxes. These are some of most regressive taxes we currently have and they are one of the biggest burdens for many of our farmers and small business persons.

4) It makes equity capital more available and affordable, because we will no longer be taxing savings and investment.

5) It will be much easier to administer—we would only need to keep track of the approximately one point six (1.6) million retail businesses in the U.S., as opposed

to the more than one hundred sixty-nine (169) million individuals who file tax returns and pay taxes.

6) The Fair Tax plan makes sense and it will work for the 21st century. I would be willing to predict that most states would piggyback on our system. We would also have a mechanism to tax Internet businesses the same as business on main street.

Understandably, the people don't have a lot of faith in Congress when it comes to tax reform. As my Dad said when he heard about it, "That will never happen—it makes too much sense."

The Fair Tax is well thought out, well researched, simple and fair. Let's show the American people that we can take bold steps and do what's right. Let's move the Fair Tax through the Congress—doing so would let the American people keep every penny of their paychecks and have some say over how much tax they pay.

Thank you, Mr. Chairman.

[Attachments are being retained in the Committee files.]

———

Chairman ARCHER. Thank you, Congressman Peterson.

Mr. Camp?

Mr. CAMP. No questions.

Chairman ARCHER. Ms. Dunn?

Ms. DUNN. Thank you very much, Mr. Chairman.

Gentlemen, thank you for coming to testify today. This is a fascinating hearing we have going on today, and I know that Ways and Means members will be moving in and out of this meeting. But it is great to be able to be at the head of the line to ask you questions. That usually doesn't happen when you are in the bottom row.

But I do have a couple of questions I would like to ask you. Could you explain to the committee how the national retail sales tax compares to the more broad-based taxes that we see on sales in Europe?

Mr. LINDER. Well, first of all, they typically have a value-added tax, which adds a tax every time you add value to a product, from the time you get the order to turn it into a bumper to put it on a car, and it is a hidden tax. It is buried in the cost of goods and services.

One of the first principles of this tax is that everything be transparent so that everyone would know when they buy something what the tax was to the Federal Government.

This tax is only retail consumption. No taxes between businesses, no taxes for farmers. If a farmer buys a tractor to work his land, there is no tax. If he buys a hat to put on his head to do so, there is a tax.

It taxes everything only one time, so a used house would not have a tax in it, but a new house would. But it is only personal retail consumption that is taxed.

Mr. PETERSON. John has explained it well. I think the thing that also should be pointed out is that in Europe, they not only have the value-added tax that is added at every level and added into the price of the product so you don't know what it is, it is also at different levels, depending on what type of goods and services it is.

But the other thing that they did is they kept the income tax, so they have two taxes. They have the income tax and the value-added tax. And I will tell you today that if we don't get rid of the income tax, I will not support this bill. The only way I support this is to completely eliminate all of the current system and replace it with this. The worst thing that we could have is to do what Europe did, and that is, have an income tax and a sales tax.

Canada did the same thing, and my district is right up alongside of Canada. That didn't work very well because they weren't able to take the cost of goods and services out of their products because they kept their income tax, they kept their Social Security tax, and they added the GST tax on top of it.

So what we are doing here has not been done any other place, and I think if we pass this, we will become the Hong Kong of the world and this economy will boom, and it will be a great thing for America.

Mr. LINDER. Let me add a point to that, if I might. Americans are paying this tax today. They are paying the embedded cost of the IRS at retail, about 22 percent, we have a study that says. They are paying all the cost of businesses, the cost of businesses, attorneys, and accountants to avoid the tax. There are payroll tax costs. There are income tax costs. There are compliance costs, all embedded at price.

Ours is the only bill that gets rid of all those taxes and gives competition the opportunity to drive out of the price of goods and services that 22 percent.

Ms. DUNN. I think it is really important to continue to make that point, that this national retail sales tax would be a replacement for the current income tax system. It would not be in addition to the current income tax system. I think we have got to say that over and over again. Mr. Peterson, you did say that, and people need to realize that there has got to be a mechanism to get rid of the old tax code before we move in a new tax code.

Is there anything like that being thought of right now?

Mr. PETERSON. Well, in our bill, we do call for the repeal or the process to repeal the 16th Amendment so that it will never rise again. So we have tried to address is, but, you know, I am a co-sponsor of the bill to scrap the code, and I have been criticized or it has been criticized that, you know, it is irresponsible to terminate the code without having a replacement. Well, we have a replacement. It is here today, and I am cosponsoring it.

You may disagree with some of the aspects of it, or you might have your own way to replace it, but some of us that feel strongly about this have come up with an alternative, and, you know, it is time to get rid of this income tax code. It is so screwed up it cannot be fixed.

Ms. DUNN. Let me ask you, gentlemen, how would your proposal affect the national and the individual rate of savings in our country?

Mr. LINDER. Well, if you don't tax—first of all, the average income earner who has a 28 percent withholding rate and a 7.65 percent share of the payroll tax will have an increase in take-home pay the next day of 56 percent. We are all going to be savers. We are all going to be investors. Because when you drive the embedded cost of the IRS out of the price of goods and services and replace it with this tax, the cost of living will be about a percent higher, but we will all have an increase in take-home pay and we will all be investors.

We believe the increase in savings is going to be huge. We think the interest rates are going to go down 25 percent because of that.

Mr. PETERSON. You know, the American people, they are smart. And when it becomes apparent, which it will almost immediately, that if they spend money they are going to pay tax, if they save money they are not going to pay tax, it is going to change the psychology of this country.

Now, we have tried to increase the savings rates with IRAs and all this other stuff. It hasn't worked. It has gone down. And I guarantee you that if this thing changes, as somebody who sat across the desk and did taxes for people, they are going to figure this out and they are going to save more. I don't know how much more but——

Ms. DUNN. So that means that every dollar that is invested or saved by an income earner is not going to be taxed under your program.

Mr. PETERSON. That is correct.

Ms. DUNN. Thank you.

Thank you, Mr. Chairman.

Chairman ARCHER. Mr. Kleczka?

Mr. KLECZKA. Thank you, Mr. Chairman.

Let me thank both of you for appearing before the committee today. In your presentation, you criticized the current tax code extensively and said little about the proposal, which I think, before we move on it, the American public has to understand much better.

It seems that you are touting this plan as a 23 percent sales tax, and I just question that calculation. Let me ask either one of you, if this were to be the law of the land and I would go and purchase a suit for $100, what would the sales tax be on that suit? The cost of the good is $100. What would be added on for this national sales tax?

Mr. LINDER. It is our design to have the sales tax included in the cost of the good. Currently, your income tax——

Mr. KLECZKA. Okay, that is fine. Let's say it is included in the good. The cost of the good is $100.

Mr. PETERSON. It is $123. It is $23.

Mr. KLECZKA. That is not what we are told. We are told it is 30——

Mr. LINDER. If it was——

Mr. PETERSON.—dollars on $100——

Mr. LINDER. Let me explain to you, Mr. Kleczka, what the current system is. You are currently taxed on a tax-inclusive basis, which is to say, the Government takes the first $36 of what you earn, within what you earn. If you treat this on a tax-inclusive basis——

Mr. KLECZKA. I am trying to compare it to the current sales tax. If I buy something in Wisconsin now, then——

Mr. LINDER. It will be 29.9——

Mr. KLECZKA. Wait, could I finish? If I buy something in Wisconsin now, there is a 5.6 percent sales tax. It is the State sales tax. It is a half percent county tax and 1 percent stadium tax, since now the taxpayers are building stadiums. Okay?

If I buy something for $100, that 5.6 is added on. Now, tell me what my total cost of a suit would be if the suit itself costs $100.

Mr. LINDER. The added-on Federal national sales tax would be 29.9 percent, and if you want to compare apples——

Mr. KLECZKA. Now, that is not the 23 percent we are told about.

Mr. LINDER. The tax-exclusive rate is 29.9 and the tax-inclusive is 23 percent. If you want to treat the income tax on an exclusive basis, which is to say, divide the amount of money you have to spend into what the Government took out of it, you would be paying an effective sales tax rate of 56 percent today, so we are still cutting it in half. You have to treat it either as an exclusive or an inclusive tax.

Mr. KLECZKA. You know, what I am trying to do is go back to my constituents and explain what this proposal is all about. And my concern is, am I to tell them that the sales tax is 23 percent or 30 percent? I suspect that in an attempt to sell this you are trying to minimize what the actual impact is, so you are saying 23; however, the effective rate to be charged on goods and services is actually 30.

So what I am going to do when I respond to any letters I get on this issue, I am going to say what they have proposed is a 30 percent sales tax rate, and we are told by the tax experts around here that to be revenue neutral, that tax rate would have to be 59 percent.

Mr. Peterson, would you like to respond to that?

Mr. PETERSON. Well, I don't know where you get the 59 percent.

Mr. KLECZKA. To be revenue neutral. As it stands, your 30 percent would cost—would deny big revenues that are, you know, coming in today.

Mr. LINDER. We have three different studies that disagree with you.

Mr. PETERSON. Yes, the people that did the studies from MIT and Harvard and Stanford estimate that, as we said, the effective tax rate is 23 percent when you figure out what the percentage is of the total price of the goods and services. That is what it comes out to be.

But we can argue——

Mr. KLECZKA. Okay. Well, the joint committee——

Mr. PETERSON. Figures lie and liars figure, but——

Mr. KLECZKA. The joint committee, which works for the committee or is assigned to the committee, did come up with that amount.

Could you explain to the committee how local units of government and State governments are going to pay this sales tax? As I read the proposal, all goods and services are taxed for governmental units. Could you explain how that works?

Mr. LINDER. Well, first of all, most governments are heavily labor-intensive and they are going to have a huge savings on their payroll tax just to begin with.

Mr. KLECZKA. Okay. How are they taxed? You forgot to finish the point.

Mr. LINDER. If they buy something that they are going to use in the business of running the city, they are going to pay a tax on it.

Mr. KLECZKA. So they are going to pay a 30 percent tax. Now, how are they to treat their payroll? Let's say the city of Milwaukee has a $50 million payroll in a month, are they taxed at 30 percent on that also?

Mr. LINDER. No, no, 7.65 percent of that payroll is going to be coming out of their side and 7.65 coming out of their employees' side.

Mr. KLECZKA. Okay. That is the FICA tax, is it not, and HI?

Mr. PETERSON. Well, yes, but we eliminate——

Mr. LINDER. We eliminate the Social Security and Medicare.

Mr. PETERSON. Eliminate the Social Security tax. Part of what this bill does, it doesn't just get rid of the income tax, it gets rid of the payroll tax.

Mr. KLECZKA. Okay. And so how is the payroll tax to be funded— I mean, the Social Security trust fund to be funded?

Mr. PETERSON. It is going to be funded out of the proceeds of the sales tax, and that——

Mr. KLECZKA. Okay. But so——

Mr. PETERSON. The economists figured that in.

Mr. KLECZKA. So is income going to be sales taxed also?

Mr. LINDER. No.

Mr. PETERSON. No.

Mr. LINDER. Only what they spend.

Mr. KLECZKA. That is unclear.

Chairman ARCHER. The gentleman's time has expired. There will be additional opportunities.

Mr. Collins?

Mr. COLLINS. Thank you, Mr. Chairman.

If I understood you right, for this to be revenue neutral, based on the estimated revenue of this year, about $2 trillion——

Mr. LINDER. 1995 is the last number we have.

Mr. COLLINS. 1995, okay. A couple of questions, then. How do you treat accumulated savings prior to the implementation of this tax?

Mr. PETERSON. They are not taxed. Savings aren't taxed under any circumstances.

Mr. COLLINS. If you take the funds out of savings and spend them.

Mr. PETERSON. Okay. If you spend them on personal consumption, new goods and services that are used in personal consumption, then you would pay tax.

Mr. COLLINS. Even though they were accumulated after tax?

Mr. LINDER. Correct.

Mr. PETERSON. Right.

Mr. COLLINS. Okay.

Mr. LINDER. Let me make a point on that, Mr. Collins. If senior citizens who have saved all their life and accumulated something and paid tax on the accumulation and paid tax on the interest earned and the capital gains earned, they are currently paying this tax every time they spend something. They are currently paying the embedded cost of the IRS. All we are saying is you get to take your money out of your IRA with no tax consequences. There will be no tax on your Social Security revenues or any income you have. But you will pay a 23 percent inclusive sales tax when you buy things, which is about what you are paying today.

Mr. COLLINS. Okay. Another question. How do you treat depreciation that businesses already have in place prior to the implementation? Because there would be no depreciation after the implementation?

Mr. PETERSON. Well, depreciation is not necessary or relevant because we don't tax income. And so one of the problems that we have had in talking to people about this is that they are so ingrained in thinking about the current system that they can't conceive of us moving away and not having to worry about all this stuff, depreciation and deductions and all of that. But because we are not taxing income, it is irrelevant. The only thing that makes any difference is what you are spending for your own personal consumption. So depreciation is important in doing your financial statements for reporting, you know, but other than that, it won't make any difference.

Mr. COLLINS. But depreciation is your way of expensing——

Mr. PETERSON. But we aren't taxing income anymore.

Mr. COLLINS. Before we run out of time, what about existing excise taxes? Do you eliminate those or replace those?

Mr. LINDER. No. We tried to draft a bill that merely replaces the current system of taxing income to another system of taxing expenses without making policy decisions. It is my view that this bill would fail on the floor of the House if we eliminated the excise tax on tobacco. We would fail on that issue alone. So we decided we will take on excise taxes at another time.

Mr. COLLINS. That would include the 12 percent excise tax on a lot of major purchases?

Mr. LINDER. Correct.

Mr. COLLINS. It is already in place. It would stay there. Okay. That is all. Thank you, Mr. Chairman.

Chairman ARCHER. Mr. Watkins?

Mr. WATKINS. Mr. Chairman, I have no questions of my two colleagues. I have for the next panel when we get to it.

Chairman ARCHER. Thank you.

Mr. Rangel?

Mr. RANGEL. Let me thank you for your efforts. I would say that this Committee has not been responsive to your legislation "over the years." But we have a few months left, and who knows what can happen.

The Social Security system, since there is no payroll tax contribution to it, would benefits be paid out of the general funds with monies that would be collected from the taxes?

Mr. LINDER. The monies would apply to the Social Security trust and the Medicare trust in the same manner they currently are because your employer would submit your income, what they paid you in salary, and your earnings would still be credited to your account, and the 40 quarters for which you get your benefits out of Social Security will still be the same as the current system. All we are doing is gathering the money a different way.

Mr. RANGEL. So would the money be paid out by the Appropriations Committee rather than by the so-called Social Security trust fund?

Mr. LINDER. The revenues that would come from the general sales tax collections would be applied to the Social Security trust and the Medicare trust in the same way they are now based on earnings.

Mr. RANGEL. Now, since your sales tax is on top of the excise tax, how would it apply to a gasoline tax?

Mr. PETERSON. Well, if you are buying gasoline for your own personal consumption, there would be this tax on gasoline like anything else.

Mr. RANGEL. On top of the excise tax?

Mr. PETERSON. On top of the excise tax, yes.

Mr. RANGEL. Now, Mr. Kleczka reviewed that. We have the Joint Committee on Taxation, which is a bipartisan effort, Republican and Democrat, and they have given an analysis of your bill. They say that the tax-neutral rate is 59.5 percent over 5 years, and neutrality over 10 years would be 57 percent. You don't argue with the Joint Taxation Committee's estimate.

Mr. LINDER. Sir, we have not seen that study yet. Is that fairly recent?

Mr. RANGEL. Yes, it is April the 7th.

Mr. LINDER. We have some economists that will argue with that, yes.

Mr. PETERSON. You know, it is hard for me to believe because the retail consumption base in this country is 20 percent higher, according to our economists, than the income base. So it is hard for me to believe that it is going to take 59 percent of a base of 20 percent higher than the current income base to raise the same amount of revenue.

Now, I don't know—I haven't seen the study, but it would be hard for me—I mean, I think we would raise so much money we wouldn't know what to do with it all.

Mr. RANGEL. Well, if this is to be considered a bipartisan effort, don't you think in 6 years that you guys would be entitled to a Joint Committee Tax estimate of the cost so that you would have plenty of time to bring in witnesses to defend it? I mean, if this is serious, these questions should not be presented to you this late in our legislative agenda.

Mr. Chairman, I ask unanimous consent that the Joint Committee's evaluation of this legislation be placed into the record.

Chairman ARCHER. Without objection, so ordered.

[The information was not available at the time of printing.]

Mr. RANGEL. This concept is complicated, and you can bet your life that most of the American people haven't the slightest idea what you are talking about. Are you saying that cities and States have to pay taxes on hiring policemen, firemen, doctors, nurses; that the health care that is provided has to be taxed; and, this is going to be fair and equitable and across the board? The whole idea of cities being able to piggyback on Federal income tax programs or States being able to attach to our system would not work because the vehicle would be no longer there. And so, therefore, they would have to now think of new ways for them to get the revenues that would be necessary for them to run their local and State governments.

It is a revolutionary concept and one that merits not only hearings but an opportunity for the American people to be educated. They then can weigh whether it makes any sense the proposal works for them, and whether for local government or State governments.

But the most important thing, in my opinion, whether or not it is a Democratic Congress or a Republican Congress, is how in God's name do you think you could possibly revolutionize the tax system unless it is bipartisan in terms of the cooperative spirit that you bring to this Committee. That bipartisanship has to come to the Ways and Means Committee and has to come from the House. Other than that, you are not realistically talking about revolutionizing the tax system. You may have an opportunity to express views, but the only way that we can bring about any dramatic change in pulling up the tax code by the roots and not increasing its complexity, as the way we have done in the last 7 years, is to make certain that at least we are reading from the same page in how we are going to present it to the American people and, therefore, to the Congress and this Committee.

So I want to congratulate you for your special effort. I wish I could give you some hope that we would be able to consider it in this Committee. But as you know, soon we will have the Easter recess in order to celebrate the resurrection of our Lord and Savior, Jesus Christ, as well as Passover, and then after that we will be moving into Memorial Day for those who lost their lives. We will go through June, probably be busy at Committee two or three days a week, and then July 4th we have to close shop to celebrate our independence.

Come August, of course, our conventions will be the main consideration, Republicans and Democrats. September we will come in for a couple of weeks, and then in October, of course, we get down to the campaign.

So how we squeeze this into our so-called legislative agenda, I don't know, but maybe, just maybe. If we can keep this idea alive, we will find the bipartisanship that you two have enjoyed and worked with over the years being conveyed to this Committee and to the House and Senate. And, we can take a hard look at the income tax system as we know it and take a look at the changes that we can make in a bipartisan way.

These hearings really complicate things because we have a lot of legislation on the House floor right now. But, again, the absence of Members should not be interpreted as an absence of concern of the serious nature in which you present this legislation.

Thank you, Mr. Chairman.

Mr. LINDER. I thank the gentleman.

Chairman ARCHER. Mr. Crane?

Mr. CRANE. Mr. Chairman, I don't have questions for our witnesses, but I would like to take advantage for an opportunity to express my appreciation to all of you for the support. I am sorry for you absence, and I can't tell you how exciting it is to be back again and contemplate an opportunity to serve my country, my district, my family and friends and colleagues. And I want to express appreciation to all of you, from my distinguished chairman here to my ranking minority member, Charlie Rangel, for all of the input I got from you folks. It was really reassuring and very helpful and beneficial, and I look forward to a very positive and dynamic future.

It is one of those things I am humbled by, but, on the other hand, we dig in our heels, fight the good fight, keep the faith, and we shall continue. Thank you again, all of you. Thank you.

[Applause.]

Chairman ARCHER. The gentleman from Illinois is to be congratulated for taking his life in his hands and moving forward in a positive way, and I know all the members of the committee share that view.

Mr. RANGEL. Would the gentleman yield?

Chairman ARCHER. Mr. Rangel?

Mr. RANGEL. I think you know the love and affection that we have had for you over the years. You gave us a chance to display it by indicating a unique type of courage for all of us. No matter what shortcomings we have, we can never wrestle the demons to the ground unless we have the courage first to admit it and then to do something about it. So it was a bad setback, but you have set a standard for all of us to follow. We welcome you back.

Mr. CRANE. Thank you.

Chairman ARCHER. Mr. English?

Mr. ENGLISH. Thank you, Mr. Chairman. I would like to also congratulate these two gentlemen for having the courage to offer a truly revolutionary tax plan. And it has a number of features that make it similar to the one that I have proposed in terms of the incentives. But the one that I think is particularly important and I would like you to comment on is the whole question of border adjustability.

We obviously, when we discuss tax reform, tend to focus on how tax simplification benefits the individual taxpayer. The individual taxpayer all too seldom recognizes that they have a big stake in tax reform because of the impact of the tax system on their job, and this is particularly true in export industries.

I wonder if you gentlemen would comment on how you think the question of border adjustability, taking the taxes off of exports and putting the tax on imports, would benefit the American economy long term.

Mr. PETERSON. Well, as I said during my statement, I think that one of the reasons we are running this huge trade deficit is because we are exporting our tax system, which is expensive, and it adds greatly to all of our products, even the farm products, the raw commodities that come out of my district.

So there is no question in my mind that if we can change this system where we can wring the cost of the Internal Revenue Code out of the system, which is 22 percent, that means that the price of goods and services are going to be 78 percent of what they are now. Obviously, we are going to sell a lot more, and it is going to create more jobs.

You know, we are also going to tax the imports coming into this country if it is used for personal consumption. So for the first time in a lot of areas, we are going to put ourselves on the same footing as these foreign countries, and we are not going to have our companies having to go overseas to manufacture products just to send it back into this country because of tax considerations, which is happening now.

You know, I can't quantify it, but I can guarantee there is going to be a significant increase in jobs and commerce if we pass this bill in the world market.

Mr. LINDER. Let me add something to that. I mentioned in my opening statement that the chairman often refers to the poll done by Princeton Group of foreign companies wanting to relocate here. In addition to that, imagine how many United States corporations dealing in overseas sales have dollars stranded all over the globe, billions upon billions of dollars, because it is cheaper to borrow here at 8 percent than it is to repatriate your dollars at 35 percent.

All that money would come home. Building on these shores would be much more attractive both for foreign companies and our domestic companies. So we would see a huge change in the global balance of trade.

Mr. ENGLISH. Certain sectors of the economy tend to be more tax sensitive in the sense that they tend to operate on thinner margins. One of those, I sense, is manufacturing. And in the recent example of the steel crisis that faced U.S. steel producers, do you feel that a border-adjustable tax in that case would have allowed America's steel industry to thrive in the face of foreign competition?

Mr. PETERSON. Well, my district doesn't include steel manufacturers, but I——

Mr. ENGLISH. That is why I am calling on you as an objective observer.

Mr. PETERSON. Well, I have got to believe that if you can take 22 percent of the cost of your production out of the price of your product and if that steel coming into this country is going to go into cars that are going to be used for personal use, it is going to be taxed, I mean, it has got to go a long way to solving this problem.

One of the reasons that we are having trouble in the world market is we are trying to export our tax system, and it is an expensive tax system, and it is a big penalty on everybody that is in the world market.

Mr. ENGLISH. Thank you, Mr. Chairman. I have no further questions. And, again, I want to compliment the gentlemen for their excellent testimony.

Mr. LINDER. Thank you.

Chairman ARCHER. Mr. Stark?

Mr. STARK. Thank you, Mr. Chairman.

Gentlemen, thank you for providing a creative approach to changing basically the whole way we handle commercial transactions in the country.

I would note that, Collin, you have introduced legislation to have a refundable dependent care tax credit to help families, but that obviously wouldn't work anymore, and you would be willing to give up helping people with their dependent care for this program.

Also, the 60 percent rate, I might add, probably comes because somebody forgot to calculate what your rebates cost. You would be giving rebates to every American in here, which amounts to about $400 or $500 billion a year, and that is about 50 percent more than we collect in taxes now.

But I am going to stick with the 60 percent rate here and discuss the impact on Medicare. This would apply to doctors' fees and pharmaceutical drugs. Now, the Republicans on this committee just voted a month or so ago to deny senior citizens a discount on their prescription drugs. We Democrats all voted for it. And now we saw in the paper the other day that senior citizens are paying 15 percent more if they are uninsured for their prescription drugs.

You guys would add 60 percent on top, so that prescription drugs for my seniors, Zocor, for instance, would go from an average retail price of $107 a month to $172 a month, or $780 a year more. Prilosec for ulcers would go up $840 a year. Procardia for people with heart problems would go up over $1,000 a year in cost. At the same time, you would raise the Part B premium on Medicare automatically from $45 a month to about $73 a month. And this is most interesting. We just celebrated the fact that the Part A trust fund became solvent to the year 2023. Under your plan, increasing the hospital cost 60 percent would make the Medicare trust fund insolvent in the year 2003. You guys just chop 20 years off the solvency of the Medicare trust fund.

If you really want to scare the seniors, then just think about those who had bought long-term care insurance. Nursing homes cost over $100 a day. You guys would kick that up to $160 a day, and the long-term insurance would no longer cover it.

While we talk about insurance, every American would have their insurance bill automatically increased by 60 percent. Not only that, they would have to increase the face amount because the repair prospects for collision damage or storm damage under a homeowner's policy would go up by 60 percent.

It seems to me that you are asking the average American to spend an awful lot of money that they are not now spending, and particularly those in the lower incomes, which I know you both understand. Congressman Peterson being an accountant knows that lower-income people spend a far higher percentage of their income in consumption than do people who are paid well like you and me. We don't spend so much. So we get a gift out of this. But people making $70,000 a year and less really get hammered because they have to spend so much more of their income.

Now, I know that we kind of forget about middle-income people and low-income people in Congress because we get these big salaries. But to think that we are going to rack them up with a 60 percent tax rate on what they spend hardly seems quite fair.

So aside from the fact that we are about to destroy Medicare with this and that is interesting—you talked about lobbyists and their costs. It seems to me, when I listened to you on National Public Radio, you did a good job. That is my commute program. I heard you guys on the radio this morning while you were on television.

The lobbyists and the doctors and the accountants are going to have to pay 60 percent of what they bill when they bill it to the Government in cash while they wait for the collectibles to come in. Now, I have a hunch that every lobbyist in Washington is going to be in here fighting this bill.

So I think that while it is interesting to talk to people about lowering their income tax and their payroll tax, I think we've got to tell them a little bit more about the other side of this coin. And I would like to know how you plan to save Medicare, which would now go broke in 2 or 3 years, when you have added 60 percent to the cost. Have you got any ideas for that?

Mr. PETERSON. Well, this was not designed to save Medicare or change Medicare. We are trying to just replace one tax system with another.

Mr. STARK. If you would yield, I understand that. But unintended consequences——

Mr. PETERSON. And I disagree—you know, I do not agree with the Joint Tax Committee, with all due respect, in this 60 percent number. Now, we asked them a long time ago for this information, and now I am getting it from the other side of the table before they gave it to us. And I think that is a little bit unfair, and, you know, we didn't need to wait 6 months to get this information.

But I can understand that because——

Mr. STARK. Excuse me, Collin. It was given to the Republicans a long time ago.

Mr. PETERSON. Well, I am not trying to get into Republicans or Democrats. This is not why I am involved in this. You know, for whatever reason, we didn't get the information. So the first I heard this is today. I cannot believe that the 60 percent figure is right. I don't know where it is coming from. You know, maybe people want to put this in as bad a light because they are concerned about protecting the current system or whatever else, you know.

But it depends on what you believe and how you believe in the marketplace. I know that some of you think that the drug companies are making a lot of money.

Mr. STARK. I know that.

Mr. PETERSON. Okay. Well, then they are paying the maximum corporate tax rate——

Mr. STARK. No. They are paying the lowest corporate tax rate of any major industry in the country through all their deductions and credit.

Mr. PETERSON. Well, but who gave them the deductions and credits?

Mr. STARK. We did.

Mr. PETERSON. Okay. So if they are making a lot of money, they are paying a lot of taxes, generally.

Mr. STARK. They should.

Mr. PETERSON. They should. But, you know, it—I think it is hard to argue that the current tax system is fair or progressive as it relates to these different companies, and I think that we do penalize people's incentive to work and all these other things. I think it is a much better policy in this country to tax people when they spend money and to not tax when they save money. I think that is in the best interest of the country, and we do exempt on the bottom end the people—if you are a family of seven, you are going to get $31,200 of your spending exempted from this tax completely.

So we have fairly well insulated the bottom end——

Mr. STARK. But you and I would get the same amount.

Mr. PETERSON. Right. Well, why not?

Mr. STARK. Well, what have we done to deserve it? I mean, the taxpayers are already paying the——

Mr. PETERSON. You have the same necessities of life as anybody else. I mean, everybody needs to have a place to live——

Mr. STARK. But I have got a lot more income than everybody else.

Mr. PETERSON. Well, and if you save it, you won't pay any tax, which is, I think, a good thing because then that money is going to be available——

Mr. STARK. Collin, I can't sell that in my district. They don't even want to pay me, much less have me go home and defend——

Mr. PETERSON. Well, I can't speak for your district, but I just think it makes sense. You know, that is where I am coming from. We can have a disagreement on that. But I really think that in the best interest of the country this is a better system, a better way to raise the money.

Mr. LINDER. Let me just say, the only thing I agree with what you said is that the lobbyists will indeed oppose this.

Mr. STARK. Because of the——

Mr. LINDER. Because 60 percent of them make their living because of their intellectual capital in the tax code that we have drafted over 88 years.

Mr. STARK. Well, whatever they are lobbying for, I mean, the interesting thing is having to pay the tax the day you send a bill to the client, and if the clients are as slow-paying as some people I know, you are going to really affect the cash flow. This would go to every lawyer and physician. Think of the doctors coming to complain how long it takes Blue Cross to pay them or HCFA to pay them. But when the doc does the operation and sends the bill, they would have to pay 60—even Collin's figure of 30, let's split the difference and say 45 percent of that fee has to be paid in cash to the Federal Government. Think about what this would do. And Collin as a CPA knows that cash flow probably is more important to these people in operating their practices. You would take a big cut out of that because for people who are carrying receivables, 30, 60, 90 days, there would be a major problem. We would all be paying——

Chairman ARCHER. The Chair notes this is a very interesting conversation, but the gentleman's time has long since expired.

Mr. STARK. I thank the Chair for his indulgence, and I thank the witnesses for——

Chairman ARCHER. The gentleman will have other time today, frequently.

Mr. Lewis?

Mr. LEWIS. Thank you, Mr. Chairman.

With a national retail sales tax, what role would the IRS play? I would assume that it would be diminished.

Mr. LINDER. We anticipate a small agency within the Treasury Department that will contract with the various States and pay them to collect the tax, just like 45 States are already doing with their sales tax now.

Mr. PETERSON. So we sunset the IRS in this in, I believe, 2005. We have 110,000 employees. We probably need, you know, 10,000 to do compliance, because one of the—the one issue where you are going to have a problem is we don't tax businesses, so you are going to have a lot of people that are going to want to say they are in business so they can buy a car or buy a plane for their business. Now, that is already happening under the current system, but, clearly, you are going to have that kind of pressure with this kind of system, so we will need people out there to police this and to try to make sure that these businesses are legitimate businesses and they are not some kind of sham just to get around the sales tax. So much diminished.

Mr. LEWIS. So the intrusion into individual lives would be greatly diminished.

Mr. PETERSON. Right.

Mr. LINDER. Everybody in America would be a voluntary taxpayer, and they would pay taxes exactly when they choose and as much as they choose by how they control their spending.

Let me speak just a little bit to the compliance question, which I think was at the edge of your question. Currently the IRS says they collect—they have a compliance rate of 75 percent. It is very easy just to cheat on your tax return, lie on your income, and you have a 99 percent chance of not being audited. Under our proposed system, you have to have someone conspire with you to cheat. And since 80 percent of the tax is going to be collected by 20 percent of the businesses, such as Wal-Mart and Home Depot, they are not going to be interested in helping you cheat because they have too much to lose.

The States that currently collect the sales tax tell us on average the compliance rate is 92 percent. So we not only capture the underground economy, but we think the compliance rate will be much higher than currently.

Mr. LEWIS. Wonderful. Thank you.

Chairman ARCHER. Mr. Tanner?

Mr. TANNER. Thank you, Mr. Chairman.

I, too, thank you all for your innovation. I have long thought that we could do some things here in Congress that would simplify the tax code and would also give us a chance to realize some of the principles of taxation that you all have expressed, and so I thank you.

I have a couple of questions about the mechanics, I suppose. There would be a 23 to, I think in your words, Mr Linder, 29.9 percent levy on the local payrolls of State and local governments under this provision.

Mr. LINDER. Not on payroll.

Mr. PETERSON. Not on payroll.

Mr. TANNER. Well, on wages. There would be a sales tax paid on wages of State and local government employees?

Mr. LINDER. On waivers? I can't hear what——

Mr. TANNER. Wages.

Mr. LINDER. Wages? No, that is not my understanding.

Mr. TANNER. It is in this bill, as far as I can read.

Mr. LINDER. Correct.

Mr. TANNER. Am I incorrect?

Mr. LINDER. You are correct.

Mr. TANNER. I am correct?

Mr. LINDER. Yes.

Mr. TANNER. You said the difference earlier that would be—that they would save money because payroll taxes would be eliminated under your proposal.

Mr. LINDER. That is correct.

Mr. TANNER. There is a difference between the 20-something percent that would be levied on the wages of the local employees, State and local government employees, and the amount of contribution they are presently making to the payroll taxes, anywhere from as much as 20 percent, depending on what number you used, to maybe 15 percent.

Now, we have passed a law called unfunded mandates. I don't know how they pay for that if we impose that on the taxpayers of the State and local governments. I am from Tennessee where we have a sales tax-based system, so I guess I am more sensitive to that than you are. Could you help me with that? Could you explain how that would work?

Mr. PETERSON. Well, I think one of the reasons that this provision is in there—and this, I guess, depends on how you come at this. But I think—I am convinced that if we take the income tax, the corporate income tax, payroll tax off of businesses, then you are going to have a reduction overall in the price of goods and services of 20 to 22 percent. So what these people buy in local governments are going to go down. The costs of goods and services are going to go down 20 or 22 percent.

So if you believe that, then you are going to have a tradeoff here basically that is going to be even if you believe that the rate is 29.6 percent.

Mr. TANNER. Do you have any data? I mean, that is the first question——

Mr. PETERSON. Well, yes. Economists——

Mr. TANNER.—that is going to be asked by State legislators and all of the government employees in the urban areas as well as the little towns like I come from. How are they going to pay it?

Mr. PETERSON. Well, the economists from Harvard, MIT, and Stanford that did the work on this say that the costs of goods and services on average are going to go down 20 percent because we are going to take the cost of the income tax and payroll tax system out of the price of goods and services.

So we are trying to leave people——

Mr. TANNER. Well, you understand my question.

Mr. PETERSON. Yes, I understand——

Mr. TANNER. When I go home and the little town I live in is going to buy a police car and they are going to pay this tax on that police car, they want to know how they are going to come up with it other than raising the local property taxes. They are going to pay a sales tax on the salary of the five or six policemen we have.

Now, if the price of the paper that they buy comes down, I guess it might make up for the tax they pay on wages of the policemen and firemen. I don't know. But I think we need to look at the unfunded mandates law if we think it is worthwhile and see how we can relate it to this law.

The other question I had is what about the case of retail sales over the Internet. Are they taxed under your proposal?

Mr. LINDER. Yes. Under this principle, we would not——

Mr. TANNER. You understand we just passed a moratorium on all Internet——

Mr. LINDER. Well, we passed a moratorium on special access charges, but the Internet is still susceptible to the same sales tax that the catalogue sales are and Sears has been paying this for 60 years.

On this principle, we think that Government ought to be neutral between competing parties, and if the fellow down the street puts up a store and sells books out of it, participates in your community, votes in your elections, and serves on your library board, he ought not to be put at a 7 percent disadvantage to Amazon. So under the principle that Government ought to be neutral, everything ought to be taxed exactly the same. And Internet sales and catalogue sales would be captured at the national level.

Mr. PETERSON. Well, and people are mixing——

Mr. TANNER. We have a moratorium until October of next year on retail sales taxation over the Internet.

Mr. LINDER. The moratorium is only on special access charges.

Mr. PETERSON. Well, the Federal Government doesn't charge sales tax——

Mr. TANNER. That is not my information, but——

Mr. PETERSON. The Federal Government doesn't charge sales taxes on anything right now.

Mr. TANNER. Under your proposal, I understand it would.

Mr. PETERSON. Well, we would. But I am just saying right now—so when people talk about this, they get this mixed up between the State issue and the Federal issue. We aren't taxing anybody retail sales at the Federal level. The only people that are taxing and where it is an issue is at the State level.

Mr. TANNER. Right.

Mr. PETERSON. And they get this mixed up, and so I think a lot of people don't even really know what this is about. You know, they are just reacting that they are against taxing the Internet, and I am, too, in terms of taxing the Internet service and making this available to people. I am against taxing that. But one of the positive things about this piece of legislation is that we will tax all sales, wherever it is, and I think that the States will piggyback on this system, because they will no longer have the income tax to base their income tax system on. I think the States are going to go away from the income tax, will piggyback on this, and then that will help solve——

Mr. TANNER. Well, let me ask you one other question, so I can explain it to people when they ask me because I am interested in it. Under your bill, do you propose to tax the Internet access?

Mr. PETERSON. No.

Mr. TANNER. Well, now, I thought you said there were no exemptions earlier.

Mr. PETERSON. Yes, there will be a sales tax on all services if it is used for personal use. So if you are using the Internet in your house for your own personal use, you will pay a sales tax, like everything else. If you use the Internet in your business, you will not pay a tax because businesses are not taxed under this at all. Businesses——

Mr. TANNER. Internet access charges to individuals, non-business, would be taxed under this provision.

Mr. PETERSON. Right, because——

Mr. TANNER. So we would have to change the moratorium on——

Mr. PETERSON. And so is your phone bill, so is any other utility.

Mr. TANNER. I am just trying to find out what we are and are not doing.

Thank you, Mr. Chairman.

Chairman ARCHER. Mr. Hayworth?

Mr. HAYWORTH. Thank you, Mr. Chairman. My colleagues from Minnesota and Georgia, I appreciate you coming down today to talk more about this, and I also take time to salute you because I hear from several people in my district who are very captivated by the notion of changing, reforming our system of collecting taxes.

My friend from Minnesota may have touched on this a little bit in his answer to a previous question, but I think there is a legitimate concern that we need to address—and if it has been touched on already, I apologize for raising the issue again—about the so-called sticker shock. When we make a transition from the current taxation policy to this form of sales tax, there are those who say, wow, take a look at perhaps a one-time escalation in price. Would you agree that is a legitimate challenge in making this transition? And what about that whole notion of sticker shock and a jump in prices?

Mr. LINDER. We have a study out of Harvard that says that the reduction in sales in the first year would decline by 8 to 9 percent, and in the fourth year we will be spending more than we are currently spending under the current system because people would have so much more discretionary income to spend with.

Mr. HAYWORTH. So the flip side is—and this was brought up at a town hall. When there was a lament about the sticker shock, somebody said, well, yes, but look at what you are taking home, because I think the epiphany for many of us comes when we enter the world of work, get a paycheck and say, "The Government has taken how much already? Gee, if I just took home what I earned."

And yet there is another question that arises, and I know our friends, the retailers, will be along to talk about this. A lot of folks tend to take the position, well, wait a minute, we have already become the tax collector for the State, for the county, for the city, all these sales taxes. Please don't make us the tax collector for Uncle Sam. That is one heck of a responsibility.

But I wonder, too, about the percentage—will there be a temptation for different businesses to say, well, let's pop the prices up to an even percentage. It not only will be easier to figure, but there will be a little bit in there for us in terms of care and handling. Is that a legitimate concern?

Mr. LINDER. Yes, but we think the marketplace works. We really trust that the competition will drive that embedded cost of the IRS out of the price of goods and services. If we didn't trust the marketplace, we wouldn't be interested in this. For every retailer that wants to put a few pennies extra in there, the guy down the street is going to take a few pennies out because his interest is market share. He is going to make more because he is going to sell more.

So we think we have a very efficient system. We think that we are in a period of time right now when everything is penny-sensitive. The competition has never been keener. And we think that will drive the price of goods and services down.

Mr. HAYWORTH. Gentlemen, how do we get from here to there? I mean, is it just take over on an arbitrary date, or is there a transition period?

Mr. PETERSON. The only transition rule in this is going to be—you know, it is on the 1st of January. The only transition rule is the inventory that you have on hand at that date you will get a credit against the sales tax for that inventory because the price—the current price of the tax system is in those goods and services. So we would, in fact, be collecting the tax twice on that. So that would be the only transition rule.

We would go cold turkey on January 1st of—I think in the original bill it was 2001. Now it is probably going to have to be delayed beyond that if we move this year. But it would be cold turkey.

Mr. HAYWORTH. One final point. I appreciate your advocacy of this plan, but I also know that you take your oaths of office very seriously and you are willing to come here as honest brokers and advocates. As you look at the plan you have introduced, in all candor, what do you consider to be the limitations or the drawbacks? Are there any things that concern you both in terms of what has been drafted?

Mr. LINDER. I have two concerns. The first one is for the States to administer and oversee the collection of taxes on services will be much more difficult than on products. And the second concern, which is very real with me, is that 15 years after this passes, we are going to have a hard time finding employees because this economy is going to grow so rapidly. Every foreign company, is going to want to build in our country because there are no tax consequences. Every investor in the world will be in our equity markets because there are no tax consequences. And we will have so much growth that I am worried about finding employees.

Mr. PETERSON. You know, any piece of legislation has got things that can be questioned or places that can be improved. And I think there has already been some issues raised here today that ought to be looked at. And I come at this with the idea that you folks can help us make this a better situation. I think we ought to look at the issue with the local units of government and see if there is a better way to address that.

But I think that the biggest concern that we are going to have in the implementation of this, as I said earlier—and we have got big problems in the current system with compliance. But we are going to have a significant problem because we don't tax businesses. You are going to have people trying to create businesses so they can avoid the tax. And that is going to be one of the biggest challenges in implementing this, is setting up a system whereby we can ferret out what is a legitimate business and give them a number and a way to control this. We are going to have to have some kind of a system whereby we can make sure that when the Federal Government gives you a number to be in business, that you are legitimate business, and then use that as an underpinning to make sure that people don't get around this law. That would be my biggest—I think that is the one place where you are going to have people trying to undermine this. And it can be handled, but it is going to have to be thought out very carefully.

Mr. HAYWORTH. Well, again, gentlemen, I thank you. You are to be commended, and there are many of my constituents in the 6th District of Arizona who have more than a passing interest in this, have a deep and abiding conviction that this could be the answer in terms of tax reform. And I pledge to you as a committee member we will take a close look at this, and, again, Mr. Chairman, I commend you for calling these hearings today.

Chairman ARCHER. Mr. Jefferson?

Mr. JEFFERSON. Thank you, Mr. Chairman.

I also would like to comment you members for taking a stab at this issue of tax reform. But I have some questions about a part of it that I think a lot of folks in the country are going to be concerned about.

We have done a lot in this committee and throughout the Congress to incentivize home ownership as a way of creating a wealth of people and a way of providing for them a chance for what we call the American dream.

We have also done a lot in our committee to try and build communities through incentives for rental property development, both rehabilitation projects and new ones, and we have done low-income housing credits for that, and we have done accelerated depreciation.

On the other hand, for home ownership, as you know, we have allowed the deduction of mortgage interest payments, and these have incentivized home ownership and have been probably the principal incentive for the ordinary person in the whole tax code.

Now, if I understand the bill correctly, it will place a 30 percent retail sales tax on purchases of newly constructed homes. It seems to leave out old homes, although I am not quite sure, but it seems to leave that out. But it also imposes a 30 percent sales tax on rentals whether the apartment is new or old. And then it seems to include sort of a new tax here under this definition of financial intermediation services, the difference between the home mortgage and the—I am sorry, the mortgage interest rate and the Federal rate, there is a 30 percent tax on whatever that difference is.

So let me ask you this: Am I correct that your bill imposes a 30 percent retail sales tax on purchases of newly constructed homes?

Mr. PETERSON. That is correct.

Mr. JEFFERSON. And let me ask you this: Do you know if any State imposes such a tax? I don't think any State imposes such a tax now, right?

Mr. PETERSON. No. But you have to, again, go back to the underlying principle that the economists tell us that 28 percent of a home, a new home, is the embedded cost of the current tax system, payroll taxes, corporate income taxes. So 28 percent of the cost of that home is going to go away if we pass this bill. Then you add 30 percent back onto it, you are about where you started off.

Mr. JEFFERSON. Again, you have the discrepancy that exists between Joint Tax and those who are putting together this legislation about what the rate will actually be.

Mr. PETERSON. Right.

Mr. JEFFERSON. But let's assume it is a 30 percent rate. If someone buys a home for $200,000, is the tax on that $60,000? Is that the way you would calculate it?

Mr. PETERSON. This is the one place—in all other instances, the tax is paid up front, but in the case of homes, we think that is a large enough purchase that it is not fair to ask the lenders to pay that tax and have to collect it back over the length of the mortgage.

And so the way that it works on a new home is you pay tax on the equity portion, whatever your down payment is, you would pay the tax on that, and then you would pay the tax on the principal part of your mortgage payment every month. So that would be spread out over the length of the mortgage.

On a $200,000 house, if you had $40,000 down, you would pay the tax on that, and then you would pay the tax on the principal as you paid off the principal of the rest of the mortgage.

Mr. JEFFERSON. So where does the taxpayer get this money from? He has to borrow the money as part of the overall loan?

Mr. PETERSON. Well, he gets it—I mean, he has to borrow the 28 percent of the embedded cost of the tax system that is in the house right now. He borrows that.

Mr. JEFFERSON. Well, you are talking about——

Mr. PETERSON. So it is the same——

Mr. JEFFERSON. Yes, but on top of that, in real terms, on top of the cost of the house, if the fellow is buying a house at $200,000, the so-called embedded cost is already there. I mean, that is what he is getting. Then he pays a mortgage on it now, and he pays his mortgage interest rate over time. This sales tax thing is a new feature here. It is something you would have to borrow, it seems to me, to add to his liability on this thing.

Now, let me ask you this: This intermediation charge, you agree that is a new charge, the difference between——

Mr. LINDER. It is simply a way to get to how to charge for banking services, and we are trying to borrow—we are only charging sales tax on the service provided. If you borrow $100,000, there is a service cost. We don't pay the sales tax on $100,000 that you are going to borrow and pay back, only on the service aspect that the bank incurs in making that loan for you.

Mr. JEFFERSON. You calculate that as the difference between the mortgage rate and the Federal rate. That is what it seems to be—and I don't know that necessarily—those two necessarily jibe in every case, but, anyway, that is the way it is calculated here. That is another issue.

Does the bill impose—on apartment rentals, are you troubled at all by the proposal that we would increase the cost of housing by 30 percent for somebody who is renting? Does that trouble you at all? Or you think it isn't a problem, especially for moderate- and low-income people?

Mr. PETERSON. The price of building that apartment building is going to be 30 percent less than it is currently because you are not going to have all of those payroll taxes and corporate income taxes to pay. So, theoretically, if the cost of that rental property is less, then the amount that you have to charge for rent would be less as well. Plus we exempt—like for a family of five, you don't pay any tax on $25,400, and part of that $25,400 is the rent that you would pay on your apartment. So you are insulated from the tax on that portion of it.

Mr. JEFFERSON. In the case of the new home purchase, you made an explanation about getting rid of embedded costs. In the case of rental, of course, it applies to old and new. So if a person is in a rental unit now and it is an old unit, won't that person just experience an increase in rent because of this proposal?

Mr. PETERSON. Yes.

Mr. JEFFERSON. I would think so. And in the case of a new one, you could say the rent rate is just being established, so it is taken off for the first time, perhaps. But in every case of—now, we have made—we try to make it easy for people to find decent and affordable home ownership, rental properties through what we have done in the tax code, through the low-income housing tax credit. We made a big deal out of that over the years, and it has been—most people say it has been effective in building communities.

I just wonder if you are going to put some housing out of the reach of low-income families and without any sort of a provision before it, because we take the low-income housing tax credit away.

Mr. PETERSON. It is a legitimate concern, and I would just say that I think that the things that are embedded in the code that we can all agree are good public policy and are needed to get people what we think they need and deserve, then they can withstand the scrutiny of this Congress, and we can set up a program to accomplish the same thing with a direct appropriation. We don't have to do this through the tax code. So the low-income housing tax credit incentives—I mean, we are wasting 50 percent of that money to have these brokers sell these credits in the first place. We could eliminate that.

I have worked with low-income housing tax credits. I see how much of it goes to the people that sell the credits and don't go to the folks that actually invest in the properties. So, again, if that is what we want to do to encourage home ownership for people in rental property, we can have an appropriation, we can have a program that spends that money directly, and we can all vote on it, and it will be out in front. And I think that is a better way to do it.

Mr. JEFFERSON. Won't you have to set up——

Chairman ARCHER. The gentleman's time has expired.

Mr. JEFFERSON.—some bureaucracy to deal with all that stuff?

Chairman ARCHER. Mr. Becerra?

Mr. BECERRA. Thank you, Mr. Chairman. And I appreciate that our two colleagues have stayed for such a long time answering so many questions, and I appreciate also their proposal and their efforts to try to reform our tax code.

Mr. Jefferson raised some of the questions I was going to ask, so let me just continue along those lines.

Inherent in your discussion is the fact that we have embedded in the cost of items that we currently sell income tax rates—or the income tax that we pay as individuals, other taxes such as the payroll tax, and that by eliminating those taxes and placing it all under a sales tax, we can have at least a simpler, cleaner understanding of what our tax really is. So we take that $200,000 home. Under your legislation there would be a tax of $60,000 on that home that could be spread over the life of a mortgage in terms of the paying of that tax.

My understanding from what you are saying as well is that because we are now eliminating income taxes, payroll taxes, all other forms of taxes, those embedded taxes now being eliminated, we can now actually reduce the cost of items that we purchase, so, therefore——

Mr. LINDER. And we think the market will do that. We think that $200,000 home will cost about $140,000 to build.

Mr. BECERRA. So you are saying it will cost about $140,000 to build, so, therefore, you are actually saving a little bit. So even though you are paying a tax, your cost really won't be much different from what it was before.

Mr. LINDER. But you are going to be paying for it with your whole paycheck. If you are the lowest-income earner right now in a rental unit with a 15 percent withholding level and 7.65 percent your share of the payroll tax, you are going to get tomorrow a 30 percent increase in take-home pay. Most people who buy homes, the first consideration they have in going to the mortgage lender is how much of your income—how much take-home pay do you have? Can you afford to make the payment? And you are going to have an increase in take-home pay.

Mr. BECERRA. Your proposal would try to put more money in people's pockets at the beginning.

Mr. LINDER. That is correct.

Mr. BECERRA. A concern I have, though, is that if you are saying that the cost of that new home will be $140,000 instead of the $200,000 now, then for someone to sell that home, a home builder to sell that home, you would have to sell that at $140,000, when before this tax may have been in place, someone would have purchased the neighboring home at $200,000. But now the home is selling for $140,000. How do you tell the neighbor that purchased the home for $200,000 under the old system that now his home is really valued at $140,000 because the neighbor next door bought it at $140,000?

It seems to me that what you have told all the neighbors is the value of your homes has just dropped quite a bit.

Mr. PETERSON. Well, no, because under our plan, one of the principles is that things are only taxed once. So we only tax new property. So that home next door is not taxed when it is sold.

Mr. BECERRA. So do you mean to tell me that someone else will now purchase the next year the neighbor's home that cost the neighbor $200,000 at $140,000?

Mr. PETERSON. Well, no, because if it was a new home, the tax would be added on to it. It would be back up to $200,000. So you would be in the same position as you were with a used home.

Mr. BECERRA. So let's take this scenario. The year 2000 a home was built, and under our current system, the homeowner purchased it for $200,000. The year 2001 we go into your new tax system, and you are saying that same home will really cost about $140,000. The neighbor would buy that new home next door—a purchaser would buy that home next door for $140,000.

Mr. LINDER. Plus taxes——

Mr. BECERRA. Plus the tax. Plus the tax.

Mr. PETERSON. $60,000.

Mr. BECERRA. $60,000. The neighbor that bought the home for $200,000 in the year 2000 now wishes to try to sell. I am a purchaser seeking a home in that neighborhood. I look at the home that cost $140,000 plus the tax, but the purchase price is listed as $140,000, and I now look at the homeowner who purchased the home for $200,000 in the year 2000, that homeowner is not going to sell it for $140,000. I am probably not going to be willing to pay——

Mr. LINDER. First of all, both of these houses have tax costs in them. One is visible and the other is invisible. But they are both going to wind up costing about the same.

Mr. BECERRA. Yes, but—and you may be right that it may be invisible, but the prices are not invisible to people shopping for homes, and I have a difficult time understanding how anyone as a neighbor is going to want to see a $60,000 reduction in the value of their home and someone else is going to, as a purchaser, be willing to shop for a home that is priced at $60,000 more than what someone else bought the home.

Mr. PETERSON. As someone who has spent 20 years advising people and spending most of my life figuring out how to get around the tax code, I can tell you what is going to happen with this. Used houses will become very popular for a while because they are not taxed. That is the psychology of the American people. If they can find something that they can buy and not pay the tax, they are going to just gravitate toward that. So I think you are going to actually see the used houses become more valuable for a while. Eventually it is going to sort out as the system goes into effect.

Mr. BECERRA. And, you know, we would have to roll the dice on that, but I think the same problems you see with real estate you would see with funeral services. You are going to tax people to go bury their deceased relatives; doctors' services, which were discussed; prescription drugs, a 30 percent tax on prescription drugs for elderly who are right now on fixed incomes; nursing homes; the Internet, which we here have agreed should not be taxed for at least a few years until we figure out what, if anything, we should do. Somehow we are going to have a total change in mind-set, and then we are still rolling the dice.

I thank you for all your efforts and your time, and, Mr. Chairman, I thank you also for the indulgence on the time.

Chairman ARCHER. Ms. Thurman will inquire.

Mrs. THURMAN. Thank you, Mr. Chairman.

Just to reiterate the comments by my colleagues, we do appreciate the work that you have put into this. I am probably one of the few members other than—well, I may be one of the only members here that has had to deal with a service tax ever before through the State of Florida when Governor Martinez was Governor and tried to impose a service tax on the State of Florida and the residents. And I have to tell you it was pretty nasty, very nasty, and it was only at 6 percent. But what it was basically doing was putting a sales tax on services, on everything that was defined through the Federal SIC codes. So it became a rather—it actually ended up being fairly embarrassing because it ended up being repealed within about a 6-month period of time.

But in saying that, there are a couple of things I would like to ask about. Florida is also one of those States that does not have a State income tax, although State income taxes would be piggybacked somewhat on our income tax. So even though yours may be 30 percent or 60 percent—whoever's numbers you agree with—what happens to a State if their income tax is no longer available to them? I mean, replacing it with a sales tax, property taxes?

Mr. PETERSON. Well, I think that, you know, first of all, I was in the State legislature in Minnesota when we tried to tax services, so I have been through that. But the thing that you need to understand is that those same people that are going to be collecting this tax are paying a huge income tax, corporate income tax, payroll tax burden, and I think a lot of them would be willing to have their services taxed with the sales tax if they can get rid of that other part of the system. So that is a new part of the equation that was not there, you know, when we were just going to put the sales tax on top of what is already there.

But in the case of the States that have income tax, I think it is unlikely that any State will be able to maintain an income tax if we don't have a Federal income tax, and I think that is a good thing. And I think what will happen is you will see States piggybacking onto our sales tax system.

For example, in Minnesota, we exempt food, clothing, medicine, you know, all of those kind of things. And because of that, we have to have a 6.5 percent sales tax. If we taxed everything, like we are doing in our bill, we could drop that to 2 percent and raise the same amount of money.

So I think you are going to see States piggyback onto this Federal system, be able to drop their rates, and still collect more money than they are collecting now.

Mrs. THURMAN. How do they piggyback onto this system? I am not sure that I understand that.

Mr. PETERSON. Well, because your merchant is going to charge you on your Federal sales tax, you know, 30 percent, whatever it is. So the State will just add on another 6 percent, and then they will get their revenue based on the same taxable sales as the Federal, and they just piggyback right on and it makes it simple.

Mr. LINDER. Let me make a comment on that, Mrs. Thurman. We have had Governors tell us that they would love to see this because they would eliminate all their exemptions and exclusions, tax everything equally just like ours does, and it is much easier for them to administer and oversee. We are making the retailers be cops today. They are picking out who gets taxed and who doesn't, and we shouldn't ask that of our retailers. They should tax everything the same.

I practiced dentistry. Why should my profession be privileged to operate in Georgia and not have pay to have a tax when the neighbor who is a jeweler has to collect the tax? So we are operating under a principle that no industry should be favored over another industry, no business section should be favored over another. Everybody should pay equally the same because they are all serving consumers.

Mrs. THURMAN. Well, but the business is not paying the tax.

Mr. LINDER. That is correct.

Mrs. THURMAN. The customer is paying the tax. You can't say that it is a privilege by the business.

Mr. LINDER. It is a privilege not to have to collect it and turn it in.

Mrs. THURMAN. However, in saying that, I mean, if I look at the constituency that I represent of about—you know, the second poorest district, maybe just above that poverty line but still one of the poorest districts, and a very old district. I mean, the three or four things that they have to depend on, which has already been mentioned: housing, food, medicine, going to the doctor. And, you know, what you are saying to them—and they are not necessarily paying or receiving or paying a payroll tax or doing any of those kinds of things. For them, what benefit is this to them?

Mr. LINDER. Well, there are two benefits. The first one is we are going to drive the embedded cost of the IRS out of those things that they are currently paying now.

Mrs. THURMAN. But is there an enforcement mechanism in this bill to make sure that those things drop?

Mr. LINDER. No, we actually trust the market. We actually trust the free market system to do that.

But, secondly, they are going to have a rebate at the beginning of every month that is going to totally rebate the tax consequences of purchasing the necessities, which the HHS determines every year——

Mrs. THURMAN. For everybody?

Mr. LINDER. For everybody. We don't need an agency determining who deserves it and who doesn't, because then we are back in the income business. Every household will get a rebate check at the beginning of every month that will totally rebate the tax consequences of spending up to the poverty line. For a household of five, that is about $25,000. Their check of about $500 a month would totally rebate the tax consequences of spending up to that. So we not only drive the current 22 percent embedded cost of the IRS out of the purchase of milk and bread, but we also add a check to that so they don't pay the 23 percent sales tax on it.

Mrs. THURMAN. So who is going to pay that difference? I mean, somewhere along the line throughout this——

Mr. LINDER. Who is going to pay the check?

Mrs. THURMAN. Well, no. I mean, if somebody is not paying and it is above this—I mean, who gets squeezed in this?

Mr. LINDER. Actually, the consumption base is a very consistent base over the last 40 or 50 years. Even in downturns of the economy, we have seldom had a turndown of more than 3 percent. So the consumption base is a far more steady predictor of revenues than is the income base.

Now, let me tell you who is going to get hurt the most: the guy who is worth $300 or $400 million and he has got all his money in tax-free municipals. He is going to have to pay taxes for a change.

Mr. PETERSON. Plus the spending base is 20 percent higher than the income base. People spend 20 percent more than they report in income. So it is a higher base to start with.

Mrs. THURMAN. But I would imagine it also depends on what you are spending on and what grouping you are in as to your needs.

Mr. PETERSON. Yes. But, again, you know, most seniors, a lot of them have their homes paid for.

Mrs. THURMAN. Sure.

Mr. PETERSON. So that is not going to be an issue. And I think with most seniors the amount that we have in here for the poverty level spending is going to cover their drugs and food and clothing, because most seniors are not spending a lot of money on clothing either, probably.

So, you know, it is going to vary between people, but, I mean, generally, I have had seniors—I have had town meetings and talked this through with seniors. And once they understand it, you know, I think most of them think it is a good thing, not so much for them but for their kids, because what most seniors are concerned about is that their kids or grandkids get a chance to make it in this world, and this takes the burden off of them. You know, they have no taxes on their payroll. They get to keep their whole check, and they decide whether they are going to spend it and pay the tax or whether they are going to save it and start a business or whatever, which I think is a better way.

Chairman ARCHER. The gentle lady's time has expired.

Mrs. THURMAN. Thank you.

Chairman ARCHER. Mr. Doggett?

Mr. DOGGETT. Thank you, Mr. Chairman.

Mr. Linder, do I understand that the idea of this legislation is to apply it to all forms of commerce with one simple rate?

Mr. LINDER. All forms of personal consumption.

Mr. DOGGETT. All forms of personal consumption. So that would include any and all purchases that are made through electronic commerce over the Internet?

Mr. LINDER. Yes.

Mr. DOGGETT. And I had thought prior to today that there were not any individuals in the Congress that were advocating using electronic commerce as a source of Federal revenues. But do I understand that it is the objective of you and all the supporters of this measure to rely on electronic commerce, as well as other forms of commerce, as a Federal revenue source?

Mr. LINDER. Yes. You were not here when I made the point. I would like to make it again. We think Government should be neutral in respect of competition between businesses, and it ought not give a 6 or 7 percent disadvantage to the fellow down the street because he is selling it door to door instead of over the Internet.

I have said for some time that in respect of being neutral, Internet commerce should be taxed, anyway. I bought a Gateway computer just recently over the Internet, and I was taxed on it. And the reason I was taxed on it is because Gateway has a store in my district.

Mr. DOGGETT. And there may well be good arguments for that point of view. But even those who have held that point of view in the past, I have not heard anyone else advocating that, in addition to State and local taxes, we should use the Internet and electronic commerce as a major Federal revenue source. Indeed, as I understand, under your proposal, almost the exclusive Federal revenue source would be to rely on taxation of all forms of consumption, including all consumption through the Internet.

Mr. LINDER. You understand the bill perfectly.

Mr. DOGGETT. Okay. And as far as the level of tax that you will impose for the Federal Government on electronic commerce and other kinds of commerce, what is the level that you think will be necessary in order to fulfill the objectives of revenue neutrality?

Mr. LINDER. Since we are replacing income tax, which is tax-inclusive of what you earn, the inclusive basis is 23 percent of what you spend. If you treat it as a sales tax, as a tax-exclusive rate, it would be 29.9 percent.

Mr. DOGGETT. So under your—it would be what, now?

Mr. LINDER. 29.9 percent.

Mr. DOGGETT. Under your best-case scenario as a sponsor of this legislation, then it would be 29, almost 30 percent that would be imposed now for the first time as a Federal revenue source on electronic commerce along with these other sources. To an Internet start-up company that is not earning any revenues at present, in fact, is having losses, this is a real change in their tax situation, isn't it? They are not paying——

Mr. LINDER. No, actually not. Actually not.

Mr. DOGGETT.—taxes now. Now they will be involved.

Mr. LINDER. No. They only collect the tax. The consumer pays the tax.

Mr. DOGGETT. I see. But if there is no income tax being imposed on many of these Internet start-ups, they don't have any tax to pass on to their consumers at present, do they?

Mr. LINDER. They are paying the payroll tax. They are paying it right now.

Mr. DOGGETT. All right. And I want to have some discussion about the payroll tax with you as well. But you do see the more we rely on electronic commerce, you feel, perhaps contrary to the attitude of those who supported the Internet Tax Freedom Act, that we should look at electronic commerce as a major source of Federal revenue.

Mr. LINDER. I think we should treat it the same as the fellow down the street. But let me repeat that the bill that we passed to delay taxation on the Internet has nothing to do with sales taxes. You can collect sales taxes on the Internet today if the local community chooses to do that. It is only the access charges we have the moratorium on.

Mr. DOGGETT. Well, there is some dispute about the Internet Tax Freedom Act and what it does and does not do. But it is pretty clear that Governor Gilmore is seeking a tax-free zone on the Internet——

Mr. LINDER. Yes, he is.

Mr. DOGGETT.—to the exclusion of any sales taxes, and you obviously disagree with him in his approach and feel that we should apply a sales tax not only for the States but for the Federal Government on all this kind of commerce, just as you would to non-Internet commerce.

Mr. LINDER. That is exactly correct. I think the Government ought to be neutral.

Mr. DOGGETT. Now, with reference to the payroll tax, if I might ask you, Mr. Peterson, about that. There are many constituents that I have had—and I am sure each of you as well—who have always viewed Social Security as a little different from other types of Government programs. In fact, I have had even a few who have said let's get the Government out of Social Security. And that is based in large measure on the feeling out there that people pay into Social Security as a form of public or social insurance and that they have a stake in Social Security and preserving Social Security as a result of their own payments—much like premiums into a private insurance program.

Isn't there a danger that if we eliminate entirely those kind of payments and rely exclusively on general revenue to finance Social Security that we will undermine that relationship between people and Social Security and perhaps permit those who have never supported Social Security to undermine and destroy Social Security?

Mr. PETERSON. Well, I guess you could make that argument, but I think a bigger concern is that down the road they are projecting we are going to have 100 percent more people on Social Security and only 17 percent more people working.

Now, I would argue that if we don't change this system, we have an unsustainable situation because, as you know, we have a pay-as-you-go system. And so, you know, if you look at that, you are talking about a payroll tax of 30 percent. And I think that is a lot bigger danger to the system than what we are talking about here.

So I would argue that one of the best things we can do for Social Security and Medicare is to change the way we raise this money. Instead of basing it on employment, which is diminishing in relation to the people that are retired, base it on what people spend. I think that is a much better way to do it.

And this whole idea that somehow or another 7.65 percent or 15.3 percent equates into exactly what the Medicare and Social Security should be is not true. We have only set those rates to cover what we projected in the future was going to be the needs of the system, which is not necessarily related to what we are actually paying people.

My grandfather retired in the 1950s. He paid in like $2,000 and lived to be 90 years old and drew out hundreds of thousands of dollars. And we have all kinds of examples of that.

So, you know, I understand where you are coming from, and there has been a lot of rhetoric that has backed everybody into this corner. But the truth of the matter is this is a pay-as-you-go system, and it is going to fall apart.

Mr. DOGGETT. I thank you for your response.

Chairman ARCHER. The gentleman's time has expired—has long since expired.

The Chair believes that it probably would be wise for the committee to stand in recess for about 45 minutes, and, gentlemen, all of the members have inquired of you, so you are excused. And when we return, we will have our first panel up as witnesses.

Mr. LINDER. Thank you, Mr. Chairman.

Mr. PETERSON. Thank you.

[Recess.]

Chairman ARCHER. The committee is not going to come to order, but just for notifying those who are here, those two buzzers mean we have a vote on the floor, and we will go vote, and when we come back, whatever members are here, we will proceed with the hearing. But we will continue to be in recess until we return from this vote.

[Recess.]

Chairman ARCHER. The committee will come to order.

The Chair invites the next witness panel to come have seats at the witness table: Mr. Linbeck, Mr. McCracken, Mr. Rooth, Mr. Kouplen, and Mr. Martin.

Mr. Linbeck, if you would be our lead-off witness, and I would ask each of you gentlemen if you will identify yourselves for the record before you commence your testimony. We will have that available. And, Mr. Linbeck, welcome to the committee. In fact, welcome to all of you. And, Mr. Linbeck, if you are ready, you may commence.

STATEMENT OF LEO E. LINBECK, JR., CHAIRMAN, LINBECK CORPORATION, HOUSTON, TEXAS, AND VOLUNTARY CHAIRMAN, AMERICANS FOR FAIR TAXATION, HOUSTON, TEXAS

Mr. LINBECK. Thank you very much, Mr. Chairman.

My name is Leo Linbeck. I am from Houston, Texas. I am chairman of Linbeck Corporation, a family-owned business engaged in the construction industry. I am also serving as voluntary chairman of Americans for Fair Taxation.

Americans for Fair Taxation was founded about 4 years ago for the purpose of doing research, both market and academic, into what could be an appropriate replacement system for the current income tax system. We devoted considerable time and resources in going to the consumer, the taxpayer, and asking them what it is they value about the current system and what it is they dislike about the current system and what they would believe to be an appropriate body of contents to be embedded in a new tax system, in a replacement tax system.

This took about 3 and a half years and it engaged an iterative process out of which we learned from the consumer what it is they valued, and then we asked the academic community to give us their analysis as to whether or not what we learned in the market research was economically efficacious.

After having done that for the period of time I described, about 3 to 3 and a half years, we then took what we considered to be the product that had been gleaned from that research and did market testing. And we went to three cities in the first instance—Bakersfield, California, Traverse City, Michigan, and Charleston, South Carolina—and did testing to determine if people know about the system, what would their attitude be in respect thereto, and we found that their attitude changed 21 points, which we were told by experts, of which I am not one, that is a significant movement in attitude.

We then tested the system in 31 different markets to discern if people would, in fact, when they learned about it, want to become involved in furthering the interest of that particular system. And from that exercise we learned that they were very interested in doing that to the extent that in a 3-week period we generated approximately 200,000 phone calls and hits on the website seeking additional information.

We then did the third level of testing to determine if when people knew about it and they were informed enough to become members of Americans for Fair Taxation, would they, in fact, contact their elected Representative to make known to their Representative their wish to bring into law the Fair Tax. We were very pleased with the results we generated from that effort, the results of which were very, very significant. A Senator from New York received over 12,000 phone calls in 2 weeks, which he reported to me was an extraordinary response.

That is basically the background. It is an effort undertaken in the private sector exclusively. There were three of us at the outset who embarked on that research journey, and we are, as I said, private citizens. We are involved in business, civic, and charitable activities. But none of us are experts in the field of taxation.

What we learned at the end of the day is that there are four essential elements to the Fair Tax. Number one is that when people understand that you eliminate the sales tax, that is by far the most important factor in garnering their support. We learned, and did not know at the outset, that a very small percentage of people itemize, less than 30 percent of the taxpayers on average itemize. And for the person who works for wages, we learned that approximately 60 percent of that non-itemizing group, the payroll tax is the largest tax. And we found that when people understood that the payroll tax would one of the elements of the existing system that would be eliminated, it greatly enhanced their enthusiasm for the total replacement of the income tax system.

The second most important feature is the rebate. The rebate is framed in a manner that permits a family to receive in advance a rebate equal to the amount of tax that will be due in that month in the purchase of essential goods and services. We examined in our research a variety of ways in which to deal with the problem of the regressivity that is perceived to be embedded in a sales tax, and found that a universal rebate on essential goods and services was the most efficient.

The third element that is most important in the hierarchy of interest is that there be no exceptions and no exclusions. People are very, very concerned about the complexity of the system they wish to replace.

And, finally, the need for a constitutional amendment to be certain that there is not both an income tax and a sales tax.

Mr. Chairman, we appreciate the chance to be here with you today. We look forward to any questions, and we urge the Committee on Ways and Means to favorably consider the Fair Tax and move it on the track after hearings to a vote on the floor.

Thank you very much, sir.

[The prepared statement follows:]

Statement of Leo E. Linbeck, Jr., Chairman, Linbeck Corporation, Houston, Texas and Voluntary Chairman, Americans for Fair Taxation, Houston, Texas

I would like to thank you, Mr. Chairman and members of the committee for the opportunity to testify before your committee on replacing the current tax system. I am the Chairman of Linbeck Corporation and voluntary Chairman of Americans for Fair Taxation (AFT). AFT is a grass roots citizens organization, based in Houston Texas, dedicated to replacing the current tax system with the FairTax. I am testifying today on behalf of AFT.

The FairTax

The FairTax was introduced on a bi-partisan basis by Representatives John Linder and Collin Peterson during the first session of this Congress. The FairTax will repeal individual income taxes, corporate income taxes, all payroll taxes (including

44

Social Security, Medicare and self-employment taxes) and the estate and gift tax. It would replace these taxes with a 23 percent national retail sales tax on all goods and services sold to consumers.

Individuals will no longer file tax returns. Businesses will collect and remit the sales tax in a manner similar to that in 45 states and the District of Columbia.

The FairTax is a tax on final consumption. Business to business transactions will not be taxed since those goods and services will be taxed when the goods and services into which they are incorporated are finally sold to consumers. Education and training expenses will be treated as an investment in human capital and not taxed. Exports will not be taxed. Imported goods will be taxed when they are sold at retail in the U.S.

The FairTax is Progressive

Unlike the present tax system which taxes many poor people, the FairTax will literally untax every poor person in America. This is because the FairTax will provide every household in America with a rebate of sales tax paid on necessities. Thus, the FairTax is progressive and every family is protected from tax on essential goods and services. Because of the rebate, those below the poverty line will have negative effective tax rates and lower middle income families will enjoy low effective tax rates. The table below shows the annual allowances and rebate amounts.

Fair Tax Rebate Amounts for Calendar Year 2000

Family Size	HHS Poverty Level (1).	Single Person Fair Tax Annual Consumption Allowance.	Single Person Annual Rebate	Single Person Monthly Rebate	Married Couple Fair Tax Annual Consumption Allowance (Married Couple).	Married Couple Annual Rebate	Married Couple Monthly Rebate
1	$8,350	$8,350	$1,921	$160	$8,350	$1,921	$160
2	$11,250	$11,250	$2,588	$216	$16,700	$3,841	$320
3	$14,150	$14,150	$3,255	$271	$19,600	$4,508	$376
4	$17,050	$17,050	$3,922	$327	$22,500	$5,175	$431
5	$19,950	$19,950	$4,589	$382	$25,400	$5,842	$487
6	$22,850	$22,850	$5,256	$438	$28,300	$6,509	$542
7	$25,750	$25,750	$5,923	$494	$31,200	$7,176	$598
8	$28,650	$28,650	$6,590	$549	$34,100	$7,843	$654

A(1) Federal Register: February 15, 2000 (Volume 65, Number 31, Pages 7555–7557).

46

The rebate will be paid monthly in advance. The total annual rebate amount will be equal to the sales tax rate times the federal poverty level. In addition, because the federal poverty level for a two person household is not twice as high as that for one person, an additional amount will be provided in the case of married couples to prevent any marriage penalty.

The FairTax effective tax rates for families of four at various consumption levels are shown in the figure below.

the figure below.

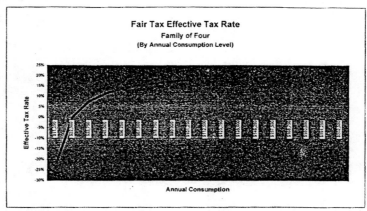

A family of four, for example, could spend $22,500 per year free of tax because they will have received over the course of the year rebates totaling $5,175. $5,175 is the amount of sales tax paid on $22,500 in expenditures. A family spending $45,000 per year will effectively pay tax on only half of their spending and, therefore, have an effective tax rate of 11% or half the FairTax rate.

It would be a mistake to emulate the states when they attempt to achieve progressivity by exempting various categories of goods or services from tax. First, this does not achieve the advertised goal. When food is exempted, for example, not only hamburger is exempted but also filet mignon; not only macaroni and cheese is exempted but also caviar and lobster. In fact, research indicates that 60 percent of the gain from such exemptions goes to the top 40 percent of taxpayers. In addition, these exemptions add complexity to the law as lines are necessarily drawn. Moreover, one set of exemptions will inevitably lead to lobbying to exempt other products. Finally, exempting particular goods or services leads to higher tax rates on those that remain taxable which is economically distorting and inefficient as well as unfair to those companies and workers in the sector that remains taxable.

Administration

The FairTax affords state governments the opportunity to administer the FairTax within their states in return for a fee. The fee will be equal to ★ of one percent of the revenue collected. Alternatively, the state could contract with another state or simply elect for the federal government to collect the tax directly. In our view, smoother administration and fewer start-up difficulties will result if the sales tax is administered by civil servants that have years of experience administering a sales tax.

Americans for Fair Taxation (AFT)

AFT worked hard to develop the FairTax. We engaged economic researchers at leading universities throughout the country. We engaged professors of law. We conducted focus group research with demographically diverse groups of citizens in many different geographic locations to determine what attributes the American people wanted in a tax system. The result of these efforts was the FairTax.

We have now begun the process of bringing the FairTax to the attention of the public. AFT now has over 250,000 members. AFT's grass roots support is growing every day. We aim to soon have an AFT chapter in every State and Congressional district in the country.

Economic Impact of the FairTax

The FairTax will have a dramatic positive impact on the standard of living of the American people and lead to higher rates of economic growth. The current tax system punishes people who are trying to improve the financial position of their families by working, saving or investing. It is a huge barrier to upward mobility. The FairTax will stop the punitive taxation of work inherent in the income and payroll tax and end the multiple taxation of savings and investment. The FairTax will end the taxation of investment in education.

Instead it will tax consumption. It has the broadest possible consumption base. Therefore, the FairTax has the lowest possible marginal tax rate in a consumption tax that protects the public from sales tax on expenditures to purchase essential goods and service.

Economists anticipate the FairTax will lead to much higher levels of savings and investment which in turn will lead to greater productivity and output. Work by Harvard economist Dale Jorgenson shows a quick 9 to 13 percent increase in the GDP.[1] Similarly, Boston University economist Laurence Kotlikoff predicts a 7 to 14 percent increase.[2] The FairTax will eliminate the present tax system's bias against savings and investment. Thus, savings and investment will increase. A larger capital stock means that people will have more capital to work with embodying the latest technology and their productivity will increase. Higher productivity, in turn, will increase real wages.

Businesses, in the final analysis cannot pay wages higher than the productivity of their workers warrants. If they do, they will quickly go bankrupt. Thus, the key to increasing real wages is higher productivity. The key to higher productivity is two fold. Education and capital investment. The FairTax makes both education and capital investment more attractive.

Education

The FairTax is the most education friendly of any tax reform proposal and is much more supportive of education than current law. The FairTax embodies the principle that investments in people (human capital) and investments in things (physical capital) should be treated comparably. The current tax system, in stark contrast, treats education expenditures very unfavorably.

Today, to pay $10,000 in college or private school tuition, a typical middle class American must earn $15,540 looking only at federal income taxes and the employee payroll tax.[3] The amount one must earn to pay the $10,000 is really more like $20,120 once employer and state income taxes are taken into account.[4]

The FairTax does not tax education expenditures.[5] Education can be paid for with pre-tax dollars. This is the equivalent of making educational expense deductible against both the income tax and payroll taxes today. Thus, under the FairTax, a family will need to earn $10,000 to pay $10,000 in tuition, making education much more affordable.[6] The FairTax makes education about half as expensive to American families compared to today.

Education is the best means for the vast majority of people to improve their economic position. It is the most reliable means that people have to invest in them-

---

[1] Dale W. Jorgenson, Economic Impact of the National Retail Sales Tax, National Tax Research Committee. See also, "The Economic Impact of Fundamental Taxing Consumption," Dale W. Jorgenson, Testimony before the House Ways and Means Committee, March 27, 1996 and "The Economic Impact of Fundamental Tax Reform," Dale W. Jorgenson, Testimony before the House Ways and Means Committee, June 6, 1995.

[2] Laurence J. Kotlikoff, Replacing the U.S. Federal Tax System with a Retail Sales Tax: Macroeconomic and Distributional Impacts, National Tax Research Committee. See also, "The Economic Impact of Replacing Federal Income Taxes with a Sales Tax," Laurence J. Kotlikoff, April 15, 1993, Cato Institute Policy Analysis.

[3] $15,540 less 7.65 percent in employee Social Security ($1,189) and Medicare payroll taxes less 28 percent in federal income taxes ($4,351) leaves $10,000.

[4] Economists generally agree that the employer share of payroll taxes is borne by the employee in the form of lower wages. This figure assumes that employees bear the burden of the employer payroll tax and that they are in a seven percent state and local income tax bracket. $20,120 less $5,634 in income tax (28 percent), $3079 in payroll taxes (15.3 percent) and $1,408 in state and local income taxes (7 percent) leaves $10,000.

[5] H.R. 2525 defines education and training to mean "tuition for primary, secondary, or postsecondary level education, and job related training courses." It excludes "room, board, sports activities, recreational activities, hobbies, games, arts or crafts or cultural activities."

[6] If the states kept their income taxes rather than replacing them with a sales tax, then the family would need to earn $10,753, about half of what they would need to earn today.

selves and improve their earning potential. Yet the tax system today punishes people who invest in education, virtually doubling its cost. Only the FairTax would remove this impediment to upward mobility. No other tax reform plan will do so.

The FairTax is More Fair than the Current Tax System

The FairTax is more fair than the present tax system. Rather than holding people down by taxing them for working, saving, investing or getting an education, the FairTax taxes people when they consume for their own benefit above the necessities of life. The FairTax eliminates special preferences, credits and deductions for politically favored interests. It treats everyone the same. It has no loopholes.

International Competitiveness

Under the FairTax, imported goods and domestically produced goods will pay the same U.S. tax. This stands in stark contrast to the present system, where U.S. companies and workers must pay income tax and payroll taxes but foreign goods enter the U.S. entirely free of any tax other than whatever modest customs duties are levied.

The FairTax will, by its very nature, be border-adjusted.[7] Exports will not be taxed since they are not sold at retail in the U.S., but imports will be taxed when sold at retail in the U.S. or when brought into the U.S. by a consumer.[8]

A national sales tax will comply with World Trade Organization (WTO) rules. WTO is the successor to the General Agreement for Tariffs and Trade (GATT). Under WTO rules, an indirect tax may be border adjusted while a direct tax may not.[9] Since a sales tax is indisputably an indirect tax, this border adjustment feature will pose no difficulty. Foreign value added taxes, also indirect taxes, are typically border adjusted. Income taxes are direct taxes and may not be border adjusted.[10] Many on this committee may find this aspect of a national sales tax of particular interest since the WTO just found the Foreign Sales Corporation (FSC) export incentives to be a violation of WTO rules.

U.S. businesses will be much less likely to locate their plants overseas and foreign companies will come to the United States. Americans will be employed building these new plants and Americans will be employed in the new plants. America will become the most attractive place in the developed world in which to do business. We will attract more and higher paying jobs.

The FairTax is less Intrusive

The FairTax will be less intrusive. Rather than having to report almost every aspect of their lives to the federal government, Americans will be relieved of such intrusions. April 15th will be just another Spring day. The privacy of the American people will be enhanced considerably when the FairTax is enacted.

The income tax is collected with a heavy hand. In 1995, the IRS assessed over 34 million civil penalties on American taxpayers in an effort to force compliance with the tax system. Of these, about 4.1 million were forgiven. The present system requires that we inform on each other. Americans must provide over one billion information returns to the IRS (primarily 1099s and W–2s). Under the FairTax, all of this would no longer be necessary.

The FairTax respects the privacy rights of the American people to a vastly greater degree than the income tax. No longer will Americans have to report the details of their lives to the federal government. No longer will they have to confess to whom they gave money, where they earned money, what medical problems they had and so forth.

The FairTax will reduce Evasion

Under the income tax, evasion is a major, continuing and growing problem. Notwithstanding a much larger Internal Revenue Service (IRS), more burdensome information reporting requirements, increasing stiff and numerous penalties and a

---

[7] Border adjusted is a value added tax (VAT) term. Since VATs, unlike the sales tax, impose a tax on all stages of production, a VAT must rebate the tax on earlier stages of production when goods are exported to achieve a zero tax rate on exports. This is called border adjustment. Because a sales tax does not impose any tax on goods unless sold at retail, there is no need for a border tax adjustment rebate.

[8] As with domestically produced goods, imported capital goods and other business purchases would not be taxed immediately. But the output of goods produced by capital goods would ultimately be taxed when consumption goods were produced and sold.

[9] See Agreement on Subsidies and Countervailing Measures, Annex 1.

[10] The status of the flat tax, which is a subtraction method value added tax but administered like an income tax, is unclear under WTO rules but it seems highly likely that it would be deemed a direct tax given its similarity in appearance and administration to an income tax.

host of legislative initiatives, the problem is getting worse. Based on IRS figures, tax evasion has increased by 67 percent during the past 11 years. As a percentage of Gross Domestic Product (GDP), tax evasion has reached 2.0 percent compared to 1.6 percent in 1981. Taxes evaded continue to be in the range of 22 to 23 percent of income taxes collected. These IRS figures *do not* include taxes lost on illegal sources of income. The tax gap now is about $200 billion.

Tax evasion will decline under the FairTax because the chance of evaders being caught will increase and the incentive to cheat will decline. The FairTax will reduce the number of tax filers by roughly 90 percent. Thus, if enforcement resources remain comparable, audit rates will rise. Moreover, since the audits will be much simpler than current audits, audit rates will rise still further. Therefore the chance of evasion being detected will increase.

Since marginal tax rates are much lower under the FairTax than under present law, especially for small businesses and sole proprietorships where disproportionate evasion occurs today, the benefit to cheating will be lower. Today, if a self-employed taxpayer fails to report $1,000 they will benefit by $433 ($280 because of the income tax and $153 due to the self-employment tax). Under the FairTax, they would benefit by $230.

In short, the gains from evasion would decrease and the potential costs of evasion from detection and enforcement would increase. Thus, the amount of tax evasion can be expected to decline markedly.

Compliance Costs will Fall

The FairTax is a simple tax. The administrative burdens placed on businesses are much less. In fact, they are comparable to tracking revenue for income tax purposes. There will be no more alternative minimum tax, no more depreciation schedules, no more complex employee benefit rules, no more complex qualified account and pension rules, no more complex income sourcing and expense allocation rules, no more foreign tax credit, no more complex rules governing corporate acquisitions, divisions and other reorganizations, no more uniform capitalization requirements, no more withholding and the list goes on. Businesses will simply need to keep track of how much they sold to consumers.

Compliance costs will, therefore, fall under the FairTax. Today, according to the Tax Foundation, we spend about $250 billion each year filling out forms, hiring tax lawyers, accountants, benefits consultants, collecting information needed only for tax purposes and the like. These unnecessary costs amount to about $850 for every man, woman and child in America. To the extent these costs are incurred by businesses, they must be recovered and are embedded in the cost of everything that we buy. The money we spend on unnecessary compliance costs is money we might as well burn for all of the good it does us. The Tax Foundation has estimated that compliance costs would drop by about 90 percent under a national sales tax.

The FairTax is Simple, Understandable and Transparent

The FairTax is simple, understandable and transparent. People understand the FairTax. They don't understand the present tax system. Even tax professionals don't understand the present system. Money magazine, for instance, each year asks 50 CPAs to fill out a relatively straight forward middle class family's tax return. Each year they get 50 or nearly 50 wrong answers. Of course, the answers are only wrong if you believe the magazine's tax advisors are better than the survey participants. Today a huge proportion of the overall tax burden is hidden from the ordinary taxpayers view. Under the FairTax, people will for the first time actually understand their tax burden and have confidence that their fellow citizens are bearing their fair share.

The FairTax will help Charities

Charities will thrive as never before—for two reasons. First, the FairTax provides the equivalent of a deduction, for itemizers and non-itemizers alike, against both the income and payroll tax. Remember, all the charitable deduction does is allow someone to make their contribution from pre income tax dollars (but after payroll tax dollars). The FairTax will enable all Americans to give to their favorite charity free of income tax, free of payroll tax and free of sales tax. Second, total philanthropy as a percentage of GDP has held steady at around 2 % for at least two decades. As people become more prosperous, they give more to philanthropic causes. The FairTax will enlarge the economy dramatically and will lead to a corresponding increase in charitable giving.

Pre-Tax Prices will Decline

Costs are one of the primary determining factors for prices. One of the costs that businesses must recover if they are to stay in business is taxes. Dale Jorgenson of Harvard University estimates that the income tax and payroll tax are embedded in the price of goods and services to such an extent that they raise prices by 20 to 30 percent. His results are shown in the figure below. When these taxes are repealed by the FairTax, costs will go down and competition will quickly drive prices down 20 to 30 percent depending on the product. In addition, although Dr. Jorgenson research did not consider these effects, higher levels of investment will make the economy more productive and the elimination of loopholes that distort the economy will make it more efficient, These effects will be seen both in the form of higher real wages and lower prices. Moreover, lower compliance costs will reduce costs and prices still further.

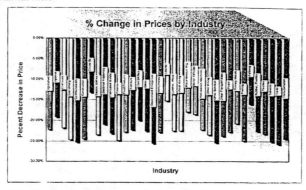

The FairTax helps Homeowners

Homeowners will do very well under the FairTax. Homeowners will have the equivalent of a supercharged mortgage interest deduction because under the FairTax mortgage interest can be paid free of sales tax and free of income and payroll taxes. In terms of the current system, it would be as if the mortgage interest deduction was allowable against payroll taxes. In addition, existing homeowners will be able to make their principal payments with tax free dollars. Buyers of newly constructed homes will have to pay sales tax, just as they must pay for their house from after tax dollars today, but the marginal tax rate is lower under the FairTax. In addition, interest rates will fall by about 25 percent because lenders will no longer have to charge a tax premium to make up for the tax on interest income. Once interest is no longer taxable nor deductible, interest rates will quickly fall toward the current tax-exempt rate. Homeownership will be more affordable and prospective homeowners will be able to save their downpayment more quickly under the FairTax.

Financial Markets

The FairTax will increase the market value of long-term financial assets such as stocks, real estate and non-callable bonds. The price of those assets reflects the fact that the future income stream of those assets will be taxed. When that tax is removed, the future income stream will increase and therefore the present discounted value of those future income streams will increase as well. Thus, the market value of the assets will increase considerably.

Conclusion

Support for the FairTax is growing rapidly. Once people understand the FairTax and grasp all of the positive things it would mean for them and for the country, they generally support it. AFT will continue to bring the FairTax to the attention of the public.

AFT looks forward to working with this committee to pass the FairTax. It is in your power to move beyond the current indefensible tax system and replace it with a tax system more in keeping with what the public wants. We appreciate the opportunity to present our views to you today. Thank you.

Chairman ARCHER. Thank you, Mr. Linbeck.
Mr. McCracken?

STATEMENT OF TODD McCRACKEN, PRESIDENT, NATIONAL SMALL BUSINESS UNITED

Mr. McCRACKEN. Mr. Chairman and members of the committee, my name is Todd McCracken, and I am president of National Small Business United, the Nation's oldest small business advocacy organization.

NSBU was founded when the income was just 23 years old, with only two pages in forms and several pages of instructions. NSBU has not grown at the exponential rate of the income tax laws, but we do now represent 65,000 businesses nationwide.

In 1997, our diverse bipartisan 32-member small business board of trustees decided it was time for NSBU to take a hard look at a new tax system rather than just continue to take easy potshots at the system we have now. After a year-long process in which the current system and various alternatives were held up and examined from all sides, our initially skeptical board finally selected the Fair Tax as the best possible system for small businesses, without a single dissenting vote.

Why? At every stage of a business' life, it faces significant tax obstacles. At the start-up level, savings are taxed and start-up costs are not deductible, and capital investments are made from after-tax dollars and then taxed multiple times, when the income is earned and when the underlying asset that generates that income stream is sold. They are taxed when growing because the Government takes an increasing share of income as more money is made. They are taxed when exporting because U.S. taxes raise the price of our goods relative to foreign goods. They are taxed when they add jobs because our extraordinarily high payroll taxes increase costs of hiring. Family businesses are discouraged because they are taxed when they are sold or passed on.

I would like to call special attention to the current payroll tax burden that small businesses and their employees must endure. It is an enormous tax that receives relatively little attention given the share of revenues it accounts for. In fact, a survey by NSBU and Arthur Andersen found that small businesses cite payroll taxes as their most significant tax burden.

Payroll taxes, after all, must be paid whether a business is making money or not, and it is a tax on workers, the lifeblood of any small business.

Finally, we have the extraordinary complexity of the current code. I would submit to you that the entrepreneurial community is more vexed by the labyrinth that our system creates than it is by the amount of taxes paid. We are the only part of the taxpaying public that sees every aspect of the tax system: tax withholding and filing, estate taxes and capital gains taxes, among others.

Since the Fair Tax abolishes all Federal income, FICA, estate, and capital gains taxes, it would allow small businesses to prosper as never before in this country. The Fair Tax would allow businesses to begin with savings put aside with pre-tax dollars. It would allow them to grow unfettered by the income tax and without an eye on the capital gains tax. It would allow them to hire without discouragement from the payroll tax. It would allow them to export, unfettered by punitive American taxes on our exports.

It would allow them to make capital investments unfettered by hidden costs in the capital assets. It would discontinue the charade of taxing income multiple times. Most importantly, it would repeal the self-employment and payroll taxes which are the most despised by entrepreneurs.

Small business owners would have greater access to capital, the lifeblood of a free economy. Small business owners would be free to pass their businesses on to their children.

Compliance costs would diminish. Individuals not in business would never have to file a tax return again, and business returns would be vastly simpler. More than 7,000 incomprehensible sections of the Internal Revenue Code would be exchanged for one simple question: How much is sold to consumers? This question is asked of retailers in 45 States in our Nation today. Ninety percent of our $250 billion annual compliance bill would just disappear.

We are often asked why retailers should support this plan. No single industry is more burdened by the multitude of State and Federal tax laws than retailers. Retailers today are both tax collectors and taxpayers. Under the Fair Tax, there will be no more uniform inventory capitalization requirements, no more complex Government rules on employee benefits and retirement plans, no more tax depreciation schedules, no more tax rules governing mergers and acquisitions, and no more international tax provisions. Retailers will have "found" money in lower compliance costs. Retailers will also receive an administration fee for complying with the greatly simplified law.

It is for all these reasons that there is increasing support for the Fair Tax among small businesses. In our most recent survey, we found that a national sales tax had surpassed a flat tax as the preferred form of tax reform among small business owners. Even more interestingly, support for a sales tax among retailers in the survey was almost a high as support among manufacturers, though small retailers still gave the flat tax their narrow support.

In conclusion, the Fair Tax would reinstate the novel concept that Americans have a right to understand the law to which they are subject. This would be a boon for small business that quite often lack the legal and accounting staffs to be in compliance with the tax code. It would enhance compliance costs so honest taxpayers pay less.

After the process that we went through, we are confident that as this committee understands the essential differences in the proposal, you will favor the Fair Tax plan. We are confident that the more you know about the Fair Tax, the more you will support it.

We want to thank you for the ability to appear here today, and especially want to thank you for holding these very significant hearings. You can do nothing more profoundly significant for the small business community and the entire Nation than to continue to push forward with fundamental tax reform.

[The prepared statement follows:]

Statement of Todd McCracken, President, National Small Business United

Mr. Chairman and Members of the Ways and Means Committee:

My name is Todd McCracken, and I am President of National Small Business United (NSBU), the nation's oldest national small business advocacy organization.

Mr. Chairman, NSBU was founded when the income tax was just 23 years old—with only two pages in forms and several pages of instructions. NSBU has not grown at the exponential rate of the income tax laws, but we now represent 65,000 businesses nationwide. We represent the varied tapestry of the America's entrepreneurs, from immigrants seeking a more fertile environments in which to grow their dreams to family businesses that have remained for generations. The average size of our membership is 12 employees. We are nonpartisan. We do not ask whether the policies we endorse are republican or democrat: we ask whether the policies enable entrepreneurs to thrive.

NSBU applauds this Committee for having the courage to explore the FairTax. In February, a national survey conducted by American Express confirmed what NSBU already knew. The survey showed that 74 percent of entrepreneurs consider tax reform a top priority. But since the vast majority of Americans share commons dislike for our present system, it is easier to demagogue the current system than to reach consensus on what a new and more ideal system should look like.

NSBU leads entrepreneurial organizations not only by defining the principles on which tax reform should be based, but lending our full support for a specific proposal: the FairTax national sales tax plan. In 1997, our 32-member small business Board of Trustees decided that it was time for NSBU to take a hard look at a new tax system, rather than just continuing to take easy pot-shots at the system we have now. After a year-long process in which the current system and various alternatives—various flat tax plans and other forms of a sales tax among them—were held up and examined from all sides, our initially skeptical Board finally selected the FairTax as the best possible system for small businesses, without a single dissenting vote. If you knew this diverse group of independent-minded entrepreneurs like we do, you would realize just how remarkable this vote was. After we all had a chance to ask our questions and have them thoughtfully answered, this decision, that many of us thought we could never reach, suddenly seemed obvious.

We would like to explain to the committee why NSBU, consisting of firms in all sectors, including service firms and retailers, endorsed a national sales tax plan. We want to contrast the FairTax with such plans as the flat tax and other sales tax plans. And last, we want to suggest the next steps this committee should take if it is serious about considering reform.

The Current System: Fundamentally Broken

Discouraging Entrepreneurs at Every Level. Most entrepreneurs—that is unless they make a career of selling tax shelters—correctly see our system as punishing each step towards the American dream. At every stage of a business' life, it faces significant tax obstacles. At the start-up level savings are taxed, and start-up costs are not deductible. Capital investments are made from after-tax dollars and then taxed multiple times, when the income is earned and when the underlying asset that generates that income stream is sold. They are taxed when growing because the government takes an increasing share of income as more money is made. They are taxed when exporting, because U.S. taxes raise the price of our goods relative to foreign goods. They are taxed when they add jobs, because our extraordinarily high payroll taxes increase costs of hiring. Family businesses are discouraged because they are taxed when they are sold. And finally, the owner gets to meet the undertaker and the IRS on the same day as the government effects a leveraged buy-out of the businesses.

The Burden of Payroll Taxes. But I think this committee is certainly familiar with the current income tax code and the many compliance obstacles it creates. So, I would like to call special attention to the current payroll tax (primarily FICA) burden that small businesses and their employees must endure. It is an enormous tax that receives relatively little attention given the share of revenues it accounts for. In fact, a survey by NSBU and Arthur Andersen found that small businesses cite payroll taxes as their most significant tax burden.

The U.S. has made a fundamental shift toward payroll taxes in the last 30 years. In 1995, 38 percent of all federal revenues came from payroll taxes, compared to just 14 percent (of a lower tax bill) 40 years ago. From 1970 to 1990, business received nine social security (FICA) tax increases totaling 60%, three unemployment (FUTA) increases totaling 94%, three FUTA base increases totaling 133%, and 19 FICA base increases totaling 677%.

54

At first glance, payroll taxes might seem to be an equitable form of taxation. The unemployed are not taxed, and larger businesses with more employees are taxed more than smaller businesses with fewer employees. However, most small businesses are much more labor intensive than their larger counterparts. Payroll taxes cause these small businesses to be taxed at a higher effective rate than larger, more capital-intensive firms. Moreover, holders of corporations organized under Subchapter "S" (which are almost always small) have been forced to pay both sides of this tax, making for a substantial tax increase.

Businesses must pay their payroll taxes whether or not they make a profit. The fact that this huge tax must be paid regardless of the financial condition of the company creates substantial problems. First, it discourages new businesses. Most new businesses lose money in their early days, and payroll taxes amount to one more debt that must be somehow financed. Second, it discourages employment. The only way that a business in a financial bind can reduce payroll taxes is to reduce payroll; this means fewer jobs or lower wages.

A payroll tax amounts to a tax on employment. Today, businesses and their employees pay about 15% out of every wage dollar (below the cap) in FICA taxes. Through this substantial hike in the cost of hiring and working, the payroll tax reverses the needed incentives in the American economy. Taxing businesses for hiring an employee clearly discourages increased employment, which is damaging to the unemployed, the business, and the economy. And, of course, payroll taxes are the most regressive taxes we have, where only earned income (as opposed to investment income) is taxed, and only earned income up to a certain, annually adjusted level is taxed.

Unnecessary Complexity. Small firms are accountable to a protean system that is so complex simply because we choose to tax savings and investment. We waste an estimated $3.70 in compliance costs for every dollar we pay in taxes. We endure the lion's share of the $250 billion in annual compliance costs, when we cannot pass these essentially fixed costs on to consumers as larger firms can. We endure the lion's share of the more than 34 million civil penalties issued.

Our current tax system is certainly a testament to the indomitable spirit of American entrepreneurs, but it is not enlightened tax policy.

The FairTax: The Best System for Small Business

The FairTax is enlightened policy. Since the FairTax abolishes all federal income, FICA, estate, and capital gains taxes, it would allow small businesses to prosper as never before in this country. By instituting a 23 percent tax on all end-use goods and services, the FairTax would sweep away the burdens of the current tax system and create a new dawn for American entrepreneurship and economic growth.

The Fair Tax would allow businesses to begin with savings put aside with pre-tax dollars. It would allow them to grow unfettered by the income tax, and without an eye on the capital gains tax. It would allow them to hire without discouragement from the payroll tax. It would allow them to export, unfettered by punitive American taxes on our exports. It would allow them to make capital investments unfettered by hidden costs in the capital assets. It would not penalize good years and bad by implementing the best of income averaging, a zero rate of tax. It would discontinue the charade of taxing income multiple times. Most importantly, it would repeal the self-employment taxes which are the most despised by entrepreneurs. The Fair Tax would tax Americans on income, but only at the point that they consume that income, not when they invest and save. Small business owners would have greater access to capital, the life-blood of a free economy. Small firm owners would be able to pass their business on to their children.

Simplicity and Lower Compliance Costs. Compliance costs would diminish. Individuals not in business would never have to file a tax return again, and business returns would be vastly simpler. More than 7,000 incomprehensible sections of the Internal Revenue Code, would be exchanged for one simple question: how much is sold to consumers? This question is asked of retailers in 45 states of our Nation today, so the additional burden on these businesses would be negligible. Ninety percent of our $250 billion annual compliance bill would disappear.

Greater Visibility and Understanding. As complexity disappears, we would reinstate the novel concept that Americans have a right to understand the law to which they are subject. Moreover, they will immediately see and understand the tax rates and any changes that occur. The mentality of "Don't tax you; don't tax me; tax that fellow behind the tree" would be gone. The current complexity of the code leaves most Americans, rightly or wrongly, feeling that they bear an unfair share of the tax burden. The poor believe that advantages must lie with those who are more well-off. The wealthy see their high marginal rates and eliminated deductions and feel singled out by the tax system. And the middle class assume that credits for the poor and loopholes for the wealthy mean that they alone should the country's tax burden. While there are both fallacies and accuracies in each group's assumptions, the unfortunate side effect is a polarization of the country and a universal feeling of victimization. And it should be clear to any rational observer that this feeling leads to tax avoidance and cheating on an unprecedented scale. If we can remove these hard feelings about the tax code, we can markedly improve compliance and give a boost to national comity at the same time.

The FairTax would do just that, by making visible the taxes now buried in goods and services. We would have a uniform tax for all the world to see and understand. How would the rich guy avoid some taxes? Only by saving and investing, which helps us all. But some day, he or his descendants will spend his profits, and taxes will be collected. At the same time, those less fortunate will receive a rebate lowering their total tax bill and effective tax rate, even if they don't save a nickel. This is a system all Americans can understand and be united behind—and voluntarily pay. The tax system would achieve greater enforceability with less intrusiveness. Today, more than $200 billion in income taxes, over 20 percent of the total collected, are not voluntarily paid.

Economic Growth. Almost every researcher who has examined the FairTax have concluded that the U.S. will experience significantly higher economic growth rates if this plan is enacted. Specifically, Harvard's Dale Jorgenson predicted a quick nine to thirteen percent increased in the GDP, while Boston University's Laurence Kotlikoff predicts a seven to fourteen percent increase. Essentially, this growth will happen because the tax code will no longer discourage work, investment, savings, and education. Even studies that start with more pessimistic assumptions, like that by Nathan Associates for the National Retail Institute, predict greater long-term economic growth, though to a smaller degree than others predict.

There are those, of course, who fear that the FairTax will discourage consumption and thereby cause a drop in economic growth. The FairTax is, after all, a tax on consumption, and we always get less of whatever we tax (like work, savings, investment, etc.). But there are several salient facts that mitigate, even eliminate, this fear. First, institution of the FairTax would mean that consumers have their entire paycheck to spend, free of any tax withholdings or FICA payments. Consumers would be able to spend this greater income on goods that cost no less than they do currently, because economists tell us that the elimination of taxes currently embedded in the price of goods and services will cause that price to go down dramatically. At the same time, the elimination of the tax on interest income will cause interest rates to drop dramatically, probably by about 25 percent. Taken together these two consequences of the FairTax should actually have the effect of increasing consumption.

But there are additional reasons why prices should fall and thereby encourage additional consumption. Since the FairTax will encourage savings and investment, greater investment dollars will be available to improve the productivity of American business, causing prices to drop still more. Greater productivity is likely to lead to greater corporate profits, which is likely to lead to improved stock market gains. The last few years have proven what stock market gains can mean for consumption and continuing economic growth. So, we have been persuaded that these very appropriate concerns are nevertheless unfounded.

Improved Work-Force. Any current survey of the small business community will show finding and keeping qualified workers is their greatest challenge. Businesses cannot find enough workers with specific educational backgrounds, nor can they find sufficient workers with broad-based educational backgrounds. To further compound matters, most small businesses cannot create and maintain their own education and training initiatives the way some larger businesses can. The FairTax comes to the rescue by essentially "un-taxing" education. Currently, a middle class taxpayer must earn $15,540 (ignoring state taxes) to pay $10,000 in tuition. Under the FairTax, only $10,000 must be earned, because education is not taxed.

Improved International Trade Position. The current tax system buries taxes in all sorts of goods and services. But this becomes an especially big problem in the international arena. These embedded taxes mean that American goods and services are more expensive than they otherwise would be, thereby hurting American exports. But it is even worse than that. Many of our competitors impose a Value Added Tax (VAT), which is rebated at the border. That means that we have foreign goods coming into the U.S. which have no embedded taxes, competing with domestic goods with very high embedded taxes. The FairTax reverse this position, creating much greater incentives for goods and services to be produced in the U.S. and making those products much more competitive abroad.

Retailers Aided by FairTax. Why should retailers support it? No single industry is more burdened by the multitude of state and Federal tax laws than retailers.

Retailers are today both tax collectors and taxpayers. Under the FairTax, there will be no more uniform inventory capitalization requirements, no more complex government rules on employee benefits and retirement plans, no more tax depreciation schedules, no more tax rules governing mergers and acquisitions, and no more international tax provisions. Retailers will have "found" money in lower compliance costs.

Under the FairTax retailers will also receive an administration fee for complying with a greatly simplified law. The FairTax actually compensates the industry for compliance burdens. Moreover, the FairTax will encourage uniformity among increasingly disparate state taxing schemes that have pitted small retailers against large direct mailers. As we have seen with state income taxes, states will face great pressure to bring their system into line with the federal standard. The FairTax could lead to a way out of the current stalemate on the internet and sales taxes.

It is for all these reasons that there is increasing support for the FairTax among small businesses. In the most recent survey NSBU conducts with Arthur Andersen, we found that a national sales tax had surpassed a flat tax as the preferred form a tax reform among small business owners. Even more interestingly, support for a sales tax among retailers in this survey was almost as high as support among manufacturers, though small retailers still gave the flat tax their narrow support.

While respected economists haggle over the dimensions of the economic benefits, they are unanimous in their view the FairTax would greatly enhance economic performance by improving the incentives for work and eliminating the current bias against saving and investment. Even the National Retail Institute's study by Nathan Associates shows that the economy would be one to five percent larger under a sales tax than in the absence of reform.

The FairTax Versus the Alternatives

The major alternative to a national sales tax is, of course a flat tax. And, while a sales tax and a flat tax are both improvements over the current system, and both are essentially consumption-based taxes, the sales tax is clearly preferable to small business for two key reasons.

The Flat Tax. First, a sales tax is vastly simpler to administer than a flat tax. While a flat tax creates uniform rates, it still leaves the question of determining income, and still leaves business owners with the need to hire tax advisers and accountants to sort through those remaining rules. And, of course a flat tax leaves in place the requirement for businesses to withhold and file taxes (of both payroll and wage taxes) on behalf of their employees. This system is the source of more civil penalties on small businesses than any other.

Second, a flat tax would have to leave in place the pillars of the income tax system we have today: tax withholding, a central enforcement agency, and the need to define and determine taxable income. Given this scenario, it is not a stretch to imagine that we could readily creep back to the same system we have now. Congress decides to allow an additional deduction or allowance for this or that. How to pay for it? Let's increase the rate, but only for people above a certain income level. Once the dam breaks, there is no turning back. With a sales tax, the entire income infrastructure is dismantled. It is very hard to conceive of it being easily reconstructed; it has an inherent integrity that is much more difficult to breach.

But not all sales taxes are created equal. The FairTax holds special appeal for the small business community for two reasons. First, it eliminates the payroll and self-employment taxes that are the most burdensome on small businesses, and which are easily the most regressive taxes this country has ever imposed. This elimination both greatly helps small business (we discussed the payroll tax burden at length above) and makes the FairTax system much more progressive than competing sales tax plans.

Second, a key pillar of the FairTax is its uniformity. Rather than picking and choosing among end-use products to tax, it taxes everything. Going down a different path, and exempting certain goods or services from taxation would be very dangerous and greatly diminish the support the FairTax has from the small business community.

Conclusions

Defenders of the income tax system fondly quote Oliver Wendell Holmes who said, "taxes are what we pay for a civilized society." But this phrase does not stoically celebrate the 'income tax' per se and was made before the income tax even existed. What Holmes should have added is that a civilized society must also collect taxes in the most civilized manner.

The income tax is the antithesis of a civilized system for entrepreneurs. Unlike many unwise state sales taxes, the FairTax would fully exempt any business inputs from taxation, i.e. all business-to-business transaction would be free of tax. In this way it would remove the mythology that businesses pay taxes as opposed to their owners, employees or consumers. It would make all taxes visible. It would convey the true cost of government to every American on each purchase they make, precluding government from raising taxes other than by changing the rate for all. Quite simply, it would allow businesses to keep the entire profit from their operation and transfer the emphasis of taxation away from income-producing activities to consumption.

The FairTax would reinstate the novel concept that Americans have a right to understand the law to which they are subject. This would be a boon for small businesses that quite often lack the legal and accounting staffs necessary to be in compliance with the tax code. It would enhance compliance so honest taxpayers pay less.

Mr. Chairman, if we can get entrepreneurs who, by genetics I suppose, are independent minded, to agree upon this plan, than your committee can do so also. But in order to do so, you must put aside politics and predilection. We are confident that, as this Committee understands the essential differences in the proposals, you will favor the FairTax plan. Now here is what I ask of you.

First, this Committee must not consider its job done in one hearing. These plans deserve further introspection. Hearings should be conducted on all relevant topics affecting tax reform. We are confident that more you know about the FairTax, the more you will support it.

Second, the Joint Tax Committee and other institutions that analyze distribution should change their means of portraying the burden of consumption taxes. Why do we persist in scoring taxation of savings and investment as a gain? Income is not income until it is consumed. Why not present distributional tables as an alternative on taxes paid over consumption?

Third, we urge all members of this committee to understand the issues presented here. One of the reasons taxes have risen in this nation is because so much is hidden from the consumers on which all taxes ultimately fall. Do not fault the FairTax because it makes these taxes visible.

We want to thank you for the ability to appear here today, and we especially want to thank you for holding these very significant hearings. You can do nothing more profoundly significant for the small business community and the entire nation, than to continue to push forward with fundamental tax reform.

Chairman ARCHER. Thank you, Mr. McCracken. Mr. Rooth?

STATEMENT OF SCOTT ROOTH, REALTOR, CASHIERS, NORTH CAROLINA, CHAIRMAN, PUBLIC POLICY COORDINATING COMMITTEE, AND MEMBER, TAX REFORM WORKING GROUP, NATIONAL ASSOCIATION OF REALTORS

Mr. ROOTH. Mr. Chairman, members of the committee, my name is Scott Rooth, and I am realtor from Cashiers, North Carolina. I am here today on behalf of 760,000 members of the National Association of Realtors, NAR. Currently, I serve as chairman of the Public Policy Coordinating Committee and as a member of the Tax Reform Working Group.

In the tax reform debate, NAR supports the goals of tax reform and substantial simplification because, as self-employed individuals, our members face significant compliance challenges. We emphasize, however, that the tax rules that apply to home ownership, especially since 1997, are among the simplest to administer in the entire tax system. NAR continues to aggressively oppose the flat tax, and as for today's hearings, the National Association of Realtors has taken no official position on H.R. 2525, the Fair Tax proposal advanced by Americans for Fair Taxation. We neither oppose nor support it at this time. We understand that we have been invited here today to share some concerns that we might have and we have identified to Mr. Linbeck.

Some may say that we are here today to protect a special interest. Even if that is true, consider the magnitude of your decisions about how to tax real estate in a new tax system. Today, more than two-thirds of all Americans own their own home. This is an all-time high. The fastest growing category of homeowners is our minority population. Last year, 43 percent of first-time home sales were to minorities and immigrants.

Individuals in every income class own homes. Notably, lower-income families have a greater proportion of their net worth tied up in the home. Federal Reserve data shows that even at the $10,000 to $25,000 income range, 51 percent own their own homes. Real estate is the most widely held asset in our economy. Thus, real estate affects the largest number of households and voters in this country.

NAR believes that changes to the tax system will inevitably have a substantial impact on the value of those homes. We urge you to be very careful in how you make decisions about the taxation of homes and other real estate.

Depending upon how you do the computation, the Fair Tax would impose a sales tax of either 23 or 30 percent on the purchase of a new but not an existing home. NAR has grave reservations about any sales tax plan that would tax the purchase and sale of a home. We embrace and salute Chairman Archer's publicly stated view about the consumption tax systems, and he has clearly stated that the purchase of a home should be treated as an investment and not be taxed.

NAR rejects any proposition that the purchase of a home should trigger a tax. We believe taxing the sale makes housing more expensive and makes it harder to afford. A tax of 23 to 30 percent, paid at the time of the sale, adds substantial costs to an already expensive transaction. In today's market and under today's tax laws, newly constructed housing is more expensive than existing housing by a factor of approximately 20 percent. Under the Fair Tax model, the sales tax cost will fall squarely on this higher cost of new housing.

To test our perceptions about sales tax on homes, we held focus groups in three cities in this country. In one such focus group in San Diego, our random sample pulled up one strong supporter of a sales tax plan. But at the end of debate at the end of the day, even that proponent was absolutely opposed to any tax on homes. And I quote his final summation, "A home is what we are, it is what we work for."

The Fair Tax imposes a sales tax on all consumer retail services, as we have already heard today, everything from real estate commissions to contract and document preparation, termite inspections, appraisals, painting and fix-up maintenance, legal advice, on and on, would be added on to the cost of this transaction.

Rental income housing we have already heard referred to. We are absolutely opposed to any tax on rental income housing as it makes moving up to home ownership even more difficult.

One very attractive feature of the Fair Tax plan is that it imposes Federal tax only once. This is a worthwhile objective. The Fair Tax model relieves all businesses from paying any payroll, income, or sales tax. Thus, investors in either residential or commercial rental property would pay no sales tax on their purchase of these income-producing properties.

Similarly, if a business occupied the building, these businesses would not be required to pay tax, and this is a good thing for our investment group of properties.

How do we get there from here? Ladies and gentlemen, transition is the key in our business. The 1986 Tax Act was a debacle in our industry. It was also a debacle that almost led to the end of the savings and loan industry in this country. We urge you to look very closely at the transition issue of this bill.

Only in the last 2 to 3 years has investment real estate regained its footing, and from 1988 to about 1992, even real estate residential values fell. And because of this depression in commercial real estate, the resulting tax credit crunch was almost the end of our industry.

We thank you very much for allowing us to speak here today. We look forward to addressing your questions, and thank you, Mr. Chairman.

[The prepared statement follows:]

Statement of Scott Rooth, Realtor, Cashiers, North Carolina, Chairman, Public Policy Coordinating Committee, and Member, Tax Reform Working Group, National Association of Realtors

Mr. Chairman and members of the Committee. My name is Scott Rooth. I am a Realtor from Cashiers, North Carolina. I appear here today on behalf of the NATIONAL ASSOCIATION OF REALTORS... (NAR) where I presently serve as Chairman of the Public Policy Coordinating Committee and as a member of the Tax Reform Working Group. NAR represents 760,000 real estate professionals engaged in all aspects of the real estate business. About 80% of our members are residential sales agents and brokers, and about 20% are principally engaged in commercial brokerage, leasing and management.

NAR and Tax Reform

Since 1995, NAR has been actively involved in the tax reform debate. Our focus then was on the flat tax. NAR continues to aggressively oppose the flat tax, because it would repeal the mortgage interest deduction (MID) and the deduction for state and local property taxes. We believe, and economic studies confirm, that eliminating the MID causes the value of homes to drop, thereby destroying equity and wealth. The loss of value nationally is about 15% and as much as 25% in high cost states such as California. The study that the respected econometric analysis firm of Standard & Poors/DRI performed indicated that the loss in home value under the flat tax was permanent. NAR viewed this as simply unacceptable and so opposed the flat tax.

In conjunction with our work on the flat tax, NAR adopted a series of tax reform principles and guidelines designed to clarify our own thinking and to enumerate the features of a tax system that would treat real estate fairly. Those principles and guidelines are attached as Appendix A of these comments. The principles and guidelines delineate the elements of real estate transactions and investment in real estate in order to assess the impact of proposed replacement-type tax systems on our industry. The flat income tax falls short under the criteria enumerated in those principles and guidelines. By contrast, Chairman Archer's publicly stated view that the purchase of a home should be treated as an investment and not subject to a consumption tax is completely consistent with those guidelines.

The principles and guidelines include elements applicable to both income and consumption tax models. NAR has no preference for one type of tax system over another. We believe that both income and consumption tax models could be crafted that would be practical for our industry.

Simplification

NAR shares Chairman Archer's perspective that the current income tax system is overly complicated and burdensome. Its complexity is particularly crushing for small businesses. We support tax reform's goals of substantial simplification, because, as self-employed individuals, our members face significant compliance challenges.

The tax rules that apply to homeownership, however, are among the simplest rules for individuals to comply with in the entire tax system. All that an individual must do in order to comply with the MID rules is to take the Form 1098 that the lender provides and transfer the MID and property tax numbers on Form 1098 to Schedule A of the Form 1040. This is no more difficult than entering an individual's wage and salary from Form W–2 or providing the amount of interest and dividends from Form 1099. Even if seller financing is involved, a settlement services provider such as a title company or attorney can usually provide an amortization schedule to the buyer and seller so that both parties can determine the amount of mortgage interest paid each year. Accordingly, we can think of no rationale based on simplification for eliminating the MID and property tax deduction in any income tax model.

The FairTax, H.R. 2525

In the context of today's hearings, the **NATIONAL ASSOCIATION OF REAL-TORS has taken no official position on the FairTax proposal advanced by Americans for Fair Taxation (AFT) (H.R. 2525). We neither oppose nor support it.** We understand that we have been invited here today to share with you the issues we have identified as NAR's Tax Reform Working Group has studied the plan and met with Mr. Linbeck and his AFT associates.

Why Does Real Estate Matter in the Tax Reform Debate?

Some may say that all we are doing here today is protecting a special interest. If so, it is a "special interest" that affects the two-thirds of all Americans who own their home. This homeownership rate is an all-time high. By contrast, during the decade of the 1980's, homeownership rates actually declined, dipping to about 62 percent. Given the progress over the past five years in not only reversing the decline, but actually reaching the highest homeownership rate in our history, it is difficult for us to understand why we would want to do anything to disrupt housing markets by changing the tax system.

Individuals in *every income* class own homes. Notably, the lower the family's income, the greater the proportion of their wealth is tied up in their homes. According to the Federal Reserve, even at the $10,000 household income level, almost 35% of households own a home, but only 8% of these households own stock. By contrast, the wealthiest 1% of households own 43% of all direct stock holdings, and their homeownership rate is 94%. The chart in Appendix B shows the rates of ownership and median values of some family assets by income and age categories. Simply stated, real estate is the most widely held asset of any category of household wealth in our economy.

It is worthwhile to compare ownership of a home with ownership of securities. In today's high-flying stock market, high Dow Jones averages mask some real turmoil. Of the 1,000 stocks tracked by the Wall Street Journal's Shareholder Scoreboard, 442 display a negative return for all of 1999. By contrast, of the 138 Metropolitan Statistical Areas (MSA) NAR monitors, only 12 showed a decline in median prices from 1998 to 1999. The worst performing housing market lost only 7% of its value. Again, it is difficult for us to understand why we would want to do anything to disrupt housing markets by changing the tax system. (Appendix C presents a series of statistics on various aspects of homeownership and some comparisons with assets such as securities.)

Even if you believe that real estate is a special interest, it is the special interest that affects the largest number of households and voters in the country. If you believe as NAR does that changes to the tax system can have a substantial impact on the value of those homes, then we believe you should tread very carefully when considering tax legislation that could negatively affect that most valuable of all possessions.

Achievements in Housing Among Minorities

The fastest growing category of homeowners is our minority population. Last year, 35% of first-time homebuyers were minorities and immigrants. Minorities and immigrants are highly motivated towards homeownership. 67% of African-Americans and 65% of Hispanics rank homeownership as a top priority. There is great understanding that homeownership is the way that Americans build wealth and savings. In 1999, NAR was a leading sponsor of the Congressional Black Caucus Foundation's Summit on Housing and Wealth Accumulation. By the end of 1999, we had achieved the highest number of minority homeowners in American history. At that time, a record 5.9 million African-American and 4.2 million Hispanic families had achieved the goal of homeownership.

Today, one in ten Americans were not born in the United States. We have made great progress in helping these families to achieve homeownership. Again, therefore, we are compelled ask why we would want to do anything to disrupt housing markets, particularly for minorities and immigrants by changing the tax system.

How Do You Get There From Here?

For NAR, the overriding question about any tax reform is "How do you get there from here?" Real estate professionals are particularly sensitive about transition because of the violent fallout from the 1986 Tax Reform Act. That bill pulled the rug out from under real estate investments, because it changed the tax rules for existing real estate investments in midstream without adequate transition. The result was a depression in real estate, a near-collapse of the financial system and a loss in value to existing assets. Only in the last two or three years has investment real estate regained its footing. From 1988 to about 1992, even residential real estate values fell or were flat because of the depression in commercial real estate and tight credit.

The FairTax provides no mortgage interest deduction (MID) because the MID is part of an income tax system, but not a consumption tax system. The loss of the MID will inevitably create additional transition problems. Contrast a home bought the day before the new tax system went in place, and a home purchased the day after. The home bought the day before the new tax system was implemented would no doubt change in value the day after the new system was implemented, because the two homes, even if they were identical, would not be on the same playing field. The MID matters a very great deal, and transition would be essential for all homes that were purchased under the current system.

What is the Tax Rate?

The FairTax is intended to replace the existing income, estate and payroll systems with a retail sales tax. Depending on how you do the computation, the FairTax would impose a tax of 23 or 30 percent on all goods and services. The tax rate under the FairTax, stated in H.R. 2525 at 23%, is what is called an "inclusive" rate. This in contrast to the way we usually think about sales taxes which today are stated in what is called an "exclusive" rate. What does this mean?

The way we are accustomed to think about sales taxes is in a tax "exclusive" manner. If a good costs $100 and the sales tax is 6%, then we pay $106.00, with $100 to the seller, and $6 to the taxing authority. The tax "inclusive" method works differently. The example that follows illustrates the inclusive and exclusive methods by using the stated FairTax rate of 23%.

Two examples based on $100 can assist in understanding the tax "inclusive" and tax "exclusive" methods. First, think of a seller who wishes to charge no more than a total of $100 for a product, including both the sales price and the tax. If the seller is to remit 23% of that total $100 retail cost to the government, then the seller will receive $77 as follows:

Price charged to purchaser $100
Sales Tax at 23% $23
Proceeds to seller $77

This is the tax "inclusive" method. The 23% tax is included in the retail purchase price the buyer pays.

Now think of a seller who wishes to realize or net $100. If we were to apply the tax "exclusive" model used today, the seller would have to charge a total of $129.87, as follows:

Total gross purchase price: $129.87
LESS: 23% sales tax $28.87
Net proceeds to seller $100.00
Effective rate for purchaser: 30%

The FairTax uses the tax "inclusive" method, so that the seller receives less than the stated $100 purchase price. Today's sales tax uses an "exclusive" method, so the seller receives the full $100.

Buying and Selling a Home

The FairTax would impose a sales tax of either 23% or 30% on the purchase of a new (but not an existing) home. AFT's theory does not include existing homes in the tax base, because today they have already borne the incidence of the income tax. In the future, if the FairTax were adopted, when a home that had been subject to the sales tax was sold, it also would already have been taxed.

We have expressed grave reservations to AFT and other sales tax advocates about any tax system that would tax the purchase of a home. We believe the imposition of a tax is a substantial barrier to affordability. A tax at 23% or 30% paid at the time of the sale, adds substantial costs to an already expensive transaction.

NAR's informal economic analysis of the sales tax model showed that the imposition of a sales tax causes the value of a home to drop. The drop is not as dramatic as under the flat tax, and, unlike the flat tax, the value of homes does eventually restore itself to where it would have been in the absence of the sales tax. (Under the flat tax, the decline in the value of homes is permanent and never recovered.) Under a sales tax, the value of homes does not decline as much when existing homes are excluded from taxation, as under the FairTax, but there is still a decline. Because homes represent so much of our national wealth, we have a fundamental question as to whether it is wise to substantially erode that wealth in the pursuit of tax reform.

We have another specific concern about taxing new homes. In today's market and under today's tax laws, newly-constructed housing is more expensive than existing housing by a factor of about 20%. Since both new and existing housing are subject to the same tax laws today, there appears to be a premium on the cost of new housing, even net of today's tax. Under the FairTax model, then, the 23% or 30% sales tax cost will fall heavily, indeed, on this higher-cost housing. The Committee will need to assess the impact this will have on housing starts and the economy.

NAR chose not to rely on future predictions of economic models (beyond our informal preliminary analysis). To test our concerns about the present, rather than make guesses about the future, we went directly to Americans, both homeowners and prospective homeowners. We conducted focus groups in Cincinnati, San Diego and Philadelphia. The focus group participants were chosen at random. In San Diego, our random sample happened to draw a man who was active in the national sales tax grass roots movement. He came to the meeting remarkably well informed about the current tax system and about the philosophy of a national sales tax. He was persuasive to the group about the merits of changing to a national sales tax. After some general discussion, the facilitator asked how the group would feel about taxing the purchase of a home. This fellow was shocked, as were other members of the group. At the end of the meeting, the group took a straw vote about supporting a sales tax that imposed tax on the purchase of a home. The vote against such a model was unanimous. Even the persuasive sales tax advocate said that he could never support a tax on the purchase of a home. Another participant summed up the feelings well: "A home is what we are, it's what we work for."

Predicting the Future

AFT responds to our concerns about a 30% increase in the cost of a home by saying that interest rates will be lower. They also say the purchaser will have more cahse, because that person will no longer be paying income and payroll taxes.

Our Working Group members have differing views about how the economy will perform and whether interest rates will really decline. This is because market performance is subject to numerous forces beyond the scope of the tax system. When Congress makes tax law changes, it is of course essential that it get the best possible economic information and forecasting on the likely outcome of the changes. Despite their sophistication, however, these prediction models have not necessarily come to fruition.

The economic models that drove the tax cuts in 1981 and 1986 assured declining deficits and more revenue collections for the government. The impact of the 1981 tax cuts was an increase in the deficit. After 1986, there was a depression in real estate and a slowdown in the economy because of problems in the financial system caused by the real estate depression. The result was even bigger deficits as the government supported the collapsing financial system. The tax rate increases in 1993 were accompanied by cries of alarm that there would be a significant recession and more deficits. Since 1996, the economy has exploded, and the government is in a surplus for the first time in more than a generation. Markets rely on more than the tax system.

Similarly, we have differences among ourselves about employer behavior in the future. To devise a crude example, say that an employer today pays an individual $50,000, for a net of $35,000 or $40,000 after all payroll, state and federal withholding. If the FairTax were adopted how much will that employer continue to pay the employee? Will the employer continue to give the employee the same net pay of $35,000 to $40,000? Or will the employer still pay the gross $50,000 salary? Will the elimination of income and payroll taxes benefit the employer, the employee or both? We disagreed among ourselves. You may, too.

Taxes on Services

We have a further concern about the impact of the FairTax 30% sales tax on real estate sales transaction. The FairTax imposes the sales tax on all retail (but not business to business) services. Real estate sales commissions would be taxed, as would services provided for title searches, contract and document preparation, termite inspections, appraisals, painting and fix-up maintenance, legal advice, tax advice and settlement or escrow fees. Each of these services would be subject to the 23% or 30% tax. Again, the cost of completing the housing transaction just went up.

In states that have attempted to impose sales taxes on services, Realtors... have joined with other service providers from dry cleaners to newspaper delivery providers to doctors and lawyers to oppose sales taxes on services. We believe that the imposition of sales taxes on the services associated with the purchase and sale of property will put a significant cost burden on prospective purchasers that would yet another barrier to homeownership.

What about Renters?

Under the FairTax, rents paid by consumers for their residences are taxed as consumption. Under the current system, we acknowledge that renters do not receive any of the tax benefits enjoyed by homeowners or landlords. Many, many renters would like to own a home, but find numerous barriers to affordability. Paying rent is certainly a form of consumption, but we are troubled about imposing such a heavy tax on one of life's fundamental necessities.

What about Investors in Real Estate and Other Business Activities?

One very attractive feature of the FairTax plan is that it seeks to impose tax once and only once on any activity or purchase. This is a worthwhile objective to pursue. The FairTax model achieves this result by relieving all businesses from either income or sales taxation. Thus, investors in real estate, whether the investment is in residential rental property or in commercial space, would pay no sales tax on their purchase of these income-producing properties. Similarly, if a business occupied the building, that business would not be required to pay sales tax on its rent, because business-to-business activities are not taxed under the FairTax model. Outside the context of real estate, the local bookstore would not pay income or sales tax on its revenues or on any of the inventory or supplies used in the business, nor would Barnes and Noble.

This single-level tax, applied only to retail consumption by end-users of goods and services (i.e., individuals) appeals to those interested in capital formation for business. A single-level tax is certainly a valid economic model. Even under current law, a significant amount of investment real estate income is taxed only once at the federal level, because real estate is often held by individuals or in partnerships. Inevitably, the Committee will have to make a political decision about whether exempting all business-to-business transactions from a sales tax is the best method of achieving the highly desirable goal of single-level taxation.

Conclusion

In the words of a former member of this Committee, America was built on real estate. We like it that way and look forward to working with the Committee to improve the tax system.

Appendix A

REAL ESTATE-BASED TAX REFORM PRINCIPLES AND GUIDELINES

Tax reform has been a major political theme since 1995. Tax reform supporters advocate complete elimination of both the current income tax code and the Internal Revenue Service. They would replace the current system with either a revised, broad-based, low-rate income tax model or a consumption tax. Advocates stress that any system adopted would be designed to be more fair and more simple than current law. Despite criticisms of the IRS, little consideration has been given to date to the mechanics of administering a new tax regime.

Anticipating that a variety of proposals will continue to emerge and that any reform process will be evolutionary, the National Association of Realtors... has developed guidelines and principles to use in evaluating proposals as they emerge. The guidelines are intended to provide a systematic means of evaluating both income and consumption taxation models. No principle would apply to every feature of any proposal. These guidelines are intended to cover a range of possibilities based on the elements of real estate transactions that potentially give rise to taxable events under current law and that could give rise to taxable events under income and consumption tax models. Not surprisingly, the guidelines list many principles that respond to features of the current income tax system, and only a limited number of applications to a consumption tax model.

A real estate investment has three distinct phases: acquisition, holding period and disposition. In addition, numerous services are associated with these phases of investment. Accordingly, these guidelines are organized to reflect those phases. Furthermore, a real estate investment is capital intensive, so the guidelines are based on the premise that the risks inherent in capital investment will be recognized in any tax system. In an income tax system, those risks would be recognized with a meaningful differential between the treatment of ordinary income and capital gains. A consumption tax system would properly recognize the risks of capital investment by treating real estate investment as a form of savings, and not consumption.

The National Association of Realtors... believes that the present income tax system, despite its flaws, has helped create a home ownership system that is unequaled in the world. Similarly, investment real estate is the most widely-held capital asset in the nation. In all income groups, the ownership of both residential and investment real estate is widely distributed.

Finally, the critical question in any tax reform effort, no matter what model is adopted, is "How do we get there from here?" Any changes to the tax system, whether incremental or sweeping, must include careful planning for adequate transition.

REAL ESTATE-BASED TAX REFORM PRINCIPLES AND GUIDELINES

Tax reform proposals generally fall into two categories: income tax models and consumption tax models. The features of those models vary, so not every principle below would apply to every proposal. The National Association of Realtors... believes that a workable tax system should:

Acquisition
• Treat home ownership as investment, and not as consumption.
• Encourage savings and tax-based incentives for home purchases.
• Eliminate penalties for using savings for home purchases.
• Treat services associated with the purchase of real estate as part of the investment costs of the transaction, and not tax those services.

Holding Period
• Preserve mortgage interest deduction benefits.
• Treat debt financing for owners of investment property as a business expense.
• Provide cost recovery rules that reflect a viable economic life for real estate investment for both owners and tenants.
• Allow netting of income from real estate activities against other income streams.

Disposition
• Maintain a meaningful tax differential between ordinary income and gain from sales of capital assets.
• Apply capital gains provisions equally among all investments, including real estate.
• Tax only true economic gain.
• Defer recognition of gain on disposition of all real estate until reinvestment ceases.
• Preserve loss carry forward principles.
• Treat services associated with the sale of real estate as part of the investment costs of the transaction, and not tax those services.

Real Estate Operations
• Preserve independent contractor status for real estate professionals.
• Preserve (or establish) the principle that ordinary and necessary business expenses, including interest, should be deductible under an income tax model, and nontaxable under a consumption tax model.

Transition
Provide transition rules to preserve owner equity and eliminate adverse effects on real estate assets in service at the time of enactment.

APPENDIX B
OWNERSHIP OF ASSETS BY INCOME AND AGE

	Stock	Retire Acct	Home	Stock	Retire Acct	Home
All Families Income	48.8%	48.8%	60.2%	$25,000	$24,000	$100,000
Less than $10,000	7.7%	6.4%	34.5%	$4,000	$7,500	$51,000
10,000–24,999	24.7%	25.4%	51.7%	$9,000	$8,000	$71,000
25,000–49,999	52.7%	54.2%	68.2%	$11,500	$13,000	$85,000
50,000–99,000	74.3%	73.5%	85.0%	$35,700	$31,000	$130,000
100,00 or more	91.0%	88.6%	93.3%	$150,000	$93,000	$240,000
Age of head Less than 35	40.7%	39.8%	38.9%	$7,000	$7,000	$84,000
35–44	56.5%	59.5%	67.1%	$20,000	$21,000	$101,000
45–54	58.6%	59.2%	74.4%	$38,000	$34,000	$120,000
55–74	58.9%	58.3%	80.3%	$47,000	$46,800	$110,000
65–74	42.6%	46.1%	81.5%	$56,000	$38,000	$95,000
75 or more	29.4%	16.7%	70.0%	$60,000	$30,000	$85,000

ASource: Federal Reserve Board, Survey of Our Summer Finance.

Tax Notes on Homeownership
- Home largest asset for most families.
- In 1998, 66% of households own a home, while only 49% own any stock, either directly or indirectly.
- Median value of home for owners is $100,000; while median value of stock holdings in only $25,000 (1998).
- Housing wealth is more evenly distributed across the income distribution than any other asset, except for vehicles. The Federal Reserve Board reports that the wealthiest 1% of households own 43% of all direct stock holdings, but only own 9% of all value of personal residences.
- Although minority households have lower homeownership rate, for those that do own, their home is an even larger share of their wealth than for majority households.
- Homeownership rate of minority households in 46.8% compared to 71.8% for white households in 1998.
- Although homeownership declines with income, for those that do own, their home is an even larger share of their wealth the lower is household income.
- For households earning less than $10,000 annually, less than 8% own any stock, direct or indirect, while 34.5% own their own homes.
- For households earning less than $10,000 annually who do own stock the median value of stock holdings is only $4,000, while those homeowners earning less than $10,000 have a median home value of $51,000.
- For much of the current elderly their largest source of retirement wealth is their home.
- In 1998, 77% of households aged 75 plus own a home, while less than 30% own any stock, either directly or indirectly.
- Median value of home for owners aged 75 plus is $85,000; while median value of stock holdings in only $60,000 for those who own stock (1998).
- High Stock Market masks many losing stocks while most housing markets share in national gains.
- Of the 138 MSA monitored by NAR, only 12 displayed a decline in median prices from 1998 to 1999. The worst performing housing market lost only 7%.
- Of the 374 IPO's issued between June 1999 and April 2000, 99 are trading below their issue price as of April 4, 2000 (that is they lost money), with an average decline of 36%.
- Of the 1,000 stocks tracked by the Wall Street Journal's Shareholder Scoreboard, 442 display a negative return for all of 1999.

Mortgage facts (from 1997 American Housing Survey):
- Of the 65.5 million homeowners in the US, 39% own their home free and clear (no mortgage). So that's 40 million with a mortgage, of which about 30 million claim take the MID.
- Over 7 million have more than one mortgage (may include home equity loans and lines of credit).

About 3 million only have a home equity line or loan without a regular mortgage

---

Chairman ARCHER. Thank you, Mr. Rooth.
Mr. Kouplen?

STATEMENT OF STEVE KOUPLEN, PRESIDENT, OKLAHOMA FARM BUREAU, ON BEHALF OF THE AMERICAN FARM BUREAU FEDERATION

Mr. KOUPLEN. Chairman Archer and members of the committee, my name is Steve Kouplen. I am a farmer from Okmulgee County, Oklahoma, where I operate a cow-calf operation on some 2,000 acres. I am president of the Oklahoma Farm Bureau and am here today on behalf of the American Farm Bureau Federation.

Farm Bureau members are ready for fundamental tax reform. They have become increasingly frustrated with the current tax system and disheartened that every attempt to change the system makes the system even more complex.

The current tax system forces farmers and ranchers to consider the tax consequences of each input purchase, commodity sale, capital asset purchase, or capital asset sale. Farmers and ranchers should be making decisions based on the economics of the situation, not the consequences of the tax situation.

After a lifetime of hard work and paying taxes, farmers and ranchers are faced with double taxation through capital gains and estate taxes. If they sell equipment, livestock, and other assets at retirement, they find the Federal Government ready to take a share as capital gains taxes. These taxes often discourage retirees from reallocating assets to a more appropriate mix for their retirement years. Young producers lose the opportunity to purchase assets that they can use more economically than current owners.

Planning for the transfer of assets at death has become a time-consuming and costly activity. Many family farms are multi-generation family farms. Transferring farms and ranches from one generation to the next without a huge tax load is critical to the financial success of these farms. Many farms are lost when death taxes force farmers and ranchers to sell part or all of their business to secure enough cash to pay death taxes.

Farm Bureau supports replacing the current Federal income tax system with a new tax that encourages, not penalizes, success and encourages savings, investment, and entrepreneurship. It should be transparent, simple, and require a minimum of personal information.

It must be fair to farmers and ranchers in payroll taxes, the alternative minimum tax, the capital gains tax, and personal and corporate income taxes. A consumption tax must not tax business-to-business transactions or services unless sold for final consumption.

The American Farm Bureau Federation supports H.R. 2525, the Fair Tax Act of 1999 and any other tax reform proposals consistent with Farm Bureau policy.

The national sales tax plan sponsored by Representatives Linder and Peterson is a bold attempt at fundamental reform. By ending the Federal individual and corporate income taxes, capital gains tax, estate tax, and payroll taxes for Social Security and Medicare, many of the concerns that Farm Bureau members have with the current tax system would be eliminated. These changes would have far-ranging impacts on day-to-day farm and ranch management and the transfer of farms and ranches from one generation to the next.

If H.R. 2525 is enacted, attention should be given to two potential problems that are of concern to farmers and ranchers. First, a national sales tax will need to be meshed with existing State and county sales taxes. Second, only the 5 percent of the farmers and ranchers who sell directly to consumers should be required to keep records and remit sales tax money to the proper collection agency in order to avoid a heavy compliance burden.

We look forward to working with you to promote fundamental tax reform that will be good for farmers and ranchers and good for the citizens of our country.

Thank you, Mr. Chairman.

[The prepared statement follows:]

Statement of Steve Kouplen, President, Oklahoma Farm Bureau, on Behalf of The American Farm Bureau Federation

Mr. Chairman and members of the committee, good morning. My name is Steve Kouplen, and I am president of the Oklahoma Farm Bureau. I have a Hereford cow-calf operation on 2,000 acres in Okmulgee County, Oklahoma. I am appearing here today on behalf of the American Farm Bureau Federation (AFBF) and the Oklahoma Farm Bureau. AFBF represents more than 4.9 million member families in all 50 states and Puerto Rico and produce nearly every type of farm commodity grown in America.

Farm Bureau members are ready for fundamental tax reform. They have become increasingly frustrated with the current tax system and disheartened that every attempt to change the system to benefit farmers and ranchers makes the system even more complex. Simple ideas, such as income averaging for farm and ranch incomes that vary greatly year to year, become almost incomprehensibly complex when changes are passed by Congress and regulations issued by the Internal Revenue Service (IRS).

The national sales tax plan sponsored by Reps. John Linder (R–GA) and Collin Peterson (D–MN), H.R. 2525, is a bold attempt at fundamental reform. By eliminating the federal individual and corporate income taxes, capital gains tax, estate tax and payroll taxes for Social Security and Medicare, they would address the hundreds of concerns that Farm Bureau members have with the current tax system. These changes would have far-ranging impacts on day-to-day farm and ranch management and the transfer of farms and ranches from one generation to the next.

The current tax system forces farmers and ranchers to consider the tax consequences of each input purchase, commodity sale, capital asset purchase or capital asset sale. Tax planning has become a normal part of everyday decision making. Farmers and ranchers should be making decisions based on the economics of the situation, not the tax consequences of the situation.

After a lifetime of hard work and paying taxes, farmers and ranchers are faced with double taxation, with the capital gains tax at retirement and the estate tax at death. If they sell equipment, livestock and other assets at retirement, they find the federal government as a silent partner ready to take a share as capital gains taxes. These taxes often discourage retirees from reallocating assets to a more appropriate mix for their retirement years. Younger producers lose the opportunity to purchase assets that they can use more economically than the current owners.

Planning for the transfer of assets at death has become a time consuming and costly activity. Many family farms are multi-generation family farms. Transferring farms and ranches from one generation to the next without a huge tax load is critical to the financial success of these farms. Asset transfer decisions that were delayed because of the capital gains tax are further complicated by the estate tax. Many farms are lost when death taxes force farmers and ranchers to sell part or all of their business to secure enough cash to pay death taxes.

These problems would all be swept away by the tax reforms as proposed by H.R.2525.

If H.R. 2525 is enacted, attention should be given to two potential problems that are of concern to farmers and ranchers. First, a national sales tax will need to be meshed with existing state and county sales taxes. State Farm Bureaus have worked for decades in their respective states to develop a state sales tax system that treats farmers and ranchers fairly. They want to avoid having to start over again on basic sales tax issues with state governments.

Second, only about 5 percent of the farmers and ranchers sell directly to consumers. These should be the only ones that have to keep records and remit sales tax money to the proper collection agency. Farmers and ranchers buy billions of dollars of inputs for production purposes that are also purchased by consumers for final use. This includes a wide range of items from pickup trucks to lumber for building repairs to hand tools. They do not want to get caught in the compliance burden that may be necessary to ensure that all retail sales taxes are properly collected.

Farm Bureau Policy

Farm Bureau supports replacing the current federal income tax system. The new tax code should encourage, not penalize, success and encourage savings, investment and entrepreneurship. It should be transparent, simple and require a minimum of personal information.

We support a replacement tax system if it meets these guidelines:

(1) Fair to agricultural producers;

(2) Implemented simultaneously with the elimination of all payroll taxes, self-employment taxes, the alternative minimum tax, the capital gains tax, death taxes and personal and corporate income taxes;

(3) Revenue neutral;

(4) Repeals the 16th amendment; and

(5) Any flat tax proposal or other reform proposal not based on gross revenue received.

We support requiring a two-thirds majority for imposition of new or additional taxes, or for the increase of tax rates. A consumption tax must not tax business-to-business transactions or services unless sold for final consumption.

At an American Farm Bureau Federation Board of Directors meeting in March of this year the board took specific action to support the Fair Tax Act of 1999 and any other tax reform proposals consistent with Farm Bureau policy.

We look forward to working with you to promote fundamental tax reform that will be good for farmers and ranchers and for all citizens.

———

Chairman ARCHER. Thank you, Mr. Kouplen.

Mr. Martin, you are clean-up hitter in this group, and if you are prepared, you may proceed.

STATEMENT OF JAMES MARTIN, HORSESHOE BAY, TEXAS

Mr. MARTIN. Yes, sir. Mr. Chairman and members of the committee, my name is James Martin, and I am grateful for the opportunity to testify today. I am the former general vice president of the Ironworkers International Union. I also served as deputy chairman of the Dallas Federal Reserve Board. I would like to ask that my written statement and a recent op-ed article that I co-authored with Gale Van Hoy, the executive secretary of the Texas Building and Construction Trades Council, be made part of this hearing.

Chairman ARCHER. Without objection, any printed material or statement by any one of the witnesses will be inserted in the record in full.

Mr. MARTIN. Thank you, sir.

The tax system is one of the primary reasons that so many people are having such a hard time getting ahead financially. The existing tax system is holding the working men and women of this country back. I believe that the Fair Tax, introduced on a bipartisan basis as H.R. 2525, is the best plan to make our tax system better.

American workers are disgusted with the present tax system. They want to see fundamental change. They see loopholes and special provisions in the tax law that benefit politically powerful interests but these are not available to ordinary people. They see accountants and lawyers putting together intricate deals that take advantage of these loopholes. They have seen tax reform after tax reform passed by Congress, and yet the situation only gets worse. In the meantime, the taxes taken out of their paycheck seem to remain about the same or even go up every year. The Fair Tax would eliminate all loopholes and all of these games. It is a straightforward tax system that would eliminate the ability to gain advantage through tax shelter deals.

Most Americans don't understand the current system. For that matter, I am not convinced anyone really understands the current tax system, including the people that try to administer it at the IRS. It is just too complex. I believe that the American people have the right to understand the tax system. A system that is so complex that virtually no one understands it is going to lead to unfairness. The Fair Tax would give us a simple tax system that anyone can understand.

The current tax system holds people down. The only way for most people to get ahead is to get an education or training, go to work, and to save. Yet this is precisely what the current tax system punishes. Work is taxed more heavily than any other form of income due to the combination of high payroll taxes and the income tax. Under the current tax system, we generally have to pay for education or training for ourselves or our children with after-tax dollars. You have to save with after-tax dollars unless you are willing to tie up your money until retirement. The Fair Tax taxes only consumption. Education and training are treated as an investment in people and are not taxed. Wages and salaries are not taxed. And savings is not taxed.

The Fair Tax would eliminate not only the income tax but also payroll taxes. For many people, the payroll tax is a bigger burden than the income tax. It is a regressive tax that taxes only wages and taxes people earning less than $76,200 more heavily than those earning more. The Fair Tax is the only tax reform plan to address this problem. No other plan would repeal payroll taxes. Workers would be able to keep their entire paycheck. There would be no withholding of income or payroll taxes. What we earn is what we would receive in our paychecks.

Americans also want more control over their own financial future. They want to be able to make choices for themselves and their families rather than have the decisions made for them in Washington. They want to be able to save or go to school or get training without having to deal with complex tax provisions or pay a large tax.

The current tax system imposes a heavy burden on American workers and businesses exporting to foreign markets and on U.S. workers and businesses competing with imported goods in the U.S. markets. In contrast, foreign goods enter the U.S. market free of any significant tax burden. This places U.S.-produced goods at a big competitive disadvantage.

Our tax system is one of the major reasons that we have such a large trade deficit. This disadvantage is made worse because most of our major trading partners eliminate a big part of their tax burden on exports since their value-added taxes are border adjusted. This disadvantage is built into our tax system, and it exports high-paying jobs to our competitors. We should be exporting goods, not good jobs.

There is nothing that can be done about this problem if we keep the income tax, but the Fair Tax fixes the problem. The U.S. will stop shooting itself in the foot. For the first time, foreign-produced goods will bear their fair share of the tax burden. U.S.-produced goods and foreign-produced goods will be subject to the same tax when they are sold retail in the U.S. Exported U.S. goods will bear no tax burden. This will make American firms and American workers more competitive both in domestic markets and abroad. It will enable us to create and preserve more high-quality and high-paying jobs, and it will improve the standard of living of American workers.

We need to rethink the tax system. It really is broken beyond repair. It is time to do something about it. The Fair Tax is legislation that deserves support, and I would urge you to pass this legislation.

I thank you, and I would be glad to answer any questions, Mr. Chairman.

[The prepared statement follows:]

Statement of James Martin, Horseshoe Bay, Texas

Mr. Chairman and members of the committee, I am grateful for the opportunity to testify today. I am the former General Vice President of the Ironworkers International Union. I also served as Deputy Chairman of the Dallas Federal Reserve Board. I would ask that my written statement and a recent Op-Ed article that I coauthored with Gale Van Hoy, the Executive Secretary of the Texas Building and Construction Trades Council, be made a part of the hearing record.

The tax system is one of the primary reasons that so many people are having such a hard time getting ahead financially. The existing tax system is holding the working men and women of this country back. I believe that the FairTax, introduced on a bipartisan basis as H.R. 2525, is the best plan to make our tax system better.

American workers are disgusted with the present tax system. They want to see fundamental change. They see loopholes and special provision in the tax law that benefit politically powerful interests but are not available to ordinary people. They see fancy accountants and lawyers putting together intricate deals to take advantage of those loopholes. They have seen tax reform after tax reform be passed by Congress and yet the situation only gets worse. In the meantime, the taxes taken out of their paycheck seem to remain about the same or go up every year. The FairTax would eliminate all loopholes and all of these games. It is a straightforward tax system that would eliminate the ability to gain advantage through tax shelter deals.

Most Americans don't understand the current system. For that matter, I am not convinced anyone really understands the current tax system, including the people that have to try to administer it at the IRS. It is just too complex. I believe that the American people have the right to understand the tax system. A system that is so complex that virtually no one understands it is going to lead to unfairness. The FairTax would give us a simple tax system that anyone can understand.

The current tax system holds people down. The only way for most people to get ahead is to get an education or training, to work, and to save. Yet this is precisely what the current tax system punishes. Work is taxed more heavily than any other form of income due to the combination of high payroll taxes and the income tax. Under the current tax system, we generally have to pay for education or training for ourselves or our children with after-tax dollars. You have to save with after-tax dollars unless you are willing to tie up the money until retirement. The FairTax taxes only consumption. Education and training are treated as an investment in people and are not taxed. Wages and salaries are not taxed. Savings is not taxed.

The FairTax would eliminate not only the income tax but also payroll taxes. For many people, the payroll tax is a bigger burden than the income tax. It is a regressive tax that taxes only wages and taxes those earning less than $76,200 more heavily than those earning more. The FairTax is the only tax reform plan to address this problem. No other plan would repeal payroll taxes. Workers would be able to keep their entire paycheck. There would be no more withholding of income or payroll taxes. What we earn would be what we receive in our paychecks.

Americans want more control over their own financial future. They want to be able to make choices for themselves and their families rather than have the decisions made for them in Washington. They want to be able to save or go to school or get training without having to deal with complex tax provisions or pay a large tax.

The current tax system imposes a heavy tax burden on American workers and businesses exporting to foreign markets and on U.S. workers and businesses competing with imported goods in the U.S. markets. In contrast, foreign goods enter the U.S. market free of any significant tax burden. This places U.S. produced goods at a big competitive disadvantage. Our tax system is one of the major reasons we have such a large trade deficit. This disadvantage is made worse because most of our major trading partners eliminate a big part of their tax burden on exports since their value added taxes are border adjusted. This disadvantage is built into our tax system and it exports high paying jobs to our competitors. We should be exporting goods not good jobs.

There is nothing that can be done about this problem if we keep the income tax but the FairTax fixes this problem. The U.S. will stop shooting itself in the foot. For the first time, foreign produced goods will bear their fair share of the tax burden. U.S. produced goods and foreign produced goods will be subject to the same tax when they are sold at retail in the U.S. Exported U.S. goods will bear no tax burden. This will make American firms and American workers more competitive both in domestic markets and abroad. It will enable us to create and preserve more high quality, high paying jobs. It will improve the standard of living of American workers.

We need to rethink our tax system. It really is broken beyond repair. It is time to do something about at. The FairTax is legislation that deserves support and I would urge you to pass this legislation.

Thank you. I would be glad to answer any questions you may have.

Chairman ARCHER. Thank you, Mr. Martin.

Mr. Rooth, you have said you are neutral on H.R. 2525. Is there any structural tax reform proposal that you positively support?

Mr. ROOTH. Not at this time, Mr. Chairman.

Chairman ARCHER. And do you have any specific recommendations that you might make to the committee as to what sort of avenues we might look into in order to get to ultimate structural tax reform?

Mr. ROOTH. As I had mentioned, our chief concerns are in any form of taxation on the first-time home buyer, on the taxing of rental rents, on the transition rules. 1986 was a devastating event in our industry because most people assume that this is a long-time investment purchase. And to change the rules in midstream can be an earth-shattering event for them.

Chairman ARCHER. Well, I certainly agree with that, as the leader of the opposition to the 1986 Tax Reform Act and citing in the debate the very things that we learn from hindsight in advance as to what would happen to real estate and the S&Ls.

Mr. Linbeck, how would you respond to Mr. Rooth's specific objections to the Fair Tax?

Mr. LINBECK. Well, Mr. Chairman, I understand the concern that he has expressed, but I suggest that the elements of the Fair Tax relating to the sale of new homes and the manner in which the producer price is predicted to go down on average by about 20 percent would suggest that the cost of that new home including the tax would not go up. But of equal importance, if I may, is that one needs to look at the purchasing power side of the equation as well. As I am sure he knows, the essential components of a person's ability to purchase a home are typically the interest rate that one has to pay, the amount of spendable income that they have to apply to the debt service on the home that they purchase, and the amount of time that one has to save in order to pay the down payment on a new home.

Under the Fair Tax, there is virtually unanimous expectation that interest rates will go down, and if interest rates go down, then that means the debt service for a comparable home would go down. If a person receives in their paycheck 100 percent of what they earn, then they are better able and equipped to pay the debt service that is applicable to the home they choose to buy.

And, finally, under the existing law, research suggests to us that it takes a person on average between 7 and 8 years to save for the down payment on a new home. Under the Fair Tax, since there is no tax on either the payroll level or the income level, a person can save for that down payment in between 4 and 5 years.

So in considering all of those factors together, it seems to us that the environment for purchasing new homes will be improved, that it will not deteriorate, as suggested by the analysis put forward earlier.

Chairman ARCHER. Are there any probative economic studies that show what we might see in the decline of long-term interest rates if the Fair Tax were adopted?

Mr. LINBECK. Yes, sir, there is a position paper that is the product of the research effort that spells out the more technical details of that. But the shorthand response is that the tax wage is eliminated between tax-exempt and taxable bonds. So it is assumed—and it seems to be appropriately so—that the interest rates will come down at least by the difference between taxable and tax-free bonds.

Chairman ARCHER. Well, would you estimate that to be 100 basis points, 150, 200? Or what range?

Mr. LINBECK. Well, in the current environment, that is probably 175 to 200 basis points, and that is leaving aside the risk issue, assuming the risk on the security is comparable as between those that are compared. But, in addition, it is commonly believed that there will be more money in the system in order to provide additional capital, thereby driving interest rates down still further.

One of the reasons driving that, of course, will be that corporations that have earned income overseas who are now deterred from repatriating it because of the tax that would apply would be able to bring it back, thereby relieving the burden that they currently place on the domestic capital markets for the need for their cap ex expenditures.

Chairman ARCHER. Thank you.

Mr. Kleczka?

Mr. KLECZKA. Thank you, Mr. Chairman.

I think the more we learn about this national sales tax bill, the more questions are raised. Mr. Rooth, you have been in the home-selling, home business, so you probably know more about it than any member of the committee. Under this proposal, it is guessed, hoped, prayed, that the price of the home is going to go down about 20 percent, a newly constructed home is going to go down by 20 percent, and so a 30 percent add-on sales tax under this proposal won't be that burdensome.

In my experience around here—and I can cite right off the top of my head—every time we put more dollars into student loans and grants, we find that the more we give the kids to help offset their educational costs, the more the tuition goes up. Okay?

In your experience or in your knowledge of this bill, is there anything that is going to guarantee that those homes are going to go down by 20, 25 percent for new construction? I just fail to believe that.

Mr. ROOTH. Well, for someone to step forward and try to crystal ball what the economic impact will be I think is next to impossible. How an employer treats their wages I think is difficult for us to predict. In certain conditions of labor, I am sure that they will be maintained because of prior contractual arrangements.

But I would say to you that in 1981, in 1986, and again in 1993, we tried to predict the outcome of changes in the tax provisions and estimate what it would do to the rental income or the residential real estate market and the commercial real estate markets, and we were wrong on all three attempts, 1986 being almost a doom-and-gloom situation.

So I think it is difficult for anyone in our business to predict the impact that this might have.

Mr. KLECZKA. Well, we know one thing. If this would become law, there would be a 30 percent add-on at closing.

Mr. ROOTH. Right, and one of the things that concerns us a great deal I alluded to in my oral comments, and that is the impact of the services fee on every aspect of the closing of the transaction, whether it be attorney's fees, title fees, impact doc fees, appraisal fees, home inspector fees. There is a plethora of different fees at closing in that transaction. And for the first-time home buyer, that is a very important component because we are looking at a down payment and what they have to put to the transaction.

Mr. KLECZKA. Are those fees taxed today?

Mr. ROOTH. No, they are not.

Mr. KLECZKA. Mr. Linbeck, what would be the business tax under this proposal?

Mr. LINBECK. The business tax? There is no tax on business-to-business transactions.

Mr. KLECZKA. So it would totally repeal the corporate income tax?

Mr. LINBECK. Yes, and also the——

Mr. KLECZKA. So businesses would pay no tax at all.

Mr. LINBECK. That is correct.

Mr. KLECZKA. How would a person be advantaged, let's say, in the 15 percent income category or even 28 percent income category? That person would not pay income taxes anymore, but he or she would be paying 30 percent at minimum, and Joint Tax tells the committee, to be revenue neutral, that tax would almost have to approach 59, 60 percent. So how does a person who currently pays 28 percent be advantaged by paying in excess of 30 percent on every good and service that person needs to survive?

Mr. LINBECK. That is a very good question, and it is one that concerned us a great deal. And we spent an enormous amount of time researching this, and we found that the person in that income category today is paying the biggest tax in the payroll tax, and the rebate tacked on top of the payroll tax in effect brings that person to the point when they have to buy products that no longer have the embedded income tax in them is completely tax free at the poverty level and below. Those that are above the poverty level continue to get the benefits on a gradated basis.

Mr. KLECZKA. That poorer person would get a rebate every month?

Mr. LINBECK. Yes.

Mr. KLECZKA. And so they would—right now I file a once a year my taxes. In fact, today I mailed them in with a check, okay? And, you know, I am not ready to commit hara-kiri. It is something you have to do as an American citizen. But under this new system, that poorer person would have to file something every month to get their monthly rebate, would they not?

Mr. LINBECK. No, sir. Under the provisions as embedded in the bill, they would make a request once a year to the Social Security Administration, which request is a postcard with their Social Security number on it. The Social Security Administration runs that through the system to make certain it is a valid Social Security number and that it has not already been used. And then based on family size as promulgated by Health and Human Services, the rebate is automatically dispatched to them at the beginning of each month.

Mr. KLECZKA. So every month they get a check, and there is no— and it doesn't bear any relationship to their actual purchases.

Mr. LINBECK. That is correct.

Mr. KLECZKA. So for that month that they received a check, for whatever reason they didn't buy much, but they, nevertheless, get that same check every month.

Mr. LINBECK. That is correct.

Mr. KLECZKA. Well, that is a heck of a deal. Could you explain to the committee how this tax on local and State government works? The authors of the bill didn't even realize that the payroll of the municipalities would be taxed as national sales tax. Now, maybe you know more about the bill than the authors, but are you aware that payroll is taxed under this proposal?

Mr. LINBECK. I am not aware of the specific mechanism by which it is taxed. I am aware of the principle that the tax on products that are consumed are taxed regardless of their origin or who produces them. And in the area of Government services, they are taxed just like if they were produced by the private sector. But I am not personally familiar with the mechanics by which that would——

Mr. KLECZKA. So you are not aware that the payroll of any municipality would have applied to it a 30 percent national sales tax?

Mr. LINBECK. There is a paper that is prepared as part of the information on the Fair Tax that deals with the technicalities of that.

Mr. KLECZKA. Well, that is more than a technicality. That is a big, big liability for our municipalities. Right now if you would exclude workmen's comp and unemployment comp, the major contribution on that payroll by local municipal government is the FICA tax. Well, that is going to be taken off, and in lieu of, we are going to be asking Milwaukee and Cleveland and all cities to pay 30 percent of their gross wages. That is one big one for the property taxpayers in this country. So they are shedding a 7 percent plus liability, and we are replacing it with a 30 percent.

Mr. LINBECK. And that is a proper concern, and that is why there was specific research done on that in order to make certain that there was a level playing field as between services provided by Government and services provided by the private sector, the intent being that there would be no differentiation between the tax outcome as between public and private services.

I apologize for not knowing the specific technicalities of it, but there is a position paper that has been prepared by researchers——

Mr. KLECZKA. Well, see, our dilemma is we are asked to support this critter, and we have to know those things because that is of big, big importance back home.

Mr. LINBECK. And I would encourage you, if there is any prospect of your support, that you become familiar with the technical side of it.

Mr. KLECZKA. Well, that is more than technical. That is one of the mainstays of this bill.

Mr. LINBECK. The principle is that there is a level playing field of taxation as between public and private service providers.

Chairman ARCHER. The gentleman's time has expired.

Mr. KLECZKA. I thank the chairman.

Chairman ARCHER. Ms. Dunn?

Ms. DUNN. Thank you very much, Mr. Chairman.

I want to welcome you, gentlemen. Thank you for coming and expressing your point of view. I think it is a fascinating discussion, and we all have lots and lots of questions. And we also have questions on behalf of the folks we represent at home, so I think it is a wonderful opportunity for us to get you all together.

Mr. Rooth, I wanted to ask you a question. In your testimony, you said that you oppose the flat-rate flat tax that has been discussed by folks as we reform the tax system, and I was going to ask you, because in some discussions of that tax, there are bills that would exempt interest deductibility, and so that would still be provided. And despite that, you still oppose the flat tax.

Mr. ROOTH. It is difficult to oppose the "flat tax" because without a bill on the floor for me to speak directly to, it——

Ms. DUNN. Well, just assume it is a flat tax with deductibility continuing for mortgage interest and charitable donations and maybe medical expenses.

Mr. ROOTH. I would say that it is an issue that we would take very serious looks at. There are economic impacts on rental income housing, and home purchase would be the most important thing that we would consider. I am also concerned about transition issues in the depreciable items.

Ms. DUNN. And then when we were talking about the national retail sales tax, did you say that you would expect a full exemption for the purchase of homes because they would be considered investments?

Mr. ROOTH. In my comments to the chairman, we feel that the purchase of a home, because of its significant nature, is an investment.

Ms. DUNN. Do you prefer the current tax system for the taxation of purchasing homes?

Mr. ROOTH. Yes.

Ms. DUNN. Okay. Thank you.

I wanted to ask Mr. Linbeck, what are you finding out there among folks you are talking with about the Fair Tax? Are you finding a building consensus behind this as people begin to understand how it works? And if you are finding that, what do you see as the movement through the Congress? Are we now in an education period? What do you see the process being for the success of your program?

Mr. LINBECK. As I mentioned, we have conducted market research for the last several years in order to discern what, in fact, was the embedded attitude of the electorate in respect to this issue.

Since we have learned what we believe that to be, we are now involved in an educational effort. We expect over the next 30 to 90 days to ratchet that up to the extent that the 50 major markets in this country will be exposed to the availability of the Fair Tax, and the whole thrust of the AFT effort is to inform the electorate and then leave it up to them to decide whether or not they wish to support it and manifest that support through their contacting of the people that they vote for.

I only vote for one Congressman and two Senators, and it would be presumptuous of me to expect a response from people for whom I don't vote.

But if they hear from enough of the people that send them to Congress and they have a persuasive enough basis on which they form their position, we think it is going to be a very strong groundswell of support for the Fair Tax. Our research suggests that. And most recently, when the four essential elements that I shared in my oral testimony are known to the electorate, over 70 percent of the people support it.

So we are very encouraged by that, but, again, we think the success or failure of the Fair Tax undertaking will be the degree to which the constituents in the grassroots in the country become energized by the prospect of its passage.

Ms. DUNN. I think that is very realistic, and I guess I would urge all of you who are involved in this discussion not to give up hope that there may not be all the members of the Ways and Means Committee here or that people aren't talking to us out in the districts. The discussion is important, and as part of the educating process, it has to be taking place now.

Frankly, I think that because we don't have a lot of time left in this year, there is not a lot of legislative time, because I am waiting for the freshness of the new administration, I think there will be great attention paid to this as we move through this year and move into next year.

But I think there are benefits of the Fair Tax, as there are benefits of other forms of tax as replacements for this totally outdated income tax system that we penalize people with today.

Let me ask one more question, and whoever on this panel can answer it, I would appreciate it. We have talked a lot about the effects of the Fair Tax on border adjustment, and I am wondering if somebody could address this once again in this panel. How would products made in the United States benefit from a national retail sales tax?

Mr. LINBECK. Well, I am not an expert in this or anything else, but I will take a crack at it based on what I have learned from our research. And it is a timely question in that there has recently been a WTO finding that the existing international trade vehicles that have been used by exporters does not conform to GATT or the World Trade Organization rules, thereby disadvantaging exporters under those rules.

It is our understanding and belief that in the regimen of the Fair Tax, all of the embedded taxes occasioned by the current system would be purged from their cost structure, and, therefore, they would be able to export their products into an international market on a much more competitive basis. And it has been suggested in some of the companies with whom we have visited who are heavily involved in export that the 20 to 25 percent lowering of their producer price would have a dramatic impact on both their ability to increase their market share and maintain their margins, but also penetrate new markets that heretofore have not been available to them because of the tax disadvantage that they are burdened with.

Mr. MCCRACKEN. If I could add just briefly, it will also encourage businesses to continue to be in the United States and to come to the United States to produce the products. It creates enormous incentives to do things here as opposed to abroad.

Ms. DUNN. That is a really good point. We have been stuck with the FSC ruling right now, and some of the other problems we have, the H–1–B visa cap and so forth that causes people to start looking toward going overseas to be competitive.

Thank you very much. Thank you, Mr. Chairman.

Chairman ARCHER. Would it not also prompt the return of all of the companies that have gone offshore for tax reasons that are currently operating in tax havens like Bermuda and the Cayman Islands and Aruba and other places?

Mr. LINBECK. Well, it is our belief that it would remove the incentive for them to take that kind of a step. Whether it would immediately cause them to return, only they could answer that. But all of the incentive for them to be located in an external domicile would be removed. And as a matter of fact, all of the advantages of being domiciled in the U.S. would return to them, which is a good skilled labor force, availability of capital, good mature markets, and a secure economic system. So my instinct is that the vast majority of those who were driven offshore by virtue of the tax system would return quickly.

Chairman ARCHER. Thank you.

Mr. Tanner?

[No response.]

Chairman ARCHER. Ms. Thurman?

Mrs. THURMAN. Thank you, Mr. Chairman.

We have been given kind of a grouping of editorials that have been written across the country in support of your tax or replacement. One of the things that I found interesting, especially because we are now sitting in a situation where we have the Joint Tax coming in and saying it could be anywhere between 30 to 57 percent, are we going to go back out and resell this? I mean, when you talk about going nationally, are you going to tell them about potentially this costing 30 to 57 percent?

Mr. LINBECK. Is that addressed to me?

Mrs. THURMAN. That would be addressed to you, and it would be addressed to the business—anybody that wants to respond to this.

Mr. LINBECK. I will try to respond. Our objective is that whatever the tax is, that it be revenue neutral. Our undertaking of this effort was totally bipartisan. We have undertaken the research on a bipartisan basis. All of our polling was doing by a joint venture of a Republican and Democratic pollster. Our commitment to the effort is that it be consistent with two principles: that it be bipartisan and, number two, that it be revenue neutral.

The research that we have received suggests the rate that we have been promulgating. If at the end of the day and if the base is consistent with what we understood to be the broadest possible base the rate is higher, that is the rate that we will use. We are not really trying to sell the rate but, rather, the principle.

Mrs. THURMAN. But it does sound much better to be able to say a 23 percent sales tax versus a 30 or a 57 percent.

Mr. LINBECK. Absolutely, it does. And, also, one ought to bear in mind that it is a replacement tax.

Mrs. THURMAN. Correct. Let me just give you some examples of some things, and any of you can talk about this. But we did some calculations quickly just to figure out, say, a couple making $50,000, using dependent care credit, with two children, and they are using standard deductions. Their income tax would be about $2,810; the employee's share on the payroll tax, $3,825; employer share, $3,825—with a total of $10,460. That sounds a little outrageous, I agree.

Then you go down, though, and you say the proposal is consuming, say, 30 percent of the $50,000, or at a rate of 30 percent, which is the lowest rate that has been given tough, is at about $15,000, and then the rebate, which would be the 0.23 times the 1,750, which would be the poverty, comes to a total of about $11,078. So what you really would be is you would have a net tax increase of about $618. So, actually, you would be ending up paying more in a tax under a sales tax than you would under the current system.

And then if you went to somebody—and then if you went to a 57 percent rate, which Joint Tax has said——

Chairman ARCHER. Would the gentle lady suspend for one moment? My presence is now being mandated on the floor of the House of Representatives, so I am going to leave for a while, and Congressman Hulshof will preside.

Mr. HULSHOF. [Presiding.] Thank you.

Chairman ARCHER. The gentle lady may commence. Sorry.

Mrs. THURMAN. So then at 57 percent at $50,000, it is $28,500. The rebate would be $3,922, with a tax of $24,578, with the net tax increase then being $9,579.

I don't know how to particularly—then if you talk about issues of taxing food and medical and drugs and all of those kinds of things, how do I sell this to either the $50,000 person a year making $50,000 and/or the senior who is now going to be picking up a cost that is not being shared by them? And then you can go on with a $30,000 single mother.

I mean, simplification is good. I understand the reason. But when you look at it from a dollar, a pure dollar, of who is going to pick up the cost of this, I have some concerns in who this is being shifted to. Maybe somebody can talk to me about that because I need to be able to explain that at home.

Mr. LINBECK. If you are asking me——

Mrs. THURMAN. Oh, whoever would like to take——

80

Mr. LINBECK. I will be glad to give you my thoughts on it, and they consist of the—if the numbers are correct and someone ought to be able to sit down with the person who understands the Fair Tax and all of its complexity and simplicity and the income tax and its complexity and simplicity and come to an understanding of what the comparison is, then we ought to have a common basis for moving forward.

In all candor, I couldn't follow all of the numbers in my head to know what the variation may or may not be as between the findings that were expressed——

Mrs. THURMAN. It is based on two very simple things. One would be the consumption of $50,000 at a 30 percent or 57 percent, depending on where we are under Joint Tax, and what payroll—and what the difference would be what they paid a day and what they pay under the—what your system would be including the rebate. And it seems to be quite different.

Mr. LINBECK. I would encourage you to invite someone in who understands the system and see if you can work through those numbers with those persons, and it does not ring true to me, based on what I have previously discerned from the research, but it is very possible that we have made an error in it. And if we have, that can be corrected. But if not, then that will inform us all.

Mrs. THURMAN. Then I would just say to you that I will be glad to open my office if you would like to send somebody and show me where we are wrong.

Mr. LINBECK. Well, I am not sure we can show you where you are wrong, but we can show you where the calculations come out.

Mrs. THURMAN. Thank you.

Mr. HULSHOF. Mr. Portman?

Mr. PORTMAN. Thank you, Mr. Chairman. And I want to commend the panel for taking the leap off the cliff, with the exception of our friend from the realtors who is not there yet, with at least coming up with what I view to be a very creative and innovative approach. I think it has problems, and I am going to ask you about some of those problems. But our current system is too complex, too complicated, and the compliance costs are a big hit on our economy and individual Americans who are filling out their taxes even as we speak. And then, finally, it does penalize savings and investment in a way that is counterproductive to economic growth. So we need a new approach to taxes.

My concerns with the Fair Tax are some of those you have already heard. I think the percentage that would be paid is the key issue. It affects really so many other issues related to it, including, of course, the compliance, the possibility that there could be enormous compliance issues with the many transactions which would occur every day. Also, of course, it affects what the States might do. The States do tend to piggyback on us. They do that with our Federal taxes. I think they would tend to do it with this tax. And so the rate that we are talking about, whether it is 24 percent or 65 percent—as Pricewaterhouse has said, there is a range, depending on compliance, depending on other assumptions about economic growth. I think you have to add what the States are going to do currently with regard to their income taxes and corporate income taxes on top of that, and you end up having a fairly onerous percentage. So that is one of the issues that I have, and I won't get into that because I think you probably heard a lot about that earlier this morning. And we can go back and forth on what that percentage might be, but I think it is important as to, again, so many other issues.

My understanding is that today about 60 percent of the taxes are paid by the top 10 percent, somewhere between 55 and 60 percent. Is that your understanding? I am talking about Federal income taxes, forgetting the payroll tax. You know, people say we don't have a very progressive system. The top 1 percent pay about 25 percent of the taxes; the top 10 percent pay about 30 percent of the taxes.

Have you all looked at the Fair Tax in terms of this analysis? And it is really building on the question from the gentle lady from Florida that you just heard. But what would the top 10 percent of wage earners in this country pay as a percentage of the Fair Tax?

Mr. McCRACKEN. Well, I understand that—actually, that is a very difficult question to answer because it is based not on what you earn or what you are worth; it is based on what you consume, on basically what you take out of the economy. So it is going to vary widely. Bill Gates could pay billions of dollars this year in taxes if he consumed that much, or he could pay nothing in taxes this year if he chose to reinvest everything he makes back into the economy into creating jobs.

So it is very different from the income tax, and it is hard to look at it in quite the same——

Mr. PORTMAN. It is very different, but although the analysis will depend on certain assumptions, it shouldn't be as difficult as you indicate because Bill Gates will still get a salary, so will Rob Portman, so will everybody else. And the question is: Of the top 10 percent of wage earners, what percentage will they pay in terms of the Federal sales tax?

Now, again, our current system is very progressive, and this is one of the issues that all of us who are interested in tax reform have to deal with. And those who think it is not, again, I believe are wrong. When you get into tax reform, you will find out it is very difficult to end up with the same distribution you have now if you really believe in fundamental reform unless you are going to go to a tiered system.

But I just wondered if you had a number on that, what the top 10 percent of wage earners would pay as a percentage of the Fair Tax?

Mr. McCRACKEN. I don't. Do you want——

Mr. LINBECK. No, I have seen no data, to my knowledge, there is no data available because it does, as Mr. McCracken pointed out, depend on the behavior of the individual in respect to their spending habits. And over a lifetime, one can make those calculations with a reasonably high degree of certainty, and it is my understanding that given the rebate and the elimination of the payroll tax and the stripping away of the tax embedded in products and services that we buy, the Fair Tax will be as progressive if not more progressive than the current system.

So, in general, that is the principle we think underlies the plan, but we cannot tell you what the idiosyncratic outcome would be for an individual taxpayer.

Mr. PORTMAN. Well, I am not looking for the idiosyncratic or individual. I am going on average. And you do have to make certain assumptions, which I know you have made, with regard to purchases, and GAO has done that and other groups have done that over the years. It is very difficult to do. I know the Treasury Department, I think under Ronald Reagan, tried to do that. And where you have to start, is purchases and income. I just think it would be helpful to know that, frankly, to be able to respond to some, I am sure, of the critique that you got this morning, and the most recent question indicates that we will be concerned about that. There is with every fundamental tax reform proposal, whether it is a flat tax, the Fair Tax, or some hybrids that are out there.

A couple other questions, if I could. One, there is obviously a compliance issue when you have got, let's say for argument's sake, a 30 percent sales tax. There is going to be an incentive for folks to figure out a way to barter or figure out a way to deal with it outside the tax system that is not there currently. In my own county, we have 5.5, 6 percent sales tax, the counties that I represent, and taking it up to 30 percent is going to change people's behavior. So there is a compliance issue there.

The bigger compliance issue that I worry about, though, is the rebate. I look at the earned income tax system, where we are told by the Treasury Department there is probably a 20 to 22 percent mispayment. Some would say that is fraud. Others would say it is error. It is probably a combination of a lot of things. But it is an enormously difficult rebate system for the IRS to enforce. They aren't structured to do it.

Who would enforce your rebate system? You know, when you get something in the mail, at the IRS now, that says I am eligible for the EITC, for the most part a check then goes from the taxpayers to that person because, frankly, it is very difficult to audit and have appropriate compliance. When there is auditing and compliance, it can get very difficult for the agency that does that because you have millions of taxpayers and, frankly, you are going into issues that are very intrusive and personal to people in terms of their income. How would you determine whether people who applied for the rebate deserve the rebate?

Mr. LINBECK. Well, first of all, there is no means test. It is a universal rebate. But the mechanism to implement the rebate is driven by the Social Security Administration and the use of the Social Security number. So if the subject person seeks a rebate, they send a card to the Social Security Administration on which they have placed their Social Security number. If there are multiple beneficiaries of the rebate they wish to claim, they list each of those Social Security numbers.

The Social Security Administration runs that through the system to see if each of those are a valid Social Security number, or if there are duplicates of that same number, that triggers an inquiry as to who is the legitimate holder of that number. That then triggers the rebate on a periodic basis every month in an amount equal to the number of the tax times the Health and Human Services determination as to the poverty level for that size family.

Mr. PORTMAN. Well, having——

Mr. HULSHOF. I must say to my friend that your time is——

Mr. PORTMAN. I am sorry. With the indulgence of the Chair, let me just finish up that point and just say that it is much simpler having just one flat rate based on whatever the poverty rate is for that number of individuals. I will say, though, there are still going to be major compliance issues, and we ought not to overlook those and we should be concerned about those.

I have lots of other questions, but, again, I want to commend you all for taking the leap and for making this innovative proposal.

Mr. HULSHOF. The gentleman's time has expired. As I yield to my friend from Texas, I know that one of the issues that he has been pursuing quite vigorously in this committee is the end of abusive corporate tax shelters, and I would suggest that were the Fair Tax to be implemented and business income no longer being taxed, it would eliminate these corporate tax shelters that you have been so——

Mr. DOGGETT. I will have to take up another agenda, and I am glad Mr. Linbeck is here to add support to that.

Mr. HULSHOF. I yield to the gentleman.

Mr. DOGGETT. Let me begin, though, with my neighbor, Mr. Martin. I appreciate the service that you provided our community in central Texas, and I know that you are approaching an age when Social Security is important to you and many of the people that you work with. And one of the concerns that I have about this, James, I was down at the Archives last week, and just down from where the Declaration of Independence is there for everybody to look at, they now have up a quote in connection with an exhibit from Franklin Delano Roosevelt. And the essence of it is that he set up a payroll contribution system for Social Security so that every American would feel that they have a stake in Social Security and that no politician would ever be able to take that Social Security system away from them.

Isn't there a danger, as you heard me ask the sponsor of this measure this morning, that if we totally eliminate what has become a burdensome payroll system, no doubt, but if we totally eliminate that system, we may set up a way that those who don't support Social Security will be able to undermine it because no longer will each American feel that they are paying in something specifically for that system?

Mr. MARTIN. Mr. Doggett, my own opinion on that is that if the transfer system is done in a proper manner and it is clear and it is able to be understood by the rank-and-file working American, that they will feel secure with it. They will be looking at overall totals, and they will be listening to Congress and various administrations tell them how much is in there and how long the fund is solvent for. And I think if those numbers are consistent, I think that they will have the same degree of either concern or satisfaction that they do now.

Mr. DOGGETT. I appreciate it.

Mr. Linbeck, I wish that we had more citizens that were as interested in affecting public policy as you obviously are, because I have heard from a number of constituents there in Austin that you have either talked with personally or others of this effort have talked to personally.

There are several concerns, and mine are similar to the ones that I raised this morning also. I gather that you envision that after this act is put into place, electronic commerce will provide a significant source of Federal revenues.

Mr. LINBECK. It is our expectation that it would. The expectation under the Fair Tax is that all terminal transactions, by whatever distributional means, will be subject to the tax. So that would be brick and mortar, Internet transactions, and mail transactions.

Mr. DOGGETT. And your goal is to try to get this tax into place just as soon as you can as a replacement for the income tax.

Mr. LINBECK. Yes, sir.

Mr. DOGGETT. And so I gather, therefore, that you would not support extending the Internet tax moratorium until 2006.

Mr. LINBECK. I would personally support not having any tax on the Internet medium.

Mr. DOGGETT. Sure, the access.

Mr. LINBECK. The access.

Mr. DOGGETT. But I am talking about taxes on transactions.

Mr. LINBECK. But to tax the transaction, I would support taxing immediately, as long as it was an evenhanded application. I think the dislocation occurs and the unfairness occurs when you have different means of distribution taxed on a different basis, or at least not enforced in a uniform fashion.

We contemplate that under the Fair Tax there would be uniform application of the tax so that everyone has a level playing field from which to embark on their economic activity.

Mr. DOGGETT. I am accustomed, from my perspective, at least, to getting advice from the majority leader, Mr. Armey, that I consider to range from bad to worse. But I was listening to his comments on Sunday about your proposal on Fox News, which I am sure you saw——

Mr. LINBECK. No, sir, I didn't.

Mr. DOGGETT. Well, he was asked if he supported your bill, and he said "no, it doesn't work and, furthermore, it is regressive and it adds inevitably to the tax code, making it equally as complex as today's income tax." And he also said that no country has ever made a successful change from an income tax to a sales tax, and that when Canada went to a higher sales tax, the use of cash in the Canadian economy tripled in just 6 months. I am quickly summarizing the latter part of his testimony. The first part was a direct quote.

I am just going to ask you if Mr. Armey has finally gotten something right.

Mr. LINBECK. Well, I must admit, if the Fair Tax had the attributes he ascribes to it, I wouldn't be for it. I don't know what he is looking at, but the provisions that are embedded in House bill 2525 do not appear, through my own observation nor the research that has been undertaken, to have those kinds of outcomes. I would certainly not be in favor of any system that didn't have a preferential option for the poor. And in my judgment, the Fair Tax is the only bill currently being considered that represents that kind of an option.

Mr. DOGGETT. What about the specific issue—my last comment, Mr. Chairman—that he raised? I know I covered a lot of it, but greater reliance on a national sales tax in Canada greatly increased the underground economy, and he specifically said the use of cash in the Canadian economy tripled in just 6 months, as an indication of too much sales tax resulting in an underground economy.

Mr. LINBECK. Well, I have no frame of reference for his data. But it is my understanding that in Canada the problem arose because they promised to eliminate the income tax and replace it with a sales tax. When they passed the sales tax, they kept the income tax as well. And if that is a correct understanding of the facts, then it is not surprising to me that people would take extreme measures to find whatever relief from the burden that was imposed on them with both tax systems that was available to them. But our research suggests to us that there is no reason to believe that there would be a higher incidence of evasion or leakage or cheating under a transparent uniform sales tax at the Federal level than there is under the present income tax system. And we have made no assumptions in the body of the research that suggests that it would be less. We have just assumed it would be the same.

Mr. DOGGETT. Thank you very much. And thank all of you.

Mr. HULSHOF. Mr. Lewis?

Mr. LEWIS. Thank you very much, Mr. Chairman.

Mr. Rooth, what would be the impact of this legislation on minority home ownership?

Mr. ROOTH. Excuse me, on which home ownership?

Mr. LEWIS. On minority.

Mr. ROOTH. Minority?

Mr. LEWIS. Right.

Mr. ROOTH. As we have stated earlier, and I have a handout that I will be happy to include to any of the members that we have done, that basically we find that minority spending is a huge part of our economy here in housing, that the priorities of home ownership are highest among minorities and far higher than all Americans combined. Anything that restricts that purchase, we are going to have great difficulty with.

The actual impact of this legislation on the first-time home buyer or on minority home buyers is next to impossible to predict. As I have mentioned earlier, we have been wrong in every other prediction we have ever made. But I am very concerned about the impact to such a large amount of our population.

Mr. LEWIS. Are you troubled by the possibility of a 30-percent increase on renter apartments, on new home construction?

Mr. ROOTH. I am absolutely concerned with it on new home construction because we have already demonstrated that there is an excess cost of new home construction of 20 percent today. So if we were to add another 30 percent to that, that could conceivably be a 50-percent impact. But the rental housing sector is probably what concerns me the most because if I can rent you an apartment today for $500 a month, there is nothing to say that I can tomorrow afford $650 or $700 a month because I can't predict what the employer is going to pass on to me in my paycheck. Unless I have a contract about my employment, I cannot guarantee that I am going to get my full paycheck.

Mr. LEWIS. Thank you, Mr. Rooth.

Mr. Linbeck, are you concerned that 2525 will impose an increase, a dramatic increase on purchase of prescription drugs, hospital bills, doctor bills, and nursing home care when home care is already going higher and higher and you come and you are suggesting that you are going to add more of a cost?

Mr. LINBECK. Yes, sir. I would be very concerned about it if I believed that would be the outcome. I am persuaded by the rigor and the intensity of the——

Mr. LEWIS. But I want you to persuade me. I want you tell me how we are going to, with 2525, how can we keep the cost of prescription drugs, doctor bills, nursing home care from going up, up, up?

Mr. LINBECK. In my judgment, the prescription drug issue, as well as other health care issues, will be subject to the same type of market forces, in terms of stripping away the costs that are currently embedded therein by the current system, thereby lowering the cost at the producer level, the net outcome of which, we believe, based on the research we have been given, is that the price that the consumer pays will not be higher, including the tax, than it is today. But on top of that, the purchaser of the products will have more money in their pay environment. Their gross pay will be their net pay. In addition, they will get the rebate in an amount equal to the tax on essentials, and in most of the Health and Human Services information, with which I am familiar, health care is a component of the cost that they use in determining what the cost of living would be for the poverty level.

So it is our understanding and belief that there will not be a disadvantage, particularly to the poor, but rather an advantage to the poor under the Fair Tax in purchasing the essentials.

Mr. LEWIS. But the costs of health care is not just something that should be the concern of the poor, but is middle income, working people, so much of their limited income is going to try to pay doctor bills, and buy prescription drugs, to provide nursing home care.

Mr. LINBECK. And it is our belief, Congressman, that those costs at the producer level will come down. Let's look at that particular doctor who is dispensing that care. They will no longer have to administer the current tax system in the management of their office. They will no longer have to keep track of any of that information, so the compliance costs will go down very substantially. It is expected that those costs will be passed along to the consumer, to the patient that they are treating.

Mr. LEWIS. But if I am doctor running an office and I have nurses and others assisting, I have to collect those taxes, right?

Mr. LINBECK. Yes.

Mr. LEWIS. But you do believe that health care should be accessible, affordable and it should not be out of the reach of any of our citizens. When you come along and put up another tax, additional costs, you are moving health care further and further away from working Americans.

Mr. LINBECK. If we believed that was the outcome, we would be gravely concerned about it. We believe the outcome will be contrary to that assumption, and that it will, in fact, not go up in cost over where it is today.

Mr. LEWIS. Thank you.

Mr. LINBECK. Yes.

Mr. LEWIS. Thank you, Mr. Chairman.

Mr. HULSHOF. Mr. Watkins?

Mr. WATKINS. Thank you, Mr. Chairman. To a couple of you, Mr. Rooth and Mr. Kouplen, I have a background in both of those areas; first, in agriculture, as Mr. Kouplen knows, and then later on in building and real estate. So I have got a couple of questions I would like to take up with both of you.

I know in the agriculture area, a lot of us have worked very hard because of blatant double taxation on estate tax, trying to get more relief and more relief in that area, and we have made some headway, but we have not got it repealed yet, and we realize that is something a lot of farm families are very interested in doing.

I also recognize, if we stop and look through I think in detail, that if we have a tremendous just total change of direction, agriculture would probably end up being in the tax structure overall we could be hurt in agriculture a great deal. So I think we have to be very careful on how we go into it.

A bill I am working on, and Ken Hulshof, my good friend from Missouri, I know probably would be interested in this bill, and I am working on it with staff and others. But one of the things in agriculture right now, we have an age problem, a population that is out there getting closer to 60 years of age, and not only with that, it is very difficult for maybe their offspring to enter, but along with that situation, many of them cannot get out. Now, let me share with you it is a capital gains situation. It is a fact that I know from experience.

I will use the example that maybe 30 years ago a farmer may have bought land at $200 an acre. Today it may be $700 an acre. He has been farming with the inflation of that land. And I understand that. I have been there. I understand. And as a result, now he is 70 years old. He cannot sell and pay capital gains tax and pay his debts. He doesn't have the money, and so he is locked. And these are some of the most patriotic, hardworking, 15-, 16-hour-a-day families, husbands and wives, out on that farm.

I am working on a bill that will allow us, hopefully, at least what we are allowing for, $500,000 on a piece of real estate—if you happen to have capital gains, you can go up there—for that to be for a farm, home, and the surrounding land. That would allow a lot of relief for a lot of farmers out there if they were allowed to do just as our city cousins were able to do with a $500,000 home. Now, I think we should get hopefully a little bit better situation worked out than that, but I am going to be going full bore trying to get something like that.

Do you feel like that would be a great help to a lot of our farmers? Now, I know you have got 2,000 acres, but you take $500,000, for a lot of farmers, they have got several hundred acres, and it would be a big help I think.

Mr. KOUPLEN. I think the Congressman is right on target with that. As you know, the most appealing aspects of this proposal is the elimination of the capital gains tax and the death tax or estate taxes. And you know, as well as those of us in agriculture, the situation that we have been in over the last couple of years, is a very tough situation. We are a very capital-rich industry and a cash-poor industry. And like you say, the age of our farmers and ranchers in this country is getting to be 60/65 years on average. When they do decide they want to sell, they find out they have a silent partner in the Government. A lot of them decide they cannot afford to sell. Instead they hold on, and sooner or later when the death tax situation arises, their heirs find out that they must sell a great portion of it. This makes that farm economically unfeasible because they have had to sell that much of it. just to keep what is left.

So that aspect of it and compliance costs are the main aspects that we like in this plan, and that is what we would look for in the Farm Bureau in any plan that comes from your committee.

Mr. WATKINS. On that, let me say that I just don't foresee an overhaul of the tax deal for some for several years. Maybe when a new President comes in, there may be some opportunity with the Congress and all to get something overhauled, but I don't see it coming down otherwise.

Let me ask you about real estate, having been a builder. I was sitting on the other side of the aisle when the Tax of 1986 came in. I told them it was probably the most un-American tax bill that ever came down through here because, really, it was nearly wiping out that opportunity of getting the home, the American dream.

What kind of happened to the real estate industry right after that? Are there any lessons that we should learn here? Do we need something on the record?

Mr. ROOTH. I think the most important thing that we learned and the thing that we have got to focus on with any new tax plan, and let me say that our membership is much in support of the simplification, whatever it might be. Transition is a word that I want each and every member of this committee to remember. Because what we did not have in 1986 was a good transition plan. Anything that happens overnight in a major investment sector like real estate has the tendency and the possibility of a severe impact and ripple on the economic climate of this country. So I would encourage you, in any bill that you do, that we have got to have adequate thought about transition.

1986 was as severe as it was primarily because of the loss of passive loss and some of the credit issues that came out. But had we had a sound transitional period of 2 to 5 years, I feel we could have survived it in a much better light.

Mr. WATKINS. I think that is a very good point, as we look at it. Thank you, Mr. Chairman.

Mr. HULSHOF. I thank the gentleman.

Mr. WATKINS. He has been wanting to do that all along.

Mr. HULSHOF. I appreciate the gentleman, and before I let the panel go, just a couple of quick comments. I was flipping through an old Farmer's Almanac recently, and I came across this passage that said, "If Patrick Henry thought taxation without representation was bad, he should see it with representation."

[Laughter.]

Mr. HULSHOF. And I think were this a town meeting back in the 9th Congressional District of Missouri, if I were to take a quick survey, as some of you talk about focus groups, probably a third of those in attendance would invariably say, "We like the ideal, Mr. Linbeck, of such as H.R. 2525"; another third might say, "We like a flat income tax"; and the other third is not yet sure of what sort of system they would like to go to. But what that says is that two-thirds of those in attendance think that we should do something radically different than the present tax code.

Mr. Kouplen, let me just echo the comments of Mr. Watkins. As the only son of a Missouri farm family, we continue to try to work within the existing tax structure to make it easier to pass that family farm on to the next generation. We put the elimination of the death tax on the President's desk last fall, as well as the capital gains rate and relief from the alternative minimum tax, and unfortunately we didn't get that tax relief to you. But we continue to work on those efforts.

Just two quick questions, Mr. Linbeck, because I need some health in that proverbial town meeting that I have talked about.

I think it makes economic sense, the argument that you have made, that were we to move to this retail-type of tax, that there would be pressure on interest rates to go down. And you and the chairman, the real chairman, were discussing how many basis points that would be, and yet I felt the same thing would happen if and when Congress began to balance its books; that is, to balance the Federal budget, that the pressure would be on interest rates to come down.

And yet as we have seen the economy continue to expand, the chairman of the Federal Reserve, and I am not being critical, but in an effort to gain, get arms around the monetary policy, the pressure has been just the opposite, that interest rates, of course, have gone up. So what can you tell me, Mr. Linbeck, that I can talk to my constituents about to assure them that were we to make this fundamental reform, that we would, in fact, see interest rates dropping rather than going in the other direction.

Mr. LINBECK. The only comfort I could suggest in respect to that, and bear in mind I am not Alan Greenspan, and I cannot talk in terms that he talks in and perhaps that is a blessing or not. You will have to make your own judgment on that. But in my judgment, the fact that there will be a lot more money in the capital markets by virtue of the issues that I raised; number one, the repatriation of the earnings of corporations who work overseas, they will be able to bring that money back and no longer have to borrow from the capital markets to meet their Cap X expenditures, the elimination of the tax wedge from interest rates that exist today. There is no reason to believe that people will not loan money at the tax-free rate that they are loaning it today if there was no consequence to them having done so.

And finally, when everybody gets their entire paycheck, let us assume for the sake of discussion that the average person has about a 23- to 27-percent withholding from their current paycheck in the combination of payroll check and income tax withholding, hereafter, they would get 100 percent of that in their paycheck. If they only save 10 percent of that increment, that is a 2-percent to 2.5-percent increase in savings on the total payroll that we currently have in the country. That is a very substantial incremental increase in funds to go into the capital markets.

For those three reasons, I think it is reasonable to assert that there will be a lowering of the interest rates coming out of the Fair Tax passage.

Mr. HULSHOF. Last question for you, and I know we have got other panelists waiting and some on time constraints, so I will cut my questioning short, but with this final question, and I recognize in your written testimony, Mr. Linbeck, you talk about charitable contributions.

Mr. LINBECK. Yes.

Mr. HULSHOF. And I agree with you to the extent that I think we are Americans, we are a charitable people. And when we see that there are those that need, we open up our pocketbooks or volunteer our time or our talents. And yet I also recognize, as someone who itemizes our family, and I muddle through our tax forms because I want the same experience that you have each April 15th, but I also believe that there are some who are motivated, perhaps to give to certain charities or certain philanthropic organizations because of their ability to take some sort of a deduction.

And so my concern is that there may be some significant charities that all of us will continue to give to, but that we might, the incentive is that perhaps there are some other charities that we do make a donation to simply because we are going to at least get at least a small tax benefit. Do you believe that is not the case?

Mr. LINBECK. Well, obviously, we are concerned about that prospect, and that is why we commissioned specific research on that issue. It was instructive to me to learn that there was a similar concern surrounding the infamous 1986 Tax Act that has been referred to lovingly earlier.

It seems to me that the evidence that was put forth then suggested from the charitable community that if they lowered the rate to the degree which they were going to lower the rate, that would have an adverse impact on charitable giving. As a matter of fact, the exact opposite occurred. There was an increase in charitable giving. There seems to be only one direct correlation: the more money people have in their pocket, the more money they give to charity.

I think it is also noteworthy that for the people who don't itemize, the people who tithe to their church, and that is the principal beneficiary of the eleemosynary activities at that level, they are giving after-tax and after-payroll-tax dollars. Just imagine how liberating it will be to them for the first time to have their whole paycheck from which they can extract those funds they wish to give to their church or the charity of their choice. Our belief is, and the evidence suggests very strongly, that if anything, there will be an uptick in charitable giving, not a depressing impact from the Fair Tax.

Mr. HULSHOF. Thank you, Mr. Linbeck.

Mrs. THURMAN. Mr. Chairman, I have to comment on a comment you made.

Mr. HULSHOF. Surely.

Mrs. THURMAN. Because, Mr. Kouplen, I just want you to know, though, in 1997—even though the last tax package did not get up to the President—the one in 1997 did, and it was a very bipartisan act, and we did lower the capital gains, and we did take care of some of the inheritance tax, and there are floating proposals out there. So I just could not let that go by.

Mr. MCCRACKEN. Can I add one more quick point on the issue of the charitable deduction?

Mr. HULSHOF. Mr. McCracken?

Mr. MCCRACKEN. It is important to realize that, in fact, charitable giving would be tax preferred under the Fair Tax; that is to say, you would not pay additional sales tax if you gave money, as opposed to spending it. So you would pay a tax if you spent the money. You wouldn't pay the tax if you gave to a charity. And that is the case for a whole range of different kinds of attributes we discussed here today, whether it is rent or other things.

It is important to realize that anything for which there is not a deduction in the Code now, it is essentially taxed because we were paying for it with after-tax dollars. And so just because it is taxed under the Fair Tax, doesn't mean it is a brand-new tax that we are not paying right now.

Mr. HULSHOF. I thank the panelists for your patience. You are excused with the thanks of this committee.

I will call the next panel to step up, and I will yield to the chairman, Mr. Archer.

Chairman ARCHER. The chair invites the next panel to be seated at the witness table.

Gentlemen, welcome to the committee. Dr. Kotlikoff, I understand you have pressing engagements elsewhere, so to accommodate that, the chair will recognize you first, and you may proceed.

STATEMENT OF LAURENCE J. KOTLIKOFF, PROFESSOR OF EC-ONOMICS, BOSTON UNIVERSITY, AND RESEARCH ASSO-CIATE, NATIONAL BUREAU OF ECONOMIC RESEARCH

Mr. KOTLIKOFF. Thank you, Mr. Chairman.

Chairman Archer and other distinguished members of the Committee on the Ways and Means, I am honored by this opportunity to discuss with you the Nation's need for tax reform and the role that consumption taxation, particularly a Federal retail sales tax, could play in enhancing the economy's economic performance and improving its distribution of resources.

Chairman ARCHER. Dr. Kotlikoff, can I remind all of the witnesses, again, if you will identify who you are and whom you represent, in that event, before you start your testimony, for the record, please.

Mr. KOTLIKOFF. I am Larry Kotlikoff. I am a professor of economics at Boston University and a research associate of the National Bureau of Economic Research.

Our Nation's economy has been performing remarkably well in recent years, but our economic success is no reason to be complacent about a tax system that is extraordinarily complex and highly distortionary and that plays a critical role in an overall fiscal system that is like to visit enormous burdens on our children and grandchildren.

I think the Congress and the administration are under the impression that our fiscal house overall, generally speaking, is in good order; that we are running large surpluses and that those surpluses are going to be enormous for as far as the eye can see and that they are going to take care of the fact that close to 80 million baby boomers are going to be retiring starting in 8 years, and then in about 11 years, starting to collect Medicare benefits on top of the Social Security benefits they will be collecting in 8 years.

Well, that is not the case. Suppose you take more realistic projections than the CBO baseline; namely, suppose you don't assume that Federal purchases, as a share of GDP, will decline by 20 percent over the next 10 years and by 30 percent over the next 30 years. If you, instead, assume that Federal purchases are going to grow with the economy, then according to a Federal Reserve and CBO generational accounting study that will be published in the American Economic Review next month, we cannot afford to cut taxes, as some of the members of this committee advocate, and we cannot afford to raise spending, as some other members advocate. Instead you need to have an immediate and permanent 25-percent hike in the Federal income tax in order to keep our children from paying even higher tax rates.

Now, why am I saying all of this in the context of tax reform? Well, the key distributional question that confronts our country is how are we going to be treating the next generation compared to ourselves. And consumption taxation has the advantage that it will place a larger burden of paying for the Government's bills onto rich and middle-class elderly, as well as middle-aged people, and place less of the burden on today's younger people as well as future generations.

Now, let me indicate why it is that a consumption tax would be generationally more equitable. The reason is that the current elderly and those who are about to retire, the baby boomers, have one primary economic activity in front of them, which is consuming. This is a fine activity, but it is not one that is subject to federal taxation, apart from some excise taxes.

So moving to a consumption tax would place a larger burden on the elderly, in general. But the poor elderly, those who are living off of Social Security, would be fully insulated from a consumption tax because the Social Security benefits are indexed to the Consumer Price Index. So what we are talking about is asking the rich and middle-class elderly, who have received enormous transfers over the years from Medicare and Social Security to help bail out their children and grandchildren.

A retail sales tax is a transparent consumption. Its adoption would greatly reduce compliance costs because you won't have an army of lawyers, and accountants, and tax planners spending their entire working lives trying to lower people's taxes. And you won't have people like me spending 3 days trying to get our tax returns together. That is a terrific plus. An retail sales tax would also reduce enforcement costs because the effective marginal tax rates will be lower.

We have had some discussion back and forth this morning about how high the tax retail sales rates would be. And I think that the number 59 percent has been cited, and the number 30 percent, and

23 percent. I think there is some comparison here of apples and oranges. The 59 percent is a tax-exclusive number, while the 30-percent number is a tax-inclusive number. I think the right number to use here is the tax-inclusive number because you want to compare it with the Federal income tax, plus the payroll tax, both of which are calculated on a tax-inclusive basis.

If you consider the Federal income tax and the payroll tax for somebody who has low income, there is a 15-percent federal income tax, plus a 15-percent payroll taxes (employer plus employee). Also, a lot of low-income people get the earned income tax credit, and when they earn a dollar, they lose roughly 20 cents on the margin. So, effectively, they are in a 50-percent marginal tax bracket.

So, the comparison is 50 percent versus 30 percent for those low-income people because the 30 percent is really what I think a comprehensive retail sales tax at the Federal level would generate in terms of a tax-inclusive rate that could be compared with the alternative that we now have. And If you also consider middle-income and high-income people, you find that they are paying close to 40- to 50-percent tax brackets at the margin.

So with a retail sales tax we would end up with a lower effective tax rate because we are going to be broadening the base. Consumption is a much bigger base than the payroll tax base, and it is also probably as big as the income tax base when you take into account all of the exemptions and deductions from the income tax base. So in some fundamental sense, it must be the case that effective tax rates if you are shifting to taxing all of consumptions.

And in the process of broadening this base, we are going to be eliminating all kinds of distortions. We talked about saving distortions and labor supply distortions, but we are also going to get rid of the lock-in effect on the sale of appreciated assets, the subsidy to health insurance, which is helping to speed up the rise in health care costs, differential tax treatment of investment in different kinds of capital, the tax advantage to debt versus equity, the marriage penalty, the subsidy to home ownership. And I could go on, but you get a sense that there are some major efficiency gains here to be had.

Chairman ARCHER. Dr. Kotlikoff, sadly enough, your time has expired sometime back. But if you want to add something for a very short period of time, the chair will be glad to receive it.

Mr. KOTLIKOFF. I appreciate that.

The knee-jerk reaction to the consumption tax by the public is that it is regressive because the public compares consumption to current income. But economists think lifetime income is the correct resource measure, and consumption is roughly proportional to lifetime income. So one should think about a consumption tax as being a proportional tax. In contrast, the payroll tax, which would be replaced under the Fair Tax proposal, is regressive relative to lifetime income. Take Bill Gates; his payroll taxes are a pittance relative to his lifetime income.

The Fair Tax gets rid of a very regressive tax. It also gets rid of the income tax, which is progressive on a lifetime basis, but has lots of exemptions for certain activities that the rich engage in more than the poor. All in all, I agree with Leo Linbeck that the Fair Tax proposal, though I have some suggestions to improve it relative to what is being proposed, would improve intragenerational equity, and as I said, it would certainly improve intergenerational equity. Hence the Fair Tax would be a lot fairer than what we have now.

Thank you.

[The prepared statement follows:]

Statement of Laurence J. Kotlikoff, Professor of Economics, Boston University, and Research Associate, National Bureau of Economic Research

Chairman Archer and other distinguished members of the Committee on Ways and Means:

I'm honored by this opportunity to discuss with you the nation's need for tax reform and the role that consumption taxation, particularly a federal retail sales tax, could play in enhancing the economy's economic performance and improving its distribution of resources.

Our nation's economy has been performing remarkably well in recent years, but our economic success is no reason to be complacent about a tax system that is extraordinarily complex and highly distortionary and that plays a critical role in an overall fiscal system that is likely to visit enormous burdens on our children and grandchildren.

The complexity of the tax code doesn't just drive taxpayers crazy. It also costs them a significant amount of time—time that could be spent working or time that could be spent enjoying life. Having just spent three days doing my taxes, I have a refreshed sense of the substantial costs to the man in the street and the nation as a whole of complying with the federal income tax code.

The distortions of our tax system also diminish the nation's well being, but in ways that are less transparent. Today, almost all American households are in combined federal, state, and local marginal income tax brackets of roughly 50 percent. Because governments are collectively confiscating half of every dollar most workers earn, most workers work many fewer hours than they would were their tax payments independent of their labor earnings. And since the government is confiscating half of every dollar of income most savers earn on their non tax-favored retirement accounts, many Americans choose to spend today rather than save for tomorrow.

Tax Reform's Importance for Fiscal Sustainability and Generational Equity

Eliminating complexity and distortions would be cause enough for reforming the federal income tax, but there is a much more pressing reason: notwithstanding recent wishful projections about future government surpluses, our fiscal house is not in order. Indeed, getting it in order would require not cutting federal income taxes, as some in this chamber advocate, but immediately and permanently raising them by over 25 percent. That assessment comes not from academia, but from the Congressional Budget Office and the Federal Reserve Bank of Cleveland. A joint CBO-Cleveland Fed generational accounting study, to be published next month in the American Economic Review, shows that such a tax hike is needed to achieve generational balance—a situation in which our children and grandchildren will face tax rates that are no higher than those we face.

The 25 percent or greater requisite tax hike is derived under the assumption that growth in federal purchases of goods and services keeps pace with growth in the overall economy. This responsible assumption can be contrasted with the irresponsible one underlying the projection of very large surpluses over the next few decades. The irresponsible projection, whose surpluses are routinely cited by advocates of tax cuts and spending hikes, assumes that, as a share of GDP, federal spending will decline by 20 percent by the end of this decade and by 30 percent by roughly 2040.

Who am I to say that the federal government won't shrink to this extent relative to the economy? Just a parent of a two and a nine year old who knows that such shrinkage is highly unlikely and that basing policy on that assumption amounts to gambling with our children's future—an enterprise worthy of neither this Congress nor this administration.

Our long-term fiscal position is bleak for one straightforward reason. Right now there are about 35 million older Americans. But waiting in the wings are 78 million baby boomers who will start collecting Social Security checks in just eight years and Medicare benefits in just eleven years. Over the next 30 years, the number of elderly will increase by 100 percent, while the number of workers will rise by only 15 percent. This enormous disparity in the growth of the number of elderly and in the number of those who will support them would be much greater still if the recently convened Technical Panel of the Social Security Advisor Board is correct in its assessment that the baby boomers will live substantially longer then the government's actuaries now predict.

What does tax reform have to do with addressing the generational imbalance in U.S. fiscal policy? Essentially everything. To see this, let's start with what a tax reform would tax. Since the federal government is currently taxing wages and capital income, the only meaningful reform would involve taxing consumption on a comprehensive basis (as opposed to levying, as it currently does, a few excise taxes). And each of the major tax reform proposals advanced in recent years does precisely that.

The retail sales tax clearly taxes consumption. But so does the Flat Tax. Just ask Robert Hall, one of the originators of the proposal, who describes his Flat Tax as, effectively, a Value Added Tax. A value added tax taxes output less investment (because firms get to deduct their investment.) Now investment equals saving, so taxing output minus investment is taxing output minus saving, which is taxing consumption, since output minus saving equals consumption.

The Flat Tax differs from a VAT in only two respects. First, it asks workers, rather than firm managers, to mail in the check for the tax payment on that portion of output paid to them as wages. Second, it provides a subsidy to workers with low wages. The first difference is one of form, not substance. The second is more important, but doesn't negate the basic fact that the Flat Tax taxes consumption.

So what does taxing consumption have to do with achieving a generationally equitable fiscal policy? Again, essentially everything. The reason is that the current elderly as well as the baby boomers, who will shortly retire, have one primary economic activity left to accomplish—consumption. And under a consumption tax, they will pay a lot more in future taxes than they would under the current tax system. Although the elderly as a group would share in the burden of a consumption tax, the poor elderly—those living exclusively on Social Security benefits—would not because their benefits are indexed to the consumer price level and are thus guaranteed in real terms.

To recapitulate, given the likely path of government spending and the inevitable aging of our society, our children and our children's children are in for extremely rough sledding. Indeed, the CBO–FED study suggests they will face lifetime net tax rates [1] that are 80 percent higher than those we face if nothing is done. This generational imbalance, rather than the treatment of the rich versus the poor within a generation, is the fundamental issue of economic justice facing us today. Consumption taxation can address that issue by asking the current and near-term elderly to do their fair share in helping to achieve generational balance.

Consumption Taxation and Economic Efficiency

Consumption taxation is needed not just to help our children. It is also needed to simplify the tax code and reduce effective marginal tax rates. The Fair Tax proposal is a case in point. This proposed reform would eliminate both the personal and corporate federal income taxes as well as the payroll tax, and replace them with a federal retail sales tax plus a rebate based on each household's demographic characteristics. Compliance costs would be vastly lower under a retail sales tax. So would, it seems, enforcement costs. The reason is that a broad based sales tax, with no exemptions for housing or any other forms of consumption, would feature much lower effective marginal tax rates than those we now face and, therefore, much smaller incentives to evade taxation.

The lower effective marginal tax rates under the Fair Tax would also mean much smaller economic distortions than currently exists. This reflects the proposition, which is well known to economists, that the welfare costs of distorting economic incentives rises with the square of effective marginal tax rates.

In addition to substantially reducing saving and labor supply distortions, a comprehensive retail sales tax would eliminate a myriad of other distortions such as the lock-in effect on the sale of appreciated assets, the subsidy to health insurance associated with the deductibility of premium payments, the differential tax treatment of investment in different kinds of capital, the tax advantage to debt over equity finance, the marriage penalty, and the subsidy to home ownership.

Is Consumption Taxation Regressive?

Consumption taxation has a bad rap among the general public. It's viewed as regressive when, indeed, it's nothing of the sort. To economists, consumption rep-

---

[1] The lifetime net tax rate is defined as the present value (to birth) of taxes paid over the lifetime net of the present value (to birth) of transfer payments received over the lifetime divided by the present value (to birth) of lifetime labor income.

resents the primary measure of economic well-being. So it makes sense to compare households' taxes with their levels of consumption to determine whether those who are better off pay more than those who are worse off. But consumption is financed not just by current income, but by lifetime resources, which consists of lifetime earnings, lifetime inheritances and gifts received, and initial net worth. So comparing a household's taxes with its command of economic resources requires comparing its taxes with lifetime resources, not current income.

Since lifetime resources are either consumed or bequeathed and since bequests will, themselves, ultimately finance consumption, taxing consumption is like taxing lifetime resources. If consumption is taxed at a fixed rate, as in the case of the Fair Tax and the Flat Tax proposals, the consumption tax will be proportional to lifetime resources; i.e., the tax would be neither progressive nor regressive, but rather proportional.

So if there were no system of taxation to begin with and we introduced a consumption tax, someone with twice the level of lifetime resources as someone else would pay twice the amount of tax. But we aren't starting from scratch. Instead, we are starting from a tax system with some very progressive and some very regressive elements. When measured relative to lifetime resources, the personal income tax is highly progressive, while the payroll tax is highly regressive. And the corporate income tax is essentially proportional to lifetime income since it reduces the net returns to all households no matter the size of their lifetime resources. The fact that the current tax system is not strongly progressive and may even be regressive is the reason that moving from the current system to the Fair Tax, with its progressive rebate, could end up raising the overall degree of tax progressivity.

The lifetime resource perspective leads naturally to comparisons of tax burdens within a cohort, since the lifetime resources of the young and old will be quite different simply because of their ages. Among the elderly, the Fair Tax would be particularly progressive because a federal sales tax would lower the purchasing power of the rich elderly who live off their assets, but not the poor elderly, whose primary means of support—Social Security benefits-would be automatically raised in response to a sales-tax induced increase in the price level. Hence, the Fair Tax features not just a demographic rebate, but also, implicitly, a rise in Social Security benefits. If government transfers to the poor young were also effectively indexed to the price level, the adoption of the Fair Tax would also trigger a rise in those transfer payments as well.[2]

Were the very staid and well established businessmen and women who advocate the Fair Tax to proclaim that their tax reform 1) levies a tax on the holdings of wealth, 2) provides a highly progressive tax rebate, and 3) implies an increase in Social Security benefits and, most likely, transfers to the poor, they would probably be viewed as members of a vast left-wing conspiracy. But this is precisely what they are recommending.

The fact that a consumption tax is, in part, a tax on wealth is well know to public finance economists, but not to the general public. The reason is that when a consumption tax is levied, it lowers the amount of actual consumption that can be purchased with a given amount of wealth since some of the wealth must be spent on the consumption taxes. Stated differently, the imposition of a consumption tax visits an immediate real capital loss on wealth holders because their assets no longer have as large a claim on current or future consumption.

My sense is that the Fair Tax would be more progressive than the current system when assessed on a cohort-by-cohort basis and measured relative to lifetime income. However, knowing the actual degree to which the Fair Tax would enhance intragenerational progressivity requires additional empirical research based on lifetime models of consumption and saving. Such research is now underway, and I would expect that a year from now we'll have a pretty clear picture of the policy's potential impact on the distribution of resources within each generation.

The Long-Term Impact of Consumption Taxation on the Economy

In contrast to the limited empirical analysis of consumption taxation that has been conducted to date, consumption taxation has been studied extensively with large-scale life-cycle simulation models. My own research and that with Alan

---

[2] This sentence and the one preceding it assume the price level will rise with the adoption of the Fair Tax. If the Federal Reserve used its monetary policy to maintain the consumer price level, the adoption of the Fair Tax would entail a decline in the level of producer prices and, thus, the nominal wages and capital income received by productive factors. Under this scenario, government transfers, if they weren't reduced in nominal terms, would end up maintaining their purchasing power, while factor payments would not. I.e., the same real redistribution toward the poor would arise.

Auerbach, Cleveland Fed David Altig, Kent Smetters, and Jan Walliser indicates that the Fair Tax would raise the economy's living standard over the long term by roughly 15 percent.[3] This long-run increase in output is generated by a major long-run increase in capital formation and a modest increase in labor supply.

Part of the reason that consumption taxation stimulates saving and labor supply is its improved incentives to work and save. But the primary reason involves the shifting of fiscal burdens away from young savers and onto old spenders. It is a little know, but extremely important fact that the elderly in our country have much higher propensities to consume out of their remaining lifetime resources than do the young and certainly than do the unborn, whose propensities to consume in the present is, of course, zero. The fact that the elderly consume their remaining resources at a higher rate than other generations is precisely what the standard economic theory of saving—the life cycle model of Nobel Laureate Franco Modigliani—predicts. This explanation for this prediction is intuitive; the elderly are closer to the end of their lives than are the young and are, therefore, running short on time to spend their resources. To compensate, they have to spend at a faster rate.

As described in Gokhale, Kotlikoff, and Sablehaus (1996), essentially all of the decline in the rate of U.S. saving in the postwar period can be traced to the government's five-decade long policy of taking ever larger sums from the young and giving them to the old.[4] This intergenerational redistribution, carried out primarily through Social Security, Medicare, and Medicaid, has led to a dramatic rise in the absolute and relative consumption of the elderly. Since 1960, for example, the elderly's share of economy-wide consumption has increased more than four times fast than has their share of the population. Typical 70-year olds are now consuming roughly twice the amounts consumed by typical 30-year olds. In 1960, by contrast, 70-year olds consumed less than three quarters of the amounts consumed by 30 year olds.

In shifting to a consumption tax, the U.S. would shift more of the tax burden onto the current middle class and rich elderly and partly reverse the postwar process of taking from the young and giving to the old. In addition to depressing national consumption and raising national saving, the switch to consumption taxation would, as indicated above, ameliorate our grievous imbalance in generational policy.

The simulation studies also show substantial long-run welfare gains for all lifetime income classes from switching to consumption taxation. Indeed, under the Fair Tax, the initial upper income elderly are the only ones to suffer welfare losses during the transition.

Tax Rates

Simulation analysis and a variety of empirical calculations suggest that the retail sales tax rate needed for revenue neutrality under the Fair Tax, assuming no decline in the real value of government purchases, would be roughly 30 percent when measured on a tax-inclusive basis. This tax rate could be expected to decline by 3 or so percentage points over time as the economy expands. Moreover, if the Fair Tax were structured to include the consumption of existing housing services in its tax base, the initial Fair Tax rate would probably be about 3 percentage points lower. This could be accomplished by assessing the tax on the imputed rent on housing, where the calculation of imputed rent is based on a fair market valuation of housing real estate. This valuation could be done by local municipalities in the course of appraising houses for local property taxes.

A tax-inclusive consumption tax rate of 30 percent translates into a tax-exclusive consumption tax rate of 43 percent. While the 43 percent rate sounds very high, proper comparison of the Fair Tax tax rate with the current payroll and income tax rates requires evaluating the consumption tax rate on a tax-inclusive basis. Even a 30 percent tax rate may sound like a high rate. But one needs to bear in mind that middle and upper income households in America are typically in combined income tax and payroll tax marginal tax brackets of 40 percent or more and that low income Americans are typically in even higher tax brackets once one considers the phase out of the earned income tax credit. Hence, given the state of U.S. marginal taxation, 30 percent is a low number.

---

[3] See Kotlikoff, Laurence J., "Replacing the U.S. Federal Tax System with a Retail Sales Tax—Macroeconomic and Distributional Effects," mimeo, December 1996 and Altig, David, Alan J. Auerbach, Laurence J. Kotlikoff, Kent Smetters, and Jan Walliser, "Simulating Fundament Tax Reform," forthcoming, *The American Economic Review*, 2001.

[4] Gokhale, Jagadeesh, Laurence J. Kotlikoff, and John Sablehaus, "Understanding the Postwar Decline in U.S. Saving: A Cohort Analysis," *The Brookings Papers on Economic* Activity, no. 1, 1996, 315–90.

Transition Issues

Shifting to a consumption tax requires thinking carefully about transition issues. In the case of the Fair Tax, one would want to make sure that the vast sums that have been accumulated tax free in retirement accounts not avoid taxation. How this could be accomplished fairly and quickly is not altogether clear. But what is clear is that the large amount of revenue to be raised here could help limit the size of the Fair Tax Rate. Note that this problem doesn't arise under the Flat Tax because the Flat Tax maintains an explicit tax on labor income and retirement account withdraws are included in the labor income tax base.

While the Flat Tax deals with this transition issue much more easily than does the Fair Tax, the Fair Tax avoids the potential for special transition rules that would favor existing business capital under a Flat Tax and, thereby, dissipate the tax's implicit taxation of existing wealth.

Transparency and Perceived Fairness

The Fair Tax would be easily understood by the general public, and it would be clear to all that everyone—rich and poor alike—pays the tax. In contrast, under the Flat Tax, wealthy individuals who have no labor income will appear to be paying no tax when, in fact, they will implicitly do so through the revaluation downward of the market value of their assets, assuming no special transition rules in behalf of those assets.

Conclusion

The Fair Tax has a lot to recommend it. It would most likely help the poor more than the rich. It would substantially improve the economy's economic performance. It would save Americans enormous amounts of time complying with the bewildering provisions our current tax code. And it would redress the grave intergenerational imbalance America still faces with respect to its fiscal policy.

———————

Chairman ARCHER. Thank you, Dr. Kotlikoff.
Mr. Wilkins?

STATEMENT OF JOHN G. WILKINS, MANAGING DIRECTOR, BARCROFT CONSULTING GROUP, ON BEHALF OF THE NATIONAL RETAIL FEDERATION

Mr. WILKINS. Thank you, Mr. Chairman. My name is John Wilkins. I am managing director of the Barcroft Consulting Group, and I am here on behalf of the National Retail Federation. My statement reports on the findings of a PricewaterhouseCoopers study, of which I was principal author.

Nine years ago, Mr. Chairman, I testified before this committee on international competitiveness, and I observed that a greater reliance on taxing consumption and a lesser reliance on taxing income would be healthy for the economy. I continue to hold that view, but I do not subscribe to abandoning the income tax altogether and replacing it with a sales tax. Our study shows that there could be very harmful results in the short run as a consequence of that action.

In the early 1990s, Coopers & Lybrand undertook to develop an economic model that combined the personal income tax and the corporate income tax models that are used by the Joint Committee of Taxation's staff and the Treasury's staff for revenue-estimating purpose, combining those with a large-scale macroeconomic forecasting model, retaining the best features of all three models.

Unlike many other models, the model includes foreign trade and other international transactions. The model permits the economy to be in disequilibrium, which is important during transition periods.

The model's database includes 100,000 households and 15,000 corporations; whereas, other models sometimes have only a handful or sometimes only one. The model tracks 85 different industries, producing 85 different products.

However, the most distinguishing feature and important characteristic of the model is that it focuses on the near term. It forecasts detailed information on the performance of the economy on a year-by-year basis as the economy makes the transition to a national sales tax regime. And the model shows that this transition may not be nearly as smooth or as simple as we may like.

Much of the discussion today surrounding the sales tax is centered on the tax rate. On the usual tax-exclusive basis of State sales tax rates, the rate for H.R. 1467 would be 18.8 percent if there were 100-percent compliance, there were no exemptions or transition rules and only revenue and not the budget were required to be kept in balance. The Fair Tax rate would be somewhat higher because it also repeals the payroll tax.

Since tax changes will affect the spending side of the budget, as well as the revenue side, a more meaningful measure of budget neutrality would raise that 18-percent rate I mentioned to 24 percent. However, that rate would still rely on what I would consider an unrealistic assumption that compliance will be 100 percent. If compliance turns out to be no better than it is under the Federal income tax, then that rate would have to go up further to 29 percent. And if financial services, rental housing and employer-provided fringe benefits are taken out of the base, as many believe would eventually be the case, then the budget-neutral tax rate goes up to 37.5 percent. Last, if States add on their income tax and their sales tax in a piggyback fashion, which would undoubtedly be the case, then the rate facing consumers would be 53.6 percent and could rise to 64 percent, if compliance slips down to the level applicable to proprietors' income.

In the long run, the economy will perform better under a sales tax. By 2010, we predict that real GDP would be up some $178 billion, real personal consumption will be up $16.5 billion, national savings will be up thanks to higher personal savings and higher corporate savings. These salutary accomplishments are similar in direction, if not magnitude, to the long-term findings of other studies you will hear about.

It is the short-term results, however, that concern me. In the short run, there will be a speed-up of consumer purchases in anticipation. This will cause a temporary economic downturn when the tax actually becomes effective. The economy will shrink by 1.1 percent in the first year of the tax and GDP will remain below the baseline until the fourth year. Personal consumption will be lower, in real terms, until the ninth year; corporate profits will be about 2 percent lower, on average—although some will be higher and some will be lower than that throughout the tenth year. After that period, we see profits rising. Employment will be lower than expected through the fourth year of the tax with 1.5 billion jobs lost; prices are predicted to rise by roughly the tax rate, although eventually the price rise will subside as the economy picks up steam; and investment will increase some 7 percent, with roughly a third of that financed by foreign capital. Corporations will finance about half of their new investment through retained earnings.

In conclusion, keeping within my 5 minutes, Mr. Chairman, while it is important, very important, to seek a fairer and simpler tax structure—as you have explained—to replace the incredibly complex code we have today, swapping the income tax for a sales tax is an experiment that could bring our flourishing economy down. It is not one we ought to be trying now.

Thank you, Mr. Chairman.

[The prepared statement follows:]

Statement of John G. Wilkins, Managing Director, Barcroft Consulting Group, on behalf of National Retail Federation

Mr. Chairman and Members of the Committee:

I am managing director of the Barcroft Consulting Group and I am here on behalf of the National Retail Federation. My statement reports on the findings of a study undertaken by PricewaterhouseCoopers ("PWC") for the National Retail Federation Foundation. I was principal author of that study, which examines the economic impact of substituting a national retail sales tax ("NRST") for the federal income tax.

Introduction

Nearly nine years ago, I testified before this committee on the issue of international competitiveness and the role of income taxation. In that statement, I noted that the United States relied less on consumption and more on income taxes to finance government than virtually all of the other industrialized nations—even when state retail sales taxes are included in the equation. Although our income tax structure is by no means a pure income tax—having some elements of a consumption tax mixed in with an income tax—I nonetheless observed that a greater reliance on taxing consumption and less reliance on taxing income, would be healthy for the economy by spurring savings and helping keep income tax rates low. That was 1991 and this is 2000. And I continue to hold that view.

While I applaud the desire of the chairman to replace the current tax code with something that is simpler and fairer, I do not, however, subscribe to abandoning an income tax altogether and replacing it with a national sales tax. As our study shows, this could have very harmful short-term and mid-term economic results. In light of the remarkable economic achievements of the past decade, it would be foolish to simply get rid of a tax structure under which the economy is flourishing and replace it with an untried system with uncertain economic consequences.

The PWC study, largely completed last year when I was director of PricewaterhouseCoopers' national economic consulting group, focuses on the economic impact of replacing the income tax with a national sales tax similar to the Fair Tax proposal. The proposal examined was H.R. 1467 rather than H.R. 2525, which had not been introduced at the time of the study. One significant difference is that H.R. 1467 does not repeal federal payroll taxes while the Fair Tax, H.R. 2525, does and consequently requires a higher tax rate.

What follows is a discussion of (1) why the PWC dynamic model is particularly capable of recognizing the effects of a national sales tax on the economy in general and on retailers in particular; (2) why the proposed national sales tax rate could eventually be much higher than proponents advertise due to likely exclusions, the need for budget neutrality, and transition rules; and (3) what impact this kind of tax would have on short-term and long-term economic growth, consumption, corporate profits, employment, and trade.

The Dynamic Estimating Model

In the early 1990s, Coopers & Lybrand undertook to develop an economic model that was missing from the arsenal of tax analysis tools available to government economists and others concerned with the potential economic impact of fundamental tax reforms. The traditional microsimulation models used by the staff of the Joint Committee on Taxation ("JCT") and the Treasury Department's Office of Tax Analysis for revenue estimating purposes are based on large samples of individual and corporate taxpayers and consequently are ideal for analyzing the impacts of tax law changes on the taxpayer population. These models are not, however, capable of analyzing the impact of fundamental tax reforms on the economy. For such analysis economists turn to macroeconomic models. Unfortunately, macroeconomic models are rarely designed for tax analysis: they frequently have only two or three producing sectors; some have only a single household or a handful of households to represent the entire population of taxpayers and consumers; and most examine the economy only when it is in equilibrium, with labor and other resources artificially restricted to be at full employment.

The PWC model was designed specifically for analysis of tax reforms, such as the replacement of the income tax with a NRST. In order to retain the benefits of the microsimulation models used by the JCT and the Treasury, the PWC model has three prongs, incorporating two microsimulation models with a macroeconomic forecasting model. The two microsimulation models are an individual income tax model with 100,000 separate tax return records and a corporation income tax model with 15,000 synthetic tax return records. The third prong of the overall model is a macroeconomic forecasting model that provides year-by-year short-term forecasts of the economy as well as mid-term and longer-term forecasts. Importantly, the PWC model has the following traits that distinguish it from most other models:

• The PWC model contains an open economy, allowing changes in foreign trade, cross-border investment flows and exchange rate adjustments. Many models are restricted to closed economies that ignore the existence of foreign trade and other international transactions.

• The PWC model permits the economy to be in disequilibrium during transition periods. Most other models artificially force the economy to always be in equilibrium, with no unemployment of labor and other resources—even during periods of transition from an income tax to a sales tax.

• The PWC model's database includes records for 100,000 households and 15,000 corporations. Most models include only a handful of households and corporations. Sometimes only one household represents the entire household sector.

• The PWC model tracks 85 different industries, producing 85 different products for intermediate and final sales.

Most models represent the entire producing economy with only two or three industries frequently producing only two or three different classes of goods.

The most important distinguishing characteristic of the PWC model is that it focuses on the near and intermediate term. The key feature is the model's ability to forecast detailed information on the performance of the economy on a year-by-year basis as the economy makes the transition from an income tax structure to a sales tax structure. The PWC model shows that this transition is not nearly as smooth and simple as some sales tax proponents would like. It is this ability of the model to provide short-term transition results on an annual basis that provided the main impetus for its construction.

The PWC model has been used successfully to evaluate a wide range of tax proposals, from the recommendations of the Kemp Commission to the national sales tax. The model was also used to produce dynamic revenue estimates for the January 1997 symposium on dynamic revenue estimating sponsored by the staff of the Joint Committee on Taxation.

Required Tax Rates

Much of the discussion surrounding national sales taxes centers on the required tax rate. This rate depends obviously upon the tax base—all consumption or some portion of consumption after certain exclusions. It further depends upon the amount of taxes to be replaced on a neutral basis. It also depends upon the degree of compliance—100 percent or some lesser fraction as is the case with the income tax. Lastly, it depends upon mitigating provisions such as increased social security benefits for the elderly designed to prevent too much double taxation of their lifetime earnings, family allowances designed to prevent some of the associated redistribution of tax burden and other transition rules designed to lessen short-term economic disruptions.

Tax Exclusive and Tax Inclusive Tax Rates. The discussion of tax rates is confused by the practice of proponents of the NRST to couch the rate in so-called tax inclusive terms. Sales tax rates are usually considered on a tax exclusive basis. Under this normal tax exclusive concept, for example, a $30 tax on a $100 item is considered to represent a 30 percent tax rate. The consumer would pay the retailer $130, $30 of which would be forwarded to the tax authorities.

Proponents of national sales taxes like to measure the tax rate in this example by dividing the $30 tax by the tax inclusive price, which is $130. The tax rate calculated this way would be only 23 percent (30/130). Under the tax inclusive rate concept, confusion is likely to arise when a customer is quoted a 23 percent tax inclusive rate on a $100 purchase and finds the sales clerk asking for $130.00 ($100 plus $30 tax) rather than the expected $123.00 ($100 plus $23 tax). The confusion will be reinforced by the fact that all state sales taxes are always quoted on the normal tax exclusive basis.

Revenue Neutral vs. Budget Neutral Tax Rates. A second concern in determining the appropriate rate for a national sales tax that would replace other existing federal taxes involves the concept of neutrality. Most believe that any replacement tax ought to be neutral: the government should be left as well off under the replacement tax as it is under the current tax structure. Independent of its political appeal, neutrality focuses the spotlight on the economic pluses and minuses that could result from restructuring the tax system as opposed to the consequences of making the government bigger or smaller, which can be done without restructuring the tax system.

There are two ways to identify neutrality (revenue and budget) and two ways of measuring neutrality (static and dynamic). Revenue neutrality means that the replacement tax raises the same revenue as the current tax. Budget neutrality means that the replacement tax leaves the overall budget surplus (or deficit) unchanged. Budget neutrality is the better measure because it recognizes that, by influencing the price of government purchases, interest rates, or transfer payments, for example, tax changes can affect the spending side of the budget as well as the revenue side.

Static measurement of budget neutrality fails to take account of how a replacement tax influences the budget by accelerating or retarding economic growth. Dynamic measurement of budget neutrality corrects this shortcoming by taking into account macroeconomic effects, such as a short-term change in the level of employment, that can affect government spending and revenue. The dynamic measure of budget neutrality is the most meaningful concept for a replacement tax.

These concepts can be illustrated as follows. According to the PWC model, a very broad-base national sales tax, such as the Tauzin-Traficant proposal to replace the current federal personal and corporate income taxes, the federal estate and gift tax, and most federal excise taxes would require a tax exclusive rate of 18.8 percent under the somewhat unrealistic assumption of 100 percent compliance and revenue neutrality. This rate would be a 15.8 percent rate on a tax inclusive basis, reasonably close to the 15 percent claimed by the sponsors. In order to maintain budget neutrality—even on a static basis—the rate would have to be raised from 18.8 percent to 24.5 percent. This is because the federal government would want to fully maintain the purchasing power of all transfers payments (social security, welfare, unemployment, etc.) in order to protect the elderly, the poor, and other transferees. In order to do so, these transfer payments must be increased by the amount of the tax on the goods and services they would purchase. Holding recipients of federal government transfer payments harmless in this manner while maintaining real federal spending on goods and services requires a budget-neutral NRST rate of 24.5 percent (or 19.7 percent on a so-called tax-inclusive basis)—still figured at an unrealistic 100 rate of compliance.

On a dynamic basis, this 24.5 percent budget neutral tax rate could be lowered slightly to 24.1 percent by the tenth year of the tax, thanks to a somewhat improved economy; however, there are still other concerns involving base erosion and compliance that need to be factored in before an ultimate budget neutral tax rate can be determined.

Compliance. Most experts concede that it is difficult to estimate the rate of compliance under a NRST. What is not in dispute, however, is that the compliance will be lower the higher the NRST rate. Moreover, while state sales tax rates appear to have relatively high rates of compliance, these compliance rates are not comparable to the NRST. State sales tax compliance is high because the sales tax rates are relatively low—typically 4 to 6 percent—and their tax bases are relatively narrow. Unlike the value added tax, there is an incentive on the part of both consumers and sellers to avoid the tax. Individuals could easily avoid the NRST in a number of ways, such as disguising personal consumption expenditures as business costs that would not be subject to tax.

If tax compliance is no better than the 83 percent overall compliance rate under the federal income tax, the budget neutral tax rate would have to be raised from 24.1 percent to 29.0 percent. If compliance matches compliance rate for proprietors under the federal income tax, then the budget neutral rate would be raised another 5.9 points to 34.9 percent. Keep in mind that the compliance rates under the income tax are strengthened by forced compliance of withheld tax on wages and by numerous checks and balances payer-provided information returns and audits.

Exemptions and Allowances. Many have observed that enactment of a NRST would encourage many special exemptions from the base. Three of the most frequently mentioned are:

• removing consumption of financial sector services entirely from the base, since the taxation of such services is, at best, extremely complicated and would be difficult to administer;

• removing rental housing services and the resale of existing homes from the tax base so as to continue a current-law tax preference and to mitigate problems arising from unequal treatments of owner-occupied and rental housing; and

• removing employer-provided fringe benefits from the tax base so as to vastly simplify the tasks of businesses, which would otherwise be untaxed.

The effect of removing these items from the NRST base would cause the budget neutral tax rate to rise to 37.5 percent with compliance equal to overall income tax compliance and to 45.1 percent with compliance equal to income tax compliance of proprietors.

Effect of State and Local Tax Piggybacking. Once states lose their ability to piggyback their income taxes off the federal income tax, it is anticipated that many would elect to instead piggyback their revenue needs by adding a state sales tax rate to the federal rate. For consumers, this would further boost the overall rate on consumption to 53.6 percent assuming overall income tax compliance and to 64 percent assuming proprietor's income tax compliance. These figures assume the above exemptions and allowances would be established.

The PWC model is not alone in estimating tax rates for the NRST that are considerably higher than proponents frequently cite. A National Bureau of Economic Research study place the tax rate at 27.3 percent if payroll taxes are not included in those taxes to be replaced and 45.4 percent if payroll taxes are also replaced. A Joint Economic Committee (";JEC") study concluded that the NRST rate would have to be at least 32 percent unless imputed items of consumption, like "rent" that the national income accounts assume homeowners pay themselves were also included in the base. Furthermore, if food, medicine, and physician's services were excluded (as is commonplace among many state sales taxes) the rate would have to rise from 32 percent to 49.3 percent. Alternatively, they found that if all services were excluded from the base but food and medicine continued to be taxable, the rate would have to rise to 64.6 percent.

Impact of the NRST on the Economy

In the long run, the economy will perform somewhat better under a NRST. The results of the PWC model show:

• By 2010 real GDP will be higher by $178 billion (1.8 percent) and will remain above baseline throughout the forecast period.

• By 2010 real personal consumption expenditures will be higher by $16.5 billion (0.3 percent) and will remain above baseline throughout the forecast period.

• Throughout the forecast period national private savings is higher than under the baseline thanks to higher personal savings as consumers delay consumption and higher corporate savings as businesses reinvest a large portion of undistributed corporate profits.

These salutary accomplishments are similar in direction to findings of other studies. Only the magnitudes may differ. It is in the short run that the PWC study finds harmful results.

Economic Growth. Gross domestic product (";GDP"), the value of all goods and services produced in the country, would increase in real terms in anticipation of the enactment of the NRST, as consumers speed up purchases they would otherwise make at a later date.

The aftermath of the speedup is a sharp economic downturn in the year the tax becomes effective. Instead of achieving an expected 2.0 percent rate of real growth in 2001, the assumed first year of the tax, the economy would shrink by 1.1 percent. Although the economy would begin to grow again in subsequent years, it would take until the fourth year of the tax for GDP to reach its pre-NRST level. Before the economy fully recovered, the cumulative loss in real GDP (measured in 1992 dollars) would reach $180 billion and annual employment would dip by 1.5 million jobs. By 2010, real GDP under the NRST would be 1.8 percent above the level that the current income tax would have achieved. Given a growth forecast of about 2.3 percent per year, the 1.8 percent of additional GDP represents only a 9-month speedup in economic growth over a ten-year period.

Consumption. Personal consumption expenditures in real terms would be below the current-law baseline until the ninth year after the NRST was introduced. During the 2001–2008 period, the cumulative decline in consumer spending (measured in 1992 dollars) would exceed $500 billion. Over the first five years of the tax, consumption would be 1.5 percent lower on average than it would be under current-law tax; and over the second five years, consumption would be down 0.2 percent from expected levels.

The overall drop in consumption and the subsequent pickup as the economy recovers masks many important details. Consumption changes will vary greatly according to income levels and according to items of consumption. Changes in consumer purchases reflect the fact that the NRST generally shifts the tax burden away from higher income families and toward lower income families. Although the poorest of the poor may be roughly compensated for their loss of the refundable earned income credit by repeal of the payroll taxes, the moderately poor and many in the vast middle class must have higher overall tax burdens in order to balance those with the highest incomes whose consumption taxes would be far smaller than their income taxes. Households with incomes in the bottom fifth of the income scale would have to reduce their purchases of durable goods by 13 percent on average for the second five years after introduction of the NRST and purchases of nondurable goods by 6 percent. In contrast, households with incomes in the top fifth of the income scale would increase their purchase of durables by an average of 2.4 percent and their purchases of nondurables by 0.3 percent for that same period.

Saving and Investment. In nominal terms, the net private saving of U.S. residents and businesses under the NRST would be about 18 percent higher than under current law for the ten-year period, 2001–2010. Government saving is assumed to be virtually unaffected (that is, the NRST is assumed to be a budget-neutral replacement for current-law taxes that would be repealed). For that same period, personal saving would be higher by about 15 percent. The nominal dollar increase in private saving would come about equally from personal saving and corporate saving. Corporations would be expected to finance about half of all induced new investment through their own saving, by retaining approximately 15 percent of the repealed corporate income tax. The remaining 85 percent of the corporate income tax would be distributed to shareholders in the form of increased dividends.

Over the ten-year period, 2001–2010, induced gross private domestic investment would add another 7 percent to the amount of nominal investment under current law. This increase in investment is nearly twice as large as the increase in gross national saving. Consequently, roughly half of all induced investment is foreign-owned investment flowing into the United States in response to lower financing costs and the elimination of the Federal corporate tax on equity income. Although most of the growth in real investment occurs in the business sector, most of the increase in nominal investment can be attributed to the rise in the price of residential investment due to the tax on new construction under the NRST.

Corporate Profits. On average, corporate profits are about 2 percent lower over the ten-year period, 2001–2010; however, there are notable exceptions for certain industries and certain years. In the aggregate, profits return to the level expected under current law by the year 2010, and are expected to improve thereafter.

Employment. Due to the near term decline in consumer spending, private sector jobs and civilian employment are expected to be lower than they would be under current law through the fourth year of the NRST. The near term estimate would indicate a drop of 1.5 million jobs. Thereafter, jobs and employment will pick up. The labor force is expected to expand by about 1 percent as potential second earners and others are lured into the workplace by vastly lower taxes on wages and salaries and entrepreneurial income.

Anticipatory Consumption Speedup. Introduction of a NRST is expected to create a speedup in purchases of goods and services between the time the tax is announced and the time it becomes effective. If the NRST were imposed as of January 1, 2001, a surge in personal consumption of both domestically produced and imported goods and services would occur in 2000. In addition, equipment investment would accelerate to take advantage of depreciation deductions in the year 2000 before the income tax is repealed. Together, these factors produce a temporary drop in personal saving and a temporary rise in the real rate of economic growth in 2000. Real GDP in 2000 is estimated to be 2.8 percent above the level that would have been obtained in the absence of a proposed NRST. Thereafter, real GDP is depressed by $180 billion from 2001 through 2003. By 2004, real GDP has recovered to pre-tax change levels, and remains above the pre-tax change baseline throughout the remainder of the forecast period.

After the speedup in spending in 2000, personal consumption expenditures remain $500 billion lower than they would otherwise be until the year 2009. In other words, during the first eight years of the NRST, consumption would be depressed as families and individuals respond to the tax by saving more and spending less. It is only after disposable income increases sufficiently that consumption picks up enough to pass the pre-tax change baseline level.

Real investment in equipment is down in 2002 from the pre-tax change baseline due to the tax-motivated speedup of investment into 2000. Thereafter, equipment investment is higher as businesses respond to a lowered cost of capital. Real investment in non-residential structures is down in 2003 and 2004, but picks up significantly after 2004. However, real investment in residential structures remains below pre-tax change baseline levels over the entire 2002–2010 period.

Prices. Prices for consumer goods and services quickly rise by the amount of the tax, and then some. The portion of the price increase in excess of the tax is due in part to the higher cost of imports (from the weaker dollar) coupled with the ability of some domestic producers of competing goods to hike their price to that of imports. Consumer prices similarly rise 25 percent—roughly the nominal rate of sales tax, unadjusted for any exemptions or transition rules—by 2002 and gradually drop from that peak to a level that remains about 18 percent above the pre-change baseline.

Examined on a year-over-year basis, these price increases generally amount to a large, one-time hike in prices as the NRST is imposed, with some moderation of this increase in the longer run. Due to a weaker dollar, merchandise import prices increase by nearly 4 percent shortly after the NRST is imposed and are 6.5 percent over baseline levels in 2010. Merchandise export prices are also above baseline levels. In 2001 and 2002 they are nearly 3 percent above the baseline. However, due to lower interest rates, which reduce business costs, export prices are only slightly greater than baseline levels for most of the remainder of the forecast period. The overall impact on prices is measured by the change in the GDP deflator, which initially rises 20 percent above the baseline price level before settling back to a 13 percent price rise relative to the baseline.

The notion espoused by some that pre-tax prices would drop some 20–30 percent under a NRST (so that after-tax prices would not rise and may even decline) is a peculiar one. This could only happen if all of the personal income tax, the corporation income tax and payroll taxes are currently embodied in retail prices. Tax incidence—that is, who actually bears the ultimate tax burden—is an elusive question that has been the focus of many economic papers, because the answer is not clear. However, the general consensus among economists is that perhaps a portion of the corporate income tax may be passed on to consumers in the form of higher prices, but that the majority is ultimately paid by corporate owners in the form of lower after-tax profits and by employees in the form of lower compensation. Most economists concede that personal income taxes and payroll taxes are ultimately borne by labor and are not passed on to consumers in the form of higher prices.

Nominal Output. In nominal terms, personal consumption expenditures are expected to be above their baseline level by $1,582.9 billion per year on average for the 2006–2010 period. This represents an increase of 18.3 percent over the average that would have occurred in absence of the NRST. Note, because prices would be 18.5 percent higher, on average, for this period, this nominal increase is consistent with a slight real decline in real consumption expenditures during this same period.

Trade. Merchandise exports and imports are both impacted by the NRST. Exports are made relatively cheaper to foreigners because the dollar is somewhat weaker under the NRST. Imports are subject to the NRST and are also more costly for U.S. consumers to buy due to the weaker dollar. As expected, in real terms, exports grow about 4.3 percent over the baseline during the last five years of the forecast period, 2006–2010; and imports drop an average of about 1.6 percent during that same period. In nominal dollar terms, both exports and imports are larger than under current law due to the sharp price increases for imports discussed above. Real net merchandise exports increase by $448 billion (in 1992 dollars) over a ten-year forecast period. However, over the same ten-year period, net merchandise exports in nominal dollars decline by $68 billion relative to the baseline. This nominal merchandise trade deficit helps to finance domestic investment.

Conclusion

If a NRST is enacted, the U.S. economy would lag behind for at least three years and employment would dip by more than one million jobs. Beneficial effects would not be felt for at least five years after adoption. While it is admirable to seek a fairer and simpler tax structure to replace the incredibly complex income tax code, trading an income tax in for a national sales tax is an experiment that could bring serious harm to a flourishing national economy. Uncertain long-run benefits are far insufficient to risk the short-run setbacks in virtually all sectors of the economy.

Chairman ARCHER. Thank you, Mr. Wilkins.
Our next witness is Dr. Metcalf. You may proceed, Doctor.

STATEMENT OF GILBERT E. METCALF, PROFESSOR OF ECONOMICS, TUFTS UNIVERSITY, MEDFORD, MASSACHUSETTS, AND RESEARCH ASSOCIATE, NATIONAL BUREAU OF ECONOMIC RESEARCH

Mr. METCALF. Thank you. I am Gilbert Metcalf, a professor of economics at Tufts University and a research associate at the National Bureau of Economic Research.

I appreciate the opportunity to speak before this committee on the topic of tax reform, and I would like to focus, first, on the issue of fairness or progressivity, and second on the issue of the relative merits of a national retail sales tax versus alternative consumption tax proposals.

First, the issue of progressivity. As has been noted before, consumption taxes look very regressive when households are distributed by annual income. People tend to earn the highest incomes in their life around middle age and the lowest incomes in their youth and old age. And consequently, in an annual income analysis, lower income groups are likely to include some young and elderly people who are not poor in a lifetime sense. Similarly, higher income groups are likely to contain some people at the peak of their age earnings profile, for whom peak earnings are a poor measure of annual ability to consume.

In previous research, I have considered the distributional impact of a replacement of the personal and corporate income tax with the national sales tax, and while the analysis does not capture the precise nature of the Fair Tax proposal, it is close enough to demonstrate a number of key points. That research, summarized in my written testimony, shows the following:

First, using an annual income analysis, a national sales tax, with family allowances similar to the Fair Tax, would look highly regressive. But when a lifetime income analysis is undertaken, when we think of people's resources over their entire lifetime, then the tax reform looks much more distributionally neutral.

And this lifetime distributional neutrality of the sales tax depends importantly upon the family allowances that the Fair Tax proposes or allowances similar to the ones that the Fair Tax proposes. And without these, the sales tax reform looks moderately regressive, even on a lifetime basis.

A second aspect of a consumption tax reform bears mentioning, and there has been some allusion to this. In the shift from an income to a consumption tax, existing wealth is subjected to a one-time wealth tax. This by itself provides a great deal of progressivity.

So let us see how this works. Existing wealth is subjected to the national sales tax at the time that it is spent. So imagine that I have a million dollars in existing savings and a national sales tax at a 30-percent rate is imposed, if I spend that million dollars immediately, I will pay $300,000 in sales tax and consume $700,000 in goods and services. The same result arises if instead of a sales tax I am subjected to a 30-percent initial wealth tax. The retail sales tax effectively taxes away 30 percent of that initial wealth, and this example generalizes. No matter when I spend that wealth on consumption or even if I die and leave that money to my children, I end up, under the retail sales tax, in exactly the same boat as under a one-time tax on initial wealth.

In addition to adding progressivity to the reform, this one-time tax adds efficiency, since this is a lump-sum tax, which is the most efficient of all taxes.

Next, let me turn to the second point, the relative merit of a sales tax versus other forms of consumption taxes. It seems to me that one of the greatest difficulties that the proponents of the flat taxed faced was the perception that rich people would avoid taxation, since they were not subject to taxation at the personal level, and that problem is eliminated under a sales tax.

And we have talked about the transparency of the sales tax as one of its virtues. This transparency extends to the problem of transition giveaways. Unlike other forms of consumption taxes, any efforts to provide advantages to certain sectors or to grandfather existing capital from the wealth tax I just mentioned, would be highly visible.

And so to the extent that Congress wishes to enact a clean tax reform, and I hope that is the intent of this committee, this visibility provides support for that effort. Avoiding the transition compensation to old capital will allow a lower tax rate, greater progressivity and larger efficiency gains from the reform.

There has been a lot of discussion of the appropriate tax rate. Let me focus on tax-inclusive tax rates to be comparable to income tax rates. The 23-percent tax rate is achieved in the Fair Tax proposal that I have seen by subjecting Government purchases to the sales tax and assuming that Federal spending will be held constant. This, in effect, subjects Government to a substantial spending cut, and I think needlessly mixes issues of tax reform with the issue of the appropriate size of Government.

I calculate a tax rate of roughly 33 percent would be required to achieve a revenue-neutral reform; yet, as Dr. Kotlikoff has noted, even a 30-percent rate or 33-percent rate leaves a middle-income worker facing a 15-percent Federal tax rate and 15.3-percent payroll tax rate unaffected at the margin.

Second, the experience at the State and local level with sales tax is that there is enormous pressure to exempt certain goods and services from taxation, and Congress must resist this temptation at the Federal level. The rebate on spending on amounts up to the poverty level appropriately addresses distributional concerns and further exemptions would only reduce the efficiency gains from the reform, while adding complexity to the administration of the tax.

So, in conclusion, consumption tax reform is one of a number of attractive options for improving the current tax system, and of course other possible options would be to simplify the current income tax. The Fair Tax proposal, here before you today, has many attractive features. But I think its success depends, importantly, on its being a clean reform with few transition rules and tax-base exemptions.

Thank you.

[The prepared statement of Mr. Metcalf follows:]

Statement of Gilbert E. Metcalf, Professor of Economics, Tufts University, Medford, Massachusetts, and Research Associate, National Bureau of Economic Research

Introduction

I appreciate the opportunity to submit written testimony to the Committee on Ways and Means on the very important topic of fundamental tax reform. Just over four years ago, I had the privilege of participating in an Issues Seminar on tax reform hosted by this committee at Airlee House in Virginia. While the bills before this committee may be different than those under consideration four years ago, the issues have not changed.

Much of my research on the topic of tax reform has focused on distributional considerations. The main result from that research is that the focus on annual income as a measure of individual welfare significantly biases distributional analyses of consumption taxes towards making them look more regressive than they are when an individual's lifetime earnings possibilities are taken into account. In this testimony, I'd like to review why annual and lifetime income perspectives lead to such different results and then to present some findings from research that I have conducted using the Consumer Expenditure Survey.[1]

II. Background

An incidence analysis attempts to answer the question of who bears the burden of a particular tax. Any attempt to evaluate the "fairness" of a tax (or a change in the tax system) requires knowing whose disposable income is changed and by how much in response to the tax. Economists often refer to taxes as "regressive" or "progressive." There is often some confusion as to the meaning of these terms and so it is worth defining them carefully. The definition that most economists use relies on the average tax rate—the ratio of tax liabilities to income.[2] A tax is said to be regressive if the average tax rate falls with income. It is proportional if the average tax rate is constant and it is progressive if the average tax rate rises with income. Low income people pay a higher (lower) fraction of their income in taxes if the tax is regressive (progressive).

Early tax incidence studies used the results of partial or general equilibrium models to inform judgments about relevant incidence results. In effect, these studies used existing research results to generate plausible assumptions about the incidence of specific taxes. Pechman (1985) represents the classic example of this type of research. The time frame for analysis is one year, and Pechman assumes that consumption taxes are passed forward and borne by consumers in proportion to their expenditures. Taking this approach, Pechman finds that consumption taxes are quite regressive. A recent study by Gale, Houser, and Scholz (1996) confirms this view. In an analysis of a shift from the current income tax to a flat tax they find that the lowest income group would see their average tax rate increase by 2.2 percentage points (81% increase) while the highest income group would see their average tax rate decrease by 7.1 percentage points (17% decrease).[3] Similarly, Feenberg, Mitrusi, and Poterba (1997) find that there would be a substantial shift in tax burden to the poor in shifting from the income tax to a retail sales tax using annual income to rank households.

An alternative approach utilizes estimates of lifetime income as a measure of the taxpaying unit's economic well-being. Invoking Friedman (1957) and the permanent income hypothesis as well as life-cycle considerations, economists have long recognized that annual income may not be a very good measure of an individual's potential to consume. With perfect capital markets, individuals should be grouped according to the present discounted value of earnings plus gifts received. This theory makes the difficulties with the annual incidence approach readily apparent. People tend to earn the highest incomes in their life around middle age and the lowest incomes in their youth and old age. Consequently in a cross section (annual) analysis, lower income groups are likely to include some young and elderly people (as well as some people with volatile incomes who have obtained a low realization) who are not poor in a lifetime sense. Similarly, higher annual income groups are likely to contain some people at the peak of their age earnings profile for whom peak earnings are a poor measure of annual ability to consume.

To see why a lifetime approach makes a difference, imagine a world with identical people with identical skills and an identical pattern of earnings over their lifetime.

---

[1] This research is presented in Metcalf (1997).

[2] More precisely, the numerator is the change in real disposable income resulting from the change in the tax law. If a new tax is imposed, the change in disposable income might occur because prices have gone up so that a given income purchases fewer goods and services or it might occur because have fallen.

[3] Table 8–2, page 290 of Gale, Houser, and Scholz (1996).

Figure 1 illustrates the lifetime income and consumption paths of a typical person in this imaginary society. Income is initially low and rises to a peak in the middle years. It than falls as this worker gradually cuts back on work and enjoys more retirement leisure. Consumption is constant over the lifetime. In early years individuals borrow against future income to finance consumption that exceeds income. Savings occurs in the middle years, first to repay borrowing from the early years and then to finance consumption in the retirement years. In this stylized example, I'll assume that all savings are consumed so that at death there are no assets remaining.

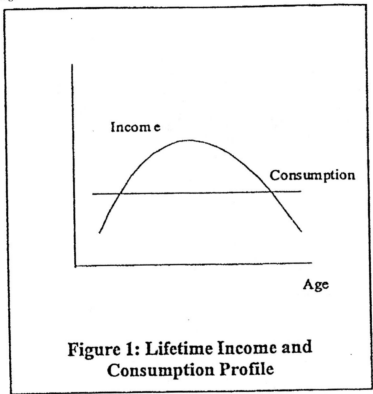

Figure 1: Lifetime Income and Consumption Profile

Next assume that there is one person of each age in this society. Otherwise people are identical. Figure 1 now has an additional interpretation. In addition to it indicating consumption and income patterns over an individual's lifetime, it also shows income and consumption patterns for our society of individuals at any one point in time. Now consider an annual incidence analysis of a national sales tax. Since consumption is constant across all individuals, tax payments will also be constant. But since income varies (based on where people are on their lifetime income schedule), the average tax rate (taxes as a fraction of annual income) will fall as income rises. The tax will look very regressive. But this is clearly wrong. Individuals are exactly the same in this hypothetical society and over their lifetimes will earn exactly the same amount of income and pay exactly the same amount of taxes. A lifetime incidence analysis will correctly conclude that this tax is proportional.

III. A Distributional Analysis of a Sales Tax Based on the Consumer Expenditure Survey

H.R. 2525 (introduced by Rep. John Linder (R–GA) and Rep. Collin Peterson (D–MN)) would replace the personal and corporate income tax, all payroll taxes, the self-employment tax, and the estate and gift tax with a national retail sales tax. The tax is levied on a destination basis, meaning that imports are subject to the tax while exports are exempt. H.R. 2525 (otherwise known as the "Fair Tax") would provide families with a rebate of sales tax on spending up to the federal poverty level.[4]

In previous research (Metcalf (1997)), I used data from the 1994 Consumption Expenditure Survey (CES) to measure the distributional impact of a replacement of the personal and corporate income tax with a national retail sales tax rate. While the analysis does not capture the precise nature of the Fair Tax proposal, it is close enough to demonstrate a number of key points. Ignoring payroll taxes in my analysis will likely bias the analysis towards making the reform appear less progressive. Thus the results I present can be viewed as lower bounds on the progressivity of the reform.

First let me note that after making adjustments for consumption expenditures that are difficult to tax, I calculated that a tax exclusive tax rate of roughly 18 percent would be required for a broadbased retail sales tax replacing the income tax to be revenue neutral. Adding payroll taxes and the estate tax to the proposal would increase the required tax exclusive tax rate to 30 percent.[5] This tax rate assumes that Congress will hold the real level of government spending fixed. This could be done by exempting government spending from the tax. If government spending is taxed (as is proposed in H.R. 2525), then nominal government spending would have to increase to keep real spending constant. (See Table 1 below for details.)

Table 1. Aggregate Consumption and Taxation

	(1)	(2)	(3)
Taxes Replaced By Retail Sales Tax			
Personal Income Tax	544.5	544.5	544.5
Corporate Income Tax	144.0	144.0	144.0
Payroll Taxes		428.8	428.8
Estate and Gift Tax		15.2	15.2
Total Income Tax	688.5	1,132.5	1,132.5
Retail Sales Tax Base			
Personal Consumption Expenditures	4,698.7	4,698.7	4,698.7
Adjustments to Personal Consumption Expenditures:			
Indirect Taxes	(266.9)	(266.9)	(266.9)
Owner Occupied Housing	(280.2)	(280.2)	(280.2)
Imputed Financial Services	(146.0)	(146.0)	(146.0)
Non-Profit Activities	(236.6)	(236.6)	(236.6)
Farm Food	(0.5)	(0.5)	(0.5)
Net Foreign Spending	19.8	19.8	19.8
Consumption Tax Base	3788.3	3788.3	3788.3
Family Allowance			(1500.0)
Net Consumption Tax Base	3788.3	3788.3	2288.3
Retail Sales Tax Rate (Tax-Exclusive)	18.2%	29.9%	49.5%

[4] The rebate is adjusted so that a married couple with no children would receive the same rebate as two unmarried individuals sharing a household (a marriage penalty elimination adjustment).

[5] Using 1991 data, Feenberg, Mitrusi, and Poterba (1997) estimate that a tax rate of nearly 29 percent would be required to replace the income and payroll taxes. Both my estimated tax rate and those of Feenberg et al. are measured as a percentage of the producer price. To compare the average income tax rate, we can re-express the tax rates as percentages of consumer prices. Expressed that way, the required tax is 23 percent.

Table 1. Aggregate Consumption and Taxation—Continued

	(1)	(2)	(3)
Retail Sales Tax Rate (Tax Inclusive)	15.4%	23.0%	33.1%

ASource: Metcalf (1997)

Those adjustments do not allow for the family rebate based on poverty level. The Fair Tax Proposal exempts from taxation spending up to the poverty level. Based on 1994 poverty levels, this rebate would (in effect) exempt $1.5 trillion from the Retail Sales Tax base. This raises the required tax rate from 30 to nearly 50 percent [6] . On a tax inclusive basis (comparable to an income tax rate), this is a rate of 33 percent.

My first analysis considers a shift from the current income tax to a broad based retail sales tax. The tax base is quite comprehensive. Housing services are not taxed per se but are taxed at the time of purchase of the house. The same approach is used for other durable goods. Medical services are included in the tax base as are other services. Table 2 (and Figure 2) shows the distribution of a shift from the income tax to a broad based income tax using both an annual and a lifetime income incidence approach. The second column shows the change in average tax rate (change in tax as a percentage of annual income) for households ranked by annual income. Based on the annual income approach, the tax reform is very regressive. Tax liabilities increase for the bottom 70% of the income distribution and decrease for the top 30%. The changes are quite substantial with the lowest income decile seeing their average tax rate increase by 64 percentage points.[7] Meanwhile the top decile's average tax rate falls by 7%. Another way to measure the regressivity of the tax reform based on annual income is to note that the Suits Index falls from 0.202 (income tax) to −0.217 (retail sales tax) as a result of the reform.[8]

Column 3 redoes the analysis using a lifetime income analysis. The variation in changes in average tax rates across lifetime income deciles falls markedly relative to the annual income analysis. The reform is still regressive—the lowest 70% of the income distribution face tax increases while the top 30% enjoy tax decreases. However the differences are not nearly as large as when measured using annual income to rank households. Moreover, the change in average tax rates is much smaller with the lowest lifetime income decile facing an average increase in their average tax rate of 5.7 percentage points while the top decile's average tax rate falls by 2 percentage points. Ranking households by lifetime income, the Suits Index now falls from 0.068 to −0.010 with this tax reform.

---

[6] Feenberg, Mitrusi, and Poterba (1997) estimate that a rate exclusive tax rate of 45.4 percent would be required.

[7] The size of the tax shift for this lowest income decile indicates one of the problems of the annual income approach. It tends so magnify average tax rates as income is likely to be poorly measured and also low relative to consumption. It is for this reason ftha tPechman (1985) dropped th ebottom half of the lowest income decile from his analysis. The median change in tax rate for this decile is 32.9%. Except for the lowest decile, median and mean tax rates are fairly similar.

[8] The Suits Index is a tax-based analogue to the Gini Coefficient. It ranges from −1 to 1 with negative values indicating a regressive tax and positive values a progressive tax. The Suits Indexc for the income tax that I report is not comprable to estimates of the Suits Index reported elsewhere for the personal income tax since I attribute the corporate income tax to households in this study.

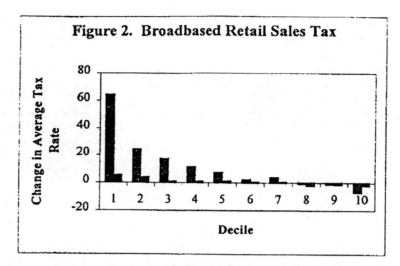

Figure 2. Broadbased Retail Sales Tax

Table 2. Distribution of a Broadbased Retail Sales Tax: No Family Allowance

Decile	Annual	Lifetime
1	64.3	5.7
2	24.4	4.0
3	17.4	1.0
4	11.5	1.0
5	7.3	1.2
6	2.3	0.4
7	3.9	0.4
8	− 0.6	− 2.0
9	− 0.9	− 1.3
10	− 7.0	− 2.0

ATable reports change in average tax rate from reform
ASource: Metcalf (1997) This analysis repeals personal and corporate income tax and replaces it with a national retail sales tax.

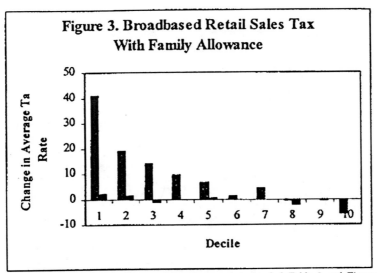

Figure 3. Broadbased Retail Sales Tax With Family Allowance

Next, I add the family allowances based on poverty levels.[9] Table 3 and Figure 3 presents the results.

Table 3. Distribution of a Broadbased Retail Sales Tax: Family Allowance

Decile	Annual	Lifetime
1	40.9	2.2
2	19.1	1.5
3	14.2	− 0.9
4	9.6	0.2
5	6.6	0.8
6	1.5	0.0
7	4.4	0.1
8	− 0.3	− 2.0
9	− 0.1	− 0.3
10	− 5.8	0.1

ATable reports change in average tax rate from reform
ASource: Metcalf (1997) This analysis repeals personal and corporate income tax and replaces it with a national retail sales tax.

[9] This analysis differs from the Fair Tax proposal in not making a marriage penalty adjustment.

114

current account deficit.

Saving and Investment as % of GDP

Saving = Income Est. of GDP less Expenditure (C+G+M-X)

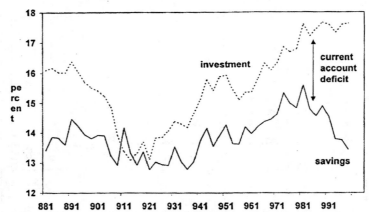

Compared to Table 2, the tax is modestly less regressive on an annual basis. However it continues to look very regressive. The Suits Index for the sales tax with rebate is −0.155 indicating considerable regressivity (relative to the income tax system it replaces for which the Suits Index equals 0.202). The story changes dramatically when I rank people by lifetime income (last column). Now there is no clear pattern to the change in average tax rates. The change ranges from a decrease of 2 percent (decile 8) to an increase of 2.2 percent (decile 1). Ranking households by lifetime income the Suits Index for the sales tax with rebate (0.054) is nearly the same as for the current income tax (0.068). If you compare Table 2 to Table 3, it is easy to see that rebates based on the poverty threshold can offset any remaining regressive aspects of a national sales tax when ranking households by a measure of lifetime income. These results indicate that it is not impossible to structure a consumption tax that is broadly progressive.

IV. Other Issues

The distributional analysis above is a "steady-state" analysis and ignores transitional considerations. In any switch from an income to a consumption tax, there is the potential for a lump sum tax on old capital. One difficulty with previous consumption tax proposals has been that these losses have been compensated through transition rules that cost significant amounts of revenue and require higher tax rates. Much of the efficiency gains from a consumption tax reform are lost if such transition rules are enacted. The benefit of the retail sales tax is that it makes it more difficult to incorporate these kinds of transition rules and so increases the probability that the reform will indeed be efficiency enhancing.

One other consideration worth mentioning is the current debate over taxation of internet sales. While this is not a distributional issue, it is an important issue of fairness and it will be important to treat internet transactions just like any other retail sales transaction. If the federal government can do this correctly, it increases the odds that state and local governments will also treat these sales correctly under state and local sales taxes.

V. Conclusion

It is quite possible to design a distributionally neutral consumption tax reform. Doing so, however, requires an understanding of the difference between annual and lifetime income. Measuring lifetime income is conceptually easy but in practice impossible. This raises hurdles to the use of lifetime income for distributional analysis in policy circles but it does not negate its importance as you take up the important topic of fundamental tax reform. Thank you for the opportunity to comment on this issue.

References

Feenberg, Daniel R., et al. "Distributional Effects of Adopting a National Retail Sales Tax," *Tax Policy and the Economy,* 1997, 11: pp. 49–90.

Friedman, Milton. *A Theory of the Consumption Function.*. Princeton, NJ: Princeton University Press, 1957.

Gale, William, et al. "Distributional Effects of Fundamental Tax Reform." *In Economic Effects of Fundamental Tax Reform,* ed. Henry Aaron and William Gale, 281–315. Washington, DC: Brookings Institution, 1996.

Metcalf, Gilbert E. "The National Sales Tax: Who Bears the Burden?," Washington, DC: Cato Institute. Cato Policy Analysis No. 289, Dec. 8, 1997.

Pechman, J. *Who Paid the Taxes: 1966–85?.* Washington DC: Brookings, 1985.

Chairman ARCHER. Thank you, Dr. Metcalf. Dr. Angell?

STATEMENT OF WAYNE ANGELL, CHIEF ECONOMIST, BEAR STEARNS & COMPANY, INC., NEW YORK, NEW YORK

Mr. ANGELL. I am Wayne Angell, chief economist at Bear Stearns, and formerly, Mr. Chairman, 8 years as a member of the Board of Governors of the Federal Reserve system.

I believe the case for fundamental tax reform rests on whether the current tax system poses a serious risk to the continuation of our current prosperity through the first decade of the 21st Century. Piecemeal amendment of our tax code cannot alter the one fundamental problem facing our economic expansion, our national shortfall of saving. Only the national undersaving or overconsumption stands in the way of our continuing prosperity.

As the chart on page 2 of my testimony indicates, just maintaining our national saving rate is far less than optimum in a new-era economy that relies on investment spending to continue to rise as a percent of GDP. Our savings shortfall has accelerated over the last 3 years to 4 percent of GDP, and of course that then would be our current account trade deficit.

Without fundamental tax reform, the gap between national saving and investment is likely to continue to widen. The new era of business focus on cutting costs by relying on increased nonresidential capital goods investment that have risen from 9 to 14 percent of GDP over the last decade is likely to continue to increase equity market wealth and to depress the household saving rate. Depressed domestic saving is currently balanced by the expectation of higher equity prices that is part of the ingredient and the inflow of saving from abroad.

Now, I do not join the scare-mongers who suggest that our rising trade deficit cannot go on forever. Our rising trade deficit can go on as long as global investors, including, in particular, U.S. investors are willing to hold an ever-increasing ratio of their wealth in the United States. Nevertheless, it is correct that our rising trade deficit makes our economic expansion more vulnerable to any adverse news, period; that is, if the Federal Reserve were to make an inflation mistake during the 5- or 10-year period ahead, the interest rate consequences would be much worse.

I hope you will choose fundamental tax reform. Take away the current tax system disincentive to save. All Americans will benefit by participating in the wealth-creating process that begins by the decision to abstain from spending income and thereby to save. Far too long, we have lived with the incorrect assumption that imposing higher tax rates on individual incomes can reduce income and equality.

If we desire equality of incomes, we need a new consumption-based tax system that will provide more encouragement to save for those who are poor and who would like to become wealthy. The acceleration of capital goods investment is a first step toward improving income equality, for it is rising capital investment that is driving the increase in labor productivity and rising real wages that directly contribute to the capacity of working families to save.

If a nation undersaves, then real interest rates will move higher. As long as our national saving does not match our spending on capital goods, real interest rates must move enough higher to offset the increased exchange rate risk faced by global investors. If global savers approach satiation by an overconcentration of loans and investments in the United States, then the full tax burden on saving must be shifted to borrowers.

Alan Greenspan is right on target in recognizing the inflation risk that would be associated with a low Fed funds rate, while real corporate bond rates are rising. Nothing would endanger this expansion more than for the FOMC to peg the Fund's rate below the level consistent with Triple B corporate bond rates. Corporate bond market yields reflect our shortfall of saving while the demand for capital goods is rising. Unfortunately, to the extent that rising real interest rates dampen investment spending, labor productivity cannot accelerate to the optimum economic equality level.

The Americans for Fair Tax Proposal—the Fair Tax—is the superior starting point for fundamental tax reform. First, the Fair Tax proposal directly deals with our, one imbalance, under-saving. The 23-percent national retail sales tax would dramatically increase household savings rates. And I would be happy to respond to questions as to why I differ from the other panelists in regard to that rate.

Second, only the Fair Tax proposal has a perfect offset for the growth slowdown that would occur if a national saving rate were to quickly rise to the national investment rate around 20 percent GDP. By eliminating the cost of Government in the prices of goods we export, the growth of exports accelerates. By subjecting imported final goods to the sales tax, domestic production of goods would crowd out imported goods. That would mean that imported goods would compete fairly and squarely under the same burden of Government cost as domestic-produced goods. Both would be subject to the 23-percent uniform sales tax rate.

During the adjustment period, consumer spending would likely fall, exports would leap upward and imports would fall. After the adjustment period, growth rates of consumer spending, exports and imports, would tend to normalize at a rate somewhat higher as is consistent with the higher capital spending induced by lower interest rates and lower interest volatility.

Without fundamental tax reform, our expansion is apt to encounter an increasing risk of being aborted by a policy mistake. Let us not wait too long to act now as the current balance between rising inflow of saving and an increasing trade deficit could change from global balance to global imbalance. The longer we delay in dealing with this tax impediment to saving the more risky our future.

[The prepared statement follows:]

Statement of Wayne Angell, Chief Economist, Bear Stearns & Company, Inc., New York, New York

Mr. Chairman, members of the committee, thank you for the opportunity to testify on the subject of fundamental tax reform. I believe the imperative case for fundamental tax reform rests on whether the current tax system poses a serious risk to the continuation of our current prosperity through the first decade of the Twenty-first Century.

The focus of my advice is (1) do not underestimate our potential for achieving a very long period of growth at a rate approaching five percent and (2) do not ignore the potential for an economic policy breakdown to precipitate an abrupt end to this expansion. Just as we have benefited enormously from new high technology capital investment, so also would an end of this expansion with a likely collapse of labor productivity growth be unusually difficult for workers and investors alike.

Although our current expansion, at nine years, is the longest expansion in our history, it is far short of achieving the 4.3 percent average annual growth rate over 36 quarters from 1963 to 1972. The estimated average growth rate over the last nine years ending in the first quarter of 2000, at 3.6 percent, is a good beginning for an expansion that has a potential to go on another nine years. If we succeed in growing another nine years by continuing the 4.4 percent average rate of the last four, then we would achieve an 18-year average growth rate of 4 percent.

Undersaving as a risk to this expansion

Piecemeal amendment of our tax code cannot alter the one fundamental problem facing our economic expansion—our national shortfall of saving. The continuation of our accelerating prosperity is dependent on the means to finance non-residential capital investment that is growing at twice the rate of growth of gross domestic product. Without fundamental tax reform our current under-saving requires an inflow of capital from abroad that has its counterpart in a rising trade deficit.

Only the national undersaving (or overconsumption) stands in the way of our continuing prosperity. As long as economic growth remains on this current track of four straight years of growth rates approaching 4-1/2% percent, the current system of tax rates will provide more revenue than projected growth of government expenditures. Some, including Alan Greenspan, seem to be suggesting that the correct approach is to rely on rising public saving to offset the adverse impact of rising equity market wealth on household saving. This is an austerity approach, which I believe actually increases the risk of difficulty in funding our under-saving.

But, as the chart below indicates, just maintaining our national saving rate is far less than optimum in our new era economy that relies on investment spending to continue to rise as a percent of GDP. Adding 1999-government investment of approximately 2-1/2% of GDP to the private investment shown in the chart brings national investment spending to 20 percent of GDP. Subtracting government investment from government spending increases national saving to 16 percent and implies an inflow of saving from abroad of 4 percent of GDP. One constant in our equation is that the balance of payment is balanced; saving (capital) inflows equals the current account deficit.

Without fundamental tax reform the gap between national saving and investment will get worse. The new era business focus on cutting costs by relying on increased non-residential capital goods investments, that have risen from 9 to 14 percent of GDP over the last decade, is likely to continue to increase equity market wealth and depress the household saving rate. Depressed domestic saving is currently balanced by the expectation of higher equity prices that is part of the ingredient in the inflow of saving from abroad.

Now I do not join the scaremongers who suggest that our rising trade deficit cannot go on forever. Our rising trade deficit can go on as long as people who live abroad are willing to finance it. However, it is correct that a rising trade deficit makes our economic expansion more vulnerable to any adverse news period that would cause global investors to lose confidence in the exchange value of the dollar.

That is, if the Federal Reserve were to make an inflation mistake during the five or ten year period ahead, then the interest rate consequences would be much worse.

I hope you will choose fundamental tax reform. Take away the current tax system disincentive to save. All Americans will benefit by participating in the wealth-creating process that begins by the decision to abstain from spending income and thereby, to save. Currently, our saving rate is too dependent on the higher income and higher wealth segment of our citizens. Why not shift to a consumption-based tax system that will enhance the incentive of all income groups to participate in the rewards of wealth creation.

For far too long we have lived with the incorrect assumption that imposing higher tax rates on high-income individuals can reduce income inequality. First, marginal income tax rates including the double taxation of corporate profits directly subtract from saving by reducing the capacity of taxpayers to save. Second, marginal tax rates, which include some very high marginal rates on low income households as the earned income tax credit is phased out, tilt the preference of households to spend a higher proportion of their disposable income. If we desire equality of incomes, we need a new consumption-based tax system that will provide more encouragement to save for those who are poor and would like to become wealthy.

It is essential to understand that in a market system economy, prices will adjust so as to correct imbalances. Scarcities lead to higher prices that ration out scarce goods and provide incentives to produce more of that good. And that includes saving as a scarce good.

The tax burden on saving is fully shifted to borrowers

If a nation under-saves then real interest rates will move higher. It is important to note that the current move toward a larger government surplus, an increase in government saving, has led to a somewhat lower interest rate on Treasury securities, while corporate bond interest rates have increased. As long as our national saving does not match our spending on capital goods, real interest rates must move enough higher to offset the increased exchange rate risk faced by global savers. As global savers approach satiation by an over-concentration of loans and investments in the United States, then the full tax burden on saving must be shifted to borrowers.

For two decades we have filled the shortfall of national saving by an inflow of investment and lending from abroad. But a continuation of the domestic saving shortfall will continue to require higher real interest rates to both attract saving inflows and to offset the adverse wealth effect on domestic saving. Eventually, an inflow of saving from abroad becomes ever more risky as foreign savers contemplate the equity and exchange rate risk of being so heavily weighted in the United States.

For a country mired in under-saving, high marginal tax rates on the return to saving must necessarily lead to higher returns on saving until either the higher return is sufficient to restore the saving balance or until the entire tax rate is fully passed forward to borrowers. In either case, higher marginal tax rates on saving are completely frustrated by none of the tax falling on savers and all of the tax falling on borrowers.

Increasing income inequality vs. increasing income equality

As long as the return on capital goods accelerates with the new technology induced productivity of capital we need more saving. That means that, one way or another, the return on capital will rise. A higher return on capital will continue to increase income inequality. Under the current tax system our income distribution pattern will continue to flow toward augmenting the income of the wealthy that have higher savings rates. This process toward inequality of incomes is likely to continue until that domestic saving imbalance is reduced.

The continuation of the acceleration of non-residential capital goods investment is a first step toward improving income equality. For it is rising non-residential capital investment as a percent of GDP that is driving the increase in labor productivity and rising real wages that directly contribute to the capacity of working families to save. This is the growth solution.

The sub-optimum growth solution

It seems to me that too many policy makers have become overly pessimistic concerning the likelihood of increasing saving by fundamental tax reform. Consequently, they are looking toward a sub-optimal growth and a sub-optimal federal debt ratio. Central banks and monetary authorities around the world are going to need more Treasury securities than are likely to be available to facilitate the dollar's reserve currency role. This committee has a wonderful opportunity to restore a more optimistic vision by recommending fundamental tax reform.

Given our current tax system there is no alternative to increasing real rates of interest. Rising real rates of interest tends to work more quickly toward limiting investment spending than in increasing saving rates. Unfortunately, to the extent that rising real interest rates dampen investment spending; labor productivity cannot accelerate to the optimum economic equality level.

Alan Greenspan is right on target in recognizing the inflation risk that would be associated with a low Fed funds rate while real corporate bond rates are rising. Nothing would endanger this expansion more than for the FOMC to peg the funds rate below the level consistent with rising Baa corporate bond rates. Corporate bond market yields reflect our shortfall of saving while the demand for capital goods is rising.

And, if this committee helps to restore policy maker's confidence that household savings could be counted on to rise sufficiently to close the imbalance, then they would be free to consider some optimum federal debt level as a contrast to the political proposal to pay down the national debt.

More importantly, Alan Greenspan should no longer be so concerned that rising household wealth from equity market gains would lower national saving. As he now sees it, rising equity prices increase wealth faster than the increase in income. Thereby consumer spending rises faster than income and the savings rate falls.

Fortunately, the revised Federal Reserve de-emphasis on the level of equity market prices has lessened the risk that global investors might, at some point, reduce the inflows of saving into the U.S. equity market and that could pull the down the dollar. Ultimately it is the dollar exchange rate risk that could jeopardize the FOMC's freedom to lower interest rates as they did in the fall of 1998 during a period of deflation risk. It is imperative that, as our inflation rate approaches zero, the FOMC maintain its domestic policy focus so as to avoid deflationary episodes such as occurred in 1986, 1990 and 1998.

Fundamental tax reform

From my perspective as a Wall Street economist, the Americans for Fair Tax proposal—the FairTax—is the superior starting point for fundamental tax reform.

First, the FairTax proposal directly deals with our one imbalance—undersaving. Household behavior responds to a change in relative prices. The 23 percent national retail sales tax would dramatically increase household savings rates.

Second, only the FairTax proposal has a perfect offset for the growth slowdown that would occur if the national saving rate were to quickly rise to the national investment rate around 20 percent of GDP. By eliminating the cost of government from the goods we export, the growth rate of exports accelerates. And, by including imported final goods in goods subject to the sales tax, domestic production of goods would crowd out imported goods. That would mean that imported goods would compete fairly and squarely under the same burden of government cost as domestic produced goods—both would be subject to the 23 percent uniform sales tax rate.

During the adjustment period, consumer spending would likely fall, exports would leap upward at about the same rate that resources can flow into export industries, and imports would fall. After the adjustment period during which saving and investment converge to the same percent of GDP, growth rates of consumer spending, exports and imports would tend to normalize. These new normal rates of growth of GDP, exports and imports would be somewhat higher as is consistent with the higher residential and higher non-residential spending induced by both lower interest rates and by lower interest rate volatility.

Conclusion

Without fundamental tax reform our expansion is apt to encounter an increasing risk of being aborted by a policy mistake. The 4.3 percent expansion over the 36 quarter period ending in 1972 came to an end as the Federal Reserve made the policy mistake of shifting its focus of monetary policy toward increasing economic growth. Undoubtedly, the Congressional stand-pat policy on leaving top marginal tax rates at 70 percent after lowering rates in the 1963–64 Kennedy round of tax rate cuts from 90 to 70 percent, contributed to the FOMC focus on using money creation to maintain economic growth.

Let us not wait too long to act now as the current balance between rising inflow of saving and an increasing trade deficit could change from global balance to global imbalance. And, if fundamental tax reform is not done, then you may end up tempting other policy makers to do what they cannot do. Surely, the FOMC cannot successfully control economic growth. Nor can the FOMC successfully control equity market asset values. The longer we delay in dealing with this tax imbalance the more risky our future.

Chairman ARCHER. Thank you, Dr. Angell. I am struggling with how to best use my time to take advantage of all of the talent that is represented at the witness table today. It is not often that we have access to this sort of economic talent.

Do you gentlemen agree with the general concept that the more you tax of something the less you are going to get of it?

Mr. ANGELL. Yes.

Chairman ARCHER. Does anyone disagree with that?

Mr. WILKINS. I am sorry. Could you repeat it.

Chairman ARCHER. Do you agree with the general thesis that the more you tax something the less you are going to get of it?

Let the record show all witnesses are nodding assent.

And do you disagree that the income tax, as a base of taxation, taxes work, savings, productivity and incentive? Does any one of you disagree with that?

No. The answer is apparently they all agree with that. Then why are we using a system that reduces work, reduces productivity, reduces savings and reduces incentive? I don't understand it? And yet is not factored in, and I will be glad to get your responses. I am going on a little here with a soliloquy, but I am curious, Mr. Wilkins, as to whether the survey, the study that you mentioned that was done by Pricewaterhouse, included any of these basic factors.

Mr. WILKINS. Yes. Income tax is certainly put in there carefully, Mr. Chairman. The argument, of course, you are making are an argument against any income tax, but it is also a good argument for keeping tax rates as low as possible. An income tax that has relatively low rates is going to have relatively lesser impact on the disincentives that you just talked about.

Chairman ARCHER. Yes, it is true that the higher marginal rates create a greater disincentive. But any taxation of income will operate the same way even if it could be done at the flat tax level. By the way, flat tax is dead. It has basically been assigned to oblivion by its own creator, Professor Hall, but even if you could do a flat tax, it would still be true that the more hours you work, the more you are going to pay in taxation. It just does not increase incrementally by the graduated tax structure. And you are still taxing work. You are still taxing at a lower rate, and I agree it would be better, you are still taxing work effort.

Mr. WILKINS. Let me just make one more comment in response to your question, Mr. Chairman, and that is our study does not differ a great deal with many of the other studies that show there are going to be positive benefits in the long run from switching from an income tax to consumption tax. What our study shows is that there are some very dangerous effects in the short run in getting there. You are giving an enormous incentive to saving and a disincentive to consumption, and by golly they both work. GDP drops and consumption drops just the way you might expect them to.

Chairman ARCHER. No, no. I did listen very carefully to your presentation, and I noted that you distinguished between the short-term and the long-term. But I am wondering, even if in the long term, these studies have any way of factoring in work effort and productivity, and how it is burdened by the income tax and how it is freed up by abolishing the income tax? And I doubt very much that those factors have been adequately put into the models. Additionally, and I want to develop a few more points and then I want to get responses from all of you. The cost of compliance with the income tax is to be $250 billion estimated and some say it could go as high as $500- to $600 billion a year. But being a conservative, I will take the lower number and work off of $250 billion. It means that some of the brightest and best minds in this country are spending full time coping with this tax code, which produces no wealth. And if those minds were freed to go into the marketplace, and their ingenuity, and use their mental capabilities were designed to produce wealth, would we not also have a bigger GDP? Is that factored into all of these studies? I rather doubt it. And so I think the studies are flawed because they are unable to cope with a lot of these intangibles as to the truth benefits that will come.

And then, finally, I want to ask each one of you, which I have done to a number of other witnesses, not today, but in previous hearings, what would you pay, Dr. Kotlikoff, not to have to deal with the IRS every year?

Mr. KOTLIKOFF. That is a good question.

Chairman ARCHER. What value, in dollars, would you assign to that, personally?

Mr. KOTLIKOFF. Probably somewhere between $3,000 to $5,000.

Chairman ARCHER. I take it you do your own income tax from your testimony, and if you do, I am there with you, and I am in the process of trying to handle that right now.

Mr. KOTLIKOFF. Right.

Chairman ARCHER. What would you pay, Mr. Wilkins, not to have to deal with the IRS every year?

Mr. WILKINS. I apparently haven't had as bad an experience as Larry Kotlikoff has had with the IRS. It certainly would be nice not to have to deal with them on a personal level, and I have had to deal both with my own taxes, my elderly mother's taxes, and other taxes, but it would not be worth that much to me. I think I have probably wasted hundreds of dollars, but not thousands of dollars of my time.

Chairman ARCHER. You must have a very cheap tax prepayer.

Dr. Metcalf, what would you assign as a value that you would pay not to have to deal with the IRS every year?

Mr. METCALF. Well, I am the wrong person to ask, I am afraid, for two reasons. One is that my income is fairly simple, as a professor. But, second, as a public finance economist, I am rather embarrassed to say I get some consumption value out of filling out tax forms. So it helps me in thinking about it to talk to my students. So I am an outlier, I am afraid.

Chairman ARCHER. So it is a learning experience, and you benefit from it.

Mr. METCALF. Yes, sir.

[Laughter.]

Chairman ARCHER. Dr. Angell?

Mr. ANGELL. Chairman Archer, I am one of those fastidious taxpayers that really wants to do it exactly right, and there is a lot of personal pride and integrity in that. I would happily pay $25,000 compensatory costs to not have to go through that process. But I would like, in addition, $80,000 of punitive costs in regard to the entire intrusion into my life. And even though I want to do it most accurately, I do not like that kind of big Government in my personal financial life.

Chairman ARCHER. Well, you alluded to what was going to be my next question. How much value do you attach to your personal freedom and privacy? Thomas Jefferson said in his second inaugural address that one of his most notable achievements while in public office was the removal of the Federal tax collector from any direct contact with the American citizen because he understood, probably more than any other American, the value of individual freedom.

Now, put that into your hopper. Dr. Kotlikoff, how much is your individual freedom and privacy worth?

Mr. KOTLIKOFF. I had one minor audit that was pretty much an even split with the Feds, so to me it is not so much an issue of private freedom. I think the Government is going to have to collect taxes no matter how we do it. I do not get exercised over the existence of the IRS, to tell you the truth. I am just concerned about the next generation, and the fact that we are not looking ahead to the retirement of all of these baby boomers and distributors. I am also concerned that tax inefficiencies have been getting worse over time.

I think that if more Democrats really looked at this tax proposal, they would see that it is really very much a Democratic proposal. It is getting rid of the regressive payroll tax. It has got a very progressive rebate. And it is going to presumably maintain the real spending power of Social Security beneficiaries, food stamp beneficiaries and people on Welfare.

I also has an implicit wealth tax, as Gil Metcalf was just describing. today, if you are Bill Gates and spend your $80 billion or so on consumption, you don't pay any taxes on it. But under the retail sales tax you would. And if you don't spend you wealth yourself, you give it to your kids, and they spend it, plus some interest, they'll pay taxes on it. And in present value, it is equivalent to a one-time wealth tax on $80 billion. That, to me, is very progressive.

Mr. Linbeck does not seem like part of a vast left-wing conspiracy, but he actually is. And it is really time, I think, for the Democrats to recognize that what is being proposed here is something they should be advancing.

Chairman ARCHER. Okay. I think there is merit to what you are saying. I also think that when you talk about the Baby Boomers and the problems that we are going to have in the next century which has not started yet we have got to be concerned about two things—savings had productivity. We have got to start presaving, and we have got to increase productivity. And those are the only two answers to the problems that are looming ahead.

Mr. KOTLIKOFF. Let me just say, if I could, respond on the issue of saving.

I have studied in simulation models with other economists the whole way consumption taxation increases saving. And part of it has to do with these economic incentives, that you are not facing a double tax on saving. But a large part of it has to do with the fact that you are putting a bigger burden on the older people who are the big spenders in this economy. Their propensity to spend, to consume, out of their remaining lifetime resources is two to three times higher than that of younger people. The reason our national saving rate is so low, to be quite honest, is because we have been spending five decades taking ever larger sums from young savers and giving it to old spenders. The consumption of old people, relative to young people, in the post-war period has roughly doubled.

This is exactly what economic theory predicts, which is older people, because they have fewer years left to go, are spending at a more rapid clip. So when you put more of the burden onto the old people and away from the young people, you are really taking from spenders and giving to savers. That is the real reason, in these simulation models, based on the standard life cycle and neoclassical model of economic growth, that you actually get a crowding in of capital, you get more saving, and you get the national output to go up by about 15 percent in the long run.

Chairman ARCHER. That is also, I think, very helpful and very interesting.

Let me just pursue with Mr. Wilkins how much value you put on privacy and individual freedom in your own life. Is it also down there around $100?

Thank you, Dr. Kotlikoff. I understand you have to leave.

Mr. WILKINS. You are speaking to someone who just got through filling out the census long form, so I have a little different view. Back to thousands of dollars on this, several thousand dollars. I really do share your view that it would be very nice not to have somebody looking over our shoulder all of the time and have some more privacy.

I will have to say that I am a little concerned about my neighbor down the street. I would just as soon they continue to look at him for a while.

Chairman ARCHER. Dr. Metcalf, is this also a learning experience for you so it really is something that you are benefitting from?

Mr. METCALF. Well, I did the short census form, so I am not so exercised.

No, I think as an individual I share your concerns certainly about privacy. As an economist, in addition, I think I share your frustration that income is enormously difficult to measure. And if we could tax consumption, a lot of that intrusion, the need for intrusion goes away. And if we were in a world without taxes, initially then, I think we would certainly want to choose a consumption tax. And the real frustration, I suspect, is that we are in a world with one tax, we want to switch to a world with a better tax. So there are clear benefits of making that shift, but there are real costs in how we get from A to B that are what you have to struggle with and how to deal with.

Chairman ARCHER. And, Dr. Angell, you said if I asked, you would explain why you disagree with the other panelists and why you believe a 23-percent rate is the appropriate rate.

Mr. ANGELL. Yes. But it is not just that disagreement. I disagree with Mr. Wilkins' notion that the short run would provide slower growth. I think just the opposite. I think we would come out of the gates very, very fast with the transition to the America for Fair Tax proposal. That would occur because consumer spending slowdown would be very significant and abrupt in the tax year that you made the transition. But that would free up resources to enable our companies to crowd out imports, and it would also free up resources to move into the export industry. And we have got American companies or global companies and they know how to do it, and they simply do it wherever it is best to do it. So I would expect to come out of the gate at 6-percent real growth rate.

Chairman ARCHER. I see.

Mr. ANGELL. Now, expecting, thereby, that we have a very strong economy, that then is going to lead to higher consumer spending. That is we are going to have an incremental increase in consumer spending because people's perception of their lifetime income will be so much higher. Alan Greenspan talks a lot about the wealth effect that comes from equity price increases that causes consumer spending income ratio to rise. But I think there is another wealth effect that has been overlooked, and that is this new technology economy develops such increases in labor productivity and such improvement in job opportunities, that the human capital that is estimated by the young worker is a whole lot different than it would be if we were in an economy that was really lost in the doldrums. So we need to be freed up to save the money, to fuel the capital spending that we are doing, and I expect that will then produce high tax receipts.

Now, I would also want to question whether the income tax is passed backward onto the wage earner or forward to consumers. I think the corporate income tax is largely passed forward to consumers. But if my firm received a thousand-dollar asset management fee and we had to put a 23-percent sales tax on it, and it would be $1,230, I don't think there's any chance that my bonus arrangement with the company would be the same as it is now, and the firm would not need to pay me the same amount they paid me now because I always take into consideration my after-tax income in deciding whether or not I wish to remain employed.

Thank you.

Chairman ARCHER. I am grateful to the responses from all of you, and I have imposed on my colleague, Mrs. Thurman. Thank goodness she is the only one that I have imposed on. Mrs. Thurman, it is your turn.

Mrs. THURMAN. Mr. Chairman, I just want you to know that the one question that I might have had, the guy left already.

[Laughter.]

Mrs. THURMAN. So you did a very good job on that.

I have a couple of questions, and, you know, Dr. Angell, I was listening, and I was sitting here thinking if I were a business person, and I am a business person in the office that I run, and I think about the cost of running my office and what this would incur if I had to have an electrician come in, and it is going to be an extra 30 percent or if I am going to have somebody check the plumbing or you are going to have an electrical bill or whatever other kinds of services that are being provided to me, that is going to raise the cost of every service that is provided.

So if you take that into effect, then this assumption that it is going to, just because the payroll taxes are going to come down and the employer might save some money there, that it is going to be passed onto the worker or not passed onto the worker, I mean, I don't know where we get into a better situation here at all, not to mention the fact that they say the accountants and all of these people are going to be taken out.

Well, you know what, I remember in the State legislature when the businesses came to us and said, "Look, you have got to raise the amount of money that we are going to—that we are collecting these taxes for you because we needed another proportion of this so that we can continue to do the paperwork and the constant thing." The same thing with the doctor's office, the hospitals. I mean, you know, they are overburdened with insurance things. Now we are going to add this idea that they are going to have to, you know, bear the cost of 30 percent on every billing that they do, and somebody is going to have to take care of that paperwork.

Mr. ANGELL. But a lot of it is passed backward already; that is, we are a Nation, using international comparison, we are a Nation of very high tax compliance. But, we are increasingly low tax compliance in regard to nannies, and craftsmen who are working and who are insisting on cash payment.

Mrs. THURMAN. Are you suggesting that would get rid of that problem?

Mr. ANGELL. No, I'm saying it is already there. What I am saying is if the Federal Reserve continues to do its job well, then people say I do not have the ability to pay more, and so consequently when the worker has a reduction of the payroll tax, the worker has a reduction of the income tax, the worker is willing to do the work at a lower rate than otherwise would be the case. And that include Government workers.

Mrs. THURMAN. I am not so sure when they have to pass along to themselves a 30-percent on every payment that they are making.

But let me go to Dr. Metcalf—or maybe, Mr. Wilkins, can you respond to that, though, as far as the paperwork and the kinds of things. I mean, you seem to be this lone voice out there suggesting that this may not be the best thing to do at this time.

Mr. WILKINS. I suggest it is not best to do this on a big-bang basis because it will hurt the economy quite a bit. I disagree with Dr. Angell, I think in degree more so than in direction. We find the incentives in a national sales tax work extremely well, so well that consumption drops, savings increases and the economy temporarily goes in the tank. That is what has us worried. That is what has retailers worried. They may like the long-run situation, but they may not be here in the long run. That is the concern.

On the paperwork, I think you are right. There is going to continue to be paperwork to do this. Unfortunately, most of that burden is going to be on retailers under this new law.

Mrs. THURMAN. And States, particularly if that is where the collection point is.

Mr. WILKINS. If States are the ones that are going to have to collect the tax, since the Feds will not be collecting any more, that is right. I would concede that it is probably not nearly as difficult or as big an overall job as we would probably have with the income tax. But the burden of collecting it is clearly shifting to States and to retailers.

If I could just mention, Mr. Chairman, one point about cutting the tax rate and pushing it on to individuals, I do not understand why we would think that cutting the income tax is all going to go ahead into prices. We don't see that happening. And the only anecdotal evidence I recall is the 1986 act, when we cut the rate from 50 percent to 28 percent, almost in half, I do not recall my accountant or my lawyer or my physician cutting his prices that I had to pay. So I guess, I only base it on anecdotal evidence, but I guess I do not see it the same way Dr. Angell would see that.

Mrs. THURMAN. Mr. Chairman, do I have time for another? Okay.

Dr. Metcalf, in your testimony that was given to us earlier on page 15, you go through it. Actually, the title of it starts with rebating the payroll tax and then goes on. And the last paragraph, you just need to explain it to me a little bit. "There are important distributional considerations that I have not considered in this analysis. Transitional gains and losses will be substantial in any tax reform, and in particular reform that shifts from income to consumption taxation. A shift without any transitional rules from income taxation to a national sales tax will [among other things] induce a transfer from the current elderly to the current young. It is also worth noting that this study does not take into consideration the broad economic gains that might be expected from converting to a consumption-based tax system. Low-income Americans may very well realize gains in after-tax income from the tax shift if the economy improves and wages rise," which is contrary to somewhat what we are hearing here, that wages actually could go down.

Can you explain that to me a little bit.

Mr. METCALF. There are a lot of ideas embedded in that, and I do not have what you have in front of you. I am not sure what it is that you have. But let me speak first to the transition issue.

Two examples, in my comments I noted that there is this windfall tax on existing—a one-time wealth tax, so to speak. And many of the problems of previous consumption tax reforms has been an effort to try to create transition rules to somehow avoid this one-time wealth tax. And to my way of thinking, that simply decreases the efficiency gains of the reform. It requires a higher tax rate because you are giving money back. This issue of transfers from the current elderly to the current young is the point also that Larry Kotlikoff was making, that if we go to a sales tax, the current elderly have a much higher propensity to consume, therefore will be paying more in taxes than under the current system.

Whereas, younger people that have more saving ahead of them and therefore will be paying less in taxes relative to the current tax system, which taxes both consumption and savings, which is what an income tax is.

Mrs. THURMAN. But it also could mean that the younger, being myself, with a mother, ending up paying for that extra consumption by that elderly, costing me and shifting that burden even further.

Mr. METCALF. Well, it is true that we go through phases of high consumption and low consumption. And my kids are teenagers, so I feel like I am in a high-consumption phase right now.

Mrs. THURMAN. I have two in college.

Mr. METCALF. Yes. But, clearly, you have years of saving ahead of you; whereas, if you were 70, you probably would not.

Chairman ARCHER. Mrs. Thurman, have you completed your questioning?

I came on this committee when Wilbur Mills was chairman of the committee, and it was operated very differently in those days. But I remember, in the middle of the afternoon, he would be here by himself and all of the other members would be absent. And I was told so often that is how he became so knowledgeable about the Code because he was always here and very few other members were present at hearings. And on afternoons like this, where I have the opportunity, without imposing on too many other members to explore in greater detail with wonderful witnesses all types of concepts, I understand the benefit that comes from it.

I thank all of you for your presentation today, and I know that I have learned, and I do wish that there had been more other members here to learn from you.

You are excused.

Our next panel is invited to come to the witness table, the final panel for the afternoon. Mr. Hamilton, Ms. Skarbek, Mr. Chapoton, and Mr. Threadgill.

As usual, all of your written statements, without objection, will be inserted in the record. And to the degree that you can, if you will synopsize those in your oral presentation, it would be appreciated. And if you will identify yourselves before you begin to testify, for the record, that would be very helpful.

Mr. Hamilton, would you commence.

STATEMENT OF BILLY HAMILTON, DEPUTY COMPTROLLER, OFFICE OF THE TEXAS COMPTROLLER OF PUBLIC ACCOUNTS, AUSTIN, TEXAS

Mr. HAMILTON. Mr. Chairman and members, I am Billy Hamilton, and I am deputy comptroller of public accounts for the State of Texas. Carole Keeton Rylander, the Texas Comptroller of Public Accounts, was delighted to receive an invitation to testify before this committee regarding the fundamental tax reform measures under consideration today. Unfortunately, her schedule didn't permit her to be in attendance, and so she asked me to testify on her behalf.

My comments today are directed only to the feasibility of State administration of the Fair Tax proposed by H.R. 2525. I do not intend to comment on the economics or any other aspects of the proposal.

The Texas Comptroller's Office has administered a sales and use tax since 1961, and I have been involved with administration of the tax since 1982. Last year, the Texas Comptroller collected about $13 billion in sales tax revenue for more than 600,000 businesses. I offer my experience with sales tax administration, as well as the size of the Texas sales tax program, as the basis of qualification to speak on the administerability of H.R. 2525.

As you know, H.R. 2525 would permit States to collect and administer the Fair Tax on behalf of the Federal Government. In my opinion, Texas would be well-equipped to administer the Fair Tax based on our experience in administering our own sales tax. Even though the base rate and other characteristics of the Fair Tax are significantly different from the Texas sales tax, it would be feasible for our office to collect the Fair Tax by expanding and enhancing the systems we currently have in place.

For example, we would expand our current system for registering Texas retailers to include registration of sellers under the Fair Tax, 615,000 businesses are currently registered as sellers in Texas. Under the Fair Tax, we estimate that about 1.5 million Texas businesses would have to be registered; expand our taxpayer assistance efforts to respond to a larger volume of telephone, letter and e-mail inquiries from sellers who collect the Fair Tax and individuals who pay it; expand our Revenue Processing Division to process more returns and tax payments on a more frequent basis and to remit tax collections to the Federal Government on an almost daily basis; expand our current audit team and train all auditors to examine businesses for both the Fair Tax, as well as the Texas sales tax; and, of course, expand our information technology systems to collect and maintain computerized records critical to the effective administration of a consumption tax like the Fair Tax.

The expansion of our systems to administer the Fair Tax in this manner I have just described would be sizable. Under the Fair Tax, we would serve approximately 900,000 more filers than we do currently. We estimate that serving that many additional taxpayers would require between 1,100 and 1,600 more full-time employees. The Texas Comptroller currently employs about 2,700 people on a full-time basis.

In spite of this expansion, the compensation for electing the Fair Tax that would be provided to the States under the terms of H.R. 2525 would likely cover our projected costs. As a first approximation, we estimate the cost to the Comptroller's Office for collecting the Fair Tax at full implementation, would be between $100- and $150 million a year. I emphasize, however, there would be significant costs to begin collection, including the cost of facilities to house the additional processing facilities, the capital costs of information technology and revenue processing equipment and the costs of notifying, registering and educating taxpayers on the new tax. However, these seem to be manageable within the amount that is allowed under provisions of the bill.

In closing, I believe that if the Fair Tax is to become a reality, the United States Government would be well-served to make use of the existing expertise of the States. Many States have administered consumption taxes since the 1930s and have developed particular capabilities in this area. We also have extensive experience in dealing with the affected businesses. As long as the administrative fee paid to the States is adequate in relation to the costs of collection, I see no reason that the State of Texas could not effectively administer this tax.

Thank you, Mr. Chairman.

[The prepared statement follows:]

Statement of Billy Hamilton, Deputy Comptroller, Office of the Texas Comptroller of Public Accounts, Austin, Texas

My name is Billy Hamilton, and I am the Deputy Comptroller for the State of Texas. Carole Keeton Rylander, the Texas Comptroller of Public Accounts, was delighted to receive an invitation to testify before this committee regarding the Fundamental Tax Reform measures under consideration today. Unfortunately, Comptroller Rylander's schedule did not permit her attendance, and she has asked me to testify here on her behalf.

My comments today are directed only to the feasibility of state administration of the Fair Tax proposed by H.R. 2525. I do not intend to comment on the economics or any other aspects of the proposal.

The Texas Comptroller's office has administered a sales and use tax since the 1960's, and I have been involved with administration of the tax since 1982. Last year, the Texas Comptroller collected $13 billion in sales tax revenue from more than 600,000 businesses. I offer my own experience with sales tax administration, as well as the size of Texas' sales tax program, as the basis of my qualification to speak to you about the administerability of H.R. 2525.

As you know, H.R. 2525 would permit states to collect and administer the Fair Tax on behalf of the federal government. In my opinion, Texas would be well-equipped to administer the Fair Tax based on our experience in administering our own sales tax. Even though the base, rate and other characteristics of the Fair Tax are significantly different from the Texas sales tax, it would be feasible for our office to collect the Fair Tax by expanding and enhancing the systems we currently have in place. For example, we would:

• Expand our current system for registering Texas retailers to include registration of sellers under the Fair Tax (615,000 businesses are currently registered as sellers in Texas; under the Fair Tax, 1.5 million Texas businesses would have to be registered);

• Expand our taxpayer assistance efforts to respond to a larger volume of telephone, letter and e-mail inquiries from sellers who collect the Fair Tax and individuals who pay it;

• Expand our Revenue Processing Division to process more returns and tax payments on a more frequent basis and to remit tax collections to the federal government on an almost-daily basis;

• Expand our current audit team and train all auditors to examine businesses for both the Fair Tax and the Texas sales tax; and

• Expand our information technology systems to collect and maintain the computerized records critical to effective administration of a consumption tax like the Fair Tax.

The expansion of our systems to administer the Fair Tax, in the manner I've just described, would be sizable. Under the Fair Tax, we would serve approximately 900,000 more filers than we do currently. We estimate that serving that many additional taxpayers would require 1,100 to 1,600 more full-time employees. The Texas Comptroller currently employs about 2,700 people on a full-time basis.

In spite of this large expansion, the compensation for collecting the Fair Tax that would be provided to states under H.R. 2525 would likely cover our projected costs. As a first approximation, we estimate that the cost to the Texas Comptroller's office for collecting the Fair Tax at full implementation would be $100 to $150 million per year. I emphasize, however, that there would be significant costs to begin collection, including the cost of facilities to house the additional processing facilities, the capital costs of information technology and revenue processing equipment, and the costs of notifying, registering and educating taxpayers on the new tax.

In closing, I believe that if the Fair Tax is to become a reality, the U.S. government would be well-served to make use of the existing expertise of the states. Many states have administered consumption taxes since the 1930s and have developed particular capabilities in this area. We also have extensive experience in dealing with the affected businesses. As long as the administrative fee paid to the state is adequate in relation to the costs of collection, I see no reason that the State of Texas could not effectively administer the Fair Tax.

———————

Chairman ARCHER. Thank you, Mr. Hamilton. Ms. Skarbek?

STATEMENT OF JANET L. SKARBEK, CINNAMINSON, NEW JERSEY

Ms. SKARBEK. Thank you, Mr. Chairman. My name is Janet Skarbek. I was asked here today to specifically address the viability of administering a national sales tax from the perspective of a professional that deals with State sales tax administration every day.

I started my career as a CPA working at the IRS Regional Inspector's Office. After receiving a Master's of Taxation from Villanova University's Graduate Tax Program, I went to work for a Big 6 accounting firm where I was responsible for the management of sales and use taxes for clients in the Mid-Atlantic region. I am currently employed by a Fortune 500 company, where I am responsible for sales tax compliance and administration.

I have not been asked to speak about the economic impact of the proposed national sales tax, nor have I been asked to provide an opinion as to the overall feasibility of such a plan. My testimony will specifically address business administration and the related concerns raised by such a tax. The views I express in this testimony are my own and should not be construed as representing any official position of my employer.

In my opinion, the administration of the national sales tax would "probably" be simpler and easier than administering the current income taxes and payroll taxes it proposes to replace. I emphasize "probably" because the detailed procedures that businesses would be required to follow, with regards to documentation, have yet to be established. These details will be essential in determining the potential administrative costs to businesses.

The national sales tax, as proposed, would not duplicate most of the larger problems that businesses currently encounter when dealing with the States' sales taxes. However, there are a few issues that will need to be addressed.

Under current State sales tax administration, businesses are required to either collect the sales tax or the appropriate exemption documentation from their customers. The documentation that most States require vendors to collect from their exempt customers includes: the purchaser's name, address and registration number, the seller's name, a description of the property being purchased, a statement that the property being purchased meets the requirements for the exemption, and a signature from the purchaser.

Whereas, the currently proposed national sales tax merely requires businesses to accept copies of their customers' registration permits in good faith. The States are very aware that their tougher documentation requirements can be defeated by individuals using copied or forged certificates. Making cash purchases with such illegal documentation generally results in the lack of any audit trail.

Due to the fact that the proposed national sales tax rate is higher than any current State sales tax rate, I strongly believe that further rules and regulations would be developed to remove the current control weaknesses. The burden that those potential rules and regulations would place upon business is unknown. The simpler solutions tend to allow more tax evaders to slip through, while the more tedious solutions tend to put a larger responsibility on businesses.

Under most current State sales tax systems, if an individual purchases a product in a State and is not charged sales tax in that State, that individual is legally required to self-assess that State's tax. For example, if you live in Virginia and you purchase a table from L.L. Bean, L.L. Bean does not currently have nexus with Virginia and is therefore not required to collect Virginia's sales tax. Upon receiving your table from L.L. Bean, you are supposed to check your receipt and make sure you paid sales tax. If sales tax was not paid, you are legally required to self-assess that tax. And I am sure everyone in this room reviews all of their receipts and makes sure to self-assess tax when legally required.

Now let's face it, the State sales tax system is not working when it comes to individual's self-assessing the tax. The proposed national sales tax would also require individuals to self-assess when sales tax was not originally paid to the seller. One such example occurs when orders are placed over the Internet and shipped from locations outside the United States into the United States.

Due to the fact that individual self-assessment does not work for the States, it is doubtful that compliance would increase at the national level. I am confident that this hole would also be plugged by future rules and regulations. The question then arises as to the burden these controls would place upon businesses.

In closing, the administration of the national sales tax would probably be simpler and easier than administering the current income taxes and payroll taxes, depending upon the procedural requirements. Every issue I have addressed in my testimony today is further addressed in my written statement.

I appreciate the opportunity to speak at this first-ever Congressional Summit on Fundamental Tax Reform. The testimony heard over the next 3 days from the members of Congress, the economists and the business leaders on improving the IRS, as well as on the various tax reform proposals, can only serve to improve our future tax system. But I am afraid you have your work cut out for you.

[The prepared statement follows:]

Statement of Janet L. Skarbek, Cinnaminson, New Jersey

I was asked here today to specifically address the viability of administering a national sales tax from the perspective of a professional that deals with state sales tax administration every day.

I started my career as a CPA working at the IRS Regional Inspector's office. After receiving a Master's of Taxation from Villanova University's Graduate Tax Program, I went to work for a Big 6 Accounting Firm where I was responsible for the management of sales and use taxes for clients in the Mid-Atlantic region. I am currently employed by a Fortune 500 company, where I am responsible for sales tax compliance and administration.

I have not been asked to speak about the economic impact of the proposed national sales tax, nor have I been asked to provide an opinion as to the overall feasibility of such a plan. Therefore, I will limit my testimony to specifically addressing business administration questions and the related concerns raised by such a tax.

In my opinion, the administration of the national sales tax will "probably" be simpler and easier than administering the current income taxes and payroll taxes it proposes to replace. I emphasize "probably" because the specific details and mechanisms of how the tax will actually be administered leaves too many unanswered questions. The simplicity of the tax itself is without question. However, the procedures and compliance requirements that still need to be drafted will significantly impact the ease and simplicity of administering this tax from a business standpoint.

Potential Costs

The costs to administer a national sales tax are unknown because the business requirements and documentation procedures have yet to be determined. However, if the procedures are similar to those imposed by states with sales taxes, the costs of administering the proposed tax should be significantly less than the costs of administering the current income taxes and payroll taxes. Between employees and accountants used to track the information and prepare the returns, and the attorneys needed to interpret and argue the gray issues contained in the massive tax codes,

American businesses spend billions of dollars every year complying with their federal tax burdens

States collect more in sales tax than they do from the combination of the individual income tax, corporate income tax, and property taxes. This fact usually surprises people because so little time and money is spent administering the sales tax. Sales taxes are generally quite simple to administer. However, some of the states have goofed up the simplicity, by adding new exceptions every year.

Also note that not all current costs associated with administering the payroll taxes would be completely eliminated under the new proposal. The proposed tax would merely change the source of funding for social security payments, but would not change how the social security payments are calculated. Therefore, companies would remain responsible for tracking wages. W–2's and yearly filing for the self-employed would still be essential.

For the businesses that are already collecting at least one state's sales tax or the necessary exemption documentation from customers, most companies are already familiar with the basics of sales tax administration. The education of these businesses on the national sales tax would be fairly straightforward (again depending upon the procedural requirements). For those businesses new to sales tax (such as direct mail and internet retailers, banks, and insurance companies), they would have a larger learning curve.

Problems encountered by businesses currently administering the states' sales taxes

The national sales tax as proposed would not duplicate most of the larger problems that businesses currently encounter when dealing with the states' sales taxes. The first and foremost complaint that businesses have with the current states' sales tax systems is that:

• —all of the 45 states that impose a sales tax have different rules regarding what is taxable, when it is taxable and the amount of tax. Even when a state's tax appears to be similar to another state's, their respective courts often interpret those laws differently.

It's fairly simple to become proficient administering one state's sales tax, but administering to several of them is a very difficult feat. The national sales tax would be just that—"national." As proposed, there are no regional or local zones that would be established with different guidelines (tax rates or exemptions) to complicate the national sales tax.

Another area that concerns many small and large businesses is nexus. Nexus, for sales tax purposes, is the minimum connection that must exist between a vendor and a state before that state can require the vendor to collect sales tax. A salesman or an independent contractor can create nexus for a business. Making deliveries to a customer in a state using a company truck can create nexus for a business. Nexus would not be a major concern for businesses if the states applied the same interpretation of what constituted "minimum connection" in the creation of nexus. However, the states are not consistent in their criteria. Some states take the position that if a company's salesman visits one customer in their state, that is sufficient to create nexus. Other states take the position that it takes 10 visits to create nexus. There is no across the states standard to easily assess whether a business has nexus with a state. As proposed, the requirement that a business collect the national sales tax is not dependent upon a business' nexus with any specific state.

The topic that raises the blood pressure of more sales tax administrators on a daily basis is the topic of drop-shipping for customers. This occurs when a business sells to one customer and that customer requests that the products be shipped directly to their customer. The problem is that many of the states take the position that if a business is not registered in a state, they cannot provide the documentation (generally a resale certificate) that would otherwise allow the sale not to be subject to the state's sales tax. The basic underlying premise for the sales tax is "the sales tax should only be paid by the ultimate consumer purchasing the product." However, this goes out the window in the states that take the position that only registered businesses can provide the necessary exemption documentation to support their stance that they are not subject to tax. When this occurs double taxation can take place on property that is drop-shipped into those states. First, it would be paid by the company that is not registered in the state. Next, it would be paid by the ultimate consumer purchasing the product.

This places businesses that have nexus with such states at competitive disadvantages with those that do not have nexus with such states. For example, assume Company A has nexus with State Q and Company B does not have nexus with State Q. Company A would have to collect sales tax on shipments for a customer that has no nexus with State Q and is not registered with State Q when shipping to their customer's customer located in State Q. However, if Company B made the same sale and shipments, they would not be required to collect the tax. As proposed, a company's nexus with a state would not put it at a competitive disadvantage with companies that did not have a minimum presence in the state.

Many states tax the property and services that are purchased by businesses. Determining what purchases are taxable in a state, which ones qualify for an exemption, and how to obtain such exemptions is an ongoing concern for many businesses. The national sales tax would not result in nearly as many problems because according to Chapter 1, Section 102 "(n)o tax shall be imposed under Section 101 on any taxable property or service purchased for a business purpose in a trade or business." However, the definition of the statement "purchased for a business purpose in a trade or business" needs to be more fully developed. The proposed definition is "purchased by a person engaged in a trade or business and used in that trade or business—(1) for resale, (2) to produce, provide, render, or sell taxable personal property or services, or (3) in furtherance of other bona fide business purposes." The definition needs to be further defined because opposing opinions on the taxability of various business purchases still remain. For example, would a business lunch be taxable? My interpretation is that they would not be taxable. However, there are those that disagree with that interpretation. All such questions and gray areas need to be eliminated.

Compliance

Under the current state sales tax systems, non-compliance will generally fall into one of three categories:

1) underpaying the tax because of a mistake,
2) underpaying the tax due to a difference in opinion from the states on the many gray areas of the laws, or
3) underpaying the tax intentionally.

The regulations that are developed in order to reduce these compliance problems could make the tax difficult or easy to administer from a business standpoint. The current proposed national sales tax is more lenient on what a seller can accept as exempt documentation in lieu of the tax, than what the states currently require. Most states require that the purchaser provide the seller an exemption certificate that includes the:

a) purchaser's name, address, and registration number,
b) the seller's name,
c) a description of the property being purchased,
d) a statement that the property being purchased meets the requirements for the exemption (i.e. resale, exempt business purpose, etc...), and
e) a signature.

The proposed national tax merely requires the vendor to receive in good faith a copy of a registration permit from the purchaser and for the seller not to have at the time of the sale reasonable cause to believe that the buyer was not registered. Due to the fact that the proposed national sales tax rate is higher than any current state sales tax rate, the controls should be at least as tough as those imposed at the state level.

The first non-compliance category listed above is underpaying the tax because of a mistake. Most mistakes made by businesses and individuals are the result of a lack of knowledge that something is taxable. The simpler a tax is the less likely that mistakes will be made.

The states have made parts of their sales/use tax laws so complex and difficult to follow, that there is close to 100% non-compliance with some sections. This is the case with the sections relating to individuals self-assessing use tax. According to most current state sales tax systems, if an individual purchases a product in a state and is not charged sales tax, the individual is legally required to self-assess that states use tax. For example if you live in Virginia and you purchase a table from LL Bean—LL Bean does not currently have nexus with Virginia and is therefore not legally required to collect Virginia's sales tax on their shipments to Virginia customers. Therefore, you would be required to self-assess the tax.

The states' sales tax systems are not working when it comes to individuals self-assessing. Most Americans don't even know that they are legally required by most states to do this. The proposed national sales tax is much simpler and this problem would be much smaller because a business' lack of nexus with a state would not effect the fact that it would generally need to collect the tax from these customers. Whether a business had nexus with a state would be irrelevant to the fact that the national sales tax would be required to be collected by the vendor in most situations. Therefore, essentially more businesses would be collecting the tax when shipping products directly to individuals' homes and fewer individuals would have the need to self-assess the tax. In addition, the marketing advantage that many direct marketers and internet retailers without nexus in a state have over other businesses physically present in a state would not exist under the national sales tax (when the direct marketers or internet retailers have a physical presence in the United States).

The second area of non-compliance falls under the category of underpaying the taxes due to a difference of opinion from the states on the many gray areas of the laws. The fact that the national sales tax as proposed is based on the presumption that many businesses would not be subject to the national sales tax and that all purchases by individuals (with very few exceptions) would be taxable eliminates most of the gray areas that would come under contention.

The third area of non-compliance is due to those individuals that intentionally underpay the tax. There will always be individuals attempting to illegally outmaneuver paying their fair share of taxes, just like there will always be individuals trying to create new and more potent computer viruses. With any tax system, it's a matter of trying to stay one step ahead of the law breakers.

There are several areas where the details of the internal controls that will be used to stop those intentionally trying to make purchases without paying tax are not currently defined under the proposed "Fair Tax Act." These internal controls will be essential to determining the ease with which businesses can meet their tax responsibility. Here are five areas that need to be further developed.

1) What controls would be established to stop importers from shipping their goods over our borders and selling them tax free on a black market?

2) What controls would be established to ensure that Americans traveling over the borders and purchasing their goods without the tax and bringing them back into the United States will self-assess the tax? Chapter 1, Section 103(b) provides that "(i)n the case of taxable property or services purchased outside the United States and imported into the United States for use or consumption in the United States, the purchaser shall remit the tax imposed by Section 101." Section 101(c) provides that if a consumer imports taxable property directly, they would pay both the sales tax and any import duty together at the same time at customs. Section 101(d) states that "(t)he person using or consuming taxable property or services in the Unites States is liable for the tax" except when the person pays the tax to the person selling the taxable property or service and receives a qualifying receipt. The compliance for individuals self-assessing the states taxes is almost non-existent. What controls would be instituted to increase compliance?

3) What controls would be established to tax goods purchased over the internet and shipped directly to customers from locations outside the United States?

4) What controls would be in place to locate individuals that register non-existent companies (where no actual business is taking place) in order to obtain the documentation to provide vendors in order to make personal purchases tax free?

5) What controls will be in place to stop individuals from utilizing their companies' certificates of registration in order to make tax free personal purchases? This is another area where states know the problem exists. However, if the person makes the purchase with cash, the audit trail is generally non-existent.

The regulations and controls that would be established in answer to the above questions could be very simple or very complex for businesses to follow. The simpler solutions tend to allow more tax evaders to slip through. The more tedious solutions tend to put a larger burden on businesses.

For example, in response to question number 5, a simple procedure could be established that:

1) a company must designate a specific employee(s) to be responsible for the tax documentation,

2) the employee would be required to register and sign a document that they will not illegally use the tax documentation to make personal purchases tax free, and

3) the employee provides a copy of the documentation to each vendor that the company makes non-taxable purchases from.

However, this simple procedure leaves open several loop holes. First, if the designated employee actually uses the tax documentation for personal purposes there would be very little in the way of an audit trail to weed out such occurrences. The records at her employers would show no indication of the misdeed. Second, what would stop a dishonest clerk at the vendors from making another copy of the tax documentation and then making tax free purchases with the documentation and cash. This would essentially be untraceable.

An example of a slightly tougher solution that would rely more heavily on businesses would establish that:

1) every company that registers receives a booklet of exemption certificates containing sequential numbers, the company's name, and identification number,

135

2) every company would be responsible to keep a log of the exemption certificate number and what vendor they gave the exemption certificates to.

This procedure, although not fool proof, would result in fewer employees utilizing such certificates for their own purposes. An audit of the log and purchases made by the company from specific vendors would show any certificates that were missing. Copying of certificates by vendors for their own use would also be less likely since the certificates would be printed by the government.

This then raises the question of "when is a seller relieved of liability when collecting documentation?" Section 103(d) provides that when the vendor accepts a copy of the registration certificate in good faith and has no reasonable cause that the purchaser was not registered that this is sufficient to relieve the vendor of liability. The issue of "what constitutes the acceptance of documentation in good faith" is an area where the states and businesses currently hold varying opinions. For example, what happens if the government establishes a set of guidelines to indicate that a certificate is valid and a clerk at a store accepts one that is missing a little identifying insignia in the bottom corner? Would the store that mistakenly accepted the counterfeit documentation be subject to the tax that they should have collected from the customer? The mere fact that vendors would now be required to look for this insignia would place a large responsibility on vendors.

You can see from the above, that the details of what would be required of a business in the day to day activities of compliance would be essential in determining the full impact a national sales tax would have on businesses.

What agency (agencies) would administer the tax?

Section 401 provides that states which maintain a sales tax and which enter into a cooperative agreement with the federal government can choose to administer the federal tax for ¼ of one percent of the revenue they collect and remit to the federal government. They also have the ability to contract out the work to another state. Title III, Section 302 would establish within the "Department of Treasury a Sales Tax Bureau to administer the national sales tax in those States where it is required." Specifically, those states that cannot or choose not to collect the national sales tax.

The current national sales tax proposal suggests that the states should administer the tax because of their previous experience administering a sales tax. Just because a state has experience, does not mean that it is good at what it does. There are states that are great administrators and states that are very poor.

It would be simpler to have all administrative responsibilities fall under the Sales Tax Bureau than under the 45 states that currently impose a sales tax. Imagine the IRS administration problems under 45 different roofs. It would be best to have one organization responsible for administering the tax and to make sure the individuals in that organization are well educated and trained. If there were several agencies administering the tax, the administrative controls would be significantly diluted. In addition, for businesses operating in more than one state, there is confusion as to which agency would have control over the returns.

Conclusion

In closing, I appreciate the opportunity to speak at this first ever Congressional Summit on Fundamental Tax Reform. The testimony heard over the next three days from the members of Congress, the economists, and the business leaders on improving the IRS, as well as on the various tax reform proposals, can only serve to improve our future tax system. I'm afraid you have your work cut out for you.

———

Chairman ARCHER. Thanks, Ms. Skarbek.
Mr. Chapoton?

STATEMENT OF HON. JOHN E. CHAPOTON, PARTNER, VINSON & ELKINS, LLP, ON BEHALF OF THE AMERICANS FOR FAIR TAXATION [FORMER ASSISTANT SECRETARY FOR TAX POLICY, U.S. DEPARTMENT OF THE TREASURY]

Mr. CHAPOTON. Thank you, Mr. Chairman. My name is John Chapoton. I am a partner with the law firm of Vinson & Elkins, and I am here on behalf of the Americans for Fair Taxation.

Mr. Hank Gutman and I have a statement that we have submitted for the record, and I would like to just give a brief summary of the points that we have made, again, focusing on the administrative points.

I think a starting point, when you assess or evaluate any tax system, is how understandable the rules are and how predictable the outcome of calculating the tax is. I think when you look at our present income tax, you have to say that it does not meet that test very well. We have all sorts of special rules, we have phase-ins, we have phase-outs, we have disputes on what has to be capitalized, what doesn't have to be capitalized, we have rules for determining ordinary income and capital gains. So it is complex and, unfortunately, efforts at simplification have failed. It absolutely becomes more complex every year.

I think it is reasonable to conclude, I think it is really cannot be doubted that the Fair Tax that is before you today would eliminate most of these complexities and would, thus, eliminate the administrative costs that those complexities bring with them. There are objections voiced to the national sales tax, the distribution issues, the transition issues. Would the rate be so high that Americans would object? There are other objections. I think the Fair Tax deals with those in a very straightforward and open manner. I want to just talk about the administrative points, however.

One thing we ought to keep in mind is that consumption taxes are used, in one form or another, very widely in the world. All of our trading partners, I guess for all of our trading partners, most of them certainly have consumption taxes, most in the form of value-added taxes. Some 17.8 percent of the OECD countries—tax rate of the OECD countries are in consumption tax form.

And of course the States, as we have heard today so many times, depend a great deal on sales taxes to raise their revenues. Six States, including the State of Texas, my State, depends on the sales tax for most of its revenues. So sales taxes are easily understood. They generally or the perception is that they work well. Most businesses selling to retail customers collect and report the tax today and it is a familiar tax. So there is strong evidence that if the Federal Government decided to do so, it could administer a national sales tax.

The Fair Tax or any other national sales tax, though, would, of course, have to be a higher rate than we have experienced in any State sales tax to this date. And as the rate goes up, we know the incentive to avoid or evade the tax goes up by imaginative interpretation or simply by cheating. The rate of tax measures the potential reward for evading or simply avoiding the tax. So the rate of the tax is an important question in administration and enforcement of the tax. We discuss several specific areas in our paper. But what jumps out at you, as you review these issues, is that for the most part, these difficult issues that will be presented in a national sales tax are areas that present huge complexities in the income tax today, and the compliance problems that go with that.

Take a single example, but a very important example. That is mixed-use property or mixed-use service; that is, where a person buys a service or a good and uses it partially in business and partially personally. That will be a difficult administrative problem in the sales tax. But it is a very difficult problem in the income tax today, determining when an expense is personal or business. It is the subject of much litigation and it is a constant thorn in the side of the income tax. So that is just one example. There are many others that the Fair Tax or any national sales tax will have problems to deal with, but they are not increased problems, they are problems that we already have to deal with. And, indeed, in many instances, I think it is possible to argue that the Fair Tax would lessen those problems.

I think the key point is that when you look at the administration and enforcement of a sales tax, it is just how many taxpayers would be taken out of the system all together. Today, everybody is in the system. We have 120 million individual income tax returns, some 22 million business returns and over 200 million total returns. Only retail businesses, only a portion of today's business returns, would be in the system, if you will, in a sales tax, and that would only be a fraction of the total returns filed by individuals, trusts, and partnerships and businesses today.

So in enforcement terms, this means there would be far fewer opportunities to evade or avoid the tax. Fewer taxpayers would have the opportunity to bend the rules or simply cheat, even if they were inclined to do so, and even if they were doing so now under the income tax. Under the income tax, everyone has the chance. You have the chance in the privacy of your own home to claim excessive deductions or ignore small amounts of income. And the more individual taxpayers hear about others bending the income tax rules, that the wealthy are not paying their share or because of tricky schemes by so-called investment schemes and investment bankers, people are less inclined to pay their own fair share. That is a problem with any uneven tax, and I am afraid an uneven tax is what we have today.

Of course, small cash-based business, the street vendor, the contractor who comes to your house for a single job will be a problem under a sales tax. They will collect the tax on what they sell and not have the incentive to pay it over or they may give you a wink and a nod and say they won't collect the tax if you will hire them to do the job. But the clarity of the rules will, under a sales tax, would make that more difficult, and probably it would make them easier to catch and penalize. Lack of understanding of the rules would not likely be a very compelling defense.

And more important for today's discussion, this is not a new problem. This is the group of taxpayers, the small cash-based businesses, that is the single largest component of the so-called tax cap under the income tax today. There is no reason to think this would be more of a problem under the sales tax, and it might even be easier to address, given the transparency of the tax.

So, Mr. Chairman, let me just conclude by saying that this committee and the Congress may decide not to go the sales tax route for any number of reasons, for economic reasons, for transition considerations, but I think enforcement and administration questions should not prevent the very serious consideration and study of the Fair Tax.

[The prepared statement follows:]

Statement of Hon. John E. Chapoton, Partner, Vinson & Elkins LLP, on behalf of the Americans for Fair Taxation (Former Assistant Secretary for Tax Policy, U.S. Department of the Treasury)

Dear Mr. Chairman and Members of the Committee:

We are pleased to have the opportunity to submit this statement on behalf of Americans for Fair Taxation. We commend Chairman Archer and the Committee for undertaking a serious study of a national retail sales tax as embodied in the FairTax. We have been asked to comment on the administration of the FairTax.

One key element in the evaluation of any tax system is whether the rules are understandable and the outcome of the calculations predictable. Our current income tax system clearly fails to meet these criteria for most individual taxpayers and for many large corporate taxpayers as well. Features of the individual income tax that increase its complexity include elections, distinctions between capital and ordinary gain or loss, valuation questions, capitalization of certain business costs, record-keeping requirements, rules restricting favorable tax treatment, itemized deductions, the alternative minimum tax, the earned income tax credit, and a large number of phase-in and phase-out provisions. Attempts to simplify the income tax have failed, and indeed, the Code annually grows more complex. The FairTax would eliminate these complexities, and the administrative costs associated with them.

In considering a national sales tax, the Committee should be aware of the important role that consumption taxes already play both within the U.S. and globally. Consumption taxes are an important source of revenue for governments generally; this is an area where the U.S. has lagged behind other nations. The success of so many other governments in administering consumption taxes should indicate to the Committee that the U.S. can successfully administer a comparable tax.

Internationally, countries ranging from Albania to Zambia, including almost all our major trading partners rely heavily on consumption taxes. These are typically in the form of value-added taxes, which have essentially the same economic effect as retail sales taxes. The administration and enforcement of these levies are not problem-free, but there is reason to conclude those problems may not be as great as we are encountering with our individual and corporate income taxes.

Of the 29 OECD countries, only the U.S. does not have a value-added tax. Among OECD members, the United States has the lowest general consumption tax collections as percentage of total taxes (7.9% in 1996) other than Japan (5.3%). The average share of taxes raised from general consumption across all OECD countries is 17.8 percent. At the federal level, the U.S. collected $70 billion in consumption taxes, in the form of excise taxes, during FY 1999.

**TAXES ON GENERAL CONSUMPTION
AS A PERCENTAGE OF TOTAL TAXATION**

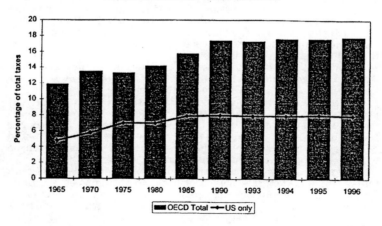

Source: Consumption Tax Trends, OECD, 1999

In the U.S. today, consumption taxes, including both general and specific sales or excise taxes, are used by every state and many local governments. In 1999, approximately 32 percent of all state and local taxes, or more than $262 billion, were collected this way. Forty-five states have general sales taxes. In 1998, general sales tax revenues accounted for more that half of total tax collections in Florida, Nevada, South Dakota, Tennessee, Texas, and Washington. When selective sales or excise taxes are included, these same states all collect more than 70 percent of their revenues through consumption taxes.

SALES TAXES AS A PERCENTAGE OF TOTAL TAXES IN SELECTED STATES THAT RELAY HEAVILY ON SUCH TAXES

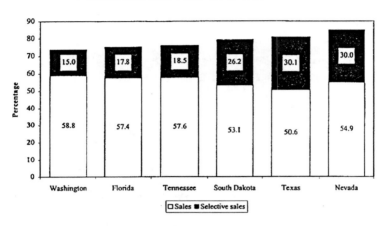

Source: Federation of Tax Administrators

Apart from some current issues with e-commerce, existing sales tax administrative systems seem to work reasonably well. Indeed, a number of significant current income tax system problems do not exist under a sales tax. The income tax and trade complexities we are currently facing with Foreign Sales Corporations (FSCs) are merely one example of the difficult issues that we must regularly address. These income tax structural problems would go away under a consumption tax system. The marriage penalty issues and corporate tax shelter concerns—two tax policy issues attracting much attention today—would largely disappear under a sales tax regime.

For tax year 1997, IRS reports that 63.5 million individual tax returns were signed by paid tax return preparers. This is more than half of the 120.8 million individual income tax returns filed. This is, of course, in addition to the substantial burdens imposed on individual taxpayers who prepare their own returns. Under the FairTax, this burden on individual taxpayers would be eliminated. The only new administrative burden would be the annual need to register families to qualify for the family consumption allowance.

Most businesses selling to retail consumers collect and report sales taxes today. While their sales tax administrative burdens would become somewhat more complex (at least until state and local tax systems are brought into conformity), this would be more than offset by the fact their income tax burdens would disappear. A variety of other new burdens would be imposed on businesses making retail sales, but many of these would substitute for burdens already required under existing state and local sales taxes. Indeed, the FairTax contemplates that the myriad of existing sales and local tax bases would over time be brought into conformity with the newly defined federal sales tax base. This by itself would be a major simplification for retailers—especially those operating in multiple jurisdictions.

Certainly there are issues of tax administration that must be addressed. A variety of services, including financial intermediation services, and other products not generally subject to sales taxes today would become taxable. Devising the appropriate tax structure will be a complex undertaking; many of our trading partners are wrestling with these issues today. Additional work will be required in this area. Another area of potential administrative difficulty is presented when property with both taxable and nontaxable uses ("mixed use property or services") is purchased. Apportionment is required under the FairTax. However, this requirement is unlikely to be any more burdensome than distinguishing between business and personal expenses under current law.

The Federal Government and state and local governments would be required to pay sales taxes on their purchases, which would be a new administrative burden. Governmental entities will be required collect tax on their sales as well.

It is reasonable to assume that total state government tax administration costs would rise under the FairTax because they would largely be responsible for collecting the new federal sales tax in addition to their own sales taxes. In recognition of this, the FairTax provides for a 0.25-percent payment to states for administering the tax. While we have not studied whether this amount would be sufficient to cover the increased costs of administration, a cost reimbursement feature is an important tool for assuring that states provide adequate support to collect all taxes that are due under the new system. There are, however, potentially significant administrative cost savings if a uniform tax base were to be adopted across all taxing jurisdictions.

It is very important to keep in mind that administrative costs in general, and compliance costs in particular, are likely to rise as the rate of tax increases. Pressure to avoid taxes—through imaginative interpretations of the rules or by simply cheating—increase as the tax rate goes up. The rate of tax measures the potential reward to a person contemplating avoidance or evasion. If the rate becomes excessive, enforceability could undoubtedly become a problem. However, these enforceability concerns may not be as significant as those that currently exist under the federal income tax.

Enforceability is more of a problem if opportunities for avoidance are presented by the mechanics of the tax, such as through exceptions and special rates. The states, for example, generally exempt a variety of goods and services. The FairTax, by contrast, has virtually no exclusion and no special rates. It contemplates a very comprehensive tax system. We want to emphasize as strongly as possible, the critical importance, from an administrative standpoint (as well as an economic standpoint), of keeping the tax base as broad as possible, and thus the rates as low as possible.

In sum, the FairTax provides the opportunity to reduce administrative burdens on taxpayers. As with the consideration of any new tax regime, and as we continually face under current law, there will be questions and problems to be solved. We believe that these administrative questions can and should be seriously addressed. Administrative issues should not stand in the way of further serious consideration of the FairTax.

Chairman ARCHER. Thank you, Mr. Chapoton.
Mr. Threadgill?

STATEMENT OF DEL THREADGILL, VICE PRESIDENT OF TAXES, J.C. PENNEY COMPANY, DALLAS, TEXAS, AND CHAIRMAN, NATIONAL RETAIL FEDERATION TAXATION COMMITTEE

Mr. THREADGILL. Thank you, Mr. Chairman and members of the committee. My name is Del Threadgill, and I am vice president and director of Taxes for the J.C. Penney Company and the current chairman of the National Retail Federation's Taxation Committee.

The National Retail Federation is the world's largest retail trade association, representing an industry of 1.4 million establishments, employing more than 22 million Americans or about one in every five workers, with sales in 1999 of more than $3 trillion.

I am here today to express the retail industry's strong opposition to a national retail sales tax, as proposed. Our principal concern is that no one really knows what the full impact of replacing the entire Federal income tax structure with a consumption-based sales tax will have on our economy. It has never been done before in any major industrialized Nation, let alone the world's largest economy. As evidenced by the comments from the previous panel, even the experts disagree over the impact from such a radical change. At a time when our economy is experiencing its longest period of sustained growth in history, do we really want to bet the ranch on some untried tax policy experiment?

Americans are truly dissatisfied with the current tax system, and rightfully so. The retail industry cannot and will not defend the income tax as it currently stands. It is entirely too complicated and cumbersome. As for fairness, it is hard to understand why a tax system that determines a person's contribution to the cost of Government based on his ability to pay is less fair than a system that is based on what he spends.

Yesterday, the National Retail Federation released a study of congressional tax reform proposals. That study was prepared by the nationally recognized economic consulting group within PricewaterhouseCoopers. PWC utilized an economic model capable of estimating both the short-term and long-term consequences of tax reform; in other words, what will happen in the short run, as opposed to 10 years from now.

Retailers thought it imperative to know what might happen to the economy and consumers in the short run as well. PWC was instructed to use their expertise to determine what they believed to be the correct answer. There was no predisposition given to PWC as to what the retail industry expected to see from the study. We simply wanted to know what the facts were.

The PWC findings should be of concern to both taxpayers and lawmakers alike. While it did show the economic gains at the end of a 10-year period under a national retail sales tax, it is the interim period that causes the heartburn. The study clearly shows that there will be short-term chaos in the economy and in the retail industry.

In the best-case scenario, the study found, one, that the required budget-neutral tax rate would range from 24 to 65 percent, depending upon the number of exemptions and the rate of taxpayer compliance.

Second, serious economic disruptions would occur under a national retail sales tax, at least in the short run. The economy would be depressed for a period of at least 3 years, consumer spending would be depressed for at least 8 years with consumer purchases down over $500 billion and up to a million-and-a-half American jobs would be eliminated. The question we have as an industry is how many smaller retailers and other small businesses would still be around to enjoy the long-term benefits of a national sales tax after this transition period.

And, third, a national retail sales tax would redistribute the Federal income tax burden from higher income to middle-income families, with the purchasing power of low-income households being down 8 to 14 percent under a national retail sales tax.

Retailers believe that a national retail sales tax would exacerbate the underground economy, become a Pandora's box of carveouts and exemptions for Washington's special interests, burden small business and require additional IRS or a like-minded agency's oversight. The retail industry would encourage lawmakers to take a measured approach to tax reform to ensure that a new system is both fair and equitable for everyone.

Thank you, Mr. Chairman.

[The prepared statement follows:]

Statement of Del Threadgill, Vice President of Taxes, J.C. Penney Company, Dallas, Texas, and Chairman, Taxation Committee, National Retail Federation

Mr. Chairman and Members of the Committee:

Good afternoon, and thank you for the opportunity to testify before this Committee today.

My name is Del Threadgill, and I am Vice President and Director of Taxes for the JCPenney Company and the current Chairman of the National Retail Federation's Taxation Committee.

The National Retail Federation is the world's largest retail trade association, representing an industry of 1.4 million retail establishments, employing more than 22 million people—about 1 in every 5 American workers—with sales in 1999 of more than $3.0 trillion.

I am here today to express the retail industry's strong opposition to a proposed National Retail Sales Tax (NRST). Our principal concern is that *no one* really knows what the full impact of replacing the entire Federal income tax structure with a consumption-based sales tax will have on our economy. It has never been done before in any major industrialized nation, let alone the world's largest economy.

As evidenced by the comments from the previous panel, even the experts disagree over the impact from such a radical change. At a time when our economy is experiencing its longest period of sustained growth in history, do we really want to "bet the ranch" on some untried tax policy experiment.

Americans are dissatisfied with the current tax system, and rightfully so. The retail industry cannot and will not defend the income tax as it currently stands. It is entirely too complicated and cumbersome.

As for Fairness, it is hard to understand why a tax system that determines a person's contribution to the cost of government based on his ability to pay is *less fair* than a system that is based on what he spends.

Yesterday, the National Retail Federation released a study of Congressional tax reform proposals. The study was prepared by the nationally recognized economic consulting group within PriceWaterhouseCoopers (PWC). PWC utilized an economic model capable of estimating both the short-term *and* long-term consequences of tax reform. Models utilized by some national sales tax proponents are only capable of estimating the long-term effects of tax reform (i.e. what happens at the end of a 10-year period.)

Retailers thought it imperative to know what might happen to the economy and consumers in the short-term as well. PWC was instructed to use their expertise to determine what they believed to be the correct answer. There was no predisposition given to PWC as to what the retailers expected to see from the study. We simply wanted the facts.

The PWC findings should be of concern to taxpayers and lawmakers alike. While it did show some modest economic gains at the end of a 10-year period under a NRST, it is the interim period that causes the heartburn. The study clearly shows that there will be short-term chaos in the economy and the retail industry.

In a "best-case" scenario, the PriceWaterhouseCoopers (PWC) study found:

1) The required budget-neutral NRST tax rate would range from 24–65%, depending on the number of exemptions and the taxpayer compliance rate.

• a seperate Congressional Joint Economic Committee report confirms PWC's findings by estimating that a NRST rate of 19–65% would be necessary.

• 2) Serious economic disruptions would occur under a National Retail Sales Tax.

• the economy would be depressed for three years—with GDP down $180 billion.

• consumer spending would be depressed for eight years, with consumer purchases down $503 billion.

• up to 1.5 million American jobs would be eliminated.

• the question arises as to how many retailers and small businesses would still be around to enjoy the modest long-term benefits of a NRST?

3) A National Retail Sales Tax would redistribute the federal income tax burden from higher income to middle and low-income families.

• the purchasing power of low-income households would be down 8–14% under a NRST while high-income households would not be affected.

Retailers believe that a NRST would exacerbate the underground economy, become a Pandora's box of carve-outs and exemptions for Washington special interests, burden small businesses, and require additional IRS or like-minded agency oversight.

The retail industry would encourage lawmakers to take a measured approach to tax reform to ensure that a new system is fair and equitable for everyone. Americans may not like the current Federal income tax or the IRS, but they may like a National Retail Sales Tax even less.

Thank you.

———————

Chairman ARCHER. Thank you, Mr. Threadgill.

The chair has no questions for this panel.

Ms. Thurman?

Mrs. THURMAN. Mr. Hamilton, were you around when the service tax was contemplated and passed in Florida?

Mr. HAMILTON. Yes, ma'am, I was.

Mrs. THURMAN. Did you have any experience in talking with the comptroller there as to the issues, or the Department of Revenue, the issues that they had and concerns of the collection of these taxes?

Mr. HAMILTON. Yes, ma'am. And one of my good friends was the commissioner of revenue until very recently there, and we actually imposed service taxes in the same period in Texas.

Mrs. THURMAN. Are yours still in place?

Mr. HAMILTON. We had the good sense not to tax advertising, and that seems to have been a very important thing not to do.

[Laughter.]

Mrs. THURMAN. So you now have services.

Mr. HAMILTON. Yes, ma'am.

Mrs. THURMAN. Everything but advertising?

Mr. HAMILTON. Well, as with most things on the Texas sales tax, it is a hit or miss. Generally, things like information services, data processing services, miscellaneous retail services, which would be like repairs of shoes and whatnot, telecommunication services, just a fairly wide range, but not all services.

Mrs. THURMAN. But those were all taxed.

Mr. HAMILTON. Yes, ma'am.

Mrs. THURMAN. Because one of the things we heard through our Department of Revenue was the burden that it was going to put on them, as well as to Mr. Threadgill on the issue of retailers of the collection.

But I want to go to Mr. Chapoton.

Mr. CHAPOTON. In the bill, actually, and I am asking these questions because actually Mr. Linbeck was in my office the other day, and he told me to ask these hard questions, so hopefully this isn't hard. In one of the parts, you talk about tax to be separately stated and charged. Now, I don't have a real big problem with some of it because even today, you know, I go into the store, I purchase something, I know it has a sales tax. If they tell me I am spending $100, I get charged my 6 percent or 7 percent. At the end of the day, I know I am going to pay $107. But there is an interesting one in here that I don't understand. And it says you pay the property or services' price exclusive of tax, the amount tax paid, the property or service price inclusive of tax, and then the fourth one, and I don't know what this means, the tax rate, which is the amount of tax paid, per paragraph 2, divided by the property or service price inclusive of tax, per paragraph 3.

Just to kind of get to the simplicity issue that everybody is going to pay this, I need to understand what does that mean?

Mr. CHAPOTON. Well, I think that is part of the danger of reading statutory language. I think what it is trying to say is it is a tax-inclusive rate. And so that, and this point was made earlier today, that when you look at the tax, it is not, if you have a dollar, it is not 23 percent of a dollar, it is 23 percent of $1.23. Do you understand that?

It is like the income tax today. It is a tax-inclusive rate.

Mrs. THURMAN. Right.

Mr. CHAPOTON. You do not pay the income tax out of other income, you pay it out of the income you are taxed on, and this is the same thing. So I am not sure I have even seen the exact, specific language you are talking about, but it is clear to me that is what it is trying to do.

Mrs. THURMAN. Is there a reason for that? I mean, why wouldn't you just put down this is the tax you are paying, end of story—I mean, just like we do today. I mean, I am just curious.

Mr. CHAPOTON. You could do it either way, really. You could do it either way. It changes the rate, but you could do it either way.

Mrs. THURMAN. Mr. Hamilton, let me go back to another question. When you said you did the services, how many additional people did you have to put on to collect the services tax that——

Mr. HAMILTON. I think we added about 20 people.

Mrs. THURMAN. That is it?

Mr. HAMILTON. Yes, ma'am. I mean, it was fairly straight—I should have mentioned earlier that the one group of services that we didn't tax were professionals, like lawyers, doctors. That might have been a problem, too, or maybe not. But at any rate, they weren't taxed. But it didn't require a lot of additional people because a lot of where the services were being delivered, people were already registered for either the Texas sales tax or the Texas corporate franchise tax or one of our other taxes. So we were able to find them.

Mrs. THURMAN. But you think there would be a lot of other people that might have to be registered under this?

Mr. HAMILTON. Yes, ma'am, about 900,000 extra. But a lot of it is because it is picking up a wider band of services than our sales tax. It picks up the professions, for one thing, the lawyers, doctors——

Mrs. THURMAN. Do you see that as an increased cost to the State?

Mr. HAMILTON. Increased in—well, the administrative costs there would definitely be a significant administrative cost to the State, if, for no other reason, than the rapid processing of the returns and the money that would be required, and I think a more extensive audit and enforcement effort to deal with what Buck was referring to.

Mrs. THURMAN. Right. And I would go to that as an enforcement issue because even today, with your flea markets and any other things that are out there, how do you deal with those issues?

Mr. HAMILTON. Well, as with most sales taxes, the majority of the tax is collected from very large retailers, the J.C. Penney's and the Wal-Marts and whatnot. The way that we deal with flea markets, and gun shows and a lot of itinerant peddlers is we have enforcement officers—that is our term—compliance officers in other States, that do routine canvasses of the shows when they are in progress. And they will go through and register every one of the taxpayers or anyone that is there that is making sales, ensure that the tax is being collected. There are marginal problems with that. It is certainly true, but that is part of the requirement on all of our enforcement offices that they do so many canvasses of those types of shows every year.

Mrs. THURMAN. But, Mr. Threadgill, that is a part of the problem that you have in those two is this underground economy that is going to start not just only in the flea markets and other areas like that, but the sale. I mean, is that the—because you raised that issue.

Mr. THREADGILL. Certainly, the concern is, in coming up with what the rate would need to be to be revenue-neutral or budget-neutral, making sure what is included or not included in the base. And I think Mr. Chapoton mentioned the fact that a lot of cash-based businesses and what happens to those, and as the rate gets higher, the chances of those going underground becomes more and more.

I know in the Canadian experience, when they instituted their GST tax, there was a study a couple of years later that a number of businesses went underground, and that was a 7- or 9-percent GST-type sales tax, on top of their income tax. But there was a study that a lot of businesses, cash-based businesses, went underground.

Mrs. THURMAN. Mr. Chairman, I appreciate the fact that you have given us the opportunity to learn a lot today. And I want to say my thanks to all of the witnesses, those who are still here, for your sincerity in trying to answer our questions and to let you all know that no matter what we are asking in questions, we all should take seriously what is before us on any of these proposals. Because I think the one thing we all do agree, that we have got to simplify for the American people, however we do that, the tax code. So I appreciate, Mr. Chairman, your time and the time of our witnesses.

Chairman ARCHER. The chair adds his gratitude to all four of you, as well as to all of the other witnesses that have been before the committee today. Thank you very much.

There is no further questioning that I know of and no further witnesses today, so the committee will stand adjourned.

[Whereupon, at 4:18 p.m., the hearing was adjourned, to reconvene on Wednesday, April 12, 2000, at 10:00 a.m.]

FUNDAMENTAL TAX REFORM

WEDNESDAY, APRIL 12, 2000

House of Representatives,
Committee on Ways and Means,
Washington, D.C.

The Committee met, pursuant to call, at 10:00 a.m., in Room 1100 Longworth House Office Building, Hon. Bill Archer (Chairman of the Committee), presiding.

Chairman ARCHER. Today we continue with our tax summit on structural tax reform and what alternatives we might look at to replace the current archaic code which we commenced yesterday.

And leading off this morning is one of our own colleagues, a member of the Ways and Means Committee and gentleman from Pennsylvania, Mr. English.

And Mr. English, we are happy to have you with us this morning on the other side of the witness table, and we will be pleased to hear your presentation as to what you think is an appropriate alternative.

STATEMENT OF HON. PHIL ENGLISH, A REPRESENTATIVE IN CONGRESS FROM THE STATE OF PENNSYLVANIA

Mr. ENGLISH. Thank you, Mr. Chairman.

I appreciate the opportunity to appear here today. I believe that the current tax system is broken. I believe it is one of the reasons why our economy is having trouble competing internationally and I believe it is one of the reasons why so many taxpayers question the legitimacy of their government.

I believe that we need to find a better way of applying taxes and generating the revenue to do what we need to do. And I want to especially congratulate you, Mr. Chairman, for raising that issue at this time. By getting involved now, I think we have an opportunity to shape the debate for the future.

A couple of years ago, when I came to Congress, I became aware of some of the problems with the current tax system simply by talking to constituents.

I was dissatisfied by many of the alternatives that were being offered including the flat tax and the idea of a national sales tax.

And I have spent a lot of time working to develop an alternative based on the old Nunn-Domenici proposal which was described at the time as a consumed income tax.

I have introduced the Simplified USA Tax Act because I want to reform the American tax system in a way sensible to the average citizen and that will pass the test of time.

Not only do we need a tax system that is fair and sensible, we need one that is stable. As bad as the current system is—and I am one of its severest critics—the last thing we need to do is enact reform that is so radical and experimental that Congress will be faced with revamping it all over again in a few years.

The Simplified USA Tax is revolutionary in that it addresses the strongest points of concern with the current system while, at the same time, addressing concerns about the equity of other tax reform proposals being considered.

SUSAT is based on principles that I feel are vital to any meaningful reform, imposing a simple tax to encourage efficiency, ensuring that income is taxed only once wherever possible, establishing trade equity for American products, taking the double tax burden off of savings so as not to discourage individuals from saving, providing incentives for investment in good-paying jobs in physical capital and in human capital. And including an accommodation with respect to the Social Security Payroll Tax, the most regressive tax of all.

In my tax reform proposal USA stands for "unlimited savings allowance." Everyone is allowed an unlimited Roth IRA in which they can put the portion of each year's income they save, after paying taxes and living expenses.

After five years, all funds in the account may be withdrawn for any purpose, and all withdrawals, including accumulated interest and other earnings and principal are tax-free.

Nothing could be simpler and nothing could give people a better opportunity to save, especially young people. Because only new income earned after enactment of SUSAT can be put into the USA Roth IRA, young people starting to move into their higher earning years are the ones who will benefit the most for the longest time.

The Tax Code should give everyone the opportunity to keep what they save and, if they wish, to pass it along to succeeding generations. Therefore, the death tax would be repealed under my proposal.

Under a new tax code, tax rates, in my view, should be lower, especially for wage earners who must now pay both an income tax and a 7.65 percent FICA payroll tax on the same amount of wages.

It is my intention that the final tax rates under SUSAT, after all adjustments are made, will be as low as possible, consistent with budget limitations.

At present, the USA Tax starts out with quite low rates, 15 percent at the bottom, 25 percent in the middle, and 30 percent at the top.

These rates are reduced even further by allowing wage earners a full tax credit for the payroll tax that is withheld from their paychecks under current law.

I do not propose to repeal the payroll tax because to do so would imperil Social Security.

However, I do allow a credit for it, and when the credit is taken into account, the rates of tax on workers' wages are very low, and the seven percent to 17 percent range for nearly all Americans.

Under the simplified USA Tax, the tax rate on the first $40,000 of taxable income from wages cannot exceed 7.35 percent which is the basic USA rate of 15 percent less 7.65 percent.

Under the current Code, the combined payroll tax/income tax rate is 22.65 percent.

On the next $32,000, the rate cannot exceed 17.35 percent which is the middle USA rate of 25 percent less the payroll tax credit.

Under the current code, the combined payroll tax/income tax rate is 35.65 percent. The Simplified USA Tax provides tax relief for all Americans, especially when they own their own home, give to their church, educate their children, and set aside some savings for a better tomorrow.

Under this proposal, everyone gets a deduction for the mortgage interest on their home and for charitable contributions they make. Child support is also deductible.

Generous personal and family exemptions are also allowed under this proposal.

The Simplified USA Tax is simplicity itself. The tax return will be short, only a page or two for most of us. But more to the point, the tax return will be understandable. For the first time in a long time, America's tax system will make sense to citizens who will file their tax returns and pay their taxes.

SUSAT also contains a new and better way of taxing corporations and other businesses, that will allow them to compete and win in global markets in a way that exports American-made products, not American jobs.

If enacted in the United States, we have some reason to believe this innovative approach to business taxation will soon become the worldwide standard by which other countries model their systems.

All businesses, corporate and non-corporate, are taxed alike at an eight percent rate on the first $150,000 of profit and 12 percent on all amounts above that small business level.

This system would be border adjustable. It would also address the territoriality problem which is at the core of our fight with Europe over FSC. If we were to pass this business portion alone of my tax system, it would address the FSC problem and, at the same time, it would allow us to import a foreign tax base.

The new revenue from the import tax will be, we estimate, about $160 billion, a large portion of which will never become a cost to the U.S. economy. We do not know exactly how much will be shifted back to the foreign companies that sell in the U.S. market, but both basic economics and common sense tell us that a large portion will be absorbed by foreign sellers and therefore will never enter the U.S. economy.

I think the point here is that the amount is large and that the Simplified USA Tax provides a correspondingly large tax cut for Americans. At the same time, it gets rid of the AMT, the death tax, and depreciation.

Mr. Chairman, wrapping up, for too long, the Tax Code has been an albatross around the neck of the economy. This is not very smart and it is certainly not fair to those citizens whose standard of living are substantially lower as a result.

It is time to restore people's faith in the integrity and competence of their tax system, and in the process take a major step toward helping U.S. companies compete in the global marketplace.

SUSAT is the product of a great deal of work by many people and I want to compliment them here. I am proud to be the sponsor of H.R. 134.

I invite the Committee to look in a bipartisan fashion at this issue and consider providing the American people the fair and sensible tax system that they deserve.

Mr. Chairman, I appreciate the opportunity to testify.

[The prepared statement follows:]

Statement of the Hon. Phil English, a Representative in Congress from the State of Pennsylvania

Good morning, Chairman Archer and my distinguished colleagues on the Ways and Means Committee. I appreciate the opportunity to testify before you today on the issue of fundamental tax reform. I commend the Chairman for scheduling these hearings as we agree that this is an issue whose time has come.

I have introduced the *Simplified USA Tax Act,* H.R. 134, because I want to reform the American tax system in a way sensible to the average citizen and that will pass the test of time. Not only do we need a tax system that is fair and sensible, we need one that is stable. As bad as the current system is—and I am one of its severest critics—the last thing we need is to enact reform that is so radical and experimental that Congress will be faced with revamping it all over again in a few years.

The Simplified USA Tax is revolutionary in that it addresses the strongest points of concerns with the current system while at the same time addressing concerns about the equity of other tax reform proposals being considered. The Simplified USA Tax is based on principles that I feel are vital to any meaningful reform:

• Imposing a simple tax to encourage efficiency
• Ensuring that income is taxed only once
• Establishing trade equity for American products
• Taking the double tax burden off of savings—so as not to discourage individuals from saving
• Providing incentives for investment in physical capital and human capital
• Including an accommodation with respect to the Social Security payroll tax—the most regressive tax of all.

In my tax reform proposal, USA stands for "Unlimited Savings Allowance." Everyone is allowed an unlimited Roth IRA in which they can put the portion of each year's income they save after paying taxes and living expenses. After five years, all funds in the account may be withdrawn for any purpose and all withdrawls—including accumulated interest and other earnings and principle—are tax free. Nothing could be simpler and nothing could give people a better opportunity to save; especially young people. Because only new income earned after enactment of the *Simplified USA Tax* can be put into the USA Roth IRA, young people starting to move into their higher-earning years are the ones who will benefit the most for the longest time.

The tax code should give everyone the opportunity to keep what they save, and if they wish, to pass it along to succeeding generations. Therefore, the federal estate and gift taxes would be repealed under my proposal.

Under a new tax code, tax rates should be lower, especially for wage earners who must now pay both an income tax and a 7.65% FICA payroll tax on the same amount of wages. It is my intention that the final tax rates under the *Simplified USA Tax Act,* after all adjustments are made, will be as low as possible consistent with budget limitations. At present, the USA Tax starts out with quite low rates—15% at the bottom, 25% in the middle, and 30% at the top. Then, these rates are reduced even further by allowing wage earners a full tax credit for the 7.65% Social Security and Medicare payroll tax that is withheld form their paychecks under current law. I do not propose to repeal the payroll tax because to do so would imperil Social Security, however, I do allow a credit for it and when that credit is taken into account, the rates of tax on workers' wages are very low—in the 7% to 17% range for nearly all Americans.

Under the *Simplified USA Tax Act,* the tax rate on the first $40,000 of taxable income from wages cannot exceed 7.35% which is the basic USA rate of 15% less the 7.65% payroll tax credit. Under the current code, the combined payroll tax/income tax rate is 22.65%. On the next $32,000 (up to the maximum payroll tax base of $72,000), the rate cannot exceed 17.35% which is the middle USA rate of 25% less the 7.65% payroll tax credit. Under the current code, the combined payroll tax/income tax rate is 35.65%.

151

The *Simplified USA Tax Act* provides tax relief for all Americans, especially when they own their own home, give to their church, educate their children and set aside some savings for a better tomorrow.

Under this proposal, everyone gets a deduction for the mortgage interest on their home and for the charitable contributions that they make. In addition, the *Simplified USA Tax Act* allows for a deduction for tuition paid for college and post-secondary vocational education. The annual limit would be $4,000 per person and $12,000 for a family.

Generous personal and family exemptions are also allowed under this proposal. On a joint return, the family exemption is $8,140 and there is an additional $2,700 exemption for each member of the family. Therefore, a married couple with two children pays no tax on their first $18,940 of income.

The *Simplified USA Tax* is simplicity itself. The tax return will be short, only a page or two for most of us, but more to the point, the tax return will be understandable. For the first time in a long time, America's tax system will make sense to the citizens who file the tax returns and pay the taxes.

The *Simplified USA Tax Act* also contains a new and better way of taxing corporations and other businesses that will allow them to compete and win in global markets in a way that exports American-made products, not American jobs. Experts who have studied it believe that, if enacted by the United States, this innovative approach to business taxation will soon become the worldwide standard by which other countries will model their systems.

All businesses, corporate and non-corporate, are taxed alike at an 8% rate on the first $150,000 of profit and at 12% on all amounts above that small business level. All businesses will be allowed a credit for the 7.65% payroll tax they pay under current law. All costs for plant, equipment and inventory in the Unites States would be expensed in the year of purchase. All export sales income is exempt, as is all foreign-source income, and all profits earned abroad can be brought back home for reinvestment in the United States without penalty. Because of a 12% import adjustment, all companies that produce abroad and sell back into U.S. markets will be required to bear the same tax as companies that both produce and sell in the U.S.

The new revenue from the import tax will be about $160 billion, a large portion of which will never become a cost in the U.S. economy. We do not know exactly how much will be shifted back to the foreign companies that sell into the U.S. market. But both basic economics and common sense tell us that a large portion will be absorbed by foreign sellers, and, therefore, will never enter the U.S. economy. A middle ground estimate would be $80 to $120 billion. The point is not the exact amount. Rather, it is that the amount is large and that the *Simplified USA Tax Act* provides a correspondingly large tax cut for Americans.

For too long the tax code has been a needless drag on the economy. This is not very smart and certainly is not fair to those citizens whose standard of living are lower as a result. It is time to restore people's faith in the integrity and competence of their tax system and, in the process, take a major step helping U.S. companies compete in the global marketplace.

The *Simplified USA Tax Act* is the product of much work by many people over a period of years. I am proud to be the sponsor of H.R. 134 , a simplified version of the USA Tax first introduced by Senators Nunn and Domenici in 1995. I hope that this committee will be able to work in a bipartisan fashion to provide the American people the fair and sensible tax system that they deserve.

Thank you Mr. Chairman for the opportunity to testify before you today. I would be happy to answer any questions you may have at this time.

SIMPLIFIED USA TAX

The Simplified USA Tax (SUSAT) would completely replace the current income tax system, both corporate and personal. SUSAT consists of two parts:
- **An 8 to 12 percent business tax paid when income is produced.**
- **A 15, 25, and 30 percent progressive rate tax paid by individuals when they receive wages, interest, dividends and other income.**

Wage income and capital income are taxed exactly the same. Income from equity capital is no longer taxed more heavily than income from debt. Incorporated businesses are no longer taxed more heavily than unincorporated ones. Most importantly, income that is saved is no longer taxed more heavily than income that is consumed. Both are taxed exactly the same.

To further assure equal treatment of wage income—whether consumed or saved—a full income tax credit is allowed for the current OASDHI (Social Security and Medicare) payroll tax. Because of the payroll tax credit, wage earners will immediately begin paying less taxes.

The business tax is internationally competitive. Imports are taxed, but export sales of American-made goods and services are not. Further, U.S. companies are no longer penalized when they make money abroad and bring it home to reinvest in America.

Both the individual tax and the business tax are extremely simple. Only a few steps exist in order to calculate the taxes. All are clearly stated and readily understandable, thereby relieving taxpayer confusion and leaving little opportunity for the IRS to interfere.

Moreover, because SUSAT repeals federal estate and gift taxes, the IRS will no longer take away a part of anyone's lifetime savings.

The Two-Level USA Tax

Business-Level Tax

Rate: 8 % on first $150,000 and 12% on excess

Tax Base: Sales Revenues from Domestic Operations (-) Exports (-) Purchases of Inventory (-) Purchases of Equipment & Services

Payroll Tax: Tax Credit for Employer-Paid Payroll Tax

Imports: 12% Tax on Imported Inventory, Equipment & Services

Wages   Interest, Dividends & Sales of Stock

Individual-Level Tax

Rates: Progressive Rates of 15, 25, and 30%.

Tax Base

Wages + Interest + Dividends + Sales of Stock and Other Assets (-) Deductions

Savings:

(1) Universal Roth IRA -- *No Deduction Allowed for Contributions, but Previously-Taxed Principal and Earnings on Principal Are Not Taxed when Withdrawn from USA Roth IRA. No Limit on Contributions and No Restrictions on Withdrawals.*

(2) Deduction for §401(k), etc. — *Preserves Limited Deductions Allowed under Current Code for §401(k), Other Employer-Sponsored Qualified Plans and Deductible IRAs.*

Other Deductions: Deduction for Exempt Amount & Deductions for Home Mortgage Interest, Charitable Contributions & Secondary Education

---

The USA Tax for individuals is simplicity itself; a truly minimalist approach that achieves a great deal without a lot of complex rules. Basically, all anyone needs to do is (1) add up their income, (2) subtract a few simple deductions, (3) apply USA's low tax rates to the balance, (4) take credit for employee-paid OASDHI payroll tax and income taxes withheld by employers, and (5) pay the additional amount, if any, that is due.

Gross Income =	Wages and salaries plus interest, dividends, pensions, etc., and amounts received from the sale of stock and other assets.
Exemptions =	A Family Allowance: . . . . . . $4,840 Single . . . . . . $8,140 Married/Joint . . . . . $4,070 Married/Separate . . . . . . $5,940 Head-of-Household Personal and Dependents: $2,700 each for taxpayer, spouse and all dependents. The total Exempt Amount for a family of four is $18,940.
Deductions =	(A) Family-based . . . . . Charitable Contributions . . . . . Home Mortgage Interest . . . . . Higher Education Tuition (B) Retirement-oriented . . . . . Deductible '401(k) Contributions . . . . . Deductible IRAs for Lower Income Families
Savings =	Unlimited USA Roth IRA from which Tax-Free Withdrawals Can Be made for Any Purpose, Not Just Retirement

Rate Schedules and Brackets

Married Individuals Filing Joint Returns and Surviving Spouses

If taxable income is:	The tax is:
Not over $40,000	15% of taxable income
Over $40,000 but not over $80,000	$6,000 plus 25% of excess over $40,000
Over $80,000	$16,000 plus 30% of excess over $80,000

Heads of Households

If taxable income is:	The tax is:
Not over $35,000	15% of taxable income
Over $35,000 but not over $70,000	$5,250 plus 25% of excess over $35,000
Over $70,000	$14,000 plus 30% of excess over $70,000

Unmarried Individuals

If taxable income is:	The tax is:
Not over $24,000	15% of taxable income
Over $24,000 but not over $48,000	$3,600 plus 25% of excess over $24,000
Over $48,000	$9,600 plus 30% of excess over $48,000

Married Individuals Filing Separate Returns

If taxable income is:	The tax is:
Not over $20,000	15% of taxable income
Over $20,000 but not over $40,000	$3,000 plus 25% of excess over $20,000
Over $40,000	$8,000 plus 30% of excess over $40,000

154

USA Roth IRA: The Centerpiece of the Individual Tax

The USA Tax would eliminate the double tax on income that is saved, and, therefore, make taxes a neutral factor in the choice between consuming income immediately or saving it in order to consume later.

USA accomplishes this feat in the simplest and fairest way possible by allowing everyone to contribute **after-tax** income to a USA Roth IRA patterned after the one in Section 480A of the current code with certain modifications. Although called an "IRA," the USA version is in reality a universal savings vehicle that can be used for any purpose, not just retirement.

• *Everyone is eligible to contribute all or any portion of their current year's taxable income to a specially denominated account (like present IRA accounts at all banks and financial institutions).*

• *Because no deduction is allowed, the person must first pay the tax on all income and then contribute to the USA Roth IRA. Further, all contributions must be made in cash.*

• *Because all money that goes into the USA Roth IRA represents post-effective date after-tax income, no additional tax is imposed either on the accumulated principal amount or on the earnings on principal inside the account.*

• *Accumulated principal and earnings on principal can be withdrawn at any time and for any purpose.*

OVERVIEW OF USA BUSINESS TAX

The USA business tax is a cash flow tax on all forms of business organization, corporate or noncorporate.[1] The calculation of a business's tax liability for the year is a simple five-step process:

1. *Add up total sales during the year from operations in the United States;*
2. *Exclude sales of goods and services for export;*
3. *Deduct all purchases from other businesses, including expensing of capital equipment, inventory items, supplies, etc.;*
4. *Apply the rate schedule to the remaining gross profit to determine tentative tax;*
5. *Subtract from tentative tax a credit for the 7.65 percent employer-paid OASDHI payroll tax.*

The "gross profit" tax base in No. 4 is the amount the business earns on a cash basis after expensing its capital equipment and paying its suppliers, but before paying its employees, stockholders and its creditors. Because the USA business tax allows no deduction for wages, dividends or interest, it collects a uniform tax on all forms of income—labor and capital. Such "neutrality" is essential to basic fairness and economic efficiency. Under international treaties, it is also an essential ingredient of the important export and import features of the USA Tax.

The most important operational components of the USA business tax, in comparison to the current code, are set forth below.

Item	Business Taxation	USA Tax	IRC of 1986
1	Corporations Taxed Separately from Individuals	Yes	Yes
2	All Business Entities Taxed as Corporations	Yes	No
3	Deduction for Dividends Paid	No	No
4	Deduction for Interest Paid	No	Yes
5	Deduction for Compensation Paid to Employees	No	Yes
6	Credit for Employer-Paid FICA Payroll Tax	Yes	No
7	Requires Depreciation of Capital Investment	No	Yes
8	Allows Expensing of Capital Investment	Yes	No
9	Deduction for Contributions to Qualified Employee Plans.	No	Yes
10	Taxes Foreign-Source Income on A Worldwide Basis.	No	Yes
11	Applies Territorial Rule to Exclude Foreign-Source Income Derived from Operations Abroad.	Yes	No
12	Taxes Export Sales of American-Made Products & Services.	No	Yes
13	Taxes Imports of Foreign-Made Products & Services.	Yes	No

[1] Like the present corporate income tax, however, the USA Tax exempts all religious, charitable and other nonprofit organizations described in section 501(c) of the current code.

The USA business tax rate schedule is as follows:

Gross Profit	Rate
$0 to $150,000	8%
Excess over $150,000	12%

REPEAL OF ESTATE AND GIFT TAXES

Not only does The Simplified USA Tax allow all Americans a fair opportunity to save and invest, it repeals the federal estate and gift taxes and, therefore, allows them a fair opportunity to pass their accumulated savings on to their children and succeeding generations.

This repeal applies across the board to everyone and to all assets presently owned and acquired in the future, whether held in USA Roth IRAs or held outside such accounts.

———————

Chairman ARCHER. Congressman English, thank you so much for bringing this alternative before the Committee. I doubt that we will have adequate time this morning to fully explore all of the details, but I look forward to examining them in great detail.

And so, at this time, I have no questions.

Mr. Rangel?

Mr. RANGEL. Mr. Chairman, I did not have the opportunity to make an opening statement.

Chairman ARCHER. Nor did I.

Mr. RANGEL. But I want to apologize to my friend and colleague, Congressman English. He has put a lot of work in trying to get a better way for us to raise the revenue that is necessary to run our government.

We can see that the timing of this type of hearing makes it very difficult for the Members to listen to his ideas. At the same time, we are trying try to protect our jurisdiction on the House Floor.

So I do not know whether this was thought out by our leadership. Yesterday, while we were here listening to the merits of a federal sales tax, there were people on the House Floor—get this, Mr. English—a Republican by the name of Mr. Terry who brought a bill up on the Floor to approve the President's increase in taxes. But, he recommended that they vote no against it.

The Republicans brought up the bill to show what the tax raises would be. When I asked why they did it, they said because the President's taxes were as a tiger in a cage, and that they wanted to kill the tiger before it got out.

So you can see, from a tax point of view, that did not make much sense.

Now, while we are here are trying to figure out the complexities of your bill, they have got another revenue-Constitutional issue, on the House Floor saying that we cannot close tax loopholes unless we have two-thirds vote in support.

Well, people may support that but we cannot do it sitting here listening to you.

Tomorrow, at long last, we get a chance to pull up the tax code by the roots. That is, to abolish it. To sunset it and say there is no more tax code for anybody. It is all over.

But then I read the fine print. It will not be the Ways and Means Committee that would be replacing the old tax code.

Guess what?

It will be a private commission, not even Congressional. They will come out and they will have the hearings. They will listen to you. They will listen to me. And, they will listen to the private sector. Maybe they will listen to our Chairman, but only four Members of Congress will be there. Then, they will report back some legislation. Guess what it is supposed to be for? For new taxes.

So they are changing the rules just when I have reached almost the top of my game. They have turned everything over to the private sector. The Ways and Means Committee's jurisdiction is being taken away on the Floor and given to outsiders.

So please do not be disappointed because the Members are not here. They are trying to protect their jurisdiction. They are on the Floor. They are listening, and it is very difficult.

But you have done a tremendous job over the years.

Mr. ENGLISH. Thank you.

Mr. RANGEL. And I just hope that we in the Congress will have a chance to listen to your ideas and that they will not get some cockamamie private sector group to study your legislation. The Constitution says it is the Ways and Means Committee, and as long as I am around, we will do the tax law.

So you keep sticking with us and not those private groups.

I want to thank you, Mr. Chairman.

Mr. ENGLISH. And I would like to thank the gentleman for being here despite all of the distractions and let me reassure him there are no caged tigers in my proposal. Thank you.

Mr. RANGEL. Thank you.

Chairman ARCHER. Well I have listened to the gentlemen's comments, and I am beginning to wonder that whatever activity we have in this room, there will always be some reason to complain about it.

I hear complaints about procedures. I hear complaints about substance. I hear complaints about me personally. It just seems to be "there you go again."

Mr. Crane?

Mr. CRANE. Thank you, Mr. Chairman.

I simply want to commend my colleague, my distinguished colleague, Phil English, for his tax proposal and we have had several and we will continue to get hearings on several, as you know, and any one of them is superior to the existing obscene code.

So any chance we have to move forward, you can count on me. And thank you for appearing and testifying.

Mr. ENGLISH. I thank the gentleman.

Chairman ARCHER. Mr. Weller?

Mr. WELLER. Well thank you, Mr. Chairman. I want to commend you for your leadership in bringing these hearings to this Committee room.

I also want to commend my colleague, Mr. English, for having the courage and the commitment of time and effort to put forward his own reform proposal. Because one thing I have learned is that in every provision in the Tax Code there is always a reason it was put there and there is somebody who wants to keep it there.

I have learned that over the last several years serving on this Committee. So I salute you for your proposal.

You know, one of the top priorities of this Congress, the Republican majority, is bringing fairness to the Tax Code. And of course I know that is your goal of your proposal is making the Tax Code more fair.

And I am just really proud that, you know, last week the President signed our effort to bring fairness to the Tax Code by wiping out the Social Security earnings penalty on seniors between the age of 65 and 70 who want to continue working or who are forced to continue working.

And I am also very proud that the House overwhelmingly passed—and in fact 48 Democrats voted with, rejected their leadership's pressures and voted with every House Republican to wipe out the marriage tax penalty with the passage of H.R. 6.

And our legislation—which eliminates the marriage tax penalty essentially wipes it out for 25 million married working couples who on average pay $1400 more in higher taxes just because they are married—is a big victory if you want to bring about tax fairness.

And I am so pleased that the Senate has moved quickly. The Senate at this moment is of course considering their proposal which is pretty similar to H.R. 6, the Marriage Tax Elimination Act, which wipes out the marriage tax penalty.

My hope is that the House and Senate can reconcile their differences relatively soon, and we can put on the President's desk another major initiative which will benefit 50 million married working individuals who suffer the marriage penalty just because they are married.

Mr. English, I was just wondering from the perspective of your tax proposal, how do you address the marriage tax penalty in your proposal?

Mr. ENGLISH. We would effectively dramatically reduce it because of the structure that we have put in place. I will leave it to others to describe where a marriage tax penalty might creep in.

I have retained multiple tax rates and the implication of that is there is always a danger of a marriage tax penalty being reintroduced.

I would welcome the gentleman to take a look at my proposal and come back to us with any suggestions he might have of addressing that problem in our code.

As the gentleman knows, because he has immersed himself in this issue more than anyone, it is very difficult to completely eliminate the marriage tax penalty and there is always a potential when you have progressive taxation that when people get married, as a couple they will end up paying more taxes than they did as two individuals.

I am not sure we have addressed that as fully as we should in this tax proposal and I would welcome the gentleman's input.

Mr. WELLER. Well, you know, Mr. English, one of the things I have observed also is, particularly in the last seven-and-a-half years, there has been a desire by some to target tax cuts, target tax relief, which means you pick and choose politically who benefits.

It usually means very few get very little in tax relief and unfortunately that targeting has caused more so- called marriage tax penalties in the last few years than any other consequence of the code.

Of course the biggest consequence of the Tax Code is for joint filers. You know, a married couple. They are both in the work force. Their combined income usually pushes them into a higher tax bracket, creating the marriage tax penalty.

But if you talk with those who are tax preparers, they will tell you that there are over 60 marriage tax penalties in the code, primarily resulting from means' testing and targeting of tax cuts because the income eligibility is never twice that for married couples filing jointly compared to that of a single filer.

And clearly as we look at bringing fairness to the tax code, not only do we want to eliminate the marriage tax penalty for joint filers, but we need to look at those so-called targeted provisions because they create a lot of consequences for those who work hard and happen to be married.

Mr. ENGLISH. I thank the gentleman. I would point out to him that what we tried to do was eliminate many of these targeted provisions which after all are adjustments for other problems in the Tax Code.

What we tried to come up with was a clean and very simple tax system that in the process does eliminate many of those marriage penalties that you discussed, and makes the Tax Code far simpler.

We found that the complexity in the Tax Code did not arise from multiple rates as much as from many of these very complicated and overlapping policies that were loaded into the Tax Code.

So as a result we think we have gone a considerable distance toward finding an equitable and global approach to these problems.

And I thank the gentleman.

Mr. WELLER. Well your point is a good one.

You know particularly in education one of our goals is to make college more affordable. That is why we have worked to expand opportunities with the student loan interest deduction. And of course for married couples, not only is there a marriage tax penalty on the income eligibility for joint filers, but if you have got a couple kids getting married right out of college, they are paying off their student loans, you know they are eligible for the full student loan interest deduction. But once they choose to get married, they discover that interest deduction is cut in half because they have to share it as if they were just one person.

And that is just not fair and that is just one more reason that as we look at tax reform, I think we really have to take a good look at the so-called targeting and preferences and means' testing and how it is created marriage tax penalties as well as other consequences that just are not fair.

Mr. ENGLISH. The gentleman makes an excellent point. Let me say that instead of providing many of the targeted tax breaks for tuition that had existed and that we have recently put into law, what we have tried to do is consolidate these into a substantial deduction that would be available per student, $4,000 per student up to $12,000 total for a family.

And we think that when you run the TRAPs on that, the tax relief is very substantial to families and makes up for some of the other adjustments that we have tried to make in the last few years to help use the Tax Code to support higher education.

Mr. WELLER. My last question——

Chairman ARCHER: The gentleman's time has expired.

Mr. WELLER. Thank you, Mr. Chairman.

Chairman ARCHER. Mr. English, thank you for the work you have done on this and giving us another alternative to look at. And unless you have something important to say, you are excused.

Mr. WELLER. Thank you, Mr. Chairman.

Chairman ARCHER. Our next panel will please come to the witness table. Congressman Frenzel, Mr. Christian, Dr. Foster, and Mr. Hufbauer.

While you are being seated, I officially welcome each of you to the Committee. Certainly some of you are no strangers to this room and to this Committee, and we are particularly happy to have you back in our presence and to hear your sage comments.

The Honorable Bill Frenzel is no stranger to any of us up here at the dias having been seated up here for many years yourself, and we are particularly happy to have you back and to listen to your wisdom which has always been present whenever you speak in this room.

And so we welcome you again, and if you will lead off, we will be pleased to hear your testimony.

STATEMENT OF THE HON. BILL FRENZEL, GUEST SCHOLAR, BROOKINGS INSTITUTION [FORMER MEMBER OF CONGRESS]

Mr. FRENZEL. Thank you, Mr. Chairman.

Chairman ARCHER. And I think Mr. Rangel also wants to welcome you.

Mr. RANGEL. I want to welcome all of you, particularly, my friend Congressman Frenzel. Please give my best to your lovely wife, Ruth, and I want tell you how much you have been missed around here.

The one thing that makes serving in Congress exciting is the memories of the good old days. Thank you for coming back.

Mr. FRENZEL. Thank you——

Mr. RAMSTAD. Mr. Chairman? Mr. Chairman?

Chairman ARCHER. Mr. Ramstad, I apologize.

Mr. RAMSTAD. Not at all, Mr. Chairman.

Chairman ARCHER. Mr. Ramstad has a very——

Mr. RAMSTAD. I just want to join in the chorus of singing the praises of my predecessor, somebody I am proud to call my mentor and my friend, and without whose tutelage, I would not be sitting here today. Somebody who distinguished himself on this panel for 16 years serving the Third Congressional District of Minnesota.

He also served as ranking member of the Budget Committee and the House Administration Committee.

Bill Frenzel is, as one person who introduced him put it best, if you look up in the dictionary, the word "statesman," you will see Frenzel's picture.

It is a pleasure, Bill, to welcome you back to the Committee.

[The opening statement of Mr. Ramstad follows:]

Opening Statement of Hon. Jim Ramstad, a Representative in Congress from the State of Minnesota

Mr. Chairman, thank you for commitment to reforming our deeply flawed tax system and for giving the American people a public forum through this week of hearings to examine the options available to us.

We already know that the current system flunks the critical tests of efficiency, simplicity, flexibility, political responsibility and fairness.

Americans spend billions of dollars complying with an incomprehensible system that discourages saving and investment. Our tax code robs Americans of time, privacy, economic opportunities and incentives to be innovators.

Our complex tax code puts American businesses at a disadvantage with their foreign competitors, robbing them of the opportunity to create jobs and find new markets for American products.

We want Americans to work and save for their family's future. But as you point out, Mr. Chairman, our tax system tells Americans that the more you work and save and succeed, the more you pay.

I appreciate the opportunity to examine alternatives which meet the important goals of rewarding work, encouraging savings and improving our competitiveness abroad.

Again, Mr. Chairman, thank you for convening these critical hearings. I look forward to hearing the testimony today.

———————————

Mr. McCrery. Mr. Chairman, I would say me too.

Chairman Archer. Let me just add one other thing since we are getting into this friendly colloquy here.

The last major battle I think that you and I and Phil Crane fought on the Floor of the House was the opposition to I think the ill-considered Tax Reform Act of 1986, and unfortunately we barely lost that battle but I think history will show that we were right.

And maybe the next major battle that we participate in, whether from the inside or the outside, we will win. So we are happy to have you before the Committee.

Mr. Frenzel. Thank you Mr. Chairman and Committee members. You have brightened the life of an old man by putting wings on the dog, and I am really pleased to be back here in this marvelous room with you distinguished Committee members.

Mr. Chairman, on this Committee all of us who have ever served here have been very frustrated with the Tax Code. We have seen the complications, the difficulties, and looked for ways to improve it. We have always been frustrated in what we have tried to do.

Size and complexity are major problems for our constituents, but they are less serious than the perverse incentives that have worked their way in the Code. They have gotten into the Code for good reasons, but there are a couple that have always bothered me, and led me in the chase for some kind of responsible tax reform.

The most prominent of these has been the inadequate incentives for savings. Secondly, I have followed international taxation for some time and been disappointed that we have had more incentives to import than to export.

I have also been concerned about regressivity and job creation disincentives in our Social Security taxes. And of course, the general layering of the Code as we try to repair it has been a problem as well.

H.R. 134, Mr. English's bill, answers these problems.

I have tried to follow this bill and its predecessors over a period of at least ten years since I left the Congress, and was interested in the original Nunn-Dominici proposal which was one of the predecessors of this bill.

It is not a simple bill but it does some things right. One of the reasons that we have had trouble in the past with any kind of tax reform bill is it presents such a big, ugly bundle that it is easy to form a majority against it.

If you are going to truly reform the Code, you have to change alot of things, and those changes hurt an awful lot of people.

I want to talk about four aspects of H.R. 134. The first one is international. H.R. 134 has the international parts right. We should not tax foreign income. We need to relieve taxes on exported goods and services and we need to assess taxes on imports to equalize the burdens that the domestic producers bear.

The FSC has been a pretty lonely incentive for us, and it is weak compared to the combination of incentives offered by many of our foreign competitors. Now, even its existence is in peril.

H.R. 134 provides powerful savings incentives. Once the taxes are paid on income going into the investment account, there is no additional tax on inside buildup or on withdrawals.

Congressman English has used the simple mechanism of the Roth IRA to solve one of he major complexity problems of the original USA Tax.

Third, H.R. 134 relieves problems of regressivity and disincentives of job formation caused by our high Social Security taxes.

We have made the Tax Code, the Income Tax Code, more progressive over the last 30 years, but because the Social Security taxes are levied on the first dollar of earnings, the overall tax burden has probably become more regressive.

And, of course, other than in times of full employment, which we are enjoying now, those taxes can be a real job creation disincentive.

So I believe that Congressman English in H.R. 134 has done a pretty good job of giving us some simple principles which can be put into a total tax reform bill.

I would like to note here that tax rates under this tax bill can be flattened or made even more progressive. Congressman English has structured it to make it roughly equal to the current burden tables. I think that is the right place to start even though you may not want to finish there.

Mr. Chairman, I commend this tax bill because it gives some promise for achieving the things that I have always thought were most important in tax reform.

It is probably an exaggeration to call it simple because life is not simple, and it does not tear the system out by the roots as you, Mr. Chairman, have always wanted to do, but it does rough up the system pretty well.

I think it can do the tax reform job, and I believe it is workable and understandable, at least for a starting place for this Committee.

And I thank you and the Committee for your kind words and for allowing me to testify today.

[The prepared statement follows:]

162

Statement of the Hon. Bill Frenzel, Guest Scholar, Brookings Institution, (Former Member of Congress)

Mr. Chairman and Members of the Committee:

It is, as always, a pleasure to return to the scene of one's former crimes. I appear here today on my own behalf and my testimony does not represent the opinions or conclusions of The Brookings Institution. I congratulate the Chairman and the Committee for holding these Tax Reform hearings. The time is ripe.

You are all, as was I, very fortunate to be able to serve on this distinguished and historic committee. I hope you are less frustrated than I was about our ability to produce a Tax Code in which our country can have more confidence.

The need for major surgery on the U.S. Tax Code has been obvious for years. Over the years, complications and "simplifications" alike have created a system of bewildering, and indefensible, size and complexity. Nobody intended that it be so cumbersome, but it got that way for a variety of reasons well known to the committee (we live in a complex society and economy; politicians run on platforms of change; its easier to amend than to delete; simplicity and fairness are sometimes in conflict). Whatever the reasons, today many taxpayers cannot comply (without help) with the Code, and tax collectors have great difficulty enforcing it.

But, size and complexity are problems that are less serious than the perverse incentives that have worked their ways into the Code. Four that I have found particularly troublesome are: (1) inadequate incentives for saving; (2) more incentives to import than to export; (3) regressivity and job creation disincentives in our Social Security taxes; and (4) the endless layering of good, and, at the time, necessary, adjustments which have led to unacceptable complexity. Each of you could list many more.

The origins of most of these policies go long way back in history. They undoubtedly made good sense when enacted. Now, the world has changed, and it will continue to change even more swiftly. Regulators are already having difficulty keeping up. Relatively small, targeted Tax policy changes, like the ones this committee has regularly made in the past, are not able to keep pace with the speed of change. I believe that you must make bold and massive changes to meet the new challenges.

But size and boldness usually mean a tax package so full of fish hooks that no one will touch it. I, myself, was, for many years in this Committee, a supporter of the theory of "creeping incrementalism." Later, I have come to believe that Band-Aids, even giant ones like TRA 1986, are more likely to extend the problems than they are to solve them.

H.R. 134, the Simplified USA Tax, appears to me to be a workable solution to the Tax Reform dilemma. In the interests of full disclosure, I must admit I was exposed to the general concept nearly 10 years ago when I attended, with about a dozen accountants, tax lawyers and economists, a series of brainstorming sessions which began with David Bradford's "Consumed Income Tax" and went through to the original Nunn-Domenici USA Tax.

That original Nunn-Domenici proposal was an important milestone in the development of H.R. 134, but, like many of its ilk, it was too complicated. The cleverest of us could not have explained it to our constituents very quickly or concisely. That kind of bill is an easy victim for interests, which want to retain the old code, or for partisan squabbling.

H.R. 134 cannnot be called simple, but it is understandable. It is a suitable vehicle for the Committee's Tax Reform efforts. I can't review the whole bill, but here are some of the aspects, which appeal to me:

1. **H. R. 134 has the international parts right. We should not tax foreign income; we need to relieve taxes on exported goods and services; and we need to assess taxes on imports to equalize the burdens on domestic producers.** We have had only the lonely FISC as an export incentive. It's a weak one compared to the combinations of incentives offered by many of our foreign competitors, and now, its existence is imperiled.

2. **H.R. 134 provides powerful savings incentives. Once the taxes have been paid on income going into the investment account, there is no additional tax on either inside build-up or on withdrawals.** Congressman English has used the relatively simple mechanism found in the Roth IRA to solve the major complexity problem of the original USA Tax. Withdrawals from these after-tax savings accounts can be made for any purpose.

3. **H.R. 134 relieves problems of regressivity and of disincentives to job formation caused by Social Security taxes.** Since I first came to Washington, the income tax Code has become more progressive as more people at lower levels of income have been taken out of the code completely. But, because the Social Security taxes are levied on the first dollar of earnings, the overall tax burden has be-

come more regressive. And, in times of less than full employment, those taxes are a real jobs disincentive for employers.

I personally support progressive income tax rates, with a couple of caveats. The present highest rate is too high. The EITC which I supported originally has been expanded to a point where it could be better managed and enforced as an appropriation entitlement rather than a tax entitlement.

It should be noted that tax rates under the Simplified USA Tax could be flattened, or made even more progressive than present rates. Congressman English has structured it to make it roughly equal to the current burden tables. That may not be the place you want to finish, but , to me, it's the right place to start.

Finally, Mr. Chairman, I recommend H.R. 134, the Simplified USA Tax, for the Committee's consideration because it gives real promise of achieving most of the things I have always sought in Tax Reform. It may be an exaggeration to call it simple, because life is not simple. It isn't perfect, because there is no such thing as a perfect tax bill.

And it doesn't tear the system out by the roots as you have always wanted to do, but it does rough up the system pretty well. Not only will it do the Tax Reform job, but its is workable and understandable. Those two virtues may be able to stand as proxies for the simplicity which has always been so elusive.

———

Chairman ARCHER. Thank you, Mr. Frenzel.
Mr. Christian?

STATEMENT OF ERNEST S. CHRISTIAN, ESQUIRE, WASHINGTON, D.C.

Mr. CHRISTIAN. Thank you, Mr. Chairman, Mr. Rangel, Members of the Committee.

Congressman English's simplified USA Tax is, in my opinion, a landmark achievement. I say that from the perspective of having spent about 25 years in the Treasury Department and in the private sector working on these concepts.

He is to be greatly commended.

His bill shows how the Tax Code can be simplified without having to repeal the deductions for either home mortgage interest or charitable contributions.

It shows how the double tax on savings and investment can be removed without enacting a consumption tax.

How tax equity for working men and women can be achieved by allowing them a credit for the payroll tax they already pay.

It shows how the archaic tax barriers to U.S. competitiveness in world markets can be removed in a way that protects and enhances American jobs.

Marginal tax rates can be lowered, a laudable goal.

Progressivity can be preserved.

Transitional dislocations can be avoided.

Congressman English's bill Simplified USA embodies some new approaches. One is to include in the tax base of the United States of America, for the first time in history, all amounts derived by foreign-owned companies from selling goods and services in our market.

The result of this shift may be to reduce, by something in the area of $100 billion per year, the tax burden borne by U.S. labor and U.S. capital, an enormous, implicit tax cut for the American economy paid for by foreign-owned companies that presently derive income from the U.S. market on nearly a tax-free basis.

The largest beneficiaries of this implicit tax cut would seem to me to be the wage earners of America. They receive a full credit for the payroll tax they now pay.

Simplified USA is a plain-language, stripped-down version of the current income tax, individual and corporate. It is concentrated on the main goals of tax reform.

The basic amendments necessary to achieve these results are neither unfamiliar nor shocking. First-year expensing of plant and equipment is already allowed under the current Code for small businesses.

It only remains for Simplified USA to make expensing universal, which it should be.

There is nothing radical about removing the double tax from personal saving and thereby taxing saved income no more heavily than consumed income.

The Roth IRA already does this under the current Code for retirement savings. Simplified USA uses exactly the same simple mechanism for all savings.

There is also nothing new or radical about the idea of not imposing U.S. tax on the income that American companies derive from developing new markets abroad, or about the related idea of not taxing exports of American made goods.

The Foreign Sales Corporation provision, commonly known as FSC in the current Code is a flawed attempt to go halfway toward these goals in the international competitiveness arena, but FSC has run afoul of the WTO. Simplified USA, Congressman English's bill, does the job correctly in a way that is consistent with U.S. tax traditions and treaty obligations.

There is also nothing radical about bringing foreign-owned companies into the U.S. tax base, and using he revenue to cut taxes on American citizens. Europeans and others have been doing this same thing in reverse to the United States for decades.

The truly remarkable thing about Congressman English's bill, Simplified USA, is that it has figured out how to level the international playing field in a way that is consistent with American tax tradition and history.

I submit, for your consideration, Mr. Chairman and members of the Committee, that the usual reasons for not proceeding with tax reform do not apply to the USA tax by Mr. English.

Genuine tax reform within the basic framework that he has outlined, which can be improved, is an available option for the Congress to choose if the Congress wishes to do so.

I strongly recommended Simplified USA to you as a great place to start on the road to genuine tax reform.

Thank you very much for your attention.

[The prepared statement follows:]

Statement of Ernest S. Christian, Esquire, Washington, D.C.

Introduction To Simplified USA Tax

The Simplified USA Tax by Congressman Philip English (H.R. 134) is a landmark achievement that shows how genuine tax reform can become a reality without resorting to radical experimentation. The tax code can be simplified without repealing the deductions for home mortgage interest and charitable contributions; the double tax on saving and investment can be removed without enacting a "consumption" tax; tax equity for working men and women can be achieved by allowing them a credit for the payroll tax they pay; the archaic tax barriers to U.S. competitiveness in world markets can be removed in a way that protects and enhances American jobs; a simple deduction for the cost of post-secondary education can, for the first time in history, help put investments in human capital on a par with investments in physical capital; marginal tax rates can be lowered; progressivity can be preserved; and transitional dislocations can be avoided.

Simplified USA embodies a new approach that has the effect of including in the U.S. tax base for the first time in history all amounts derived by foreign companies from selling goods and services in the U.S. market. It seems to me that the result is an enormous tax cut for the U.S. economy—perhaps $100 billion per year or more—paid for by foreign companies that presently derive income from U.S. markets on a nearly tax-free basis.

The biggest beneficiaries of this tax cut would seem to me to be the wage earners of America who receive a full credit for the payroll tax they pay now.

How Simplified USA Works—Structural Framework

Like current law, Simplified USA consists of a business tax and a personal tax with multiple personal rates. The illustrative tax rates below trace back to H.R. 4700 in the 105th Congress and were carried over without change into H.R. 134 when Simplified USA was reintroduced in the 106th Congress.

(1) *A Business Cash Flow Tax* is paid by corporations and other businesses. The rate is 12% of gross profit. Profit is computed using cash accounting; capital equipment is expensed because the income it produces is fully taxed when received; no deduction is allowed for interest or dividends paid for the use of capital, or for wages paid for labor, but a full credit is allowed for the 7.65% OASDHI payroll tax which is the equivalent of a deduction for about 65% of wages up to $72,000 per year for each employee. Export income and all foreign-source income is excluded from tax. A 12% import tax is collected when foreign-based companies sell into the U.S. market.

(2) *A Progressive-Rate Personal Tax* is paid by individuals when they receive interest, dividends, wages, salaries, and gains. The two bottom rates are 15% and 25% and the top rate is 30% on taxable income computed after deducting a Family Allowance of $8,000, personal exemptions of $2,700 per family member, home mortgage interest, charitable contributions and post-secondary education expenses of up to $4,000 per family member. Individuals are allowed a full tax credit for the employee's share of the 7.65% OASDHI payroll tax withheld from their wages and, if the amount of that credit exceeds their USA income tax for the year, the excess is refunded. All individuals are also allowed an unlimited USA Roth IRA for personal saving—except that, unlike the current Roth IRA, saving is not limited to retirement and can be withdrawn for any purpose. Because tax is paid on the money going into this special savings and investment account, there is no additional tax on the inside build-up in the account or on withdrawals from the account. For the first time in history, the double tax on all personal savings will be removed and everyone will be allowed to save for whatever purpose they desire.

Simplified USA is a plain-language, stripped-down version of the current income tax (individual and corporate) that is concentrated on the main goals of tax reform—which are (1) to be evenhanded as between labor income and capital income; (2) to be neutral in a person's choice to consume income or save; (3) to remove the archaic barriers to international competitiveness; and (4) to be neutral as between equity and debt financing and evenhanded among all forms of business organization.

The basic amendments necessary to achieve these results are neither unfamiliar nor shocking. First-year expensing of plant and equipment is already allowed for small businesses and probably would have been made universal long ago except for revenue limitations under the current code.

The idea of removing the double tax from personal saving—and thereby taxing saved income no more heavily than consumed income—has been around a long time. Since the enactment of the Roth IRA in 1997, the simple yield-exemption approach to removing the double tax is now familiar and standard fare. With the Roth IRA already very much part of the tax landscape, it only remains for Simplified USA to make it universal by eliminating the dollar caps, the income limitations and the restriction to retirement savings.

For decades, Treasury reports and bipartisan Congressional studies on corporate/shareholder tax integration have recommended uniform treatment of all forms of financing and all forms of business.

There is nothing new about the idea of excluding foreign-source income from taxation or about the related idea of not taxing exports. The Foreign Sales Corporation (FSC) provision in the current code is a flawed attempt to go halfway, but FSC has run afoul of the WTO and it remains for Simplified USA to do the job correctly in a way that is consistent with U.S. tax traditions and WTO requirements.

166

The Road to Simplification

Once the basic amendments necessary to achieve neutrality and international competitiveness are made, some of the most complex portions of the code become moot. Substantial simplification automatically occurs. Simplified USA also undertakes to eliminate an array of miscellaneous deductions, credits, exceptions and exceptions to exceptions that are unnecessary when the basic rules are correct to start with. But Simplified USA does not make a fetish out of repealing long-standing and familiar deductions under the misguided belief that they are the source of complexity in the code.

The existing and long-standing exclusions from income for parsonage allowances, combat pay, municipal bond interest or employer-paid health insurance are not the reason that Form 1040 is monstrously long and incomprehensible. Simplified USA retains these and several other exclusions and deductions that are easily understood and of nearly universal application without any special eligibility requirements and that do not require any side calculations. What, for example, is complicated about the deduction for home mortgage interest? All the homeowner does is take one number off the annual statement from the mortgage lender and put that one number on one line of the tax return.

Simplified USA will reduce the size and complexity of the tax code by about 75 percent and the personal tax return (long Form 1040) will be only a few pages—about like it was in 1960 before four decades of complexity ruined it.

Neutrality Between Saving and Spending

Simplified USA taxes income (whether saved or consumed) only once. It does that by taxing income when received (first tax) and then excluding the earnings on after-tax savings from a second tax.

The current code's bias against income that is saved is easily illustrated by a simple example: Mr. Jones earns $100, pays a $40 income tax, and has $60 after-tax income left over. If he uses the after-tax $60 to buy a car to drive to work (in lieu of paying bus fare), he will not have to pay tax on the value of the transportation services the car provides him; nor should he. After all, he has already paid tax on the $60 once. On the other hand, if instead of buying the car, Mr. Jones saves the after-tax $60, he will have to pay bus fare (having no car) and he will have to pay tax on the interest earned by the $60 of savings. This is not a correct result. It biases Mr. Jones's choice against saving.

Simplified USA produces the correct result: once Mr. Jones has paid his tax, he is not taxed again, either on the interest earned by his after-tax savings or on the value of the transportation services provided by the car.

International Competitiveness

Simplified USA is carefully crafted to allow American companies to compete and win in world markets without in any way providing a tax incentive for American companies to move their plants and jobs offshore. In fact, it makes the United States of America a very attractive place to be for the purpose of conducting a worldwide business.

Simplified USA does this by the combination of three things. First, it replaces the current archaic and inconsistent worldwide tax rule with a territorial rule consistent with modern practice in other countries. Thus, when necessary, U.S. companies will be able to invest and compete directly in foreign markets without having to pay U.S. tax on the profits they make in some other country's economy and bring home for investment in America. Second, export income will be excluded from U.S. tax. Thus, a U.S. company can stay home, manufacture in the U.S. and sell into a foreign market without paying U.S. tax. Third, an import tax will be imposed at the same rate as the regular USA business tax rate—12%. Thus, while a company may operate abroad when necessary to gain foreign-market sales that cannot be reached by exports from the U.S., if it goes abroad for the purpose of selling back into the U.S. market, it will have to pay a U.S. tax at the border without the benefit of any deductions.

International competitiveness will flourish under Simplified USA, but there will be no runaway plants.

The Way Border Tax Adjustments Work—A Major Shift in the Tax Burden

The border tax adjustments in USA have been borrowed from the European VAT (which is a form of sales tax) and appended to the business portion of the USA Tax in a WTO-permissible way—but when appended to a business cash flow tax like the USA business tax, the border tax adjustments operate quite differently from they way customarily are thought of in the VAT context.

Because the USA business tax is a tax on net cash flow instead of a tax on goods, USA excludes from tax the revenues derived by a business from exports. This full exclusion of export revenues is similar to the partial exclusion provided by the Foreign Sales Corporation (FSC) rule in the current corporate income tax which the USA business tax resembles in many ways.

Except for exports, USA includes in the tax base all GDP—which, in turn, is equal to the sum of all returns to labor (wages and salaries) and all unreinvested returns to capital (interest and dividends).

By means of an import adjustment, USA also includes in the tax base an additional amount which represents the amount of goods and services that are produced by foreign-sited labor and capital but sold into the United States market. The 12 percent import tax might appear to make imported products more expensive, and, in some cases, it will, but both neoclassical economic theory and common sense say that in many more instances involving a very large portion of the total dollar value of imports, the foreign companies who sell these imports into the U.S. market will have to absorb all or a major part of the 12% import tax. They will do this by adjusting their pre-tax price downward so that the after-tax price to the U.S. purchaser is the same or nearly the same amount that purchasers had previously been paying. When foreign companies do lower the pre-tax prices, they are, in effect, paying the U.S. tax and when a company pays a tax (whether it be U.S. tax or home country tax), the burden of that tax will ultimately be borne by its employees (in the form of lower wagers or fewer jobs) and its shareholders and debtholders (in the form of lower returns to capital).

As of the end of 1999, imports were $1.3 trillion involving an almost uncountable number of U.S. buyers and foreign sellers of an almost uncountable variety of imported goods and services. Out of all this, no one knows how many of the foreign companies will be "price takers" who will absorb all or part of the import tax or how many will be "price setters" who will not absorb any of the import tax. Therefore, no one knows the precise dollar value of the import tax that will be passed back to foreign labor and capital, but we do know that much of it will be. The U.S. market is, after all, the largest market in the world and the pressure on foreign companies to absorb at least a part of the tax will be large. Only those who sell a unique product for which there is no substitutable alternative will be totally immune from that pressure, but there are not so many of those situations and, even when they do exist, what may be a unique product today may not be tomorrow.

The point is not to be precise about the exact amount of import tax that will be borne by foreign labor and capital. Rather, the point is to know that the dollar amount is large and that even if 60 percent of the $160 billion import tax revenue increase is borne by foreign labor and capital, that mans that the U.S. economy has received roughly a $100 billion per year tax cut.

Payroll Tax Credit—An Offset to Implicit and Explicit Taxes on Wages

Not only is the payroll tax credit an historic breakthrough in fairness, it is essential to the evenhanded treatment of labor and capital that is the hallmark of Simplified USA and the foundation on which genuine tax reform must be built.

A. Implicit Withholding Tax Offset by Payroll Tax Credit

Like the current corporate income tax, the USA business tax is an implicit withholding tax on dividends. (Unlike the current corporate income tax which favors debt over equity, the USA business tax also serves as an implicit withholding tax on interest as well.) This implicit withholding on interest and dividends arises because the business pays tax on its as gross profit without any deductions for interest paid or dividends paid.

Like the current employer-paid OASDHI payroll tax, the USA business tax also serves as an implicit withholding tax on wages—because the business pays tax on its gross profit without deducting wages.

But for the credit that Simplified USA allows for the 7.65% employer-paid payroll tax (which reduces the implicit withholding), the implicit withholding on wages up to $72,000 per employee per year would be 19.65% (12% + 7.65%); whereas the implicit withholding on wages in excess of $72,000 and on interest and dividends would be only 12% (the USA business tax rate).

With the payroll tax credit, the implicit withholding tax is uniform as follows:

Wages up to $72,000	Wages above $72,000	Interest and Dividends
12%	12%	12%.

168

B. Explicit Tax Offset by Payroll Tax Credit

When wages, interest and dividends are received by individuals, the remainder of the tax on that income is collected from the individual, and, in the case of wages, all or part of that tax may be withheld at the source by the employer as under current law.

In the case of wages up to $72,000, however, current law imposes an additional 7.65% employee-paid OASDHI tax that is explicitly withheld at the source by the employer.

Simplified USA allows the employee a credit for the 7.65% OASDHI tax explicitly withheld from wages. With this credit, wages, interest and dividends are all taxed equally, the only variation being the rate bracket of the particular individual—15%, 25% or 30%.

Resisting Analogies—Simplified USA Is Sui Generis

The Simplified USA Tax combines some elements that may also be found, variously, to some extent, and in different forms, in taxes said to be based on cash flow, net income, consumed income or business value added, but because Simplified USA is a hybrid, none of those analogies is altogether accurate or especially illuminating.

Simplified USA is best understood as the current income tax amended to allow (1) first-year expensing of capital equipment, (2) an unlimited Roth IRA for everyone that applies to all saving (not just retirement saving) and (3) a credit for OASDHI payroll taxes. Internationally, it adopts a "Super FSC" for outbound transfers (exports) and a "Super § 482" adjustment on inbound transfers (imports).

If one insists on putting Simplified USA into some preexisting generic category, the USA Tax on individuals is an "income tax" and the USA Tax on businesses is a "business cash flow tax" (a concept which is well-known and long-standing in the tax literature).

Chairman ARCHER. Thank you, Mr. Christian.

Our next witness is Dr. Foster. We will be pleased to receive your testimony.

STATEMENT OF J.D. FOSTER, PH.D., EXECUTIVE DIRECTOR AND CHIEF ECONOMIST, TAX FOUNDATION

Mr. FOSTER. Thank you, Mr. Chairman. It is a pleasure to appear before the Committee again.

Tax reform obviously raises a great many issues. I am going to focus on two in the international area.

The U.S. currently imposes tax on our citizen's foreign earnings and allows a limited tax credit against foreign income taxes paid.

Most tax reform proposals, such as Simplified USA, wisely drop this policy, taxing instead only economic profits earned at home, a system known as territoriality.

In the global economy, companies hire, produce, and sell globally. The companies that best integrate these activities over functions, product lines, and geographic areas, are the most successful.

Current tax policy distorts our companies' pattern of investment so they cannot maximize their global efficiency. The price of this lost efficiency is jobs at home and abroad, and the price gets higher every year.

If current policy is so wrongheaded, why do we keep it? Because of misperceptions and misleading statements.

Our international tax policy is a tax based form of protectionism and nothing more.

Protectionism seeks to bar foreign production that out-competes domestic production. Recognizing that protectionism is unsound, we have had a long history in this country in support of free trade.

However, our tax policy erects tax barriers to international investment by our citizens in the usually mistaken belief that it would otherwise occur at home. This tax barrier to international investment is solely intended to protect jobs at home. The result, however, is that our current policy prevents our companies from maximizing their productivity, thereby costing us jobs.

Worse, the lost jobs are most likely to be higher-wage, high-productivity jobs because therein lies our competitive advantage. So we protect a few relatively low-wage jobs at the expense of other higher-wage jobs—the typical result of protectionism.

Most tax reform proposals, including the English proposal, embrace free trade by allowing U.S. companies to achieve their greatest efficiencies globally and so create more high wage jobs at home.

Fundamental tax reform also opens the way for border tax adjustments or BTAs in the form of an export rebate and a new import levy.

An export rebate excludes from tax the profits made on the export of domestic production. If the United States adopted territoriality, then export rebates naturally address concerns that territoriality would induce U.S. companies to shift operations overseas. A company would pay no U.S. tax on goods and services sold abroad, whether those goods are produced at home or abroad.

Once markets adjust to the new tax regime, the value of the tax rebate would shift back to U.S. labor in the form of higher wages or back to U.S. capital in the form of higher returns, permitting an expansion of the capital stock and therefore increasing employment and output for foreign markets.

The counterpart to the export rebate is the import levy. Initially, some of this levy would increase the price of imports. The vast majority of these price increases would quickly disappear, however, as U.S. consumers and businesses substituted domestic for foreign production.

This in turn would force foreign suppliers to absorb much of the tax. Thus, both the export rebate and the import levy would encourage the creation of high wage jobs at home.

Business taxes, in almost all instances, fall on labor and capital, but especially capital. If we imposed a BTA import levy, it would also fall on capital and labor. However, if would fall on the capital and labor of the countries producing goods and services sold into the United States.

In other words, a BTA import levy effectively imports tax base from abroad, shifting some amount of the domestic tax burden to foreign workers and foreign capital owners.

For example, if the U.S. had a trillion dollars, of imports a year, and we imposed a 12 percent import levy, that would raise $120 billion in receipts. Even if the net shift of this tax liability to foreign taxpayers were only half the suggested amount, that would still mean a $60 billion annual cut in taxes for U.S. citizens.

The important point here is that the BTA import levy shifts U.S. tax burden onto foreign taxpayers, providing U.S. citizens with a very significant effective tax cut, without reducing revenues to the U.S. Treasury one cent.

One might expect that the Europeans and our trading partners would not care for our shifting our tax burden onto their citizens very much.

I would note, however, that many of our trading partners have tax systems that allow them to do that very thing to us, and they have been doing it to us for decades. One way to look at this is we are recapturing tax base that they have been stealing from us for decades.

Tax reform creates a welcome occasion to abandon a counterproductive protectionist tax policy and allow our workers and our companies to maximize their productivity. It also means that we can implement border tax adjustments that would further improve the competitiveness of U.S. labor and U.S. companies.

In both cases, the clear result is higher employment and higher wages.

Thank you.

[The prepared statement follows:]

Statement of J.D. Foster, Executive Director and Chief Economist, Tax Foundation

My name is J.D. Foster and I am the Executive Director and Chief Economist of the Tax Foundation. The Tax Foundation is a non-partisan, non-profit research and education institution. It was established 63 years ago to provide the American people and policy makers with relevant, timely, and accurate information and analysis on fiscal policy matters at the federal, state, and local levels.

The sustained interest in tax reform should come as no surprise. More than any other aspect of government the federal income tax directly and repeatedly influences Americans' lives. We may be most aware of this now during the tax season, but every week our lives are touched and our decisions colored by the income tax. How much should I save in my 401(k)? Should I sell some stock and pay the capital gains tax to buy the stock I would prefer? Should I go to college, to graduate school or night school to get a better job and earn a higher salary if it means a much higher tax rate? Should I take out a home equity loan to buy a car? Should I buy a home or rent? If I rent and lose the home mortgage interest deduction, can I afford to make as big a charitable contribution to my church, synagogue, or mosque?

The income tax is like an old machine tilling the fields of the economy, reaping a harvest of revenue for the federal government. Fourteen years ago the Congress performed a major overhaul through the Tax Reform Act of 1986. In the intervening years the Congress has passed hundreds of changes in the nature of ongoing maintenance. But it has also passed scores of changes asking the old machine to do even more: To supplement welfare spending, to encourage saving for education, and so on. Meanwhile the fields have changed steadily as has the pressure to produce, putting ever greater demands on the tax machine. Even under ordinary circumstances, another major overhaul would be past due today.

Circumstances are far from ordinary, however. The growing breadth of the economy combined with the rapid escalation of computing power have spawned a degree of complexity in the tax code affecting both individuals and businesses that was unthinkable not long ago. This complexity has led to a growing animus and distrust of the tax system, the Internal Revenue Service, and the federal government in general.

It is unwise to impose upon citizens any system that is torturously complex and affects so many areas of their lives. This complexity of the code leads to a sense of imbalance and unfairness. Some instances are obvious, like the marriage penalty which the Congress is seeking to address this year. Others are a matter of perception. We come to believe our neighbor knows of some twist to the tax code that allows him to pay less tax than we do.

Circumstances are also extraordinary because there is a growing sense that an income tax is not the best type of tax for any country. At issue is not whether the income tax machinery can be made to work better, but whether it is the right machine for the job. When the income tax was advanced and adopted, it was well understood that it overtaxed saving and investment. It was also understood that this bias would reduce economic growth, but this was considered a reasonable price to pay for the redistribution of income and wealth for which the income tax is so adept.

Today, the prosperity foregone is unacceptable and the transfer of income and wealth can be achieved by other means. Further, the income tax's deleterious effects on international competitiveness that could essentially be ignored fifty, forty, or even twenty years ago cannot be ignored today.

To be sure, the federal income tax is not about to collapse. There is no crisis. We could skip fundamental tax reform, choosing instead to make repairs minor and major and keep this old machine running a while longer. We could also have set aside welfare reform, and foregone its many benefits. We could postpone Social Security Reform and Medicare reform. We could choose to do all these things, but that would not be the wise or rational choice, not when the lives of millions of Americans can be bettered by sound reforms.

What Is "Fundamental" Tax Reform?

The phrase "fundamental tax reform" is now code in tax policy. To some it stands for a specific proposal, like the Flat Tax or the National Sales Tax or the Simplified USA Tax. To some it stands for a threat to stability and the status quo. To others it stands for an alternative set of principles that should guide tax policy and that undergird most tax reform proposals: principles such as simplification, fairness, and economic neutrality. As these principles are nearly universally applauded, it is immediately clear how extensive the changes must be for legislation to rise from being a run-of-the-mill tax bill to the level of "fundamental" reform. The 1997 Taxpayer Relief Act, for example, included a great many provisions, but no one would argue that this constituted "fundamental" reform.

Neutrality and Saving

One distinguishing feature of fundamental tax reform is the meaning of the word "neutrality." Does one mean neutral within the framework of a classical income tax, or neutral in some other sense? Our current system is a mutated income tax that often taxes the returns to saving even more heavily than would be appropriate under a normal income tax. The unintegrated corporate income tax, the capital gains tax, and the gift and estate tax are monuments to excessive taxation. On the other hand, the federal income tax contains many features consistent with a consumption tax, such as the pension and savings provisions that effectively ensure that only one level of tax is paid at the individual level on labor income that is saved.

Given its current usage, at the individual level "neutrality" today clearly means taxing all labor income once and only once, uniformly and consistently. In other words, for individuals fundamental tax reform means shifting the tax base from a combination of labor and capital income, to labor income. For businesses, it means taxing only profits earned in the United States. Neutrality for businesses also means only taxing economic profits rather than financial profits, which is achieved by allowing businesses to expense their purchases of plant and equipment. Thus, it means changing a fundamental principle on which the tax system is based.

Neutrality and Education

Neutrality also means imposing no higher a tax burden on human capital income than on physical capital income. In the e-world, a well-educated work force is vital. The "e" in e-commerce could just as well represent "education" as "electronic." The New Economy is built on technology, communications, and information, all of which have value only to the extent employees, investors, entrepreneurs, and managers can use the technology to communicate and process the information productively. In other words, it depends on people with the education to use the tools effectively.

The tax code should not create a bias in favor of education, neither should it have a bias against education as it often does today. Neutrality means businesses should be able to expense their physical capital acquisitions. It also means individuals should be able to deduct in full the costs associated with their education. We already do this to an extent insofar as local school systems are funded with federally tax-deductible property taxes. This same treatment should extend to all reasonable expenses incurred by individuals seeking to invest in their own human capital.

Pursuing Fundamental Tax Reform

Defining the goal of tax reform leaves a remarkable number of options from which to choose. For example, one can "scrap the code" as many advocate, suggesting that remedial action is infeasible or impractical, and replacing the income tax with some apparently new system. I say apparently new because, in fact, none of the main proposals advanced to date are truly as new and revolutionary as their advocates would have us believe.

The Congress could achieve the essential substance of the Simplified USA Tax, for example, by allowing an unlimited Individual Retirement Account and other pension savings, while allowing businesses to expense all of their purchases of plant and equipment. Similarly, while the Federal government has no experience with broad sales taxes, it collects numerous targeted excises while most states collect general sales taxes. Thus even a National Retail Sales Tax, clearly the most radical of the popular proposals, and the most problematic, is not entirely alien. The "revolution" in fundamental tax reform is not the novelty of the new tax system, per se, but the shift in the tax base from a mutated definition of income to consumption.

An alternative to "scrapping the code" would be to "clean the code." It is entirely possible to achieve all the goals of fundamental tax reform by radically amending the existing system. For example, step one would be to allow people to save as much as they want in tax-deferred accounts, without regard to their current incomes or to when they choose to take the money out of the accounts for consumption. Alternatively, one could tax all labor income however employed, and forego taxing all forms of future capital income.

Step two would be to eliminate the Alternative Minimum Tax and all the other horrors of current law. The true source of complexity in the tax code is not the home mortgage and the charitable contribution deductions, and the others listed on Schedule A. For individuals the true complexity lies in the phase-in and phase-out of the Earned Income Tax Credit, the phase-out of the other tax credits and other bells and whistles enacted in recent years, the phase-out of itemized deductions, the phase-out of personal exemptions, the Alternative Minimum Tax, and the modern nightmare that is Schedule D for capital gains and losses. For businesses the true complexity lies in the system of depreciation allowances, the taxation of foreign source income, and the special rules and rulings that go into defining taxable income.

Step three would be to allow individuals a deduction for personal expenses associated with education—to put human capital formation on par with physical capital formation.

Step four would be to allow businesses to expense their purchases of plant and equipment.

Step five would be to tax only income earned in the United States, rather than seeking to cast an extraterritorial net in a feat of veiled protectionism.

A great many other steps would be needed to "clean the code" properly. The federal income tax is very much like a vast mansion that has collected dust and all manner of rubbish over decades of relative neglect, and in many areas may have fallen into disrepair. It is possible to clean the mansion again, to repair the walls, and to modernize the facilities. Whether one should level the income tax edifice and start over or just give it a thorough cleaning is a tactical and political decision. The former may be more unsettling though more thorough; the latter may appear easier, but it is less certain to achieve the desired result.

A No-Cost Tax Cut

Some level of compliance and administrative costs are inevitable with any tax system. Any amount in excess of the minimum wastes the nation's resources. It is, in effect, a tax with no offsetting benefit. Reducing those costs is therefore equivalent to a tax cut in that it leaves more resources in the private sector. But it is a tax cut that, at worst, leaves the Federal government with no fewer resources than it had before.

Estimates of the compliance costs associated with the Federal income tax often reach into the hundreds of billions of dollars. Four years ago the Tax Foundation concluded that a lower-bound for such an estimate was $157 billion. Today, that figure might be closer to $175 billion. This is a lower bound, so the actual figure is almost certainly much higher. For argument's sake, suppose it is $200 billion.

Using the same methodology employed to find the lower bound for compliance costs for the income tax, in 1996 the Tax Foundation estimated the compliance costs associated with the Flat Tax and the National Retail Sales Tax. In both cases the analysis showed that compliance costs would fall by about 95 percent once the new plan was fully phased-in, assuming the new tax system was enacted in its pure form. The reduction associated with the Simplified USA Tax would be comparable. Thus, even if transition issues and political considerations caused the percentage reduction in compliance costs to drop to 50 percent, that still means an effective tax cut of $100 billion annually, or $1 trillion over 10 years. That is an enormous amount of saving and should by itself be enough to compel legislative action.

The International Dimension of Tax Reform

The foregoing discussion reveals many sound reasons for pursuing fundamental tax reform, including simplification, reducing compliance costs, improving the neutrality of the tax code so that it is less of a hindrance to economic growth, and reducing the intrusive aspects of the tax system into citizens' lives. Each of these has been discussed extensively in numerous forums, including this Committee. However, the international dimensions of tax reform, particularly the change in the tax treatment of foreign source income and the imposition of Border Tax Adjustments have until recently received far less attention than they deserve.

Protectionism and the U.S. Tax on Foreign Source Income

Subject to a vast array of special provisions, tests, and rules, the essential features of U.S. international tax policy are that the U.S. imposes federal income tax on U.S. citizens' foreign earnings. The U.S. also allows a limited tax credit against any resulting tax liability for foreign income taxes paid. This policy goes under many names, the most common of which is "worldwide taxation," the most accurate of which, however, is "extraterritoriality." Most tax reform proposals wisely move away from extraterritoriality to a system whereby only economic profits earned in the United States are subject to U.S. taxation, a system known as "territoriality".

Extraterritoriality violates tax neutrality as the term is commonly used. A non-neutral tax system is hurtful to wage and job growth because it directs our national resources of land, capital, and labor away from their most productive and beneficial uses. A driving motivation for tax reform must be the recognition that a more neutral tax system is in our best interests, and this is true whether the issue is economic risk-taking, education outlays, the level of saving, the level of investment, the forms of investment, or the locations of investment.

The immediate effect of extraterritoriality is to distort the pattern of international investment by U.S. companies and therefore to reduce their competitiveness at home and abroad. This loss of international competitiveness translates into lower shareholder returns, but it also means a loss of jobs and lower wages at home. One obvious consequence of the global economy is that companies must hire, invest, produce, and sell globally. The companies that are best able to integrate each of these activities across product lines, across functions, and across countries are the most successful. A U.S. tax policy that distorts the pattern of activity of U.S. companies inhibits them from maximizing their efficiency. Space limitations prevent me from elaborating on these points. However, I have written about these matters elsewhere in greater detail, (See "Promoting Trade, Shackling our Traders," Tax Foundation Background Paper No. 21).

If extraterritoriality is so harmful to U.S. interests, it is reasonable to ask why it remains the basis for U.S. international tax policy. The answer is that its true nature has largely been hidden behind fear mongering claims and misleading statements. Extraterritoriality is a sophisticated, tax-based form of protectionism. Tariffs, quotas, and other devices seek to erect a wall against foreign goods that are in some way less expensive or of better quality than domestically produced goods. The only motivation for such policies is to protect the businesses and the their employees who cannot compete fairly with foreign goods. While some benefit from such policies, consumers and other businesses that buy these goods must accept either lower quality or higher prices and, on balance, the nation suffers a loss.

The United States has long and consistently been the world leader in the fight for free trade and open markets. This has been a bi-partisan policy and a sound policy as history has proven time and time again. Free trade countries prosper; closed economies stagnate. Free trade encourages each nation to do those things it does best while giving consumers the widest array of choices at the lowest possible prices. There are, of course, always bumps in the road and occasional backsliding. But the broad support for free trade is remarkable, and well-founded.

The essential goal of extraterritoriality is to ensure that U.S. companies pay at least as much income tax on their foreign activities as they would if those activities had taken place in the United States. This sounds reasonable at first blush, but if this principle is reasonable, why should we not require U.S. companies to be subject to the same labor laws abroad as at home? Certainly our stricter labor laws protect our workforce, but they also raise labor costs and therefore put U.S. workers at a competitive disadvantage. Why not subject these companies to the same environmental laws they face at home? Again, our more stringent rules generally protect the environment, but they also raise producers' costs. Indeed, we have in recent years heard calls for exactly such policies, and it is no coincidence that these same voices have also consistently been at the forefront of the fight against free trade.

Proponents of extraterritoriality will argue that if the U.S. fails to tax the foreign income of U.S. companies, then the tax code will create an incentive for those companies to shift their operations to lower-taxed, foreign jurisdictions. The proper way to express this, however, is that eliminating the tax would eliminate a disincentive for companies to invest globally and most efficiently, unfettered by U.S. tax policies.

Classic protectionism seeks to erect barriers to the importation of goods and services to protect jobs at home. Extraterritoriality seeks to erect barriers to international investment by U.S. citizens in the usually mistaken belief that this investment would otherwise occur at home. Thus this tax barrier to international investment is also intended to protect U.S. jobs.

Perhaps the most unfortunate aspect of the protectionism of extraterritoriality is not that it unfairly protects U.S. jobs, but that it may cost U.S. jobs, on balance, and reduce wages, on balance. As noted above, U.S. companies organize their operations on a global basis. Each element, subsidiary, and division performs a specific set of roles and company management strives to optimize the efficiency of each piece of the corporate whole. The effects of a lost or foregone opportunity in one area will negatively affect the efficiency of many of the company's operations, including those based in the United States. Sometimes these secondary effects are minor and can be overcome; sometimes they are highly significant. Thus a lost or foregone opportunity due to the U.S. imposition of a protectionist, extraterritorial tax policy will often reduce employment in a company's other operations throughout the world, including in the United States.

The U.S. has one of the best educated, most productive work forces in the world. If a U.S. company were considering an increase in its foreign operations, it is very likely those operations would represent lower-wage, less productive jobs. On the other hand, the U.S. operations that would support these low-wage jobs would tend to be higher wage, high productivity jobs, such as those associated with research and development, and support functions such as accounting, finance, marketing, and management. Thus extraterritoriality protects a few low wage jobs at the expense of other, higher-wage U.S. jobs.

The Many Roles of Border Tax Adjustments

Fundamental tax reform permits the adoption of Border Tax Adjustments (BTAs), in the form of a rebate upon export of the U.S. business tax and the imposition of the U.S. tax on the value of imports. BTAs are a common feature of many national tax systems and are an important feature of the Simplified USA Tax.

The importance of BTAs to tax policy is better recognized today in the United States thanks to the recent World Trade Organization (WTO) ruling against the U.S. Foreign Sales Corporation (FSC) provisions. The FSC is an important, though relatively modest attempt to grant an income tax rebate on U.S. exports. Fundamental tax reform and BTAs solve the FSC problem by, in effect, making the export rebate total, universal, and WTO compliant.

The role and consequences of BTAs, however, go well beyond replacing the FSC. Their major effects are to enhance prospects for U.S. companies and U.S. workers to compete globally; to offset similar provisions adopted by our trading partners, further enhancing our international competitiveness; and effectively to "import" tax base from abroad, thereby reducing the federal tax burden on U.S. citizens without reducing revenues to the Federal government. I will address each of these, briefly, in turn.

Export Rebates

An export rebate allows a U.S. producer to exclude from taxable income the profits made on the export of domestically produced goods and services. If the United States adopted territoriality, then export rebates naturally address any remaining concerns that territoriality would induce U.S. companies to shift some operations overseas. If the United States adopted both territoriality and export rebates, then a company would pay no U.S. tax on goods sold abroad whether those goods are produced at home or abroad.

Business taxes are generally and ultimately borne by the factors of production, namely labor and capital. To be sure, there are instances in which a new tax can be shifted, at least temporarily, onto consumers. But in an increasingly global and competitive world economy, consumers have a great ability to opt for alternative, lower-priced goods and services, and this is especially true in the United States because there is very little we do not ourselves produce in quantity. Consequently, consumers can effectively resist bearing business taxes, and hence they are shifted back on to labor and especially on to the owners of capital.

Upon initial introduction, an export rebate would allow U.S. exporters either to enjoy higher profits on their exports or to charge lower prices in an effort to capture a greater market share. Once markets at home and abroad have adjusted to the new tax regimes, the relative prices of U.S. exports would largely return to their previous levels, and the value of the tax rebate would be shifted back to U.S. labor and U.S. capital. Any shift of the rebate to U.S. labor would be in the form of higher wages. Most of the shift of the rebate, however, would be in the form of higher returns to capital that the market would translate into a larger capital stock permitting more output for foreign markets. In other words, the export rebate would be immediately beneficial, but it would be even more so in the long run by raising wages, increasing jobs, and increasing the competitiveness of U.S. exporters.

Import Levies

The counterpart to the export rebate is the import levy on the full value of all imported goods and services. When first introduced, some of this rebate would doubtlessly appear as an increase in the price of imports. The vast majority of these price increases would quickly disappear, however, as U.S. consumers and U.S. businesses substituted domestically produced goods and services for foreign goods and services. In large measure, the ability to substitute domestic for foreign production would force foreign suppliers to absorb much of the tax.

As with the export rebate, once markets have fully adjusted, most domestic prices would return to their pre-tax reform levels at least insofar as the effects of BTAs are concerned. Once the adjustment has been completed, importers of foreign goods and services would have shifted some of their demand to U.S. producers, with obvious beneficial effects for domestic job and wage growth. Thus both the export rebate and the import levy have the same effects in terms of raising U.S. economic activity by increasing the international competitiveness of U.S. labor and U.S. companies.

On Offsetting Exchange Rate Adjustments

One counterargument against the foregoing analysis is that exchange rates would adjust to offset any price effects of Border Tax Adjustments. I believe this argument is essentially correct. What I do not know, and what nobody knows, is how long this exchange rate adjustment would take to occur. It could be instantaneous or, more likely, it could take many years.

Economists know a great deal about the fundamental forces of exchange rate determination over the long run. They also know a great deal about many of the forces that cause exchange rates to evolve over time. For example, we know that exchange rates move to clear the markets for foreign exchange and that these markets are buffeted by changing international capital and trade flows, by changing expectations about how these flows will adjust in the future, by changes in tax policies, and by changing expectations of relative inflationary pressures.

Given all these factors it should not surprise that economists enjoy little success predicting exchange rate movements over the next day or two, and they do no better forecasting when exchange rate movements will take place and how far they will move in the short and medium terms. This is especially true within the context of fundamental tax reform. Whatever influences BTAs might have on exchange rates would almost certainly and for a long time be overwhelmed by the shifting patterns of trade and capital flows into and out of the United States in response to changes in the incentives to save and invest.

What we can say is that if exchange rates move to offset fully the competitive benefits of BTAs, then the worst that can happen is that these benefits will not materialize. Such an adjustment would likely take a long time to occur, however, and unless and until it does the benefits will manifest themselves and they could be very substantial.

"Importing" Tax Base

The tax base is the amount that is subject to tax. In the case of the income tax, for example, the tax base is the total of labor and capital income generated in a year. The federal gasoline excise tax base is the amount of gasoline purchased by consumers in a year. The tax base is often manipulated to exclude certain items and in the case of the income tax to include others more than once. The net of these manipulations yields an amount which, when subjected to the tax rates, produces tax revenue. The growing Federal tax take in recent years primarily result from the growth in the economy, which is another way of saying it results from the growth of the tax base.

Repeating a basic principle, business taxes in most instances fall on capital and labor, the factors of production. If the U.S. were to impose an import levy in the form of a Border Tax Adjustment, this levy would also fall on capital and labor. However, it would fall on the capital and labor of the countries producing the goods and services for importation into the United States. In other words, a Border Tax

Adjustment import levy effectively imports tax base from abroad, shifting some amount of the domestic tax burden to foreign workers and foreign capital owners.

To give some idea of the magnitude of these effects, suppose once tax reform has been enacted with its Border Tax Adjustments that the U.S. imported $1 trillion of goods and services a year. Assuming a 12 percent levy, that would imply $120 billion in import levy receipts. If, when all adjustments were completed, U.S. consumers resisted all efforts by foreign exporters to raise prices to compensate for the import levy, then the U.S. would have effectively imported $1 trillion of tax base and shifted $120 billion of tax liability onto foreign taxpayers.

Of course, in some instances foreign producers would be able to force U.S. consumers to bear some of the tax in the form of higher prices, and in rare instances U.S. consumers would bear all of the tax. Clearly, however, such situations would create powerful incentives for affected consumers to shift consumption toward lower-price domestic goods and services. Thus much of the expected decline in imports from imposing an import levy would occur in precisely those areas where consumer resistance to the tax-induced price hikes was incomplete.

Even if the net shift of tax liability to foreign taxpayers were only half the amount of the hypothesized upper-bound, this would still imply a reduction in taxes paid by U.S. citizens of $60 billion annually. Whatever the figure in a given year, the important point is that the Congress has within its means the ability to shift tax burden onto foreign taxpayers, providing U.S. citizens with a very significant effective tax cut, without reducing revenues to the U.S. Treasury one cent.

Given the reaction of many of our trading partners to our Foreign Sales Corporation provision, one might reasonably expect them to object to the adoption of Border Tax Adjustments. True, they would not likely be happy over this development, but they would have no cause for complaint. Many of our trading partners, especially the Europeans, have employed such BTAs for decades as part of their consumption tax systems. In other words, they have been importing tax base from the United States for many years, effectively imposing their tax burden on U.S. citizens. By adopting BTAs, the U.S. would simply be recapturing U.S. tax base these trading partners have claimed for all these years.

Conclusion

There is a great deal to commend comprehensive, fundamental tax reform. Most of the problems associated with the federal income tax are well established and virtually all of them can be effectively addressed through sound reform. Fundamental tax reform can dramatically reduce complexity and compliance costs. It can free individuals from much of the intrusiveness that is the hallmark of the income tax. It can put people and education at least on par with machines by making the tax system neutral with respect to human and physical capital formation. It can free the economy to create more and better jobs, higher wages, and more wealth.

Fundamental tax reform also creates a welcome occasion to abandon a counterproductive protectionist policy of taxing foreign source income in favor of a policy that will allow U.S. companies to maximize their international competitiveness and thereby contribute even more to the promise of greater prosperity at home.

It goes even further by creating the opportunity to consider implementing Border Tax Adjustments that would further improve the competitiveness of U.S. labor and U.S. companies.

And, not to be overlooked, it creates a powerful opportunity to provide American taxpayers with an effective tax cut, both in the reduction of compliance costs and in the importation of foreign tax base. This tax cut potentially could total in the hundreds of billions of dollars annually, without reducing receipts to the Federal Treasury. This is literally, money left on the table that the Congress can sweep up and bestow on the U.S. taxpayer.

Chairman ARCHER. Thank you, Dr. Foster.

Our last witness, Gary Hufbauer, welcome back to the Committee. We will be pleased to hear your testimony.

177

STATEMENT OF GARY HUFBAUER, REGINALD JONES SENIOR FELLOW, INSTITUTE FOR INTERNATIONAL ECONOMICS

Mr. HUFBAUER. Thank you very much, Chairman Archer and members of the Committee. Thank you for inviting me to testify this morning.

Chairman ARCHER. Mr. Hufbauer, would you just briefly identify yourself for the record?

Mr. HUFBAUER. Sure. I am Gary Hufbauer at the Institute for International Economics here in Washington, D.C.

The United States has a dysfunctional tax system for business activity and in other areas as well, but I am going to concentrate on business activity.

Our system poses burdens that are unknown to competitor firms based in Europe, Asia, Latin America. It is true today that the U.S. economy is the marvel of the world. Every place you travel, you hear this.

But our magic ingredients are being adopted by our competitors abroad. Those ingredients are an open economy, a flexible labor force and the Internet.

Meanwhile, we continue to be handicapped by our tax system. We follow an antiquated and impractical general rule. We tax the worldwide income of our firms, but we do not tax the income of firms abroad which are shipping goods and services into the United States.

This rule dates from the earliest days of the Internal Revenue Code when international commerce was in its infancy and of course multinational corporations were unknown.

Successive Congresses, in their wisdom, have modified that general rule, at least in terms of U.S. business operating abroad, so we have the foreign tax credit and we have deferral and we had the DISC and we have the FSC. But these tensions, which date back to 1918, have created the extraordinarily complicated tax system that we are coping with today.

The problems were highlighted by the recent ruling by the WTO against the Foreign Sales Corporation.

As my colleagues on this panel have pointed out, European countries routinely shift their tax burden abroad. They routinely exempt their exporters from value added tax, which amounts to about $100 billion a year. And of course European firms use foreign sales subsidiaries, saving at least another $10 billion a year.

By comparison, the Foreign Sales Corporation, as Congressman Frenzel pointed out, was a tiny little measure, saving about $3.5 billion a year for U.S. exporters.

Meanwhile, we face the problem of international tax competition. At one time that was called "the runaway plant problem." Ross Perot, with his gift of sound bytes, rechristened it "the great sucking sound." That was exaggeration, but it is true that we live in a world where international tax competition is growing more important. We also face the new issue of Internet sales, especially business-to-business sales which our present tax code is incapable of handling.

The Simplified USA business tax would eliminate the steep tilt against U.S. exports because U.S. companies, like their European competitors and their Asian competitors, would pay no tax on exported goods and services.

And it would eliminate the tax motive for "runaway plants" and that motive may get stronger in the years ahead. Under the simplified USA business tax, any firm that produced abroad, whether it is an American firm or a Latin American firm or whatever, would be taxed when it sells goods and services into the U.S. market.

Following these general principles, the simplified USA tax would handle the very rapidly growing business-to-business E-commerce.

At a stroke, the Simplified USA Tax would deal with some of our most pressing international competitiveness problems.

Thank you very much.

[The prepared statement follows:]

Statement of Gary Hufbauer, Reginald Jones Senior Fellow, Institute for International Economics

Chairman Archer and members of the Committee, thank you for inviting me to testify. The United States has a dysfunctional system for taxing business activity. The corporate income tax is enormously complex, it invites firms to establish production abroad and sell goods and services back into the U.S. market, it discourages U.S. exports, it is an open sesame for international tax shenanigans, and it is not equipped for E-commerce. Like learning Latin, learning the Internal Revenue Code is great mental discipline for young lawyers. Otherwise, it is a curse.

The U.S. system imposes burdens on business unknown to our competitors in Europe, Asia, or Latin America. Today the U.S. economy is the marvel of the world. But other countries are learning the magic ingredients: a flexible labor force, an open economy, and the internet. To stay competitive in the world, we need a dramatically simplified system of taxing business activity. Representative Phil English (R.–PA) has pointed the way with his Simplified USA Tax, drawing on the concepts pioneered by former Senator Sam Nunn (D–GA) and Senator Domenici (R.–NM). My testimony concerns the international aspects of business tax reform.

The United States follows an antiquated and impractical general rule: it taxes worldwide business income. This rule dates from the earliest years of the Internal Revenue Code, a time when U.S. international commerce was in its infancy, and the term multinational enterprise had not been coined. Under the general rule, when a U.S. company makes and sells products in France, the U.S. taxes the income. In the converse case, France does not tax the income of French firms operating in the United States.

The worldwide tax approach was born in a different era as a method of administrative convenience, but it is defended today by emotion not logic: "Every U.S. corporation should pay U.S. tax, whether it operates in Indiana or India, New Mexico or old Mexico." Carried to its extreme, the general rule would render U.S. firms totally non-competitive in a global economy, both as exporters and producers.

Successive Congresses, in their wisdom, have modified the general rule with practical exceptions, ranging from the foreign tax credit, to deferral, to the Domestic International Sales Corporation (DISC) and the Foreign Sales Corporation (FSC). But the tensions stretching back to 1918 between the impractical general rule of worldwide taxation and the practical exceptions have generated an extraordinarily complex system for taxing the international income of U.S. firms and the U.S. income of foreign firms. The administrative burden is a nightmare for the IRS and business alike.[1]

These problems were brought into focus by the recent WTO Appeals Court decision against the Foreign Sales Corporation. Elsewhere, I have severely criticized this decision.[2] It ignores legal history and it misreads the WTO text. But Congress must now reckon with a WTO decision that tossed aside the tax bargain painstakingly negotiated between the United States and Europe twenty years ago.

[1] Gary Clyde Hufbauer assisted by Joanna M. van Rooij, *U.S. Taxation of International Income: Blueprint for Reform*, Institute for International Economics, 1992.
[2] Gary Hufbauer, "A Critical Assessment: The World Trade Organization Panel Report (dated 8 October 1999) and Report of the Appellate Body (dated 24 February 2000), *United States—Tax Treatment for "Foreign Sales Corporations'"*, Institute for International Economics web site *www.iie.com*, March 11, 2000.

European countries (and many others) routinely exempt their exports from value added tax. This saves European exporters about $100 billion a year of tax payments on export sales. European firms routinely sell these same exports through tax-haven sales subsidiaries located in exotic places like Bermuda and Hong Kong. This saves European exporters another $10 billion a year of corporate income tax. By comparison, the Foreign Sales Corporation saves U.S. exporters about $3.5 billion a year. Most of the 6,000 firms that use the FSC are small and medium-sized exporters with little or no production abroad.

As the FSC decision illustrates, the WTO honors an archaic tax distinction that has no economic basis. WTO rules allow corporate taxes measured by value added (Europe) to be excused on exports and imposed on imports. But WTO rules forbid similar adjustments for corporate taxes measured by income (United States)—even though the distinction between the two tax bases is more form than substance.[3]

Meanwhile, old and new problems fester in the world of international taxation. One old problem is the "runaway plant," re-christened by Ross Perot as "the great sucking sound." Will U.S. firms pull up stakes and move abroad, and then sell back into the United States—free of U.S. corporate tax? Legislators in many countries understand that low business taxes are a good way of attracting investment, and econometric evidence bears out their sentiments. Perot exaggerated for political effect, but the possibility of fierce tax competition in a global economy cannot be lightly dismissed.

A new problem is E-commerce. Will U.S. firms be taxed on their internet sales to customers abroad? Can foreign firms sell into the U.S. market free of tax?

Congress could, in a single historical stroke, level the field of export taxation, end anxiety about runaway plants, resolve much of the looming debate over E-commerce, and discard volumes of tax complexity. It could achieve all these goals by replacing the corporate income tax with the Simplified USA tax.

Under the Simplified USA business tax, taxable income would be determined by subtracting permitted deductions from taxable receipts. Taxable receipts cover revenue from sales in the United States, but not exports or production abroad. Permitted deductions cover all costs of business purchases from taxpaying U.S. firms. Payments for imports are either not permitted as a deduction or are taxed directly. By excluding exports from taxable receipts, and by either excluding imports from deductible expenses or taxing them directly, the Simplified USA business tax provides "border tax adjustments"—just as in Europe, but without adopting a sales tax.

When U.S. firms sell into foreign markets, their receipts would not be counted in taxable income, and therefore would not be taxed by the United States. *The steep tilt in export tax practices would be leveled because U.S. companies, like their European, Asian and Latin American counterparts, would pay no tax on exported goods and services.*

The Simplified USA business tax would eliminate the tax motive for runaway plants. Any firm that produces abroad and sells in the U.S. market would effectively pay the same tax as a competitor located in the United States. When U.S. or foreign firms sell goods and services into the U.S. market, the U.S. importer would be liable for the Simplified USA tax (alternatively, no deduction would be permitted for the purchase of imported goods and services). For example, shoes made in Brazil and retailed by Walmart in Denver would pay Simplified USA tax, and so would sophisticated software written in Bangalore and sold to Citigroup in New York. The United States would collect the Simplified USA business tax on about $1.3 trillion annually of imported goods and services.

When U.S. firms both produce and sell abroad, they would pay tax to the host country, not the United States. In fact, under current law, the U.S. Treasury collects practically no corporate tax revenue on active business conducted abroad by U.S. firms. But this practical outcome results from the interaction of outlandishly complex rules dealing with foreign tax credits, foreign losses and deferral. The same outcome would be a straightforward result of the Simplified USA tax. U.S. firms would compete on a level tax playing field, whether they produced in China, Germany, Mexico, or anyplace else.

How would the Simplified USA tax handle E-commerce? As explained, business-to-business E-commerce (B2B) would not be included in taxable receipts, and B2B imports would be taxed directly (or deductions for imports disallowed). B2B is by far the largest dollar volume of E-commerce transactions. At a stroke, the most immediate E-commerce tax problem would be resolved.

America's first income tax began 1861 to pay for the Civil War. The Union imposed a 3 percent tax on incomes over $800.00 a year, which exempted most wage

---

[3] Gary Clyde Hufbauer and Carol Gabyzon, *Fundamental Tax Reform and Border Tax Adjustments*, Institute for International Economics, January 1996.

earners. The tax rate was raised to 5% in 1862 on incomes over $10,000.00. Shortly after the Civil War the income tax was repealed, the Bureau of Internal Revenue remained in existence. Budget-balancing statement have turned to income tax even in peacetime to replace revenue lost by import and export duties. That was the purpose of the income tax passed by congress in 1893 and ruled unconstitutional by the Supreme Court in 1895. President Taft pushed a constitutional amendment to revise that decision, and an income tax was passed as soon as the 16th Amendment was ratified in 1913 by only 31 states.

The new income tax was a luxury tax. Top rates remained below 10 percent and most Americans didn't pay at all. Then came World War I, which raised the federal budget from $1 billion in 1916 to $19 billion 1919; income tax rates rose to 3 percent on $2,000 and 70 percent on $1 million. After the war, Treasury Secretary Andrew Million reduced the top rate to 25 percent and got most taxpayers off the rolls by raising the minimum income subject to tax. But he also cooperated with the Congress to create preferences, exemptions, deductions and other tax breaks. The income tax had gotten the federal government deeper into the business of allocating economic resources, mostly out of public view.

During World War II, as federal spending rose from $9.6 billion in 1940 to $95 billion in 1945, income tax rates were raised 19 percent on $2,000 and 88 percent on $220,000, and the number of taxpayers rose from 14 million to 50 million.

The World War II tax is recognizable ancestor of today's federal income tax. The $500 per dependent exemption of 1944, raised to $600 in 1947, was a generous allowance no income tax. Over time, inflation eroded the value of the exemption. The Republican leaders of the 1950's feared voter's resentment of the rich and did not reduce top rates. In the 1960's, JFK stimulated the economy by reducing taxes significantly.

The experiment in maintaining the wartime's high tax rates during peacetime in order to pay for the cold war and redistribute money to the middle class and poor worked-both economically and politically-for a generation and then stopped working economically. In the 70's, runaway inflation, fueled in part by Lyndon Johnson's refusal to raise taxes to pay for the Vietnam War, propelled ordinary families into tax brackets intended for the rich, while the myriad tax breaks available to the wealthy made a mockery of fairness. As state, local, and other tax rates also rose, a middle-class tax revolt helped fuel the Reagan Republic victories of the 1980's and 1994. Politicians have been struggling ever since to reduce income tax rates to peacetime levels that the public and the economy will tolerate.

Quoting the Federalist papers #35 penned in 1788 by Alexander Hamilton, "There is no part of the administration of government that requires extensive information and a thorough knowledge of the principles of political economy, so much as the business of taxation. It might be demonstrated that the most productive system of finance will always be the lest burdensome."

In a few days, I have been able to gather signatures from disgruntled American's who support the Fair Tax plan. Be it known that these signatures cross all lines of division in that they represent ditch diggers to lawyers, truck drivers to stockbrokers, Black, White, Hispanic, and Asians. To further discern a more accurate consensus of the people, all you need do is refer to the petition filed by the people of Arizona. On Thursday, July 2, 1998, 170,000 Americans required of this congress to abolish income tax and establish a National Sales Tax. The Fair Tax Plan before you at this time is what the people want and require of you now.

One thing that amazes me is that the national news media has all but ignored this legislation. The rhetoric we as Americans have been subjected to implied that the wealthy in this country do not pay taxes, and that the tax burden has been shouldered by the "working poor and middle class." To this I quote the designed Commander of Bastognne in his response to the Nazis to surrender in World War II "Nutz." Figures recently released by the National Revue project quiet a different notion. The quintile of taxpayers from lowest to highest to outlined as such:

Lowest −2%
Low 1%
Middle 7%
High 16%
Highest 78%

When confronted with the truth in these matters of income tax and this Administrations quest for an America steeped in fairness, it is apparent that we are trying to shoot a game of pool with a nylon rope.

I would like to thank the members of this committee for the opportunity to address you regarding the Fair Tax plan, and close with another quote from Alexander Hamilton's Federalist Papers #36:

181

"It has been asserted that a power of internal taxation in the national legislature could never be exercised with advantage, as well from the want of a sufficient knowledge of local circumstances, as from as interference between the revenue laws of the union and of the particular States. The supposition of a want of proper knowledge seems to be entirely destitute of foundation. If any question is depending in a State legislature respecting one of the countries, which demands a knowledge of local details, how is it acquired? No doubt from the information of the members of the county. Cannot the like knowledge be obtained in the national legislature from the representatives of each State? And is it not to be presumed that the men who will generally be sent there will be possessed of the necessary degree of intelligence to be able to communicate that information?" I hope so!

If William Jefferson Clinton so feels the pain of the American people, let him with unanimous consent of US Congress and Senate sign the Fair Tax Plan now. I implore you to preserve our freedom, our liberty, and Save this Union by Passing this legislation NOW!!

Thank you.

[Attachment is being retained in the Committee files.]

———

Chairman ARCHER. Thank you, Mr. Hufbauer.

Again, my thanks to each one of you.

I have several questions. I had not intended to get into this today but you have prompted my inquiry.

The USA Tax was originally designed as a consumption tax, as I recall, and introduced by Senator Domenici, is that not correct.

And is it under the revisions that have been presented today still a consumption tax?

Mr. CHRISTIAN. It, Mr. Chairman, it does not double tax saving, and by an economist's definition, that is what a consumption tax is.

The difference between the original USA and the simplified USA in this respect is straightforwardly as follows:

Under the proposal sponsored by Senator Domenici and Senator Nunn, a deduction was allowed for personal saving. When income was earned, if that income was saved, the tax was deferred because a deduction was allowed, and then the tax was imposed when the original amount saved——

Chairman ARCHER. Mr. Christian, because time is limited today, I personally do not feel that I have the time to get into all of those details.

I just simply wanted to know whether this is still a consumption tax?

Mr. CHRISTIAN. By an economist definition, yes.

Chairman ARCHER. But it does tax savings once?

Mr. CHRISTIAN. That is correct.

Chairman ARCHER. Which, by my definition, would not be a straight out consumption tax.

The mere fact you eliminate double taxation means that there is still a single tax on savings, and a true consumption tax does not tax savings at all.

And I am not trying to make an argument against it; I am just trying to understand it.

The payroll tax credit that is a part of the system, as it is presented today, I assume that is refundable?

Mr. CHRISTIAN. That is refundable, that is correct.

Chairman ARCHER. All right. So in effect, what you are really doing is you are replacing payroll taxes with general income tax revenues coming out of the Treasury?

Mr. CHRISTIAN. There is no change in the payroll tax itself.

Chairman ARCHER. No. I understand that. But you are offsetting the burden of the payroll tax with general Treasury money?

Mr. CHRISTIAN. That is correct.

Chairman ARCHER. Okay. Why not simply abolish that part of the payroll tax and let the general Treasury make a contribution each year in an amount equal to what the payroll tax would have been directly into the Social Security fund?

Would not that be much simpler than having everybody have to deal with a refundable tax credit? Because that is the end result.

Mr. CHRISTIAN. You could do it that way.

Chairman ARCHER. You are reducing the revenue in the general Treasury fund by your tax credits, which is the equivalent of the Treasury writing a check to the Social Security Trust Fund.

And it just seems to me that would be far simpler, the end result is the same.

Rather than going through all of this bit of the tax credit, having the payroll tax withheld, so people foregoing that amount of their paycheck until the end of the year when they can get a refundable tax credit, why not just wipe out the employees' side of the payroll tax, and at the end of the year, have the payroll records which are being sent in determine the amount of money and let the Treasury just write a check to the Social Security Trust Fund?

Would that not be much simpler?

Mr. CHRISTIAN. You could do that, Mr. Chairman.

The thought behind this approach was to not mess with Social Security at all, not touch it, and not get into the business of the Treasury writing checks out to people that are not related to their incomes—other than as part of what amounts to a tax refund——

Chairman ARCHER. Okay, but the Treasury will be writing checks to people in this refundable tax credit. But the people will have to wait for the entire year before they get their check.

And it just seems to me that in the name of simplicity, which we are always searching for in the Tax Code, that rather than dealing with all of these multiplicity of tax credits that have to be enforced and administered by the IRS, that we just simply abolish that. Workers would love it, and simply make the transfer in one transfer, rather than a multiplicity of transfers coming out of the general Treasury.

That is just a thought that I had.

I must say to my friend and counselor and comrade-in-arms, Bill Frenzel, that one comment that you made disturbs me a little bit. And that is when you said there can be open upward mobility for the marginal tax rates. That strikes terror into my heart because we saw exactly that happen after the '86 Act reduced the rates, and then there was upward mobility for the rates in '90, and then there was further upward mobility for the rates in 1993, and I just worry a little bit about deja vu all over again, so you might want to comment on that.

Mr. FRENZEL. I do want to comment on that, Mr. Chairman. You are right. That was one of the reasons we opposed the Act, because with the bubble in there, we knew that top rate was going to go up again. And, as you suggested, it did go up a couple years later.

I have indicated in my testimony that I believe the top rate is too high now, but also I have indicated that I believe in a system of progressive taxation.

And I only suggest that any tax rate can be raised or lowered and of course is that kind of a system. You can structure it anyway you want.

Mr. Chairman, if I could go back to your original question to Mr. Christian?

Chairman ARCHER. Sure.

Mr. FRENZEL. About whether it is an income tax or a consumption tax. One of the early developers of this bill was a David Bradford, a professor at Princeton who served in the CEA, I believe. He always called it a "consumed income tax" and I do not know if that is a euphemism, or whether it helps, but that was his description of some of his early thinking.

Chairman ARCHER. I do remember that. I thank you for reminding us of it.

Can you tell me what deductions under the current law are eliminated in the USA Tax?

Mr. CHRISTIAN. One very prominent deduction that is eliminated is the deduction for state taxes.

Chairman ARCHER. State income taxes?

Mr. CHRISTIAN. All state taxes, yes, sir.

Chairman ARCHER. Well, sales taxes are already non-deductible.

Mr. CHRISTIAN. They are non-deductible.

Chairman ARCHER. But would it also eliminate property taxes?

Mr. CHRISTIAN. Yes.

Chairman ARCHER. Okay. So no state income taxes or local property taxes would be deductible?

Mr. CHRISTIAN. That is true.

Chairman ARCHER. All right. What else?

Mr. CHRISTIAN. There are a number of miscellaneous deductions. I cannot recall any further right now, Mr. Chairman. There are quite a few small ones. Everything other than charitable and home mortgage interest, I believe, of the miscellaneous itemized deductions is repealed.

Chairman ARCHER. What about the child credit the Hope Scholarship credit, the EIC credits?

Mr. CHRISTIAN. All of the credits, those that you mentioned, the child credit, the earned income tax credit, and the others are repealed. There are only two credits under the bill. That is for the payroll tax paid and income tax paid through withholding or estimated tax.

Chairman ARCHER. What about deduction for health expenses? You did not mention that?

Mr. CHRISTIAN. The personal itemized deduction or the business deduction?

Chairman ARCHER. No, personal.

Mr. CHRISTIAN. Personal. The medical deduction is not there under this version of the bill.

Chairman ARCHER. So the deduction currently in the Code for medical expenses to individuals is no longer available?

Mr. CHRISTIAN. It is replaced by the Roth-IRA savings mechanism. It is no longer available.

Chairman ARCHER. Okay.

Can you think of any other salient deductions under the current code that are not available?

Mr. CHRISTIAN. No, Mr. Chairman, not at the moment.

Chairman ARCHER. What portion of the stream of federal tax revenues is border-adjustable under your plan?

In other words, today the entire cost to the federal government is included in the price of the products that are exported which has been estimated to raise the price of those products by 20 to 25 percent on average.

What portion of that cost that is represented by the federal tax burden has become border adjustable under the USA proposal?

Mr. CHRISTIAN. The business taxes are approximately, including unincorporated business, about $320 billion. Personal income taxes are about 8.5 or 9.

It is the business tax that is border adjusted. The business tax does not apply to exports.

Chairman ARCHER. Can you just roughly say what percentage of the total stream——

Mr. CHRISTIAN. About 25 percent, I believe.

Chairman ARCHER. How much?

Mr. CHRISTIAN. It would be, the numbers I gave, the mathematical result is about 25 percent.

Chairman ARCHER. About 25 percent of the federal cost of taxation will not be passed through in the price of the product?

Mr. CHRISTIAN. That is certainly correct.

Chairman ARCHER. Okay. Thanks.

And I assume you still have tax exempt foundations?

Mr. CHRISTIAN. The organizations, such as universities, schools, et cetera, that are exempt under present law, continue to be exempt from the business tax under the USA.

Chairman ARCHER. And how do you go about taxing foreign imports mechanically?

Mr. CHRISTIAN. The mechanics under this version, the English Bill, is there is an import tax imposed at the border on the importation of goods from abroad.

Chairman ARCHER. So then the Customs Service then does that when the product enters the country?

Mr. CHRISTIAN. Well, it is primarily the importer. The importer or the importer's agent is a U.S. taxpayer subject to U.S. tax jurisdiction. They are the ones who owe to the Internal Revenue Service the import tax.

Chairman ARCHER. So mechanically it becomes a burden of the importer?

Mr. CHRISTIAN. It becomes a payment responsibility of the importer.

Chairman ARCHER. All right. And lastly, how do you avoid the double taxation of corporate income, or am I mistaken? I think that is what the presentation was that you eliminated the double taxation?

Mr. CHRISTIAN. The double tax on saved income is eliminated by means of the Roth-IRA mechanism. I think you are asking about the two-tier tax where——

Chairman ARCHER. What about dividends? You have got your new uniform business tax type operation on corporations to replace the current corporate income tax which, by the way, I think is a very positive step forward.

What about the taxation of corporate dividends to the owners of the corporation?

Mr. CHRISTIAN. Those are taxed, as are interest payments and as are wages——

Chairman ARCHER. Okay, okay. So you do not eliminate the double taxation of corporate earnings?

Mr. CHRISTIAN. In the sense you are asking it, that is true, Mr. Chairman.

Chairman ARCHER. Okay, all right. I am not trying to pick at you. I am just trying to understand this bill.

Mr. CHRISTIAN. I am grateful for the attention, Mr. Chairman.

Chairman ARCHER. I need to know what the proposal is.

Mr. Rangel?

Mr. RANGEL. Mr. Chairman, I have to go on the House Floor to protect our Committee's jurisdiction. But, before I leave, I want to ask Bill Frenzel a question, since he enjoys the expertise of former Members, as well as an advocate of tax reform.

If we were going to dramatically change the tax system, would you agree that the American people should first be educated about the replacement proposal before they would expect the Members of Congress to have the political courage to eliminate the code?

Mr. FRENZEL. Mr. Chairman, Congressman Rangel, I agree with that. I do not think you can make major changes in the tax code without some kind of a national debate and without the pretty full cooperation between the Executive and the Legislative branches of the government.

Mr. RANGEL. Now, assume we accept, as a matter of fact, that the composition of the Congress currently gives the Republicans a very slight margin for the Majority. And, that if there are any changes as a result of the election in November and the Democrats win the Majority. Our advantage too would be slight. Would you agree, if we are going to make any progress at all towards reforming the existing system, that it has to be done in a bipartisan way?

Mr. FRENZEL. It has been my observation, Congressman Rangel, that your statement is correct. It is very difficult to pass a major piece of tax legislation without cooperation between the parties and the Congress, and between the branches of government as well.

Mr. RANGEL. Well, I do not know really what is going to happen, and no one else does in November. But there is one thing I can tell you as a friend that Democrats have learned in being in the Minority. That is: we can be in the Majority and not cooperate and do absolutely nothing, or we can reach out to the minority and work with the other side in trying to find out how we can move the country and the Congress toward a better system.

I think that, no matter who wins, the best thing for the country and the coming campaign is to state upfront that we cannot do it alone. There is not going to be any Democratic way to reform the tax code and there certainly is not a Republican way to do it.

But working together, we can find a way. And I think if we had the confidence of the American people, then it is no profile in courage to do the right thing in this Committee and on the Floor and the Senate.

But we miss people like you because we could differ and we could fight and then when it was all over. We could still talk about the areas that we agreed on and how we can make progress, and that has been missing.

And while we miss it from a friendship point of view. I think, more importantly, the lack of talking together the lack of cooperation means really that the Congress has not been productive. We have taken advantage of that for political purposes on both sides of the aisle. No one knows what impact that will have in November, but it certainly has not done well for us as a body.

The whole idea that we would turn over our tax writing authority to a non-congressional committee bothers me a great deal.

But in any event, please do not go too far away. We always need you to remind us when we were working well together. And I thank you for hanging in there always.

Mr. FRENZEL. Thank you, Mr. Rangel. If I could comment just briefly. The three largest tax reforms that I can remember were '54, '69, and '86, and in each case we had a president and a Congress of different parties, and they both managed to work together. In '86, even when the Congress did not take my good advice on that bill, there was very close cooperation between the parties, as you will recall. I hope we can get back to that kind of cooperation. Maybe this is an issue that will help draw us back to that kind of working arrangement.

I thank you very much, but I assure you that other than an occasional bit of testimony, I am not looking to threaten any member's position on this Committee.

[Laughter.]

Mr. CRANE: [PRESIDING]. Thank you.

Mr. Collins?

Mr. COLLINS. Mr. Chairman, the only comment I have is to the previous member who questioned, and that is talk is cheap.

Mr. CRANE. Any responses?

[Laughter.]

Mr. CRANE. Mr. Portman?

Mr. PORTMAN. Thank you, Mr. Chairman.

I have got so many questions and I appreciate the comments from my friend from New York. I do not know why he is against the Commission, but as I told him earlier, I think it is exactly the way to do what he wants to do which is educate the public, which is to make it bipartisan and which is to get outside expertise, and then give it as a recommendation to Congress and this Committee just like IRS reform and other things would go through the normal process.

And I think it would be a tremendously positive and helpful step in getting tax reform.

I want to commend all four of you. It is great that you have come up with this plan. I have talked to Ernie a lot about it and J.D.

some. And I have been, as you know, struggling with some of these issues too since IRS reform because you cannot reform the IRS without a simpler tax code.

I do not come out quite with this proposal but I think there are positive things in it.

I have a few questions, and I guess the two key issues of course are first, what would the rate be. You have got some rates here.

I guess my question to you would be, and you all have impeccable integrity. So many of these folks who have come before us have come up with rates that just are not accurate, and without knowing what the rate is, whether you are for a Fair Tax or a flat tax or a USA tax, or something that I have talked to you about Ernie, more that I am thinking about that has to do with a VAT tax and some other aspects, the rate is absolutely critical.

The rate is absolutely critical, and I wonder about these rates. So without questioning you about them today, I would just say I hope that you can come up with current estimates of the rates. Maybe these are them. They seem a little low to me based on what we have done with some other analysis.

I hope you will use Joint Tax models so that we can compare apples to apples.

The second question I would have is border adjustability. Do you have good legal analysis which shows you that somehow we would be able to tax imports at 12 percent, that we would be able to cut out the export tax, and not have it be considered by the WTO to be discriminatory.

There is no precedent for this. No other country does it. And as you know, the VAT tax is something that is tested, battle-tested, and we know that we can border adjust, and why do you think this would be border adjustable.

Mr. HUFBAUER. Congressman, I wrote a little monograph on this and I will send a copy to you.

Mr. PORTMAN. I would appreciate that.

Mr. HUFBAUER. It is called Fundamental Tax Reform and Border Tax Adjustments.

Of course, you do not know how the WTO will rule until the case is actually before it. Nobody can say with 100 percent confidence.

But the Simplified USA Tax, in its business aspects, as proposed by Congressman English, is very similar to existing systems which have been ruled to be border tax adjustable. Thus I think the chances are very good that the U.S. would prevail in any litigation that occurred on this issue.

Mr. PORTMAN. Well those are two sort of fact issues. I mean, it is difficult to know factually when there is not a precedent. As you said, the chances are it would but it is a big risk because it is an incredibly important part of the proposal. And the second is it at an $80,000 level where you have to kick in the 30 percent tax rate?

These are obviously going to be the deciding points on what kind of tax reform makes sense.

If I could ask a couple of other questions quickly that go to some of the things that Chairman Archer was I think trying to get at.

The refundable tax credit experience with the EITC has been miserable. And I would appreciate, Ernie, your response to that, whether you could look at something where maybe you have a more sort of honest direct transfer, as the President's proposing now in Social Security. Everybody has a transition cost in the Social Security proposal.

Because to have the IRS in the position of enforcing a refundable payroll tax credit I think would be very difficult.

Also, what do you do with folks who are on the EITC now? I assume you eliminate the EITC?

Mr. CHRISTIAN. Mr. Portman, the earned income tax credit, as it exists today, is eliminated. The earned income tax credit, as it exists today, is a great problem of complexity, it is a great problem of fraud. None of those considerations seem to me to, in any way, apply to the credit that exists under the English Bill. It is very straightforward. There are no threshold requirements or anything of that nature, and the big difference is as follows:

Under the English Bill, a credit is given for a tax that has been paid. That tax is fundamental to the system. It has been around a long time. It is well-tracked. The payroll tax is a simple mechanism for tracking——

Mr. PORTMAN. Ernie, if I could because my red light is already on.

The challenge here, as I see it, is I think there will still be some compliance issues but I agree with you, it would be better because you will have a record of what the FICA tax would have been.

But as you know, with the EITC, about 85 percent of it is refundable as to payroll, about 50 percent as to income. You still end up with some people who pay no payroll taxes in effect, no income taxes in effect, and get the EITC.

How do you take care of those people, the working poor who currently get EITC?

Mr. CHRISTIAN. I do not know how anyone would be working and not paying payroll tax, but perhaps that is possible.

Mr. PORTMAN. No. I am saying the EITC is so generous that it takes care of all of the payroll taxes, it also credits all of the income taxes that some individuals pay and yet those people get a transfer from the government. They are working people but you are not covering those people. And I just wonder how you would cover them?

Mr. CHRISTIAN. The welfare element is definitely not present in this credit.

Mr. PORTMAN. I am sorry?

Mr. CHRISTIAN. I said the welfare element that is present in——

Mr. PORTMAN. No, I am not talking about welfare, I am talking about the EITC. You need to address that problem, or you need to say you are not addressing it, I guess.

Mr. FOSTER. Mr. Chairman, I would like to take a quick shot at this to put it in a framework.

The refundable part of the EITC is often considered to be a tax-based system of welfare. And in fact, that is how CBO scores it. It is not treated as a tax, it is treated as an outlay.

This tax system, like many tax systems, provides a framework within which we can make changes.

The Chairman was asking earlier about deductions that might be in or out of the system. If a deduction was deemed politically necessary or worthwhile, it can be put back in.

The system as current designed does not have the earned income tax credit. There is absolutely no reason in the world it could not be added on, much as one adds on an extra piece of equipment on a car.

This is a frame work for taxing within which we can make adjustments with rates, higher rates, lower rates, more progressive, less progressive, adding in deductions, taking them out, or adding in credits or taking them out.

Mr. PORTMAN. I understand that, J.D., and we need to do that. With the indulgence of the Chair, I looked at the '86 experience, what has happened since then, and that is the great fear the Chairman has, and again, I really applaud you and Congressman English for taking the leap and proposing this.

On the EITC, it is just a very simple question really and not a simple answer, but you are covering most of the current recipients of EITC because you are covering payroll.

You are not covering, though, folks who currently not only have their payroll taxes offset by EITC, but also their income taxes, and some folks who have both income and payroll tax, and still get a transfer from the government under this Program for the Working Poor, and I think you need to address that. There are lots of ways to do it and I will not make suggestions, but I think it needs to be addressed. Otherwise you have a hole that I think the states and localities and others are not going to be able to fill.

I have some questions on the pension side and on the health care side that maybe we can talk about later. I think they are very important because you do not have an employer match here, so you do not have a 401K type proposal, although you say in the materials, it preserves the 401K.

Mr. CHRISTIAN. It is preserved.

Mr. PORTMAN. I would like to talk to you about the fringes, as well.

Thank you.

Thank you, Mr. Chairman.

Mr. CRANE. Thank you.

Mr. English?

Mr. ENGLISH. Thank you.

And on that point, Mr. Christian, do you want to comment on the 401K situation?

Mr. CHRISTIAN. Yes, sir.

Your bill, as you know, following up Mr. Portman's point, the bill does retain the 401K provision. And it retains the ability for the employer to match. The difference is that the contribution to the 401K under the English approach is not deductible, whereas it is presently. That is the difference between—the employer match is not deductible under this proposal.

But the 401K and that mechanism still exists and employer matching is encouraged.

Mr. ENGLISH. And I thank you.

Mr. Frenzel, you heard the exchange with regard to EITC and the excellent points that my colleague from Ohio made with regard to the hole that he identified that I frankly have been very much aware of, because I have a lot of people on the EITC in my district.

In your testimony, I believe that you commented that perhaps rather than treating this as a tax program, we should—and I hate the notion of tax program—rather than trying to deal with this through the Tax Code, maybe this could be most efficiently administered as a program through the federal government, an expenditure.

Can you comment on that

Mr. FRENZEL. Yes. I was a strong supporter of the EITC when it was first effected here, and I thought the concept was wonderful. But it was a very small program at that time.

Nowadays, because the program has gotten big and because people have found out how to game the system, it has been my judgment that we would do far better to make that into an appropriations entitlement, rather than a tax entitlement, where it could be enforced much better, and probably managed better.

That is a personal comment on my part.

Mr. ENGLISH. And one that I agree with.

Thank you, sir.

Mr. Foster, in your testimony, you touch on the notion that by establishing this border adjustable system, which I believe, having researched it, is GATT consistent, that we are, in effect, importing a foreign tax base.

Would you care to comment on that further?

Mr. FOSTER. Yes, sir.

If you start from the proposition, as I do and most economists do, that business taxes ultimately fall on labor and capital, when you have a border tax adjustment import levy, that levy, too, falls on labor and capital. The question is on whose labor and whose capital.

Now some of this import levy obviously gets translated into higher prices to consumers, and in some cases, that is permanent. But in most cases, consumers will substitute domestic for foreign production so that they are able to resist the attempt by the importer to raise prices. When they are able to effectively resist those price increases, the tax then gets pushed back onto the foreign producer of those goods and services sold into the United States.

Well, if they are being pushed back into the foreign lands, that obviously means that the BTA import levy is paid by the foreign labor and capital. Another way of expressing that is we are importing their tax base.

Mr. ENGLISH. And on that point, Mr. Portland made the excellent point that none of our tax competitors have quite this kind of a tax system as is being proposed here, but many of them do have border adjustable systems.

How many of them, would you say that we compete with, what proportion of our industrialized competitors have border adjustable systems?

Mr. FOSTER. Well, probably 90 percent or more because we are talking all of Europe, Japan, and Canada.

Mr. ENGLISH. And we are at a competitive disadvantage with them.

Finally, Mr. Hufbauer, you make an excellent point that this tax system would eliminate the tax motive for runaway plants. That is something that resonates in a district like mine.

Would you care to elaborate?

Mr. HUFBAUER. Sure.

The runaway plant phrase, as you well know, Congressman, dates back to the Burke-Hastke bill of the early seventies.

The idea was that a U.S. firm would shut down its operation, for example, in Ohio, and would move to, for example, Mexico or Singapore, and would ship exactly the same goods back to the U.S. And it would do this for a lot of reasons. Wages were often cited. Other reasons as well. Taxes were often mentioned as part of that business decision.

To the extent that taxes are part of that business decision, under the simplified USA tax no firm escapes taxes in the U.S. market by moving its production to a foreign country, because when the goods are shipped back into the U.S. market, they would be taxed just as if they had still be produced in Ohio. That is, in my view, a huge improvement over the situation that we have today.

Mr. CRANE. I thank you gentlemen, and I am impressed with the quality of the testimony today. We appreciate your participation.

Mr. Hulshof?

No questions from Mr. Hulshof.

Well, then, this panel has concluded its work and I want to thank you all and congratulate you for your presentations.

And any additional material you may have, submit in writing and it will be part of the permanent record.

Now, with that, I think we are going to change the schedule as it was originally presented, because we are going to break for lunch.

So I would like to call our last panel up first, because our next two panels—well our next one in line is not available, and the one after is going to be longer in session than we have left before the lunch break—so I would like to invite Mr. Steven Worley from Lawrenceville, Georgia, and Mr. James Moore from Smithtown, New York, and Frank L. Davis, Alexandria, Virginia. I do not think he is yet here, but if he appears after you two have made your presentations, we will listen to his.

And gentlemen, we will proceed in the order I presented you, and if you can limit your oral presentations to roughly five minutes, any additional remarks will be made a part of the permanent record, and we will start with you, Mr. Worley.

STATEMENT OF STEVEN WORLEY, COLBERT, GEORGIA

Mr. WORLEY. Thank you, Mr. Chairman.

My name is Steven Worley. I am actually from Colbert, Georgia. I am a horse breeder and I am also in the construction industry.

America's first income tax began in 1861 to pay for the Civil War. The Union imposed a three percent tax on incomes over $800 a year, which exempted most wage earners.

The tax rate was raised to five percent in 1862 on incomes over $10,000. Shortly after the war, the tax was repealed but the Bureau of Internal Revenue remained in existence.

Budget balancing statesmen have turned to income tax even in peace time to replace revenues lost from imports and export duties. That was the purpose of the income tax passed by the Congress in 1893 and ruled unconstitutional by the Supreme Court in 1895.

President Taft pushed a constitutional amendment to revise that decision and an income tax was passed as soon as the 16th Amendment was ratified by only 31 states.

The new income tax was a luxury tax. Top rates remained below ten percent and most Americans did not pay at all, and then came World War I, which raised the federal budget from $1 billion in 1916 to $19 billion in 1919.

Income tax rates rose three percent on $2,000 and 70 percent on one million dollars.

After the War, Treasury Secretary Andrew Million reduced the top rate to 25 percent and got most taxpayers off the rolls by raising the minimum income subject to tax. He also cooperated with Congress to create preferences, exemptions, deductions, and other tax breaks. The income tax had gotten the government deeper into the business of allocating economic resources, mostly out of public view.

During World War II, as federal spending rose from $9.6 billion in 1940 to $95 billion in 1945, income tax rates were raised 19 percent on $2,000 and 88 percent on $200,000. The numbers of taxpayers rose from 14 million to 50 million Americans.

The World War II tax is the recognizable ancestor of today's federal income tax.

The Republicans of the 1950s feared voter resentment of the rich and did not reduce top rates.

In the 1960s, John Fitzgerald Kennedy stimulated the economy by reducing taxes significantly. The experiment in maintain the War-time high tax rates during peace time in order to pay for the Cold War and redistribute money to the middle class and the poor worked both economically and politically for a generation, and then it stopped working economically.

In the 1970s, runaway inflation, fueled in part by Lyndon Johnson's refusal to raise the taxes to pay for the Vietnam War propelled ordinary families into tax brackets intended for the rich, while the myriad tax breaks available to the wealthy made a mockery out of fairness.

As state, local, and other taxes rose, the middle class tax revolt helped fuel the Reagan Republican victories of the 1980s and 1994.

Politicians have been struggling ever since to reduce the income tax rates to peace time levels that the public and the economy will tolerate.

Quoting the Federalist Papers Number 35, penned in 1788 by Alexander Hamilton, "there is no part of the administration of government that requires extensive information and a thorough knowledge of the principles of the political economy so much as the business of taxation. It might be demonstrated that the most productive system of finance will always be the least burdensome."

In just a few days, I have been able to gather signatures from disgruntled Americans who support the Fair Tax plan. Be it known that these signatures cross all lines of division in that they represent ditch diggers to lawyers, truck drivers to stockbrokers, Black, White, Hispanic and Asians.

To further discern a more accurate consensus of the people, all you need to do is refer to the petition filed by the people of Arizona on Thursday, July 2, 1998. One hundred and seventy thousand

Americans required of this Congress to abolish income tax and establish a national sales tax.

The Fair Tax before you at this time is what the people want and require of you now.

One thing that amazes me about the national news media has all but ignored this legislation. The rhetoric we, as Americans, have been subjected to implies that the wealthy in this country do not pay taxes, and the tax burden has been shouldered by the working poor and the middle class.

To this I quote the besieged Commandeer of Bastognne in his response to the Nazis to surrender in World War II "Nutz." Figures recently released by the National Revue project quiet a different notion. The quintile of taxpayers from the lowest to highest is outlined as such:

The lowest wage earners pay—2 percent.

The low 1 percent.

The middle 7 percent.

The high 16 percent.

The highest wage earners 78 percent.

When confronted with the truth of these matters of income tax, and this Administration's quest for an America steeped in fairness, it is apparent that we are trying to shoot a game of pool with a nylon rope.

I would like to thank the members of this Committee for the opportunity to address you regarding the Fair Tax plan, and close with another quote from Mr. Alexander Hamilton's Federalist Papers Number 36.

"It has been asserted that a power of internal taxation in the national legislature could never be exercised with advantage, as well as from the want of a sufficient knowledge of local circumstances, as from as interferences between the revenue laws of the union and of the particular States. The supposition of a want of proper knowledge seems to be entirely destitute of foundation. If any question is depending in a State legislature respecting one of the counties, which demands a knowledge of local details, how is it acquired? No doubt from the information of the members of the county. Cannot the like knowledge be obtained in the national legislature from the representatives of each state? And is it not to be presumed that the men who will generally be sent there will be possessed of the necessary degree of intelligence to be able to communicate that information?"

I certainly hope so.

If William Jefferson Clinton so feels the pain of the American people, let him with unanimous consent of this Congress and Senate sign the Fair Tax Plan now. I implore you to preserve our freedom, our liberty, and save this Union by passing this legislation.

[The prepared statement follows:]

Statement of Steven Worley, Colbert, Georgia

America's first income tax began 1861 to pay for the Civil War. The Union imposed a 3 percent tax on incomes over $800.00 a year, which exempted most wage earners. The tax rate was raised to 5% in 1862 on incomes over $10,000.00. Shortly after the Civil War the income tax was repealed, ominously, the Bureau of Internal Revenue remained in existence. Budget-balancing statesmen have turned to income tax even in peacetime to replace revenue lost by import and export duties. That was the purpose of the income tax passed by congress in 1893 and ruled unconstitutional by the Supreme Court in 1895. President Taft pushed a constitutional amendment to revise that decision, and an income tax was passed as soon as the 16th Amendment was ratified in 1913 by only 31 states.

The new income tax was a luxury tax. Top rates remained below 10 percent and most Americans didn't pay at all. Then came World War I, which raised the federal budget from $1 billion in 1916 to $19 billion in 1919; income tax rates rose to 3 percent on $2,000 and 70 percent on $1 million. After the war, Treasury Secretary Andrew Million reduced the top rate to 25 percent and got most taxpayers off the rolls by raising the minimum income subject to tax. But he also cooperated with the Congress to create preferences, exemptions, deductions and other tax breaks. The income tax had gotten the federal government deeper into the business of allocating economic resources, mostly out of public view.

During World War II, as federal spending rose from $9.6 billion in 1940 to $95 billion in 1945, income tax rates were raised 19 percent on $2,000 and 88 percent on $200,000, and the number of taxpayers arose from 14 million to 50 million.

The World War II tax is the recognizable ancestor of today's federal income tax. The $500 per dependent exemption of 1944, raised to $600 in 1947, was a generous allowance to the parents of the baby boom generation. It meant the average family paid almost no income tax. Over time, inflation eroded the value of the exemption. The Republican leaders of the 1950's feared voter's resentment of the rich and did not reduce top rates. In the 1960's, JFK stimulated the economy by reducing taxes significantly.

The experiment in maintaining the wartime's high tax rates during peacetime in order to pay for the cold war and redistribute money to the middle class and poor worked-both economically and politically-for a generation and then stopped working economically. In the 70's, runaway inflation, fueled in part by Lyndon Johnson's refusal to raise taxes to pay for the Vietnam War, propelled ordinary families into tax brackets intended for the rich, while the myriad tax breaks available to the wealthy made a mockery of fairness. As state, local and other tax rates also rose, a middle-class tax revolt helped fuel the Reagan Republican victories of the 1980's and 1994. Politicians have been struggling ever since to reduce income tax rates to peacetime levels that the public and the economy will tolerate.

Quoting the Federalist Papers #35 penned in 1788 by Alexander Hamilton, "There is no part of the administration of government that requires extensive information and a through knowledge of the principles of political economy, so much as the business of taxation. It might be demonstrated that the most productive system of finance will always be the lest burdensome."

In a few days, I have been able to gather signatures from disgruntled American's who support the Fair Tax plan. Be it known that these signatures cross all lines of division in that they represent ditch diggers to lawyers, truck divers to stockbrokers, Black, White, Hispanic, and Asians. To further discern a more accurate consensus of the people, all you need do is refer to the petition filed by the people of Arizona. On Thursday, July 2, 1998, 170,000 Americans required of this congress to abolish income tax and establish a National Sales Tax. The Fair Tax Plan before you at this time is what the people want and require of you now.

One thing that amazes me is that the national news media has all but ignored this legislation. The rhetoric we as Americans have been subjected to implies that the wealthy in this country do not pay taxes, and that the tax burden has been shouldered by the "working poor and middle class." To this I quote the besieged Commander of Bastognne in his response to the Nazis to surrender in World War II "Nutz."Figures recently released by the National Revue project quiet a different notion. The quintile of taxpayers from lowest to highest is outlined as such:

Lowest   –2%
Low   1%
Middle   7%
High   16%
Highest 78%

When confronted with the truth in these matters of income tax and this Administrations quest for an America steeped in fairness, it is apparent that we are trying to shoot a game of pool with a nylon rope.

I would like to thank the members of this committee for the opportunity to address you regarding the Fair Tax plan, and close with another quote from Alexander Hamilton's Federalist Papers #36:

"It has been asserted that a power of internal taxation in the national legislature could never be exercised with advantage, as well from the want of a sufficient knowledge of local circumstances, as from as interference between the revenue laws

195

of the union and of the particular States. The supposition of a want of proper knowledge seems to be entirely destitute of foundation. If any question is depending in
a States legislature respecting one of the counties, which demands a knowledge of
local details, how is it acquired? No doubt from the information of the members of
the county. cannot the like knowledge be obtained in the national legislature from
the representatives of each state? And is it not to be presumed that the men who
will generally be sent there will be possessed of the necessary degree of intelligence
to be able to communicate the information?" I hope so!

If William Jefferson Clinton so feels the pain of the American people, let him with
unanimous consent to the U.S. Congress and Senate sign the Fair Tax Plan now.
I implore you to preserve our freedom, our liberty, and Save this Union by Passing
this legislation NOW!!

[The attachment is being retain in Committee files.]

Mr. CRANE. Thank you, Mr. Worley. That was a very good history lesson, too.

Mr. WORLEY. Thank you, sir.

Mr. CRANE. Mr. Moore.

[Pause.]

Mr. Moore?

STATEMENT OF JAMES O. MOORE, SMITHTOWN, NEW YORK

Mr. MOORE. Oh!

I am not here to castigate you guys for what you are doing in
Congress. I am here to offer some solutions for the problems of us
taxpayers which I am sure is within the realm of possibilities of
what you fellows do in writing the laws that govern how we operate in the United States of America.

Good morning, Mr. Chairman. I want to thank you and your
Committee for having this much-needed hearing and for the privilege of my having the opportunity to offer ways in which to possibly achieve its stated purpose "to make taxes fair and as easy as
possible," which is an almost universal desire of every taxpayer in
our country.

People with whom some items have been discussed have called
them radical in their diversity, but since there is a connotation of
negativity in it "extensive changes" should be more appropriate.

Our Constitution is generally thought to be possibly the best document human beings have ever written. One reason had to do with
its intent. freedom for people's self help with minimal government
interference. As President Eisenhower is credited with having said,
a government should do for its people only those things they cannot
do for themselves.

And was based on the fact that our Constitution does not require
government to feed, clothe, house, educate, nor provide health care
for its people. However, ours does so today in some ways with
funds collected from people equitably but too often unfairly distributed.

Particularly, if not living to receive the benefits paid for. Two examples: Social Security and Medicare, Monies are collected equitably in that the same appropriate percentage is applied to each
person up to the same earning limit but only on wages.

Unfairness is due to the fact that monies paid by a great many
people for promised benefits but who do not live to receive them
but is kept by the government.

In other cases, some of the monies goes to spouse and/or children meeting some requirements but there is no provision for any other beneficiary. That is taxation without recompense.

This is my second trip to Washington to testify to a government entity. The first was an IRS hearing on December the 4th, 1987, at which I proposed changes in IRA withdrawals which correctly requires withdrawals to commence at age 70-and-a-half.

As explained in my written statement which has been sent to you, it enable selective withdrawals if owning two or more IRAs and eliminate the requirement that custodians make sure withdrawals were made from each one.

Provisions of Notice 88–38 effected this change and was signed 12 years ago today, and thus coincidentally I am celebrating it in the City where it was signed.

Although that trip benefitted a great many people and custodians, what this Committee intends to do is very much more important; that it would benefit every citizen in this country and possibly even non-citizens who pay income tax.

It would change April 15th from a dreaded day to just one that happens to be the day the easily-done-tax-return is due in the amount fair assessment has required to be paid.

What a relief. I am absolutely sure it is a doable government operation provided fair is a must.

Again, thanks for this opportunity to testify and I feel sure others who testify will have proven same thing I feel is certain. Fair and easy taxes will come sooner than later. Income tax is the only way to correctly collect from people fairly because it is based on one basic fact. ability to pay. No other tax reaches that commitment.

I have asked two gentlemen to come to see me in a telephone call to Al Crenshaw yesterday afternoon, and to Howard Gleckman this morning, because I know them both from my twelve-years-ago visit to Washington, and they both promised to be here but they had commitments elsewhere that's made them uncertain as to whether or not they could.

But anyway, the complete story is told in the statement that I sent you previously, and originally I was going to bring with me two other supporting documents. The statement says there are no enclosures, which was true. However, the staff told me the two things that I wanted to bring with me to give to you today they felt it better that I send them to you. So therefore, those two addendums are also in the package that was received by you folks from me recently.

Gentlemen, it's up to you. We want fair taxes, properly assessed, and so simple that the one that I proposed I believe could be prepared on two 8½ × 11 sheets of paper with all the instructions necessary and the forms required to be incorporated in that. And a kid who is in the 4th grade and knows how to add, multiply, subtract, and divide can do it without a calculator.

Thank you, very much.

[The prepared statement follows:]

Statement of James O. Moore, Smithtown, New York

Mr. Chairman and the committee members, I am Jim Moore from Smithtown, New York but born in Birmingham, Alabama 84 years ago last Wednesday. And as a Financial Planner, the difficulties of my clients regarding tax returns have served to make me aware of the need for reforms intended to be achieved by this committee resulting in both simplification and fairness in income tax laws. Therefore I am grateful for this opportunity to offer some suggestions for your consideration and action which might be analogous to the statement credited to Mark Twain, "Everybody talks about the weather but nobody does anything about it." The analogy to you would be *almost* everyone COMPLAINS about income taxes but this committee is proposing to 'DO' something about it." As a patriotic citizen concerned about my fellow taxpayers, I want to congratulate Congressman Archer and this committee for that "DO SOMETHING" attitude and attempt!

Although not considering myself to be a tax expert, the following brief biographical sketch may serve to explain how this patriotic citizen has developed some suggestions for tax revision to do what Congressman Archer stated as basis for this hearings to "make taxes fair and easy as possible" and also to have said "to examine proposals to replace the current tax code." As I will explain in my summary, I am against replacement.

My high school diploma was received in 1932 at age 16 from Lyman Ward Military Academy in Camp Hill, Alabama. My graduation at age 34 in 1950 from NYU as a night school student after returning in 1945 from overseas service during WWII and also have a continuing 60 year connection with the 7th regiment in New York as first an active member and then in its Veterans Association including seven years on its Governing Board and a 44 year working career, the last 37 with a large international oil company before retirement in preparation for an active retirement in that field of endeavor.

Activity as a Financial Planner made me greatly aware of the need for revisions to provide the "fair and easy" income tax laws called for by the Congressman Archer. One such needed change had to do with IRS regulations for the requirement that persons who are owners of IRA's must commence withdrawals upon reaching age 70 ½ in which I concur but did NOT agree that those with multiple IRA's had to withdraw from each of them. Therefore, at an IRS hearing on December 4, 1987, with support from ICI, AARP, ACLI, Senator D'Amato, Congressman Carney and mutual fund companies, etc. I proposed that investors could aggregate their value and based on age, determine total required to be withdrawn and then make withdrawal from one or more to maintain the best investment resulting balance. The IRS Notice 88–38 issued on April 12, 1988 effected that procedure. And, the 100% vote of congress eliminating the $1 penalty reduction of Social Security for wage earners would have been a non-starter if my suggested tax revisions had been in effect as set forth in the following summary:

SUMMARY:

The varied tax problems of my Financial Planning clients gave me a much broader knowledge of intricacies of the tax laws than I would have gotten in just preparing my own tax returns. That resulted in proposed revisions set forth in the below verbatim copy of the statement I made at the tax hearing of Congressman Carney and Senator D'Amato on September 5, 1985. The notes thereon show the continuing effort to get public and then hoped for Congressional interest in effecting the much needed revisions of personal tax laws. Although affecting businesses, problems of its taxation are not addressed. Its monetary items must be increased to reflect inflation over the last 15 years to get to their equivalents of 1985 amounts.

Statement for tax hearing of Congressman Carney and Senator D'Amato at Ward Melville High School, Setauket, NY on thursday, September 5, 1985—by James O. Moore, Smithtown, NY

My name is Jim Moore from Smithtown and I am on Social Security. (Will be 70 on April 5 next year).

Almost everyone agrees (1) the current Tax System is ridled with inequities that favor special interests (2) is so voluminous and confusing that experts in the IRS sometimes give different rulings on he same question and (3) now feel tax simplification is essential.

Many tax simplification proposals are being considered. Some include proposals that are anathema to Elected Officials and Legislators of this State. Understably, they want to comply with the wishes of their Constituents BUT, when Legislators are Congressmen and Senators, they have a *HIGHER* duty to Legislate for the whole country even to the extent of voting for programs that are good for the country but not liked by local Constituents!!

With this as basis for your decisions in House and Senate on Tax simplification, herewith is a program for personal tax returns on a basis that treats *EVERYONE* equally and fairly. The proposed exemptions and tax rates may require adjustments to assure they are revenue neutral and do not *RAISE* taxes in totality.

First: all income received would be repotable *including social security,* SSI, Welfare (including value of housing allowance and clothing) but *payments from social security would not be reportable until all contributions by individual and spouse have been recovered.* Cola's would be included at full rate and *the special social security calculations would be eliminated.* Municipal bond interest, capital gains, tax shelters, etc. would be reportable fully as income. however, income *credited but not withdrawn* would not be reported until withdrawn as is now done with IRA accounts return of principal, of course, would not be reportable. This would apply to savings accounts, mutual funds, cash and stock dividends held in brokerage accounts etc etc.

Second: *no deductions for anything!!!!* including contributions to religious & charitable groups, interest, taxes, etc etc.

Third: states should eliminate sales tax on any item costing less than $25, and neither they nor the Federal government should consider value added tax as it is the most harmful to the poor.

Fourth: eliminate *all* tax shelters, (not just those the administration deem bad) so that *economic viability* rather than tax advantages would be basis for investments.

Fifth: *family* income should be basis for personal exemptions and currently suggest $5,000 for first. $4,000. Second, $3,000. Third and $2,000. All others. A family of four would pay no tax until income exceeded $14,000. approximating *current* poverty income level. A suggested flat 20% rate or better still, graduated scale of 10 to 40% might be used or whatever is needed to give a revenue neutral income. Social security taxes may also require adjustment. But, in order to have *everyone* contribute to this great country for the privelege of living here, assess ½ of 1% on gross income so that the family of four would pay $70, on its $14,000. Exemption. This would be returned to the states from which taxpayer files his return to offset no sales tax on $25.00.

This is an eminently fair and even handed program which should eliminate the feeling that "That guy makes X number of dollars and pays no taxes. Why should I pay so much?" Also, it would end confusion on tax laws, reduce the volume upon volume of tax laws; Myriads of pamphlets, files and paperwork, cut irs staff considerably and save money for government, business and individuals in the multi-millions of dollars. I believe such a program would be welcomed by all taxpayers and businesses except those whose livelihood depends on the present *unfair* system!!!!

Note: Subsequent to this statement, a 6–5–86 letter to 8 people (Congressmen, Senators & Pres. Reagan) added provision for a $5,000 allowance for fringe benefits. Thus any amount paid by employers for pensions, INS, etc. would be reported on W–2's BUT only any amount in excess of $5,000 allowance would be taxable income. However, if amount paid by employer is less than $5,000 or none at all, the taxpayer could purchase protection desired or invest in IRA's etc. and deduct up to $5,000 on tax return. Senator Bradley's 10–9–86 reply called this an "intriguing idea!!!" Seniors could apply this against medical expense as well as insurance premiums.

Added in 1994: If health care revisions provide for deductibility of health care costs, they would be eliminated from fringe benefits allowances for everyone *not* just seniors.

The first note refers to a 6–5–86 letter to 8 addresses on adding fringe benefits deduction and the "added in 1994" item on Health care relates to my 8–25–94 article on "Declaration of Independence from Socialized Medicine" printed in local Smithtown Messenger. It proposed 100% deductibility of medical expenses, including health insurance premium less reimbursement by the insurance company for claims. Then in 1999, I offered some ideas to economic Security 2000 to be discussed at its January Forum in D.C. but suggested tax revisions would solve some of the problems of Social Security for which forum was being held.

Referring only to items in the 9–5–85 statement, everyone with whom I have discussed items therein have agreed they WOULD provide the fairness intended but said IMPOSSIBLE!! Why? Because they felt politicians would not agree to them and said the effort was as useless as Don Quixote jousting at windmills. I have never felt that way. Instead, I believe such revisions ARE possible, and like the Lone Ranger, want to help people in distress. Taxpayers?

My optimism is based on the fact that the IRS amended its regulations on IRA withdrawals as covered above while I was continuing this now 15 year effort at tax revision.

In connection with the vexing tax problem, I have recently initiated an effort towards formalization of an organization to be called COFEHATT, which is the acronym for "Citizens Organization For Equitable Health and Tax Treatment." However, we intend to go one step further than "equitable" which can apply by treating everyone the same at inception but be UNFAIR in distribution. Thus, our additional requirement is "FAIR." Implementing the suggested revisions, while keeping the laws FAIR, the biggest benefit is the simplification which enables everyone to prepare tax returns perhaps by IRS using the equivalent of two 11 by 8 ½ sheets of paper to explain and provide form on which to prepare the return.

It is our view that the ability to pay is the only criterion on which to base taxes and that ability is predicated on income which should be generic and include in it every source which would be wages, commissions, profit from self-employment, profit from sale of material assets or securities, dividends on investments and interest on savings and finally ALL bonds whether commercial or municipal.

We feel absolutely sure that neither a FLAT nor National Sales Tax is fair. If we are wrong, please let us know since we do NOT want COFEHATT to provide erroneous information and lose our credibility. The flat and sales tax could be instantaneous but our proposal cannot be done in one "fell swoop" prohibited by contractual termination dates and some must be put into effect incrementally or they would be calamitous disaster to our economy.

If the committees's review of proposals received from all participants in this hearing finds ours to be FAIR, we hope some of our suggestions will be incorporated in laws that will provide the intended benefits to ALL OF US.

However, should any proposal be either NOT "doable" for reasons other than fairness or NOT considered fair we would also appreciate being advised accordingly just as we hope for your opinion regarding our position on FLAT and NATIONAL SALES TAX.

It has been gratifying to make a second trip to Washington on thus two matters so important to every citizen and also even to every non-citizen taxpayer and much appreciated.

My thanks to your staff as well for "squeezing me in" after initially being told there was no vacancy.

Our is a wonderful country and I am proud to have served it militarily and as a contributor to some degree in other ways.

[The attachments are being retained in the committee files.]

Mr. COLLINS: [presiding] And thank you, Mr. Moore. You can be assured that your full statement and any other accompanying documents that you have presented will be entered into the record.

Mr. Hulshof, do you have any questions, please?

Mr. HULSHOF. Thank you, Mr. Chairman.

Let me first extend my appreciation, Mr. Worley and Mr. Moore, for your efforts in being here today.

Mr. Worley I think you, if I am not mistaken, were here through the entirety of yesterday's hearing as well.

Mr. WORLEY. Yes, sir.

Mr. HULSHOF. I noticed you probably had better attendance than many of us did, but I appreciate the fact. Just as a general point, let me say that even as we are here discussing fundamental tax reform, that elsewhere on the Capitol grounds about 10,000 American citizens are gathered to express their viewpoints about certain matters that Congress will be taking up.

It just reminds me again of what an awesome thing that we have, a representative form of government, that citizens are allowed to come before a Committee such as this, or to stand on the steps of the United States Capitol and to express their opinion freely.

Whether it means petitions, Mr. Worley, as you have submitted for us and gathered here, I think again it is just an extraordinary testament to the type of government that we have.

Let me say—and, Mr. Worley, I am going to ask you a couple of questions because there was something in your written testimony, and as you mentioned it today, that really struck me.

You pointed out that one thing that amazes you, as it does me, is that some that report the news nationally have not really given a full focus of attention as we are of these series of hearings.

In fact, let me just quote you again because I think it bears repeating.

"The rhetoric"—and this is you writing, I assume?

Mr. WORLEY. "The rhetoric we as Americans have been subjected to implies that the wealthy in this country do not pay taxes and the tax burden has been shouldered by the working poor and middle class" to which you paraphrased the word "nutz."

Let me ask you about that. Because we have had a variety of different opinions already over this day-and-a-half talking about, for instance, whether we should have the fair tax as you support, Mr. Worley.

We have had flat tax proponents. I suspect Congressman Armey will be here to talk about that.

Mr. Moore, as I understand it from your testimony you do not support a national sales tax or a flat tax, but a different type of tax. I know my colleague, Mr. English, has got his idea.

Again I think it is useful that we debate and discuss these things. One thing that is frustrating for me especially, Mr. Worley, being on this Committee, having the honor of serving on this Committee, is the rhetoric that seems to percolate among other Members, that if we try to provide tax relief, for instance, we are "giving tax breaks to the wealthy," when in fact we may be trying to simplify the tax code.

Can you give us any guidance as a—and I do not mean this in a derogatory term—but as a common, ordinary citizen who watches what we do, how do we pierce that rhetoric so that we can have an honest discussion about the best policy?

Mr. WORLEY. If I knew that, I would probably be the President of this Nation.

I do not see, without a grassroots organization, or just by citizens like myself stepping forward and talking to other citizens, and saying this is what is going on and this is what we can do if we will take it upon ourselves to do that. I do not know that the national news media is going to give us any kind of regard in this.

I do not know what we could do to cause them to do this other than a revolt. Now that certainly, if a million Americans came to the Halls of this Congress and said we demand tax reform, it would certainly gather some sort of attention from the national news media.

Mr. HULSHOF. Let me ask you, how did you first get involved, or have your interest peaked by this piqued by this and the fact that you would try to collect signatures on a petition, and then come from Georgia, or your home to come to the Halls of Congress?

I mean what has motivated you to become an activist in this area?

Mr. WORLEY. As an American Citizen, I have been abused by the Internal Revenue Service. I purposely left out my personal problems with them from this because I did not want to make it just a personal matter.

My personal problems with the Internal Revenue Service are neither here nor there. This is a total problem throughout the country and it affects every American. And we have got to do something.

If you have a car and it breaks down, you fix it. Well we have been fixing our problem with the Internal Revenue Service and our taxation of income for years now, and we are still broken.

So maybe it is time that we junk the old car and go buy a new one.

Mr. HULSHOF. Well again I see my time is up. The red light is on. Let me just again—and I see Mr. Davis has also joined us here with the panel. But let me just again express my appreciation that each of you would take the time, and probably at your own expense, too, to come here to help enlist our support on these various different ideas of the way we collect revenue in this country.

Again, I think it is just testament to the type of Nation that we have that you would have the opportunity to come here and have your voices heard.

So thank you for that.

Mr. WORLEY. Thank you.

Mr. MOORE. Thank you.

Mr. COLLINS. Thank you, Mr. Hulshof.

I know Chairman Archer will be back in just a few moments, but I wanted to take the time and the opportunity to extend my appreciation to Mr. Worley, being a fellow Georgian, for coming and bringing a lot of common sense with him to address this Committee, and also the list of names who signed your petitions.

And I am sure if you had more time and had travelled a lot more throughout Georgia you would have had a stack that would have been much, much taller because I hear about this quite often as I am travelling throughout the Third District of Georgia, which goes from Clayton County down to Muskogee County, which you are very familiar with.

I also understand from your opening that you are in the concrete business?

Mr. WORLEY. Yes, sir.

Mr. COLLINS. And you have had 18 years of experience in the ready-mix concrete business. And having pushed many a wheelbarrow of concrete and finished some myself, too, I appreciate the work and the hard work that you have endured.

We will take Mr. Davis' testimony at this time, and Mr. Chairman will be back very shortly.

Mr. Davis?

STATEMENT OF FRANK L. DAVIS, JR., ALEXANDRIA, VIRGINIA

Mr. DAVIS. Thank you, Mr. Chairman.

Mr. Chairman, Members of the Committee, my fellow Americans: It is a privilege to be asked to testify this morning. My name is Frank Davis. I am a retired Naval Reserve Aviator, having spent 28-and-a-half years in Active and Reserve Service to my country.

I consider myself still serving, albeit in a somewhat different capacity, but with the same goal in mind. Protect my country from all enemies foreign and domestic.

As you might expect, I consider that the duty of every citizen.

I am co-founder and Executive Vice President and National Director of Legislative Affairs for the National Retail Sales Tax Alliance.

The National Retail Sales Tax Alliance is a nonpartisan, nonprofit, grassroots organization working to replace the federal tax system with a National Retail Sales Tax and abolish the Internal Revenue Service.

I cannot think of a more fitting goal in life than to bequeath my country, my children, and my grandchildren a free society without an income tax and without an IRS.

I am a citizen activist. I speak as a very concerned private citizen. My remarks reflect both my own thinking in this matter and the advice and counsel of countless thousands of American citizens who are likewise concerned about the ship of state.

For example, the Internet has proven very helpful to the National Retail Sales Tax Movement and tax reform in general.

FReeRepublic.com is an especially helpful site for keeping a pulse on the American public with respect to fundamental tax reform.

A number of prominent public servants have provided outspoken leadership for the National Retail Sales Tax tax reform movement and are noted in my extended remarks.

I want to personally thank you, Chairman Archer, for your foresight and leadership these past five years. Notice, if you will, ladies and gentlemen, that this is a bipartisan movement. It is not about partisanship. It is about doing what is right for America.

In addition, articles published in influential opinion journals have contributed to the dialogue. I highly recommend Dr. Allen Keyes' article "The Case For Repealing The 16th Amendment To The United States Constitution. Abolish The Income Tax!" published in Human Events Magazine on April the 17th, 1998.

I also commend to the Committee the testimony for the record of Mr. Charles Adams, Historian.

A number of well-known organizations are invaluable in our work and are noted in my extended remarks.

The National Retail Sales Tax Alliance supports both H.R. 2001 and H.R. 2525. We know that neither bill will pass in its present form. We also know that there may well be additional NRST bills added to the mix and that there will be provisions added and subtracted until such time as the Committee has reached consensus and a measure goes to the Floor of the House.

My promise to all Americans, to you Mr. Chairman, to the Committee and the Congress and to all interested parties is this:

The National Retail Sales Tax Alliance will work to ensure that America gets a modern, national retail sales tax system which will meet America's needs for the 21st Century and beyond.

Mr. Chairman, there are at least three fundamental reasons why the Income Tax System must be replaced with a national retail sales tax:

Freedom.

Economic Growth.

And a quality of treatment under the law.

America is the only nation in world history whose founding was based on the notion that certain unalienable rights are handed down from God to the People and then are loaned to government.

Since the dawn of man, governments have claimed that rights are handed down from God to government, the Divine Rights of Kings, and then loaned to the people. And this is a very important distinction.

To the degree that America has become the great Nation is it today and has the capacity to even become greater, the concept of a citizen's unalienable rights is very important. This concept differentiates the United States from every other country in the world. Every U.S. Citizen's unalienable rights are guaranteed by our Founding Fathers in the Declaration of Independence and the Constitution.

Why then does the United States have a tax system which severely restricts its citizens' Constitutional rights, artificially limits their ability to work, save, and invest and exacerbates class warfare by dividing them one from the other on the basis of types and amounts of income?

These perverse disincentives to succeed and resultant lower-than-it-should-be U.S. economic growth in recent years are fueled by our oppressive Income Tax Code.

It defies comprehension.

The United States of America has a Tax Code based on the 19th Century Marxist class warfare notion of "from each according to their ability, to each according to their need."

Do we really want to begin the 21st Century with a tax system based on class envy and warfare? Which punishes those who work, save, and invest and rewards those who do not?

Do we want to retain a tax system that annually invades our privacy and usurps our Constitutional rights?

Or do we truly want to be free people?

Mr. Chairman, I would submit that we can never be a truly free society so long as we allow the income tax and the Internal Revenue Service to exist.

If we are to restore to American Citizens those freedoms guaranteed by the Constitution, we must replace the federal tax system with a national retail sales tax and, in the process, abolish the Internal Revenue Service.

And while we are at it, we must also repeal the 16th Amendment to the Constitution to complete the tax reform process and to ensure that America will never have to suffer another tax.

Dr. Keyes refers to the income tax as a slave tax inherently incompatible with freedom. Abolishing it is therefore not just economically feasible; it is a moral imperative if we are to meet our obligations to bequeath liberty to future generations.

Mr. COLLINS. Mr. Davis?

Mr. DAVIS. Yes.

Mr. COLLINS. I hate to interrupt you, but your entire statement will be entered into the record. You have kind of exceeded your time already, but we will give you about another minute to wrap it up if you could, please.

Mr. DAVIS. Well let me go straight to a letter that I have, an anonymous letter, which will take about a minute to read that was sent to me:

Dear Friends and Buddies,

Most of you know that one of my most treasured beliefs is that we are a free people. I am deeply saddened that every day we lose more of those freedoms as the government usurps them in the name of protecting us from ourselves.

Our current tax code is extremely damaging in that it punishes success—the very thing this country was founded on and so many lives were lost over—and it requires disclosure of every aspect of our lives for public consumption.

My spirit is personally so broken by this that, after doing our taxes, I realize I am chipping my—and she said it in French—joy of life; I can't pronounce it—and very life away and have become enslaved by the government.

I have decided to end it.

I am selling our business and will not continue to contribute to this folly. It was a grim realization. Although we have a lot to contribute to this country and its future with our technology information and teaching, it is not worth the payback anymore.

I give up.

The American dream has vanished. I am joining the ranks of the crushed in spirit, the squashed, the oppressed. And yes, if you are wondering, I am depressed about the whole thing. A good cry sometimes helps, but that has been way too common of late.

And in a short note to Mr. Archer:

"Please record my support FOR the National Retail Sales Tax to replace the tax code in this country. We must abolish the oppressive tax code and REPLACE it. The FLAT TAX does not accomplish replacement of the complexities of the code; it merely masks them and simplifies computations. Therefore I urge you to please support the FAIR TAX/National Retail Sales Tax.

"I also urge you to abolish the illegal agency known as the IRS."

I will close with that.

Thank you, Mr. Chairman. Thank you, Members of Congress, for your time.

[The prepared statement follows:]

Statement of Frank L. Davis, Jr., Alexandria, Virginia

Mr. Chairman, Mr. Rangel and Members of the Committee; my fellow Americans. It is a privilege to be asked to testify this afternoon. My name is Frank Davis. I am a retired Naval Reserve Aviator, having spent 28 ‡ years in active and reserve service to my country. I consider myself still serving, albeit in a somewhat different capacity, but with the same goal in mind: protect my country from all enemies, foreign and domestic. As you might expect, I consider that the duty of every citizen.

I am a co-founder and the Executive Vice President and National Director of Legislative Affairs for the National Retail Sales Tax Alliance. The National Retail Sales Tax Alliance is a nonpartisan, non-profit grass roots organization working with like-minded individuals, think tanks, other public interest advocacy groups and businesses to replace the federal tax system with a National Retail Sales Tax (NRSTA) and abolish the Internal Revenue Service.

I cannot think of a more fitting goal in life than to bequeath my country, my children and my grandchildren a free society without an income tax and without an IRS.

I am a citizen activist. In my testimony today, I will relate to the committee the viewpoint of a very concerned private citizen. My testimony reflects both my own thinking in this matter, and the advice and counsel of countless thousands of American citizens, who are likewise concerned about the ship of state.

For example, the Internet has proven very helpful to the NRST movement; we are able to mine a rich field of pertinent research, communicate with and share opinions with expert economists and political scientists and more important, find each other. In this regard, FReeRepublic.com is an especially helpful site for keeping a pulse on the American public with respect to fundamental tax reform.

A number of prominent public servants have provided outspoken leadership for the NRST tax reform movement. I want to personally thank you, Chairman Archer, for your foresight and leadership these past five years. Also, now retired Congressman Dan Schaefer, who was the primary sponsor of the first NRST legislation introduced on March 7, 1996. Senator Richard Lugar has long been an advocate of the NRST. In the present Congress, leaders such as Congressmen. W.J. "Billy" Tauzin, Jim Traficant, John Linder and Colin Peterson, along with the cosponsors of their respective Bills, are to be congratulated. Congressmen Largent and Cox also deserve recognition for their efforts in tax reform.

Notice, if you will, that this is a bipartisan movement. It is not about partisanship, it is about doing what is right for America.

In addition, articles published in influential opinion journals have contributed to the dialogue. I highly recommend Dr. Alan Keyes' article, The Case for Repealing the 16th Amendment Abolish the Income Tax! published in Human Events magazine on April 17, 1998.[1]

Well known organizations such as The Americans For Fair Taxation, the Tax Foundation, the Tax Education Association, Heritage, the CATO Institute, The Argus Group, Citizens for an Alternative Tax System, Citizens for a Sound Economy, and the National Taxpayers Union have proven to be invaluable in our work. And there are others.

Curiously enough, the article that constitutes my "defining moment" in respect of fundamental tax reform was also published on April 17th—in 1991. Pat Buchanan's nationally syndicated column that day was entitled "A tax whose time has gone?"[2] That is the day I became a tax reform citizen activist. Mr. Buchanan has since published two more articles favorable to the National Retail Sales Tax.[3]

A quick word about the National Retail Sales Tax Alliance. NRSTA does not support either H.R. 2001 or H.R. 2525; we support both bills. We know that neither bill will pass in its present form. We also know that there may well be additional NRST bills added to the mix, and that there will be provisions added and subtracted until such time as the Committee has reached consensus and the measure goes to the floor of the House.

Our promise to all Americans, to you, Mr. Chairman, to the Committee and to all interested parties is this: The National Retail Sales Tax Alliance will work to ensure that America gets a modern National Retail Sales Tax system which will meet America's needs for the 21st Century and beyond.

Mr. Chairman, there are at least three fundamental reasons why the income tax system must be replaced with a National Retail Sales Tax: freedom, economic growth and equality of treatment under the law.

America is the most envied nation in the world. Not only are we envied by the world's governments, we are envied by the world's people. America is the only nation in the history of the world whose founding was based on the notion that certain unalienable rights are handed down from God to the people, and then are loaned to government. Since the dawn of man, governments have claimed that rights are handed down from God to government [Divine Right of Kings] and then loaned to the people, a very important distinction.

How important? To the degree that America has become the great nation it is today, and has the capacity to become an even greater nation, the concept of a citizen's unalienable rights is very important to keep in mind as we consider fundamental tax reform. This concept differentiates the United States from *every other country in the world.* Every U.S. citizen's unalienable rights are guaranteed by our founding fathers in the Declaration of Independence and the Constitution.

Why, then, does the United States have a tax system which severely restricts its citizen's Constitutional rights, artificially limits their ability to work, save and in-

---

[1] Dr. Alan Keyes. The Case for Repealing the 16th Amendment. Abolish the Income Tax! *Human Events,* April 17, 1998.

[2] Patrick Buchanan, "A tax whose time has gone?," *Tribune Media Services,* April 17, 1991.

[3] Patrick Buchanan, "Brave new world: no tax forms, no IRS," *Tribune Media Services,* April 15, 1994; Patrick Buchanan, "Sales tax alternative," *The Washington Times,* July 14, 1997, p. A12.

vest and exacerbates class warfare by dividing them one from the other on the basis of types and amounts of income?

These perverse disincentives to succeed, and the resultant lower (than it should be) U.S. economic growth in recent years, are fueled by our oppressive income tax code. It defies comprehension—the United States of America has a tax code based on the Nineteenth Century Marxist class warfare notion of "from each according to their ability, to each according to their need." Do we really want to begin the 21st Century with a tax system based on class envy and warfare, which punishes those who work, save and invest and rewards those who don't? Do we want a tax system that annually invades our privacy and usurps our Constitutional Rights? Or do we truly want to be a free people?

We can never be a truly free society so long as we allow the income tax and the IRS to exist.

If we are to restore to American citizens those freedoms guaranteed by the Constitution, we must **replace** the federal tax system with a National Retail Sales Tax (NRST), and in the process abolish the Internal Revenue Service. While we are at it, we must also repeal the 16th Amendment to the Constitution to ensure complete tax reform and to ensure that America will never have to suffer another income tax.

Dr. Keyes refers to the income tax as a. . . "slave tax—inherently incompatible with freedom. Abolishing it is therefore not just economically feasible, it is a moral imperative if we are to meet our obligation to bequeath liberty to future generations." [4]

Under the NRST, Americans would no longer have to annually divulge to a faceless bureaucrat their most private and personal financial information. How much money an American earns becomes his or her own private business. Taxes will be paid on the basis of how much a person "takes out" of the economy rather than how much a person earns. Under the NRST, those who consume the most, will pay the most in taxes. All Americans will be encouraged to work, save and invest, and government interference in their personal economic activities will cease. That, my fellow Americans, is Freedom.

The next question before us is: Why does the United States have a tax system that discourages and penalizes those activities which grow the economy?

The progressive income tax system punishes those personal and business activities that encourage economic growth. The more a person works, saves and invests, the higher his or her taxes become. Likewise, the more successful his or her business, the higher his or her tax bill (which is passed along to the consumer in the form of higher retail prices).

And there is the matter of hidden taxes and compliance costs in the business income tax. The current tax system holds both people and business back, rather than encouraging them to move forward and become even more successful.

The change to a National Retail Sales Tax will cause (and these are very conservative estimates) the Gross Domestic Product rate of growth to double and the national personal savings rate will triple. [5] America will become the investment "sponge" of the world—attracting billions of dollars invested elsewhere, further expanding the investment pool of capital available for business expansion and job growth. Interest rates will decline by 2 basis points, making it easier and less expensive for business to borrow money for growth and expansion and for individuals to qualify for home loans and other big ticket items. [6] The NRST will eliminate compliance costs for individuals and reduce business compliance costs by a factor of 90%. [7] And, those who chose to participate in the underground economy will pay taxes at the check out counter, just like everyone else.

And the economic benefits of a switch to the National Retail Sales Tax do not stop with these gains. Picture even lower unemployment, more and better jobs for people willing to work, higher wages, and more robust export markets.

In respect of exports, let me say that the recent WTO ruling declaring the Foreign Sales Credit provision of the current tax code illegal presents a challenge to America that the National Retail Sales Tax handles very well. The National Retail Sales Tax is a territorial border adjustable tax; meaning it is not applied to exported goods and is applied to goods imported for sale in America. The NRST is legal under the

---

[4] Keyes, op. cit.

[5] Laurence J. Kotlikoff, "The Economic Impact of Replacing Federal Income Taxes with a Sales Tax," CATO Policy Analysis No. 193, April 15, 1993.

[6] Americans for Fair Taxation Policy Paper, "The Impact of a National Retail Sales Tax on Interest Rates," April 21, 1997.

[7] Tax Foundation Special Brief, "Compliance Costs of Alternative Tax Systems II, House Ways and Means Committee Testimony," March, 1997, pp 8, 9.

terms of the WTO. The NRST levels the playing field between domestic and foreign companies in respect of tax policy—it treats them exactly the same.

The NRST, when implemented, will cause America, in your own words, Mr. Chairman, to become "the economic juggernaut of the world."[8] Foreign capital will flow into America and expatriated capital will return to America. As you know, with a NRST, jobs and companies that have "gone offshore" will relocate to America. Foreign businesses will locate new facilities here. In your words, Mr. Chairman, the NRST will "allow our nation and its people to soar to unparalleled prosperity in the next century."[9]

The final point I'd like to make is that America's founding fathers guaranteed that the Rule of Law (as opposed to the Rule of Man—the "Divine Right of Kings"— prevalent throughout the world prior to America's founding) would apply in America. The phrase "Equal Justice Under the Law." is chiseled in granite over the entrance to the Supreme Court Building, reminding us of the absolute importance of this founding principle.

The progressive income tax makes a mockery of the Rule of Law. The Rule of Law provides for equality of treatment before the bar of justice. We are violating one of America's basic founding principles by continuing to keep a progressive income tax system in place.

The progressive income tax system, which divides us into economic classes for the purpose of levying taxes, is conceptually wrong and at its core, un-American. You will recall that the founders were opposed to income taxes, and insisted that the country finance itself through excise taxes and tariffs.

In 1913 the 16th Amendment to the U.S. Constitution, the single worst piece of legislation ever passed by any Congress, was adopted. It fundamentally altered the relationship of the American people and their government, as the founders in their infinite wisdom knew would happen. The government became the master, and the people became the slave. Dr. Keyes addresses his remarks about the morality of the slave tax to this very point.

But it got worse. The instigators of the first legal U.S. income tax could have adopted a flat rate income tax, but they chose a different course and thereby changed the American political landscape. They accepted the second plank of the Communist Manifesto as the core principle of the U.S. tax system in 1913, and adopted a progressive rate income tax system. Thus, the progressive income system, with its built in appeal to those who practice the art of divide and conquer by encouraging class warfare became institutionalized in America. The progressive income tax intentionally pits Americans of different economic classes one against the another, and is used by demagogues for their own political gain.

How can America enter the 21st Century with a 19th Century Marxist tax system in place? And why would we want to?

Eighty seven years of tinkering has produced an unknowable tax code full of social engineering experiments. This social engineering has served only to make the code more complex and further disunite the American citizens. Tax policy should be focused on raising the funds necessary to operate government, not as a laboratory to "fix" this or that perceived social problem.

Americans are the most generous people on the face of the earth; social programs that we agree upon (within Constitutional bounds, of course) should be funded from the spending side of the federal ledger, not the taxing side.

As we are guaranteed equality of treatment before the bar of justice, all Americans must be guaranteed equality of treatment before the bar of economic justice. The best way to do that and to put an end to class warfare is to tax consumption, not earnings. With, and only with a consumption tax such as a single rate National Retail Sales tax, can we Americans be guaranteed equality of treatment under economic law.

I call upon the Congress to eliminate the social engineering in the tax code by adopting the National Retail Sales Tax. With the NRST, the economic class warfare that has so divided this country over the past 87 years will eventually go away— everyone will be working, saving and investing and we won't have time to be envious of "the Joneses."

Americans believe that all men are created equal by their Creator, and have an unalienable right to be treated equally by their government. The progressive income tax violates that fundamental principle.

---

[8] Rep. Bill Archer (R–TX), Chairman, House Ways and Means Committee, "Opening Statement of Chairman Archer Fundamental Tax Reform Hearing," June 6, 1995.
[9] Ibid.

Mr. Chairman, we are all stakeholders in America. As such, we should be enjoying equality of treatment under the law. As I have gone to great lengths to point out, we are not.

The NRST, because it is applied uniformly and taxes everyone at the same rate, will be a constant reminder to each of us that we are a stakeholder, and that taking an interest in the affairs of this nation is an important duty of citizenship. By demolishing the myth that there is a "Free lunch," the National Retail Sales Tax can become a unifying theme for all Americans.

Accordingly, I call for all Americans to unite, to come together and demand of our elected officials that the income tax system be replaced with a simple, fair, flat National Retail Sales Tax and that the IRS be abolished.

Mr. Chairman, I have in my possession (Appendix 1) an eloquent message from a taxpayer, who prefers to remain anonymous, that neatly sums up the frustrations millions of Americans have about our tax and regulatory system. I would like to read it for the record.

America will never be a truly free society so long as we allow the income tax and the IRS to exist. America will never realize its true economic potential so long as we allow the income tax and the IRS to exist. Americans will never be treated with equality so long as we allow the income tax and the IRS to exist.

What better way to restore Americans' Constitutional freedoms, invigorate America's economy through more robust economic growth and ensure that every American is treated with equality?

Isn't that what our Grand Vision of America is? One Nation, under God, with liberty and justice for all?

Thank you, Mr. Chairman for allowing me to testify.

Dear Friends and Buddies,

Most of you know that one of my most treasured beliefs is that we are a free people. I am deeply saddened that every day we lose more of those freedoms as the government usurps them in the name of protecting us from ourselves. Our current tax code is extremely damaging in that it punishes success (the very thing this country was founded on and so many lives were lost over) and it requires disclosure of every aspect of our lives for public consumption.

My spirit is personally so broken by this, that after doing our taxes I realize I am chipping my [joy of life] and very life away and have become enslaved by the government. I have decided to end it.

I am selling our business and I will not continue to contribute to this folly. It was a grim realization. Although we have a lot to contribute to this country and its future with our technologoy info and teaching, it is not worth the payback anymore. The exhaustion of teaching, the aching legs and feet, the sleepless nights waking up with leg pains after teaching all day, the stress of it, the technology "Keep-up" issues have all mounted too high unless there is big bucks in it. Running our own business has meant learning too much about regulations, forms, accounting etc. and handing over in excess of 63% of our earnings. And that is before property and gas and sales tax, let alone how to finance retirement and pay for college and all that.

I give up. The American Dream has vanished. I am joining the ranks of the crushed in spirit, the squashed, the oppressed. And yes, if you were wondering, I am depressed about the whole thing. A good cry sometimes helps, but that has been way too common of late. Oh well.

[The following is a personal letter to the Committee, from the same taxpayer]

To the House Committee on Ways and Means:

Please record my support FOR the National Retail Sales Tax to replace the tax code in this country. We must abolish the oppressive tax code and REPLACE it. The FLAT TAX does not accomplish replacement of the complexities of the code; it merely masks them and simplifies computations. Therefore I urge you to please support the FAIR TAX/National Retail Sales Tax.

I also urge you to abolish the illegal agency known as the IRS. It was not properly established according to our constitution and has powers way beyond those ever envisioned by our forefathers. The IRS simply MUST be eliminated, as everyone in good conscience must admit.

May this committee please take this challenge to right the wrongs perpetuated for many years by this agency called the IRS. We need a constitutional, non-invasive, and non-"targeted" tax code, that treats us with equality. And enact a tax code that preserves life, liberty and the pursuit of happiness. . . not one that causes us to fear running afoul of the IRS and requires keeping every scrap of evidence from every sector of our lives, should it ever be demanded.

Thank you for your time

Why Scrap the Code?

- Families pay more in taxes than food, clothing, and shelter combined.

- Americans work 1 hour, 57 minutes of each day to pay federal taxes.

- Taxes are at peacetime record highs.

- $200 billion in annual compliance costs.

Why Scrap the Code?

- Americans will spend 6.1 billion hours filling out IRS forms -- equal to 2.7 million workers doing nothing but IRS paperwork.

- The IRS has 4 times as many employees as the FBI and US Marshals combined.

- In 1999 the IRS was only able to answer 73 percent of inquiries correctly.

The Flat Tax: Fairness

- Everyone pays the same rate.

- No exceptions for special interests.

- That's fair.

- If your neighbor earns 10 times more than you, he will pay ten times more in taxes.

Life in the Flat Tax World

- No intrusive IRS.

- No double taxation.

- No death taxes or marriage penalty.

- No Social Security benefit tax.

- Expanded IRAs.

- Eliminates 94% of compliance costs.

How the Flat Tax Works

- Scraps the current code and IRS.

- Grants a generous personal exemption ($36,800 for a family of four).

- 17 percent tax on all income.

- No loopholes for special interests.

Life in a Sales Tax World

- April 15 would be just another day.

- No more IRS tax audits.

- You get first crack at your paycheck, not the IRS.

- You decided how much to pay in taxes.

- Save and invest without being penalized.

- Leave an estate without being penalized.

The Sales Tax: Fairness

- Everyone pays the same 15 percent on the purchase of any retail good or service.

- Those who spend more, pay more taxes. Those who spend less, pay less taxes.

- That's fair.

How the Sales Tax Works

- Abolishes all federal income taxes and the IRS.

- Imposes 15 percent national retail sales tax on goods and services.

- Everyone pays the same rate; no loopholes for the rich.

- Protects the poor (no one pays sales tax up to the poverty level).

Mr. COLLINS. Thank you, Mr. Davis. I expect by the close of day next Monday when people, when most people finalize their tax forms and write their checks, that we will be able to get many, many more letters and also a lot more signatures on petitions.

Mr. English?

Mr. ENGLISH. Mr. Chairman, I have no questions. But I want to thank these gentlemen for taking the time to exercise their sacred right to petition Congress and to testify.

We appreciate your willingness to come forward and share your views. And, frankly, I hope you are able to motivate many more of our fellow citizens to get involved in this debate, to provide their ideas, but to push this institution to reform a tax code which has become an octopus which has reached into virtually every part of our life.

I thank you for being here.

Mr. DAVIS. Thank you.

Mr. COLLINS. Thank you, Mr. English.

Mr. Hulshof, do you have any further questions for Mr. Davis?

Mr. HULSHOF. No. Thank you.

Mr. COLLINS. Thank you.

Mr. Archer, do you have any questions, sir?

Chairman ARCHER: [presiding] No, sir.

I simply want to thank all of the witnesses for coming and presenting their views. We are very grateful for that. We know some of you have come from a long way and together, some way or another, we are going to work our way through and find an answer.

Mr. COLLINS. [presiding] Thank you, gentlemen.

Mr. Worley, we do appreciate you sitting through the entire service of yesterday and today.

Gentlemen, that concludes this panel and we will now recess for lunch. Thank you. For those of interest, 1:00 o'clock will be our time to reconvene.

[Whereupon, at 11:55 a.m., the Committee recessed, to reconvene at 1:23 p.m., the same day.]

Chairman ARCHER. The Committee will come to order.

Continuing with our hearing, we have our next panel of our colleagues: the Honorable Dick Armey, and the Honorable Billy Tauzin, and the Honorable James Traficant, to talk about their individual perspectives and potential alternatives for the current income tax.

Welcome, gentlemen. We will start off with our friend Dick Armey. We will be pleased to hear your testimony and your recommendations.

STATEMENT OF HON. RICHARD K. ARMEY, A REPRESENTATIVE IN CONGRESS FROM THE STATE OF TEXAS, AND HOUSE MAJORITY LEADER

Chairman ARCHER. Thank you, Mr. Chairman.

First let me appreciate you and your leadership in this whole area of tax law. I have said many times, and I am happy to say again, never could we have had a finer Chairman of the Ways and Means Committee more devoted to a professional commitment on the tax code.

I have had my own interest in the matter for some time, and particularly in January of 1994 when I focused on the issue at a level I had not done before.

I wrote the Flat Tax Bill. He later wrote his National Sales Tax. We teamed up, as you know, and have spent the better part of the last two years travelling across the country speaking frankly to very large audiences where we have had a clear commitment to end this nightmare called the current tax code.

In our presentations before those audiences, we always start off with a discussion of the burdens of the existing code. I have on the billboards up here an example of how we make the presentation.

For example, we divide the difficulties of the existing code up between myself and Billy, and we point out that families pay more in taxes, food, clothing, and shelter, and now we also add transportation, combined.

Americans work an hour and fifty-seven minutes of every day to pay federal taxes. Taxes are at peacetime record highs. And I think one of the very big issues. $200 billion in annual compliance costs for the current tax code.

Billy, when he opens his presentation, then will present further facts. And by this time what we see in the audience is a congealed understanding. Yes, this current tax code is a horrible mess in our lives. It confounds us. It complicates our lives. It costs us time, money, and energy, and it is generally all-around depressing and we want to be rid of it.

I think, Mr. Chairman, you yourself have seen in your own travels that there is a fairly clear agreement among the American people. We want to be rid of this current tax code.

The next part of our presentation then focuses on:

All right, once we agree that we want to get rid of the current tax code and replace it with something that is of better service and less intrusion in our lives, where do we go?

It is at that point that I present what I still will argue is the best alternative, the flat income tax, based on my desire to have a tax code that does not intrude government organization into the affairs of the family or the business.

No family or business decision about how to use your income—whether it be consumption, savings, or investment—should be made on the basis of tax considerations but should be on family and business considerations.

So our tax code to be correct in my estimation should be fair. It should be simple. It should be easily understood and easily complied with.

It should eliminate double taxation and accept a standard of fairness that I believe is the unique American definition of "fairness."

"Fair" is when you treat everybody the same as everybody else.

And it should forsake the sophistry that underlies so much of what we have in our current tax code, overburdened as it is with efforts of social control and income redistributions, a sophistry that we hear pronounced so many times as the false distinction between earned and unearned income that would give rise to a justified sense of it is fair to treat some forms of income differently than others.

The flat tax is very simple. It says to the individual. Take your total income earned in a given accounting period, deduct from it a generous family allowance—for a family of four that could be as high as $33,800—multiply the remainder by 17 percent, and your taxes are filed.

If you are a business, you take your total business income, deduct your business expense, multiply the remainder by 17 percent, and your taxes are filed.

We can cut that compliance cost down by 95 percent with this.

Now let me just say, the flat tax is filed on a form like this, the size of a postcard, 10 lines. In the original iteration of the flat tax I had written it so that we would put an end to withholding tax.

Your joint tax scorekeepers whacked me for $10 billion on that. In those deficit days, that seemed like a terrible burden. I took it out. But I would tell you, Mr. Speaker, when you mark up the flat tax in your Committee to bring it to the Floor, I would encourage you to follow my original advice and drop the withholding tax.

You will have a chance in this Committee—and this is very important for us to understand—by Constitutional authority we will write the modern, up-to-date, civilized respectful tax code for the American people in this Committee.

When this Committee does that work, you will find the flat tax is a bill easily written, congenial to the taxpayer, and one that you will get a fulfillment of what I think is one of the great, heroic American ideals. voluntary tax compliance.

I look forward to your proceeding with this. I encourage this Committee to move forward. Certainly you will be fair and you will be judicious as you judge all of the alternative ways in which you might write a new tax code for America. And I stand fully confident that when you begin this prospect in earnest you will find, as I have found, the only way to do this job is to do it with the flat income tax.

Thank you.

[The prepared statement follows:]

Statement of the Hon. Richard K. Armey, a Representative from the State of Texas, and House Majority Leader

Mr. Chairman, I appreciate your affording my colleague Representative "Billy" Tauzin and me the opportunity testify together. We have traveled to over 40 "Scrap the Code" debates to educate the American people on tax reform. Our effort has been intended to elucidate the details of two major alternatives to our current tax system to the public. I commend you for your own commitment to this cause. I know from our years of hard work together on this issue and our many conversations that we share the same goal for tax reform. I want to take this opportunity to thank you again for your leadership, friendship and advice on this issue.

The Tax Code is Broken

Mr. Chairman, there is an emerging consensus among the public policy community, members of Congress, and the public that our current tax system is broken and needs to be scrapped and replaced with a system that is fair, simple, low, and honest. This growing consensus centers around the belief that the current tax code is complex; inhibits saving, investment and job creation; imposes a heavy burden on families; and pollutes Washington's political culture. It cannot be fixed or replaced. It must be scrapped.

At the beginning of the 20th century, federal taxes accounted for less than 3 percent of U.S. gross domestic product (GDP) and the entire tax code and regulations filled just a few hundred pages. Today, federal taxes account for 20 percent of GDP, and a complete set of federal tax rules spans over 46,000 pages. I'd like to focus my remarks today on the problems with the current tax structure and how my bill, H.R. 1040, The Flat Tax, corrects these problems.

Current Code: Complex

This year, the tax code itself is 2,840 pages and about 2.8 million words. Taxpayers have to choose from 481 forms, a rise of 20 percent from 403 forms in 1990. The system is steadily growing more complex, causing over half of individual taxpayers to use a tax preparer for their income tax return, up from less than 20 percent in 1960.

Even the well trained are stumped by the complexity. Unsurprisingly, the IRS receives over 110 million phone calls a year from taxpayers asking for assistance. In 1999 the IRS was only able to answer 73 percent of the phone calls correctly. The inability of the IRS to answer over 25 percent of calls signals an inherent failing of the current system.

In 1998, Americans spent 5.7 billion hours filling out IRS forms—equal to 2.7 million workers doing nothing but IRS paperwork. With spring in the air, my family wants our time together to be better spent than digging deep in drawers searching for receipts or trying to make sense of complicated forms. I am confident there are many families like mine who are forced to sacrifice time with their loved ones to spend time making sense of the maze of forms and paperwork.

The Tax Code is Unfair

The unfairness of receiving a penalty for a wrong answer given the tax codes' complexity strikes at the heart of the American principles of fairness, justice, and equality before the law.

In one typical case, according to the non-partisan General Accounting Office, it took the IRS 18 months to correct an erroneous $160,000 assessment to an individual who was actually due a refund. The American people deserve fairness and they deserve to be rewarded for their honesty, integrity, and responsibility.

Yet the current tax code gives rise to legions of tax lobbyists fighting for their own particular deduction, credit, or other special preference in the law. Besides contributing vastly to the complexity, taxpayers with similar incomes can pay vastly different amounts. How much you pay in taxes is correlated to how much time you have to study and learn the tax code, and whether or not you have a lobbyist in Washington.

Record Peacetime Tax Burden

The total tax burden is at 20.7 percent of GDP—a post-World War II high. In fact the tax burden is a major impediment to our new digital economy. Some may argue that rising tax burdens as real incomes increase is the appropriate outcome of our current tax system. However, a progressive tax system is designed to make the rich pay a higher amount than the poor—not to increase the total tax burden on all citizens. The disincentives imposed by implicit and explicit marginal tax rates are growing and these disincentives reduce savings, investment, and growth.

The only legitimate purpose of a tax code is to raise revenue, and do that while doing the least harm to the economy and to the people. Yet the high burden imposed on us by the tax code also punishes us financially for activities and values that we should encourage.

—If we marry, we pay higher taxes than when we were single. We save for our children's education, only to pay taxes on savings from those earnings. We work hard to do more for our family, only to pay a higher tax rate on every new dollar that we earn. We die and pass our farm or business to our family, only to have them break up the business due to the punitive "death tax."

The Flat Tax Solution

The legislation I reintroduced this year with Senator Shelby of Alabama, (H.R. 1040) scraps the entire income tax code and replaces it with a flat-rate income tax that treats all Americans the same. This plan would simplify the tax code, promote economic opportunity, and restore fairness and integrity to the tax system. The flat rate would be phased-in over a three-year period, with a 19—percent rate for the first two years and a 17-percent rate in subsequent years.

Individuals and businesses would pay the same rate. The plan eliminates all deductions and credits. The only income not subject to tax would be a generous personal exemption that every American would receive. For a family of four, the first $35,400 in income would be exempt from tax. There are no breaks for special interests. No loopholes for powerful lobbies. Just a simple tax system that treats every American the same.

Simplicity

The flat tax replaces the current income tax code, with its maze of exemptions, loopholes, and targeted breaks, with a system so simple Americans could file their taxes on a postcard-size form. The Tax Foundation estimates that a flat tax would reduce compliance costs by 94 percent, saving taxpayers more than $100 billion in compliance costs each year.

Fairness

The flat tax will restore fairness to the tax law by treating everyone the same. No matter how much money you make, what kind of business you're in, whether or not you are married, or even when you die, you will be taxed at the same rate as every other taxpayer.

Prosperity

Because the flat tax treats all economic activity equally, it will promote greater economic efficiency and increased prosperity. When saving is no longer taxed twice, people will save and invest more, leading to higher productivity and greater take-home pay. When marginal tax rates are lower, people will work more, start more businesses, and devote fewer resources to tax avoidance and evasion. And because tax rules will be uniform, people will base their financial decisions on common-sense economics, not arcane tax law.

Lower Taxes

The flat tax was not designed to be revenue neutral. It reduces unfairness. Because of the high tax overpayment, there is room to provide tax relief. And the flat tax would provide significant tax relief. When the rate is reduced to 17 percent in the third year of the proposal, there would be significant further tax reduction.

But the flat tax does have a progressive element. Under the flat tax, the more you earn, the more you pay. In fact, because of the high family exemption, the more a taxpayer earns the greater the share of his income he pays in tax. A family of four earning $35,000 would owe no tax under the proposal. A family of four earning $50,000 would pay only six percent of its income in income taxes while a family earning $200,000 would pay 14 percent.

The flat tax is pro-family. The flat tax eliminates the marriage penalty and nearly doubles the deduction for dependent children. By ending the multiple taxation of saving, the flat tax provides all Americans with the tax equivalent of an unlimited IRA. This will make it easier for families to save for a home, a vacation, a college education, or retirement.

The flat tax also has a powerful political virtue in that it excites the public. The crucial importance of this should not be underestimated. Policy experts can and do sit in a room and write their version of the ideal tax code but it will remain a purely academic exercise if they cannot rally public enthusiasm for change.

In fact, a Zogby poll shows that the following breakdown:

	Percent Favorable	Percent Unfavorable
Democrats	60	31
Republicans	75.1	19.1

To the many Americans who have grown profoundly skeptical of the federal government, politicians, and lobbyists, the flat tax has spectacular appeal because it offers the American people a straightforward deal. It also rids Washington of many of the special interests' reason for existing: the current, unfair tax system.

The flat tax scraps the current code and gives taxpayers a new code that is simple, low, fair and honest. America deserves no less.

Chairman ARCHER. Thank you, Congressman Armey.
Congressman Tauzin, you may proceed.

STATEMENT OF HON. W.J. "BILLY" TAUZIN, A REPRESENTATIVE IN CONGRESS FROM THE STATE OF LOUISIANA

Mr. TAUZIN. Thank you, Mr. Chairman.

Mr. Chairman, you asked us to focus today on three points.

The first was the fairness and simplicity of the alternative plans.

The second was the impact on trade and commerce.

And the third was the compatibility with state tax collection systems.

Let me first acknowledge that I am accompanied today by Jim Traficant, my chief Co-Sponsor, who I am always pleased to share a podium with. He will also be available to answer any questions you might have.

Let me touch upon those three points. Without going into all the great reasons why we need to scrap the code, I adopt your great admonition that it is time to pull it out by its roots and destroy it so it never returns again.

Moving to a consumption tax does that. It allows us to get rid of the income tax code completely, to abolish the IRS, and to move to a simple, fair tax code.

Why is consumption taxes on retail sales fair?

First of all, let me suggest to you that there is something about an income tax code that is hidden from the American public that is not very apparent until you examine it closely.

At your desk, in addition to the wonderful little book I have written entitled the National Sales Tax. April 15th Just Another Day, is also a copy of an article by Dale Yargenson, the Chairman of the Department of Economics of Harvard University, in which Dale Yargenson points out something that I think Americans are not aware of. That is, that the income tax, the fact that we currently tax income on individuals and corporations and businesses, adds about 25 percent to the finished product cost of everything made in America.

So the pervasive effect of income taxes, however you style them— complex, simple, or flat—is that they add to the cost of products made in America.

So the perverse effect of an income tax code is that it punishes an American worker for buying his own products. It punishes those products in export trade, and it rewards him only when he buys a foreign product that comes in very often exempt from foreign VAT, value added taxes.

So when you think about income taxes in comparison to consumption taxes, you need to think about a single consumption tax at the retail level compared to not one but two taxes on the same money. the tax we pay from our paycheck that comes out as withholding, and the tax we pay in higher American prices for everything we make because income taxes have added 25 percent to the cost.

Take local bread for example. Studies indicate that 35 percent of a loaf of bread is income-tax related. If you get rid of the income tax, according to Dale Yargenson, you reduce the cost of a loaf of bread by that much in a competitive marketplace.

A loaf of bread, instead of costing $2, should rightfully cost $1.30. When you put a sales tax on the back of it at the retail sale, you still have a much lower price for bread than you have in America today. It is eminently.

In our plan that Jim Traficant and I have devised, you remember that this is a plan that we introduced years ago and have reintroduced every Congress. In this plan we go even further to make it fair.

We also repeal all of the payroll taxes that are collected from a worker's income up to the poverty line so that all income under the poverty line is not only free of income taxes under our plan, but also free of the payroll tax.

Now that is an extra 15 percent that goes into the workers' income and fully makes up for the effect of the sales tax on all the products you buy to take care of your family with income earned under poverty.

Now think about that. You have got more money to spend. you have got all of your paycheck, plus your payroll taxes that are no longer going to the government. And you are buying products made in America that can cost as much as 25 percent cheaper. That is pretty fair. Pretty simple. It puts you in charge of how much taxes you pay instead of a government that writes a code and regulatory structure of 7 million words and nobody can understand anymore.

On trade, Dale Yargenson points out that if we got rid of the income tax and so reduced the cost of American products by 25 percent, the export trade from the United States would jump 29 percent annually and would be at least 15 percent higher than it is every year thereafter.

In short, we would eliminate the trade deficit. American products would go out tax free. No income tax effect on them. And they would be taxed once in the place of destination instead of being taxed in America and also taxed there. A 29 percent jump in exports.

Dale Yargenson also indicates if we were smart enough to do what we recommend in a consumption tax at retail sale, we would also increase investment in jobs and manufacturing in this country by a factor of 80 percent. A huge increase in jobs, in manufacturing, a huge increase in exports, a simple plan that works for Americans that is fair, it is decent, it cuts the cost of American prices, and also rewards workers for buying their own products instead of punishing them.

That is a pretty good deal and one we ought to consider in this room. What a great gift we could give to this country if we ever pull that off.

Now you asked also about compatibility with state collection systems. The good news is that 45 states currently have sales tax collection systems. Under our plan, those states do the collecting. We would encourage the last five to put up a collection system, but if they do not we of course would set one up in those five states.

But in 45 states, the states would do the collecting. Our bill provides them with a one percent commission to cover the cost of the collection. Our bill rewards the retailer with a half of one percent to make sure the retailers' cost are covered in the collection system, and the balance is then remitted to the Federal Treasury.

Here is the good news on the collection system, how easy it works. In most sales tax jurisdictions, 80 to 90 percent of the sales taxes are paid by 8 percent of the retailers. The bulk of it is done by the big national retailers.

Under our plan, they can remit directly to the Federal Treasury if they want it on a national retail basis. In short, the minimum amount of sales tax collection is then left to the states for which they are paid a commission and for which the retailers are paid a commission.

One final thought and then I know my time is up. We even in our bill make provision to help the retailers with the software they might need to make their collection systems for the federal sales tax compatible with whatever plan may exist in their states for state sales tax collection.

Mr. Chairman, I yield back.

[The prepared statement follows:]

Statement of the Hon. W.J. "Billy" Tauzin, a Representative in Congress from the State of Louisiana

Mr. Chairman, it is my honor to address the Committee on the benefits of a national retail sales tax and my proposal, H.R. 2001, the National Retail Sales Tax Act of 1999. I first introduced this legislation, along with my friend, former Congressman Dan Schaefer in the 104th Congress. Since then I have been joined in this effort by Congressman James Traficant and others, that understand the economic benefits of a national retail sales tax. I look forward to working with you and the members of the Committee to overhaul our current system and lift the burden of the income tax from the shoulders of all Americans.

The federal government's outdated, flawed and unfair income-tax system has become a nightmare for all Americans. It has grown from 14 pages in 1914 to more than 2,000 pages of law, 6,000 pages of regulations and hundreds of thousands of rulings and interpretations. Tax preparers and income-tax experts who routinely testify before Congress admit that even they do not fully understand all of the provisions and ramifications of the Internal Revenue Code.

Since I last appeared before this committee in 1997, Majority Leader Armey and I have taken our message of tax reform to tens of thousands of people in over thirty cities on the "Scrap the Code" tour. At every stop on our tour we have been met by hundreds of Americans yearning to learn more about the major alternatives to the current code.

While Congressman Armey and I may differ on which tax-reform bill is best for America, we agree that Americans work too hard for their money, have too little to show for it and should not have to tolerate our inherently-unfair and overly-complex federal income tax code. What's worse is that the federal income tax code tells Americans how to live their lives—encouraging some types of actions and discouraging others.

Mr. Chairman, you have asked that these hearings focus on: whether our respective fundamental tax reform proposals are simple, fair and enforceable; the relevance of these proposals to the increasingly global marketplace; and, their compatibility of our proposal with State tax laws. First, let me briefly explain my proposal, H.R. 2001, the Tauzin-Traficant National Retail Sales Tax Act of 1999 (NRST).

My legislation would eliminate the personal and corporate income tax code—including taxes on capital gains and savings, inheritance and gift taxes, and all non-trust funded excise taxes, abolish the Internal Revenue Service and replace them with a 15 percent national sales tax on the retail purchase of all goods and services.

Simple, Fair, Enforceable

Unlike the current income tax code or even the flat tax, the national retail sales tax requires no federal individual tax returns of any kind. Americans are forced to spend in excess of 5 billion hours trying to calculate the amount of income taxes owed to the federal government. This is absurd. Individual Americans will pay their taxes when they make purchases of retail goods and services. No receipts, no tax returns, no audits, no hassle.

All goods and services for consumption would be taxed at the same rate—no exceptions. If we exempted food, clothing, and housing—which represents a substantial amount of the American economy—the rate would have to be significantly higher. The broader the NRST base the lower the rate. Exempting entire categories of goods or services would inevitably lead to an administrative nightmare of definitions.

The NRST will empower all Americans by giving them the choice as to how much tax they pay. Our present income tax system takes our money through withholding before we even receive it. Most of us now consider that our wages are really the "take-home pay" that we get net of all the deductions. Under the present system, it doesn't matter if one of us is more frugal than the other because we all pay the same amount of tax. In fact, if we are more frugal than our neighbor we are actually going to pay more and more tax because our earnings on our savings will be taxed each year.

With the national retail sales tax we receive all of the money we earn. Our checks are increased by the amount previously deducted for federal income tax. With this money in hand, we have the power to determine the amount of federal tax we pay based on how much we choose to spend. The more you consume the more you will pay in taxes. The less you consume the less you will pay in taxes. The American people, not Congress or the IRS, will have the power.

Also because of the way that the present income tax system hides the amount of taxes we pay in the price of goods and through withholding, I don't think any of us can really tell how much tax we are paying to the federal government. By eliminating the individual and corporate income tax, the estate and gift tax and all non-trust fund excise taxes and replacing them with a simple national retail sales tax, all of us will see the amount of federal tax we pay each time we make a purchase.

Critics of the NRST often claim that it is regressive—that the poor have to devote a greater percentage of their income to pay the NRST than do the rich. Under H.R. 2001, a tax credit would be allowed for thousands of households with incomes below the poverty line. This assures that all workers below the poverty level will pay no taxes. The formula will be made adjustable for non-working spouses and children by reducing FICA deductions on every paycheck.

Enforcement is an serious issue for any tax plan. Will there be people who try to evade the national retail sales tax? Yes. There are always going to be people who refuse to pay any tax. The current code has become so complex that it makes it easier for people to cheat the system..

Under the NRST there will be dramatically fewer collection points to watch. Instead of having to audit and collect information on 250 million taxpayers and millions of businesses, the government will have to watch a smaller number of collection points. All but five states levy state sales taxes. The other 45 states and the District of Columbia already have the mechanisms and experience in place to enforce the sales tax. Local administration and collection will translate into better compliance rates. States will also have an incentive to enforce the tax because the more they collect, the more they receive to cover their administrative costs.

The NRST would ensure that the underground economy, those individuals and businesses that don't file income taxes, would pay their fair share. The underground economy encompasses not only illegal sources of income, such as drug dealing, gambling, and prostitution, but also the ordinary citizen who accepts a lower price for cash payments and doesn't report the income or the businessman who keeps two sets of books and pockets a portion of the sales or takes improper deductions.

Relevance to the International Marketplace

Currently, Americans, in effect are taxed twice by the IRS. Americans pay a federal tax on their income, and pay what amounts to a "hidden" sales tax (believed to be as high as 15 to 20 percent) on the retail purchase of all goods and services. The federal government calls this the "corporate income tax"—as if it were really paid by corporations. But, in reality, consumers pay this tax in the price of goods they buy. So under the present code, American income is literally taxed coming and going. The net effect of the NRST, is to eliminate two taxes and replace them with one clearly defined tax on goods and services sold at the retail level.

This "hidden" sales tax makes it harder for American goods to compete overseas. Due to the income tax and its burdensome compliance costs, American products produced for export leave the U.S. at a 15–20 percent competitive disadvantage.

What's worse is that products imported into the United States enjoy a 15–20 percent competitive advantage over our American-made products. Most industrialized countries simply exempt products for export from most of their taxation. This exacerbates our trade deficit and translates into millions of lost American jobs. Mr. Chairman, that's unfair to American workers, products and companies.

Members of this committee are well aware that the World Trade Organization (WTO) has determined that the Foreign Sales Credit (FSC), a portion of the income tax code created to mitigate the effects of the income tax code, constitutes an illegal subsidy. In its October 8, 1999 Panel Report on FSC's, the WTO found that "...the United States is free to maintain a world wide tax system, a territorial tax system or any other type of system it sees fit. This is not the business of the WTO. What it is not free to do is to establish a regime of direct taxation, provide an exemption from direct taxes specifically related to exports, and then claim that it is entitled to provide such an export subsidy because it is necessary to eliminate a disadvantage to exporters created by the US tax system itself.."[1]

There will also be what some economists call the "sponge effect." The U.S. is the world's largest market and has the best infrastructure of any country on earth. When the income tax is replaced with the national retail sales tax, it will become the world's largest tax haven and a "sponge" for capital from around the world.

Compatibility with State Tax Laws

Currently, 45 States and the District of Columbia levy sales taxes (Alaska, Deleware, Montana, New Hampshire and Oregon do not). These states have the experience and mechanisms in place to administer the NRST. Under the Tauzin-Traficant plan, States would collect the 15 percent national sales tax from the retailers within the state and remit the tax to the United States Treasury. Participating States may keep 1.0 percent of their collections to offset their collection expenses. Similarly, any business required to collect and remit the sales tax would be permitted to keep 0.5 percent of tax receipts to offset compliance costs.

In closing, I believe that we should re-examine the basic ideas on which this government was founded. Our Founding Fathers insisted on the use of indirect taxes on individuals and specifically forbade direct taxes like the income tax. We have an opportunity to eliminate the income tax, the IRS, tax returns, audits, and the penalties on our work, savings and investments and replace them with a national retail sales tax. We must free Americans from the trappings of the income tax code.

The beauty of the national retail sales tax is its simplicity and fairness. Those who spend the most will pay the most. Those who spend the least will pay the least. No more income tax forms. No more compliance costs. No more hidden taxes. No more loopholes for the corporations and the rich.

What's important now is to begin a national dialogue and a dialogue within this committee on tax reform. This debate isn't simply about a flat tax vs. a national sales tax. This is about fundamental tax reform vs. preserving the status quo. Revolutionary change, such as scrapping the federal income tax and abolishing the IRS, will never happen unless Americans demand it.

Mr. Chairman, thank you again for holding these hearings and for your leadership on this critical issue.

———————

Chairman ARCHER. Thank you, Congressman Tauzin. Congressman Traficant.

STATEMENT OF HON. JAMES A. TRAFICANT, JR., A REPRESENTATIVE IN CONGRESS FROM THE STATE OF OHIO

Mr. TRAFICANT. I would just like to amplify upon Mr. Tauzin's statement and commend you, Chairman, for your leadership.

I believe if there is a possibility of changing a tax code that is un-American, it has the greatest shot with Bill Archer as Chairman.

I want you to know that your reform bill made a dramatic impact in America. I want to thank you for working with me on two of those issues, in changing the burden of proof and judicial consent.

I wanted to give you one statistic before I give you my statement: Seizures of farms, homes, and businesses in 1997 were 10,037. In 1999, they were 161. Thanks to you, Chairman Archer. And I want to thank the Republican Party for working with me.

---

[1] Adoption of a national retail sales tax would eliminate the need for Foreign Sales Corporations. Under the NRST, no tax will be placed on a product exported from the United States. In addition, since the NRST is designed to only tax consumption, all purchases made for business purposes would NOT be subject to the 15 percent tax. As our country becomes more and more dependent on foreign markets for our goods and services it is becoming increasingly clear that we must fundamentally modernize our tax code to increase U.S. competitiveness around the world.

One point I would like to amplify upon Billy's statement is that the Consumer Price Index plays a big part in the analysis of this particular bill. If there is any upward trend in cost, then there would be a reciprocal upward allotment in the cost of living allowance for seniors which are going to be very much panicked over this legislation.

Where I can help I believe Mr. Tauzin and the Congress is in trying to get hardcore democrat opposition to look at the salient points of this legislation, because it will have to have some Democrat support or they will continue to be at the back of the bus in the minority for many, many years, because the time has come.

I want to talk about attitude. General tax attitude.

If you fix up your home, you pay more taxes. If you let it run down in America, you pay less. I am not talking about a federal system, am I? But if you work real hard and you are very industrious, you get hit over the head and pay more taxes.

If you do not work, you get a check.

We must reward people for industry and work. But here is a point I would like to amplify upon what Mr. Tauzin has stated I think very eloquently. Let me say this. I have great respect for the Majority Leader. I believe a flat tax is absolutely necessary—not an income tax, but a flat tax on final retail sales consumption—for the following reason.

In my District we make the Cavalier, and Phil English is right across the border and his people work there as well. That Cavalier carries a 25 percent disadvantage against the Toyota that is imported from Japan.

For the first time in history you would have a border-adjusted tax. My Cavalier is made with a 25 percent overload from the tax code, gets shipped to some other country overseas and they put a value-added tax on that baby.

Then they come in under an agreement of some trade of some sort with basically free access to our market, and then we are worried about keeping our Cavalier plant in Lordstown, Ohio, Mr. Chairman.

So I think when you look at the final retail sales tax, here is a big issue. And here is one concern I have. I support that 15 percent national retail sales tax, but ask you to ensure that is going to be enough.

Now I heard this 30 and 50 percent crap, and this opposition crap I think is distorting it to the American people, but I think you will come up with that particular number that is necessary.

But I think what is most important that we all take a look at is that FICA and senior citizens. I think if there can be an improvement to our bill, and I would ask the Chairman to look at these machinations as you look at changing the code, that rather than have the opportunity to politically scare seniors, which I believe will be an opposition tactic and I predict it, to leave FICA alone as we do and put a study in there with that transition that would allow for a study and a natural transition to, if it in fact proves to be worthy in that regard.

But I think we leave open the opportunity to quantify income. And that is how we in fact evaluate those that are in hard times and those that are in good times. So I know that you are working on that, and you are working on many of those issues. But I would like to just close by talking about the attitude of our tax scheme.

When people work hard, they get penalized in America. That is not the type of scheme we need. We should be rewarding industry and industrial strength.

And finally, I think American companies will come back home. I think they will relocate in districts like mine, and I would ask for special legislation to help my District.

With that, I thank you for allowing me the opportunity to appear with two of the most distinguished Members of Congress, and I am glad Mr. Portman has shown.

Thank you, Mr. Chairman.

[The complete statement of Mr. Traficant follows:]

Chairman ARCHER. I am grateful to all three of my friends who are at the witness table today because all three of you want to put your shoulder to the wheel to drive this tax system to where it is not an odium on the American people, and rather that it can be transferred into a position to where it can be a strength.

All taxation, no matter how we collect it, is not a happy thing for the American people. There is no tax system that is going to be perfect without complaint. But the system should be fairer. It should be simpler. And what you, Congressman Tauzin, and you Congressman Traficant said, it should be one that is designed to improve our competitiveness in the world marketplace which in the next Century is going to be essential to meeting the needs of the American people.

It must furthermore level the playing field between foreign products and services entering this country and those that are manufactured and produced and ideated in this country.

And if we go through tax reform and we do not do the latter, we will have missed the golden opportunity for future Americans. And so I thank you for what you have presented today, all of you.

I say to my friend, Dick Armey, you have designed a system that is much, much better than the current income tax system and I applaud you for that.

I do wonder if—and I would like your response to this—is there upward mobility on the rate structure in your system?

Mr. ARMEY. Well, Mr. Chairman, let me just say, no. There is a single rate. Now if I make $100,000 a year, I pay 17 percent of that. If my good friend Sam Donaldson makes $500,000 a year for talking about what I do, he pays 17 percent of that. Now he will pay more in taxes than I will, but we will pay the same rate.

There is an adjustment at the low end in that the standard deduction is a larger share of the percentage of total income for low income earners than it is for high income earners, so there is some progressivity put in there. But it must be understood. When I wrote the flat tax, I said somebody has got to be stubborn about this.

The first point about which you must be stubborn is it can only be one rate. Immediately upon trying to introduce two rates, you will bring complexities to the tax code that will make it an unbearable thing.

And if I might say one other thing, when I tried to write a tax code I wanted to fulfill a variety of objectives. simplicity, honesty, fairness, neutrality. I have not found any effort to put border adjustability into any tax code that does not first violate the principle of neutrality and does not also simultaneously trespass against all the other principles, and would not in fact in the long run be eliminated and made ineffective by adjustments and exchange rates.

So I do not place a lot of store in efforts to achieve border adjustability in the tax code. I think that is—I think it is an objective that is, first of all, errant, and secondly comprises the rest of your effort.

Chairman ARCHER. But relative to my specific question, there is no provision in your bill to prevent future Congresses from raising the rate and going to marginal rates in your system, is there?

Mr. ARMEY. No. Let me just say that first of all as we saw in 1986, it is impossible for any Congress to protect America from a future Congress.

We do put a provision in that says it takes a two-thirds vote of both the House and Senate to either increase the rate, reduce the family exemption, or add any complexities back into the system. But that is about the best protection you can get, and in the end it stands upon the ability of the American people to hold their Congress's feet to the fire.

As we saw in 1986, future Congress's can fowl up anything.

Mr. TAUZIN. Mr. Chairman, might I——

Chairman ARCHER. Mr. Tauzin, I know you were a little nervous there in wanting to get into this question of border adjustability, so what is your response?

Mr. TAUZIN. Well first let me agree with Dick on this two-thirds provision. We have it in our bill as well.

Let me say, this is how it works today under GATT. Many of our trading partners have value-added taxes in their tax system. If you go buy something today in London you will be charged a value-added tax. But if you bring it to America, you get that value-added tax back. It is rebated.

The effect of that is to allow those countries under GATT to sell their products in the American market value-added tax free.

Chairman ARCHER. Will you suspend for a moment?

Mr. TAUZIN. Yes.

Chairman ARCHER. When the gentleman mentions GATT, he is talking about currently the WTO.

Mr. TAUZIN. The General Agreement on Trades and Tariffs.

Chairman ARCHER. Yes, which has been replaced by the WTO.

Mr. TAUZIN. Yes, the WTO.

Chairman ARCHER. Correct.

Mr. TAUZIN. The bottom line is that under these trade agreements, value-added taxes can be rebated back when the sale is made to another country.

So in effect the foreign product comes in and is purchased value-added-tax free. We can't do that with our income tax code under those agreements.

Our income tax code adds this 25 percent to the cost of the automobiles made in America to any product we make in America. It is shipped overseas and, guess what, the value-added tax is then assessed on those products overseas.

So they pay both the income tax in America and the value-added tax overseas. Whereas the foreign product pays whatever income tax they have in that country with the value-added taxes rebated. That is a natural advantage to the foreign product.

And let me say it again, Mr. Chairman. When you get rid of the income tax, you get rid of that 25 percent hidden tax on American products both consumed in America and shipped overseas.

So suddenly if you do this, if you go to a national sales tax, the American exported product gets taxed only once with the VAT tax overseas, instead of being taxed here in America first for the 25 percent burden, as Mr. Traficant pointed out, and then getting taxed twice.

You do achieve border adjustability.

Now let me concede to Mr. Armey. Nobody can say what is going to happen in future trade agreements, future exchange rates, but it is inconceivable to me that we can suffer this huge trade deficit with 19,000 American jobs lost for every $1 billion of that trade deficit, and not adjust our own tax code to deal with it. And we can and we should, if we adopt a national sales tax.

Chairman ARCHER. Do you believe—and, Mr. Traficant, I will recognize you in a minute—do you believe that it is fairer for foreign products to be able to enter this country under an income tax system and pay no share of our cost of government or to have to hear some of the burdens of this society?

Mr. TRAFICANT. Absolutely not, Mr. Chairman. This is a Final Retail Sales Tax Act. That Cavalier made in Lordstown is only taxes at 15 percent if it is bought in America.

If that baby is exported, it carries no 15 percent and would only be subject, as Billy said, to the VAT or the taxes of those particular countries.

I know you are working feverishly on leveling the playing field, but that is an awful big part of that. But let us also look at the double taxation.

Now we sell that Cavalier, or we sell that Toyota that is made overseas. It comes in. It carries now that 15 percent tax just like the Cavalier.

Now we pay $20,000 for the car. Now it is $23,000. We sell it in four years for $12,000. Now $12,000 of that car we did not use. So there is a deduct for the unused portion of the consumption that we originally paid.

So we are not taxing everybody twice, which we are also doing. We take that dollar on income. We pay an income tax on it. We put it in the bank. We take it out to buy the car, pay a tax on the interest, then pay a sales tax on the car with a 24 percent cost factor due to the tax code.

So I think the only reasonable tax scheme that has to be thoroughly investigated is one which adjusts that border-tax issue, or our trade deficit will continue to balloon because our free enterprise system is designed to produce at the lowest cost, thus forcing our manufacturers into Mexico, forcing them over into China to produce an item which we could perhaps produce in America competitively by reducing that heavy load.

Chairman ARCHER. I am trying to understand the disconnect between what Mr. Armey is saying and what the two of you are saying.

He says that he is leveling the playing field with his proposal. You are saying I take it that he is not leveling it?

He is further saying that your proposal creates an unlevel playing field which benefits the United States of America, and that unlevel playing field runs contrary to what he is attempting to achieve in his tax proposal.

I am just trying to understand the difference between you.

Mr. TAUZIN. Let me try. Mr. Armey's proposal does level the playing field of paying taxes in America. It is a flat rate. Everybody pays the same once you take your family deduction.

I applaud that. I think it is a much better plan than our current income tax code.

But there is another playing field outside of the one that we play on here in America. That is the global economy. In that playing field, simply flattening income tax rates will not do anything about the inequity of American products being taxed twice in global trade, and foreign products only being taxed once when they are brought to America.

That is the second playing field, if you will, that ought to be leveled.

Now you can argue about whether our bill levels it fairly or not, but it aims at leveling it. It aims at not only leveling the playing field inside our country with the simple flat rate everybody pays above the poverty line because we take care of income under poverty, but it also levels the playing field at the border which is the second one that as you pointed out, Mr. Chairman, may be the most important in the long run as this country goes more and more into global economic trade.

Mr. TRAFICANT. Mr. Chairman, I would like to amplify on that. There is a third playing field. And let me say this. I think Mr. Armey has done a great service, and it may be his legislation enacted into law, because I do not know if America is progressive enough yet to take a hard look. It takes years to make changes.

But there is a third playing field no one is looking at, and Mr. Armey's tax scheme does not even attempt to challenge it let along our current system. That is. The underground economy that avoids the payment of income tax, that many times is selling drugs on the street and getting an SSI check, where we are sponsoring literally with our tax dollars, subsidizing individuals who are paying no taxes.

Remember this. If that drug dealer buys a car, he is going to pay the same tax as Mr. Armey will, or Mr. Archer will. Every final retail sale is taxed with provisions to protect those on the bottom, and with the Consumer Price Index being calculated each year and adjusted for a COLA increase for those at the top.

So are we concerned about our seniors? We must be. We must be very careful.

Second of all, we are concerned about those at the bottom end of the ladder. I have many of them. But why should I continue to have an underground economy that goes untaxed with the continuing complication of submitting any forms when we can do away with forms and truly simplify it and raise revenue from all transactions.

That is the third playing field that I think is not being addressed by Congress and should be a salient point in the discussion.

Chairman ARCHER. Mr. Armey, you are outnumbered there. You certainly deserve to have an opportunity to respond.

Mr. ARMEY. Let me comment on both things.

I know this Committee is going to seriously undertake the task of writing a new tax code and I applaud you for that. I think this Committee should try to write a national sales tax, or even try to write a national value-added tax. I think you ought to try.

But in this process of doing that, I think you ought to take a hard scholarly look at border adjustability. It is a very complex and difficult subject fraught with a lot of misconception, almost mysterious at times, and you should have if you are going to try to sacrifice one of the what I think precious principles of tax law and engage in social engineering and income redistribution scheme called border adjustability, then I think you ought to have some very sober assessment as to whether or not it would work.

Because border adjustability is about trying to redistribute income between Americans and foreigners, and trying to encourage Americans specifically to buy American-made products as opposed to foreign. Those are social engineering objectives.

I think you will find when you study it thoroughly that it is ill advised and does not achieve the desired results.

Now the question of the underground economy must also be understood. It is wrong to say that you will capture the underground economy with a sales tax and you will not do so with an income tax.

In a world of income tax, a person who otherwise earns his income honestly pays income tax on his income and then buys cocaine from someone who earns his income dishonestly who does not in turn pay income tax on his ill-gotten gains through the peddling of cocaine.

In a sales-tax world, a person who otherwise earns his income honestly does not pay sales tax on his purchase of cocaine and the person who receives the income dishonestly may in fact pay sales tax on his purchase of an automobile.

But I can tell you, if the guy is smart enough to figure out how to acquire and sell cocaine and avoid taxes in that, he will figure out how to avoid paying his sales tax. Indeed, empirically speaking, we know as a matter of fact that every nation state in the world that has ever tried to implement a national sales tax has found the size of their underground economy has in fact grown.

The most recent case is Canada where they found that the use of cash in the Canadian economy doubled within six months of their implementing a national sales tax. Because the fact of the matter is, a national sales tax does not capture the underground economy; it encourages it to grow larger.

Now I too am concerned about the underground economy. There are two aspects of the underground economy. I think my flat tax addresses the one that breaks your heart the most.

The first part of the underground economy, the one we like to talk about, is people dealing in illegal transactions—contraband, dope dealers, bank robbers, people like that. Well obviously that is a question of criminal law not tax law.

The second, and the one that breaks your heart, is the guy who looks at the current tax code—he is otherwise normally very honest in his dealings in life and would love to be a person who would fulfill all of his contract with America by saying, yes, I will voluntarily pay my taxes but the tax code is so unfair in the way it gives breaks to people other than myself that I have a right to give myself a break.

It is so complex in terms of all the data points it must track, that they are never going to find me if I do give myself that tax break.

And that person succumbs to the temptation to, while otherwise is almost perfectly honest in his life, cheat on his taxes because it is a corrupt system and administered in a nonfair way by mean-spirited people. And besides that, they are treating my brother-in-law different than they are treating me, so I have got a right to give myself a break.

The flat tax ends that. The flat tax, you know I have a simple, decent, honest, fair tax code that is perfectly well understood not only by me but by my 8th grader, and it treats my brother-in-law exactly the same as it treats me so I have no excuse to cheat on such a fair system. And besides that, it has to track so few data points they would catch me if I did.

And you will get rid of most of the underground economy, but you will have to take care of the drug dealers with another method.

Chairman ARCHER. I have got one last question to ask for both of you, and then I have presumed too much on the time of the other Members.

Mr. Armey, what percent rate on your flat tax is required to give us revenue neutrality, to raise the same amount of revenues we currently raise from the income tax?

Mr. ARMEY. Let me say first of all, I appreciate that. I never strived for revenue neutrality when I wrote the flat tax. I wrote the flat tax in 1994, and I was perfectly content to get within $30 billion of total expenditures. That is based on my personal belief that the Federal Government is already too big and spends too much of our money and spends it too wastefully.

So given the formula the formula that I worked out at the time and the size of the personal exemption that I chose to give to the family, I came up with 17 percent. That is something that would be wholly in the discretion of the Committee of course as you wrote the bill.

I believe that if I went back in these surplus times and went through the scoring process to rewrite the flat tax, that I might come up with a different rate and it might be lower than 17 percent.

It troubles me a little bit. As you know, you can read about the flat tax on my web site at flattax.house.com, or you can buy and read my book in which case we would both profit, or you can find out.

There is a tendency on the part of people to believe that a flat tax must be 17 percent. I know the Canadians are talking about that and one or two other countries are talking about it. So we should never get ourselves fixed to a percentage as the necessary percentage.

My own view is in these surplus times we could get the level of revenue neutrality we have found acceptable, given our other budgetary patterns and still be under 17 percent, but that would have to be something the Committee would have to work out.

Chairman ARCHER. Well, Mr. Armey, that is all very interesting, but on that basis, Mr. Tauzin could say, well, we are only have a ten percent sales tax. We are going to arbitrarily pick that, and give a tax reduction to everybody.

And do not bother us with trying to duplicate current revenues. But as this Committee begins to pursue alternatives to the current tax system, we must put them all, as you say, on a level playing field.

Mr. ARMEY. Umm hmm.

Chairman ARCHER. So we must know what the rate is on your proposal to duplicate current revenues, which is the level playing field on which we compare every proposal.

Mr. ARMEY. I would be more than happy to have you apply that test with the apparatus of your joint tax committee and your scoring apparatus. When you mark up the flat income tax, I know you will apply that test, and you will come up with a rate. Whatever that rate is, it will be still welcomed by the American people.

By the same token, should you decide to mark up a national sales tax, or a national value-added tax, again, this committee making that mark would have to determine what that rate would have to be.

Chairman ARCHER. Well, it just so happens that the Joint Committee has done an updated analysis of your proposal, and the rate on that is somewhere around 26 percent to duplicate current revenues.

If we went with a 17 percent rate, which I continue to still hear promoted by the advocates of the flat tax, we are going to run massive deficits and we will more than use up the amount of tax relief that is provided for in the budget that we are voting on tomorrow.

Mr. ARMEY. Well, the first thing I would ask you, Mr. Chairman, is give me the joint tax committee's report, and I will, within a day or two, find out what their mistakes are. I do not believe they have evaluated my flat tax. We will take a look at it but I have not seen any scorekeeping on the flat tax that has ever come anywhere near that figure.

Treasury, a few years ago, came out with a figure like that. Within a day-and-a-half, we showed them their mistakes and they retracted their study because in fact, under their study, they found out that they could get—when made the adjustment for the errors, they came back to 17 percent.

Chairman ARCHER. Your proposal is in statutory language and it has been specifically been submitted to the Joint Committee.

Mr. ARMEY. Well, I will have to go over their work.

Chairman ARCHER. And the Joint Committee's estimates in the end, whether it is the AFT proposal, whether it is a Tauzin-Traficant proposal, whether it is the USA proposal, will be judged based on the Joint Committee's estimates.

Mr. ARMEY. No doubt about it.

Chairman ARCHER. And I have debated with them for many, many years about their estimates on capital gains and a lot of other things and I have always lost.

And whatever they say will be the criteria for what we do in this Committee. And the proponents of the flat tax have got to get honest with the American people, along with the proponents of every other proposal, and admit to a rate that will duplicate current revenues.

And to make comparisons on rates that do not do that is not level playing field.

Mr. ARMEY. Well, Mr. Chairman, let me just say I have not seen the joint tax committee's evaluation of it. I have not seen any evaluation like this from them or anyone else except the errant one that the Treasury Department retracted three or four years ago.

I would be happy to look at it.

The last thing that I want in arguing for a decent, honest, simple, neutral tax code is for me to make arguments that are not themselves honest.

I reserve the right, when joint tax works, to look at that. It is possible they have not in fact scored my bill as I wrote it or think I wrote it, and if they point some error in the interpretation of the bill that causes such an aberration in the scoring, I would be happy to address that in a rewrite of the bill, as I am sure the Committee would be.

But I do not think it is appropriate for you to suggest that I have not been honest on the bill based on some scoring made by the Joint Tax Committee that I have not seen.

Chairman ARCHER. Well, the Treasury scoring is not what we abide by in the Congress, as you well know. So that needs not be referred to.

What we do abide by is the Joint Tax Committee scoring, and they have never scored your proposal as being revenue neutral at 17 percent.

Mr. ARMEY. I have never asked them to.

Chairman ARCHER. From the beginning until today. And the argument in the past has been, no, we know it is not revenue neutral, we wanted to give tax relief to the American people.

That is fine. But if we are going to compare on a level playing field, then we have got to have a percent that will duplicate current revenues. Then if want to give tax relief, we can make an adjustment.

Mr. ARMEY. Mr. Chairman, I have never at any time since I first rewrote the flat tax in 1994 ever suggested it was my objective to be revenue neutral. I have always allowed that it would be the Committee's objective to do that, should they ever decide to mark it up.

And I have always been more than willing to work with any agency or persons that wanted to try to score this code.

If the Joint Tax has scored my proposal and come out with a conclusion that it would take 26 percent to get revenue neutral, I would like to look at that. I believe they have made a mistake.

I think I have a right to challenge their scorekeeping. You certainly exercise that right. But I do not appreciate having it suggested in here that I have been out before America being dishonest about this proposal, especially in light of the fact that I have not even seen this scorekeeping and have not had a chance to evaluate it.

Four years ago, when the Treasury Department made these pronouncements, in a day-and-a-half, we had them retracting their study because they were wrong. And I fully accept the possibility that the Joint Tax Committee has as much chance to be wrong as I do, but I certainly will not have my integrity impugned on the basis of a study I have not seen.

Chairman ARCHER. Let me say to my friend, I am not impugning your integrity because I think you have honestly said that the 17 percent is short and that you want to give a tax relief to the American people.

But if we are going to compare alternative plans before this Committee, then we cannot have every proponent say, oh, well I intended to give tax relief.

We have got to have a rate that compares on a level playing field. And the ultimate determinator of that will be the Joint Tax Committee, not the Treasury. And irrespective of what arguments any of us might have with them, they will be the supreme court, as they always are.

And we must follow that and go with it.

Mr. ARMEY. I think, Mr. Chairman, if you do not mind, we find ourselves in perfect agreement. I am offering you a form, a structure within which to write the tax code. It will be scored by Joint Taxes, as will everybody else's.

And I am going back to where I began this conversation, when this Committee sits down and goes about the business of writing a new tax code, you will, even if you try to write a national sales tax or a national value-added tax, quickly come to the conclusion that your time is better spent forsaking that impossible task and writing the flat tax.

Chairman ARCHER. Mr. Tauzin, what percent on your sales tax will duplicate current revenues?

Mr. TAUZIN. Here is how we calculate it, Mr. Chairman?

Chairman ARCHER. Do you have a Joint Committee estimate yet?

Mr. TAUZIN. I do not think we do. But it is a very simple formula. I will describe it to you, and I would do what Mr. Armey has suggested it, submit it to the Joint Tax Committee.

Chairman ARCHER. Yes, I think that would be very helpful.

Mr. TAUZIN. Yes. I think they have done some work on the Fair Tax you heard yesterday.

Ours does not repeal all the payroll taxes, nor does it contain an extra rebate, so it will differ dramatically from any scoring you already have on the Fair Tax.

Let me tell you how we came to it.

We took the total amount of taxes we repealed, the income tax, the gift tax, inheritance taxes, certain amount of excise taxes, we added to it the commissions that would be paid to the state and the retailers for collecting our tax, we divided that total into the total consumption as reported by the Department of Commerce, and we came up with a percentage.

Pretty simple formula. The percentage you come up with, if you do that work, will be 12.9 percent, 12.9 percent national retail sales tax would duplicate the income lost from all the taxes we repealed.

We did not stop there. Because our plan also repeals the payroll savings tax on all income earned under poverty.

We took that amount of taxes, divided that into the amount of total consumption, and you get a two percent rate. That is the amount of sales tax it would take to compensate Social Security, Medicare for the loss of payroll taxes collected on all income under poverty.

That two percent was added to the 12.9 percent to arrive at our 15 percent national rate. That is the rate that according to this simple math, replicates the amount of income that would be produced from the following totals.

The income tax repeal on individuals and corporations, from the gift taxes we repealed, from the death taxes we repealed, from the commissions we pay to the states, and for the payroll taxes we repeal under the poverty line.

Add up all those totals, divide it into the total consumption as reported by the Department of Commerce, and you will get a little less than a 15 percent rate.

Chairman ARCHER. I would appreciate it if you would get a copy of your proposal to me so that I can get it scored by the Joint Tax Committee.

Mr. TAUZIN. Count on it, Mr. Chairman. We will do that immediately.

Chairman ARCHER. And then just finally, before I yield to other members, Mr. Armey, does your proposal repeal the death tax too?

Mr. ARMEY. Yes, it does. It ends all forms of double taxation.

Chairman ARCHER. Okay, thank you.

Okay, Mr. Doggett.

Mr. DOGGETT. Thank you very much.

Mr. Armey, if I understand correctly, despite your obvious affection for Mr. Archer and Mr. Tauzin and Mr. Linder, you are unalterably opposed to their proposal for a national sales tax.

As you told Fox News on Sunday, "it does not work and furthermore it is regressive and it inevitably adds to a tax code that is equally as complex as today's income tax."

Does that remain your opinion?

Mr. ARMEY. My opinion is that, first of all, the current tax code must be forsaken, we have got to get rid of it, get behind it. The best way to do that, the most effective way to do that is the flat tax. It is the only proposal I know of that can be written, can be enacted, and can be complied with by the taxpayers.

Mr. DOGGETT. But I have accurately quoted your interview with Fox. And that remains your position.

You think that their idea is a very bad idea that this Congress should reject?

Mr. ARMEY. I think their idea is a much better idea than the current tax code as we know it. I believe that in the effort to actually sitting down, writing it out, enacting it, that you will find it is an impossible task.

Mr. DOGGETT. Thank you.

And there was some reference to a Joint Tax Committee analysis of your proposal. The only one I have seen, Mr. Chairman, is the one yesterday that said that this sales tax would have to be at a 59 percent level.

Is there one now available analyzing this flat tax too?

Chairman ARCHER. I am told that three is and I am requesting a copy of it in writing which I will be happy to.

Mr. TAUZIN. Mr. Doggett?

Mr. DOGGETT. Thanks. I am going to get to you in just one minute because I have got some questions I want to ask you too, Billy.

And as far as you mentioned a markup, has a markup been set on this flat tax yet. Mr. Armey was referencing a flat tax markup.

Chairman ARCHER. I am not sure to what he refers.

Mr. DOGGETT. Okay. Well, let me move on to something else then. Am I correct in understanding, Mr. Armey, that you remain opposed to requiring the Section 527 political bank accounts, like Mr. DeLay has set up to disclose their contributors and expenditures on the same basis that all of us, as federal candidates and political action committees already do?

Mr. ARMEY. No. I have never said I am opposed to that. I think I would be happy to have that kind of disclosure and for the 527, for the labor unions, for any number of other organizations that are out there now mucking around in our world with relative anonymity spending other people's money.

What I am opposed to is just taking part of the issue to the floor without this Committee exercising its jurisdiction on it.

Mr. DOGGETT. As far as 527 political organizations, whether the money comes directly out of a labor union treasury from the Chinese government, from a corporate treasury, or from anyone else, do you think that this problem of them taking unlimited amounts of money and not telling what the source was is a problem that requires prompt action by this Congress and a floor vote?

Mr. ARMEY. I have mixed emotions about that. For the most part, if the 527 complies with the performance requirements of such an establishment, that is, does what is legally done under the law given their charter, I am not sure that I have a need to know where they receive their resources.

If in fact though, we want to make that disclosure requirement, I would be happy to live with it, as long as it was evenly imposed on all such organizations.

Mr. DOGGETT. But basically you do not think the fact that they hide their contributors is a problem that this Congress needs to deal with soon?

Mr. ARMEY. From my point of view, I do not care who is paying your bills if you are minding your manners.

Mr. DOGGETT. Okay. And with reference to another issue that you have expressed an opinion on, do I understand it is your view that instead of the House acting promptly to address the problem of abusive corporate tax shelters, as recommended by the American Bar Association Tax Section and the Treasury Department, that it remains your view that this Congress should instead encourage corporate tax, I believe in your words, "avoidance is necessary and legal and legitimate."

Mr. ARMEY. Tax avoidance is legal; tax evasion is illegal. This government writes the laws. We ask the American people, whether through individual or corporate behavior, to comply with the laws. If they comply with the laws that we write, we have no complaint about them.

If we want to rewrite the law, we should do so. That is why we have a Ways and Means Committee, that is why we have a Senate Finance Committee, and it is our prerogative and our duty to write the law.

Mr. DOGGETT. But, again,——

Mr. ARMEY. But as we write the law, we should never exercise any prerogative to complain about the legal compliance with the law we write.

Mr. DOGGETT. In terms of your priorities, you do not see abuse of corporate tax shelters as something this House needs to move on promptly to address?

Mr. ARMEY. I believe that is addressed. Chairman Archer has addressed that repeatedly and recurringly and consistently throughout all his efforts——

Mr. DOGGETT. You see nothing further that needs to be done in——

Mr. ARMEY. I did not say that. I am saying that I am not on this Committee and I am not an expert of it. I have a Chairman though that is distinguished in the respect that he commands across the nation is unparalleled in his understanding of the Tax Code, and I am more than happy to work with him and this Committee as they move forward.

Mr. DOGGETT. As far as tax avoidance, does your proposal that you are advancing here in front of the Committee, repeal those sections of the Internal Revenue Code that currently prohibit tax avoidance?

Mr. ARMEY. Tax avoidance is legal, is a legal activity. Anybody has a right to minimize their tax burden within the existence of the law. This accounting 101. Everybody knows that.

Tax evasion is illegal activity. I do not believe that tax evasion should be tolerated, and tax avoidance is a basic right of every taxpayer.

Mr. DOGGETT. You indicate that your concern in your written testimony with the many pages and the millions of words that are in the Tax Code.

Can you advise us of how many hundreds or thousands of pages have been added to the Tax Code during the time you have been majority leader?

Mr. ARMEY. I have no idea, but I can tell you it is impossible to do much of anything with this existing code except to abolish the separate parts like we did with the marriage penalty or like we did with the earnings limitation, cut it out. It is like cancer. You cut out the lump completely and throw it away.

But this is one of the problems with the existing Tax Code. You cannot either lower it or raise it without making it more complex.

Mr. DOGGETT. Is the number of pages or sections or pounds or words that have been added to the Tax Code during the time you have been majority leader something you could advise the Committee on?

Mr. ARMEY. I do not know the answer to that. It is roughly the same as the number of pages that have been increased since you have been on this Committee.

Mr. DOGGETT. Well, I have only been on it for about a year-and-a-half. But in the last six years, you have added much more than that, have not you?

Mr. ARMEY. I have no idea.

Mr. DOGGETT. No idea?

Mr. ARMEY. I do not count such things.

Mr. DOGGETT. Mr. Tauzin, let me see if I can get one idea from you, and I only have one question for him, Mr. Chairman.

Do I understand that under your proposal, that you would view as a significant federal revenue source, particularly in future years, electronic commerce?

Mr. TAUZIN. No, we have not addressed the issue of electronic commerce.

Mr. DOGGETT. Well, you are going to tax, as a federal revenue source, all the sales over electronic commerce, are you not?

Mr. TAUZIN. No, we have not addressed that issue at all in the plan. The plan was written before electronic commerce even began. If you will let me answer.

Mr. DOGGETT. You cited some testimony and then you can elaborate on that. Your written testimony——

Mr. TAUZIN. Well, I am trying to answer you, Mr. Doggett, give me the courtesy of an answer.

Mr. DOGGETT. Sure, if you would, sir. Your written testimony indicates you do not want to exempt anything, that it is important that it be a broad-based tax. So if you would tell us if you plan to or to not impose a sales tax on electronic commerce?

Mr. TAUZIN. Let me try it again. Let me try it again.

When the Joint Taxation Committee reviewed the Fair Tax plan you heard yesterday, they stated very clearly that the estimate did not assume that retail Internet sales would be subject.

We have not made an assumption one way or the other because Internet retail sales now amount to less than two percent and 80 percent of those are in services that are not subject to sales taxes today.

So let me make the point to you. The plan we wrote was written to the advent of the beginning of this electronic commerce technology phenomenon.

If the decision of this Congress is, at any point, to subject Internet sales, goods or services, to taxation by any jurisdiction, that is a decision we will make separate and apart from the decision we make on changing the income tax code to a consumption tax code.

We did not assume Internet commerce sales in our numbers. They were not in our 15 percent projection. If Internet commerce becomes a major part, as it certainly will be, we will have to address that as a separate issue as written——

Mr. TRAFICANT. Will the gentleman yield.

Mr. DOGGETT. Mr. Tauzin, as written, and as presented to the Committee today, your bill contains no exemption for Internet commerce sales, does it?

Mr. TAUZIN. Let me say it again. The bill was written prior to the advent of Internet sales and sales taxes on the Internet even becoming an issue.

Let me make a point to you. If the decision of our Congress, at some point, was to reject a recommendation of the Commission that we created, that is, recommended no taxes on Internet, if we reverse that decision and decided that the states and localities did have a right to collect the sales tax on those, or if we wanted to impose the national sales tax on those numbers, those numbers would then be calculated——

Mr. DOGGETT. I appreciate that. But you understand, of course, since you referred to the Joint Tax Committee, that when scoring the Fair Tax, they included Internet sales and said it would be substantially higher than 59 percent sales tax if you did not include Internet sales.

And if we passed your bill as you presented it today, it would impose a sales tax on every bit of E-commerce in this country today.

Mr. TAUZIN. Let me say it again. The assumptions we made in our bill were based upon the current economy. The current economy without the advent of substantial——

Mr. DOGGETT. In what year?

Mr. TAUZIN. I am sorry?

Mr. DOGGETT. In what year?

Mr. TAUZIN. We started the bill in 1996, I think it was.

Mr. DOGGETT. We had pretty good E-commerce going down our way in 1996.

Mr. TAUZIN. Yes. No. You did not have any E-commerce?No, sir. In fact, a browser was presented to the American public in 1995. If you had a lot of E-commerce going in 1996, Texas was substantially ahead of the world.

Mr. DOGGETT. It usually is.

Mr. TAUZIN. It usually is. And guess what Texas did, sir? Texas does not have any income tax, it has a sales tax. And when Mr. Armey talking about there being no great country in the world that has ever gotten rid of the income taxes and adopted a sales tax and done well with it, he neglected to say that the great country of Texas has made that decision and has done fairly well with it.

In fact, the states that have gotten rid of their income taxes and have gone to sales taxes do substantially better economically than the states who either have income taxes or a combination of the two. Texas is a good example why we ought to do this for the country.

Why does it make sense to locate in a state which has an income tax that is going to add to the cost of doing business, when you can locate in the great State of Texas and pay no income taxes, and simply have others pay the taxes when they buy your products?

Texas understands that.

Mr. Doggett, you ought to understand it too, sir.

Chairman ARCHER. That is a good place to terminate this.

Mr. TRAFICANT. Mr. Chairman, I want to make one quick response, if I could, to my fellow Democrat.

Our bill would repeal corporate income taxes, shelters would not be a big problem.

Second of all, if this Committee would ever decide to tax the Internet, it would raise more revenue with our bill.

And I think that the numbers you are throwing around are very arbitrary, and I do not think they come from sound, pragmatic information.

Now let me just close by saying this. You had about ten minutes. One thing I think is important in this process, whether you are Democrat or Republican. We are trying to help the American people. And one thing we do not want to do is scare the American people by pushing partisan concepts.

And I would just like to say that I believe that our plan, at 15 percent, is tentative. And I have talked to the Chairman myself. I believe that it is something we can work out and make manageable at a figure much lower than a flat income tax.

Chairman ARCHER. Let me speak just briefly to what my colleague, Mr. Doggett, alluded to which appeared to me to be an effort to say that Republicans have complicated the Tax Code.

Now maybe I am misreading the inquiry.

First, the number of pages that we have to comply with and the number of words that we have to comply with is primarily being churned out by regulations out of the Treasury and the IRS. And they are spewing out by the hundreds of thousands.

The number of additional pages to the Tax Code that have occurred in the last six years, I regret. But the gentleman from Texas realizes that the only tax bill that has been passed was the one in 1997 that was negotiated with the Administration which insisted on provisions that I could not prevent that thoroughly complicated the Code and required many, many extra pages.

Now you cannot have it both ways. On the one hand, you cannot say the Administration is responsible for the wonderful economy, but the Congress is responsible for extra pages in the Tax Code. That does not wash.

And so let the record be very clear about that.

Mr. English?

Mr. ENGLISH. Thank you, Mr. Chairman.

And Mr. Chairman, I want to compliment your performance chairing this hearing in that you have given a great deal of time for a variety of views to be heard and you have not strictly honored the time limits.

I am going to keep my remarks brief. I want to compliment these two gentlemen for the exceptional job they have done and the majority leader has done of framing the issues of tax reform.

You were not present earlier today when we heard testimony with regard to my tax proposal which has some similarities to yours.

And on the business side, there are some clear similarities that I would like you to comment on.

Mr. J.D. Foster from the Tax Foundation described the value of border adjustability very clearly.

And Mr. Tauzin, you and Mr. Traficant have also made a strong case for it here.

Mr. Foster talked about, in effect, importing the tax base of our competitor countries when exports are taxed.

Mr. Hufbauer, on the second panel, talked about how a border adjustable tax eliminates the tax motive for runaway plants.

I know, Mr. Traficant, that has been the source of a lot of your interest in some of these issues.

I wonder if either of you could comment on the effect that your plan would have on the cost of capital for businesses trying to compete in the international marketplace?

Mr. TAUZIN. Well, let me turn your attention, Mr. English, to the study done by Dale Yargenson at Harvard University.

Mr. ENGLISH. I am familiar with it.

Mr. TAUZIN. He indicates in there that, in the long term, in the long run, producer prices in America would fall by almost 25 percent relative to prices under an income tax code.

Now, when producer prices fall and you are shifting away from a tax code that penalizes savings and investment to one that rewards savings and investment, and only taxes consumption, the combination of consumer prices falling, which means lower cost to produce products, and the combination of an incentive for savings and investments, because there are no taxes on interest earned or investment portfolios or capital gains any more, both combined to increase savings rates and to lower the cost of capital to those people who want to invest and dramatically increase manufacturing opportunities in the country.

In fact, his conclusion is, production would increase in all industries and the rise of production of investment goods would be much more dramatic.

The combination would be, according to Dale Yargenson, absolutely phenomenal.

Mr. TRAFICANT. I would like to just quickly respond thereto, Mr. English, and appreciate all your efforts that you have done on this.

Mr. ENGLISH. And we appreciate yours, sir.

Mr. TRAFICANT. I think that our bill will send a clear message to the world that if you are going to play in the biggest marketplace, the flea market of the world, it might be good to put some roots in there, rather than look at 15 or 16 or 17 percent when the Chairman is done, ultimately looking at the numbers and the prices.

And that Toyota may not be shipped into America, it is going to be built in America because they are going to want to take that competitive advantage away that American firm is going to have.

When we drop the prices, the capital and the use of capital will raise. When you are not taxing savings and investment, there is going to be more savings, thus there is going to be more capital, thus we are going to have a downward spiral on inflation with a built-in hedge against inflation which will provide more capital the normal way, through commercial loans that are caused by savings, not by borrowing and foreign debt.

Mr. ENGLISH. That make excellent sense.

Let me also quickly, gentlemen, ask you one last time so we can clarify.

Neither of you are here advocating Internet taxation, are you?

Mr. TAUZIN. Let me say that again. No, we have not.

Mr. ENGLISH. That is all you need to say.

Mr. TAUZIN. No, we have not.

I do want to correct the record that the Tax Committee report that the gentleman referred to on the Fair Tax, that is not our plan. That is a plan that was presented yesterday did make an assumption that Internet sales taxes would apply to the Internet.

We made no such assumption.

We leave it to the good sense of your Committee in drafting a national sales tax plan along with the other members of Congress who are going to have to make that difficult decision to decide it.

But if we decide it as a Congress, that goods and services sold on the Internet were going to unfairly compromise in competitive terms, goods and services sold within our states and that are currently taxed, if we wanted to rationalize a system, you can do it within a national sales tax context a lot easier than you can trying to let 1700 jurisdictions tax the Internet.

So while we make no judgment on that, Phil, we do not recommend it. We make the point that at least if you want to make a decision on that, the national sales tax is a place where you can reasonably and rationally make those decisions.

Mr. TRAFICANT. One thing I would just like to add briefly is if that ever did happen, and we were to tax that Internet sale activity, it would be very hard to avoid the tax and to have an underground economy, would not it?

So I think that is a decision your Chairman and your Committee makes, and our bill would be, in my opinion, an enhancer for revenue, but we do not have it as a part of our construct.

Mr. ENGLISH. Mr. Chairman, I have plenty of other questions, but I think out of courtesy, I will leave them to another time. Thank you.

Chairman ARCHER. I overlooked, in my preliminary comments, a compliment to our colleague, Mr. Traficant, who was kind enough to compliment me on the IRS Reform Act, and without his persevering efforts, I do not believe we would have shifted the burden of proof, because he drove that issue or the levying on someone's homestead without a court order.

And those two vital provisions in that reform were driven by Congressman Traficant, and I was pleased to be able to be a vehicle to carry his ideas into law.

Mr. TRAFICANT. Thank you, Mr. Chairman.

Those were some of those additional pages too, were not they?

Chairman ARCHER. Yes.

Mr. TRAFICANT. Those very good things.

Chairman ARCHER. Yes. Yes.

Mr. Collins?

Mr. COLLINS. Thank you, Mr. Chairman.

You know, Mr. Chairman, I think it is interesting and good that we have the dialogue among members especially as we have seen here this afternoon. I have enjoyed listening to three Texans in the dialogue. I have always heard that things are big in Texas. Some people produce big ideas, some people produce big talk.

You know, I came here in the elections of '92. I remember the first yea here, the approach to the budget and deficit reduction was a large tax increase. I do not how many pages it added to the Tax Code, but I do know it some somewhere around $250 billion over five years, and it taxed additional benefits on Social Security. It took the cap off the Medicare earnings for tax. It added an additional marginal rate. It also added a surtax in retroactive taxation for the first time in history and a 4.3 percent fuel tax increase for deficit reduction. That was the approach of that budget of 1993.

I also know that in the beginning of 1995, when a new majority was formed in this town by the people across this country, that the CBO, the Congressional Budget Office, reported that based on the way the government was running, based on the previous majority, the deficits over the next ten years from that date would be somewhere around $3 trillion negative cash flow.

Spending was wild. It was about as wild as the approach to the '93 tax reform and budget.

I also know that the only tax relief that the American people have seen was in 1997 and then our seniors last week with the signing of the earnings limit repeal.

But I do know too that at the beginning of 1999, the Congressional Budget Office came back to the Congress and said, look, based on the way the government is now operating, the approach that we have taken to the budget process and to attempted taxation relief, a strong economy that has made by the people of this country that the projections were over the next ten years, we would have $3 trillion positive cash flow. Now a lot of people use the word "surplus," but it is a positive cash flow.

And even came back the first of this year and said there would be another trillion, a $4 trillion positive cash flow.

I think that is quite substantial in comparison to any type of regulations the IRS may have added to the pages of the Tax Codes.

You know, I hear a lot and receive a lot of E-mail about the proposed Internet tax.

I think one of the reasons the people get up in arms so about a proposed Internet tax is because they do not want an additional tax. It is not that they are not looking for a fair tax, they just do not want an additional tax. They are already taxed too much as it is.

And I have always felt like that excessive taxation comes from excessive spending. We still have some spending that we need to address, even as the majority.

Mr. Chairman, I appreciate the gentlemen that have been here to offer their proposals on a flat income tax and a flat national sales tax.

And to quote a good friend of mine from my district that used to serve in the Congress of the United States, at home I have friends for the flat income tax and I have friends for the flat sales tax. And, Mr. Chairman, I am for my friends.

We thank you for this dialogue, we thank you for this hearing, and we appreciate our colleagues coming with their comments and their proposals.

Thank you, Mr. Chairman.

Chairman ARCHER. Thank you, Mr. Collins.

Mr. Becerra?

Mr. BECERRA. Thank you, Mr. Chairman. And let me thank my friend, Mr. Tauzin, for being such a sturdy character and being able to sit there and take all the questions. We thank you for your patience.

Mr. TAUZIN. Thank you, sir.

Mr. BECERRA. Let me go back to the Internet tax because I think it is an important point to make. And I think you were trying to be thoughtful in your response to that. That at the time you were proposing this, we did not know the impact that the Internet would have and the growth of sales on the Internet.

I think everyone agrees that it is going to continue to grow. And right now, Congress has agreed on a moratorium on taking any action with regard to taxing the Internet.

In your written statement, in your testimony, you do say exempting entire categories of goods or services would inevitably lead to an administrative nightmare of definitions.

If now, if what you are saying is that because we were expecting the Internet to become such a major player in retail sales, you did not take it into account, can you reconcile that with your statement that if you start having exemptions of categories of goods or services, that this will inevitably lead to an administrative nightmare of definitions.

How do you reconcile that now?

Mr. TAUZIN. Well let me explain to you what we meant by that, what we mean by that.

The concern was that there are categories of purchases, like food and drugs, that might or should be subject to an exemption. Because those are items that are used by all of us regardless of our income and because those items tend to be necessities in life that the people at the bottom there has been a disproportionate share of their income in order to purchase.

Many states give exemptions for food and drugs and other items. All of those states have experienced bureaucratic nightmares with their exemption program. Is Cheetos a food or an entertainment? Who knows what it is?

So they have come with some bizarre descriptions of what is a food that is exempt and what is not. And we have tried to avoid that by simply providing the 15 percent rebate into a worker's salary for the amount of money that otherwise would have gone into the Social Security Medicare Trust Fund from payroll taxes.

We make that up with a two percent add-on to the retail sales tax.

In effect, we found a simple way of compensating people at the bottom for the taxes they would pay on necessities like food and drugs.

Mr. BECERRA. Now, let me keep you focused at this stage, and I am not asking you this is what you would do in your legislation. But at this stage, now knowing what you know about the Internet——

Mr. TAUZIN. Let's talk about it.

Mr. BECERRA.—yeah, what is your sense right now. How would you treat the Internet in your legislation?

Would it be taxed so that there are no exemptions, or at this stage, are you saying that maybe there is a need for an exemption for Internet retail sales.

Mr. TAUZIN. Let's talk about it.

First of all, understand that one of the reasons for a national sales tax that I think is superior to a flat income tax is the border adjustability question. The problem is that American workers are penalized when they buy their own products and rewarded when they buy foreign products.

If you want to keep to that border adjustability you have to at least make room in your plan for the notion that you cannot let American consumers buy foreign goods over the Internet and escape the border adjustable tax.

So you probably have to take that into the consideration in the context of a formal plan that we would eventually adopt taking into account Internet sales.

Mr. BECERRA. But then how would you account for the difference between prescription drugs that are produced here in America versus abroad? Would you now make an exemption for seniors on Medicare who are on fixed income who have to purchase drugs to now have the exempted from the tax, or will they have to pay a tax?

Mr. TAUZIN. I do not think that is the issue because our plan provides a rebate whether you buy a foreign drug or a domestic drug. You still get the 15 percent rebate, and we are still producing products in America, according to the Harvard study, at 25 percent less cost than we are producing them today.

In effect, we are producing products in America that cost less and you have more money to buy them with, so you still come out better.

The issue you raise, though, which is a real one, is if you go to a national sales tax base, in order to achieve border adjustability, you must apply the tax to foreign imported product, then must you simultaneously apply it to a domestic product that is purchased over the Internet as opposed to purchased in a brick and mortar store?

And the answer is, you may well have to. You may end up with that conclusion. Because to exempt it might create a problem with WTO.

Mr. BECERRA. So what I hear you saying is. Probably look at an exemption so that you can compete with foreign sales, but not an exemption if it is a retail sale over the Internet domestically?

Mr. TAUZIN. No, what I am saying is I think you have to apply the same rule to both.

Mr. BECERRA. But then you would exempt domestic sales as well?

Mr. TAUZIN. If you ended up deciding you wanted to exempt all domestic sales on the Internet from the national sales tax, I think you would have to exempt the foreign imported purchases as well.

Therefore, I think you would probably have to do what the Joint Tax Commission did. You would probably have to assume that they are all either subject to taxation or not.

And that is, as I said, is a decision we are going to collectively have to make.

Mr. BECERRA. But then what you are going to end up with is a higher tax rate on your sales tax because, as the Joint Tax Committee has said, that with the AFT proposal, which is similar to yours, as a consumption tax, they assume that the Internet retail sales will be taxed, and if they are not, that means the tax rate you would have to impose on sales would have to be even higher.

So you are going to have to impose a higher rate which is a higher rate for that drug purchase by that senior for those prescription drugs or for funeral services or for medical services.

If I go have a surgery, a lifesaving surgery, I will have to pay taxes on that, that someone who has got the good fortune to be able to purchase on the Internet will have those particular purchases exempted from the tax.

Mr. TAUZIN. That is my point. I think you either have to come to the conclusion that you exempt them all, in which case you have a reduction in income not just to the federal system, but to all the state and local jurisdictions.

You have to come to a conclusion that you have to rationalize the tax collection across the board. I think we end up, at some point, deciding the latter, but that is a decision we all have to make.

If you do exempt them across the board, of course you need higher rates on that which is not exempted. That is why we start with the proposition that you ought to at least start with the notion that the fewer exemptions the better, because that applies a uniform treatment to all parties in the marketplace.

And secondly, that you ought to keep the rate as low as possible so that you spread the burden across the spectrum of consumers. Always keep in mind that we protect those at the bottom.

And I appreciate your reminding me of that because my friend from Texas asked Mr. Armey to reiterate his quote on the news show this weekend.

I heard him this weekend, and I almost called him up because he is never said that in any of our debates, because he knows better than to say that the plan we have presented is a regressive tax plan.

You can have a sales tax that is regressive if you do not take care of people under poverty. But we do. It is not regressive.

You know what is regressive? What is regressive is an income tax code that adds 25 percent to the cost of every drug, every piece of bread, every bottle of milk that a family buys to take care of themselves. That is what goes on today.

Mr. BECERRA. And that is a notion that ultimately, if we were to move towards a different system, would be tested because it still stands to be seen if rates, prices on goods or services would actually go down.

Mr. TAUZIN. Let's talk about that for a second.

Mr. BECERRA. Well, I know I am running out of time.

Mr. TAUZIN. I think we got time.

Mr. BECERRA. All right, but before we go there, let me ask you this.

When do you think you will have some sense about what you will do when your legislation with regard to Internet retail sales?

Mr. TAUZIN. Well, first of all, I would not do anything in the legislation to make that decision until we collectively make it as a Congress.

You would have to decide whether, if you were going to national sales tax, whether you wanted higher rates on the goods you do not exempt in order to exempt goods on the Internet.

I do not think you would make that decision. I think we would end up deciding to cover them all equally at some point, but that would be a decision we would make jointly.

Let me mention, let me answer the question you asked about whether prices would fall. The answer is at your local Wal-Mart today. Wal-Mart and K-Mart compete bitterly right now for your and my dollars.

I understand they are operating on extremely small margins. And if it was not a competitive marketplace, they could probably raise their prices 25 percent, and you and I would have to pay it if the only place we could go is to one or the other.

But because we have a competitive marketplace, they have to operate on small margins. They cannot gouge us. Competition does that.

If Wal-Mart all of a sudden tomorrow, because we repealed the Income Tax Code, is now able to buy goods for substantially less than they did last week, and they try to sell them to us at the same price as they did last week, they will find out that K-mart is taking their business away.

Mr. BECERRA. But how are they purchasing them for less if they are going to have to pay to purchase the goods that they are going to sell are taxed?

Mr. TAUZIN. Ah, but they do not. Read the bill. The bill is only a retail sales tax. There is no tax on the wholesale, there is no tax on the purchase of raw materials.

Mr. BECERRA. Where is the savings on the goods that was produced?

Mr. TAUZIN. I am sorry?

Mr. BECERRA. Where is the saving on the good that is produced?

Mr. TAUZIN. Here is where it comes from. In an income tax world, even a flat income tax world, the two professors who devised Mr. Armey's plan, Dr. Holland Rebushka have admitted this I think in testimony to this Committee.

When you apply a tax on the earnings of individuals and the earnings of corporations, you are effecting applying a VAT tax. You are taxing the value added to the product as it goes through the various stages of production.

At the very end, the consumer pays it all. It all ends up in the price of the finished product. And you and I pay that tax at the end.

Mr. BECERRA. Right. But you are talking about a wholesale product that has not gone through that whole——

Mr. TAUZIN. But this is my point to you. If you repeal income taxes, and you only apply the tax in our plan at the very finished product retail end, there are no taxes collected along the manufacturing process.

For example, the farmer does not pay a tax on the purchase of seed and fertilizer because that is a tax for the purpose of producing a product. There is no tax on those things under our plan.

There is no tax on the purchase of the tractor designed for business or the rental for office space. The tax does not apply to the miller, it does not apply to the baker, it does not apply to the wholesaler. The tax is only collected, under our plan, at the very end of the retail point of purchase.

Mr. BECERRA. Well, let's take food.

Mr. TAUZIN. Okay.

Mr. BECERRA. Anything grown in a field that is picked. Say there is some——

Mr. TAUZIN. Let's take wheat.

Mr. BECERRA. Wheat, or any kind of crop. There are only so many taxes that will be charged and that is only a certain percentage. In the case of particular states, whatever it might be, whatever the sales tax might be in that process.

How do you get to the point where you are reducing the price by the 30 or so percent——

Mr. TAUZIN. Twenty-five percent.

Mr. BECERRA. Twenty-five percent. You are ultimately still going to have a price for that product which you are expecting to be able to lower as a result of the elimination of income taxes along the stream are all these various taxes.

But ultimately you are talking a lot about being able to reduce wages to make up a lot of the difference since employees are no longer paying income taxes. You are assuming you will be able to reduce wages of employees to reduce the cost of employers in providing a particular good or service.

Mr. TAUZIN. No, we are not. And that is what—you have got to look at Dale Yargenson's study to see that. He does not calculate a loss, a reduction in the wages. In fact, under our plan, the wages go up by 7.5 percent.

Because you not only get your total wage, you also get the 7.5 percent your employer was formerly sending to the payroll system.

Mr. BECERRA. I thought you kept the payroll system? I thought you kept the payroll tax?

Mr. TAUZIN. Pardon me?

Mr. BECERRA. I thought you kept the payroll tax?

Mr. TAUZIN. You keep it above the poverty line. We only repeal it below the poverty line. So if all income earned up to the poverty line, the worker gets his full paycheck plus that 7.5 percent his employer was sending in.

See, you have got a lot more money now to go buy your bread and your milk and your drugs.

In addition, because the businesses will no longer be paying taxes on the income earned on the raw materials, the wheat, eventually the flour, eventually the bread, eventually the packaged bed products, eventually the donuts at Krispy Kreme, wherever you are going, because none of the taxes are collected on the value-added to those products and all the compliance cost is done away with, all the lawyers and accountants the businesses have to hire to comply with the Code.

That saves you 25 percent——

Mr. BECERRA. But where are the taxes on strawberries? How many levels of taxation are there on, say, strawberries that are picked and then shipped directly to a grocery store?

Mr. TAUZIN. They are processed. Strawberries are first, you know, there are farmers who grow them. They have to buy fertilizer, they have to own land, they have expenses. Farmers pay taxes.

If a farmer does not have to pay a tax on the income he makes from the sale of his strawberries, that reduces the cost of the strawberries to the consumer.

If the guy——

Mr. BECERRA. Where I think the disconnect between what you are proposing and what will ultimately happen is that you are saying a quarter of the cost of all goods and services will be eliminated by this particular change in the Tax Code?

Mr. TAUZIN. Yes.

Mr. BECERRA. And I think that is a big leap of faith. That folks are out there saying, well, if I am going to pay this new higher tax for a prescription drug, to bury my father, to have that medical surgery that I need to stay alive, I want to know how I am paying for it.

And you are asking a lot of folks to believe that all of a sudden, we are going to see major drops in the cost of a lot of these products and services.

I know I have taken up a lot of time, Mr. Chairman.

Mr. TAUZIN. All I can tell you, Mr. Becerra, is that is the nature of our free market competitive system.

Let me be honest with you. If there is a product out there and if it is a cable service, and you have got no competitor to it, you know, there is no direct broadcast satellite with local programming into your town, and so you are bound to buy a cable if you want your local program, I say that is a monopoly provider of service, and our bill will not lower the cost there. Because any monopolist can charge whatever he wants all the time in our marketplace.

But whenever you reduce the cost to any competitive player in a competitive marketplace, you will eventually reduce the cost to the consumer. Otherwise, somebody will take his business from him.

That is the nature of competitive bread businesses and strawberry businesses.

Let me make a final——

Mr. BECERRA. Before you make that final point, I agree with what you just said.

If you can reduce the cost to the producer, certainly in a competitive world the charge for that product will be lower for the consumer.

Mr. TAUZIN. I think that is correct.

Mr. BECERRA. But the consumer's saying, you are telling me to swallow, in some cases, a 30 to 60 percent tax on these products and I am wondering if producers are going to be able to reduce the cost that much so that I will not pay more.

That is where the leap of faith comes in.

Mr. TAUZIN. That is a fair question. The only thing I can tell you is, again, that it is going to be different depending upon how many stages of production are in a product.

For bread, it is about 35 percent. That is not my number. That is numbers derived by people who have studied this carefully.

Dale Yargenson is not—the School of Economics at Harvard is not the bastion of conservative thought. We are talking Harvard University here.

They are telling us the average reduction in producer prices is 25 percent of you get rid of the Income Tax Code.

Do you know what that says to you and I? That says that we are being punished, as workers in our society, for buying the products we make in America by 25 percent.

That is terrible.

Mr. BECERRA. You know, and we can always cite studies that show that it would be different than the 25 to 30 percent drop in the price.

The difficulty I think a number of folks have is that when you need an operation, you cannot ask, well did the price drop on the cost of that operation, which will now, under your tax scheme, be taxed?

I will have to pay a tax on the $7,000 charge for that hospital bed, the $7,000 charge for that surgeon, the $5,000 charge for that anesthesiologist and all of that is going to be taxed at a very high rate, and I have got to hope for my life threatening surgery that I need, the lifesaving surgery that I need, that in fact the prices will have dropped.

And that could apply to the senior on fixed income who needs prescription drugs.

That could apply to my father who passes away and I have got to pay for funeral expenses if I do not have money. That is the difficulty I think folks have.

And you have been gracious and I thank you for the——

Mr. TAUZIN. Let me, let me just say one final thought.

Mr. BECERRA. Sure.

Mr. TAUZIN. You see, the perniciousness of our current Income Tax Code is that it hides the truth from all the folks you have just described who go buy those services today.

The ugly truth is that they are buying those services with after-tax dollars. They have already paid taxes on their income, they have paid it on their savings, they have paid it, in some cases, on their Social Security even. And then they go buy those services.

And the ugly truth is they are paying the same taxes all over again, because the services and the goods they are buying made in America contain all this hidden income tax cost.

That is the ugly truth, and if you face that ugly truth that we are paying twice on the same dollars every time we buy necessities of life in this country, unless you buy a foreign product, then you come to the realization that you would be much better off paying it only once at the end instead of paying it once on your income, and then once on the purchase.

Mr. BECERRA. I do not think any American is deceived by the notion that we are going to be able to just get rid of the Tax Code and not have to pay taxes.

I think every American believes that it is an obligation to keep this country a civilized society.

Mr. TAUZIN. I agree with you. But if you had a choice of paying once instead of twice, what would you choose?

Mr. BECERRA. I choose to pay the lower, whichever is lower, and I think most people will say, at the end, I do not care which system it is, it is the one that reduces my taxes most.

Mr. TAUZIN. That is right.

Mr. BECERRA. And I do not know if the consumer will say that it is fairer to pay it one time at a high rate versus many times at a smaller rate.

I think we have to ultimately assure the American people that they are not going to be further taxed by having gone to a system, even if it is simpler.

Mr. TAUZIN. That is a fair evaluation. I thank you for it.

Mr. BECERRA. Thank you.

Thank you, Mr. Chairman, for the time.

Chairman ARCHER. Thank you, Mr. Tauzin.

Mr. TAUZIN. Thank you, Mr. Chairman.

Chairman ARCHER. We appreciate your input.

The colloquy you just had with Mr. Becerra I think is fundamental and is very constructive and important for us to hear.

If I may just engage my colleague a moment further, the points you are making are matters of concern that we have got to address if we go in this direction.

I think it is important to note that fundamentally what we all should try to achieve I think in how we tax is to create the greatest opportunity for the greatest productivity and the greatest competitiveness in the world marketplace so that we can have an economy that not only grows, which it is currently doing nicely today, but which creates better jobs, better paying jobs.

We have full employment today. Hopefully, that will continue for a long period of time.

But the important thing now is how do we elevate these jobs, how do we have more in the family paychecks for all Americans, and how much less does our tax system create inefficiencies, nonproductivity, waste, as it were.

We talk about waste in federal spending, but we have to also talk about what waste there is in our tax system. We need to come to grips with all of these and to make sure how it is going to affect an individual product is important but perhaps not subject to precise quantification.

I would add a couple of things, and I will be glad to have a response from you because this will all go in the record and I think that will be very helpful to consideration in the future:

That when we pay taxes, both the cost of the tax and the compliance costs are a cost of doing business. They must be recovered one way or another. They are either going to be recovered by the investor getting a lesser return on their investment, or by labor being paid less, or by the consumer being paid more.

There are really only three places for this to go.

Most people believe that in most products that it will be passed on to the consumer in the price of the product rather than going back against the investor and lowering wage rates.

To that degree, it must be recovered. But when we say there is an average 20 to 25 percent, that does not mean that is the same on every product. And the loaf of bread might be different than medical care. And medical care might be different than purchasing an insurance policy or whatever the rest of the activity is.

And yet when we talk about a loaf of bread, which is a good one because it is a staple in all of our lives, what the farmer gets in the wheat is minuscule compared to what the expansion of that price is through all of the middle men, the processor, and everything else. And those people really are on the front line in bearing the burden of the income tax, both compliance costs as well as the tax itself.

I cannot, nor can Mr. Tauzin, for sure tell you what it is going to be on a loaf of bread. But we can tell you some averages. Because the one thing that is pretty basic is that compliance costs for the current income tax which must be borne by our society are a minimum of $200 billion a year.

Fortune Magazine says they could be as much as $500- to $600 billion a year.

Now that is all wasted effort and somebody has got to pay for it. It is not creating wealth. It is not creating bread, or any other thing of real value in our lives. It is just a part that has to be administered under this tax system.

If we can cut that down by 90 percent, then the burden of anywhere from $180 billion to perhaps $2- or $3- or $4 billion dollars is going to be removed as a cost in the total economy. How it will relate to any individual product we cannot absolutely be sure.

But I think as we seek, and this would be my overall objective, and I think most of us would agree with it. We may not agree how to get there. But that we should be very careful as we spend the taxpayers money to assure that it is being spent efficiently.

By the same token, we should have as efficient a tax system as we possibly can. That is a long number of words that I have put out there, but I would be glad to have your response.

Mr. BECERRA. Mr. Chairman, I think most folks who may have just heard your remarks would be nodding right now in full agreement.

Certainly any time that we are using money in the stream of the economy just to pay for administration, above and beyond what is necessary to get that product to market, is certainly an inefficiency and we should try to eliminate the total cost, or at least reduce it to the degree possible.

In fact, I think Mr. Tauzin and everyone else who has come before this Committee is completely genuine in their efforts to try to come up with a system that just works better, whatever it might be.

Obviously there are different beliefs about how we best do that. My concern with any system, including the one we have now which I agree is extremely cumbersome and every year we talk about its cumbersomeness but we make it more cumbersome, my belief is that whatever we do we have to be able to face every American and say we have tried to do it by a change in the Code so that it helped you.

I am not certain yet that I have heard a proposal yet that lets me say it helped you—and by the "you" be able to reference as many Americans as possible. I am not sure if I have heard a proposal that includes as many "you"s as possible.

That is where I would be concerned. Because we get into this notion of what is on paper. It looks good on paper, but when you play it out the terms we use ultimately are very different. As I always say, it looks really good in the war room when the generals move the war ship here and the tank there, it looks really good, but on the battlefield the folks that have to fight the war look at it a little bit differently.

A quick example. I know that many folks, the Chairman referenced this full employment. Full employment means that we have some 7—8 million Americans right now who are not working because about 4 percent of America is not employed, and that includes only those who are actively searching.

I mention that because my father when he was still employed— now he is retired—used to be among those folks who would only be partially employed because his work in road construction was temporal. During rainy seasons he could not work because there was no road construction that would take place.

So for three months out of the year, or sporadically throughout the year whenever it would rain he could not work. He would always work. He would find something else to do to earn some money. But he could not work in the field that he most practiced.

And while he was unemployed and had to either get unemployment compensation or try to find a second job, he really was not unemployed. He was seeking out work. So those who are out there meaningfully trying to find a full-time, well-paying job should not be lost in the shuffle when we talk about full employment.

There are a lot of folks out there.

And in the same vein, as we try to reform the tax code to make it better and fairer and more efficient, I think we have to remember that the bottom line is the guy that does have to go in for the surgery. Are we going to make it easier for him to survive not just the surgery but the cost of the surgery afterwards?

And as we buy the loaf of bread or buy the dental service or bury our deceased loved ones, have we made the tax code work better for them?

I do not think anyone approaches this without a real thoughtfulness and desire to improve our taxation system. But it is a lot bigger bear than most people would believe.

Chairman ARCHER. Well you have stated I think very well what we should all strive for. My comment about full employment was based on the economists saying we now have full employment. Not to think that individuals are not sometimes covered up by the average and are still out there looking for work.

But the important thing is that we give the greatest economic opportunity to all Americans who want to get out and work, to be able to work, and then not be content to simply have a job but to improve——

Mr. BECERRA. That is right.

Chairman ARCHER.—The quality of that job and the amount of pay.

Mr. BECERRA. That is right.

Chairman ARCHER. I feel so strongly that we must win the battle of the global marketplace to be able to do that in the next Century.

Mr. BECERRA. I agree.

Chairman ARCHER. Thank you very much. You are excused.

[Laughter.]

Chairman ARCHER. The next panel, and the final panel for the day, is Mr. Rogstad, Mr. Howard, Mr. Mack, and Mr. Rose who will please come to the witness table.

256

A hearty welcome to each of you. Thank you for your persever-
ance in waiting in the back of the room until you come and give
us the benefit of your input. We are most happy to have you.

Mr. Rogstad, if you would, lead off. I think all of you know the
general rules under which we operate, which is please identify
yourself for the record before you testify and, if possible, do not follow in the Chair's footsteps. Try to limit your oral comments to five
minutes, if at all possible and, without objection, your entire printed statement will be inserted in the record.

Mr. Rogstad.

STATEMENT OF BARRY K. ROGSTAD, ECONOMIST AND PRESIDENT, AMERICAN BUSINESS CONFERENCE

Mr. ROGSTAD. Thank you, Mr. Chairman. I am Barry Rogstad, an
economist and President of the American Business Conference. The
ABC is a nonpartisan coalition of chief executives of fast-growing
American businesses.

I applaud this Committee for conducting these hearings and
highlighting recent progress toward fundamental tax reform, and I
thank you for the opportunity to comment here today in particular
in support of Congressman English's Simplified USA Tax Bill.

My comments are made from two perspectives:

First, as an economist and as a member of the team who worked
with Senators Domenici and Nunn in the development of the first
USA Tax legislation introduced in 1995.

And, as a representative of mid-size growth companies who have
a keen interest in tax restructuring and the contribution that it can
make to the growth and competitiveness of the American economy.

Today I am more convinced than ever that the USA Tax is the
best and most workable framework for achieving fundamental tax
reform.

I say that because:

One, it specifies the correct tax base, assuring that all income is
taxed and it is taxed once and only once.

Secondly, I think it drastically improves the neutrality in the tax
code with respect to the impact of taxes on the behavior of individuals, households, and businesses.

And thirdly, and I know this is controversial, it allows for a progressive rate structure and other provisions that, quite frankly in
my judgment, are necessary to achieve the political consensus required for final passage of any tax reform legislation.

I am here to support the bill introduced by Congressman
English, H.R. 134. Congressman English recognized the USA Tax
is a vastly superior method for treating international business
transactions and, most importantly, incorporates the correct treatment of individual saving and business investment.

The English Bill improves upon the original proposal by addressing provisions that were viewed by some as overly complex. These
concerns focused on the need to assure that saving was taxed once
and only once. Congressman English avoids this perceived complexity while removing the double tax on savings by relying on the
now well established Roth IRA framework.

We want to thank Congressman English and look forward to his
continued leadership of the USA Tax Reform.

From the perspective of American growth companies, I would like to mention five important issues that basic tax reform must address, and how the USA Tax succeeds in addressing each.

Of greatest importance is the level of saving and investment as the foundation of continued economic growth and improved standard of living of our citizens. The current income tax, as you well know, is biased against saving and investment and in favor of the consumption uses of income. We continually ask ourselves as citizens and businesses, what is the rationale for a national policy that reduces the level of our Nation's seed corn that determines how our country, its businesses and its citizens, prepare for the future?

Secondly, it is increasingly important in our "new economy," that we correctly tax human capital. We have come to recognize that it is the skills and knowledge of our citizens that underscore productivity growth and our competitive advantage as a Nation.

Thirdly, the international implications of the USA Tax are very significant to American businesses and their ability to compete on a level playing field. Tax policy should seek to ensure that these businesses make decisions based on market and operating conditions and not features contained in national tax regimes. Congressman English's bill achieves this result.

Fourthly, moving towards a simpler and understandable tax system is an important objective of the business community. By moving from accrual accounting toward cash flow accounting, the USA Tax reduces the complexity and compliance costs which businesses now face. Expensing of all investment outlays not only assures the correct specification of net income from capital in the tax base but would be the single most important step in my judgment to the simplification of our tax code.

Finally, growth companies, many of them knowledge intensive and with little collateral on which to borrow, are critically dependent on equity financing. The current tax code, as you know, by favoring borrowing over equity investment generates a higher cost of capital for growth companies. Bringing neutrality to debt and equity financing is a significant forward step achieved by the English bill.

A couple of final comments just about the ramifications of the first three of these points on the international marketplace.

First of all, on the saving question it is very difficult to argue today in this rather remarkable economy that the low level of personal saving is a key problem. However, it certainly is. It is now and will continue to be the core determinant of long-term growth.

I would suggest to you that one way of looking at the roughly $340 billion current account deficit we incurred in 1999 is that we are dependent to that amount on foreign saving. If we want to remove that dependency, tax reform is in order.

Secondly, this question of correctly taxing labor income can be a great opportunity for tax reform. Tax reform is about getting the tax base correct. By proposing to expense capital outlays, the USA tax correctly specifies the net return to capital.

Neutrality in tax reform requires that we focus on taxing net income to human capital as well so that we tax the returns to capital and labor equally.

I would suggest to you that the net income to human capital is gross income minus the cost of producing that which are essentially outlays for training and investment.

Congressman English's bill allows up to $12,000 a year per household for deductions for education outlays. I would suggest to you that at some point in the deliberations about tax reform you will see fit to deduct all expenses for investment in human capital, the same way that we do for physical capital.

Finally, I just want to mention the international tax provisions of this.

As you know, the English bill is territorial in nature. I think territoriality provides a generic approach to dealing with the FSC dilemma that we now face.

I think border-adjustability is an appropriate way for us to unilaterally level the playing field with foreign competitors.

I thank you, sir.

[The prepared statement follows:]

Statement of Barry K. Rogstad, Economist and President, American Business Conference

Mr. Chairman and Members of the Committee:

I am Barry Rogstad, an economist and president of the American Business Conference (ABC). ABC is a nonpartisan coalition of chief executives of fast growing midsize companies. The American Business Conference has never been a recipient of a Federal Government grant or contract.

I applaud the Committee's actions to hold this series of hearings on fundamental tax reform, and its current focus on the effects of our tax code on the functioning of American businesses in the international market place. By holding this series of hearings you recognize that the current tax code remains a failed instrument. Nobody understands it. Everybody thinks it is unfair. It is systemically biased against saving and investment. It extracts revenues from the economy in a hideously inefficient and expensive way. And through the specific focus of this hearing, the Committee highlights the blindness of the code to the competitive realities of our fast moving global economy.

I was pleased to testify before this Committee in 1995 during an earlier series of hearings on fundamental tax reform. At that time my remarks focused on the path breaking efforts of Senators Domenici and Nunn with the introduction of the USA Tax. The ABC is very proud of its role in the development of that proposal.

Congressman Phil English has improved upon this original formulation by introducing the Simplified USA Tax, H.R. 134. As an alternative to our current tax system, Congressman English recognized the USA Tax is a vastly superior method for treating international business transactions, and most importantly, incorporates the correct tax treatment of individual saving and business investment.

The original USA Tax, in attempting to assure that saving was taxed once and only once, was perceived by some as overly complex. The English bill avoids this perceived complexity while removing the double taxation on saving by relying on the Roth IRA framework. This approach in H.R. 134 is technically correct and fully understandable to the taxpayer. It provides a workable blueprint from which to address the core challenges of tax reform. We also recognize that there is additional detail and refinement required before the Congress can achieve final consensus. We applaud Congressman English for his efforts and look forward to his continued leadership in tax reform.

My remaining comments reflect the perspective of midsize growth companies toward basic tax reform.

First and foremost, American business leaders understand the singular importance of saving and investment to continued national economic growth and an improved standard of living for our citizens. The current income tax is biased against saving and investment and in favor of consumption. They ask, "What is the rationale for a national policy that reduces the level the "seed corn" that determines how our country, its businesses and its citizens prepare for the future?".

H.R. 134 removes that bias by taxing the consumption and saving uses of income in the same manner. It accomplishes this by taxing all income once and only once.

The English bill does not, and this is a key point, offer a subsidy to saving, it merely removes the double taxation on saving that now occurs.

Concern over a low level of national saving is a tough argument to make during these remarkable economic times. Yet it is, and will remain, a core determinant of the nation's future economic performance.

Given the international focus of this hearing, a comment on the contribution of foreign saving to the current U.S. economic expansion is in order. In 1999 the current account deficit of the United States was approximately $340 billion. This deficit was "financed" through net foreign saving being invested in this country of an equivalent amount. If our objective is to lower or eliminate the trade deficit, we must address the serious shortfall in our own saving behavior. The shortfall in our national saving could become severe and obvious in the face of any significant reduction in foreign saving and investment. Said more directly, the correct tax treatment of saving and the trade deficit are directly related.

Business leaders also support the integrated structure of the Simplified USA Tax, and the correct specification of the tax base contained in the proposal.

The structure of H.R. 134 provides for an integrated alignment of the business and individual elements of tax system. Tax revenues are the returns to capital and labor services. Taxes can be collected where these factor incomes are produced, at the business level; where they are earned, at the individual level; or as is done under the Simplified USA Tax, at both levels. This two-tier, split-rate approach, combined with a credit for both the employer and employee shares of the payroll tax, assures that all sources of taxable income are treated equally. Income from wages is treated the same as income from interest, dividends, and asset sales. And all forms of income are treated the same in both the business and individual components of the Simplified USA Tax. This treatment assures both fairness and understandability by the American people.

I believe the true revolution in tax reform is to achieve the correct tax base. The properly defined tax base is the net return to capital and labor services: or the gross returns less the costs of producing these returns. Tax policy has been replete with discussions on how to achieve the right definition of net returns to capital. The approach taken in the English bill correctly incorporates the best of these by expensing investment outlays immediately.

However, economic efficiency and fairness require that we achieve the same neutral treatment in the taxation of labor services. Investments in human capital, primarily outlays for education and training, are costs of producing higher gross returns to labor and should be expensed. These and other intangible investments are, as you know, becoming the core of our "new economy" and our comparative advantage as a nation. The English bill recognizes that tax reform must include the expensing of these investments in human capital. It provides for up to $12,000 in annual deductions for education per household. I would suggest future deliberations by the Congress on this issue may well remove limitations on qualified training and education outlays entirely.

The international implications of the USA Tax are very significant to American businesses and their ability to compete on a level international playing field. Public policy should seek to insure that businesses, both US and foreign-based make decisions based on market and operating conditions only, and not on the subsidies contained in national tax systems. Congressman English's bill achieves this result.

The USA Business Tax is territorial. An American-based business would not include in its gross tax base the proceeds from sales made by subsidiaries outside the United States. It would also not deduct the purchase of goods or services outside the United States. For their part, foreign businesses with a commercial presence in this country would include in their tax base amounts received for goods sold or services provided in the United States and would subtract amounts paid for goods acquired and services provided in the United States.

To repeat, for an American company, territoriality would free entrepreneurs to base their international strategies on business opportunities rather than on tax considerations. From a public policy standpoint, adopting a territorial system would be the best approach to resolving the current dilemma regarding the Foreign Sales Corporation (FSC) provisions in the code. It would also vastly simplify the tax structure and the agenda of this Committee.

The USA Business Tax is also border adjustable. Goods made here and shipped abroad would receive a tax rebate. Goods made abroad and imported and sold in the United States would be subject to tax. This provision would align the tax system of the United States with that of most of our major trading partners while insuring that all products sold in this country carried their appropriate share of the tax burden.

Simplification of the tax code is a longstanding objective of tax reformers. By moving from accrual accounting towards cash flow accounting, the USA Tax eliminates the maze of complexities and the high compliance costs which businesses now face. H.R. 134, by providing for expensing of all investment outlays, leads to the correct and desired impact on the cost of capital for American businesses. Its adoption would achieve a greatly simplified tax structure.

The English bill would have other positive effects on the cost of capital. The current tax code, by favoring borrowing over equity investment, generates a higher cost of capital for growth companies. These companies, frequently knowledge-intensive and with little collateral on which to borrow, are critically dependent on equity financing. Bringing neutrality to debt and equity financing is a significant forward step achieved by the USA Tax.

The Simplified USA Tax introduced by Congressman English explains why tax reform is both necessary and possible. Perhaps now the USA Tax will get the second look it so richly deserves.

Congressman English has championed a plan that does not discriminate against saving and investment, is simple, efficient, and understandable, is easy to administer, readily accommodates a progressive rate structure, offers a full credit for the FICA tax, and reflects international competitive realities by excluding from taxation export sales and income from foreign sources. It is fully worthy of further consideration by his colleagues on this Committee and in the Congress.

I would be happy to answer any questions you may have.

———————

Chairman ARCHER. Thank you, Mr. Rogstad.

Mr. Howard.

STATEMENT OF JERRY HOWARD, VICE PRESIDENT, TAXES, USX CORPORATION, PITTSBURGH, PENNSYLVANIA

Mr. HOWARD. Thank you, Mr. Chairman.

My name is Jerry Howard and I am Vice President of Taxes for USX Corporation. Though I currently reside in Pittsburgh, I worked for the USX Marathon Group in the 7th Congressional District in Texas, and we found the 7th District to be one of the best represented districts in the country.

I appreciate having the opportunity to have worked with you and members of your staff for an extended period of time.

This is an opportune time to discuss fundamental tax reform. I appreciate the opportunity to address the Committee on this issue.

USX Corporation operates primarily in the integrated energy and steel businesses. Our 1999 sales of over $29 billion ranks us within the top 25 industrial companies in the United States.

Both our energy and steel businesses are capital intensive and face strong foreign and domestic competition. U.S. tax laws have an important bearing on our ability to compete in world markets.

We have several serious concerns with the current Federal Income Tax on businesses. We believe the current tax system is anti-competitive, acts as a disincentive to investment, and is unduly complex.

We support fundamental tax reform that addresses these concerns. Any new tax system should be a replacement for the current income tax system and should not result in additional taxes on business.

The Simplified USA Tax proposed by Representative English is a significant move in the right direction. We agree with the fundamental concepts of his proposal since they address many of our concerns.

For example, most industrialized countries rely mainly on border-adjustable taxes in which export income is exempted and imports are taxed.

In the U.S., however, export income is taxed and imports are not. As a result, U.S. companies are at a disadvantage both at home and abroad.

The Simplified USA Tax corrects this inequity by exempting export income and taxing imports.

The present U.S. income tax system acts as a disincentive to making capital investments because of the long cost recovery periods. Since real capital costs are not fully recovered, there is a tax on the capital investment itself. This makes capital acquisition much more costly for U.S. businesses.

The Simplified USA Tax eliminates the increased cost on capital by allowing an immediate writeoff of capital investments.

The current U.S. income tax system is overly complex, requiring companies to hire a large number of accountants and attorneys in order to determine the amount of taxes owed and to resolve disputes with the IRS.

While there will always be some complexity and uncertainty in any tax regime, the Simplified USA Tax will be significantly easier to understand and administer than the present income tax law.

The aforementioned provisions of the Simplified USA Tax represent significant improvements to the current U.S. tax system. However, the following issues require further study:

As I mentioned, the Simplified USA Tax includes a tax on imports which will help make U.S. companies more competitive in the global marketplace. That being said, it must be recognized that there are certain items that must be imported since domestic supply cannot meet demand.

One notable example that directly affects USX is crude oil. The imposition of a new nondeductible tax on imported crude oil could cause the cost of refined products to increase and result in higher costs to consumers.

Due care should be taken to ensure that consumers and U.S. companies are not unduly harmed by this measure. A national energy policy which promotes increased domestic oil and gas production and enhances refining capacity in the United States would lessen our demand on imports.

A major issue in developing any new tax system to replace the present income tax law involves transition rules for costs that have been incurred or credits generated during the period that the present system has been in effect but that will not be deducted or taken into account by the time the new system is put in place.

Accordingly, transition rules should be fair and equitable.

In conclusion, a new tax system modeled around the Simplified USA Tax would be a significant improvement over the present system. It would eliminate the competitive disadvantage inherent in the current system and allow U.S. companies to compete more effectively with our foreign competitors.

We believe that a national energy policy that promotes increased domestic oil and gas production and enhances refining capacity, coupled with fair and equitable transition rules, will cause the new system to achieve its intended results.

USX welcomes the opportunity to participate in the process. Thank you.

[The prepared statement follows:]

Statement of Jerry Howard, Vice President, Taxes, USX Corporation, Pittsburgh, Pennsylvania

Mr. Chairman, my name is Jerry Howard, and I am Vice President-Taxes for USX Corporation. Though I currently reside in Pittsburgh, I worked in the 7th district of Texas for a number of years and found it to be one of the best represented districts in the country. I have appreciated the opportunity to work with you and members of your staff over an extended period of time. We also applaud the members of this Committee who announced their opposition to the Administration's budget proposal to impose a tax on the recipients of tracking stock. This ill-conceived measure would cause severe harm to companies with tracking stock outstanding and reduce business expansion while generating no benefits.

This is an opportune time to discuss fundamental tax reform and I appreciate the opportunity to address the Committee on this issue.

USX Corporation operates primarily in the integrated energy and steel businesses. Our 1999 sales of over $29 billion rank us within the top 25 industrial companies in the United States.

Both our energy and steel businesses are capital intensive and face strong foreign and domestic competition. U.S. tax laws have an important bearing on our ability to compete in world markets.

We have several serious concerns with the current federal income tax on businesses. We believe the current tax system is anti-competitive, acts as a disincentive for investment, and is unduly complex.

We support fundamental tax reform that addresses these concerns. Any new tax system should be a replacement for the current income tax system and should not result in additional taxes on business. The Simplified USA Tax proposed by Representative English is a significant move in the right direction. We agree with the fundamental concepts of his proposal since they address many of our concerns.

Competition Concerns

For example, most industrialized countries rely mainly on border-adjustable taxes, in which export income is exempted and imports are taxed. In the U.S., however, export income is taxed while imports are not. As a result, U.S. companies are at a disadvantage both at home and abroad.

The Simplified USA Tax corrects this inequity by exempting export income and taxing imports.

Incentive for Investment

The present U.S. income tax system acts as a disincentive to making capital investments because of the long cost recovery periods. Since real capital costs are not fully recovered, there is a tax on the capital investment itself. This makes capital acquisition more costly.

The Simplified USA Tax eliminates the increased cost on capital by allowing an immediate write-off of capital investments.

Complexity of Current Tax Law

The current U.S. income tax system is overly complex, requiring companies to hire a large number of accountants and attorneys in order to determine the amount of taxes owed and to resolve disputes with the IRS because the laws are so difficult to interpret and administer. While there will always be some complexity and uncertainty in any tax regime, the Simplified USA Tax will be significantly easier to understand and administer than the present income tax law.

The aforementioned provisions of the Simplified USA Tax represent significant improvements to the current U.S. tax system. However, the following issues require further study.

Oil and Gas Imports

As I've mentioned, the Simplified USA Tax includes a tax on imports, which will help make U.S. companies more competitive in the global marketplace. That being said, it must be recognized that there are certain items that must be imported since domestic supply cannot meet demand. One notable example that directly affects USX is crude oil.

The imposition of a new non-deductible tax on imported crude oil could cause the cost of refined products to increase and result in higher costs to consumers. Due care should be taken to ensure that consumers and U.S. companies are not unduly harmed by this measure. A national energy policy which promotes increased domestic oil and gas production and enhances refining capacity in the U.S. would lessen our demand for imports.

Transition Rules

A major issue in developing any new tax system to replace the present income tax law involves transition rules for costs that have been incurred or credits generated during the period that the present system has been in effect, but that will not be deducted or taken into account by the time the new system is put into place. Accordingly, transition rules should be fair and equitable.

Finally, a word about compatibility of the USA Tax with other tax regimes.

Compatibility with Other Tax Regimes

Presently, the tax base for most state income taxes uses federal taxable income as the starting point. Thus, any new federal tax regime developed to replace the current federal income tax will not be compatible. States should be able to modify their tax systems to use the new federal tax base as the starting point, making modifications and other adjustments necessary to generate the same tax revenues from businesses as are currently collected.

Conclusion

In conclusion, a new tax system, modeled around the Simplified USA Tax, would be a significant improvement over the present system. It would eliminate the competitive disadvantage inherent in the current system and allow U.S. companies to compete more effectively with our foreign competitors. We believe that a national energy policy that promotes increased domestic oil and gas production and enhances refining capacity, coupled with fair and equitable transition rules, will cause the new system to achieve its intended results. USX welcomes the opportunity to participate in the process.

Mr. KLECZKA [presiding]. I have no questions of this panel, and the Chair is going to be right back.

Has Mr. Mack testified? Oh, I am sorry.

Mr. Mack, welcome. You do not win the prize for coming the longest distance, you know, being from McLean, Virginia. Welcome to the Committee and we look forward to your remarks.

STATEMENT OF JAMES H. MACK, VICE PRESIDENT, GOVERNMENT RELATIONS, ASSOCIATION FOR MANUFACTURING TECHNOLOGY, MCLEAN, VIRGINIA

Mr. MACK. Thank you, Mr. Chairman.

I am Jim Mack, and I am here representing U.S. producers of machine tools and related manufacturing technology.

Our industry is the principal enabler of America's high productivity levels which are the key to our current prosperity and its continuation into the foreseeable future.

Our industry translates the dizzying advances in information technology into the design of new manufactured products and the factory floor automation that more efficiently produces them.

However, our current tax code actually discourages American manufacturing companies from acquiring new manufacturing technology and from producing new products in the United States.

It encourages international mergers and acquisitions that transfer to foreign sources the ownership of technology, the development of future technology, and decisions as to whether American jobs will stay in America. The territoriality and border-adjustability features of the USA Tax would reverse that trend.

Some have criticized the USA business tax because, in order to make it border adjustable in conformity with WTO rules, labor costs would no longer be deductible.

The fact is, Mr. Chairman, that labor costs are not entirely tax free today. The current payroll tax is a heavy burden on businesses and on their employees—most particularly on skilled craftsmen and skilled factory workers. It acts as an incentive against hiring new workers. By providing a credit for the 7.65% employer-paid FICA tax, the USA Tax actually reverses the regressive impact of the payroll tax.

Congressman English's USA Tax is good sound tax policy and AMT—The Association for Manufacturing Technology, strongly supports it passage.

The USA Tax also meets all the requirements that the WTO laid out in requiring you to repeal the Foreign Sales Corporation (or FSC) and, therefore, would be a good starting point when looking for solutions as FSC replacement.

FSC helps make U.S. exports more competitive in world markets. Many AMT members, both large and small, have FSCs. However, unless you act by October 1st, or unless a settlement is reached with the European Union by that date, billions of dollars in U.S. exports will be subject to retaliatory compensation by the EU and possibly by others.

Simply repealing the FSC would deprive U.S. companies of a powerful incentive to export and effectively amount to a $4 billion a year tax increase on U.S. exports.

On the other hand, simply replacing FSC with a slightly different version could be inconsistent with the WTO decision and could lead to European retaliation.

Mr. Chairman, we know that coming up with a replacement for FSC that is consistent with the WTO ruling will be extraordinarily difficult. Therefore, we believe that the best possible solution is to move to a territorial, border-adjustable system of taxation like the USA Tax which would not tax export income at all but would impose a tax on imports.

This is the system used by all of our major trading partners. The WTO Dispute Resolution Panel clearly pointed the way in that direction when it stated that we could not couple territorial treatment of exports with a system of taxing the worldwide income of our companies.

Now we are not naive enough to believe that fundamental tax reform like the USA Tax can be enacted by the first of October. However, if you can achieve a bipartisan momentum for the USA Tax approach, you and the Administration would have a powerful incentive—a powerful club, if you will—to persuade the European Union to reverse its current headlong dash toward an October 1st trade war with the United States.

Absent such bipartisan momentum, the Administration unfortunately has very little negotiating leverage, and the prospects for averting disaster on October 1st are very bleak.

Passage of a border-adjustable cash flow territorial cash flow tax that allows for expensing of capital purchases like the USA Tax is one of AMT's top legislative priorities. We strongly support Congressman English's USA Tax as the best possible tax system for

U.S. manufacturers and their workers in an increasingly competitive (and even hostile) global trading environment. It is also the best possible replacement for FSC.

The time for fundamental tax reform is long overdue. The need to replace the FSC provides an excellent opportunity to begin the process of real reform rather than simply searching for a short-term fix. Thank you.

[The prepared statement follows:]

Statement of James H. Mack, Vice President, Government Relations, Association for Manufacturing Technology, McLean, Virginia

I. INTRODUCTION

My name is James H. Mack, Vice President of Government Relations at AMT—The Association For Manufacturing Technology—a trade association whose membership represents over 370 machine tool building firms with locations throughout the United States. Pursuant to House Rule XI, clause 2(g)(4), I am obligated to report to you that AMT has received $219,000 in fiscal years 1997–2000 from the Commerce Department's Market Co-operator Development Program to help pay for our export offices in China and Mercosur.

I appreciate the opportunity to testify before the Committee in support of Fundamental Tax Reform. My comments will also address how Congress could use fundamental tax reform to respond to the World Trade Organization's (WTO) dispute resolution panel ruling that the Foreign Sales Corporation (FSC) violates WTO rules and must be repealed by October 2000.

II. STATUS OF THE U.S. MANUFACTURING TECHNOLOGY INDUSTRY

The majority of AMT's members are small businesses. According to the 1997 U.S. Census of Manufacturers, 69% of the companies in our industry have less than 50 employees. They build and provide to a wide range of industries the tools of manufacturing technology including cutting, grinding, forming and assembly machines, as well as inspection and measuring machines, and automated manufacturing systems.

Everything in this hearing room, except for the people, was either made by a machine tool or made by a machine made by a machine tool. Several years ago, the Reagan and Bush Administrations, responding to strong encouragement of over 250 Members of Congress, provided temporary import relief for our industry, based on the threat posed to our national security from Asian machine tool imports. They did so because of their recognition that a strong machine tool industry is vital to America's military and economic security.

Our industry is very cyclical. Price pressures are very strong, and profitability is relatively low—even in good years. Today, despite the extraordinary performance of our overall economy, domestic consumption of machine tools is nearly 30% lower than a year ago. Imports represent about half of domestic consumption. And American-made machine tools comprise only 13% of world supply. About 30% of our industry's output is exported. If, as we believe, successful competition in the global marketplace is the key to a strong and healthy economy, then we need U.S. policies that reflect that goal. I think most would agree that our current business tax policy is inconsistent with that goal.

III. THE USA TAX

The anti-investment, anti-export biases of the current tax code are well documented. Our tax code discourages saving and productive capital investment in the United States; it discourages exports; and it makes it hard for U.S. companies to directly compete in foreign markets. America urgently needs a tax system rebuilt from the ground up around a new set of design principles to compete and win in world markets.

Your colleague, Cong. English (R–PA), has introduced legislation which replaces our current tax system with a cash flow tax that would be both border-adjustable and territorial and would provide for the expensing of capital purchases. Its enactment would, for the first time, truly level the international playing field for U.S. companies in world markets, including the United States.

The USA tax combines a low-rate business tax which allows expensing of capital equipment with border-tax adjustments and territoriality to produce an ideal result—a neutral, evenhanded tax that treats all business alike (whether corporate or noncorporate, capital intensive or labor intensive, financed by equity or by debt, large or small) and which, for the first time, is tilted in our favor when we compete in our own and foreign markets.

The key to our current prosperity, and its continuation into the foreseeable future, is improved productivity. Our industry is the principle enabler of America's high productivity levels. Our industry translates the dizzying advances in information technology into the design of new manufactured products and the factory floor automation that more efficiently produces them. However, our current tax code discourages American manufacturing companies from acquiring new manufacturing technology and from producing new products in the United States. It encourages international mergers and acquisitions that transfer to foreign sources the ownership of technology, the development of future technology, and decisions as to whether American jobs will stay in America. The territoriality and border-adjustable features of the USA tax would reverse that trend.

Some have criticized the USA business tax because, in order to make it border adjustable in conformity with WTO rules, labor costs would no longer be deductible. The fact is that labor costs are not entirely tax-free today. The current payroll tax on wages up to $72,000 is a heavy burden on businesses and their employees—most particularly on skilled craftsmen and factory workers. It acts as an incentive hiring new workers.

By providing a credit for the 7.65% employer-paid FICA tax, the USA Tax reverses the regressive impact of the payroll tax. Under current law, the first $72,000 of employee compensation is taxed. Under the USA Tax, employee compensation under $72,000 would be partially taxed (at a 4.35% rate) and employee compensation over $72,000 would be fully taxed (at a 12% rate).

Cong. English's USA Tax is good sound tax policy, and AMT strongly supports its passage. The USA Tax also meets all the requirements that the WTO laid out in repealing the FSC, and would, therefore, be a good starting point when looking for solutions to FSC replacement.

IV. FSC REPLACEMENT

As I stated earlier, a WTO dispute resolution panel has ruled that the FSC law, which allows U.S. exporters to exclude part of their export income, violates WTO rules and must be repealed by October 2000.

FSC helps make U.S. exports more competitive in world markets. Many AMT members—both large and small—have FSCs. However, unless Congress acts by October 1, or a settlement is reached with the European Union (EU) by that date, billions of dollars in U.S. exports will be subject to retaliatory "compensation" by the EU and possibly by others. Simply repealing the FSC would deprive U.S. companies of a powerful incentive to export and effectively amount to a $4 billion per year tax increase on U.S. exports. On the other hand, simply replacing FSC with a slightly different version could be inconsistent with the WTO decision and could lead to European retaliation.

Mr. Chairman, we know that coming up with a WTO-compatible replacement for FSC that is consistent with the WTO ruling will be extraordinarily difficult. But we do believe the best possible solution is to move to a territorial, border-adjustable system of taxation, like the USA tax, which would not tax export income at all but would impose a tax on imports. This is the system used by all of our major trading partners. The WTO dispute resolution panel clearly pointed the way in that direction when it stated that we couldn't couple territorial treatment of exports with a system of taxing the worldwide income of our companies.

Now, we are not naïve enough to believe that fundamental tax reform, like the USA Tax, can be enacted by October 1. However, if you can achieve a bipartisan momentum for the USA Tax approach, you and the Administration would have a powerful incentive to persuade the European Union to reverse its current headlong dash towards an October 1 trade war with the United States. Absent such bipartisan momentum, the Administration has very little negotiating leverage, and the prospects for averting disaster on October 1 are very bleak.

V. CONCLUSION

Passage of a border adjustable, territorial cash flow tax, like the USA Tax, is one of AMT's top legislative priorities. We strongly support Cong. English's USA Tax as the best possible tax system for U.S. manufacturers and their workers in an increasingly competitive (and even hostile) global trading environment. It is also the best possible replacement for FSC. The time for fundamental tax reform is long overdue.

The need to replace the FSC provides an excellent opportunity to begin the process of real reform rather than simply searching for a short-term fix.

Thank you.

Chairman ARCHER. Thank you, Mr. Mack.

Mr. Rose, you are cleanup hitter today.

STATEMENT OF JAMES E. ROSE, JR., SENIOR VICE PRESIDENT, TAXES AND GOVERNMENT AFFAIRS, TUPPERWARE CORPORATION, ORLANDO, FLORIDA; AND BOARD MEMBER AND CHAIRMAN, TAX AND BUDGET POLICY COMMITTEE, NATIONAL ASSOCIATION OF MANUFACTURERS

Mr. ROSE. Thank you, Mr. Chairman, and Members of the Committee:

I am very pleased to have the opportunity to testify on the need for fundamental reform of our federal tax laws. My name is Jim Rose. I am Senior Vice President for Taxes and Government Affairs at Tupperware Corporation. I also serve as a Board Member of the National Association of Manufacturers and chair its Tax and Budget Policy Committee.

I am testifying today on behalf of NAM, 18 million people who make things in America. The NAM is the Nation's largest and oldest multi-industry trade association representing 14,000 members, 10,000 of which are small and mid-sized companies, and 350 member associations serving manufacturers and employees in every industrial sector and in all 50 states. Headquartered in Washington, D.C., the NAM has 10 additional offices across the country.

The NAM has long supported fundamental tax reform. The NAM has a long-standing belief that our current tax system is fundamentally flawed and is a major obstacle to realizing the full potential of our economy.

The solution calls for a new tax system that encourages work, investment, and entrepreneurial activity. Importantly, the new tax system should be competitive with our foreign trading partners.

Specific changes should include:

Incentives for savings and capital formation;

Avoiding multiple tax system like the AMT;

No net tax increase on businesses;

Elimination of double taxation of corporate earnings;

And fair and equitable transition rules.

NAM members generally favor a system in which only income sourced within the United States is taxed by the United States.

This is commonly referred to as a territorial tax system. Any territorial tax system should embody simple sourcing rules to determine where income is earned. Importantly, a territorial system should encourage U.S. activities including R&D and headquarter functions. This is accomplished, among other ways, by not taxing foreign royalties.

These priorities reflect the significant challenges U.S. manufacturers face in today's world economy.

While U.S. manufacturers enjoy a stable political environment and a creative and energetic workforce, they are at a significant disadvantage in the highly competitive world economy.

For example, the cost of borrowing in the United States is often higher than that of other countries, reflecting our remarkably low U.S. savings rate.

The high cost of borrowing, when combined with our relatively slow depreciation schedules, result in a less attractive recovery of U.S. invested capital. Over time, this will result in a less competitive U.S. asset base and, ultimately, the loss of U.S. jobs.

Other signs of an uneven playing field have emerged.

A significant negative trade balance exists that continues to increase. While NAM is a staunch advocate of open trade and is certainly not looking for protective trade barriers, U.S. manufacturers need and deserve a tax system that is competitive with those of our major trading partners.

In a nutshell, their tax systems are all border adjusted and many are territorial. Our tax system is neither. That is, it is neither border adjusted nor territorial.

The need for a new tax system has been heightened in recent months with the World Trade Organization's finding that Foreign Sales Corporation constitute an illegal export subsidy.

An example might be helpful in understanding how U.S. exporters are disadvantaged in the global marketplace. Let us take a hypothetical Country A.

Country A's tax burden consists of an income tax and a VAT. Companies that manufacture in Country A receive rebates of its 15% VAT when their goods are exported to the U.S.

Conversely, an exporting NAM member, and around 80% of its 14,000 members do export, does not receive a tax rebate when its products are exported from the U.S. Instead, it finds that its products are subject to the 15% VAT of Country A when they are imported into Country A.

Incidentally, the 15% may actually exceed the normal profit margin of the exported item.

Since the U.S. does not have a VAT system, and thus does not impose a VAT on imported goods, imported goods from Country A into our market come in tax free.

The Country A example incidentally has been adopted by virtually all of our major trading partners. As you can well appreciate, this tax environment significantly favors foreign imports and discourages U.S. exports.

The story gets worse. Foreign companies competing with U.S. manufacturers often operate with a territorial tax system that does not tax foreign source income.

Territorial systems of our competitors can essentially eliminate the home country income tax burden on export sales. It is important to note that FSC-type benefits would be allowable under WTO rules in the context of a territorial tax system.

Furthermore, our U.S. tax system subjects foreign earnings of U.S. companies to U.S. taxation when these earnings come back to the U.S. and in certain other circumstances.

While the U.S. Tax Code does include a foreign tax credit system to reduce this burden, the very complicated foreign tax credit rules typically result in incremental U.S. taxation when these funds come back to the U.S.

Accordingly, U.S. companies are inevitably discouraged from investing in the U.S.

The U.S. world-wide taxation system is having another negative effect on our economy. Increasingly, U.S. companies often large and well known, are being acquired by foreign companies.

While nontax business reasons often exist in these transactions, the more favorable tax systems of the acquiring foreign companies heavily influence the structure of these mergers.

For example, an NAM member last year testified before this Committee that the U.S. tax system was an important factor in why their U.S. company was acquired by its German-based merger partner.

Among other factors, the German-based acquirer benefitted importantly from Germany's territorial tax system.

The scenario has been repeated at an alarming rate in recent years. A recent study covering 1998 acquisitions involving U.S. and foreign entities concluded that approximately 85% of the combined value of the acquisitions resulted from foreign entities acquiring U.S. entities.

This trend will result in a loss of American jobs as, after an acquisition or merger, the headquarters of an the acquiring entity typically survives and expands while the headquarters of an acquired entity often is reduced in size and sometimes eliminated, effectively moving jobs offshore.

Furthermore, R&D facilities and even plant locations can be affected by these decisions.

In summary, American companies have well trained employees, products, and technology to win in the global marketplace, but the U.S. Tax Code has stacked the deck against us and in favor of our foreign competitors, both here at home as well as abroad.

The NAM is very pleased to participate in this dialogue over restructuring the U.S. Tax Code and applauds this Committee's efforts to fundamentally rewrite our tax code.

While NAM strongly supports fundamental tax reform, at this time it has not endorsed any specific proposal. However, the proposals under consideration have many attractive features.

Mr. Chairman, we certainly welcome the opportunity to work with this Committee to develop a new tax system which is simpler and encourages work, investment, and entrepreneurial activity and, importantly, one that is competitive with the tax systems of our foreign trading partners.

Thank you, Mr. Chairman.

[The prepared statement follows:]

Statement of James E. Rose, Jr., Senior Vice President, Taxes and Government Affairs, Tupperware Corporation, Orlando, Florida; and Board Member and Chairman, Tax and Budget Policy Committee, National Association of Manufacturers

Mr. Chairman and members of the Committee, I am very pleased to have the opportunity to testify today on fundamental reform of the federal tax laws. My name is James Rose and I am senior vice president for Taxes and Government Affairs at Tupperware Corporation. I also serve as a board member of the National Association of Manufacturers (NAM) and chair its Tax & Budget Policy Committee.

I am testifying today on behalf of the NAM—"18 million people who make things in America." The NAM is the nation's largest and oldest multi-industry trade association, representing 14,000 members (including 10,000 small and mid-sized companies) and 350 member associations serving manufacturers and employees in every industrial sector and all 50 states. Headquartered in Washington, D.C., the NAM has 10 additional offices across the country.

The NAM has long supported fundamental tax reform, reflecting our belief that the current tax system is a major obstacle to realizing the full potential of our economy. The solution calls for a new tax system that is simpler and encourages, rather than penalizes, work, investment and entrepreneurial activity, and importantly, a tax system that is competitive with our foreign trading partners. Specific changes endorsed by the NAM include incentives for savings and capital formation; a single tax system for businesses, with no additional components like the alternative minimum tax and no net tax increase on businesses; elimination of the double taxation of corporate earnings; and fair and equitable transition rules.

Moreover, our members generally favor a system in which only income earned within the United States is taxed within the United States. This is commonly referred to as a territorial tax system. However, as increasing globalization of the economy often makes it difficult to determine the point where income is "earned," any restructuring proposal should embody simple sourcing rules. Importantly, such a proposal should also encourage U.S. activities, including R&D and headquarters functions.

These priorities reflect the significant challenges U.S. manufacturers face in the world economy in which they must compete to survive. U.S. manufacturers enjoy many advantages including a stable social and political environment and a creative and energetic workforce. Nonetheless, U.S. manufacturers are at a significant disadvantage in the highly competitive world economy. In particular, the cost of borrowing in the United States often is higher than that of other countries. This differential reflects the remarkably low U.S. savings rate, as compared to that of other countries. A higher cost of borrowing, when combined with relatively slow tax depreciation schedules, results in a less attractive recovery of U.S. invested capital. Over time, this will result in a less competitive U.S. asset base and ultimately a loss of U.S. jobs.

Other signs of an uneven playing field have emerged, including a negative trade balance that continues to increase. The NAM is a staunch advocate of open trade and is not looking for protective trade barriers. What is needed, however, is a U.S. tax system that is competitive with those of our major trading partners. The need for a new system has been heightened even more in recent months with the World Trade Organization's finding that foreign sales corporations constitute an illegal export subsidy.

Let me give you an example of how U.S. exporters are at a disadvantage in the global market. The tax burden on a foreign product often consists mainly of a combination of income tax and a Value Added Tax (VAT). A foreign exporting company that manufactures products in Country A typically receives a rebate of the 15 percent VAT when its goods are exported. The tax burden of a U.S. product consists mainly of income tax. An exporting NAM member (and around 80 percent do export) receives no tax rebate when its products are exported from the United States but finds that these products are subject to a 15 percent VAT when they are imported into Country A. In some cases, the 15 percent tax on the value of the goods may actually exceed the normal profit margin of the item. As the United States does not use a VAT and therefore does not impose such on imported goods, domestically produced goods that are exported sustain the full effect of the U.S. tax burden plus the VAT of Country A, while imported products sustain only a portion of this heavy tax burden. This has the effect of significantly favoring foreign products within the United States and discouraging U.S. exports.

The story gets worse. Foreign companies competing with U.S. manufacturers often operate within a territorial tax system that does not tax foreign source income. Accordingly, the territorial systems of our competitors can essentially eliminate the home country income tax burden on export sales. The U.S. tax system subjects foreign earnings of U.S. companies to U.S. taxation when this money comes back to the United States and in certain other circumstances. The federal tax code does include a foreign tax credit system to reduce this burden. However, too often the very complicated foreign tax credit rules result in incremental U.S. taxation when these funds are returned to the United States. In this environment, U.S. companies are inevitably discouraged from investing in the United States.

The U.S. worldwide tax system is having another impact on our economy. Increasingly, U.S companies, often large and well known, are being acquired by foreign corporations. Last year a representative from a well-known NAM member company testified before this Committee that the U.S. tax system was an important factor in why their U.S. company was acquired by its German-based merger partner. Among other factors, the German-based acquirer benefited from Germany's territorial tax system.

This scenario has been repeated at an alarming rate in recent years. For example, a recent study covering 1998 acquisitions involving U.S. and foreign entities concluded that approximately 85 percent of the combined value of the acquisitions resulted from foreign entities acquiring U.S. entities. Why should we be concerned? One reason is the loss of American jobs. After an acquisition or merger, the headquarters of the acquiring party typically survives and expands, while the headquarters of the acquired entity often is reduced in size, and sometimes eliminated, effectively moving jobs off-shore. As part of this restructuring, R&D facilities and even plant locations can be affected by these decisions.

In summary, American companies have the well-trained employees, the products, and the technology to win in the global marketplace, but the U.S. tax code has stacked the deck against us and in favor of our foreign competitors—here at home as well as abroad.

The NAM is pleased to participate in the dialogue over restructuring the U.S. tax code and applauds Congressional efforts to fundamentally rewrite the tax code. At this point in the debate, the NAM has not endorsed any specific proposal. However, we welcome the opportunity to work with you to develop a new tax system that is simpler and encourages not penalizes work, investment and entrepreneurial activity and one that is competitive with the tax systems of our foreign trading partners.

Thank you.

———

Chairman ARCHER. Thank you, Mr. Rose.

The Chair is grateful to each of you for your outstanding contribution to our deliberations on fundamental tax reform.

The points that you have made I think are pertinent, and I am hopeful that the Committee will take them under advisement and ultimately into implementation.

Mr. Kleczka?

Mr. KLECZKA. No questions, Mr. Chairman.

Chairman ARCHER. Thank you very much, gentlemen. You are excused.

The meeting will stand adjourned.

[Whereupon, at 3:40 p.m., the hearing was adjourned, to reconvene on Thursday, April 13, 2000, at 10:30 a.m.]

FUNDAMENTAL TAX REFORM

THURSDAY, APRIL 13, 2000

COMMITTEE ON WAYS AND MEANS,
HOUSE OF REPRESENTATIVES,
Washington, D.C.

The Committee met, pursuant to recess, at 10:35 a.m. in room 1100, Longworth House Office Building, Hon. Bill Archer (Chairman of the Committee) presiding.

Chairman ARCHER. The Committee will come to order.

Today is the final day of our hearings on structural reform, and I believe it is going to be an interesting one.

We begin by receiving testimony from our own colleague, Mr. Portman, who has a deep interest in tax reform. Then we will hear from two pollsters, one republican and one democrat, on what the American people are thinking about structural reform. Thirdly, we will receive testimony from Mr. William Helming and one of my long-time friends, Jimmy Powell, about a very interesting tax reform proposal that Mr. Helming has developed. Finally, we will hear the views of the U.S. Chamber of commerce and testimony on the death tax and on the elements of fundamental tax reform.

Mr. Rangel?

Mr. RANGEL. Thank you, Mr. Chairman.

I don't know how we slipped up and let a Democrat get on one of these panels, but I will have to stick around and see that. This is going to be the most exciting hearing, because my dear friend and fellow Committee member, Mr. Portman, will be testifying. I say that not just out of a sense of affection but because, realistically, he probably is the only one that will be around here, as relates to witnesses, in order to do something about the tax code. Most of the other people are just giving some ideas of their frustrations before April the 15th.

I have known about Mr. Portman's concern about the structure of our tax code and the constant contributions he makes to make it a better instrument to guide the collection of revenue. I really look forward to his testimony this morning and look forward to working with him no matter what the political composition will be of this committee next year.

Thank you.

Chairman ARCHER. Mr. Portman, welcome to a new position at the witness table, but not to a new presence in this room. We will be happy to receive your testimony.

STATEMENT OF HON. ROB PORTMAN, A REPRESENTATIVE IN CONGRESS FROM THE STATE OF OHIO

Mr. PORTMAN. Thank you, Mr. Chairman. It is a little daunting, but I appreciate your words and Mr. Rangel's and my colleagues who have the patience and fortitude to be here this morning.

I am delighted to get a chance to testify briefly. I have sat through, as you know, a number of the witnesses' testimony with this series of hearings on tax reform, and I think it has been very informative, I think it has been very thoughtful, and I want to commend the chairman for having these hearings and opening up a discussion. I have learned a lot about various alternatives, and I guess what I hope is that we can at least all agree that we must replace our current code with one that is simpler, one that is fairer, and one that is less intrusive.

This morning, Mr. Chairman, I would like to switch gears just a little bit even from the testimony I had planned to present and talk a little bit more about why we need to change our process, maybe how to get to structural tax reform, rather than focusing so much on why a specific tax reform plan does or doesn't make sense. I think over the next two to five years we have a tremendous opportunity to move forward on tax reform. Unlike some in this room and elsewhere, I believe it can happen. In fact, I believe it must happen if America is to be prosperous in the increasingly-competitive new century.

In 1996 and 1997, thanks to the chairman's support and others, I had the opportunity to serve as co-chairman on the National Committee on Restructuring the IRS. I served on that with Bill Coyne, who is with us this morning. It was a blue ribbon panel of experts, as you know, convened by Congress to recommend reforms to improve taxpayer service at the IRS.

I want to touch on this commission only because I think it relates the to the topic here today in two regards.

First of all, the Commission in its work found the complexity of the tax code was one of the major—and I would say the major—problem facing the Internal Revenue Service. It is consistent with the hearings that we have had and the focus of this committee on tax reform.

Second, because I think it says a lot about process—that is, how to achieve reform—in the Commission we rolled up our sleeves, spent literally a year auditing the IRS, kind of turning the table and getting to the root of the key problems at that agency.

It was a complex and very difficult task, but after careful, thorough review we recommended the most comprehensive overhaul of the IRS in 45 years. And, although some of those recommendations were viewed as controversial at the time, and although the Administration was initially opposed to our findings, at the end of the day, I think, based on the Commission's work and the credibility that the Commission's research brought, we were able to enjoy broad, bipartisan support and we got these important reforms enacted into law.

Throughout our work on the IRS Restructuring and Reform Commission, there was one cross-cutting problem that kept resurfacing. Of course, I am talking about complexity of the tax code.

It was an evolutionary process. When we first started out, folks weren't focused too much on the complexity. We were focused more on the inner workings of the IRS. But on a bipartisan basis, Mr. Chairman, commissioners came to conclude that the code, itself, was the greatest problem facing a very, very troubled agency.

This isn't news to members of this committee, but it provided, I think, a clear basis for reform because we found convincing evidence that there were enormous organizational challenges that the tax code poses to the IRS.

Again, although tax simplification was not our mandate, I think we pushed the envelope a bit in our recommendations, because the problem was so pervasive.

As you know, our recommendations included the tax complexity analysis because of that which subjects all perspective tax bills to a Joint Tax Committee analysis to determine complexity for the taxpayer and for the IRS. We also recommended getting the IRS formally involved in the tax-writing process, to comment on the administrative challenges, which we are trying to get even today from the IRS as an independent agency looking at this issue.

We also made recommendations—some members of this committee remember those, because some were controversial—on 60-odd specific code sections that could be simplified, including the alternative minimum tax, to reduce needless complexity. Some of these reforms, incidentally, were included in the 1997 Taxpayer Relief Act.

And, finally, we recommended and passed in law that there be an annual meeting of the seven committees with IRS oversight coming together with Ways and Means and Finance on both sides of the Capitol to ensure this agency gets more consistent guidance from the Hill.

So these reforms underscored the connection we saw between the problems with the IRS and complexity of the tax code.

Now, my thinking today is, you know, how do we get from point A to point B. How do we get to this fairer, simpler tax code?

I think a Tax Reform Commission makes a lot of sense, and the purpose of this commission would be to keep the ball rolling, to help educate the public about the problem—and Mr. Rangel talked about that yesterday—and the alternatives, and also take some of the rough and tumble of partisan politics out of the process to bring some non-partisan expertise to bear on the problem in a focused way with a specific time table.

I do urge my colleagues to support the legislation on the floor today because it does have this commission as part of the so-called "sunset the code" idea. I think it is a much more responsible piece of legislation this year as a result of that. It is an 18-month commission.

I know, again, some commissions have had a checkered past in this town, but others have worked very well, and the IRS Commission is the model upon which the commission we will vote on today is based—15 members appointed by both parties, both Houses, and the President, short time table, and report to Congress. It does not take away, in any sense, the responsibility of the Ways and Means Committee or the Finance Committee to work through a tax reform. Just like the IRS Commission, it makes a recommendation.

We then go through normal procedures, subcommittee and committee, to come up with a proposal that the Ways and Means Committee and the Finance Committee think is appropriate to bring to the floor.

But I think we need to have this kind of outside expertise brought to bear on this issue. Obviously, before we even have the recommendation, the committee has a lot of work to do, and it is doing it well this week, in laying out the framework for tax reform we can all agree on.

I think part of this framework must be broad support, and that means it must be bipartisan. And this is really for two reasons. First, it is reality. It is going to be difficult for either party to ramrod a tax reform plan through Congress on its own. But second, and very importantly, is stability. We need to ensure that future Congresses and administrations don't throw out the tax code every time party control switches.

I think if there is anything in the code that is worse than the complexity, it is the changes to code, and we have seen thousands of them since 1986. People are looking for certainty and consistency, so that kind of a broad-based, two-thirds support I think is absolutely critical.

Revenue neutrality—I would just urge that any tax reform plan we come up with must deal with the current revenue estimates.

We have heard, as you know, Mr. Chairman, lots of testimony here this week on various estimates of what rates could be, but I think we have got to be able to compare apples to apples, which is, let us deal with the issue of reducing the scope and size of the Government separately, which I support, but, with regard to tax reform, I think we have got to focus on keeping it revenue neutral and how do we come up with the best way to raise the revenue to meet our needs.

And finally, of course, fairness. I think we have to recognize the progressivity of the current code. It is extremely progressive, and the top 10 percent pay 60 percent of the income taxes in this country. For political reasons, I think a very regressive tax has no chance of passing, so I don't think that we can throw the distribution tables too far off. At the same time, we must deal with the reality that our current code does penalize savings and investment, our current code does add enormous complexity, which is a waste of time and money and energy, and this is where, frankly, we have, I think, the most potential to make a huge difference in terms of economic growth in this country and, again, moving into the next century with prosperity.

I think, Mr. Chairman, again, all of us have different ideas. You know I have some specific ideas on tax reform. I thought about talking about them today, but I think that is less useful, frankly, than it is talking about process at this point and moving the ball forward.

I appreciate your allowing me to testify here today and I urge us to take that next step, move forward on a bipartisan basis to put together a plan for reform, and I thank you for your patience this morning.

Chairman ARCHER. Thank you for your input. The committee, I think on a bipartisan basis, welcomes it.

[The prepared statement follows:]

Statement of Hon. Rob Portman, a Representative in Congress from the State of Ohio

Thank you, Chairman Archer, for holding this series of hearings on tax reform. It's been an informative and thoughtful discussion, and I've appreciated the opportunity to learn about the various alternatives to the current tax code, which I hope we can all agree should be replaced by a simpler, fairer and less intrusive system.

This morning, though, I would like to focus, not so much on **why** a specific tax reform plan does or doesn't make sense, but on the process of *how* we might bring structural tax reform about within the next two to five years. Unlike some, I believe it *can* happen-in fact, I believe it must happen if we are to continue our current prosperity into an increasingly competitive 21st Century.

In 1996 and 1997, thanks to the Chairman's support, I had the opportunity to serve as co-chairman of the National Commission on Restructuring the IRS—a blue ribbon panel of experts convened by the Congress to recommend reforms to improve taxpayer service at the IRS. We rolled up our sleeves and spent a year literally auditing the IRS—to get to the root of the key problems at the agency. It was a complex and difficult task, but after careful, thorough review, we recommended the most comprehensive overhaul of the IRS in 45 years. Although some of the recommendations were controversial at the time, and although the Administration was initially opposed to our findings, at the end of the day, based on the Commission's work and the credibility it brought, we enjoyed broad bipartisan support and got these important reforms enacted into law.

Throughout our work on the IRS Restructuring Commission, there was one cross-cutting problem that kept resurfacing. I'm talking, of course, about the overwhelming *complexity* of the tax code. On a bipartisan basis, Commissioners came to conclude that the tax code ITSELF was the greatest problem facing a very, very troubled agency. This isn't news to the Members of this Committee. But it provided another clear basis for reform, because the Commission found convincing evidence of the enormous *organizational challenges* the tax code poses to the IRS.

Although tax simplification was not our mandate, we pushed the envelope a bit with our recommendations because the problem was so pervasive. Among our recommendations:

1) Tax complexity analysis-subject all prospective tax legislation to a Joint Tax Committee analysis to determine its complexity for the taxpayer and the IRS.
2) Get the IRS formally involved in the tax writing process to comment on the administrative challenges posed by the proposed tax law changes.
3) Recommendations on 60-odd specific code sections that could be simplified to reduce needless complexity-some of these reforms were implemented in the 1997 Taxpayer Relief Act.; and
4) An annual meeting of the 7 committees with IRS oversight responsibility to ensure that the agency gets more consistent guidance from the Hill.

These reforms underscored the connection between the problems of the IRS and the complexity of the code itself. But I believe they've also had the effect of helping to convince Members of Congress and the public that we'll never get at the real root of the problems at the IRS unless we address the tax code itself.

Now, I know what you're thinking—despite the amount of rhetoric devoted to tax code reform, little seems to get done (raise your hand if you remember the Tax Reform Act of 1986). While the general notion of tax reform has broad bipartisan support the devil, as always, is in the details. So how do we get from Point A—the current code—to Point B—a simpler, fairer tax code that actually makes sense for a 21st Century economy? Let me offer a few suggestions.

First, let's establish a *Tax Reform Commission*. The purpose of the Commission would be to keep the ball rolling, to help educate the public about the problem and the alternatives, to take some of the rough-and-tumble of partisan politics out of the process and to bring some non-partisan expertise to bear, in a focused way and with a specific timetable.

That's why I urge my colleagues to support the legislation that's on the floor today—which not only contains the "sunset the code" idea that we've debated in the past—but in the meantime also establishes a non-partisan NATIONAL COMMISSION ON TAX REFORM AND SIMPLIFICATION. It is modeled on the successful National Commission on Restructuring the IRS.

I know that Commissions have a checkered past in this town, but we proved that they can work. The Commission will have 15 members—three appointed by the President, four each appointed by the Senate Majority Leader and the Speaker, and two each appointed by the House and Senate Minority Leaders. It will have a short timetable −18 months—to complete its work and make a report to Congress on ways to fundamentally reform and simplify the tax code. The Commission's recommendations will cut through some of the clutter and give the Ways and Means Committee a specific starting-point for more general debate.

But even before we have a specific plan before us, this Committee should take the lead by laying out a framework for tax reform that we can all agree on. Any framework for tax reform should include these three elements:

1. **BROAD SUPPORT**, meaning, of course, it must be **BIPARTISAN:**Taxes are some of the most intensely partisan issues we consider in this Congress—and there are real and legitimate differences between the tax policy viewpoints of both parties. But, as we consider structural tax reform, we need to have a plan that can draw bipartisan support. Why? (1) **Reality**—neither party has the ability to ramrod a tax reform plan through Congress on its own; and (2) **Stability:** Ensure that future Congresses and Administrations don't throw out the tax code when party control switches. There have been thousands of changes to the Code even since 1986, and it's the constant changes—as well as the complexity—that causes such compliance headaches.

2. **REVENUE NEUTRALITY:** Any tax reform plan that stands a realistic chance of becoming law cannot significantly increase or decrease federal tax receipts. I'm not going to mention specific plans, but there have been tax reform plans that have advertised a certain rate that is predicated on significant reductions in the federal budget. Our focus should be on developing a vehicle for reforming the tax code—we can find plenty of other opportunities to have the debate over reshaping the size and shape of the government.

3. Finally, **FAIRNESS:** I think we have to recognize the *PROGRESSIVITY* of the current code and—for both fairness and for political reasons—I just don't see a regressive tax passing. We can't have a plan that throws the distribution tables too far off by shifting too great a percentage of the overall tax burden onto one income level or another. An important, but overlooked, part of ensuring tax progressivity, in my view, is to reduce compliance costs and burdens for taxpayers—particularly lower-and middle-income taxpayers. If we can lower or *eliminate altogether* the costs of complying with the code for a substantial number of taxpayers, we'll have a much fairer and less intrusive system.

As some of you know, I've been working on my own ideas for how we might accomplish those goals. And I know other Members of this Committee have offered thoughtful plans for reforming the tax code. I commend Chairman Archer for having these hearings to increase the awareness and understanding of the challenge of tax reform.

Now, let's take the next step—on a bipartisan basis—to make tax reform a clear policy goal for this Congress.

Thank you.

———————

Chairman ARCHER. I have no questions.

Mr. Rangel?

Mr. RANGEL. I am a little afraid of the idea of a commission having such broad powers in determining philosophically how we should collect the revenues that would run our country.

With Social Security, I joined with the Chairman in believing that a commission was the right way to go. Philosophically I don't think there is that much diversity in terms of how do you fund a system once you have already decided the health care that you want to provide. But whether we are talking a value-added tax, a Federal sales tax, or a progressive income tax, I think we are elected to make those type of decisions.

But I am attracted to the idea of bringing together groups of professionals, excluding Members of Congress, have them review and analyze the different systems that have been offered to the Congress, and to report back to the Ways and Means Committees the pros and cons of it.

But it just seems to me that I would not want presented to the Ways and Means Committee, to the House, or however you work this out, something that philosophically may be diametrically opposed to what I think should be happening. Members are elected to express their views of their constituents, are would need to know what direction the commission would be going and have an impact.

There is enough good ideas in what you are saying and I think that your presentation is positive. We should have more outside views, so that we don't waste a lot of times just with hearings, where experts can come together, study a situation, and then report back to the Congress.

I want to thank you for your thoughtfulness. We will continue to rely for you for direction in assisting us. We hopefully will move forward in bringing some resolution to this problem.

Mr. PORTMAN. Thank you. I will.

I would just make one quick comment, and that is that the educational element to this that you mentioned—I believe it was at yesterday's hearing—I think would be a tremendous benefit that would come from a commission.

In the IRS Commission case, as Mr. Coyne knows, we held hearings around the country, and I think that would be appropriate.

A lot of it is going to be exactly what you say, which is bringing experts in and also bringing people from everyday life who are affected by these massive changes that are being recommended to talk about the impact it would have on our businesses, on individuals, families, and so there would be an educational aspect to this and there would also be a lot of analysis, and at the end of the day there may not be a consensus recommendation. It may be just that—it may be just information that Congress can use.

Ultimately, of course, I said earlier—which is obvious—this committee and the elected representatives would have the final say.

Mr. RANGEL. Thank you.

Chairman ARCHER. Does any other Member wish to inquire? Mr. Neal?

Mr. NEAL. Thank you, Mr. Chairman.

Mr. Portman, you know of my regard for your opinions, and I am delighted with much of your testimony, but let me ask you a couple of specific questions that I think might focus part of this discussion.

A certain amount of the tax reform debate relies upon the old notion that the grass is always greener on the other side of the fence. Certainly, retail sales tax supporters found that out when joint tax Tuesday estimated that it would take a 60 percent sales tax to replace all Federal taxes.

I react favorably to Mr. English's philosophy when he said yesterday that the last thing we need is to enact reform that is so radical and experimental that Congress will be faced with revamping it all over again in but a few years.

Let me ask you this. I know you have an interest in simplification, especially in the pension area. I have introduced a bill, which even Mr. Archer has commented on favorably, that would eliminate 200 lines from individual income tax forms. Mr. Houghton has another version of that and has worked on international tax simplification, as well.

Do you think it is really possible that the committee, or at least some of us, could hammer out a practical, reasonable, wide-ranging tax simplification proposal? And do you think that would satisfy many of the complaints about complexity in the current system?

The 1986 Tax Act was intended to promote fairness, simplicity, and economic efficiency. Regardless of how well the committee achieved any of these goals, it has spent the last 15 years unraveling at least part of it.

Do you think that we would be any more successful this time, or do we need a completely different tax system?

Mr. PORTMAN. I guess I think both. I have always believed that it is worth the committee's time and the Oversight Subcommittee, on which I serve, to focus on simplification. Every day we ought to be trying to simplify the tax code. At the same time, and I think this gets to your question maybe more directly—if we just do that, we will not have done enough. Because of the forces in this town and elsewhere to find special breaks and provisions in the tax code that help individuals and help businesses, we will end up with the same complexity problems, which is why we need, also, to have debate on and movement toward a more fundamental tax reform measure which would, indeed, replace the current code.

I also think we have to realize that, as long as we are just taxing income, we are, in effect, taxing success and taxing productivity, and all the economists with whom I have talked and you have talked, right, left, or center, agree that moving from something that penalizes savings and investment and the next dollar earned to a system that taxes consumption more would make sense from an economic perspective.

In our current code, with all the simplification you or I might want to do, you can't get at that economic reality. What we can get at is the compliance cost, which I salute you for. I think your bill is a movement in that direction. But I think we need to go on both tracks.

Mr. NEAL. Thank you, Mr. Portman.

Thank you, Mr. Chairman.

Chairman ARCHER. Mr. Thomas?

Mr. THOMAS. Thanks, Rob.

One of the concerns I have is that all of our focus is on the hated IRS, for a lot of good reasons, and a lot of the programs look at the domestic picture and the internal role of the tax code, because we have structured ourselves so long in that way.

You and I and others know that our tax code, vis-a-vis other countries, has significant impact on trade.

It used to be that no one really wanted to look at Medicare or other major Federal programs because it was, as they used to say, the "third rail." Although President Clinton probably doesn't want to have credit for starting the debate by putting out a plan that was examined in great detail and wound up being found lacking, I think a significant education process went on among Americans and those institutions—the media and others—in examining an area that had not been at the forefront of exploration, the Medicare system, and, beyond that, the health care system and the delivery structures that go with it.

My concern about not wanting to put something forward—and you always do the best you can—is not so much to worry about failing, but that, absent something concrete about which debate could turn, we aren't going to get the kind of educational process among the American people that I think we need. A sterile, academic discussion of options isn't the same as, "This is what we have. This is what you are going to get. What do you think of the difference?" That focuses the debate.

The fact that we would fail, say, the first time around is less important to me than how far have we advanced the American people's understanding that we need something new, notwithstanding what it was they just lost.

Having been on a commission recently dealing with Medicare—yours was a bit more successful than ours—we, nevertheless, I think, elevated to a degree the discussion, because we put forth a specific plan.

Commission, us, somebody—esoteric, academic debates don't create the intensity to choose. Something out front that could be an alternative does.

Reaction?

Mr. PORTMAN. I couldn't agree with you more. It is an action-forcing event. And let me say I didn't use Thomas-Breaux, which was the Medicare Reform Commission, as my example, I used the IRS one because I am closer to it, but it is a perfect example of what I am talking about. A major difference, as you know, between the IRS Commission and Thomas Breaux was the two-thirds requirement. Wasn't it a two-thirds requirement for a recommendation to be made from the Commission?

Mr. THOMAS. Yes. It was 11 out of 17.

Mr. PORTMAN. We had a different set of rules under which we worked. Now, in the end we did get a two-thirds majority, but I think it was too bad that at the end that effort was torpedoed by representatives from the Administration.

But, by the same token, it certainly focused debate and it certainly moved the ball forward, and I think it is a good example.

People, again, say commissions don't work. Well, they have a checkered past. Some have, some haven't. But I can tell you these two examples of the IRS Commission and the Medicare Commission I think would lead us to be favorably disposed toward a commission approach to this.

IRS reform is difficult and Medicare reform is extremely controversial and can become very political, but nothing is bigger than tax reform because it is going to affect every single person in America, every business, and how we transact every business transaction.

As Mr. Rangel said, it is fundamentally government how we collect our taxes.

I think Chairman Archer has, through the last few years, done incredible work in moving the ball forward, because we wouldn't be here at these hearings. We wouldn't have the headlines that we are getting. But we need to now move it to the next level, and I think it is helpful to take it out of this politically-charged environment.

Frankly, the Administration hasn't been able to come to the plate on it.

If you look to the history of tax reform, it has always been led by Treasury. They have the expertise. They have the ability to understand how it would be implemented. This Administration has not taken the lead on that, unlike the Reagan Administration in 1986. That may or may not happen in the next Administration.

The wonderful thing about this commission is that, while it includes the Treasury Department—and actually the Secretary of the Treasury would make an appointment—and includes the Administration, it does not rely on them. Instead, it relies on Congress and the Administration, bipartisan, bicameral, moving ahead on it.

So I agree with your observation, and I think the Medicare Commission is another good example.

Chairman ARCHER. Mr. Portman, thank you very much.

Mr. PORTMAN. Thank you, Mr. Chairman.

Chairman ARCHER. Our next panel is Frank Luntz and Jefrey Pollock.

Welcome, gentlemen. If you will identify yourselves for the record, you may proceed with your testimony. And, if possible, we would appreciate your holding your verbal testimony to five minutes. Your entire printed statement, without objection, will be inserted in the record.

Dr. Luntz?

STATEMENT OF FRANK LUNTZ, PRESIDENT AND CHIEF EXEC-UTIVE OFFICER, LUNTZ RESEARCH COMPANIES, ARLING-TON, VIRGINIA

Mr. LUNTZ. Mr. Chairman, for the record, my name is Frank Luntz. It is an honor to be here. Having had the opportunity to present to a number of you in your offices and in various places on the Hill and now being before this tremendous chamber, I can tell you that distance only makes the heart grow fonder.

I am sorry that the ranking member is not here. I would have informed him that in our polling for New York, on more than one occasion, he is the most popular and respected political figure in the State. When we asked him why, the number one reason was his voice. I was looking forward to hearing his voice after we spoke today.

I begin with a single finding from my—

Chairman ARCHER. Dr. Luntz, would you identify your official position in our world, for the record, before you commence?

Mr. LUNTZ. My official position is the president of the Luntz Research Companies. Thank you, sir.

I begin with a single finding from a survey my firm completed just last week. When asked to choose the one government agency or institution Americans hated the most, it should come as no surprise that they chose the IRS. In fact, the IRS was chosen more than every other Government agency combined.

Mr. Chairman, that is just one reason why up to 80 percent of Americans want fundamental tax reform and why so many Americans want to rid themselves of this complicated, confusing, and corrupt tax system.

I ask the members of this committee to answer one question that we asked the American people—which would you rather have happen to you, have your wallet or purse stolen or be audited by the

IRS? Of Americans, 45 percent chose the wallet or purse stolen, 45 percent chose the IRS audit, and 10 percent actually said they couldn't tell the difference between the two.

Now, if you ask the American people to set a fair tax rate, most Americans would agree to something around 20 percent. But what frustrates Americans the most is not the income tax rate so much as it is the complexity of the system and the perception that the rich have expensive tax attorneys and fancy accountants to navigate the IRS code.

In public opinion research we have done in terms of tax reform, Americans have four essential requirements

Number one, fairness. Americans want to know that the family with the expensive mansion on top of the hill is paying his or her fair share. Fairness does not mean soak the rich, but it does mean the wealthy must pay their fair share.

Number two is simplicity. People do not want to pay accountants to prepare their taxes, yet an increasing percentage of working class families now need to because the system is so complicated and so frustrating.

Number three, uniformity. Working families dislike having tax advantages parceled out to those who hire expensive lobbyists and tax lawyers. Americans want a Federal tax system that treats billionaires like Bill Gates exactly the same as bus drivers like Ralph Cramden.

Consistency—Americans hate how the tax code changes from year to year. With all due respect, they want a tax code that you all up there can't tinker with from year to year.

Tax reform is a middle class issue because it is the middle class who work the longest and hardest and feel the most short-changed by not finding all the tax deductions they are entitled to. I ask you to think about just how often you all are affected by the tax code.

When you wake up in the morning and drink your first cup of coffee, you pay a sales tax. You start your car, you pay a gas tax. You drive to work, you pay an automobile tax. At work you pay an income tax. You turn on the lights, you pay an electricity tax. You flush the toilet, you pay a water tax. You get home at night, you pay a property tax. You turn on your TV, you pay a cable tax. You make a phone call, you pay a telephone tax. Even when you die, you pay a death tax.

Two-thirds of Americans believe that they are over-taxed and they want a break, and that is why tax reform, Mr. Chairman, is so universally popular and that is why, in particular, they want an end to the marriage penalty and an end to the death tax.

It doesn't matter whether you are a republican or democrat. Americans believe that a recently-married couple should not pay more in taxes just simply because they decided to get married. It is one of the most sacred and important institutions in our society, and you are going to have a difficult time finding anyone who believes that they should have to pay more just because a man and a woman tie the knot.

Similarly, it was Benjamin Franklin, my favorite founding father, who said, "There are only two certainties in life—death and taxes." But I don't think even Ben Franklin would have known that both those occurrences would have come at the same time.

My colleague, Jef Pollock, has more numbers to share with you, so I will close with the following observation: most Americans believe you can fix the tax code, instill fairness and consistency, and still maintain and strengthen programs like Social Security and Medicare. They believe you have got the power to do it all, and they want you to do it all.

And the people that I polled are not the Internet paper billionaires, they are not the high-priced lawyers. They are struggling to make ends meet. They sacrifice their own needs and give everything they can to their children. All they want to know is that you hear them and that you care, so prove it with a new tax code that is consistent, flat, fair, and tinker-proof.

Thank you, Mr. Chairman.

Chairman ARCHER. Thank you, Dr. Luntz.

[The prepared statement follows:]

Statement of Frank Luntz, President and Chief Executive Officer, Luntz Research Companies, Arlington, Virginia

I begin with a single finding from a survey my firm completed just last week. When asked to choose the one government agency or institution they hated the most, it should come as no surprise they chose the IRS. In fact, they chose the IRS more than every other government agency—**combined** In fact, according to a colleague of mine, Democratic pollster Peter Hart, few things frighten Americans more than receiving an IRS notice in the mail.

Mr. Chairman, that's just one reason why up to 80% of Americans want fundamental tax **reform**, and why so many Americans want to rid themselves of this complicated, confusing and corrupt tax system. In fact, for most Americans, the point of least favorable contact between them and Washington occurs sometime late in the afternoon of April 15 when they deliver their tax return to the *friendly* local post office.

I ask this Committee to answer a question I put to the American people: would you rather have your wallet or purse stolen or be audited by the IRS? Among Americans, 45% would rather be audited, 45% would rather have their wallet or purse stolen, and 10% said there was no difference!

Now, if you asked Americans to set a fair tax rate, most would readily agree to something around 20 percent. But what frustrates Americans most is not the income tax rate so much as it is the **complexity** of the system and the perception that the rich have expensive tax attorneys and fancy accountants to navigate the Internal Revenue Code.

In the public opinion research we have done in regard to tax reform, Americans have four essential requirements for any new tax code:

1) *Fairness.* Americans want to know that the family in the mansion at the top of the hill is paying his fair share. Fairness does not mean soak-the-rich, but it does mean the wealthy must pay their fair share.

2) *Simplicity* People do not want to pay accountants to prepare their taxes, yet an increasing percentage of working class families now need to because the system is so complicated and frustrating.

3) *Uniformity* Working families dislike having tax advantages parceled out to those who hire expensive lawyers and lobbyists. Americans want a tax system that treats Bill Gates no better than Homer Simpson.

4) *Consistency* Americans hate how the tax code changes from year to year. With all due respect, they want a tax code that stops all of you from tinkering with it.

Tax reform is a middle class issue, for it is the middle class who work the longest and the hardest and feel the most shortchanged by not finding all the tax deductions they are entitled to. I ask you to think about just how often the working men and women of America are taxed in their day-to-day livesa...

When you wake up in the morning and drink that first cup of coffee, you pay a sales tax. When you start your car, you pay an automobile tax. Drive to work, you pay a gas tax. At work, you pay an income tax—and a payroll tax. You get home at night, you pay a property tax. Flip on the light—you pay an electricity tax. Turn on the TV—you pay a cable tax. Call a friend, you pay a communications tax. Brush your teeth, you pay a water tax. Even when you die, you pay a death tax.

In short, two-thirds of hardworking American believe they are overtaxed, and they want a break. That's why tax reform is so universally popular, and why, in particular, Americans want an end to the so-called marriage tax and the death tax.

It doesn't matter whether you are a Republican or a Democrat. Americans believe that a recently married couple should not pay more in taxes simply because they decided to get married. The institution of marriage is one of the most sacred and important in our society, and you would have a difficult time finding anyone who believes the government should penalize a man and a woman simply because they choose to tie the knot and start a family.

True, it was Benjamin Franklin, my favorite Founding Father, who said there were two certainties in life: death and taxes. But I do not believe even Dr. Franklin could have told us that both would occur at the same time. Perhaps that is why only a fraction of Americans believe they will ever be impacted by the death tax, and yet a clear majority want that tax eliminated—now.

My Democratic colleague has more numbers to share with you, so I will close with the following observation. Most Americans believe you **CAN** fix the tax code, instill fairness and consistency into the system, and still maintain and strengthen programs like Social Security and Medicare. They believe you have the ability and the power to do it all.

And the people I poll are not the Internet paper billionaires. The people I poll don't have the high priced lawyers and fancy CPA's at their beckon call. The people I poll still struggle to make ends meet. They still burn the candle at both ends to put food on the table and keep a roof overhead. They still sacrifice their own needs and giving everything they've got to make sure their children have every opportunity for a brighter future. All they want to know is that you hear them and that you care. So prove it, with a new tax code that is consistent, flat, fair and "tinker proof."

WAYS AND MEANS

Now, if they truly wanted to, do you think it is possible or impossible for Congress to cut taxes for working Americans while at the same time strengthening Social Security?

What is your overall view of the federal tax system. Does it work...

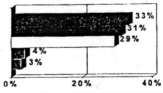

●	Possible
◎	Impossible
○	DK/R

- ● Not Well/ Major Changes
- ● Fairly Well/ Minor Adjustments
- ○ Very Badly/ Overhaul
- ● Don't Know/ Not Sure
- ● Very Well/ No Changes

The Luntz Research Companies

Please tell me whether you believe each form of taxation is completely fair, somewhat fair, somewhat unfair or completely unfair.

(% people saying unfair)

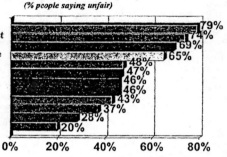

Soc. Sec. Benefits	79%
Savings Acct. Interest	74%
Death/ Inheritance	69%
Long Distance Phone	65%
Capital Gains	48%
Property	47%
Income	46%
Payroll	46%
Gas	43%
Sales	37%
Cigarette	28%
Alcohol and Beer	20%

The Luntz Research Companies

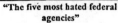

Congress should support a complete overhaul of the federal tax system that includes abolishing the IRS and replacing the five different income tax rates that now exist with a single rate.

"The five most hated federal agencies"

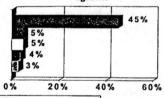

	45%
	5%
	5%
	4%
	3%

- Agree
- Disagree
- DK/R

- ● The IRS
- ● OSHA
- ○ The Pentagon
- ● The FBI
- ⊕ The Post Office

The Luntz Research Companies

Chairman ARCHER. Mr. Pollock?

STATEMENT OF JEFREY POLLOCK, PRESIDENT, GLOBAL STRATEGY GROUP, INC., NEW YORK, NEW YORK

Mr. POLLOCK. Thank you, Mr. Chairman.

My name is Jef Pollock. I am the president of Global Strategy Group, a public opinion research firm for the democrats.

Hemlines go up. Hemlines go down. Los Angeles has forsaken the martini lunch for a sobering shot of oxygen. Public opinion waxes and wanes. But what is the one thing everyone has consistently agreed upon since Truman beat Dewey? Taxes, Mr. Chairman, are too high, and the system we endure too complex.

Over 40 percent of Americans have considered Federal income taxes to be too high since the 1940s, and for the last 30 years that figure has risen to 60 percent, though admittedly it is down from its high of 69 percent in 1969.

How much is too much? As my republican colleague, Dr. Luntz, has stated, almost two-thirds of Americans say the highest percentage we should have to pay for all taxes combined—that is Federal, State, and local—should be less than 20 percent of their income. And who is getting their free ride? According to most Americans, it is the rich.

Fully two-thirds of the Nation believe that those in the upper income bracket pay too little in taxes, and almost half of all Americans say this is the aspect of our tax system that bothers them the most.

Still, on a more personal level, less than half of the population believes that the amount of taxes they will pay this year is "fair."

Americans are focused on their persistence that our tax code needs overhaul. Dr. Luntz is correct to demonstrate that Americans are frustrated with their increasing reliance on accountants. The middle class think they are being squeezed by a complex system. An impressive 61 percent of Americans believe the Federal income tax system needs major changes or a complete overhaul.

The components of this overhaul encompass cutting taxes, simplifying the process, and regulating the power of the IRS, but, while these suggestions sound succinct, they come with strings attached, further complicating the process of reform.

Simplicity—two-thirds of Americans find the Federal system too complicated; yet, although the system of taxation is considered too complex, Americans are unwilling to give up deductions to simplify it, and they oppose, by a 57 to 34 percent margin, replacing the system with a simpler nationwide sales tax.

Regulation—a vast majority of Americans, 68 percent, believe the IRS has more power than it needs. There is no "other side" to this issue. Right or wrong, they feel the IRS should be better regulated.

Tax cuts—Americans are equally in support of a tax cut for all Americans, as well as a cut for moderate to low income households. However, while 72 percent of Americans favor a cut in Federal income taxes, it is not their highest priority. A plurality, 39 percent, placed a high priority on Congress passing a significant Federal income tax, but only 21 percent say it is the top priority. And more than a third, 38 percent, say it should be a low or not a priority at all.

In addition, when our firm, Global Strategy Group, frames the question pitting tax cuts against generic spending, Americans prefer tax cuts. But when you ask people about cutting tax as opposed to spending on programs, Americans choose, of course, to fund the programs they most enjoy.

288

So, although they are concerned about their own purse, the point of contributing to the Government's coffers is clearly understood and accepted.

The task that lies before you all is great. Americans are not happy with the current tax system, and, although they do offer solutions, the solutions are not without their own complexities.

While Americans overwhelmingly want reform, they do not want it at any cost. They will not trade tax reform for a cut in specific spending programs, and they will not sacrifice deductions for a simplification in the tax codes; however, they will likely be receptive to a discourse on how to reform the code, and we can be pretty certain they will embrace a plan to equalize the tax contributions of all Americans and certainly to reduce the power of the IRS.

As we approach April 15th, Americans are struggling to complete their tax forms accurately and on time. There is no better time to reassess the tax code and deliver a simpler, fair system that addresses the perceived inequality of taxation and the inappropriate power of the IRS.

Let us put last century's opinion on this issue to rest forever.

Thank you, Mr. Chairman.

Chairman ARCHER. Thank you, Mr. Pollock.

[The prepared statement follows:]

Statement of Jefrey Pollock, President, Global Strategy Group, Inc., New York, New York

Hemlines are up, hemlines are down. La Vida Loca replaces Duck & Cover. L.A. has forsaken the martini lunch for a sobering shot of oxygen. The Watergate has become just another fashionable address. Public opinion waxes and wanes.

But what's the one thing everyone has consistently agreed on since Truman beat Dewey? Taxes, Mr. Chairman, are too high. And the system we endure, too complex.

Over 40% of Americans have considered federal income taxes to be too high since the late 1940s. And for the last thirty years, that figure has risen to 60% (though it is down from it's high of 69% in 1969).

How much is too much? As my Republican colleague, Dr. Frank Luntz has stated, almost two-thirds of Americans say the highest percentage we should have to pay for all taxes combined—that's federal, state and local—should be less than 20% of their income.

And who's getting the free ride? The rich. Fully two-thirds of the nation believes that those in the upper income bracket pay too little in taxes. And almost half of all Americans say this is the aspect of our tax system that bothers them the most. Still, on a more personal level, less than half of the population believes that the amount of taxes they will pay this year is "fair."

Now, although everyone likes to gripe vaguely about situations they perceive to be out of their control, Americans are focused in their persistence that our tax code needs an overhaul. Dr. Luntz is correct to demonstrate that Americans are frustrated with their increasing reliance on accountants: the middle class think they're being squeezed by a complex system.

An impressive sixty-one percent of Americans believe the federal income tax system needs major changes or a complete overhaul.

The components of this overhaul encompass cutting taxes, simplifying the process and regulating the power of the IRS. But while these suggestions sound succinct, they come with strings attached—further complicating the process of reform.

Simplicity: Two-thirds of Americans find the federal tax system too complicated.

• Yet, although the system of taxation is considered too complex, Americans are not willing to give up deductions to simplify it. And they oppose (57% to 34%) replacing the system with a nationwide sales tax.

Regulation: A vast majority of Americans (68%) believe the IRS has more power than it needs.

• There is no "other side" to this issue. Right or wrong, they feel the IRS should be better regulated.

Tax Cuts: Americans are equally in support of a tax cut for all Americans as well as a cut for moderate to low income households.

• However, while 72% of Americans favor a cut in federal income taxes, it is not their highest priority. A plurality of Americans (39%) place a *high* priority on Congress passing a significant federal income tax cut; *but only 21% say it is the top prority*. And more than one third (38%) say it should be a low priority or not a priority at all.

• In addition, when our firm, Global Strategy Group, frames the question pitting tax cuts against generic spending, Americans prefer tax cuts. But when you ask people about cutting taxes as opposed to spending on programs, Americans choose to fund the programs they enjoy. So although they are concerned about their own purse, the point of contributing to the government's coffers is clearly understood and accepted.

The task that lies before you all is great. Americans are not happy with the current tax system and although they do offer solutions, the solutions are not without their own complexities.

While Americans overwhelmingly want reform, they do not want it at any costs. They will not trade tax reform for a cut in specific spending programs, and they will not sacrifice deductions for a simplification of the tax codes. However, they will likely be receptive to a discourse on how to reform the code, and we can be pretty certain they will embrace a plan to equalize the tax contributions of all Americans and reduce the IRS's power.

As we approach April 15th, Americans are struggling to complete their tax forms accurately and on time. There is no better time to reassess the tax code and deliver a simple, fair system that addresses the perceived inequality of taxation and inappropriate power of the IRS. Let's put last Century's opinion on this issue to rest forever.

All polls cited in this testimony were conducted nationwide, and all polled only adults. Thus, the opinions cited are representative of voters across the country.

Sources include:
ABC News/*Washington Post* Poll, 3/9 −3/11, 2000, M of E 3%.
AP Poll conducted by ICR, 3/26 −3/30, 1999, M of E 3.1%.
Gallup Poll, 4/17 −4/19, 1998.
⎯⎯⎯, 3/5 −3/7, 1999, M of E 5%.
⎯⎯⎯, 7/17 −7/18, 1999, M of E 5%.
⎯⎯⎯, 1/13 −1/16, 2000.
Gallup/CNN/USA Today Poll, Margin of Error 3%.
⎯⎯⎯, 4/6 −4/7, 1999, M of E 3%.
⎯⎯⎯, 7/16 −7/18, 1999, M of E 3%.
FOX News/Opinion Dynamics Poll, 3/10 −3/11, 1999, M of E 3.3%.
NBC News/WSJ Poll, 7/24 −7/26, 1999, M of E 3.2%.
Pew Research Center Poll, 2/9 −2/14, 2000, M of E 3.5%.

Public Opinion on Taxes and Tax Reform

Prepared for Testimony Before the Committee On Ways and Means, U.S. House of Representatives

April 13, 2000

GLOBAL STRATEGY GROUP, INC.

611 BROADWAY
SUITE 206
NEW YORK, NY 10012
212.260.8813 VOICE
212.260.9058 FAX

1424 16TH STREET, NW
SUITE 400
WASHINGTON, DC 20036
202.265.4676 VOICE
202.265.4619 FAX

The proportion who believe the income tax they pay is too high is roughly the same as it was 30 years ago.

Do you consider the amount of federal income taxes you have to pay to be too high, about right or too low?

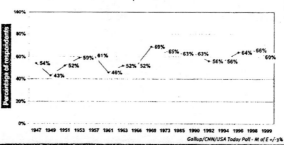

Gallup/CNN/USA Today Poll - M of E +/-3%

GLOBAL STRATEGY GROUP, INC.

291

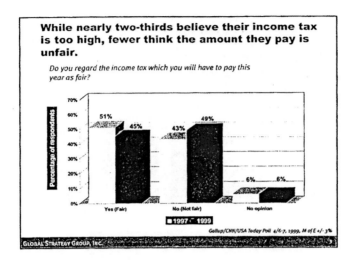

292

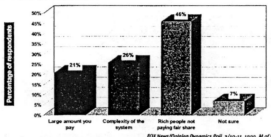

In fact, Americans say that the most bothersome characteristic of the tax system is that it allows the rich to get away with not paying their fair share.

Which of the following bothers you most about taxes: The large amount you pay in taxes, the complexity of the tax system, or the feeling that some rich people get away with not paying their fair share?

FOX News/Opinion Dynamics Poll 3/10-11, 1999, M of E +/-3.3%

GLOBAL STRATEGY GROUP, INC.

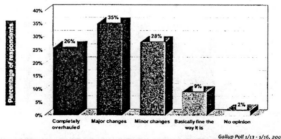

Most Americans believe the federal income tax system needs major changes or a complete overhaul.

Which of the following statements best represents what you feel about the federal income tax system -- needs to be completely overhauled, needs major changes, needs minor changes, is basically fine the way it is?

Gallup Poll 1/13 - 1/16, 2000

GLOBAL STRATEGY GROUP, INC.

293

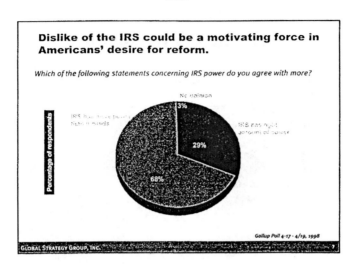

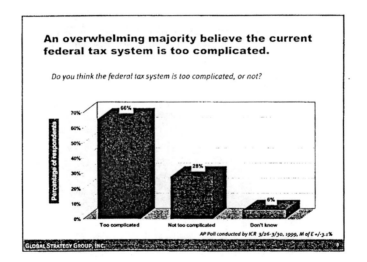

294

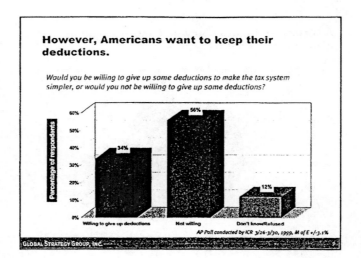

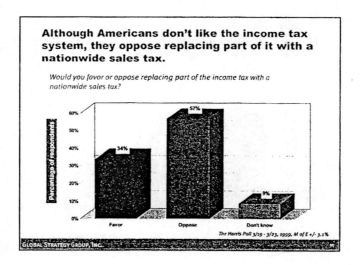

295

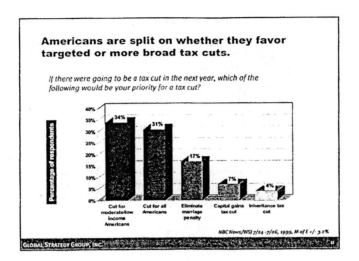

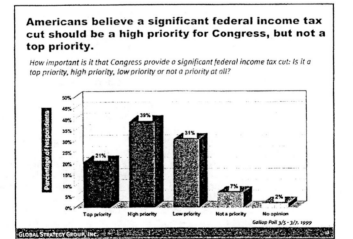

Chairman ARCHER. If I may inquire, where did you grow up?

Mr. POLLOCK. I grew up in Mr. Coyne's home State of Pennsylvania, northeast Philadelphia.

Chairman ARCHER. Well, as a Texan, I greatly enjoyed your statement that "the task that lies before ya'll is great." And I thought perhaps you might have grown up in Texas.

Mr. POLLOCK. Too many clients in the south, Mr. Archer.

Chairman ARCHER. I would like to ask both of you what, if any, difference exists between the polling data that each one of you has been able to put together.

Mr. LUNTZ. I would say that, for the most part, it is actually quite similar, though on some of the details it does differ because the focus does differ, and I would acknowledge to the Members that, depending on how you word the question, you can get a different result.

I think we would both agree that the IRS is quite unpopular. I think we would both agree that the public does support the concept of tax reform. The question is always in the details of that tax reform.

Today, more than at any other time, Americans believe that there should be a consistent rate, rather than this progressive rate, and that opinion did not exist five years ago, but it has existed for about the past two or three years, and that opinion continues to grow.

And I think we also would agree that the public does want to ensure that any tax reform not subject programs like Social Security and Medicare to any kind of disruption.

Mr. POLLOCK. I would agree with Dr. Luntz and say that the devil is in the details. When you look at questions about things like a flat tax, for example, that is when things get very complex, because when you ask Americans straight out they tend to like it, but once you ask them any single question that starts to whittle way at deductions, they basically flip out. They say, "No. Forget it." And so it just takes one little push to push them over the edge, so the simplicity sometimes is deceptive in the questions.

Mr. POLLOCK. And the surprise is actually republicans and democrats, alike, whenever we test the death tax, it is one of the taxes that Americans hate the most, even though it is a tax that very few Americans feel that they will ever face. That is what makes it quite interesting. They are not responding from their own personal benefit; they are responding from the principal belief that Americans should not be taxed at death.

Chairman ARCHER. I am a little bit curious as to what appears to be a dichotomy between the results that Americans don't think higher-income people are paying enough, number one, and the comment that today a majority of them don't like the progressive rate structure. How do you explain that difference?

Mr. LUNTZ. It is very easy, actually. It is all the deductions that you all have passed for various people that frustrate Americans. It is not the rate; it is the idea that the rich will have accountants and lawyers and people that can find in the loopholes within the current tax code that enable them to avoid having to pay taxes.

Mr. POLLOCK. And it is interesting, Mr. Chairman. Among Americans, 45 percent say that the taxes they pay are fair, so it is not as if it is 70 percent saying that it is unfair, or something like that.

I would agree with Dr. Luntz that it is the deductions, and that is the complexity that they feel.

Frank had a very good line about Bill Gates and Ralph Cramden, that Bill Gates has all these attorneys and accountants and etc. who can get him out of taxes. I am not picking on him particularly, but that is the concept that Americans feel.

Chairman ARCHER. Thank you.

Mr. Thomas and Mr. Neal.

Mr. THOMAS. Actually, I believe it was Bart Simpson, wasn't it? Ralph Cramden is someone I recognize. I figured you were trying to go for the now generation with Bart Simpson.

Thanks to both of you, but I, too, like the chairman, am kind of puzzled by the presentations, and then am curious about why and how questions are asked.

Do you have any relevant poll data if you ask American people whether rich people are happier than poor people?

Mr. LUNTZ. In fact, sir, we have looked at that, and the most happy people in America are the middle class.

Mr. THOMAS. And would you say that people are worth a million dollars that find themselves in the middle class, often?

Mr. LUNTZ. The people who are worth a million dollars would probably define themselves as being upper middle class.

Mr. THOMAS. Well, you can put all kinds of descriptive terms in front of it, but I think even Bill Gates thinks he is middle class, so I have difficulty, again, to deal with that kind of description.

Do you think people believe that the rich people get breaks—that is, it is easier to beat the system if you are rich rather than poor?

Mr. POLLOCK. Absolutely.

Mr. THOMAS. I think you get the point. You can go through a series of stereotypical statements, and people will ascribe a certain profile to the rich.

I think I could save you a lot of money and tell you without polling that people think rich people don't pay their fair share of the taxes.

Looking at this other chart—and I am using yours. Yours is Powerpoint and it has a few more. That is the only reason.

Although Americans don't like the income tax system, they oppose replacing part of it with a nationwide sales tax. Well, I don't like one, and now you are going to give me two. Did you try a question that said "replacing it in its entirety," an either/or question, rather than, "If you don't like one, how about two?"

Mr. POLLOCK. It is a good question, but, to be very clear, none of these are—I am pulling from independent polling data, so, as you will see, this is, you know, Gallup or—

Mr. THOMAS. Yes, but it is the same fraternity.

Mr. POLLOCK. That is true. I agree.

Mr. LUNTZ. Mr. Chairman, you know that fraternities right next to each other never get along.

Mr. THOMAS. And then, of course, as you said, Mr. Luntz, in terms of the way you asked the question, if I said, "Would you like to get rid of the income tax which would do away with the IRS and replace it with a different tax," you have now loaded the question, I think, sufficiently that people would go for whatever the rest of the sentence was if you threw in getting rid of the IRS.

So I am just kind of curious as to what you could provide us with that would be slightly less entertaining, perhaps, but a bit more enlightening, because when people don't like the current tax system, don't like the complexity, don't like the IRS, but want to hang on to their deductions, you kind of just say, "Don't wet your finger." We had better sit down and build the best scientific economic revenue package we can, and then go out and have people all agree that the unknown is not as acceptable as the known, notwithstanding the fact that I absolutely hate the known.

You folks are going to be in the boat with us, and we are going to be using you, but I would really love to see somebody try to cipher a series of questions with pull-out sections that substitute back in, that, in essence, asks the same question with variables, and then repeat it in different circumstances to try to begin to build a base of at least relative directional signals.

To your knowledge, has anybody begun doing this, or are we going to have to pay for it?

Mr. LUNTZ. We have done this, to some degree, and what we get, quite frankly, are mixed signals—that the public is frustrated with what they have now, they are scared about what you may give them. The problem, quite frankly, is their lack of faith in people here to give them a system that truly is flat, simple, and fair. They believe that, because of the outside influences, they are afraid that the actual new product might be more disruptive than what they have now, even though they fundamentally don't like what they have now.

Mr. THOMAS. Well, Mr. Luntz, you made the assumption the flat tax is the one that we would look at. What about one that got rid of all income taxes and allowed us to be competitive in the arena of today, and especially tomorrow, in world trade.

Mr. LUNTZ. I used the word "flat" to indicate both a sales tax and an income tax. I am not speaking just of the income tax. Flat rate means that everybody pays the same rate, regardless of whether it collects it based on what you spend or what you earn.

Mr. THOMAS. Even that, from a semantical point of view, makes it difficult because of the identity of the various plans and the terms that we use, so we are even more into a semantic jungle.

Thank you very much, Mr. Chairman.

Chairman ARCHER. Just very quickly, to piggy-back on the line of questioning of Congressman Thomas, I notice in one of the charts that you have given us, Dr. Luntz, that you ask the question, "Should Congress completely overhaul the Federal tax system that includes abolishing the IRS and replacing the five different income tax rates with a single rate." It seems to me that is an oxymoron, because if you have still got an income tax, even with a single rate, you still have the IRS. I don't know how you can do both.

Mr. LUNTZ. We were trying to get at not making a choice between income tax and the sales tax. The way the you read the question, you have assumed that it is an income tax rate.

One of the challenges in polling and to present to you all is to be neutral in terms of the income tax or the sales tax and try to judge the public's generic support for a fundamental overhaul of the system. So perhaps we have not achieved that by the question.

Chairman ARCHER. But if I were to answer the question—and, as you know, I want to abolish the income tax, which I have publicly stated for a long time, and I want to get the IRS completely and totally out of every individual's life, but if I were to answer this question and say that the IRS forever will be out of my life and I only have to pay a single income tax rate, I might be intrigued to embrace that. But I can't get both. I can't have a single income tax rate and have the IRS out of my life, because I have still got to keep the records for seven years, and they are still going to audit me, and I have still got all of the exposure, although in a more simple form than the current code.

Mr. Neal?

Mr. NEAL. Thank you, Mr. Chairman.

Dr. Luntz, I agreed with much of your testimony, but I want to ask you a question.

You said that the American people view the IRS as "corrupt." Did you use that term when you tested the question?

Mr. LUNTZ. No.

Mr. NEAL. No?

Mr. LUNTZ. We asked them, "What institution do you dislike the most? What Federal Government institution or agency do you dislike the most?"

Mr. NEAL. Let me just, if I can, address that question and the use of that term "corrupt." That word did more to poison the way that we talk to each other in this institution than any other word I have witnessed in the 12 years I have been in the House. That word was used to poison the well of the institution across the way and the way we talk and treat each other in the House.

Now, if we use that word all of the time around here to speak to each other or use that word when we wish to change an institution and its behavior, we only bring the debate to a new low, and that is the danger of using that term.

I would recommend to everybody here Joe Kline's piece in the New Yorker about a year ago, "The Town That Ate Itself," in which he went back and talked to Republican Members who used that word and now say they regret using that word because of what happened in the institution.

So if we didn't test that word, I don't know why we would throw that word into the testimony today.

Mr. LUNTZ. Because, Mr. Congressman, I would invite you, because this is not a partisan issue, to join me in focus groups and face-to-face sessions with Members, and the words that they use, not to describe the IRS but to describe the tax code.

Mr. NEAL. Right. I don't dispute that. I don't dispute that, Doctor.

Mr. LUNTZ. It is the language—

Mr. NEAL. It is the word.

Mr. LUNTZ. But it is the word that is used by the American people to describe what they perceive as a system that is out of control. And I invite you to join me in—

Mr. NEAL. I would like to do that. But let me ask you a quick question here. There is a Wall Street transaction called "exchange funds" that exactly accomplished that. Ralph Cramden's wife, Alice, has to sell her stock and then pay capital gains tax. What happens when Bill Gates goes into an exchange fund and, in effect, trades stock and pays no tax? Is this exactly the situation you referenced when you were speaking earlier about the way the American people perceive the tax code?

Mr. LUNTZ. No. I was merely using Ralph Cramden as a pop culture figure, although I would correct you. Ralph Cramden and Alice were so poor that they could never own stock, so they could never sell it and have to pay the capital gains.

Mr. NEAL. They were just blue collar democrats.

Mr. LUNTZ. Actually, they were the first blue collar republicans. They were just before the Reagan democrats came into being. [Laughter.]

Mr. NEAL. I would suggest, Mr. Chairman, that the transaction I made reference to—maybe Mr. Pollock could comment upon it, if he would.

Mr. POLLOCK. There is no doubt, Congressman Neal, that there is a feeling that the rich do get benefits. I don't think that is exactly—I mean, in terms of questioning, that is not something that hits them.

When you do focus groups—and I am sure you have seen this up north—people, especially the middle class more and more, are angered by the capital gains tax and that it is no longer a tax on the rich, exclusively.

But, from a rhetorical battle, if we were taking it out of the policy and into the rhetoric, it hasn't crossed the threshold yet where they say, "Oh, yeah, that is a tax where we, the middle class, really need to change it," but it is coming. It is coming. There is no doubt about it.

And with ever-increasing use of Ameritrade where the middle class and everybody is getting involved in trading, you are absolutely correct, that tax increases in prominence to them.

Mr. NEAL. I will close on this note, Dr. Luntz, that the Reagan democrats, which I represent, have come back home.

Thank you.

Mr. LUNTZ. I will allow you to have the last word. I hope so.

Chairman ARCHER. I am hoping that we can wrap up this panel before we go to vote, so that when we come back we can take the next panel.

Ms. Thurman has requested time and Mr. Coyne has requested time.

Well, I guess we can't do that. All right. Ms. Thurman?

Ms. THURMAN. I will try to make this quick, and maybe you all can just give us these answers in writing.

One, I would like to know, from both of you, what the demographics were of your poll, who the people were that you polled—you know, income, where they are.

Mr. POLLOCK. They are all nationwide. They are all general population.

Ms. THURMAN. But it would be good to have that information available to us.

Mr. POLLOCK. Sure.

Ms. THURMAN. Secondly, Mr. Pollock, when Dr. Luntz made the statement that everybody agreed that we ought to get rid of the death tax, your polling does not show that. Can you give me just a brief explanation of what you found, because it also would be counter to what Dr. Luntz has shown about the high-paying person.

Mr. POLLOCK. They are not mutually exclusive, unfortunately, and, unfortunately, one question doesn't cover it. What Dr. Luntz is talking about is, in a series of questions, when you ask people, "Would you like to get rid of X tax, Y tax, Z tax," when you put them all together at once you will see that inheritance taxes and also the marriage penalty, both of which Americans favor, in general, getting rid of, don't rank higher, of course, than getting rid of an income tax or getting rid of a local property tax, which bothers them much more than do those. Of course, they hurt them a lot more financially, so it makes sense.

So it is not dichotomous. You can have both in Americans' minds. It is just, when you put them all together, if I have to choose one or two, inheritance tax or, as they like to call it, "death tax," and the marriage penalty, they are not going to be number one and two. But when you ask them individually, certainly people do think it is unfair.

The marriage penalty to me, when I have seen things, tests even more egregiously, where people say, "Just because I am getting married doesn't mean I should have to pay more in taxes."

Ms. THURMAN. Okay.

Mr. POLLOCK. Did that adequately address, Frank?

Mr. LUNTZ. And I would just say that we actually have tilted the question, because I could not believe that Americans would actually believe that someone like Bill Gates should not have to pay a higher percentage of his savings and investment, and we tilted questions so anti-death tax. But if you go out—and, again, I invite you, as well, to come to these sessions that I do—Americans just believe it is a matter of principle that, even if you are rich, you should not lose up to half of your savings and income just because you die.

Ms. THURMAN. And then, I think, maybe taking off on Mr. Archer's last question, when he talked about getting rid of the IRS and then the different income tax rates, but also then to the polling that Mr. Pollock saw that says, "But don't take away my deductions," so rate would be one issue. And then, if you added in to that same question, do you think you would get a different result if you said, 'but don't take away my deductions,' as well?

Mr. LUNTZ. When you start to mention deductions, home deduction being the most popular of all, you start to—

Ms. THURMAN. Child credit.

Mr. LUNTZ. Yes. You start to see people begin to peel away. But in the end they are prepared to pay more if you could simplify the system. If you could say to Americans that we will guarantee that this will take you either no time, in the case of a sales tax, or 15 minutes, in the case of—

Ms. THURMAN. As long as it only goes to 20 percent.

Mr. LUNTZ. Once you start getting above 20 percent in taxation, you start to have Americans chafe at it. That is correct.

Ms. THURMAN. Okay.

Mr. LUNTZ. But simplification is so important.

Ms. THURMAN. I think we all agree on simplification. I think that is the one thing that we do agree on.

Chairman ARCHER. We are clearly not going to have time for the Members who do wish to question to do that, so the Chair is going to have the committee stand in recess so that we can go vote, and then we will return.

[Recess.]

Mr. CRANE [presiding]. We will resume.

We apologize for the interruption, but that is the way this place is run.

I now would like to yield to our distinguished colleague from Pennsylvania, Bill English.

Mr. ENGLISH. Thank you, Mr. Chairman. I appreciate the chance to pursue a line of questioning that occurs to me, reading with interest the testimony of these two witnesses.

You have provided some very interesting insights on how the public views tax reform and where it sees it as a potential priority. I wanted to get a sense of whether either of you had done any polling on international taxation.

I know, Mr. Luntz, you have done more polling on trade issues than, I think, anyone in your profession of my acquaintance, so I am wondering, have you polled on the idea of a fair and equal tax on the imports and stop taxing exports—in other words, border adjustability?

Mr. LUNTZ. Yes. Of course, no American will understand it as border adjustability. It is much too complicated. But when you begin to explain to them the defensive position that our products are put in by the Federal tax code and the advantage that foreign products have, again because of our tax code, not only do they become frustrated with it, they demand immediate change.

I would acknowledge that it is not one of the highest priorities, but, in terms of your question, the public believes that, at a minimum, our products should not be put at a disadvantage, and preferably our products should have an advantage over foreign products, and nothing in our Federal tax code should undermine that advantage.

Mr. ENGLISH. Mr. Pollock?

Mr. POLLOCK. I wish I had more to add, Congressman English, but Dr. Luntz has done much more on the subject than I have.

Mr. ENGLISH. Let me say one of the keys to broadening the debate and broadening the support for fundamental tax reform, in my estimation, is starting to include international tax issues framed in terms that working people understand.

My colleague, Mr. Traficant, who testified yesterday, I think has done a good job of taking that message back to Youngstown, Ohio. I have tried to do the same thing in Pennsylvania.

I think that international taxation, specifically border adjustability, moves people, and I have gotten that sense from discussing it at town meetings and actually just unscientifically trying to get a reaction in terms of a show of hands.

I would invite both of you to consider polling on this point, and also polling on the question of, as one of our witnesses yesterday testified, my proposal specifically would end the tax incentive for run-away plans. I think that is something that would resonate very much with the general public.

On a separate point, Dr. Luntz, I see from the polling that the Luntz Group did that the fairness quotient of the taxation of alcohol and beer is perhaps in a different category from other taxes. Only 20 percent feel the taxation of beer is unfair.

I wonder, in polling, have you communicated to the people you poll the fact that 43 cents on every dollar that they pay for the draft of beer in a place like Eerie, Pennsylvania, is taxed? This gets to the question of the visibility of taxation. I wonder, if people are aware of what the level of excise tax is, would those numbers change?

Mr. LUNTZ. They probably would change. In fact, in my presentation, in my testimony I spoke of all the different areas that we are taxed. Mr. Congressman, most Americans aren't aware that, from the moment they wake up in the morning until the moment they go to sleep at night, everything they do, everything they consume, every part of their lives are taxed. If they were made aware of just how much they were taxed, they would say, "To heck with everything."

Mr. ENGLISH. And do you think that insight would convert into opposition, potentially, to a value-added tax if it were applied? Most people don't know what a VAT is, but if it is described to them, how would you expect them to react? Or do you have any polling on this point, imposing a very broad and visible tax on the public?

Mr. LUNTZ. In fact, if it were consistent, if it were obvious, if it were clear, if it were applied evenly, and if it got rid of the IRS, the American people would support it.

Anything that simplifies, makes more consistent, makes flatter and fairer, any type of tax like that would be supported over the current system.

Mr. ENGLISH. So people don't view it as a priority to know how much they are being taxed, as long as they have a sense that the tax system is fair?

Mr. LUNTZ. One of the great reforms that I would wish this committee would consider would be to remove withholding. If Americans knew exactly how much they paid in taxes, this committee would be cutting taxes every single year.

Mr. ENGLISH. Thank you, Congressman.

Mr. POLLOCK. Congressman, I have done focus groups in Westmoreland, close to your home, and in that county I have talked to people about taxes. The fact is, we also have to remember that there is mass confusion about what all of their taxes are. I don't know what I am paying in property. Add the property tax into this mix, which is, to many people, extraordinarily egregious, property tax, income tax, sales tax, whatever it is, they are confused as to what tax they are paying at any given time, so certainly they don't know that 43 cents of their draft is going to a tax.

Mr. ENGLISH. Very good.

Mr. CRANE. The time of the gentleman has expired.

Dr. Luntz, I have given up on alcohol, but I have increased, escalated my consumption of sugar, but that is still a better deal, right, tax-wise? [Laughter.]

Mr. LUNTZ. I am not sure how much they put on sugar. I do know that people have paid millions of dollars to keep that sugar tax either lower or higher than it is today.

Mr. CRANE. Okay.

Ms. Dunn?

Ms. DUNN. Thank you very much, Mr. Chairman.

I wanted to make one comment, based on Mr. English's question, and that is that politics has become so personal these days, and communicating is also required to be personal for people to be able to connect government policy to what really happens in their everyday lives. And it seems to me that, if we ever began talking in terms of the number of dollars that people pay in taxes, whether it is that huge gas tax or the beer tax or property tax or death tax, and we have got people thinking about what they could purchase for their families' better quality of life for those dollars, that we could end up with a mutiny. I hope that never happens.

It is shocking, Mr. Luntz, when you go through your list of the taxes that people pay. I mean, if they are confused about what taxes they pay, they pay every tax on everything every hour of every day. It has really gotten to be way too much, I think.

I want to ask you a couple of questions. One, I would like to ask you gentlemen what you have learned, either from your survey research or from focus groups, what single people are thinking about our tax system.

For example, we have succeeded in reducing taxes in lots of areas. We have provided for education credits when dollars are set aside in education accounts for their children, we have provided for capital gains taxes to be relieved on the purchase of a house. For a single person, that house is still the same amount of money and it still takes the same number of people mowing the lawn and trimming the trees and to pay for all the costs of owning a home. We provide for a child tax credit. We have provided for a child care credit. We have provided for an end to the marriage penalty. It goes on and on and on what we have done for families who have children.

Are the singles starting to feel a little left out on this tax system?

Mr. LUNTZ. Congresswoman, you have done a lot for hard-working taxpayers, and I can assure you that they appreciate it. The great frustration for single taxpayers now can be summarized in two words, "payroll tax."

Americans, particularly those who are just starting off their careers, are shocked when they find out just how much money is taken out of their paycheck every two weeks and how little confidence they have that they will actually get that money back at the end of their careers when they are receiving Social Security or other benefits.

It is not surprising that more young Americans believe in the existence of UFOs than believe that Social Security will exist by the time they retire, and that payroll tax every two weeks is a frustration to them and they would like some relief.

Mr. POLLOCK. There is also the current—I wish Congressman Johnson were here, because the current fad, of course, is to talk about the gas taxes. And when I say "fad," it is only to say that they are talking about it right now. People really want to talk about the gas tax. It is impacting them. They are seeing it. They are seeing it on a daily basis. In Connecticut, people are seeing prices over $2. So the gas tax right now, which single people are looking at, also, because many of them are commuters—young people using a lot of their car—the gas tax is something that bothers them. It bothers them more on a State level, though, certainly.

Ms. DUNN. Well, if I could have one change in our tax system— and the chairman is not here right now to hear this—but for all singles, the group of which I am one, I wish we could just make one exemption in capital gains for the sale of a home, because the huge difference between 250,000 and 500,000, which is what the couple gets, means that somebody like me, if I choose to sell my house—and there are many of "me's" around this Nation—that we pay a capital gains, especially if we have been living in an inflationary period for any length of time.

Let me just ask you to augment what you both have said about the death tax. I am very interested in public perception of this, and I am very intrigued by the fact that folks you have researched are fair about this tax. I am wondering, as we consider whether this should be brought up as a stand-alone bill—and somebody every now and then will question the Bill Gates factor—I wonder if you could talk more in-depth on why death tax needs to die.

Mr. LUNTZ. We have done this specifically. In fact, because of the challenges that have been raised by people in both parties, we attempted to weight the question as strenuously against death tax as we could, emphasizing that these people probably have avoided taxes, that they have got high-priced accountants and lawyers to help them avoid taxes, that they are so rich that they can afford not to have to pay it. No matter how hard we weight it, by two to one, at a minimum, Americans want to get rid of this tax, because they just don't understand why you should be prevented from handing down the things that you have saved and invested to the next generation of Americans, and how in this country you should have to lose up to half of your savings and investments just because you have been successful.

Congresswoman, I can't weight it any more against it. By at least two-to-one, people want the total elimination of the death tax.

Mr. POLLOCK. It is more of a common sense thing for Americans. When they are thinking about the death tax, and also, as I brought up before, the marriage tax, it just seems to them to be silly. Why? Why, on X occasion, one of great happiness and one of great sadness, does the Government get the opportunity to then come in and tax them on that occasion?

In that respect, that is where Americans are looking and saying, "You know, this just isn't fair," whereas the other things—as I point out, Americans will say, "Okay, we understand we have to

fund Government programs. We understand that our taxes do go
to something," but those, in particular, stand out as things that
just don't seem right.

Ms. DUNN. Thank you very much.

Mr. CRANE. Thank you.

Mr. Coyne?

Mr. COYNE. Thank you, Mr. Chairman.

Dr. Luntz, I was wondering, does it surprise you that your findings of last week indicate that the least-liked Government agency
is the IRS, when politicians of every stripe, in order to make political points, continue to malign the work and the function of the Nation's revenue collection agency? Does that surprise you?

Mr. LUNTZ. It has nothing to do, quite frankly, with what is said
here or with politicians; it has to do with the fact that when Americans get that IRS tax form it scares them.

Mr. COYNE. Yes. So that is your explanation?

Mr. LUNTZ. Americans are afraid of the IRS. Absolutely. They
are scared of the IRS. Even today, even with the work that you
have done to change the system, Americans are still afraid of the
IRS.

Mr. COYNE. So if people were to say things about you going
around the country, that you were stealing money out of their
pocket and they were over-loading the U.S. Treasury by their collections, how popular do you think you would be?

Mr. LUNTZ. Maybe a little more popular than I am without people saying that.

Mr. COYNE. Well, I just think it is, in large part, a result of the
maligning of the function and the role of the collection agency in
this country that they are the least-popular agency in the Government, if that is what your findings show.

Mr. LUNTZ. I think I should make this as a formal offer to this
committee, that I would be happy—and we can't do it within the
beltway. We have to do it a little bit outside, but maybe a place
like Baltimore, which "American Demographic" has labeled as the
most representative city in America. I and my colleague will make
this offer to you, at our own expense, to bring you to the public and
have you listen to how they articulate their fear of the IRS. It is
not the way, in this case, that we word the questions, and it is not
what you say about them. It is how Americans fundamentally believe that there is an agency that can penetrate their lives and do
things to them that they have no control over in an unjust and immoral fashion.

I would invite this committee, for each of these issues—the death
tax, the marriage penalty, the IRS—to bring Members out there so
you can watch from behind the mirror as real, live people respond
to these questions. I think you might find it useful.

Mr. COYNE. Well, it might surprise you to know that everyone in
this Congress goes back to their Districts every weekend.

Mr. LUNTZ. I am sure.

Mr. COYNE. And that we mix with the people, and we know what
the people are saying, and we know that, as you pointed out in
your testimony, no one likes to pay taxes, but most people, the majority of the people, recognize that it is a necessity if we are to have
any kind of civil society, and that when you continually malign—

whether it is the IRS or the Defense Department or whoever it is, seem to me naturally they are not going to have a very high rating in public opinion tolls like you took.

Mr. Pollock, in your testimony you cite Dr. Luntz' survey showing that two-thirds of Americans say that the highest percentage we should have to pay for taxes, combined, all taxes combined, should be less than 20 percent of income. Do you know of any survey that tells us what services taxpayers are willing to give up to achieve a 20 percent rate?

Mr. POLLOCK. Congressman Coyne, that is an excellent question. And the point, of course, is nothing. And Americans are hypocritical in public opinion. There is no doubt about it. They don't make that rationalization. They want cuts, but not at the expense of their government programs. So the question is correct. And, unfortunately, that is the way the American public responds.

Mr. COYNE. Well, do you have any specific programs that Americans choose to fund rather than getting a tax cut, in your surveys?

Mr. POLLOCK. Absolutely. The ones that have been bandied about—and I believe that these have become prominent because, as you are pointing out, politicians all over are talking about them—but shoring up Medicare and Social Security certainly come before a tax cut in the voters' minds, improving spending on education, for example, as long as it is targeted spending, as long as it makes sense and not wasteful spending on education, and certainly some spending on health care. Those are the four that have come up that I have seen in the last six months in terms of both surveys and focus groups where people are saying, "Okay, we have got to spend on these things no matter what."

Mr. COYNE. Does either of your polling show what are some of the reasons that Americans oppose a national sales tax?

Mr. LUNTZ. No.

Mr. POLLOCK. No. I haven't seen any.

Mr. COYNE. Thank you.

Mr. CRANE. Mr. Portman?

Mr. PORTMAN. Thank you, Mr. Chairman.

I want to thank Frank Luntz for the information that he is giving us today and has given us over the years on this and other issues, because it is very helpful, and these polls and the focus groups do focus us a little bit more on what the key issues are and what our constituents care about.

I want to ask a question about tax reform, since that is the focus of the hearings.

I understand that when you ask people whether they agree or disagree that overhaul of the Federal tax system, including the abolishing of the IRS, and replacing five different income tax rates with a single rate, that is popular, people agree with it. But when you do your polling, Frank, about what people care about, tax reform never shows up near the top. Why is that? I mean, is it the good economy? Is it the sense of frustration, that they know that nothing will happen with it? Or is it that for most people it is just not a very important part of their daily lives?

Mr. LUNTZ. Half of it is the good economy, but there is another half. It bothers me. It troubles me to even say this, but they have heard about tax reform and they have heard about tax cuts for so long that they feel that they will never receive it.

We talk about these things and make these promises, and then, when we don't deliver, it undermines the credibility of the institution and the promise, so that most Americans believe that if the President or Congress were to offer them a tax cut or tax reform, it would never actually happen.

It is one way that you could instill a sense of confidence in this institution and in this body, to actually deliver on making their lives easier, simpler, and providing them with more money at the end of the day than they otherwise would have had.

Mr. PORTMAN. Over the last few years, you know, as we have helped to provide some relief, including the child tax credit, significantly, we have, in essence, begun to push the progressivity of the code even further so that the top 10 percent of income earners are paying something like 60 percent of the Federal income tax now. Again, it doesn't include payroll tax, although that is also somewhat progressive because of the cap. But it is an issue that, frankly, republicans, I think, are probably of two minds about. One is we want to provide tax relief to middle income Americans, but second is, as you increasingly move middle Americans to a lower and lower Federal income tax rate and you increasingly move folks who are at the bottom of the economic ladder off the tax rolls altogether—I think it is about six million Americans who don't pay income taxes today who did a few years ago, because of the changes that we have made—and as you enrich the EITC program where more and more folks are getting a refund rather than paying not just payroll taxes but income taxes—and some folks, as you know, are paying income tax, payroll tax, then getting a check from the Government in the form of the EITC that covers both of those, plus. They are actually getting something back. You begin to lose kind of a constituency for tax reform, or at least for tax relief.

I don't know if my question to you is do you agree with me or not on that. That would be the one question, I guess. Is that one reason that there isn't as much interest in tax reform, as well as maybe tax relief?

Second is: what does that mean for the prospects of tax reform going forward?

Mr. LUNTZ. Americans tend to respond to big ideas in terms of great change, and it seems very difficult to ask Americans to accept the same tax structure today that they had 50 years ago, when we have new technology and great inventions that are changing the way things operate; that Americans would expect that their laws and the things that govern them would be updated as times change.

If you can attach yourself to that outlook towards the future, I think you would be much more successful.

Support for tax reform will increase significantly in our next economic downturn as Americans become frustrated and their wallets and purses become tighter. It would be nice if you could pass tax reform before they were demanding it of you.

Mr. POLLOCK. To be very clear about one thing that Frank said, this concept that Americans are upset, or when they think about the concept of a tax cut they don't actually believe it will happen,

309

there is a lot of talk of it, but it doesn't happen, I conducted a bunch of focus groups in Connecticut where Governor Rowland gave back to all Connecticut individuals basically a per child, you got $50 a head, and even though it seems like a trivial amount— and even the voters were saying that it is silly to get a $50 check— they were all incredibly satisfied just because somebody had actually delivered upon giving them a check, getting them an actual refund, and they gave him a lot of credit for it, even though they thought the amount was trivial.

So I think Frank is absolutely right when he says it is about 50 percent good economy and 50 percent they don't believe it is going to happen.

Mr. PORTMAN. Again, thank you all very much. We look forward to continuing to get your input as we try to pursue reform and simplification.

Mr. CRANE. Well, Dr. Luntz and Mr. Pollock, we appreciate your testimony. I think that is—unless Mr. Thurman has a question yet?

Ms. THURMAN. Did you all test the debt versus taxes at all? It just has not been talked about much, and I am just kind of curious how that plays in this.

Mr. LUNTZ. I have not done it but it has been done, and the public right now is more concerned about the debt.

Mr. POLLOCK. Right now, when you look at it, the public will take paying off the national debt over tax cuts on a numerical level, and if you need the numbers I can get them to you.

Mr. CRANE. Very good. Well, we thank you for your presentations. That will terminate this panel.

The committee, however, will now stand in recess until 1:00 p.m.

Mr. LUNTZ. Mr. Crane, welcome back.

Mr. CRANE. Thank you.

The committee will come to order.

The Chair apologizes for being a couple of minutes late, but we will commence at this time.

I welcome each one of you. We are delighted to see you, and we will look forward to your presentation.

Mr. Helming, would you lead off?

Mr. HELMING. I would be more than happy to, Mr. Chairman.

STATEMENT OF BILL HELMING, ECONOMIST AND BUSINESS CONSULTANT, BILL HELMING CONSULTING SERVICES, INC., OLATHE, KANSAS

Mr. HELMING. I assume that it is appropriate to suggest that my written document will be submitted for the record, and I will just—

Mr. CRANE. Without objection, your entire written statements will be included in the record, and you can synopsize verbally, if you will.

Mr. HELMING. Yes. I will do so.

It is, indeed, an honor and a pleasure to be here. I have been self-employed for 27 years, a business consultant and economist. I work out of my home, along with my wife, in Olathe, Kansas. We have been working on this tax plan, the Helming national consumption tax plan, for 16 years. We have been advancing it with the help of a lot of people, including the two other panelists here, and literally thousands of people across the country.

We have been working on it as private citizens, paying our own bills to get it done.

I think the most important introductory thing, Mr. Chairman, would be that, as a practical matter, I have been conducting focus groups for 16 years, literally a major cross-section of the U.S. public, finding out what they liked and what they didn't like about this plan and the other plans.

Bottom line: why fundamental tax reform?

Basically, the present tax code penalizes or greatly restricts success, hard work in human capital, saving and investment, economic growth, productivity, risk-taking, and the transfer of family-owned small businesses from one generation to the next. I have designed this plan to try to send the right signal and to reward each of those things as opposed to penalizing them.

As you know, Mr. Chairman, the marginal tax rate on labor, under the current Federal tax code, is 35.6 percent. When you put it all into one pot, it is 35.6 at the margin. The Helming two-tiered consumption tax plan is 30.4, or 15.2 in tier one at the business level, 15.2 on tier two at the retail level, times two is 30.4. That is basically a 14 percent differential. I tend to be real conservative. Let us say it is a 10 percent differential.

That means that the economy would double in growth in 10 years, compared to the way we are operating now under the present tax code, or the cost of goods and services would come down by 10 percent. In the real world, it would be some combination of the two.

Basically, the major benefits of such an approach would be a stronger growth economy; more jobs; higher wages; more take-home pay; lower cost of goods and services; lower interest rates by a significant margin—15 to 25 percent—eliminates the IRS from the wage-earner's perspective; major simplification; and major advantages—in this case, competitive advantages in the global market and trade arena; and a very visible tax.

Why is this possible? Well, it is very fundamentally because, under such a plan, we are no longer double taxing income, investment, or saving, while at the same time we are taxing labor and capital pretty much equally, which Aldona Robbins is going to speak to in a few minutes, which, obviously, under the present tax system, we do not do.

It is also possible for you to get these many benefits for the economy and the working Americans of this country because it has a much broader tax base and a uniform tax rate.

The Helming NCT plan is specifically designed to achieve all of these specific benefits. This will particularly benefit lower-and middle-income wage earners.

I came to the conclusion some time ago, and certainly believe it strongly today, that the status quo in terms of our current tax code is unacceptable. If we can accrue such tremendous benefits for the common working person in America and the working families, as well as for the business community, then it is clearly time to seriously embrace fundamental tax reform.

Very honestly, all of these competing plans are going to have essentially the same impact on the economy, in terms of favorable benefits. Where the real differences come in is how they are structured as it relates to how they specifically are perceived to impact businesses, wage-earners and consumers, and that comes in the structure of the tax reform proposals.

So, basically, the Helming NCT plan represents an excellent and viable compromise, Mr. Chairman, and a common ground for real fundamental tax reform because of its structure. It reflects many of the best aspects and strengths of the other competing proposals, while avoiding their weaknesses relative to perceptions in fairness, political viability, simplicity, and compliance issues.

Very simply stated, my plan is a two-tiered plan. Tier one is a uniform and border adjustable activities tax at 15.2 percent, wherein the tax is levied on what businesses add to output—i.e., internal labor costs and the return to capital (profit). It applies to all businesses, the self-employed, and nonprofit organizations and institutions and all Federal, State, and local government agencies, and accounts for 57 percent of all Federal Government revenues raised.

Tier two is a 15.2 percent sales tax levied on consumer purchases except for the necessities of life, which I will define briefly in just a moment. The tier-two sales tax raises 43 percent of the total federal taxes.

I also want to emphasize that this plan envisions the entire repeal and replacement of the complete federal tax code as we know it today. All income taxes, the payroll taxes, the self-employment taxes, and all excise, railroad retirement, gasoline—in other words, nothing is left out.

It is essentially revenue neutral at two levels at 15.2 times two, to raise the same amount of revenues.

John Meagher just informed me today that the joint committee on taxation did complete the scoring on my tax plan, and their numbers came out very close to the numbers that we have been using.

We deal with regressivity specifically by exempting the necessities of life. I define those as food at the grocery store, food mart, and vending machine, all prescribed medical costs, and all home purchases and/or those who rent.

On the business side, all capital purchases and exports would be tax exempt for the business. The competitive position of U.S. businesses and the U.S. economy in the global marketplace would be substantially improved over what it is now. The reason for this is that we would be exempting exports and taxing, as I know you very well understand, imports on a border-adjustable basis. That, itself, would raise 10 percent of the total revenues. Basically, it would encourage many multi-national companies to come home, stay home, and hire more U.S. workers.

Progressivity and freedom of choice are primarily an outcome of how much and when consumers choose to spend, save, invest, or reduce debt with their income over and above the necessities of life.

Bottom line, Mr. Chairman, in terms of my verbal comments—and I am looking forward to any possible questions that you might want to ask—I come to this conclusion: if we can benefit the U.S. economy in such a dramatic way and also benefit the common wage-earner no positively in the United States and, the working families of America, which clearly all the studies, including Aldona Robbins and her husband, Dr. Robbins, and a number of others who have helped me with this long and involved process and helping me get to this point then, I simply ask this rhetorical question. If so many people can be benefitted, then why don't we embrace fundamental tax reform along these lines?

Thank you very much.

[An attachment is being retained in the Committee files.]

Mr. CRANE. Thank you, Mr. Helming, Mr. Powell, we will be pleased to receive your testimony.

STATEMENT OF JAMES L. POWELL, LIVESTOCK PRODUCER, FORT MCKAVETT, TEXAS

Mr. POWELL. Mr. Chairman, I come here today as a livestock producer. My interest in the Helming national consumption tax is to seek its passage and produce change in the method that Federal and State governments tax the hard-earned incomes and lifetime savings of individuals and families.

Unless income, State, gift, and capital gains taxes are eliminated, the small business owner, the family farmer will continue to be liquidated at a precipitous rate.

The evidence provided by the U.S. Census Bureau, the USDA National Statistical Service, each decade is compelling. These numbers bear serious consideration.

In 1940, the rural population, those living in communities of 2,500 or less citizens, was 43.5 percent of the total. In 1990, the rural population was 24.8 percent of the total.

The employment status of civilian workers employed in agriculture in 1940 was 17.1 percent of the total workforce. By 1990, the number of agricultural employees had decreased to 1.6 percent of the total population. The number of farms producing agricultural products had been reduced from 65 percent from 1940 to 1990. The size of those farms had increased 163 percent—corporate farms on the increase. In the last five years, those farms have increased 6 percent, while the individual, family, and partnership farm have decreased in number.

This benign trend began in the 1930s and will continue until some time in the future. Population increases in this country and a disruption in foreign nations that import agricultural products into the U.S. will create the beginning of food shortages, much like the oil shortage that developed in the 1970s.

The loss of population in agriculture and the large increase in size of farms reflect a deterioration in U.S. agriculture.

There are a number of indicators of deterioration. It is clear that agriculture is not the preferred choice of many youths. The minimum economic unit today in my area is about 6,000 acres, a value of about $1,800,000. In 1940, the minimum economic unit was about 2,250 acres, a value of less than $50,000. Today, to transfer this unit to heirs after exclusions requires a heavy estate tax. An education can equip the young heirs with an opportunity for employment in industry that now offers a much higher income than agriculture. That is more appealing to them than coming back to the farm for an inheritance that will burden them with an enormous estate tax after they have paid a hefty income and/or capital gains tax.

This country is losing its agricultural young, as is shown by the increase in the average age of the person in agriculture from 53.3 years to 54.3 years of age in only five years, from 1992 to 1997.

Another indicator of deterioration of agriculture is the parity index of farm commodities. The index is based on farm goods sold in 1914 equalling 100. That index has declined in the last eight years from 51 in 1990 to 42 in 1998, a reduction in the dollar return on goods produced of 5 percent.

That loss of income and persistent demand for payment of death taxes has caused the operating debt of the farm community to increase from $77 billion in 1980 to $80 billion in 1997, an increase of 3 percent.

Yet another indicator is an increase in agricultural imports for consumption. Food imports have increased 63 percent during the current Administration from 1990 to 1995. Imports will compete with domestic products and require those products to sell at a price close to or below production cost. The future of this country's food supply will gradually become questionable.

With these negative trends confronting agriculture, it is easy to understand the exodus of productive people from family farming and the subsequent development of corporate farming and increased importation of farm products to supply to U.S. consumers.

The solution for agriculture and small business to the problem that has just been described is the National Consumption Act. It will release the unbearable income, estate, capital gains tax from those few who now pay and place the tax more fairly on a much broader-based population.

All imported products will bear a fair share of the tax burden and release all U.S. exports, agricultural and industrial, from taxes, thereby stimulating the economy.

All the citizens of the United States would be better served by State and Federal governments if the Helming national consumption tax were implemented.

If I might be permitted, might I quote one brief vignette? Before coming here this week, an employee, after hearing the explanation that my mission was to encourage the elimination of the income, State, and capital gains taxes so that many of us would not eventually join the ranks of the defunct, said to me, "Tell them I never received a paycheck from a poor man."

Thank you.

Mr. CRANE. Thank you, Mr. Powell.

[The prepared statement follows:]

Statement of James L. Powell, Livestock Producer, Fort McKavett, Texas

Mr. Chairman, ladies and gentlemen of the Ways and Means Committee I come here as a livestock producer. My interest in the Helming National Consumption Tax is to seek its passage and produce a change in the method that federal and state governments tax the hard earned incomes and lifetime savings of individuals and families. Unless income, estate, gift and capital gains taxes are eliminated the small business owner and family farmer will continue to be liquidated at a precipitous rate.

The evidence provided by the U.S. Census Bureau and U.S.D.A National Statistical Service each decade is compelling. These numbers bare serious consideration. In 1940 the rural population, those living in communities of 2500 or less citizens, was 43.5% of the total. In 1990 the rural population was 24.8% of the total.[1] The employment status of civilian workers employed in agriculture in 1940 was 17.1% of the workforce. By 1990 the number of agricultural employees had decreased to 1.6% of the population.[2] The number of farms producing agricultural products had been reduced by 65% from 1940 to 1990. The size of those farms had increased 163%.[3] Corporate farms are on the increase. In the last 5 years those farms have increased .6% while the individual, family and partnership farms have decreased in number.[4]

This benign trend began in the 1930's and will continue until sometime in the future. Population increases in this country and a disruption in foreign nations that import agricultural products in the U.S. will create the beginning of food shortages, much like the oil shortage that developed in the 1970's.

The loss of population in agriculture and large increase in size of farms reflect U.S. agriculture deterioration. There are a number of indicators of deterioration. It is clear that agriculture is not the preferred choice for many youths. The minimum economic unit today in my area is about 6,000 acres, a value of $1,800,000. In 1940 the minimum economic unit was about 2,250 acres, a value of less than $50,000. To transfer this unit to heirs after exclusions requires a heavy estate tax. An education can equip the young heirs with an opportunity for employment in industry that now offers a much higher income than agriculture. That is more appealing to them than coming back to the farm for an inheritance that will burden them with an enormous estate tax after they have paid a hefty income and/or capital gains tax. This country is losing its agricultural young as is shown by the increase in the average age of the person in agriculture from 53.3 years to 54.3 years of age in only 5 years, from 1992 to 1997.[5] Another indicator of the deterioration of agriculture is the parity index* of farm commodities. The index is based on farm goods sold in 1914 equaling 100. That index has declined in the last eight years from 51 in 1990 to 42 in 1998, a reduction in the dollar return on goods produced of 5%.[6] That loss of income and persistent demand for payment of death taxes has caused the operating debt of the farm community to increase from $77 billion in 1980 to $80 billion in 1997, an increase of 3%.[7] Yet another indicator is an increase in agricultural imports for consumption. Food imports have increased 63% during the current administration, from 1990 to 1995.[8] Imports will compete with domestic products and require those products to sell at a price close to or below production costs. The future of this countries food supply will gradually become questionable.

With these negative trends confronting agriculture it is easy to understand the exodus of productive people from family farming and the subsequent development of corporate farming and increased importation of farm products to supply the U.S. consumer.

The solution, for agriculture and small business, to the problem that has just been described is the National Consumption Tax. It will release the unbearable income, estate and capital gains tax from those few who now pay and place the tax more fairly on a much broader base of the population. All imported products would bear a fair share of tax burden and release all U.S. exports, agriculture and industrial

---

[1] U.S. Census Bureau. "Statistical Abstract of the United States." 27 July 1999. Online. *http://www.census.gov/prod/www/statistical-abstract-us.htm.* Table #1412. 4 April 1999.
[2] U.S. Census Bureau. "Statistical Abstract of the United States." 27 July 1999. Online. *http://www.census.gov/prod/www/statistical-abstract-us.html.* Table #1430. 4 April 1999.
[3] U.S. Census Bureau. "Statistical Abstract of the United States." 27 July 1999. Online. *http://www.census.gov/prod/www/statistical-abstract-us.html.* Table #1100. 4 April 1999.
[4] U.S. Census Bureau. "Statistical Abstract of the United States." 27 July 1999. Online. *http://www.census.gov/prod/www/statistical-abstract-us.html.* Table #1441. 4 April 1999.
[5] U.S. Census Bureau. "Statistical Abstract of the United States." 27 July 1999. Online. *http://www.census.gov/prod/www/statistical-abstract-us.html.* Table #1102. 4 April 1999.

*__Parity Price__—"price for a commodity or service that is pegged to another price or to a composite average of prices based on a selected prior period. As the two sets of prices vary, they are reflected in an index number on a scale of 100. For example, U.S. farm prices are pegged to prices based on the purchasing power of farmers in the period from 1910 to 1914. If the parity ratio is below 100, reflecting a reduction in purchasing power to the extent indicated, the government compensates the farmer by paying a certain percentage of parity, either in the form of a direct cash payment, in the purchase of surplus crops, or in a NONRECOURSE LOAN.

The concept of parity is also widely applied in industrial wage contracts as a means of preserving the real value of wages. (Barron's definition of parity price as written in the Barron's Financial Digest)

[6] U.S. Census Bureau. "Statistical Abstract of the United States." 27 July 1999. Online. *http://www.census.gov/prod/www/statistical-abstract-us.html.* Table #1116. 4 April 1999.
[7] U.S. Census Bureau. "Statistical Abstract of the United States." 27 July 1999. Online. *http://www.census.gov/prod/www/statistical-abstract-us.html.* Table #1113. 4 April 1999.
[8] U.S. Census Bureau. "Statistical Abstract of the United States." 27 July 1999. Online. *http://www.census.gov/prod/www/statistical-abstract-us.html.* Table #1441. 4 April 1999.

from taxes thereby stimulating the economy. All of the citizens of the United States would be better served by state and federal governments if Helming National Consumption Tax were implemented.

If I might be permitted may I quote one brief vignette. Before coming here this week an employee, after hearing the explanation that my mission was to encourage the elimination of the income, estate and capital gains taxes so that many of us would not eventually join the ranks of the defunct, said "Tell them I never received a pay check from a poor person."

———————

Mr. CRANE. Ms. Robbins?

STATEMENT OF ALDONA ROBBINS, VICE PRESIDENT, FISCAL ASSOCIATES, AND SENIOR RESEARCH FELLOW, INSTITUTE FOR POLICY INNOVATION

Ms. ROBBINS. Thank you, Mr. Chairman.

I am Aldona Robbins, vice president of Fiscal Associates and senior research fellow at the Institute for Policy Innovation. I want to thank you for the invitation to appear at these hearings.

As the committee has heard during the last two days, there are lots of ways to implement fundamental tax reform. While the proposals have important differences, I would like to focus on some of what they have in common.

First, the tax bases of most reform proposals are basically the same. Now, someone might say, "Wait a minute. Doesn't a sales tax tax consumption, a business tax business, an income tax income?" The short answer is yes, but those distinctions really refer more to where the tax is collected than to what is ultimately being taxed.

Government gets its revenue by taxing the income going between households which provide labor and capital services and businesses which provide goods and services. Because the two flows—the value of the goods and services that businesses produce and the value of the labor and capital services provided by households—are made up of the same dollars, all taxes can be viewed as being paid out of income earned by labor and capital.

A second area of commonality is the tax rate. To raise a given amount of revenue and holding exemptions constant, most reform proposals should yield similar effective rates.

What is more, those that look to replace Federal revenues should, likewise, end up with average rates close to the current system.

I would like to highlight some findings from a project in which we have rearranged the national income and product accounts to analyze the current tax system, as well as alternatives, on the basis of factor incomes.

Currently, the effective average Federal tax rate—and this includes all Federal taxes—on the income of private business, labor, and capital is 26.5 percent. The marginal rate on factor income is 36.2 percent.

Suppose we were to replace the entire system of Federal taxes with a comprehensive sales tax, which provides every family with a refundable credit equal to the poverty line. In that case, the effective average Federal tax rate on the income of private business, labor, and capital would be about 24 percent and the marginal rate would be about 29 percent.

What about a generic business cash flow tax with or without border adjustment in the same refundable credit? Again, the average rate on factory income would be about 24 percent and the marginal roughly 29 percent.

The effective rates of the alternatives are lower than current law because the proposals have broader, more uniform tax bases and a single rate. The rates of the alternatives are the same because they both end up taxing the same dollars but at different collection points.

Compliance is assumed to be the same as under current law. The effective tax rate would be the same, regardless of what the stated rate might be.

If the Joint Tax Committee says that the required rate is really going to be 30 percent instead of 24, it simply means that the current law rate must be higher than the 26.5 percent that we had calculated.

Doing so, however, would not change either the conclusions regarding the effective rates or the relative comparisons.

I would like to close with some comments about economic effects. There are efficiency gains to be had in reform of the current system. Both capital and labor pay higher rates on the next dollar of income than on the average dollar, and—although I didn't present verbally these results, they are in my written remarks—capital is taxed more heavily than labor.

A single rate which would treat capital and labor the same, as well as lower marginal rates, would encourage greater saving and investment, lead to a more efficient use of resources, and result in increased output.

There are, to be sure, important differences among competing proposals for fundamental tax reform, but we should not lose sight of the fact that the economic ramifications of proposals that broaden the base, remove the bias against capital, and lower marginal rates are essentially the same.

Thank you.

Mr. CRANE. Thank you, Ms. Robbins.

[The prepared statement follows:]

Statement of Aldona Robbins, Vice President, Fiscal Associates, and Senior Research Fellow, Institute for Policy Innovation

Mr. Chairman and members of the Committee, I am Aldona Robbins, Vice President of Fiscal Associates and Senior Research Fellow at the Institute for Policy Innovation (IPI). Thank you for the invitation to appear at these important hearings on tax reform.

Calls for tax reform stem from growing dissatisfaction with record tax burdens, the complexity of the present code, and worries that Americans aren't saving enough. As the Committee has heard during two days of testimony, there are a myriad of ways to implement fundamental tax reform. Some, like a national sales tax, represent a radical departure from the current system. Others, like a factor payment or generic business cash flow tax, are less so.

While fundamental tax reform proposals have important differences, they also have much in common. My remarks today will focus on some key similarities.

First, the tax bases of most reform proposals are basically the same. Someone will undoubtedly protest, wait a minute, a sales tax taxes consumption, a business tax taxes business, and an income tax taxes income. Those distinctions, however, really refer more to the point of collection than to what is ultimately being taxed.

Anyone who takes an introductory economics course usually goes through an accounting exercise called the *circular flow* describing the workings of a market economy. Businesses acquire the services of labor and capital from households to produce goods and services. Households exchange their labor and capital services for the goods and services produced by businesses. But, it is important to remember that the same people who make up households also own and operate the businesses. Labels merely serve to distinguish among economic activities.

Government gets its revenue by taxing the income going between households and businesses. Here it is important to note that the two flows—(1) the value of the goods and services that businesses produce and (2) the value of the labor and capital services provided by households—are made up of the same dollars. A tax on the sale of goods and services reduces the income that would otherwise be paid to labor and capital. A tax on factor income reduces what workers and owners of capital can buy. Because both flows measure the same thing, that is, total economic activity, all taxes can be viewed as being paid out of income earned by labor and capital.

A second area of commonality is the tax rate. To raise a given amount of revenue, and holding exemptions constant, most reform proposals should yield similar rates. What is more, those that look to replace federal revenues should likewise end up with average rates close to the current system.

Demonstrating these propositions requires some complex accounting to attribute all taxes to factor income.[1] Some taxes easily translate into this framework while others require more work. For example, people pay personal taxes on income received for labor and capital services in the form of wages, interest, dividends and so forth. The employer and employee shares of payroll taxes come out of labor compensation. Less obvious are taxes seemingly levied on business, but they, too, affect the dollars flowing to factors. For example, the corporate income tax reduces the pool of money available to pay dividends or other forms of capital compensation to shareholders. Even sales and excise taxes, which are seemingly levied on the purchases of goods and services, come out of factor income because they reduce the funds available to pay the factors.

Table 1 summarizes the average and marginal tax rates on labor and capital in private businesses. Accounting for three-fourths of the economy, the private sector pays close to 90 percent of U.S. taxes.[2] Table 2 contains average and marginal rates for the rest of the economy.[3]

On average, taxes at all levels of government claim about a third of labor income in the private sector. Federal taxes amount to 25.9 percent and state and local taxes to 7.4 percent.[4] Private business capital pays almost half its income in taxes. The average tax rate at the federal level is 27.6 percent and 21.6 percent for states and localities.[5]

Private business capital and labor pay even higher marginal tax rates. Out of the next dollar of income, labor pays 44.4 percent in taxes − 35.6 percent to the federal government and 8.8 percent to states and localities. The marginal rate on capital is 60.6 percent − 37.6 percent to the federal government and 23 percent to states and localities.

Combining capital and labor, taxes claim an average 38.5 percent of private business income. Federal taxes claim 26.5 percent while state and local taxes take 12.1 percent. That implies that any proposal aiming to replace all federal taxes would need a tax rate of somewhere between 25 and 30 percent on all U.S. income, depending on the level of personal exemptions.

Summarized below are tax rates for current law and two general approaches to tax reform—a comprehensive sales tax and a generic business cash flow tax, with and without border adjustment—which are assumed to replace all federal taxes. Average and marginal rates are expressed as a percent of private business income.

Tax Rates on Private Business Income

Tax Regime	Average Federal [1]	Marginal Federal [2]	Total Marginal [3]
Current Law	26.5%	36.2%	49.8%
Comprehensive Sales Tax	23.9%	29.2%	42.7%

---

[1] This requires rearranging the Commerce Department's National Income and Product Accounts to better reflect taxes. Details will be forthcoming in a study by Gary and Aldona Robbins entitled Road Map for Tax Reform from the Institute for Policy Innovation this spring.

[2] In 1999, private businesses produced 75.8 percent of the $9.3 trillion in GDP.

[3] This includes federal, state and local government, government enterprises, domiciles (which is people employed in domestic service and the value of home ownership) and nonprofit institutions.

[4] Table 3 contains the components of labor income for 1999.

[5] Capital income is gross capital compensation less capital consumption allowance. Table 3 contains the components of capital income for 1999.

Tax Rates on Private Business Income—Continued

Tax Regime	Average Federal [1]	Marginal Federal [2]	Total Marginal [3]
Generic business Cash Flow, border adjustment	23.9%	29.2%	42.7%
Generic Business Cash Flow, no border adjustment	23.9%	29.2%	42.7%

AThe three proposals assume each family receives a refundable credit equal to the poverty line times the tax rate. The revenue collected is based on a single rate on private business income and labor compensation in the rest of the economy. There are no special tax breaks and all double taxes are eliminated.

[1] Federal taxes as a percent of private business income (gross labor income plus gross capital income less capital consumption allowance).

[2] Federal taxes on the next dollar of private business income as a percent of private business income.

[3] Federal, state and local taxes on the next dollar of private business income as a percent of private business income.

Because the tax bases for the three proposals are the essentially the same, the effective tax rates needed to raise the same amount of federal revenue as under current law also would be the same. Replacing all federal taxes would require an effective average rate on private business income of about 24 percent and a marginal rate of about 29 percent under either the sales tax or the business cash flow tax, with or without border adjustment. These effective rates are lower than the 26.5 percent under current law because the proposals have broader, more uniform tax bases.

Even though the rate is flat, the system is progressive. In this example, each family would receive a refundable credit equal to the poverty line. While families below the poverty line would face the same marginal rate as everyone else, they still would better off than under current law. Because they would get money back, their average tax rate would be negative, and they would not have to pay FICA taxes.

A last point about the summary table. The calculations assume that compliance would be the same as under current law. The effective tax rate would be the same regardless of what the stated rate may be. If the Joint Tax Committee says the required rate is 30% instead of 24%, it simply means that the current law rate must be higher than the 26.5% calculated in the table. Doing so would not change either the conclusions regarding effective rates or the relative comparisons.

I would like to close with some comments about economic effects. There are efficiency gains to be had in reform of the current system. First, both capital and labor pay higher rates on the next dollar of income than on the average dollar. Second, capital is presently taxed more heavily than labor. A single rate, which would treat capital and labor the same as well as lower marginal rates would encourage greater saving and investment, lead to a more efficient use of resources and result in increased output.

There are, to be sure, important differences among competing proposals for fundamental tax reform. But, we should not lose sight of the fact that the economic ramifications of proposals that broaden the base, remove the bias against capital and lower marginal rates are essentially the same.

Table 1.—Components of Average and Marginal Tax Rates on Private Business Labor and Capital, 1999

All Government	Labor		Capital	
	Average	Marginal	Average	Marginal
Total	33.3%	44.4%	49.1%	60.6%
Personal [1]	14.2%	25.3%	19.5%	28.0%
Corporate profits	0.0%	0.0%	11.3%	14.3%
Indirect business [2]	5.7%	5.7%	18.3%	18.3%
Payroll [3]	13.5%	13.5%	0.0%	0.0%
Federal				
Total federal	25.9%	35.6%	27.6%	37.6%
Personal	11.4%	21.1%	15.6%	23.0%
Corporate profits	0.0%	0.0%	9.5%	12.2%
Indirect business	1.2%	1.2%	2.4%	2.4%
Payroll	13.3%	13.3%	0.0%	0.0%
State and local				

Table 1.—Components of Average and Marginal Tax Rates on Private Business Labor and Capital, 1999—
Continued

All Government	Labor		Capital	
	Average	Marginal	Average	Marginal
Total state and local	7.4%	8.8%	21.6%	23.0%
Personal	2.8%	4.2%	3.9%	5.0%
Corporate profits	0.0%	0.0%	1.8%	2.1%
Indirect business	4.4%	4.4%	15.9%	15.9%
Payroll	0.2%	0.2%	0.0%	0.0%

*Taken from Gary and Aldona Robbins, Road Map for Tax Reform, Institute for Policy Innovation, forthcoming Spring 2000. Basic data from the National Income and Product Accounts, April 2000 release.
[1] Personal income taxes for labor are on wages and salaries. Personal income for capital include taxes on interest, dividends, capital gains, rent, royalties and so forth and estate taxes.
[2] Indirect business taxes levied on output, like sales taxes or excise taxes, are apportioned roughly two-thirds to labor and one-third to capital based on their respective shares in the production process . Indirect business taxes levied specifically on capital like property taxes are attributed only to capital.
[3] Employer and employee contributions for social insurance.

Table 2.—Average and Marginal Tax Rates by Major Producer, 1998 & 1999

Average Tax Rates

	Private Business [1]		Households [2]		Institutions [3]		Govt enterprises [4]		General govt [5]	
	1998	1999	1998	1999	1998	1999	1998	1999	1998	1999
Capital	47.5%	49.1%	8.1%	8.0%	26.2%	26.4%	na	na	na	na
Federal	26.3%	27.6%	-10.1%	-10.2%	3.6%	3.7%	na	na	na	na
State and local	21.2%	21.6%	18.2%	18.2%	22.6%	22.7%	na	na	a	na
Labor	33.2%	33.3%	22.4%	30.9%	28.1%	27.6%	14.8%	14.9%	15.2%	15.3%
Federal	25.8%	25.9%	19.3%	27.8%	25.2%	24.8%	12.2%	12.3%	12.5%	12.6%
State and local	7.3%	7.4%	3.1%	3.1%	2.9%	2.9%	2.6%	2.6%	2.7%	2.7%
Total Producer Income	38.0%	38.5%	8.5%	8.8%	28.0%	27.6%	na	na	na	na
Federal	26.0%	26.5%	-9.2%	-8.9%	24.1%	23.7%	na	na	na	na
State and local	12.0%	12.1%	17.7%	17.7%	3.9%	3.9%	na	na	na	na

Marginal Tax Rates

	Private Business [1]		Households [2]		Institutions [3]		Govt enterprises [4]		General govt [5]	
	1998	1999	1998	1999	1998	1999	1998	1999	1998	1999
Capital	58.5%	60.6%	-1.4%	-1.9%	28.7%	29.0%	na	na	na	na
Federal	35.8%	37.6%	-18.4%	-18.8%	5.8%	6.0%	na	na	na	na
State and local	22.6%	23.0%	17.0%	16.9%	23.0%	23.0%	na	na	na	na
Labor	43.9%	44.4%	35.5%	43.5%	39.6%	39.5%	24.7%	24.9%	25.5%	25.8%
Federal	35.2%	35.6%	30.7%	38.8%	35.2%	35.1%	20.8%	21.0%	21.5%	21.8%
State and local	8.7%	8.8%	4.8%	4.7%	4.4%	4.4%	3.9%	3.9%	4.0%	4.0%
Total Producer Income	48.8%	49.8%	-0.3%	-0.4%	39.0%	39.0%	na	na	na	na
Federal	35.4%	36.2%	-16.9%	-17.0%	33.7%	33.6%	na	na	na	na
State and local	13.4%	13.5%	16.6%	16.5%	5.3%	5.3%	na	na	na	na

[1] Corporate and noncorporate businesses.
[2] Labor services supplied by domestics and the imputed value of capital services received by those who own their own homes.
[3] Mainly the nonprofit sector including hospitals, schools and churches.
[4] Government-operated businesses which provide commercial services such as the Postal Service, Tennessee Valley Authority and state-controlled liquor stores.
[5] Functions normally associated with government including defense, police, education, and welfare.

Table 3.—Sources & Uses of Private Business Funds, 1999

Sources	$billions	As % of Priv. Bus GDP
Total sources of private business funds	7,062.3	100.6%
Private business GDP	7,018.5	100.0%
Taxable private business GDP	7,007.9	99.2%
Untaxable, in kind compensation	10.6	0.2%
Subsidies	43.8	0.6%
Uses		
Total uses of private business funds	7,062.3	100.6%
Gross labor income	4,195.2	59.8%
Compensation of employees	3,967.2	56.5%
Untaxable employee payments in kind	10.4	0.1%
Compensation of private business employees	3,956.8	56.4%
Wages and salaries	3,386.5	48.3%
Employer contributions for social insurance	279.9	4.0%
Other labor income	290.4	4.1%
Indirect business taxes on labor	228.0	3.2%
Gross capital income	2,867.1	40.9%
Corporate profits with IVA and CCA	763.3	10.9%
Profits tax liability	225.3	3.2%
Dividends	331.6	4.7%
Undistributed profits	162.1	2.3%
Inventory valuation adjustment (IVA)	(13.0)	−0.2%
Capital consumption adjustment (CCA)	57.2	0.8%
Net corporate interest paid	140.8	2.0%
Proprietors' income with IVA and CCA	646.7	9.2%
Untaxable in kind proprietors' income	0.2	0.0%
Proprietors' net interest paid	93.8	1.3%
Other proprietors' income with IVA and CCA	3.7	0.1%
Rental income of persons with CCA	62.4	0.9%
Other private business net interest paid	57.7	0.8%
Consumption of fixed business capital	796.4	11.3%
Business transfer payments	39.4	0.6%
Payments to persons		
Payments to rest of world		
Indirect business taxes and fees on capital	387.8	5.5%
Statistical discrepancy	−125.1	−1.8%

A U.S. Department of Commerce, National Income and Product Accounts, Tables 1.9, 1.15, 1.16 & 8.21, April 2000.

Mr. CRANE. The Chair applauds and congratulates and is grateful to each of you for the work that you have done, for coming to the committee today and sharing with us your ideas, but Gary and Aldona Robbins have been well-known to me for many years and do excellent work in modeling what impact our decisions are going to have on the economy and on jobs, and James Powell is a tough Texan rancher, the kind of vibrant individual this country was founded on, and Bill Helming, you have spent many years in the vineyards developing your program, and without any desire for personal gain, but to do something for the good of this country. I respect all three of you, and I am grateful that you are here before us today.

Tell me, let me ask you a couple of questions. I don't have time to examine all the details, but we have it in writing and we can, at another time, look through it. But can you synopsize why you believe your plan is better than AFT?

Mr. HELMING. Mr. Chairman, better than what?

Mr. CRANE. Than the Americans for Fair Taxation that we heard the first day of this week?

Mr. HELMING. Yes. Well, I would simply say two major reasons— and, again, from the perceptions of the common person that I interface with, Mr. Chairman.

Number one, the rate differential is a dramatic difference in terms of the perception on the part of the taxpayer. The AFT Tax rate is simply too high.

And then, secondly, the consumer and at the J.C. Penney level, the consumer is under the impression, and rightly so, that businesses aren't paying their fair share. That is the perception, and that is a major problem from a structural standpoint, not from an economic standpoint, but from a structural standard, in terms of political viability of what I am proposing versus what is being proposed under the AFT plan.

Those are two major, critical issues.

Mr. CRANE. All right. Thank you very much.

Mr. HELMING. Could I just add one thing?

Mr. CRANE. Sure.

Mr. HELMING. In my findings over the last 15 or 16 years, when it is all said and done, taking the typical taxpayer across America, it is very clear to me after that period of time that the removal of the entire tax code, including the FICA payroll taxes and the self-employment taxes and getting the IRS out of the lives of the wage earner—not the business owner, but the wage earner—those two things are very popular among the common people in this country.

Mr. CRANE. Yes. All right. Thank you.

Now I am going to ask you a more difficult question. What are the flaws in your program?

Mr. HELMING. Well, I think perhaps a potential concern that might be raised would be the exemptions that I build into the plan to deal with regressivity. In other words, a potential concern or question might be, well, okay, if we start out with food and shelter and medical, then who is to say that your committee and others in Congress might suggest something else?

Well, my response to that is as follows: first of all, there is a very well-established precedent at the State level, basically all 50 States, that for some time at the State level they exempt the very things that I am talking about, so it is a well-established precedent.

Secondly, I would envision that the tax—if you go to manipulating, if you will, the social engineering issue and Congress says, "We are going to build in another exemption, or another two or three," well then that is going to raise the rate, and every American from Watts to Harlem is going to know what change in the tax rates is and that is under consideration and there will be a lot of negative response to that.

Lastly, to the potential concern that I raised, my response and suggestion would be that any change in the new Federal tax code be required by a super majority of the U.S. Congress.

Mr. CRANE. Well, I think you have been very up front. I know, when I talk about structural tax reform in my town meetings, I have to say up front there is no tax system that is perfect.

Mr. HELMING. That is right.

Mr. CRANE. No matter how we collect taxes, there are going to be objections, there are going to be flaws, there are going to be problems, and one day when I spoke very strongly, as I do, about the need to get rid of the income tax in one of my town meetings and suggested the concept of an alternative, a man got up in the back of the room, raised his hand, and I recognized him, and he said, "I don't like your ideas." And that is the first time anyone had ever said that to me. And I said, "Well, I am curious. Why?" And he said, "Because we still have to pay taxes." And I said, "You are right. We would love for that day to come when we didn't have to pay taxes, but the Government has bills to pay, and therefore we have to collect taxes."

So we should continue to seek the best way, and I thank you for your input.

I am now going to recognize Mr. Coyne for any questions that he might like to make.

Also, I have got to excuse myself for a very few minutes, and if you will preside during my absence I will return shortly.

Mr. HELMING. Thank you.

Mr. COYNE [presiding]. Thank you, Mr. Chairman.

Ms. Robbins, your testimony notes that the fundamental proposals for tax reform do not make poor families pay more taxes. What about middle class and high-income families? What happens with their total tax bills, the middle class and upper-income families?

Ms. ROBBINS. When I refer to proposals, I am really talking about the example that we structured here with the refundable credit up to the poverty line.

I don't have distributional information with me at this point. I think, as you know, Congressman, when we are talking about broadening the base, there are going to be some deductions that are going to be lost and some people are going to be worse off. Others will be better off.

I think, overall, though, the objective of tax reform is to try to get out as many of the distortions that exist in the current system and broaden the base, bring down the tax rates, and generate more—ultimately, the greater growth that would result, I believe, from tax reform would, long run, make everyone better off, but certainly starting out of the gate there are going to be winners and losers.

Mr. COYNE. So you have no data that would show that middle class—

Ms. ROBBINS. We have not constructed that information as yet. This project is still under way, so we will eventually have distributional tables.

Mr. COYNE. Okay. The economy is in its longest period of expansion in the Nation's history, and the current tax system doesn't seem to have hampered that amazing achievement for all of us, or most of us. Do you think a sudden fundamental change to the tax code could threaten that prosperity that we have been experiencing?

Ms. ROBBINS. I have done some looking at the current recovery and have compared it, for example, to the 1960s, which, up until February, when we passed, I think, 106 months in the 1990s, the

324

1960s had been the previous longest expansion. It is interesting on the tax issue that the average tax rates in the 1990s are higher than they were in the 1960s. That is because we have programs like Social Security and Medicare that are larger today, and also because State and local governments have expanded over time.

So the average rates in the 1960s were actually lower, but what was interesting is that during the 1990s the marginal tax rates had been lower than they were in the 1960s, but they have been trending up, so right now we are getting close to marginal rates of where they were in the 1960s.

I guess what I am concerned about and keeping an eye on are leading indicators, such as the stock market and investment, to see if perhaps this recovery might not be starting to stall. If it is, then I think the tax rate issue is certainly one area that needs to be revisited.

I would argue that anything you can do to bring down marginal rates will be added insurance to keep this recovery going even further.

Mr. COYNE. Well, I guess I am not speaking so much of rates as I am any structural change in the code that would come about by saying that in the year 2003 or 2004 we are going to have an altogether different method for revenue collection.

Ms. ROBBINS. Right.

Mr. COYNE. And aside from the progressive income tax that has served us very, very well over the years.

Ms. ROBBINS. I guess, again, it would matter on what kind of disruptions that are being discussed, although I think if you look historically, when there have been changes to the tax code, the economy is remarkably resilient and does make adjustments pretty quickly.

Mr. COYNE. Thank you.

Ms. ROBBINS. You are welcome.

Mr. COYNE. John?

Mr. TANNER. I am sorry I got here late.

Mr. Helming, I was reading your proposal, and in it do you—we had a hearing two days ago, I guess it was, and there was a proposal for a national sales tax—

Mr. HELMING. Yes.

Mr. TANNER.—that would apply to the cities and counties and States in this country on not only their purchases, but also on the wages paid, as a service.

I was reading yours. Is yours similar to that, that you tax local—

Mr. HELMING. No, sir. The plan that you have before you and that I presented here today is for the Federal level, only, but I can speak to the State level, if you would like me to.

Mr. TANNER. Yes.

Mr. HELMING. The 15.2 tax rate at tier one and tier two is required to achieve revenue neutrality for raising the same amount of revenues as we do now.

I don't know if you were here when I spoke to that. The marginal tax rate on labor under the current code is 35.6 percent, and under this plan it is 30.4, about a 14 percent differential.

If you were to take the same formula and applied the tier one and tier two to be revenue neutral—in other words, strip out all income tax for those States that have income taxes and sales taxes, property and real estate and property taxes—you would basically have a 7.6 percent total, or divided by two, 3.8, so you would add 3.8 to 15.2, and you would basically have a 19 percent rate to cover and replace all federal and state government taxes.

You see what I am saying? That would replace all Federal and State taxes.

Mr. TANNER. I think I heard you say that you favor the super majority bill to raise taxes?

Mr. HELMING. Well, to change anything in the tax code.

Mr. TANNER. To change anything.

Mr. HELMING. I mean, what I am suggesting, assuming our Nation and our American people are so fortunate to have a fundamental tax reform embraced, my suggestion would be then part of the law which you and your colleagues would be writing would be a requirement that any structural change or change in the rate in any manner would require a super majority of the U.S. Congress.

Mr. TANNER. What about foreign money, raising the debt ceiling? Would you also favor super majority to do that?

Mr. HELMING. I am sorry. I am having a hard time hearing you.

Mr. TANNER. To borrow money to raise the debt ceiling, would you favor a super majority to borrow money?

Mr. HELMING. I guess I probably would, but I haven't thought about that one near as much.

Mr. TANNER. Well, would you agree that there is pressure in the here and now to not raise taxes more so than the pressure in the here and now from those yet unborn who are getting the debt that we are leaving them to just simply borrow more money, rather than paying for our consumption today? Would you have a problem with that?

Mr. HELMING. Yes, sir, I sure would.

Mr. TANNER. So if one believed that the pressure to not raise taxes today is greater than the pressure from those that are not here yet to not borrow from them, it seems to me the super majority that we ought to be talking about as relates to the tax code ought to be to borrow money rather than to pay for what we do today.

I think we should think about the efficacy of what we are doing with respect to our Nation's debt rather than what we are doing with respect to the tax code as it relates to the here and now, but that is just another—

Mr. HELMING. I guess my emphasis, Congressman, is that, when we look at a structural change and a fundamental change in the revamping of the current tax code, as many others have already said and as I have been saying for some time, if it is done properly, you know, everybody in the economy essentially wins. I mean, certainly the common wage-earner is going to benefit from a faster-growing economy, lower interest rates, lower cost of goods and services.

Mr. TANNER. I agree.

Mr. HELMING. And so I don't think we can walk away from that. I think, as long as we can do it and raise the required amount of money to stay within the budget limitations, it seems to me we ought to be doing it.

Mr. TANNER. I agree. It is curious this super majority thing keeps coming up, but no one wants to talk the fact that—

Mr. HELMING. The reason I bring that up is that, you know, one of the very nice features about the structural aspect of this two-tiered system is that it is levied across the entire economy—the business sector and obviously the consumer sector—and if Congress decides, for whatever reason or reasons at some point, assuming we were to implement such a plan, that it wanted to change it, it seems to me that ought to require a major hill to climb before it was changed. That is all I am trying to suggest.

Mr. TANNER. I understand the super majority thing. The process, though, has always intrigued me because no one talks about it in relation to borrowing money. They only talk about it in relation to raising taxes.

Would you require a super majority to declare war?

Mr. HELMING. Well, I think the Constitution says that is up to the President in one sense—

Mr. TANNER. No, it is up to the Congress to declare war.

Mr. HELMING. It is really up to the Congress. Yes.

Mr. TANNER. When you go down that road, what about a super majority to elect people to come here to make these decisions? I mean, when you start talking about super majorities—we had a vote on it this week, and I don't want to argue about it, but it has just always caught my attention when people talk about a super majority as it relates to the tax code but not to borrow money or do anything else around here. I wish—

Mr. HELMING. I wouldn't quarrel with you that a super majority conceptually is a good idea.

Mr. TANNER. You think it is?

Mr. HELMING. Yes, I do for my tax proposal

Mr. TANNER. Well, that is an interesting conception.

I yield back the balance of my time.

Mr. ARCHER [resuming Chair]. Mr. Coyne, thank you for presiding in my absence.

Again, we thank all three of you for coming and presenting your proposal. It is clearly a well-thought-out proposal, and it is going to be very helpful to us as we try to find our way through to the final solution of what we can get past in structural tax reform.

Mr. HELMING. Mr. Chairman, my next step is to get it introduced into Congress, but it is a pleasure to be here.

[The following was subsequently received:]

May 3, 2000

Congressman John Tanner
1127 Longworth Building
Washington, D.C. 20515

Dear Congressman Tanner:

Let me start by thanking you for being present during my presentation at the Tax Reform hearings conducted by the House Ways and Means Committee on April 13th. I am writing to clarify an answer I gave to you regarding having a two-thirds majority rule as it pertains to the tax code and specifically my proposal.

I need to tell you that I was having difficulty hearing questions coming from the committee. I had to have Chairman Archer repeat himself a couple of times earlier during the Q & A. Upon review of the written transcript, I saw that I missed the concern you were trying to convey in the context of your question. I'll briefly make a couple of points that hopefully will better answer your question.

I am aware that some in congress have advocated a two-thirds rule for raising taxes. I am sure there are many motivations that cause these individuals to take their positions. For those who sincerely think that such a move would help solve the inequities in the current system, I think they would be disappointed by the results. I am in the camp that believes the current code can't be fixed by tinkering with it and that we should take advantage of the good times to phase in a new, revenue-neutral code.

As a two-thirds rule could pertain to a new tax code, I think one could argue for it. As it might pertain to my proposal, the two-thirds rule would be used to primarily keep the overall structure in tact for a longer period of time. Should an industry lobby for special treatment or exempt status, for example, the overall tax rate levied at the business and retail levels would go up. The two-thirds rule would make it harder for that kind of change to occur and there would be a good chance the voters would take a more active role in letting their positions be known. The rule would apply to raising taxes, but under my plan, the rule also applies to lowering the tax rate.

My motivation for having a two-thirds rule as part of my proposal, is to ensure that the tax code will not change too much or too often. The idea is to enact a code for the citizens, businesses and government that will be predictable and consistent, that will remain in tact through the rigors of political and economic change.

I hope this better explains my position. Again, thank you for your time at the hearings and I hope well have an opportunity to talk more about my proposal in the future.

Sincerely,

BILL HELMING

cc: Bill Archer
    John Meagher

Mr. CRANE. Thank you so much. You are excused.

Our next panel is Dr. Regalia, Ms. Soldano, and Mr. Entin, if you will come to the witness table.

We are glad to have all three of you with us today. I think you probably, having sat in the room, know the general format that we try to follow, which is that your entire written statements will be put in the record without objection, and if you will attempt to synopsize verbally within the five-minute limit, we would appreciate it.

Dr. Regalia, if you would start off.

STATEMENT OF MARTIN A. REGALIA, VICE PRESIDENT AND CHIEF ECONOMIST, U.S. CHAMBER OF COMMERCE

Mr. REGALIA. Mr. Chairman, my name is Marty Regalia, and I am vice president and chief economist of the U.S. Chamber of Commerce.

The Chamber appreciates the opportunity to comment on fundamental tax reform, and I will summarize my testimony briefly.

Over the years, dissatisfaction with the Federal tax system has resulted in the enactment of significant code changes in about 11 of the last 25 years. Even these changes, however, have not really fixed anything, and the discontent over the code continues.

The current tax system is plagued by a number of shortcomings. The system is cumbersome and excessively complex and results in high compliance costs and produces a perception of unfairness, as well as a lack of trust that not only undermines compliance with the law, but respect for the Government.

The system levies multiple layers of tax on income, capital acquisitions, savings, and investment, and, as such, it is biased against savings and investment that is crucial to our continued economic growth.

It contains relatively high marginal rates, which are economically distorting, foster tax avoidance, and reduce compliance.

It suffers from a multitude of exclusions, exemptions, deductions, and credits, which often cause decisions to be tax driven, rather than made on the basis of sound economic reasoning.

Clearly, the system is in need of substantial reform, or even replacement.

The Chamber's members are currently evaluating a number of the proposals, and, while they have not yet selected a single approach or endorsed a specific proposal, they believe that, whatever system is developed, it should address as many of the following issues as possible:

The tax system needs to be simple and clear, understandable, and relatively easy to apply.

It should eliminate or substantially reduce the incidence of confiscatory multiple levels of taxation on capital savings and investment and on productivity growth.

The system should have low marginal rates which imply a relatively broad base with relatively few exemptions.

It should level the playing field in terms of our international competitiveness. It should do this by avoiding duplicative taxation and other jurisdictional problems and by adopting a territorial approach that is border adjustable.

Fundamental changes to our tax system must also be accompanied by appropriate, sensible transition rules. They must be clear-cut, of sufficient duration to allow a chance for the change to be properly interpreted, understood, and applied, and provide an orderly movement into the new tax structure without the application of undue costs.

The business world and our whole economic environment are rapidly evolving, in part due to new technologies and electronic commerce. Whether the system is reformed or replaced, it must be consistent with this new economy and afford sufficient flexibility to accommodate change with a minimum of tinkering.

The task of designing and implementing a substantial reform is daunting, but the rewards are continued economic growth and a higher standard of living. We look forward to working with you and the other members of the committee to achieve this end.

Thank you.

Mr. CRANE. Thank you, Dr. Regalia.

[The prepared statement follows:]

Statement of Martin A. Regalia, Vice President and Chief Economist, U.S. Chamber of Commerce

The U.S. Chamber of Commerce is the world's largest business federation, representing more than three million businesses and organizations of every size, sector and region, and we appreciate this opportunity to comment on reforming or replacing the federal tax system.

INTRODUCTION

Over the years, dissatisfaction with the federal tax system has resulted in the enactment of major tax code changes in 11 of the last 25 years: 1976, 1978, 1981,

1982, 1983, 1985, 1986, 1990, 1993, 1997 and 1998, with other changes in between. Yet, perhaps due in part to the sheer frequency of changes, taxpayer discontent seems to have mounted. Not only do critics cite the weight of the overall tax burden, but they also point to the way the tax is collected—specifically, the system's high marginal tax rates; its double, triple and sometimes quadruple taxation of the same income; its high level of complexity; its inherent anti-saving bias; its special provisions for certain economic activities; its high cost of compliance; and its hindrance of faster long-term economic growth.

As a result, from time-to-time, tax reform proposals have been put forth that range from relatively straightforward alterations of the current tax code to complete replacement of the income tax system with an entirely new system of taxation.

GENERAL OBSERVATIONS

The primary purpose of a tax system is to raise revenue to provide for essential public goods and services. While there may be some debate over what constitutes an essential public good or service, and thus over how much an economy should be taxed, most would agree there are certain principles that a "good" tax system should embody:

Efficiency—A tax system is efficient when the cost of collection and compliance is low relative to the amount of revenue raised. *For example*, spending $10 to collect $100 in tax revenues is more efficient than spending $50 to raise $125.

Neutrality—The distortion to economic decision-making should be minimal. How is economic decision-making altered by the tax consequences of a particular activity? Are sound economic fundamentals driving economic decisions, or are individuals basing their decisions largely on the tax ramifications?

Simplicity—Ease of understanding and fulfillment should be widespread, allowing ordinary citizens to handle their own taxes with a minimum of outside assistance. Firms, large and small, should be able to easily understand and accurately apply the tax code to their businesses.

Fairness—Are those in similar economic circumstances paying similar taxes? This notion, termed "horizontal equity," is relatively straightforward. Another type of fairness that is more difficult to measure, "vertical equity," suggests that those who are in dissimilar circumstances should pay appropriately different amounts of tax. These are very

Certainty—Are changes to the tax code capricious, frequent or unanticipated? Do households and businesses know much will be due and when? Can they readily project their tax liability in coming years under various sets of circumstances? Are they responding to the current tax code or arranging their affairs in anticipation of the next change to the tax laws?

At times, some of these principles may be at odds, but, in general, the best tax systems would score reasonably well on these criteria.

In addition to the above characteristics, the designers of a new tax system must also address a number of questions; *for example*, the degree of "progressivity" or "regressivity." A regressive tax structure exists when lower-income individuals pay a higher proportion of their income in taxes than do higher-income taxpayers. Conversely, in a progressive tax structure, higher-income individuals pay a greater proportion of their income in taxes than do individuals with lower incomes.

A key issue to understanding and redesigning our tax system is to recognize that it provides incentives for businesses and households to behave in particular ways. As such, it can be used to promote specific social goals or advance political agendas. Often, these social or political goals run counter to the aforementioned principles and force tradeoffs. The result can be a tax code that violates the principles of sound taxation and imposes numerous unintended consequences. This can cause significant economic damage. In designing a tax system for the new millennium, we should be aware of any incentive structure we may create and the likely response from the dynamic marketplace.

Another key point for those wishing to construct a new system, or significantly alter the existing one, is the choice of the tax base. Should we, *for instance*, tax income or consumption? If we choose income, should it be income less a personal exemption (of how much?), or income less a personal exemption less savings? Should we subtract out charitable contributions? Mortgage interest? State taxes? If we believe that consumption should be taxed, should we tax sales (some, all, or retail?) or "consumed income"?

Moreover, choices made about the tax base will have a significant influence on the tax rate. As we narrow the tax base—*i.e.*, as we exclude more and more activity from taxation—tax rates will have to rise to garner the same amount of tax revenue, at least in a conservative, static sense (i.e., ignoring any impact on economic

330

growth). Other questions also arise: Should a single tax rate be used, or are multiple tax rates preferable? Should different rates apply to households and businesses?

Finally, another important consideration for any tax proposal is how to get from "here to there," and over what period. Regardless of the long-term benefits that may accrue from a new tax system, making the transition from the current income tax to a different tax regime will undoubtedly create "winners" and "losers." How these winners and losers are treated could make the difference between moving to a new system and keeping our current system. Transition rules in many proposals have not been developed yet, but they will be of paramount importance and should be examined closely, prior to adopting any new system.

CURRENT TAX CODE

The current tax system, overall, is steeply progressive. Families who find themselves in the highest quintile (top 20 percent) of pretax annual income bear 77 percent of the income tax burden, and 53 of the overall federal tax liability when income, social insurance and excise taxes are included. At the same time, families who are in the lowest 20 percent have an effective income tax burden of negative two percent, due to refundable tax credits, and those in the second lowest quintile have an effective income tax burden of only one percent. Together, those in the lowest two quintiles, while making up 40 percent of the population, bear only 12 percent of the overall tax liability, *i.e.*, income, social insurance and excise taxes. (Congressional Budget Office, *Budget Options, p. 43, March 2000.*)

A degree of progressivity may achieve some measure of "fairness" in the eyes of some, *via* certain social goals, such as redistribution of income or wealth, or be reflective, in part, of ability to pay. However, just as taxes are necessary to operate our "government of the people, by the people, [and] for the people," from which everyone derives benefits, good government is founded upon input and involvement from the citizenry. When so many pay so little, if anything, towards the operation of our government, they are not very concerned as to how the revenues are spent—after all, it is not "their" money; it's someone else's. They feel disinterested in, and disenfranchised from, "the system," at the same time as those who pay a disproportionately high rate of taxes fell cheated and oppressed by the system. A *good example* of this apathy is reflected in low voter turnout for political elections, and pervasive ignorance of political processes. A tax system that requires some fair, material participation from all segments of society in the funding of government invites their interest and participation in how our government and our country operate. Government is enhanced by an engaged citizenry. A system designed to replace the current federal tax code and structure should reflect these ideals.

The current federal tax system is cumbersome and too complex. A tax system cannot be perceived as fair if it is overly complicated. Unless the average person can understand how the tax system works and prepare necessary tax paperwork without an undue amount of education and research, it will be held in disdain. A tax system that is so cryptic that only the privileged few can understand it does not gain the trust of the people—it seems to be written in a secret language by, and to serve the purposes of, an elite minority. Most people are unable to understand the tax laws and complete their own tax returns—well over one-half of all tax returns are prepared by tax professionals. This results in a lack of trust that not only undermines respect for government and compliance with the law, but renders the law more difficult to interpret and enforce. Difficulty in interpretation and enforcement breeds uncertainty and problems in administering the law, and results in a drain on the revenues, either through direct reduction due to non-compliance, or exorbitant expenses incurred in educating people in proper reporting and treatment of transactions; drafting and issuance of lengthy regulations; auditing of tax returns; and litigation of disputes. A new tax system needs to be simple and clear, understandable and easy to apply, and with a minimum of computations to undertake and tax forms to complete.

Currently, our federal tax system levies multiple layers of taxation on capital acquisition, savings, and investment. As such, it is biased against savings and investment that is crucial to sustaining our economic growth. Take, *for example*, a business owner who operates his or her own corporation, For that individual, such layers of taxation can include: the income tax on corporate earnings; the personal income tax and FICA taxes on wages paid by the corporation; personal income tax on the sales of the investor's corporate stock; capital gains tax on subsequent reinvestments made with those funds; and gift, estate, and transfer taxes levied upon the remaining assets transferred by this unfortunate taxpayer to others. When added together, some income faces an effective tax confiscation in excess of 90 percent, a truly draconian figure. A new tax system should reduce the incidence of such confiscatory cumulative taxes, and encourage productivity, savings and investment. A fair tax system must encourage and reward those who help grow our economy.

INTERNATIONAL COMPETITIVENESS

On the international competitiveness front, a tax system should be "border-adjustable" and mesh well with international tax treaties entered into with our trading partners. *For instance*, U.S. corporations doing business outside our borders should not be placed at a competitive disadvantage by multiple taxation of the same transactions or activities, or being subject to tax rates which are unfavorable when compared to those levied upon our foreign competitors. If the United States taxes its domestic businesses on their world-wide income, *i.e.*, taxes the income of transactions or acitivites occurring in foreign countries in which U.S. corporations conduct their business, and they are also subject to tax by foreign jurisdictions, it places those entities at a competitive disadvantage *vis-a-vis* their foreign competitors. If the United States taxes those transactions or activities at a competitively unfavorable rate, our companies are disadvantaged. And, when our companies are disadvantages, their employees, owners and our country, overall, are likewise disadvantaged. A business, whether a corporation, partnership, sole proprietorship, or in some other legal form, is nothing more than people, and when the business is hurt, the people that "make it up," are also injured.

Our current federal tax system protects certain of our businesses from international competitive disadvantage through the Foreign Sales Corporation ("FSC") rules. Likewise, many international tax treaties provide for elimination or reduction in the effect of duplicative taxation. However, recently, the World Trade Organization ("WTO") has ruled that the Internal Revenue Code's treatment of FSCs violates the WTO's conventions, constituting an illegal subsidy to U.S. firms. The underlying bases of this dispute and preservation of border-adjustability must be addressed and resolved in any replacement tax system to make the playing field level in terms of international competitiveness. Accordingly, our federal tax system must either be crafted in such a manner to integrate with existing international treaties or be coordinated with the drafting and adoption of new ones.

CONCLUSION

While proposals have been advanced for the reform or replacement of our current federal tax code, neither our membership, nor the public, has yet reached a consensus as to which approach makes the most sense for America. Accordingly, we advocate additional study of these proposals and their expected impact on the taxpayers, and our economy, as a whole, before any one "best" system can be devised, embraced, and advanced. Nonetheless, one thing we can says it that the current system offers much room for improvement, whether that be through major retooling or redesign, to achieve: simplicity; fairness; low marginal rates with a broad tax base with few deductions; reasonable progressivity; incentives for productivity, savings, and investment and the fostering of international competition. At the same time, the government must control its spending appetite so as to require the smallest amount necessary to provide the goods and services demanded by the public, and collect the taxes in a reasonable, cost-efficient and effective way.

Fundamental changes to our tax system must be accompanied by appropriate, sensible transition rules. They must be clear-cut; of sufficient duration to allow a chance for the changes to be properly interpreted, understood and applied; and provide an orderly movement into the next tax structure without undue costs.

We must also keep in mind that the business world and the ways which we structure and conduct transactions are evolving at a frenetic pace. The advent and development of new technologies, including electronic commerce, are altering the playing arena and the rules of the "game" with dizzying speed. A new tax system must be carefully crafted to encompass and accomplish its intended purposes. At the same time, it must be sufficiently flexible to accommodate change with a minimum of tinkering. Reasoned study and foresight must be applied to designing the system, so that in the winds of change we do not have to face the prospect of scrapping that system and returning to square one. Let's not rush to judgment; let's do it right.

Vital to reaching a broad consensus on the outcome of this debate, is the principle that everyone who is able to, should contribute to our system of government, in return for its benefits and protections, and have a stake and interest in the government. Only through the expression of such interest can the consensus we seek be discovered.

Mr. CRANE. Ms. Soldano will you now give us your testimony?

STATEMENT OF PATRICIA M. SOLDANO, PRESIDENT, CENTER FOR THE STUDY OF TAXATION, COSTA MESA, CALIFORNIA

Ms. SOLDANO. Mr. Chairman, I am Patricia M. Soldano, Center for the Study of Taxation. I am here today as president of the Center for the Study of Taxation, but, more importantly, as someone who has heard from numerous families about the effect of the gift, estate, and generation skipping tax, also called the "death tax," has had on them and their businesses. Allow me to share some death tax facts and some horror stories with you today.

To pay a tax because someone dies at the highest rate in our tax system on assets that have already been taxed before is the reason that 69 percent of the general public believes that the death tax is unfair—more unfair than payroll tax, income tax, gasoline tax, sales tax, property tax, cigarette tax, alcohol/beer tax, and even capital gains tax.

Why is the death tax so unpopular? Because it is a tax on the American dream. Hard-working entrepreneurs who build their family businesses and support our Nation's economy hope that some day they will be in a position to will their life's work to their children and not pay a 55 percent tax. Within the last few years, new voices have called for the elimination of the death tax, including the National Association of Women-Owned Businesses, the National Black Chamber of Commerce, the National Indian Business Association, U.S. Hispanic Chamber of Commerce, U.S. Pan Asian American Chamber of Commerce, National Association of Neighborhoods, and the Texas Conference of Black Mayors.

These minority groups have just started to build their businesses and they want to be able to pass on their assets to their children, the benefit of years of hard work, without a 55 percent tax or an 80 percent generation-skipping tax if they wish to give to their grandchildren, and these people are represented by 47 percent of the female Members of Congress, who have supported repeal of the death tax as cosponsors of the bipartisan Dunn-Tanner bill, and I would like to thank Congresswoman Dunn and Congressman Tanner for their work on H.R. 8 and their tireless effort to repeal the death tax.

These women and minorities are real people who are adversely impacted by the death tax. Money that they could use to send their children to college or pay their family's expenses is, instead, snatched by Washington. One unlucky victim of this tax is Lynn Marie Hoopingarner of West Hollywood, California, who writes to me, "My family has recently experienced a triple tax. My grandfather paid income taxes on his income when he earned it. When he passed away two years later, it was taxed again. My mother than suddenly passed away this past spring, and it was taxed again—effectively, an 88 percent tax."

In addition to the inherent unfairness and inappropriateness of the death tax, it actually costs the American economy a job. Yes, the death tax does eliminate jobs. How many? In a survey recently done by the Center for the Study of Taxation and the Policy Institute of New York, 365 businesses responded to a survey that they had already lost 14 jobs per business in the last five years due to the cost of planning for this tax and actually paying the tax. That is 5,100 jobs in the last five years just within the 365 survey base. In the next five years, they anticipate losing, on average, 80 per business jobs. That is 80 jobs for 365 businesses—that is 15,000 jobs in the next five years.

In a recent survey of the National Association of Women Business Owners, NAWBO, there were similar results. Within the survey respondents of 272, on average 39 jobs have been lost in the last five years per business, again for paying and planning for this tax, and in the next five years, on average, 103 jobs will be lost per business. That is 28,000 jobs just within that survey respondent group.

Carri Bell, a NAWBO member who owns a business in Oklahoma City, wrote in her response to us, "I just settled my father's estate and paid three-quarters of the total estate for taxes and fees. Sold all of our stock and bonds and had to borrow. When I die, there are no more disposable assets left, so the business will have to be sold."

The death tax also impacts our global competitiveness. Since the United States has the second-highest death tax rate of any country in the world, second to Japan at a 70 percent rate—which you should know doesn't kick in until a $15 million exemption—the death tax affects the competitiveness of U.S. companies. Family businesses have to plan for the death tax by buying expensive life insurance, selling assets, borrowing or restructuring their business. It is expensive, time-consuming, energy-wasting, and constant, year after year.

Many small-to mid-size family businesses sell out early to corporations who are not faced with the death tax, ending the opportunity of the family to carry on with the business and the livelihood of the family.

In closing, I would like to tell you the story of Ida Prichard of Seattle, Washington. In her own words, she writes: "I am 77 years old. My history of work, thrifts, and efforts to save money is unbelievable. Here is my reward. All of my Social Security, plus more, goes for income taxes. I live off my teacher's pension, as I do not want to cash my investments. If I died today, I would pay about $200,000 in death tax. I am helping a great niece go to college. I have two great nephews coming up. All are bright children. I would like to help them, not the IRS.

"I had a newspaper route in college. I worked for 50 cents an hour doing office work under the program of President Roosevelt. I have lost money in investments.

"I went to work when I had a death sentence with lung cancer in 1967. I didn't miss a day when I was told that I was only going to live three months.

"I am still working. I have a tenant and I tutor ESL students. I do almost all my own work and cooking. I have never had a bill I didn't pay. The way things are now, what the nursing home doesn't get—if i am that unfortunate—the IRS will. What did I make all this effort for? Our laws need to be changed, but I have no clout."

Gentlemen and gentlewomen of this committee, I urge you to repeal the death tax. As the committee continues to actively consider proposals to reform the tax system, I urge the committee to recognize that outright repeal of the death tax should be a principal component of any proposal. Let us show the American people that their Government has a heart. Let us show the hard-working American people like Ida Prichard that they can pass away knowing that their life's hard work will benefit their families. Finally, let us show them, the so-called "little guys," that they do have clout and their Government is listening.

Thank you.

[The prepared statement follows:]

Statement of Patricia M. Soldano, Center for the Study of Taxation, Costa Mesa, California

I am here today as the President of the Center for the Study of Taxation, but more importantly as someone who has heard from numerous families about the effect that the gift, estate and generation skipping tax ("the death tax") has had on them and their businesses. Allow me to share some death tax facts and horror stories.

Most of you are already familiar with how the death tax effects mid to small sized businesses because you have heard from those families but you may not be aware of just *how much* it hurts. The facts show that *88% of the revenue generated by the death tax comes from estates $20 million or less!* So yes, the very wealthy are generating some of this revenue but most of it comes from families who own small and medium sized businesses that cannot afford to pay the tax upon the death of a family member without selling off most of the bequeathed assets.

To pay a tax because someone dies, at the highest rate in our tax system, on assets that have *already been taxed* is the reason that 69% of the general public believes the death tax is unfair. **More unfair than payroll tax, income tax, gasoline tax, sales tax, property tax, cigarette tax, alcohol and beer tax, or even the capital gains tax**. Why is the death tax so unpopular? Because it is a tax on "the American dream."

Hardworking entrepreneurs who build their family businesses and support our nation's economy, hope that someday they will be in a position to will their life's work to their children without paying a 55% tax.

Within the last few years many new voices have called for the elimination of the death tax including:

National Association of Women Business Owners
National Black Chamber of Commerce
National Indian Business Association
U.S. Hispanic Chamber of Commerce
U.S. Pan Asian American Chamber of Commerce
National Association of Neighborhoods
Texas Conference of Black Mayors

These minority groups have just started to build their businesses and they want to be able to give to their children the benefits of their years of hard work without a 55% gift tax or an 80% generation skipping tax if they wish to gift to their grandchildren. And they are represented by (among others) **47% of the female Members of Congress who support repeal of the death tax,** as co-sponsors of the bipartisan Dunn-Tanner bill, HR–8.

These women and minorities are real people who are adversely impacted by the death tax. Money that they could use to send their children to college or to pay other family expenses is instead snatched by Washington. One unlucky victim of this tax, Lynn Marie Hooopingarner of West Hollywood, CA writes to us, "My family has recently experienced a triple tax. My grandfather paid income taxes on his income when he earned it. When he passed away two years ago it was taxed again. My mother then suddenly passed away this past spring and we were taxed again. Effectively an 88% tax rate."

In addition to the inherent unfairness and inappropriateness of the death tax, it actually costs the American economy and jobs. Yes, the death tax eliminates jobs. How many?

• In a survey done last year by the Center for the Study of Taxation and Public Policy Institute of New York, 365 businesses that responded to a survey have already lost 14 jobs per business in the past five years due to the cost of planning and paying the death tax, that is 5,100 jobs just within those 365 businesses and they anticipate losing on average 80 jobs per business in the next 5 years, or in excess of 15,000 jobs just within the survey group.

• In a recent survey of members of the National Association of Business Owners, (NAWBO) there were similar results. Within the survey respondents of 272, on average 39 jobs have been lost in the past five years per business or 1,000 jobs in total and 103 are expected to be lost in the next five years for a total of 28,000 jobs.

Carri Bell, a NAWBO member, who owns a business in Oklahoma City, wrote on her response, "I just settled my father's estate and paid ¾ of the total estate for taxes and fees. Sold all of our stock and bonds and had to borrow. When I die there are no disposable assets left—so the business will have to be sold."

The death tax also impacts our global competitiveness. Since the United States has the second highest death tax rate in the world, second only to Japan at 70%, the death tax affects the competitive advantage of U.S. companies. Family businesses have to plan for the death tax by buying expensive life insurance, selling assets, borrowing, or restructuring their businesses. It is expensive, time consuming, energy wasting and constant, year after year. Many small to mid sized family businesses sell out to larger corporations who are not faced with the death tax ending the opportunity of the family to carry on the business and livelihood of the family.

In closing I would like to tell you the story of Ida Pritchard of Seattle, Washington in her own words. She writes: "I am 77 years old. My history of work, thrifts and efforts to save money is unbelievable. Here is my reward! All of my social security (plus more) goes for income tax. If I died today, I'd pay about $200,000 in death tax. I am helping a great niece to go to college. I have two great nephews coming up. All are bright children. I would like to help them—not the IRS. I had a newspaper route in college. I worked for 50 cents an hour doing office work under the program set up by President Roosevelt. I have lost money in investments. I went to work when I had a death sentence with lung cancer in 1967. I didn't miss a day when I was told I could only live three months at the most. I am still working. I have a tenant and I tutor ESL students. I do almost all my own work and cooking. I have never had a bill I didn't pay on time. The way things are now what the nursing home doesn't get (if I'm that unfortunate) the IRS will! What did I make all this effort for? Our laws need to be changed but I have no clout."

Gentlemen and gentlewomen of this committee, I urge you to repeal the death tax. Let's show the American people that their government has a heart. Let's show the hardworking American people like Ida Pritchard that they can pass away knowing that their life's hard work will benefit their families. And finally, let's show them, the so called "little guys" that they do in fact have clout and that their government is listening.

Thank you.

Mr. CRANE. That lady sounds like my kind of American.

Mr. Entin?

STATEMENT OF STEPHEN J. ENTIN, PRESIDENT AND EXECUTIVE DIRECTOR, INSTITUTE FOR RESEARCH ON THE ECONOMICS OF TAXATION

Mr. ENTIN. Thank you, Mr. Chairman, members of the committee. My name is Stephen Entin. I am the president of the Institute for Research on the Economics of Taxation. Thank you for this opportunity to discuss fundamental tax reform.

I am speaking on my own behalf, but I will present to you today a tax system developed by the Institute's late founder, Dr. Norman B. Ture. It is a simple saving-deferred cash flow tax for individuals, which he called the inflow-outflow tax. It has two chief attributes.

First, it gets the tax base right, using the correct measure of income for tax purposes, one that maximizes economic efficiency and yields the optimal growth of income.

Second, it shows the taxpayers the cost of government more clearly than any other system.

Other advantages of the tax are that it uses concepts familiar to most taxpayers, it easily incorporates tax relief for the lowest-income citizens, and it greatly simplifies the tax system.

A good tax reform would have two main objectives—namely, economic neutrality and high visibility. The current income tax is biased against saving and investment. The bias depresses productivity and wages and keeps people's income some 10 percent or more below their potential.

Neutrality requires that the tax system treats saving on par with consumption in one of two ways: saving should be tax deferred until it is withdrawn for consumption, as with the deductible IRAs and pensions; alternatively, income saved should be taxed, but the earnings should be tax free, as with Roth IRAs and tax-exempt bonds. All saving should get one or the other treatment.

In addition, the extra layers of tax on saving imposed by the corporate income tax and the estate and gift tax must be eliminated.

Visibility requires that the tax system show the voting public what they are paying for government so that they may make an informed decision as to how much government spending to support. Ideally, all citizens, except the very poor, should pay something to help fund the outlays of the Federal Government in order that they understand that the resources used by the Government are not free or costless.

Taxes should be collected directly from individuals, not be hidden at the business level. In fact, all taxes are paid by individuals, not by businesses and not by goods.

There should be an annual filing that lets taxpayers see their total tax payments for the year. People will not know their total tax bill if it is collected in dribs and drabs at the cash register.

Of the several tax plans you have looked at this week, an individual cash flow tax is the best way to achieve the dual objectives of neutrality and visibility. The inflow-outflow tax is based on a few clear principles that determine what is and is not taxed.

The tax would be imposed on individuals at a flat rate, with a basic exempt amount to protect the poorest citizens. There would be deductions to assure neutral treatment of saving and to properly attribute income for tax purposes to the people who ultimately receive and consume it.

All forms of labor compensation would be taxable.

Saving would be deductible—that is, tax deferred—and the reinvested earnings would grow on a tax-deferred basis. All distributions from saving would be taxed at the individual level when the saver or the heir sold the assets to raise money for consumption.

Transfer payments made to other people, either voluntarily, as with gifts or charitable contributions, or involuntarily, as with alimony payments or State and local taxes, would be deducted from taxable income. Gifts and transfer payments received would be added to the recipients' taxable income.

Cost of acquiring human capital, such as tuition, and other costs of earning income would be deductible.

The inflow-outflow tax would be far simpler than the current tax system. Expensing saving and taxing all returns would eliminate capital gains calculations. There would be no corporate income tax or estate tax. Investment by unincorporated businesses would be expensed, not depreciated, eliminating complicated capital cost recovery rules.

The tax would be territorial, both for simplicity and to end the tax disadvantages that American firms encounter when they compete abroad. Savings invested abroad would not be deductible. There would be no tax on foreign-source income and no complicated foreign tax credit.

Fundamental tax reform should replace the individual and corporate income taxes, the estate tax, and the excise taxes.

The payroll tax should be addressed by Social Security reform. The two reforms would reinforce one another. Social Security reform would increase private saving. Tax reform would encourage the investment of the added saving in the United States rather than abroad, giving Americans the twin benefits of greater income in retirement and higher productivity and wages while they are working.

Thank you.

Mr. CRANE. Thank you, Mr. Entin.

[The prepared statement follows:]

Statement of Stephen J. Entin, President and Executive Director, Institute for Research on the Economics of Taxation

Mr. Chairman, members of the Committee, I appreciate the opportunity to discuss fundamental tax reform with you today. The tax system presented in this paper was the last work of Dr. Norman B. Ture before his death in August, 1997. It is his concept of an ideal, highly visible, and reasonably simple income tax that is neutral in its treatment of saving and consumption uses of income. It is a simple cash flow tax imposed on individual income. the tax is saving-deferred to account for the cost of earning capital income. The multiple layers of tax on estates, gifts, and corporations are eliminated. These correctly measure net income, eliminate the current income tax bias against saving and investment and provide substantial tax simplification. Dr. Ture developed this proposal with the help of his staff at IRET.

Two purposes of a good tax system—raising revenue and "pricing" government

Any restructuring of the nation's tax system should be based on a set of clear tax principles, which should be uniformly applied to the exercise. Those who would redo the tax system should start by recognizing the two key purposes of a tax system, 1) to obtain revenue to pay for government goods, services, and activities, and 2) to let the citizen-taxpayers know how much they are paying for government, so that they may decide in an informed manner how much government activity the wish to support with their votes.

Four principle attributes of a good tax system—neutrality, visibility, fairness, and simplicity

A good tax system should fulfill its first objective, raising revenue, in a manner that does the least damage to the economy. The attribute required to achieve that objective is "neutrality." A neutral tax must be unbiased across economic activities, and especially, not overly penalize work in favor of leisure, nor tax income used for saving and investment more heavily than income used for consumption.

The second objective, letting voters know the cost of government, may be achieved by a tax system with the attribute of "visibility" or transparency to the taxpayers. A very large segment of the population must be made keenly aware that government costs money if government spending is to be held to levels at which its benefits match its costs. Toward that end, taxes should be paid directly by individuals. Taxes should not be hidden by being levied on business and buried in the prices of goods and services where voters may not see them. Nor should taxes be collected piecemeal, a few cents or dollars at a time, as with sales taxes, because doing so hides the annual total from the voters and disguises the cost of government.

Additional principles or attributes of a good tax system include fairness (properly defined), and reasonable simplicity, clarity and understandability. These features lead to a low cost of compliance and enhanced willingness to pay on the part of the taxpayers and to easy administration and enforcement of the tax rules by the government.

Neutrality. Neutrality means measuring income correctly and levying taxes evenly on all uses of income by all income producers, without bias, to avoid distorting economic activity.

A neutral, unbiased tax system would begin with a sensible definition of income subject to tax. Income is a new concept, revenues less the cost of generating those revenues. It is well understood that a business cannot reasonably be said to have a profit until its revenues exceed its costs of production (properly measured). It should be just as obvious that a worker cannot be said to have income until his earnings exceed the amounts he spent on acquiring the education, skills and tools that enable him to perform his job. Nor can a saver be said to have income until his returns on the saving exceed the amounts he spent to acquire the assets that generate the revenues. The full value of all costs of earning revenues should be subtracted from revenues before any tax is imposed.

Once income is accurately measured and allocated among taxpayers, it should be taxed even-handedly. Neutral treatment requires that all income be taxed at the same rate. It is improper to tax some income at a higher rate than other income, either through graduated tax rates or by imposing multiple layers of tax on some types of income but not on others.

No tax system can easily avoid penalizing labor relative to leisure. However, keeping tax rates as low as possible and avoiding graduation avoids the worst of this distortion.

Making the tax system even-handed or neutral across various types of saving and investment, and between saving and investment and consumption, requires several steps. Multiple layers of tax on capital must be avoided, and the basic income tax bias against saving and investment must be eliminated by correctly treating saving and investment as costs of earnings income. In particular:

• The tax system must either allow savers to deduct saving or to exclude the returns on saving from taxable income.

The income tax, by taxing both income that is saved and the returns on that income, taxes saving and investment more heavily than consumption. There are two ways to restore neutrality. One approach is to exclude all saving from taxable income while taxing all returns on the saving—a saving-deferred tax. This is the treatment currently allowed to a limited degree with pensions and deductible IRAs and tax exempt bonds. Other costs of earning income must also be expensed as incurred. Investment outlays must be deducted in the year the outlay is made (expensed), rather than depreciated over time or otherwise delayed or ignored.

• The dual taxation of Schedule C corporate income at the corporate and individual level must be eliminated.

Corporate income should be recognized as belonging to the shareholders, and should be taxed either on individual tax returns or corporate tax returns, but not both. One way to eliminate the extra layer of tax on corporations is to pass corporate earnings on to share-holders for tax purposes as is done for income generated in proprietorships, partnerships, and sub-Chapter S corporations. Alternatively, shareholders could be given a credit against the personal income tax for corporate taxes paid on the income of their shares. These arrangements are called "corporate-individual income tax integration". Another solution is to switch to a non-income type of tax system, such as a VAT or sales tax.

• The transfer tax on estates and gifts must be eliminated.

Most of an estate is saving that has already been taxed, often repeatedly. If there is tax-deferred saving in an estate, such as assets in a decedent's IRA or 401(k) plan, current law makes the heirs pay income tax on those assets beginning shortly after the inheritance. Therefore, the estate tax is always an extra layer of tax on saving. The estate and gift tax should be eliminated, and any part of an estate that was tax-deferred saving should remain tax-deferred as long as the heirs continue to save it.

Several types of tax systems would serve to exclude saving and investment or their returns from tax, end the bias against saving and investment, and simplify the tax system. These "neutral" taxes include the unbiased income taxes (saving-deferred and yield-exempt) described above, retail sales taxes that exempt investment goods and business supplies from tax, and value added taxes that allow expensing of investment goods and other intermediate products and services purchased from other businesses at each stage of production.

Since several types of taxes are equally "neutral", choosing among them requires an assessment of their other characteristics and how well they stack up against other important attributes of a good tax system.

Visibility. Visibility requires that the tax system reveal clearly to the citizen/taxpayer what he or she must pay for government goods, services, and activities. Taxes are the "price" we pay for government; taxes "cost-out" government for the taxpayer. Ideally, all citizens should pay something to help fund the outlays of the federal government in order that they understand that the resources used by the government are not free or costless. However, compassion dictates that the very poor should not be subject to tax. Therefore, taxes should be levied on the largest number of people consistent with compassionate treatment of those who cannot afford to pay.

At what stage in the flow of income should taxes be collected? At the business level, after it has made its payments to other firms but before its remaining revenues are paid out to its workers, savers, and investors? When the revenues are received by the workers and owners of the capital as earnings? Or when some portion of their income is spent on consumption?

Goods and services do not pay taxes. Businesses do not pay taxes. Only people pay taxes. All taxes, in fact, are taxes on income. Sales and excise taxes either depress sales of the taxed products, reducing the incomes of the people who provide the labor and capital used to make them, or they reduce the purchasing power of that income when the workers and savers attempt to spend it. Taxes collected by businesses fall in reality on the income of the businesses' shareholders or other owners, lenders, workers, or customers in the form of lower returns or wages or higher prices.

Since taxes are really paid by people out of income, they should be collected from people out of income. People see their tax liability most clearly when they pay an individual tax on the (properly defined) income that they have received, with a clear accounting, annually, at tax time. Taxes should not be hidden from taxpayers by being imposed on businesses as either corporate taxes, manufacturers excise taxes, or value added taxes. Similarly, taxes should not be hidden by being collected in bits and pieces over the course of a year as the taxpayer goes shopping, as either sales taxes or value added taxes.

Fairness. Fairness is often stated as making the rich pay a higher share of their income in taxes than the poor. Most people would agree that there should be some amount of income exempt from tax to shelter the very poorest citizens. Such an exempt amount imparts progressivity to the tax system. Only people above the exempt amount pay tax, and the more one's income exceeds the exempt amount, the greater is the tax as a percent of total income (which is the definition of progressivity). However, imposing further progressivity by means of graduated rates above the exempt amount is not consistent with fairness if one considers the effort it takes to earn additional income. Income is correctly understood to be the earned reward for supplying labor and capital services to the market. Except in rare cases, income closely matches the contribution of the effort and services provided by individuals to additional output. Therefore, graduated tax rates hit people harder the more they contribute to the production of goods and services. The added effort required to earn additional income, and the notion of equal treatment under the law, strongly urge that a proportional (single rate) tax on income (above the modest exempt amount) is the fairest.

Simplicity. Ideally, a tax system should be easy for the government to administer and enforce and should be easy and inexpensive for taxpayers to comply with. Such a tax system would have to be simple enough for people to understand and to follow.

A simple tax system must start with a simple, clear and logical definition of income. A simple and logical definition of income would make it possible to write clear regulations and instructions for taxpayers to follow and tax collectors to enforce. Furthermore, if people understood clearly what is and is not taxable, and agreed with the logic of the system, they would feel comfortable that they and their neighbors were paying the appropriate amount of tax. They would have a greater sense that the tax system was fair, and a greater willingness to comply.

Unfortunately, the current tax system is neither simple, nor logical, nor understandable. Much of the complexity in the current tax code stems from its ad hoc approach to defining taxable income. The code is not based on any clear understanding of what constitutes income or an accurate measurement of income, nor any set of coherent principles regarding the imposition of tax. Additional complexity arises from the multiple layers of tax to which some types of income are subject and the multiple points of collection at which the taxes are imposed. The lack of guiding principles and resulting chaotic definition of income make for difficulties in administration and compliance, because neither the IRS nor the taxpayer can figure out clearly what is in or out of the tax base.

Most complexity is found at the business level or with respect to specialized investments of individuals. Taxation of wages and ordinary individual interest and dividends is fairly straightforward. Simplification should not go so far as to eliminate tax filing by individuals, as with a sales tax or VAT; that would sacrifice visibility to an unacceptable degree, and is not necessary to achieve significant simplification.

A tax proposal that conforms to the attributes and principles of a good tax system.

As mentioned, there are several types of (largely) neutral tax systems. Most achieve varying degrees of tax simplification. Unfortunately, most fail to do a good job with respect to visibility, which is one of the most critical attributes of a good tax system.

The following is a tax proposal that conforms to all the attributes and principles of a good tax system. It is called the inflow-outflow (I–O) tax.

Overview. The I–O tax system is an individual-based saving-deferred tax with a number of additional deductions from revenue necessary to properly measure and allocate the income for tax purposes. Inflows—an individual's revenues from work, saving, and transfer payments received—would be taxable. Outflows associated with earning the revenues (such as net saving, investment, and some education outlays), and income transferred to others (either voluntarily by gift or as mandatory tax payments) would be deductible. Net taxable income would, in effect, consist of revenues utilized for the individual's own consumption.

For neutrality and visibility, net labor and capital income would be taxed once and only once on individual tax returns. For fairness, there would be personal allowances to shelter the poor from tax. For neutrality and fairness, there would be a single tax rate imposed on income above the exempt amount. The single rate would eliminate the graduated tax rate bias against work, education, risk taking, and success, and would treat all individuals alike under the law.

The I–O tax attributes income to the correct taxpayer. For visibility, income should be taxable to the final recipient of the income. People should be taxed only on the income over which they retain control and of which they enjoy the benefit. If one taxpayer gives revenue to another, either voluntarily (as by gift or charitable donation), or due to legal obligation or government coercion (alimony, fines, taxes), the donor should deduct that revenue from his or her taxable income, and the recipient should add that revenue to his or her taxable income.

The I–O tax defines income properly. Income is a net concept, revenues less the cost of generating those revenues. Among the costs of generating income are: training and education in the case of labor income; the cost of acquiring income earning assets (saving and investment) in the case of income from capital. Costs of generating income must be deductible in full—expensed, not deferred (unless compensated by payment of interest to maintain present value).

Details of the I–O system follow. An illustrative sample tax form is appended.

Labor income. Individuals would pay tax on labor income (wages, salaries, self-employment income, and the value of non-pension fringe benefits) and pension receipts. The employer would report the total to the taxpayer on a W–2 form, as it does for cash wages and pension withdrawals under current law.

Transfers received. Individuals would pay tax on the taxable portion of social security. (All payroll taxes would become deductible in this tax system; therefore, over a phase-in period equal to a full working lifetime, all social security benefits would eventually become taxable.) Individuals would also pay tax on welfare and other transfer payments received from state and local governments and charities, insofar as they exceed the exempt amounts. (In practice, those who receive charity would usually be too poor to owe tax, and would not have to file a return.)

Income from saving and the net saving deduction. Individuals would deduct their saving (a cost of earning future income) from taxable revenues, and pay tax on all returns on saving (whether principal or earnings on the principal or earnings of an unincorporated business) when withdrawn. Reinvested returns would be tax-deferred.

In effect, all saving would be treated like current-law tax-deferred pensions or IRAs. All income that individuals transfer to financial intermediaries or other businesses through lending or the purchase of shares would be deductible by the savers. Only those earnings withdrawn or received by lenders, shareholders, or owners of an unincorporated business (and not reinvested) would be taxable, and would be reported on the individual tax returns. The "inside build-up" of the saving in saving accounts, brokerage accounts, mutual funds, corporate shares, or unincorporated businesses would not be taxable. There would be no separate calculation of capital gains; they would be covered in the proceeds from the sale of assets (whose full cost was deducted at the time of purchase). The proceeds would remain tax-deferred if reinvested. For example, trades within a brokerage account would not be reportable unless money was withdrawn from the account.

Pension contributions by employers and employees currently excluded from employees' incomes would remain deductible saving. Since all saving could be deducted in this system, all current-law restrictions on the amounts allowed as contributions and withdrawals under employer-sponsored pension plans would be eliminated.

The deduction for saving would be for net saving. Borrowing would be considered "dissaving" and be considered taxable revenue to be netted against amounts saved. However, borrowing would result in an immediate tax liability only if used for consumption. Borrowing used to buy assets such as stocks or a machine for one's business would not result in more taxable income because the investment outlays would be deductible saving. Also, repayment of debt and interest paid on debt would be part of deductible saving. (But see alternative treatments of home purchases, below.)

Each financial institution with which the taxpayer had dealings would report the taxpayer's net saving or dissaving for the year as a single number on a 1099 form, like those currently in use to report interest or dividends on Schedule B. There would be no need for the taxpayer to track all of his or her deposits and withdrawals over the year to calculate the net amount. There would be no separate Schedule D for capital gains.

Deductions of transfers paid. Charitable contributions would be deductible by the donor. (As indicated above, the charitable gifts would be taxable to the ultimate recipient, who would seldom have sufficient income to owe tax. Current law simply allows the charitable deduction and ignores the other side of the calculation.)

All payroll and state and local taxes would be deductible as income over which the taxpayer has lost control and transferred to others. State and local taxes are involuntary outflows. They largely fund welfare and other aid to the poor (income transfers akin to charitable contributions to persons below taxable levels of income) or education (a transfer that pays for the cost of the recipient's acquisition of human capital), all of which could be considered to be reasonable deductions. Law enforcement and fire protection are services to the taxpayer, but constitute remedies for or protection from casualty losses, and ought not to be considered beneficial income. There are some local government services that accrue to the individual taxpayer or homeowner, such as water, sewer, and trash pick-up, but these are often billed separately, in which case they would not be deductible.

Deductions of cost of acquiring human capital. Individuals would deduct some portion of the cost of training and education. Tuition and other training costs are already largely deductible in the form of property taxes at the local level that pay for primary education, and state income taxes that assist state universities. Tuition paid directly by the student could be considered for similar treatment. However, there is also a "consumption" or general living element of education; it is not all a cost of earning future income. Some rough adjustment must be made in what will always be a gray area.

Treatment of home ownership. We do not recommend "pure" inflow-outflow treatment of the owner-occupied home, which would be to treat it (as in the national GDP accounts) as an investment yielding income in the form of shelter. Pure treatment would include the imputed rent from the owner-occupied home in taxable income, plus the mortgage borrowing that financed the home; it would allow a deduction for the purchase price of the home, the repayment of mortgage principal and interest, and outlays on maintenance.

This pure approach to the treatment of owner-occupied homes is difficult to calculate. The alternative approach to neutral treatment of saving—no deduction for the purchase of the asset, but no tax on the returns, is an easier alternative, and the I–O tax would adopt it in this instance. Neither the imputed rent nor the mortgage borrowing would be taken into the homeowner's income. In exchange, there would be no deduction of the purchase of the home, outlays for maintenance, nor repayment of mortgage principal and mortgage interest.

Treatment of businesses. There would be no separate taxation of businesses in a saving-deferred tax. Taxation of business income would be completely "integrated" with the taxation of other income received by the savers, be they corporate shareholders or partners or proprietors of non-corporate businesses. Businesses would be treated like pensions or IRAs owned by the savers: income that individuals transfer to businesses through lending or the purchase of shares would be deductible by the savers; only those business earnings distributed to lenders and shareholders (and not reinvested) would be taxable and would be reported on the individual tax returns. "Inside build-up" of saving in the business would not be taxable.

The non-tax status of business in the inflow-outflow tax is not arbitrary. The rules of the inflow-outflow tax naturally render a business a non-taxable entity. Businesses would not be taxable because their deductible outflows would always equal their inflows.

Business inflows include revenues from sales of goods and services and income on financial investments, plus borrowing from lenders and sales of new shares to stockholders. Business outflows include operating costs—wages, purchases of materials, inventory, outlays on research and development, rent and royalties paid, and all outlays for investment in plant and equipment, structures, and (unlike current law) land—plus state and local taxes and federal payroll taxes, interest payments to lenders and dividend payments to shareholders. These outflows are all costs of earning income or transfers of capital income to lenders and shareholders for taxation on their returns. Any left-over revenues saved by the business should be considered tax-deferred saving by the shareholders. Nothing would remain to be taxed at the business level. Consequently, there would be no need for businesses to file income tax returns, eliminating most of the accounting, auditing, and costs of enforcement and compliance in the current tax system.

In this system, the deduction for business investment would effectively be passed along to the savers who lend money to, buy shares in, or otherwise invest in the business. Savers would fully deduct their purchases of stocks and bonds. These proceeds of stock and bond issues, plus what we now call retained earnings, would just equal the operating costs and (deductible) capital investment and net saving of the business, eliminating taxable business income. This pass-through of the deduction for investment would be an advantage for start-up businesses that have little income as yet from previous investments against which to take a deduction. It effectively eliminates the problem of net operating loss carry forwards that delay and reduce the value of deductions for investment and raise the cost of capital under current law.

Territoriality. The I–O tax would be territorial, imposed on income generated within the United States, not on income earned abroad. There would be no deduction for saving invested abroad, and no tax on the returns. There would be no credit for foreign taxes paid on foreign income repatriated to the United States. Territorial taxation would greatly reduce the confusing treatment of foreign source income that cripples American firms attempting to compete abroad.

The I–O tax would not be "border-adjustable", that is, it would not be forgiven on exports and imposed on imports, because it is collected at the individual level on individual income. The producers of U.S. exports worked and earned their income in the United States, and should be taxed just as all other U.S. producers, while the producers of U.S. imports worked and earned their income abroad, where it is subject to foreign taxes.

Conclusion

The inflow-outflow tax is a neutral, highly visible tax system. It correctly measures income, providing revenue to the government with minimal disruption to the economy. It allocates income for tax purposes, appropriately, to the final recipients of the income, thereby informing the citizen-taxpayer of the tax cost of government. The I–O tax also achieves a significant degree of tax simplification compared to current law, and reduced costs of administration and compliance. The I–O tax achieves these results in a superior fashion compared to most other major tax reform proposals. It is deserving of serious consideration by policy makers and students of political economy.

Form 1040: Individual Tax Form, Inflow-Outflow Tax	
1. Sum of: labor compensation, pension receipts, taxable social security, transfer payments (from W-2 forms)	$33,000
2. Net saving (+) or net withdrawals from saving (-) (from Schedule B)	$3,000
3. If line 2 is net saving (+), subtract the dollar amount from line 1; if line 2 is net withdrawal from saving (-), add the dollar amount to line 1.	$30,000
4. Other itemized deductions from Schedule A	$10,000
5. Subtract line 4 from line 3.	$20,000
6. Personal allowance times number of taxpayers and dependents: $5,000 x _2_ =	$10,000
7. Subtract line 6 from line 5. This is your taxable income.	$10,000
8. Tax from table (or, line 7 times 20%).	$ 2,000
9. Amount withheld, from W-2, plus estimated tax payments.	$ 2,100
10. Amount due (+) or amount overpaid (-) (line 8 less line 9). If amount is due, pay Internal Revenue Service.	- $ 100
11. If overpaid, fill in: Amount to be refunded _$100_ ; or Amount to be applied to estimated tax _____.	

Schedule A: Itemized Deductions	
1. Sum of individual payroll tax (from W-2), state and local income tax withheld (from W-2) and estimated state and local tax less refunds from previous year, and local property taxes.	$ 5,000
2. Gifts, contributions.	$ 1,000
3. Qualified tuition, training expenses.	$ 4,000
4. Total. Enter on Form 1040, line 4.	$10,000

Schedule B: Saving	
List net saving (+) or withdrawals (-) from financial institutions reported on 1099 forms.	
First National Bank	-$1,000
Merrill Paine Schwab	+$4,000
Total (if greater than zero, this is net saving; if less than zero, this is a net withdrawal). Enter on Form 1040, line 2.	$3,000

Mr. CRANE. Are there inquiries of this panel? Mr. Coyne? Mr. English?

Mr. ENGLISH [presiding]. Thank you, Mr. Chairman. I am sorry I wasn't here for the entire testimony, but I did read the written testimony previously, and I must say this is an enormously distinguished panel.

Dr. Regalia, I was particularly intrigued by your comments on border adjustability, and I am especially pleased to see the Chamber's support of border adjustability, given the fact that I sense that the business community is not monolithic on this issue, but your testimony, I think, points the way that, on balance, trade fairness is an important component on tax reform.

Would you care to elaborate on that?

Mr. REGALIA. Well, Congressman English, I think, having worked for the Chamber for seven years, the one thing that I could testify to unequivocally is that the business community is not monolithic on anything, but on the area of border adjustability I think that the recent problems that have occurred with the FSC and with the WTO have heightened the concern of this issue tremendously, and that there is perhaps a greater understanding now of the issues that arise because of a lack of border adjustability, the conflicts between a world-wide tax system and a territorial tax system, and the implications that can have, not just for the businesses that trade directly abroad, but for everyone that deals with those businesses and with businesses that deal with those businesses. It is truly a broad-based economic issue at this point.

I think that the various—I mean, all in the business community are waiting to hear, with bated breath what solutions will be proposed to the current situation, and I think we are heartened to see, in many of the specific tax proposals that are out there, the willingness of all the authors of those proposals to address this problem in a very clear-cut and economically-sound manner.

Mr. ENGLISH. Mr. Entin, I saw you took the contrary position. Given your public policy pedigree, that should give me second thoughts about my own support for border adjustability. Why is it that you feel that taking the tax off of exports, the embedded tax, and placing it on imports tilts the playing field in any way? Doesn't it level it?

Mr. ENTIN. I have discussed territorial tax in my plan, but I haven't specifically stated anything about border adjustability. This has to do with the point of collection.

For example, in your plan you have a business level collection and an individual level collection. Your business level collection is border adjustable. It is natural, when you have taxes on that level, that it be border adjustable. If, however, you are taxing the individual before the individual goes to the store, it is natural for it not to be explicitly border adjustable because the very mechanics of where you have collected it more or less arrive at the same point.

Let me explain that a little bit more clearly.

These taxes are generally taxes on income less saving, which equals consumption, or, if it is at the business level, it is on revenues minus investment, which equals consumption.

To measure consumption by taxing individuals, I want you to take your income, subtract your saving, pay tax on your consumption, then take your after-tax money to go shopping, and when you arrive at the store you may buy a domestic product or an imported product. There is no added tax on either one. I am being neutral.

If, however, I make the individual wait until he goes shopping to take out my tax, he is taking his pre-tax money to the store, and at that point I levy a consumption tax on the sum of his purchases of domestic goods and his purchases of imports. The two together equal, again, the amount he has consumed, and I am taking the exact same tax from the exact same people. So I am being neutral in either case.

Whether something is border adjustable or not in an explicit manner depends on where you have chosen to make the collection point more than on anything else.

Mr. ENGLISH. I guess my concern is, when you show up in a store and there are two products on the shelf and one of them has in the pricing the embedded tax of doing business in the United States and the tax of whatever jurisdiction you are in, and the other item does not have those taxes built in, isn't there at least some price advantage to the foreign-produced product as opposed to the domestically-produced product?

Mr. ENTIN. I don't think so, for three reasons. In the length of time allowed for any response, I am not sure I can go through all three.

Mr. ENGLISH. I am chairing the meeting, so I will give you a little extra time.

Mr. ENTIN. Okay.

Mr. ENGLISH. I am very interested.

Mr. ENTIN. If you are thinking about Europe and its VAT, remember, they have a corporate income tax, a personal income tax, payroll taxes, and VAT. If you take out VAT, what is left is still as big a tax burden as our total tax burden because they tax a lot more than we do, so there are still taxes embedded, if you want to think of it that way, in the imports.

If, however, you take a slightly different look at what is going on in the production process, you have to realize that workers work for an after-tax wage. Let me take two workers. One works for Boeing on planes that are exported, and one works in the corner grocery store and sells to the local population. They both know they are paying tax when they go to the store. When you impose a sales tax or a consumption-based tax, either one, the workers know they are paying tax on what they consume.

Since they want to work for a satisfactory after-tax wage, they have conveyed that attitude toward their employer and they have asked for a wage that reflects the fact that when they go shopping they have to pay tax. And that is as true for the export worker as for the domestic worker. So there are taxes imbedded in exports, even with a border-adjustable tax. All of this stuff gets passed around.

I come back to the basic point I made earlier. If I am taxing an individual's income minus his saving, either before he goes to the store or after he goes to the store, I am probably taking just the same tax liability from the worker under the two systems.

The third point is that exchange rates adjust and washout the effect of border adjustability sooner or later. If you remove the tax on business, that added layer of tax on capital formation that occurs when you tax the corporate level and the individual level, and if you end the bias against saving and investment, then I think we are going to be a lot more competitive because we are going to have so much more investment in plant and equipment in this country we are going to be the more efficient producers of a lot of things.

But suppose we did become the most efficient producers of a lot of things. Would we be running a big trade surplus? No, because for people to be able to buy our goods they would have to sell to us.

The objective of tax reform should be to make us very, very efficient, very productive, and give us very high wages and very high incomes, and that is true whether we were the only country in the world or whether there were other countries with which we were trading across the border.

Mr. ENGLISH. And, Mr. Entin, I have to say on that particular point I entirely agree with you. And this is a side of trade policy that really doesn't get introduced into the debate.

Dr. Regalia, would you like to respond to Mr. Entin's points with regard to border adjustability?

Mr. REGALIA. Well, not having reviewed all of them in detail, I would have to say I think I probably agree with them. I think that the issue of border adjustability comes up more when you have two vastly different tax systems. If you were to institute a truly territorial tax system in the U.S., tax income once and only once, that there would be less of an issue of border adjustability, given the various taxing points.

Mr. ENGLISH. I agree.

Mr. REGALIA. But when we go down the road of two very different tax systems, two very different or multiple collection points, many of which are layered on top of each other, then these issues become much more important.

As you start to correct one issue, I think it helps to correct the other, and I think that I would not disagree.

Mr. ENGLISH. I have one concern on the exchange issue, and I am not sure I can articulate this very well, but I am concerned that the tax burdens fall disproportionately on certain sectors of the economy.

For example, tax differentials have more of an impact on manufacturing and certain kinds of manufacturing than they do on certain kinds of services, and that, whereas much of the economy might not be affected dramatically by the border adjustability issue, I, who represent a largely manufacturing District, still have got to be concerned that manufacturers, where you produce a large volume of products with very thin profit margins, would be particularly sensitive to tax differentials, and the border adjustability argument might be stronger in arguing that this is a policy we need in order to maintain our manufacturing base.

I hope that is an articulate argument. Do you care to react to it? Does that make any sense?

Mr. ENTIN. I think you are right to point out that we have been seeing somewhat of a shift away from manufacturing towards services and that some of the manufacturing industries have appeared to be struggling. That is a valid point.

I think one of the reasons they are struggling, aside from just the general drift of technological advance being stronger in the intellectual property area than in the heavy manufacturing, is that we have a tax bias particularly against heavy manufacturing.

The depreciation allowances that we have in place today are so seriously damaging to investment incentives for long-lived assets, the very sorts of assets that steel and railroads and the manufacturing sector employ, that we put a bias in the economy against producing those goods in this country and in favor of importing them.

If you move to any of the consumption-based taxes, where business investment is expensed rather than depreciated and where the corporate tax layer is stripped off, you would be moving to a system where the change from current law is greatest for those heavily-impacted sectors. I think they would improve more than the other sectors under this type of tax reform. That may solve your problem.

Mr. ENGLISH. That is an interesting argument.

One of the common points I have seen between a number of leading tax reform proposals—Mr. Armey's flat tax, for example—I have a simplified USA tax. One of the common points is moving to expensing as an alternative to depreciation.

Would both of you agree that this expensing issue may be probably one of the most important things we do from a competitive and growth standpoint in tax reform?

Mr. REGALIA. I would think it would, and I also think it is going to be one of the areas that require the most innovation when it comes to transition rules because of the relationship between old capital and new capital.

Mr. ENGLISH. That is right.

Mr. REGALIA. And when you are disadvantaging—when old capital is so disadvantaged, if you were then to remove those impediments to the new capital, you would create a situation where you could significantly impair the ability of the older firm to grow, and I think it is one of the areas that is most important.

I look through much of the testimony the last couple of days and almost everybody mentioned—the savings and investment disincentives in our current code—one of the primary things that you want to fix, and it is one of the most—as I said, it will require the most innovation in constructing transition rules to address that.

Mr. ENGLISH. I have always adhered to the radical thesis that the savings rates would be affected by changes in tax policy. Do all three of you agree with that?

Mr. REGALIA. I think, contrary to a long bit of what I have read in economic theory, I think, in practice, I would have to say yes, I think that it would affect the savings rates, and I think that while we empirically have been unable to verify that it is a result of the fact that we are drawing our sample from a system that has had this corruption for years and years and years, and so the data is unable to tell us the real answer.

I think it would make a difference. I think we saw that with IRAs. Originally, when I worked at the Federal Reserve Board, we contended that IRAs would change how you saved but not how much you saved, and I think we have seen over the years that even the very small IRAs that we have allowed have probably boosted savings more than any of us thought early on, and that after an initial phase we would have to say the switching was minimal and the amount of net new savings was more than we had anticipated, and I think that would be proven for fundamental innovations to the tax code, as well, that we would improve savings more than any of our economic models would lead us to believe.

Mr. ENGLISH. Ms. Soldano, any comment?

Ms. SOLDANO. Congressman English, our issue is death tax only. It is the only thing that our organization focuses on.

Mr. ENGLISH. Okay. And I agree with your position and I recommend to you the writings of one of my constituents, Professor Hans Senhold, who is retired from Grove City College, whose book, "Death and Taxes," is still the most succinct argument and one of the best for repealing the tax.

Ms. SOLDANO. I agree.

Mr. ENGLISH. Mr. Entin?

Mr. ENTIN. One reason that economists have failed to understand the effect of the tax burden on saving is that they got mixed up between levels of saving and the rate of saving.

If saving goes up, the level of saving goes up, incomes rise, and, as incomes rise, so does consumption. Both saving and consumption tend to rise. The saving rate as a percent of the higher income may not be much higher, but the level of saving is going to be a great deal higher under these tax systems, and for some years the rate will be higher, as well.

I think economists got confused between levels and rates, and a lot of the people who said that better tax treatment of saving would not be a significant incentive are simply mistaken. You would see a result.

Mr. ENGLISH. Doctor?

Mr. REGALIA. I was just going to say one of the most, I think, interesting aspects of the simplified USA tax is the deduction for investment in human capital, not just physical capital. In today's economy, there is a whole theory of economics on endogenous growth theory that speaks to this issue of saving rate and growth rates in the economy versus levels of savings and level of growth in the economy.

I think that one of the things we are beginning to see is that the new economy, the information age, if you will, which uses and relies so heavily on intelligence, training, human capital attributes will find that the benefits to increasing our human capital may exceed even the benefits from increasing our fiscal capital, and I think that is a very innovative and important aspect of some of these proposals that are outstanding right now.

Mr. ENGLISH. Thank you. I think not only is it good economics, but it is also good as a selling point for the plan.

I want to thank all three of you for participating today. I have just had an experience similar to what Mr. Archer had on a November morning in 1994. I have awakened to discover myself chairing the Ways and Means Committee, so I want to take this opportunity to adjourn.

Thank you very much.

[Whereupon, at 2:14 p.m., the hearing was adjourned.]

[Submissions for the record follow:]

Statement of Charles Adams, Historian, Williamsville, NY

Mr. Chairman and Members of the Committee:

The economics of our income tax is under assault by some of our best economists and tax men, and for good reason. We have learned much about how best to tax to collect public revenues. The clear consensus of the unbiased economic studies demonstrate our income and payroll taxes are a drag on the economy, slow economic growth, produce chronic inflation, discourage savings and enterprise, and put America at some disadvantage in world trade with those nations, especially the miracle economies, who have moderate, simpler tax systems-systems that encourage and promote capitalism.

Our criticism should not stop there, however. While there is just about nothing right with our current system economically-speaking, not everything wrong with our current system has to do with relatively recent science of economics. Instead, it has to do with the spiritual values that were at the core of the founding of America. The current system denigrates these values in several respects. It has trampled on our liberties, it is wasteful, and it is destructive of economic and personal rights.

A national sales tax, if it replaced the income tax, would rid the nation of the evils our income tax has produced. It will also comply with the Constitutional command of uniformity. If we were to pursue this course, our descendants in centuries to come would look back upon us, as we look back upon our Founders, with admiration for delivering future generations from a tax that was oppressive, tyrannical, and corrupt.

Let us place the current tax system in historical context. We do not need to go too far for our research. Adam Smith in *The Wealth of Nations,* sets forth four signs of a bad tax system:

• a large bureaucracy for administration.
• a system that puts taxpayers through "odious examinations...and exposes them to much unnecessary trouble, vexation, and oppression."
• a system that encourages evasion.
• a system that obstructs the industry of the people, and discourages enterprise which might otherwise give "employment to great multitudes," i.e. jobs.[34]

How well has our tax system adhered to the admonitions of Adam Smith? Does it pass Adam Smith's test for a bad tax system? The answer is clearly "yes." His test defines our system today. The FairTax national sales tax would return us to these core values that have stood the test of time.

Looking at a Distant Mirror

Taxes were at the core of the world's great uprisings. And taxes and the onerous methods of collecting them were at the core of the founding of America.

The Statue of Liberty was a gift from the French to commemorate the 100 year anniversary of American independence. She stands at the entrance to New York's harbor as an inspiration to the nation and the millions of immigrants who arrived from Europe by ship before the jetage, "yearning to breath free." She was really a gift from the Romans. The same Goddess of Liberty was depicted on Roman coins, just like she was on our gold coins and early 50's piece; she was honored with a number of temples, and Roman writers proclaimed, "Liberty is a possession on which no evaluation can be placed," and "Freedom is beloved above all things."[1] Yet the coins and temples disappeared almost 200 years before Rome's official demise when the Emperor Diocletian enslaved the Roman people to ensure tax compliance, and he achieved this end by chaining every taxpayer to his land, shop, or job. One leading Roman historian acknowledged that Diocletian's tax system did indeed save Rome, but he never asked "whether it was worth while to save the Roman Empire in order to make a vast prison for scores of millions of men. "[2]

The Romans did not submit to this tax enslavement without resistance, so the Roman state resorted to brutal, savage punishments. Zisimos, a Greek writer during this period, tells us that the scourge and rack were used against taxpayers; and to make the system work, fathers were compelled to prostitute their daughters, and even children were sold into slavery.[3] As one Roman declared, "Let us flee to some place where we may live as free men."[4]

This viciousness of the Roman state towards its citizen taxpayers is what we need to focus upon, because it soon infected the relation of the people with one another. Salvian, the Bishop of Marseilles at Rome's fall, describes the evil, the decadence and cruelty that the tax system had created. As he said, any individual with any sense of human decency would seek out another homeland.[5] "Rome was like a mother cancer cell that passed its vicious propensities on to its children."[6]

A similar pattern appeared in Imperial Spain a thousand years later. Spain, like Rome, taxed itself to death. To enforce a similarly abusive, excessive tax system,

350

Spain fell back on "applying the screw" to reluctant taxpayers.[7] "Applying the screw" was not a figure of speech, like the Roman scourge it was an instrument of torture. Unlike Rome Spanish taxpayer resistance was disastrous for the state. Over six major tax revolts erupted during the height of Spain's glory and there is little doubt these revolts drained the strength of the Crown and permitted Britain, France, and the Netherlands to take over much of what was the greatest empire of all time.

Spanish taxpayers responded with the same brutality meted out by the tax bureau. In 1520, taxpayer deputies, summoned by the Crown, promised their constituents there would be "no new taxes." However, the financial goodies promised by the king were too tempting so they voted for new taxes. Riots erupted throughout Spain. In Segovia, an angry mob seized the local deputy and as they led him off for execution, his plea to receive the last sacraments was denied-there was to be no forgiveness in this life nor the life to come. I wonder, what would these angry taxpayers have done to members of Congress who approved Clinton's taxes? Or to George Bush who breached his promise of "no new taxes?"

The response of Spanish taxpayers included evasion and emigration. The Spanish operated the most massive system of tax fraud and evasion ever known, notwithstanding that the Crown threatened evaders with the death penalty. All trade from the New World was engaged in one gigantic smuggling operation. If that wasn't enough, people fled from Spain in great numbers. As one historian observed, "In place of wondering at the depopulation of villages and farms, the wonder is that any of them remain."[8]

The use of cruel and savage punishments to enforce taxes has repeated itself often throughout the course of Western history. In France a hundred years of violence against taxpayers and even tax collectors, culminated in the French Revolution in which the tax man came out on the short end-indeed, the whole lot of them were shortened about 10 to 12 inches apiece after the man who ran the guillotine had finished his work-no tears were shed when their heads flopped into the basket.

In the 18th Century, Sir Robert Walpole, Britain's first prime minister, used "vicious punishments" to enforce his tax system. He was, as one biography described him, "In no way squeamish about the liberties of the individual," and he used "savage punishments, and the full authority of the Crown to make the public conform to his system [of taxes]." Eventually, riots spread throughout Britain, as an "expression of a profound and cumulative hatred of a system oppressive, tyrannical, and corrupt [with power]."[9] When Sir William Blackstone wrote his great treatise (still in print), *Commentaries on the Laws of England* (1765), there was no praise for Walpole's tax enforcements, they were "arbitrary" and "hardly compatible with the temper of a free nation."[10] That same condemnation would easily apply to our income tax laws today. It was less than 25 years after the riots in Britain over Walpole's tax laws that the British colonists in North America sensed the same sort of tax policy coming their way, and they were willing to resort to violence and even treason against the Crown's taxes.

The Founders of America were well aware of the history summarized above. The great sage of the Enlightenment, Montesquieu, in his *The Spirit of Laws* (1751), inspired the Framers of the Constitution, and much of its form can be traced to this great book. He was a tax-philosopher historian. If our current tax makers and we as a people had been schooled in his studies, as the Framers of our Constitution were schooled, we may not be having the tax troubles that now infect our whole social order. He taught emphatically that excessive taxation produces slavery; noting that men living in a liberty oriented society will foolishly submit to excessive taxation. He added a further observation, that excessive taxes will require, "extraordinary means of oppression." And from that, "the country is ruined."[11] This conclusion of Montesquieu was not a theory, it was plainly visible to him as a fact in the governments of his day and of those in history. With Montesquieu we are not dealing with logic, we are dealing with what Oliver Wendell Holmes had in mind when he said, "A page of history is worth a volume of logic."[12]

The leading writer for the American Revolution was Thomas Paine. "Without the pen of Paine, " said John Adams in poetic rhyme, "Washington would have wielded his sword in vain." Washington had Paine's pamphlets distributed to his troops to read when they were in Winter Quarters during the dark days of the war. America was a land of liberty, wrote Paine, because it was a land of low taxes. Excessive taxes produced tyranny, he wrote, caused by the foolish and naive attitude of the people toward their government by believing that "government is some wonderful mysterious thing." And when the people believe that illusion, "excessive revenues are obtained."[13]

What drove men to revolution was simply overtaxing and overblown governments. In short, when a government is just, "taxes are few." And revolution was necessary and justified to bring about a government "less expensive and more productive," which would bring about "peace, civilization and commerce. "[14]

Direct Taxes: the Most Burdensome Type

The most pernicious of all taxes are the arbitrary," said David Hume, the great Scottish philosopher, "They are commonly converted, by their management, into punishments on industry...It is surprising, therefore, to see them have place among any civilized people."[24] Alexander Hamilton, a leading proponent of the Constitution who favored broad taxing powers, had no use for arbitrary taxes. "Whatever liberty we may boast of in theory, it cannot exist in fact while [arbitrary] assessments continue."[25]

The Framers of the Constitution thought they had provided against any arbitrariness in taxation by commanding that all tax laws be UNIFORM, i.e. the same for all. But the uniformity command disappeared in the 20th century when the justices who upheld this condition, all died and were replaced with justices willing to make that provision an "empty shell" as legal scholars have described the present state of affairs.[26] The Congress can now adopt abusive, discriminatory, arbitrary taxation to the extreme, thus fulfilling James Madison's fear expressed in *The Federalist*, No. 10;

Yet there is, perhaps, no legislative act in which greater opportunity and temptation are given to a predominant party to trample on the rules of justice. Every shilling with which they overburden the inferior number is a shilling saved to their own pockets.

Madison concluded by arguing that "The Majority...must be rendered unable to concert and carry into effect schemes of oppression." The Constitutional command of uniformity for all taxation was one means to achieve that end, but once the Court made that command an "empty shell" the U.S. Congress has with impunity "trampled on the rules of justice," with tax rates deliberately made unequal, and with exemptions and other tax favors for the best lobbyists, just as Madison had predicted.

Besides the disastrous consequences of both arbitrary taxation and excessive taxation, Montesquieu focused on another archenemy of liberty-direct taxation, which he described as being "natural to slavery, " unlike indirect taxes, or a "duty on merchandise is more natural to liberty, because it is not so direct a relation to the person."[27]

This observation was over two thousand years old. The Greeks discovered it by observing the many empires of the world—all were despotic, tyrannies. And all had direct forms of taxation, like wealth taxes, income or production taxes, poll taxes, and the like. The Greeks concluded, tyranny was the consequence of direct taxation. Except in times of war, direct taxes must be avoided if liberty is to be preserved.

Cicero, the great Roman lawyer, also condemned direct taxes as a danger to Roman liberty. He said:

Every effort must be made to prevent a repetition of this [direct taxes]; and all possible precaution must be taken to ensure that such a step will never be needed...But if any government should find it necessary to levy a direct tax, the utmost care has to be devoted to making it clear to the entire population that this simply has to be done because no alternative exists short of complete national collapse.[28]

Why, you may ask, is direct taxation so bad? Why did the Greeks and Romans have so much contempt and hatred for what we have lived under most of this century? They came to this conclusion from history. They saw the tax system of the Pharaohs of Egypt and the enormous oppressive bureaucracy the Pharaohs maintained to collect taxes; they may also have noticed that no word even exists in the Egyptian languages that means freedom or liberty. Freedom and liberty just didn't exist where direct taxes were in operation. In the past century, with the income tax, the people of America have seen their liberties slip away, one by one, year in and year out. Even in the socalled protaxpayer Reagan years, the power of the IRS over everyone's life increased dramatically. Over 150 penalties were put in operation to increase the tax, almost double the tax, for the slightest slipup by the taxpayer. Reagan and the Congress of his era may have reduced rates, but they increased IRS muscle in the process. Their process of ever increasing powers, creating a musclebound bureaucracy, reminiscent of so many ugly tax bureaucracies of the past, is what the Greeks and the Founders were warning us about.

This concept did not go unnoticed by the Framers nor by Montesquieu. At the Constitutional convention, Madison echoed the Greeks on the matter of direct taxes. He said, almost as a matter of fact, they would only be introduced during an "extraordinary emergency."[29] It was inconceivable they would ever be a permanent, peacetime measure, for the reasons both Montesquieu and the ancient Greeks propounded.

What was inconceivable then, has not been inconceivable in the 20th century. We have made direct taxation the order of the day and we have reconfirmed, for future generations, that the Greeks were right. Direct taxes do produce tyranny. When the *Readers' Digest* wrote a series on the abuses of power by the IRS, they entitled the series, "The Tyranny of the IRS." Unlike wise men, we have had to learn from history the hard way-by reliving what others warned us about.

One of the high points in Thomas Paine's life was his arrest and charge of seditious libel while in Britain. The charge came about because of his book, *The Age of Reason,* in which he condemned kingships, especially Britain. To his defense came one of the world's greatest lawyers, Thomas Erskine. He paid dearly for the defense of Paine, having been dismissed by the King from his post as AttorneyGeneral. The following is taken from his speech in 1792, which seems to explain how our liberties have been lost to enforce our income tax system.

...arbitrary power has seldom or never been introduced into any country at once. It must be introduced by slow degrees, and as it were step by step, lest the people see its approach. The barriers and fences of the people's liberty must be plucked up one by one, and some plausible pretenses must be found for removing or hoodwinking, one after another, those sentries who are posted by the constitution of a free country, for warning the people of their danger.[30]

Our Current Tax System: Vexatious, Odious, Heavy and Direct

Let us leave the past and the Founders and see what shadows of the past are cast upon us with our income tax.

Are our taxes arbitrary? There never was a tax law more arbitrary than our current income taxes. In the 1950's, Congress decided that the top bracket should be 91%; Kennedy thought 70%; Reagan 28%; and Clinton wants to jack it back up to around 40%. And as for exemptions, tax credits, and other tax goodies, they vary from legislature to legislature-arbitrariness to the utmost extreme making a field day for tax lobbyists and a joy to the tax makers on the Ways and Means Committee.

Are our taxes direct? Today we have nothing but direct taxes, which make everyone both a tax collector and a taxpayer. The IRS with more than 112,000 employees it largest tax bureaucracy in the world since ancient Rome. Its tentacles reach out and have hold on more than 200 million people.

In the 1950s it was routine for an IRS agent to begin his audit by telling the taxpayer, "Ours is an honor system, which is the only way it will work in a free society." Supreme Court Justice Jackson, a former chief counsel for the IRS, said at this time that instances of selfserving mistakes and outright evasion were rare-and that was at a time when the infamous "Information" returns were nonexistent.[15] Banks did not report anything to the IRS about the affairs of their customers. Nothing that went through a bank account was photographed and held in storage for Big Brother to see. Interest income was not reported; dividends were not reported; real estate transactions and income was not reported; stock transactions were not reported; income from independent workers was not reported. Only wages were reported and that was done to enable workers to file for a tax refund. U.S. Customs did not demand to know how much money or travelers checks you were carrying, nor did they punish and confiscate amounts in your possession which were unreported. The tax system was an honor system, and it worked.

The danger that income taxes may produce a massive espionage system and destroy much of the liberty of the people was a distinct possibility at the time America adopted its first income tax. Even the experts were aware of the risk, but they were quick to argue it would not be a possibility with the long traditions of freedom of the American people. The danger became apparent because of the income tax system in Prussia, which, according to one German legislator who opposed the system, covered the country with "a perfect system of espionage.[17] In an income tax audit, a taxpayer who was involved with securities, would be asked "How many stocks did you sell this year? On what day and at what exchange did you sell them? What is the price of each? What is the name of each company in which you have securities?" This was considered oppressive, the "espionage" that income tax advocates in America in 1914, assured the people, would never happen here.

We have also have had to resort to savage punishments to make the income tax system work. Backing up the espionage is the fear of punishment—severe, long term prison terms which hang over the heads of all taxpayers. Every March and April prosecutions are published as front page items, to put terror and to intimidate every taxpayer as the tax return season is in full force.

Some punitive measures are, at times necessary for tax enforcement, but have we gone too far? Are we outofstep with a free society? With the rest of Western civilization? Outside of the former Soviet Union no nation treats its tax offenders with such harshness.

The destruction of these values by our income tax would come as no surprise if, in our education, we had learned that most great empires taxed themselves to death, spiritually as well as economically. The Founders as well as the ancient Greeks and Romans warned future generations about the tyranny that would befall any nation that adopted a tax system like we have endured. Their words speak from the past, like the ancient prophets from Biblical times.

The evolution of our direct income tax system from an honor to a spy system has taken almost 50 years, in slow degrees, "as it were step by step," under plausible pretenses used to hoodwink the sentries "posted by the constitution," i.e., the Supreme Court decisions, like *Boyd v. United States,* a tax case which declared unconstitutional a statute that gave the revenue bureaucracy the power to order a taxpayer to bring in his books and records for examination. Said the Court:

And any compulsory discovery by extorting a party's oath, or compelling the production of his private books and papers, to convict him of a crime or to forfeit his property, is contrary to the principles of a free government. It is abhorrent to the instincts of an Englishman; it is abhorrent to the instincts of an American. It may suit the purposes of despotic power; but it cannot abide the pure atmosphere of political liberty or personal freedom.[31]

That was in 1885. The case has been cited over 3000 times. Finally, in 1983 it took a the Supreme Court acknowledge that the Court had "sounded the death knell for Boyd."[32] Year in and year out, with each new piece of tax legislation, the IRS has been given increasing powers to spy, punish and intimidate taxpayers on a level associated with a totalitarian state. The Supreme Court, like Pontius Pilate, had the duty to prevent this abuse of power-but like Pilate, the justices have washed their hands before the multitude.[33]

Finally, not long ago on the MacNeilLehrer news hour on PBS, an essayist was finishing what would otherwise have been a fine talk, except he concluded his remarks with an assertion I have heard frequently since early grammar school days- "America is the freest country in the world." That may have been true in times past, but it is not true today, not by a long shot. There are many countries in the free world that grant their citizens far greater freedoms than we enjoy in America. Not only are we slipping to some degree in world commerce, we have slipped a great deal more in matters of liberty and freedom. And the reason? Our income tax and our government's zeal to enforce it at all costs, including our liberty if it gets in the way. As a free nation, we are a third string operation, thanks to our tax system.

How Does the FairTax Address these Problems if the Direct Tax?

What needs to be done to restore our leadership and ranking among free nations? The answer is easier than you may think. We need to go back to our roots, to the ideals and passion for liberty that was the driving force behind the formation of this nation. The Founders had no use for direct taxation as a permanent revenue device. They believed, as did the ancient Greeks and Romans, that it was a great danger to liberty. They were right and we are living proof of how right they were.

Without an income tax there would be no need to photograph everything going through your bank account; no need for your bank to notify the government about your cash account or other financial dealings; no need for your interest, dividends, stock sales, real estate transactions, and baby sitters to be reported to Big Brother. No need for Customs to search travelers to make sure they were not carrying too much money with them; no need for judicial terrorism, savage punishments, and psychopathic judges. The laundry list of government intrusions would be minimal. In one fell swoop, the totalitarian muscle behind our tax system would disappear.

1. Justinian Digest, L.xvii; Naphtali Lewis and Meyer Reinhold, ed., *Roman Civilization, Sourcebook II, The Empire* (New York, 1966) p. 539

2. M. Rostovtzeff, *The Social and Economic History of the Roman Empire* I (Oxford, 1971) p. 53132.

3. Salvian, *On the Government of God,* ed. Eva M. Sanford (New York, 1930) pp. 141–49

4. Rostovtzeff, *Roman Empire,* I. p. 398

5. Ferdinand Lot, *The End of the Ancient World and the Beginning of the Middle Ages* (New York, 1961) p. 175

6. Charles Adams, *For Good and Evil: The Impact of Taxes on the Course of Civilization* (Lanham, MD, 1993) ch. 11

7. *ibid.,* p. 187

8. Martin Hume, *Spain, Its Greatness and Decay (1479–1788)* (Cambridge, 1898) p. 221

9. J. H. Plumb, *Sir Robert Walpole,* vol. 2 (Clifton, NJ, 1973) p. 238–39

10. William Blackstone, *Commentaries on the Laws of England* vol. I (London, 1765), ch. 8, p. 308

11. Baron de Montesquieu, *The Spirit of Laws,* vol. 1 (Dublin, 1751) Book XIII, ch. 8, p. 261

12. New York Trust Co. v. Eisner, 256 U.S. 345, 349 (1921)

13. Thomas Paine, *The Rights of Man* (Pelican, N.Y., 1969) p. 206

14. *The Writings of Thomas Paine,* vol. III (New York, 1906) pp. 81, 183, 189

15. Gerald Carson, *The Golden Egg* (Boston, 1977) p. 252

16. D. Saunders, ed., *The Portable Gibbon, The Decline and Fall of the Roman Empire,* (New York, 1973) p. 375

17. Edwin Seligman, *The Income Tax* (New York, 1914) p. 264

18. *ibid.* pp. 27172

19. Diogenes, *The April Game* (Chicago, 1973) pp. 12021

20. Thomas Paine, "Dissertation on the First Principles of Government," *Common Sense and Other Political Writings* (New York, 1953) p. 174

21. Blackstone, *Commentaries,* I, 307

22. Adam Smith, *The Wealth of Nations* (Harvard Classics, 1909) p. 563

23. See Adams, For Good and Evil, p. 386

24. David Hume, *The Philosophical Works,* vol. 3 (London, 1882) pp. 35660

25. Harold Syvelt, ed., *The Papers of Alexander Hamilton* vol. III (New York, 1962) p. 104

26. "The Uniformity Clause," 51 *U. of Chicago Law Review* 1193 (Chicago, 1984); 44 *Tax Law Review* 563 (New York, 1989)

27. Montesquieu, *Spirit of Laws* I, Bk. XIII, ch. 14, p. 266

28. Cicero, *On Duties* Il; see Cicero, *On the Good Life,* trans. Michael Grant (New York, 1971) p. 162

29. James Madison, *Records of the Debates in the Federal Convention of 1787, Documents Illustrative of the Formation of the Union of the Amerlcan States* (Government Printing Office, Washington, 1927) p.

30. James L. High, ed., *Speeches of Lord Erskine,* vol. 1(Chicago, 1876) p. 536; also found in 22 How St. Tr. 358, 443 (1792)

31. Boyd. United States, 116 U.S. 616, 63132 (1885)

32. United States v. Doe, 464 U.S. 606, 618 (1984)

33. Matt. 27:24

34. Smith, *Wealth of Nations,* p. 500

Statement of W. Henson Moore, American Forest & Paper Association

Mr. Chairman and Members of the Ways and Means Committee, I am very pleased to have the opportunity to address this Committee concerning the issue of fundamental tax reform.

The American Forest and Paper Association (AF&PA) is the national trade association representing producers of paper, pulp, paperboard and wood products, as well as growers and harvesters of this nations forest resources. As President and CEO of AF&PA, I see evidence on a daily basis of how the U.S. tax code negatively impacts the forest products industry as we compete in the global economy.

The members of AF&PA encompass the full spectrum of US businesses. They range from large integrated corporate operations to small private tree farms long held within a family. All our members are dedicated to business practices that foster responsible environmental stewardship at home and abroad. Many of our members, large and small, strive to maintain a competitive presence in the global market.

As good as our economy is, the provisions of the current tax code are a major obstacle to a level playing field between the U.S. forest products industry and our competitors around the world. Our taxes are higher than those of competing nations. When added to trade barriers to exports of our products, the US worldwide system of taxation functions as a major obstacle to competition.

We are fortunate in this country to possess vast forest resources that have actually been growing over time. Our nation's 500 million acres of timberland contain over 36% more wood fiber today than they did fifty years ago despite continuously growing demand. Unfortunately, in recent years, a greater proportion of our national wood and paper needs have been supplied not from our own industry, but from imports.

The importance of our forest products industry is reflected not only in our record of environmental stewardship but also in the fact that we supply more than $230 billion to the nations gross domestic product; we rank sixth among domestic manufacturing sectors. We employ 1.5 million people and rank among the top ten manufacturing employers in 46 states. The forest products industry represents more than seven percent of U.S. manufacturing output, and provides a basic renewable resource that supports a unique and vital forest-based economy.

However, the U.S. forest products industry faces serious international competitive threats, particularly from countries where new capacity growth exports are not taxed and where forestry, labor and environmental regulatory requirements are not as strict as those in the United States.

Our industry has an enviable environmental record. Members of AF&PA subscribe to the *Sustainable Forestry Initiative*, a program that assures the practice of sustainable forestry through the perpetual growing and harvesting of trees while protecting wildlife, plants, soil and water quality. However, unless we can improve the investment climate for forestry in our own country, more trees will be grown and harvested in other countries, many of which have less environmentally sensible practices than we do in the US. Improvements in our tax system will be beneficial not only to U.S. workers and U.S. companies—they will support U.S. environmental goals as well.

Our industry is one of the most capital intensive industries in the world. For the last 10 years, the pulp and paper industry has been the most capital-intensive sector in the United States. Extensive capital requirements for environmental protection cost 13 percent of the capital investment. This percentage is expected to more than double in the coming five years.

Unfortunately, the US tax system discourages investment by the domestic forest products industry. Moreover, competing countries are using their tax codes to foster the growth of the industry, benefiting non-US competitors. Our US tax system raises greater disincentives to corporate investment in manufacturing and corporate forestry activities than that of any major competitor country. Our effective corporate tax rate is the second highest among these competing countries. Corporate capital gains are taxed at higher effective rates in the US than in most competitor countries. And even within the U.S., the identical asset—timber—is taxed as widely disparate rates, creating disincentives for holding timber in corporate form.

And it is not much better for our members who operate their businesses in the non-corporate form. Some 9.9 million private individuals and firms own over 390 million acres of forestland in the United States. It typically takes anywhere between 30 and 80 years to grow and nurture trees before they can be harvested and converted to useful products. To make and maintain investments in forestry necessitates tax treatment that recognizes the long-term nature of growing trees. Under the current tax system that excludes capital gains treatment for corporations and imposes onerous passive loss rules on individuals, the effective tax rates for forestry investments are a disincentive to domestic investment. I don't believe we should be sending investment and jobs overseas, not when we have immense unrealized opportunities at home.

Passive loss limitations intensify the capital drain during the long period of growth of trees. These rules force many landowners to carry these costs until they have a timber sale, instead of deducting these costs annually. For some landowners, these passive loss provisions require landowners to carry these expenses for more than 25 years.

US estate tax laws, with rates as high as 55%, force many who inherit family-owned tree farms either to sell these properties for commercial development, or to prematurely cut their trees in order to pay the tax bill.

Our association has not endorsed any specific tax reform proposal. We applaud efforts to simplify our US tax structure. The real question is how to get there from here. In the end, any system of taxation is a formula. The preference for one tax system or formula over others is dependent on what is included in the tax base and where the rate of taxation is set. The other important element of any new system will be whether the transition rules necessary if we move to a new tax base enable taxpayers to make the transition gradually and in a way that is perceived to be economically fair.

Our industry supports the work of the committee in setting out to reform the tax code and to institute a system that is fairer and simpler for the American taxpayer. As this effort moves forward, we will work with you to accomplish those goals and to assure that any new tax system supports U.S. workers and companies in our efforts to remain successful in increasingly global markets.

Statement of American Petroleum Institute, Michael Platner, Washington, DC

INTRODUCTION

Background

This testimony is submitted by the American Petroleum Institute (API) for inclusion in the printed record of the April 1 1, 12 and 13, 2000, Ways and Means hearings on fundamental tax reform proposals introduced since the last set of hearings on the subject in 1997. API represents more than 400 companies involved in all aspects of the oil and gas industry, including exploration, production, transportation, refining, and marketing .

Several new consumption tax proposals have been introduced recently as complete substitutes for the current federal income tax system. This statement will focus on the business tax aspects of 1) the Simplified USA Tax Act ("USA Tax") offered by Rep. English; 2) the Fair Tax Act, or national sales tax ("NST"), offered by Reps. Linder and Peterson; and 3) a European-style credit-invoice value added tax ("CIVAT"). API takes no position at this time as to whether the current income tax system should be completely replaced, but there is no doubt that as presently codified, it imposes wasteful and unnecessary burdens on the economy. We commend the Committee and the sponsors of these and previous proposals for their efforts to improve our tax system and for moving toward the taxation of consumption rather than the taxation of income.

Problems with Current Income Tax System

Over the years, changes to the Internal Revenue Code ("Code") and accompanying regulations have created the most complex income tax system in the world. Because of this complexity, unreasonable compliance and collection costs (both to the government and to taxpayers) impair the efficiency of the system; obscure or conflicting aspects of the Code and regulations fail to operate as intended; and administrative implementation of complex provisions often takes years, creating long periods of uncertainty for taxpayers as to their tax obligations.

The current income tax system is biased against savings and investment, and in favor of consumption. Income generated by corporations is taxed twice. For example, in the case of a dividend, once when the income from which the dividend is generated is earned and again when the dividend is received by the shareholder. Moreover, because recovery of capital costs is spread over time there is effectively a tax on the capital investment itself.

Our income tax system is neither "territorial" nor "border adjustable." Therefore, it does not allow domestic and foreign produced goods' to compete on an equal basis in domestic or foreign markets. Rather, the U.S. foreign tax system acts to inhibit American competitiveness. U.S. corporations are taxed on worldwide income, while many foreign corporations are not. U.S. anti-tax deferral rules are the most restrictive in the world; unnecessarily complicated mechanics of the foreign tax credit limitation further reduce the effectiveness of the credit as to a means to avoid double taxation; and the volume and frequency of changes in the foreign tax area continue to add compliance costs and destabilize the ability of U.S. businesses to compete worldwide.

Most of our trading partners have some form of value added tax ("VAT")—almost exclusively a CIVAT-that permits the tax, under the rules of the World Trade Organization ("WTO"), to be rebated on exports. Our income tax cannot be rebated on our exported goods (domestically produced goods must bear the imbedded costs of our income tax as well as local taxes imposed in foreign markets), while goods imported into the United States do not bear the VAT imposed in their country of origin. Attempts to remedy this disparity in the tax treatment of U.S. versus foreign exporters within the confines of the current U.S. tax system have been mostly unsuccessful. The recent decision of the WTO, which held that certain tax breaks offered to U.S. foreign sales corporations ("FSCs") constituted illegal export subsidies, only served to highlight the difficulty in preserving the global competitiveness of U.S. businesses under our income tax system. Whatever comes out of this tax reform process should have as one of its goals enhancing the ability of U.S. companies to compete internationally.

Guiding Principles in a Properly Designed Tax System

In general, API believes that properly designed consumption taxes are preferable to income taxes. In studying consumption taxes over a number of years, we have developed a set of principles by which we evaluate alternative consumption tax proposals. They include the following:

• Minimize economic distortions;
• Ensure that foreign and domestically produced goods compete equally in the marketplace;
• Permit the current deduction of capital expenditures;
• Impose only one rate or as few rates as possible;
• Facilitate recovery of taxes in the marketplace;
• Exclude from the base separately stated excise taxes, including sales and use taxes, royalty payments to federal and state governments, and non-cash exchanges;
• Be relatively easy to comply with and administer; and
• Make the tax rate or amount of tax clear to the ultimate consumer.

Concerns with Changing to a New Tax System

While we are supportive in principle of moving towards the taxation of consumption, we urge the Committee to proceed with caution. Because the income tax has been embedded in our economy for more than eighty years, business decisions have been, and continue to be, premised on economic assumptions spawned by that system. Therefore, any radical change will have profound implications on business structure, business financing, and business operations themselves, and these implications must be thoroughly understood before moving to any new system. This is especially true in the capital intensive oil and gas industry, where the results of decisions may take a decade or more to manifest themselves.

For example, the tax treatment of imports of all basic commodities for further manufacturing will have significant ripple effects on the economy. Because more than half of the crude oil used in the United States is imported, this issue is of major concern to our industry. One of the proposals, the Simplified USA Tax Act, imposes a nondeductible import tax that would increase the price of energy to consumers. We believe that any import tax should be imposed in a manner that is designed to put the new tax system in parity with the VATs of our trading partners.

In order to survive, our industry must operate where we have access to economically recoverable oil and gas reserves. Since the opportunity for domestic reserve replacement has been substantially foreclosed by both federal and state government policy, the tax treatment of international operations is critical to our continued ability to supply the nation's hydrocarbon energy needs. In addition, since our industry's projects require large amounts of capital and are high risk, long lead-time ventures, the tax treatment of the financing and structuring of these ventures is an essential element of decisions whether to proceed. We are concerned about the impact of these proposals on our access to efficient sources of capital, whether through traditional capital markets or through partnerships, joint ventures, or other business structures.

Not only must the federal tax implications of any proposal be considered, but state tax integration, U.S. financial accounting treatment, and securities market effects must also be thoroughly understood. Finally, consideration must be given to the United States' role in the global economy. A unilateral change in the basic taxation of inbound and outbound transactions by the United States will require that new treaties be negotiated in order to maintain the protections afforded U.S. companies by the current income tax treaty system. These protections include: elimination of double taxation due to overlapping exercise of authority; facilitation of business transactions between countries that might otherwise be inhibited by overly intrusive national taxation; reduction of high rate withholding taxes imposed by many countries on payments to foreigners of items such as dividends, interest, rents and royalties; and other provisions designed to lessen the burden on international commerce of varying national taxation systems.

The USA Tax, NST and CIVAT, all of which are different forms of consumption based taxation, fully or partially satisfy several of API's eight evaluation criteria outlined above. However, each also falls short in meeting some of the criteria or leaves issues of concern unresolved. A discussion of each of these specific proposals follows.

358

THE SIMPLIFIED USA TAX ACT OF 1999 (H.R. 134)

General Characteristics

The USA Tax satisfies several of the API criteria for evaluating taxing systems. It would encourage the investment in durable business assets by allowing the immediate deduction of capital expenditures. API also favors this proposal for recognizing that excise taxes should be excluded from the tax base and for establishing one tax rate for business.

Several aspects of the USA Tax appear easier to comply with and administer than the present income tax system. Allowing immediate expensing of capital equipment is a great simplification compared to the current complex depreciation rules. Since the USA Tax is also a "territorial" system, businesses would no longer have to incur many of the administrative and compliance costs of the current system relating to foreign operations. In certain respects, the USA Tax would help to minimize economic distortions as compared to the current system. Our present income tax system contains a large number of complex deductions and credits, many of which create competitive distortions in particular business sectors. Different rules apply depending upon whether a business operates in corporate or partnership form. The USA Tax is more neutral because it would allow far fewer deductions and would apply to all business sectors and forms of business organizations, but there is considerable uncertainty as to how the taxation of partnerships would affect the industry practice of forming joint ventures for high cost, high risk projects.

Deductibility of the Import Tax

There are also several areas in which the English proposal does not meet API's criteria. The proposal would impose a 12 percent tax on the value of imports. Because the proposed tax would not be deductible, when an importer sells an imported good in the United States, the importer would be subject to the 8 to 12 percent consumption tax on the already paid import tax. This double taxation would create an unwarranted economic distortion by precluding foreign and domestic goods from competing equally in the marketplace. Consideration should be given to whether the imposition of an import tax is appropriate at all on intermediate purchases of goods that will be incorporated into a final product. This is especially the case for raw materials, such as crude oil, that generally have already been subject to high foreign taxes (which would no longer be creditable against U.S. tax obligations under the USA Tax proposal).

The USA Tax system is particularly detrimental to importers by failing to allow the import tax to be either deducted in arriving at the taxable base, or fully credited against net liability as is the case with most credit-invoice VAT systems. While most commentators focus on the payroll tax credit as the key to border adjustability, the real focus should be on the national tax treatment provisions of the WTO because, as currently drafted, the USA Tax appears to penalize imports. If a destination-based system such as the USA Tax is ultimately adopted, this major error must be corrected.

Tax Visibility

API is concerned that the USA Tax is not structured in a manner that would facilitate recovery in the marketplace. As is the case with the current income tax, the USA Tax would be imposed on the net income of a seller of goods, rather than on the product sale. Such a system also makes the amount of tax less clear to the ultimate consumer than would be the case with a tax that could be separately stated as a specific percentage of gross sales price.

Treatment of Non-Cash Exchanges, State Taxes, Payroll Tax Credit

Further analysis and discussion is warranted regarding many other aspects of the USA Tax proposal. For example, API believes that non-cash exchanges should be excluded from the tax base. Under current law, tax-free exchanges are a common and important part of the oil and gas business. Inventory exchanges of equivalently (or nearly equivalently) valued barrels of oil or product are everyday occurrences involving extremely high volumes that permit the efficient transportation and supply of crude oil and product throughout the country. Certainly, compensatory cash payments for value differences on these exchanges should be taken into account for tax purposes, but the full value of the exchanged products must not be considered as a taxable transaction. In addition, careful consideration must be given to the consequences of the proposed elimination of deductions for state income taxes and the replacement of the wages-paid deduction with a payroll tax credit.

CREDIT-LNVOICE VALUE ADDED TAX

In General

A CIVAT on sales of all goods and services appears to more closely adhere to the principles API has identified for a properly structured consumption tax. A CIVAT is imposed as a multistage sales tax collected at each point in the production and distribution process. A business subtracts the tax paid on its purchases, including capital goods, from the tax due on its sales. If the difference is a positive number, the business remits that amount to the government. If it is negative, as may occur in the case of exported goods, the business claims a refund. Compared to the current income tax, the CIVAT has the advantage of encouraging saving and investment. It does not burden capital outlays, nor does it discriminate against U.S. industry either in the U.S. or abroad.

Effective and Neutral Revenue Source

From an economic standpoint, a separately stated CIVAT on the sale of goods and services appears to be the least damaging way of raising revenue. It does not burden capital outlays, nor does it discriminate against U.S. industry either in the United States or abroad. It does not favor either capital or labor intensive industries. Wages, rent, interest and profits, i.e., the return of entrepreneurship, each bear the same direct tax burden. A CIVAT levied at the same rate on all consumption should not cause a significant distortion in consumption choices since the relative cost of goods and services would be the same after imposition of the tax as before. A broad-based CIVAT would not unduly burden the products of any one sector of the economy. Any regional distortions would tend to be minimized since no specific product or geographic region of the country would be the focus of the tax. A uniform CIVAT applied to goods and services would induce fewer distortions within particular industries than other taxes.

Border Adjustability

A CIVAT is neutral with respect to goods produced domestically and abroad. Not only are U.S. manufactured goods not burdened with the tax when they are exported, but imports must also bear the same tax as comparable domestically produced goods. This border adjustment feature of the CIVAT-permitted under WTO rules-means that the tax does not handicap U.S. manufacturers, nor does it act to distort consumer's decisions whether to buy domestic or imported goods. Some economists argue that border adjustable taxes are not necessary because monetary exchange rates will adjust to accommodate the change in U.S. taxation. While this may be true in the long run (and not everyone agrees), in the short run the adjustment period could be very harmful to U.S. competitiveness.

Differences with Other Tax Systems

Under the CIVAT, the tax liability of a firm is equal to the tax imposed on its sales net of a credit for the tax it has previously paid on purchases for business use. Under a subtraction-method consumption tax system like the USA Tax, liability is determined by applying the tax rate directly to the firm's value added, or the difference between its sales and its purchases. CIVAT is a tax on a product while a subtraction-method consumption tax system is based on a business's books of account, similar to the current income tax system. From that underlying distinction flows a number of practical differences that API concludes favor the CIVAT.

Most commentators agree that while a single rate consumption tax, without exemption, is preferable, the overwhelming weight of political experience shows that the United States would not adopt a single rate consumption tax with no exceptions. Not one of the 45 countries that currently collect consumption taxes has a single-rate, no-exemption tax. Most have both exemptions and multiple rates. The CIVAT readily accommodates these features. Because the tax a business pays on purchases is credited against the tax it owes on sales, businesses. are encouraged to register as taxpayers and to get invoices from their supplier to document the tax paid. Also, a CIVAT would reach previously untaxed income in the underground economy, since all consumer consumption would be taxed when goods and services are purchased.

NATIONAL SALES TAX PROPOSAL (H.R. 2525)

In General

Most NST proposals are relatively easy to understand since they are similar to the various sales tax systems in place in 45 out of the 50 states. The NST is intended to replace the current income tax, estate and gift tax, and most general revenue federal excise taxes. Under the plan offered by Reps. Linder and Peterson, the tax would be imposed at a 23 percent rate on the sale of goods, including both tangible personal property and real property, and services, including financial intermediation services such as brokerage fees, banking fees, and insurance fees. Although the NST is intended to be compatible with current state sales tax systems, none of the 45 states currently utilizing such a system tax services as extensively as is envisioned under H.R. 2525. A great deal of work will have to be done with the various state taxing authorities before they will become convinced to administer a uniform NST on behalf of the federal government.

Businesses would collect tax on all their taxable sales of goods and services and remit the tax to the government. Since purchases of inventory for resale are not taxable, the complex inventory rules of the current income tax system would be eliminated. Purchases of equipment and real property used in the production of taxable goods and services would also not be taxable, so there would be full expensing of capital assets. As noted above in the discussion of the USA Tax, the ability to immediately expense capital assets is extremely important to a capital-intensive business like the oil and gas industry.

Border Adjustability and Territoriality

Like a CIVAT, the NST is neutral with respect to goods produced domestically and abroad. Not only are U.S. manufactured goods not burdened with the tax when they are exported, but imports must also bear the same tax as comparable domestically produced goods. This border adjustment feature of the NST, which like the CIVAT should be permitted under WTO rules, means that the tax does not handicap U.S. manufacturers, nor does it act to distort consumers' decisions whether to buy domestic or imported goods. The NST, like the USA Tax and CIVAT, is a territorial system, which would help put U.S. multinationals on a level playing field with their international competitors.

Definitional Problems

Although it appears to be the intent of NST proponents that businesses above the retail level will be outside the tax system, this likely will not happen. While H.R. 2525 improves on prior national sales tax legislative proposals in its attempt to define what constitutes a tax exempt good or service "purchased for a business purpose in a trade or business," uncertainties remain. For instance, while the proposal would exempt purchases used in a trade or business "(1) for resale, (2) to produce, provide, render, or sell taxable property or services, or (3) in furtherance of other bona fide business purposes," it is unclear whether items such as financial services, pollution control, environmental remediation, or many other kinds of purchases would be covered by that definition. Such questions would then have to be resolved during the often- confrontational audit process between the taxpayer/tax collector and the sales tax administering authority.

Excise Tax Concerns

H.R. 2525 would not repeal the retail and manufacturer excise taxes, which include a federal excise tax of 18.4 cents per gallon on gasoline, 19.4 cents per gallon on aviation gasoline, 24.4 cents per gallon on diesel fuel and kerosene and 21.9 cents per gallon on aviation fuel. In addition, the proposal would not repeal the environmental trust fund taxes, many of which are imposed on products produced by the oil and gas industry. The preservation of these excise taxes in conjunction with the adoption of the NST is of particular concern to our industry because these excise taxes constitute a significant portion of the retail price of our products and would be included in the base upon which the sales tax is calculated. State excise taxes would also be included in the base, as proposed, and this would again be a major problem for our industry.

TRANSITIONAL ISSUES

In General

While transitional issues will arise in the context of all tax reform proposals, they become especially critical where, for example, there is a significant shift in the basis of taxation from income to consumption. Capital intensive industries, such as the petroleum industry, have made long-term investment decisions relying on the existing tax structure. Changes in that structure would impact different companies, often in direct competition, in an arbitrary and often inequitable manner. The most obvious examples of transitional issues occur in the areas of capital outlays and borrowings.s For example, a capital asset (or inventory) purchased immediately prior to the enactment of certain of the consumption-based taxes would be denied recovery of all but a miniscule fraction of its cost, whereas the same asset purchased immediately following enactment would be permitted an immediate 100 percent recovery against the tax base. In a similar manner, borrowings based on the anticipation of an interest deduction could become a significant burden on a highly leveraged business after enactment of a consumption tax.

Depreciation

The proposed USA Tax partially addresses the transition issue but stops far short of providing the equitable relief necessary for business taxpayers. The issue of unrecovered basis is addressed in the Simplified USA Tax Act through a system of amortization that substantially lengthens the recovery period under current law. This lengthened and arbitrary classification of unrecovered costs into four groups appears to be based on misconceptions regarding complexity and revenue costs. Continuing the current method for unrecovered basis of assets placed in service prior to tax reform would be preferable to inserting another new capital cost recovery regime. Permitting current law business deductions to be carried out, thus honoring prior business plans and commitments, is necessary to avoid inequitable distortions.

Interest on Pre-Reform Debt

Transitional rules that consider only lost depreciation deductions fall far short of measures necessary to ensure the success of tax reform. A continuation of current law interest deductions for pre-reform debt can be as vital to a business as cost recovery. If the interest deduction is offset by interest income on the particular pre-reform debt (i.e., pre-reform obligations continue to be both tax deductible to the debtor and taxable to the lender), there would be no significant revenue impact to the Treasury. Ignoring a continuation of the interest deduction results in arbitrary windfall gains and losses without any apparent justification.

Carryovers of Other Tax Attributes

Among other items of significant impact to business are net operating loss and capital loss carryovers, business, foreign tax and minimum tax credit carryovers, as well as other pre-reform adjustments, such as those required under Section 481 of the Code. The USA Tax attempts to solve this problem with a further complex overlay to the depreciation recovery rule. Operating and capital losses are simply a result of the annual accounting convention for tax payment determinations. Their carry forward is a valid claim on future tax payments that would take into consideration the length of business cycles in various industries and other issues of timing. There is no valid distinction between unused business credits and future deductions for depreciation and, in fact, credits are a specific and distinct congressional incentive upon which businesses have relied. The Alternative Minimum Tax was intended as an advance payment of federal income tax. Therefore, unrecovered credits require a reimbursement mechanism. Transitional rules must include a provision clearly permitting the Internal Revenue Service to make appropriate adjustments to ensure that no taxpayer takes a double deduction for any cost, nor suffers double inclusion of any income.

SUMMARY

Reform of the current U.S. tax system is a worthy goal, especially the movement from taxation of income to taxation of consumption. Each of the alternative consumption tax proposals makes important contributions to the reform effort. Any major upheaval such as complete replacement of the current income tax system will, however, require careful analysis of all possible implications. We have lived with the present tax system for over eighty years, and businesses have structured their affairs within it. Any fundamental change, unless carefully orchestrated, could cause massive turmoil, particularly in the transition period from the old system to the new. At the same time, it should be emphasized that while API has identified a number of concerns regarding the prospect of comprehensive tax reform, none of these problems are insurmountable.

Statement of Associated General Contractors of America, Alexandria, VA

Mr. Chairman and Members of the Committee on Ways and Means:

The Associated General Contractors of America (AGC) has endorsed the FairTax national sales tax (currently embodied in H.R. 2525) that is promoted by the Americans for Fair Taxation. This federal legislation would eliminate the death tax, self-employment taxes, corporate and individual income taxes, the alternative minimum tax, the capital gains tax and replace these taxes with one simple, single rate, national sales tax on the personal and final consumption of goods and services at the retail level only. It would not affect social security benefits, but simply change the funding mechanism. It would not affect those Federal excise taxes used to fund construction programs. In this endorsement, AGC joins other significant national business groups including the National Small Business United (the nation's oldest small business organization) and the American Farm Bureau Federation among other notable groups.

AGC is the nation's largest and oldest construction trade association, founded in 1918. AGC represents more than 33,000 firms, including 7,500 of America's leading general contracting firms. AGC's general contractor members have more than 25,000 industry firms associated with them through a network of 101 AGC chapters. AGC member firms are engaged in the construction of the nation's commercial buildings, factories, warehouses, highways, bridges, airports, waterworks facilities, waste treatment facilities, dams, water conservation projects, defense facilities, multi-family housing projects, site preparation, and utilities installation for housing developments.

SUMMARY:

The FairTax national sales tax will, in one broad stroke, accomplish the entire Federal tax agenda for the AGC. The FairTax eliminates the methods of accounting and long-term contract accounting problems faced by contractors. No earnings would be taxed and, equally important, once the FairTax is in place, no business-to-business transactions would be taxed.

The fundamental reform will provide the legislative vehicle for total elimination of death taxes. The death tax is one of the most onerous obstacles to family business continuity and growth. At a minimum, an estate over $675,000 (*gradually* increased to $1 million by 2006) will be subject to a federal death tax rate of 37% and an estate over $3 million will be taxed at 55%. In the capital intensive construction industry, most firms easily have assets of the current death tax exemption amount. More than 70% of family businesses do not succeed to the second generation and 87% do not survive to the third generation. Few have the liquid assets to pay death taxes if their heirs were to inherit the business today. Comprehensive tax reform of this magnitude is a strong vehicle for full elimination of the death tax.

Additionally, several beneficial economic consequences would follow from the FairTax. Replacing the income tax with a national sales tax will dramatically improve the standard of living of the American people. The FairTax would significantly enhance economic performance by improving the incentives for work and entrepreneurial activity and by raising the marginal return to saving and investment. Entrepreneurs and small business owners would be given greater access to capital, the life-blood of a free economy. Investment would rise, the capital stock would grow, productivity would increase and the output of goods and services would expand. The economy would create more and better paying jobs for American workers and take-home pay would increase considerably.

The cost of construction supplies will fall. Today, construction materials bear a heavy, hidden component of tax. Approximately 25 percent of the cost of materials are taxes that have been imposed upstream in the companies producing those materials, according to Dale Jorgenson, who is the President of the American Economics Association and Chairman of Harvard University's Economics Department. When taxes are removed, competition will drive material costs downward.

The cost of capital will fall, enabling construction firms to make greater investments in productivity and inducing further infrastructure investments. The construction industry is capital intensive, requiring large investments in heavy equipment. For instance, a 150-ton crane used in bridge construction can cost more than $1 million. A scraper can cost $700,000 and a large bulldozer can cost more than $800,000. By eliminating the capital gains taxes and any tax on investment and savings, the FairTax will enable contractors to make the needed investments in equipment and supplies before tax, not with what remains after the government has exacted a toll.

Workers would benefit. Because the FairTax repeals both the income tax and payroll taxes, workers would enjoy the full fruits of their labor. What an employee earns would be what the employee would receive in his or her paycheck. Workers would respond to a national retail sales tax by increasing the amount of work effort they want to undertake. A reasonable projection is that if the current federal income tax system were to be replaced by a national retail sales tax, total hours worked that people in the United States would choose to work would increase by 8.25 percent.

There are more advantages. The FairTax would reduce fixed compliance costs by as much as 90 percent. By imposing taxes at the cash register, the FairTax would wholly exempt individuals from ever having to file a return. *Business-to-business transactions would be fully exempt.* The Tax Foundation estimates that the FairTax would reduce compliance costs by 90 percent—more than any other tax plan. In addition to reducing compliance costs, The FairTax would reinstate the principle that Americans have a right to understand the law to which they are subjected.

In sum, AGC believes that the FairTax is good for construction and good for America. We strongly support this proposal and urge Congress to seriously consider the FairTax as a replacement to our current tax code maze.

ADDITIONAL DISCUSSION:

Construction is as vital to our economy as it is has been to our historic growth as a nation. While statistics are always moving targets, there were 487,783 construction firms in 1997. Total civilian employment based on IRS records was 142,836,000; construction directly accounted for more than 6.1 million civilian employees who paid salary and wages of $28 billion. There were $593 billion in total receipts. Construction firms had assets of $315 billion in 1997, broken down roughly as indicated below.

Relative Percentage of Minor Industry Groups

☒ General building contractors and operative builders

■ Heavy construction contractors

☐ Special trade contractors

What is Wrong with Our Tax System?

Apart from paying high direct and indirect taxes, our current tax regime places disproportionate burdens on construction, stemming from the unique nature of the our industry as a capital intensive, long-term, high-risk and often family-owned and operated effort.

Through the income tax, behavior that is essential to building—work, saving and investment—is punished. High marginal tax rates weaken the link between effort and reward. Multiple layers of taxation on work, saving and investment reduce capital for new investment. A regressive levy of payroll and self-employment taxes frustrates expansion. Finally, although families own most construction firms, estate taxes (at rates as high as 55%) due at death prevent owners from passing their firms on to their children.

While construction is inherently capital-intensive, firms are hampered by the capital gains tax, which doubly taxes investment income while punishing losses which cannot be predicted. Capital gains taxes discourage reinvestment to keep businesses growing and operations competitive. Moreover, because the industry is largely investment and reinvestment in capital assets over many years, capital gains can result more from inflation than appreciation, even when a firm is sold.

The tax system through inadequate capital cost recovery allowances, the alternative minimum tax and the passive loss limitations, makes investment in structures more expensive and reduces demand for structures being built.

The cost of capital will fall, enabling construction firms to make greater investments in productivity and inducing further infrastructure investments and allowing their customers to make greater investments in structures and other products of the construction industry. The construction industry is capital intensive, requiring large investments in heavy equipment. For instance, a 150-ton crane used in bridge construction can cost more than $1 million. A scraper can cost $700,000 and a large bulldozer can cost more than $800,000. By eliminating the capital gains taxes and any tax on investment and savings, the FairTax will enable contractors to make the needed investments in equipment and supplies before tax, not with what remains after the government has exacted a toll.

The FairTax would exempt the poor from paying any federal income, payroll or sales tax altogether. In fact, this means that poor people that spend less than the

364

poverty level amount on taxable goods and services will enjoy a negative tax rate. For three quarters of Americans, payroll taxes are a larger burden than income taxes. Payroll taxes are imposed from the first dollar of wage income earned, although the earned income tax credit mitigates this burden to some degree. The AFT plan would repeal the Social Security and Medicare payroll taxes

The sales tax imposes tax on the private use of economic resources, not on social use. When an individual buys a good or service for personal consumption purposes, he will pay tax. When that money is used for a social purpose such as investing in a job producing plant, conducting research to develop new technologies or find new medicines or is given to a charity, the individual will not pay tax. If an investor liquidates his investments to fund consumption, a tax is imposed.

Virtually all economic models project a much healthier economy if a national sales tax replaces the current tax system. These models typically project that the economy will be 10 to 14 percent larger in 10 years.[2] Real investment also will spike upward. Harvard University economist Dale Jorgenson forecasts that "real investment would leap upward. As a direct result of this dramatic increase in real investment, the capital stock will rise as well. Kotlikoff forecasts that by the fifth year after replacement, the capital stock will be eight percent larger. By the 10th year, the capital stock will be 15 percent greater. Over the long run, the capital stock will be a full 29 percent larger than under the current income tax regime.[3]

The federal tax will point the direction to sound state sales tax policy Many state sales tax schemes improperly tax business inputs and therefore cascade. When states repeatedly tax purchases between and among firms, all firms are disadvantaged, but especially disadvantaged are small firms. The more small firms are utilized in the chain of production—from raw materials to consumption—the more they will pay in taxes. Under such an ill-advised scheme, a company has every incentive to vertically integrate, rather than contract out—even if contracting out were more efficient. The normal tendency of small firms who have struggled under such cascading tax schemes would be to associate this negative characteristic with all plans that are called "sales" taxes—even a national sales tax. However, the AFT believes it wholly inappropriate to adopt a system that has cascading taxes. If a business buys a good or service from another business, such a purchase would not be taxed. Since no business to business inputs are taxes, and no profits or income is taxed, businesses pay an effective rate of zero.

While these are the highlights, there are more advantages. Hidden taxes would become visible and more difficult to raise. By placing the tax on the receipt for consumer purchases and by repealing upstream taxes, it would convey the true cost of government to every American on each purchase they make. This not only adds integrity to the tax system, but it will also keep taxes lower.

One of the best attributes of the FairTax is that it will cause a drop in interest rates and reduce the carrying costs of debt. Under the FairTax, conservative estimates predict that mortgage interest rates will fall by 25 to 30 percent or about two points on a 30-year conventional mortgage. To put this in the context of housing, for a $150,000 thirty-year home mortgage at an interest rate of 8 percent the monthly mortgage payment would be $1,112.64. On that same mortgage at a 6 percent interest rate the monthly payment would be $907.64. The two-point decrease in interest rates in this instance would result in a $73,800 cost savings to the consumer.

Conclusion

The true tax reform debate will not take place in Washington. Rather, it will take place at the grass roots level. A consensus is growing that America can and must adopt a better system of collecting the revenues necessary to fund the federal government. Which alternative is best is the question now on the national agenda. The FairTax would be simple, inexpensive, understandable, administrable, visible, equitable, pro-growth and respectful of privacy rights. The AGC has endorsed the FairTax as the most sensible alternative to a broken system. We encourage you to help make this tax plan a reality by becoming actively involved.

[2] See, "The Economic Impact of Fundamental Tax Reform," Dale W. Jorgenson, Testimony before the House Ways and Means Committee, June 6, 1995; "Looking Back to Move Forward: What Tax Policy Cost Americans and the Economy," Gary Robbins and Aldona Robbins, September, 1994, Policy Report Number 127, Institute for Policy Innovation; "The Economic Impact of Taxing Consumption," Laurence J. Kotlikoff, April 15, 1993, Cato Institute Policy Analysis. Also see "The National Sales Tax: Moving Beyond the Idea, Tax Notes, March 21, 1996, David R. Burton and Dan R. Mastromarco.

[3] Kotlikoff also simulated an economy in which income taxes at all levels of government were replaced by a comprehensive retail sales tax and found that the stock of U.S. capital would increase by as much as 49 percent.

Statement of Hon. Jim Barcia, a Representative in Congress from the State of Michigan

Thank you for the opportunity to submit this statement on the FairTax national sales tax plan. I am a cosponsor of H.R. 2525—a bill distinguished in its Congressional support by an equal balance of Democrats and Republicans.

Mr. Chairman, our Congress is one of the most prodigious legislative bodies in the world, but one would be hard pressed to find any public law more despised than our Internal Revenue Code. If we assembled ten different individuals in Bay City or Saginaw, Michigan—the heart of the Midwest—and asked them what they thought of the tax system today, we would get ten different answers. None would be favorable and none would be incorrect. The answers that I have heard are that our system is too invasive of our privacy, heavy-handed, too costly, overly complex, burdensome, punitive, invisible, anti-competitive, unfair, destructive of our collective and individual prosperity.

What would the FairTax do for the American people in my view? It would reduce the wasteful administrative overhead of our system: record keeping, the cost of advice, the cost of filling our returns, and the cost of audit. Under any tax system, we have to have tax collectors and payers. However, the FairTax would eliminate entirely the collection, record keeping and reporting responsibilities of individuals. This is much better than filing a postcard sized return as the flat taxers boast. In fact, most taxpayers now file a return very similar to a postcard sized return in the Form of the 1040EZ. Under the FairTax, 112 million taxpayers can simply let April 15th pass as a beautiful Spring day. Congress will give them a permanent extension. No returns, ever. No other tax plan can claim this.

The FairTax would repeal the payroll tax, which is the most regressive tax of all. It takes a 15.3% bite out of every single dollar earned, but only applies to the middle class wage earner; at high incomes it falls to 2.9 percent. Moreover, it only applies to wages, not dividends and interest.

The FairTax is the plan that will restore the fundamental notion of fairness, notice of the law, and privacy rights on which this country was based. Our nation deserves better than the monstrosity of law we created in the last century. As we look to the next millennium, we should have a clear vision of what an ideal tax system should look like. The FairTax is that system.

Statement of Council of Smaller Enterprises, Cleveland, OH

Good morning Chairman Archer and members of the committee. Thank you for hosting three days of hearings on Fundamental Tax Reform proposals. Please allow this document to serve as written testimony supporting Fundamental Tax Reform and the Fair Tax, or the national retail sales tax proposal (HR 2525).

This testimony is submitted on behalf of the nation's largest chamber of commerce. The Greater Cleveland Growth Association and it's small business division, The Council of Smaller Enterprises (COSE), represent over 16,000 businesses in Ohio and over 250,000 lives in its health insurance plan. Based in Cleveland, Ohio, our health insurance plan was adopted over 25 years ago to give our members, their employees and families access to high quality, affordable health care benefits. We are often cited and studied as a national model for health insurance purchasing cooperatives. We support the Fair Tax model because it promotes fairness and simplicity, improves the competitiveness of American businesses, and will increase the standard of living for the American people.

The Fair Tax plan as introduced in HR2525 (Linder, (R–GA) and Peterson, D–MN) would repeal the federal personal income, corporate income, estate, gift, capital gains, self-employment, payroll, social security and Medicare taxes and replace them with a 23% sales tax on all new goods and services. This tax would be collected at the point of final purchase for consumption. Every taxpayer will be subject tot he same tax rate with no exceptions and no exclusions. Since the Internal Revenue Service would be abolished under the Fair Tax plan, the 23% rate is intended to raise the same amount of federal funds as raised by the current federal tax system. In addition, the rate is calculated to pay for a universal rebate for essential goods and services and pay for a fee to retailers and state governments collecting the tax.

The universal rebate to all registered in the Social Security system would replace, in effect, the exclusions on clothing and food, for example, that states make for their sales taxes. The universal rebate is proposed to be calculated as the sales tax rate times the poverty level income adopted by the government for different family sizes.

Proceeds from the Fair Tax would become the primary general revenue source for the United States government. Social Security and Medicare would be funded from this revenue stream. The bill as proposed is estimated to be revenue-neutral for its first full year in effect. The new tax system will then go into effect one calendar year after the repeal amendment is ratified, with a transition phase beginning with the ratification of the amendment.

The COSE Board of Directors endorsed the Fair Tax on October 12, 1999 (see attached Resolution). Our members, primarily entrepreneurs and business owners, agreed that the current system cannot be reformed. It must be replaced. COSE believes HR 2525 is a positive non-partisan proposal that will fix the current system by taxing citizen on what they spend, not what they earn.

Thus, the time for change has come. Even former IRS Commissioner Shirley Peterson acknowledged that the current tax system should be changed. Head of the IRS in 1992, Commissioner Peterson noted that "we have reached the point where further patchwork will only compound the problem. It is time to repeal the Internal Revenue Code and start over."

COSE believes there are valuable member benefits to the adoption of the Fair Tax. Employees will be able to take home their entire paycheck. Businesses will not have to pay capital gains, payroll, income taxes or many other taxes which hurt business growth. The elimination of the estate tax burden will help family businesses grow. Finally, more capital will be available to business owners since investment will not be taxed.

On behalf of over 16,000 businesses in Ohio, we urge you to support the Fair Tax proposal. COSE believes it is the most sensible method to revise our current complex and ever-changing tax code. Thank you for your time and consideration.

Attachment is being retained in the Committee files.

Statement of Herman Cain, Godfather's Pizza, Inc., Omaha, NE

Thank you Mr. Chairman and members of the committee. I appreciate the opportunity to testify before your committee about fundamental tax reform. I am Chairman of Godfather's Pizza, Inc.

The current tax system is broken and no amount of tinkering around the edges is going to fix it. It is too complicated. It is too unfair. It holds people down economically. It destroys hope and opportunity. It needs to be replaced.

A replacement system should satisfy six principles. First, it should promote economic growth by reducing marginal tax rates and eliminating the tax bias against savings and investment. Second, it should promote fairness by having one tax rate and eliminating all loopholes, preferences and special deductions, credits and exclusions. Third, it should be simple and understandable. Fourth, it should be neutral rather than allowing the government to manipulate and micromanage our economy by favoring some at the expense of others. Fifth, it should be visible so people understand their actual tax burden and so it clearly conveys the true cost of government. Sixth, it should be stable rather than changing every year or two so people can plan and so the system remains simple and understandable.

In my view, there is more than one plan that would satisfy these principles to varying degrees. There is more than one way to vastly improve over the current tax system. One proposal that would be highly constructive is the flat tax. It would improve the tax system in all six areas. I, however, have concluded that the FairTax, introduced on a bi-partisan basis by Reps. Linder and Peterson as H.R. 2525, meets the six principles that I outlined.

The FairTax would repeal individual income taxes, corporate income taxes and the estate and gift tax. It is the only proposal to repeal all payroll taxes (including Social Security, Medicare and self-employment taxes). These taxes are a regressive tax on jobs and upward mobility and it is time to address them. The FairTax would replace these taxes with a 23 percent national retail sales tax on all goods and services sold to consumers.

Individuals would no longer file tax returns. April 15th would be just another day. Businesses would collect and remit the sales tax. In addition, the FairTax would provide every household in America with a rebate of sales tax paid on necessities.

The FairTax would encourage Economic Growth

A national retail sales tax would significantly enhance economic performance by improving the incentives for work and entrepreneurial activity and by raising the marginal return to saving and investment. Entrepreneurs and small business owners would be given greater access to capital, the life blood of a free economy. Investment would rise, the capital stock would grow, productivity would increase and the output of goods and services would expand. The economy would create more and better paying jobs for American workers and take-home pay would increase considerably.

Although the magnitude of the economic growth generated by a flat rate, neutral tax system causes lively debate among economists, virtually all agree that the large marginal tax rate reductions in the FairTax combined with neutral taxation of savings and investment, will have powerful positive effects on the economy.

The FairTax would be Fair

The FairTax would provide every household in America with a rebate of sales tax paid on necessities. Thus, the FairTax is progressive and every family is protected from tax on essential goods and services. Because of the rebate, those below the poverty line would have negative effective tax rates and lower middle income families would enjoy low effective tax rates.

The burden of paying the FairTax is fairly distributed. It is, in fact, much more fairly distributed than the income tax. Wealthy people spend more money than other individuals. The FairTax will tax them on their purchases and as a result, they pay more in taxes. If, however, they use their money to build job creating factories or stores, or to finance research and development to create new products, (all of which help improve the standard of living of others), then those activities will not be taxed. The FairTax is premised on the notion that it is fairer to tax individuals when they consume for themselves above the essentials of life, rather than when they invest in others or contribute to society.

The FairTax in effect gives a supercharged charitable contribution deduction because people can give to their favorite charity free of any income tax, payroll tax or sales tax. The charitable deduction today allows people to make their contributions with pre income tax dollars (but after payroll tax dollars). For the three-quarters of Americans that do not itemize, most must today earn $155 to give $100 to their favorite charity or to their church.[1] Under the FairTax, they must earn only $100 to give $100 since under the FairTax what you earn is what you keep and charitable contributions are not taxed.

Education is one of the keys (along with savings and hard work) to an improved standard of living. That certainly was true in my case. The FairTax is education friendly and is dramatically more supportive of education than current law. The FairTax embodies the principle that investments in people (human capital) and investments in things (physical capital) should be treated comparably. The current tax system, in stark contrast, treats education expenditures very unfavorably.

Education is the best means for the vast majority of people to improve their economic position. It is the most reliable means that people have to invest in themselves and improve their earning potential. Yet the tax system today punishes people who invest in education, virtually doubling its cost. Only the FairTax would remove this impediment to upward mobility. No other tax reform plan would do so.[2]

Today, to pay $10,000 in college or private school tuition, a typical middle class American must earn $15,540 looking only at federal income taxes and the employee payroll tax.[3] The amount one must earn to pay the $10,000 is really more like $20,120 once employer and state income taxes are taken into account.[4]

The FairTax does not tax education expenditures. Education can be paid for with pre-tax dollars. This is the equivalent of making educational expense deductible against both the income tax and payroll taxes today. Thus, under the FairTax, a family will need to earn $10,000 to pay $10,000 in tuition, making education much more affordable (not considering state income taxes on education). The FairTax makes education about half as expensive to American families compared to today.

The FairTax would improve upward mobility but no longer punishing work, savings, investment or education. It would better enable people to improve their lives. It would no longer hold people back.

---

[1] $155.40 less 7.65 percent in employee Social Security ($11.89) and Medicare payroll taxes less 28 percent in federal income taxes ($43.51) leaves $10,000.

[2] Neither the flat tax nor the USA Tax would remedy the current bias against education.

[3] $15,540 less 7.65 percent in employee Social Security ($1,189) and Medicare payroll taxes less 28 percent in federal income taxes ($4,351) leaves $10,000.

[4] Economists generally agree that the employer share of payroll taxes is borne by the employee in the form of lower wages. This figure assumes that employees bear the burden of the employer payroll tax and that they are in a seven percent state and local income tax bracket. $20,120 less $5,634 in income tax (28 percent), $3079 in payroll taxes (15.3 percent) and $1,408 in state and local income taxes (7 percent) leaves $10,000.

The FairTax would be Simple

The FairTax is a simple tax. Individuals who are not in business would have absolutely no compliance burden, nor would they be subject to the discretionary interpretation of the current convoluted tax code. As for businesses, it puts much fewer administrative burdens on businesses. In fact, filling out a FairTax return is comparable to filling out line one (gross revenue) of an income tax return. There would be no more alternative minimum tax, no more depreciation schedules, no more complex employee benefit rules, no more complex qualified account and pension rules, no more complex income sourcing and expense allocation rules, no more foreign tax credit, no more complex rules governing corporate acquisitions, divisions and other reorganizations, no more uniform capitalization requirements, no more complex tax inventory accounting rules, no more income and payroll tax withholding and the list goes on. Businesses would simply need to keep track of how much they sold to consumers.

Compliance costs will, therefore, fall under the FairTax. Today, according to the Tax Foundation, we spend about $250 billion each year filling out forms, hiring tax lawyers, accountants, benefits consultants, collecting information needed only for tax purposes and the like. These unnecessary costs amount to about $850 for every man, woman and child in America. To the extent these costs are incurred by businesses, they must be recovered and are embedded in the cost of everything that we buy. The money we spend on unnecessary compliance costs is money we might as well burn for all of the good it does us. The Tax Foundation has estimated that compliance costs would drop by about 90 percent under a national sales tax.

The FairTax would be Neutral

Under the FairTax all consumption would be treated equally. The tax code punishes those that save and rewards consumption. Under the FairTax, no longer would the tax system be in the businesses of picking winners and losers. The tax code would be neutral in the choice between savings and consumption, neutral between types of savings and investment and neutral between types of consumption.

The FairTax would be Visible

The FairTax is highly visible, and because there is only one tax rate Congress would be raising the rate on all taxpayers at the same time. Moreover, all citizens would be subject to the tax increase, not just a targeted few. It will be much harder for Congress to adopt the typical divide-and-conquer, hide-and-disguise tax increase strategy it uses today. The FairTax would explicitly state the contribution to the Federal government each and every time a good or service is purchased.

The FairTax would be Stable

The FairTax would be more stable than the present system for two reasons. First, because it is so simple and transparent, it would not invite tinkering in the way that the current system with its thousands of pages of code and regulations does. People will resist attempts to make it more complex and attempts to favor special interests because they will understand what is going on. Second, taxing consumption is a more stable source of revenue than taxing income. There are fewer ups and downs in the consumption base.

A recent study showed that for the years 1959 to 1995, the FairTax base was less variable than the income tax base. Why? When times are unusually good, people will usually save a little more. People tend to smooth out their consumption over their lifetime. They borrow when young, save in middle age and spend more than their income in retirement.

Impact on Restaurants and Retailers

I would like to discuss briefly the impact of the FairTax on my industry, restaurants in particular and retailers in general. The FairTax could have a positive impact on these industries.

Like other firms, retailers will enjoy a zero corporate tax rate and their shareholders will not be taxed on dividends received from the retailer or capital gains on their investment in the retailer. Compliance costs could be lower. Moreover, over time, most states will conform their sales taxes to the federal sales tax, reducing the costs of complying with multiple rules in each state and their political subdivisions.

If people are willing and able to purchase more goods and services in a healthy economy, then they will spend more money at retailers and eat out more. There is nothing that hurts restaurants more than a slow economy and nothing that helps them more than a good economy. In this sense, the FairTax could help restaurants and retailers.

Consumption is taxed once under both an income tax and a national sales tax. Consumption purchases must be made from after-income-tax and after-payroll-tax dollars today. The primary difference between a sales tax and an income tax is that the income tax double or triple or quadruple taxes on savings. Consumers will see their paychecks increase by nearly two trillion dollars. Since the FairTax is not a tax increase but is revenue neutral, the repeal of the income and payroll taxes will provide consumers with the money necessary to pay for the sales tax.

Instead of having to comply with the complexities of the income tax, payroll tax, and various other taxes, there will be one sales tax on all goods and services. The firm will simply need to calculate on a monthly basis its total retail sales. Retailers will receive an administration fee for complying with the sales tax. The fee is equal to ★ of one percent of the revenues collected and remitted.

In summary, this is what the Fair Tax could mean for retailers:

No more uniform inventory capitalization requirements;

No more complex rules governing employee benefits and retirement plans;

No more tax depreciation schedules;

No more complex tax rules governing mergers, acquisitions and spin-offs;

No more international tax provisions;

No more income tax or payroll tax withholding;

No more employer payroll tax; and

No more corporate tax.

I would also point out that restaurants in particular have grave concerns that any national sales tax would treat restaurant food differently from food purchased at a grocery store. Food consumed away from home is no longer a luxury, it is an essential part of the American lifestyle. The FairTax would not discriminate between the two.

Conclusion

People want to be able to dream and to pursue their dreams. As Dr. Benjamin E. Mays, late President Emeritus of Morehouse College said, "It isn't a calamity to die with dreams unfulfilled but it is a calamity not to dream." The current tax system not only destroys the ability of people to achieve their dreams, it causes many people to give up dreaming altogether.

We need a better tax system—a tax system more appropriate for a free society. The current tax code can not be reformed to achieve the stated objectives, it MUST be replaced. Please use the power of the Congress to correct a tax code that has simply gotten out of control and taken away people's freedom.

———————

Statement of Hon. Ralph M. Hall, a Representative in Congress from the State of Texas

Thank you for allowing me to submit my testimony to the Committee on Ways and Means on the important subject of reforming our nation's tax system. I am a cosponsor of H.R. 2525, the FairTax Act of 1999, legislation introduced by our colleagues, John Linder and Collin Peterson.

H.R. 2525 would repeal the federal income tax in its entirety, including all individual, corporate, payroll taxes, self-employment taxes, capital gains, gift and estate taxes. It would impose a revenue neutral national sales tax on all new goods and services at the point of final consumption. Most importantly, the FairTax would provide for a rebate in an amount equal to the sales tax on essential goods and services. No American would pay taxes on their purchase of these necessities.

Mr. Chairman, I support H.R. 2525 because it is fair to all Americans, it eliminates the complexity of our current system, it encourages savings and investment, and it is a much more efficient way to raise federal revenues than the current system.

Under the FairTax, every taxpayer starts out on a level playing field. There are no advantages to be gained by gaming the system. Those who profit from the current complexities in our tax code by sheltering income will no longer have an unfair advantage. Essentially, all taxpayers will make their own decisions about how much in taxes they will pay, in that they are only taxed when they purchase a product.

The FairTax would help improve the economic security—and thus the standard of living—for most Americans because it rewards savings and investment. Today, our country has one of the lowest rates of savings in the world. Under H.R. 2525, our rate of savings should dramatically improve because the money Americans choose to save or invest will no longer be subject to any tax. This economic incentive to save should result in more taxpayers saving and investing in our economy. Additionally, lower income families also will benefit because they will be able to keep all of their paycheck, without any costly tax deductions.

Finally, Mr. Chairman, the FairTax is a tax that every American can easily understand. It eliminates the enormous complexity that is inherent in our current tax system while providing a stable and efficient means to raise the necessary revenues to fund federal programs. And most importantly, because it is so understandable, H.R. 2525 will help restore integrity to our country's tax system.

I urge this committee not only to review the FairTax and other proposals that will be discussed during these hearings, but also to act to change forever a system that is overly burdensome, impossibly complex and inherently unfair. In short, our current system does not work for the average taxpayer. Mr. Chairman, the hearings this week are critical if we as policy makers are serious about restoring confidence in the federal tax system. I welcome this debate of the various proposals to reform our present system, and I thank you for holding these hearings.

Statement of Jospeh M. Kahn, Stanford University, Palo Alto, CA

Thank you for the opportunity to contribute to these hearings on replacing the income tax. I am providing this statement on behalf of the Stanford University Decisions and Ethics Center. From 1996 to 1997, I had the privilege of coordinating a team of economic researchers within the Decisions and Ethics Center analyzing the impact on households of a change from the current income tax regime to the National Retail Sales Tax (NRST) proposed by the group Americans for Fair Taxation. This proposal is now embodied in H.R. 2525.

Herein, I present the main findings of our study. The study was based on the 1996 income tax code, and assumed that the tax regime change would take place in 1998. Though the income tax code continues to change each year and the proposed date of changeover to the NRST remains in the future, I would not expect any major changes in the study's general conclusions.

1. Summary of Main Findings

The Decisions and Ethics Center at Stanford University investigated the impact on households of a change from the current tax regime to the national retail sales tax (NRST) proposed by Americans for Fair Taxation. Under this proposal, all federal income and payroll taxes would be repealed, federal revenues would be replaced by the NRST at a (tax-inclusive) rate of 23%, and all families would be granted a rebate for the amount of taxes paid at the federal poverty line. Our study focused on individual families over their remaining lifetimes rather than statistical aggregates in a single year. Our analysis yielded several major conclusions regarding the impact on families of a change to the NRST tax regime.

The current tax code is complex and there is probably no change which can guarantee that everyone would be better off. However, we find that most families would enjoy higher real lifetime consumption under the NRST than under the current regime. This is due to several factors, including lower tax burdens on many households, lower compliance costs, lower marginal tax rates, and increased economic growth and efficiency.

Some wealthier seniors may experience a reduction in purchasing power under the NRST. However, their own financial well-being may not be the only issue they consider in their decision to support a particular tax regime. Other factors, such as the effect on their grandchildren or on the poor, may take precedence in their decision.

This statement highlights the following points:
• Incentives to work and to save tend to be higher under the new regime—over 20% higher for many households. This is primarily due to the replacement of high marginal income tax rates with a flat rate on consumption.
• Middle-class families tend to be financially better off under the change. A combination of factors including lower compliance costs, lower marginal tax rates, and increased economic growth and efficiency contribute to improve their prospects.
• Existing homeowners tend to benefit under the change, despite the removal of the mortgage interest deduction. This is because existing owner-occupied homes would increase in value, while existing mortgages would become more affordable.

- Low-income families tend to be significantly better off financially under the change. They would effectively pay none of the national sales tax under the change because they would receive rebates which cover the amount of taxes paid at poverty level. In addition, any federal benefits they receive would be indexed to match possible increases in after-tax consumer prices.
- Younger households tend to be financially better off after the change, benefiting from improved economic conditions over their entire careers.
- Middle-and lower-income seniors tend to do better financially under the change. Social security payments would be indexed to a tax-inclusive price index, holding recipients harmless against any changes in after-tax prices. Additionally, the NRST rebate would more than make up for any losses in after-tax purchasing power of pension benefits for these seniors.
- Some wealthier seniors would tend not to benefit from the redistribution of the tax burden. This is because wealthier seniors have a larger portion of financial assets whose after-tax purchasing power may decline under the new regime. However, for many seniors the removal of income taxes from asset earnings and retirement account disbursements, the exclusion of their existing homes from the NRST, and the repeal of the estate tax would more than make up for any initial loss in asset values.
- Considered over a lifetime, the progressivity of the NRST would be similar to that of the current income tax regime. The progressivity of the NRST would be achieved through use of a rebate and replacement of regressive payroll taxes.

2. Study Methodology

Our goal was to translate the economic effects of a change in the tax regime into understandable impacts on individual households. Traditional methodologies, which examine statistical averages for a single year and aggregate very different households, lack vital data and often do not reveal important and key information.

In our analysis, we focus on specific households, considering the impact of the actual tax code. Further, we examined households over their entire remaining lifetime rather than focusing on a single year. Examining a variety of family profiles, we develop critical insights into the effects of a change in the tax regime. We then varied individual household characteristics and economic assumptions to ensure that our conclusions are robust.

Taxes affect the household either directly, or indirectly through the economy (see Figure 1 below). Direct taxation on the household includes individual income taxes (including the earned income tax credit), property taxes, and the employee portion of payroll taxes.

Indirect taxes are collected from businesses (including corporate income taxes, the employer portion of the payroll tax, sales and service taxes, excise taxes, and corporate property taxes). Businesses serve as intermediaries between workers, investors, and consumers. So all indirect taxes and other costs on business are ultimately paid by households: through reduced wages and benefits, lower investment returns, and higher prices. Economists cannot agree about how the indirect tax burden is allocated among these three economic activities. However, it is certain that all indirect taxes and other costs are ultimately paid by households.

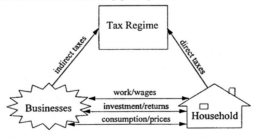

Figure 1. All Taxes Fall on Households

In addition to the visible tax revenues collected by government, there are several effects of taxation which are hidden, or less visible. These include seigniorage (the inflation tax), compliance burden of the tax code, economic distortions, and slower economic growth.

Our method accounted for the combination of direct, indirect, and hidden taxation in an integrated framework. Differences in direct taxes were computed by applying the tax code to a household's financial situation, directly affecting the funds available for investment and consumption. Changes in indirect and hidden taxes were distributed to household economic activities of work, investment, and consumption. The taxes' magnitude and incidence result in changes to the after-tax market prices, wages and investment returns available to the household.

Resulting changes in the household's annual finances lead to different levels of real consumption and investment, which carry through to affect the household's finances over its remaining lifetime. These changes are then integrated to produce a summary measure of the effect on a household's remaining real lifetime consumption.

3. Economic Assumptions

We compared the effects on real lifetime consumption of replacing the 1996 Federal Income Tax code with the National Retail Sales Tax proposed by Americans for Fair Taxation (AFT). Throughout, we attempt to match AFT's proposed tax rate of 23% (tax-inclusive)[1] on all final goods and services, to exclude from taxation any resale of existing consumer-owned housing, and to include a rebate to all families based on federal poverty levels for a given family size. We have also followed AFT's proposal that Social Security is indexed to a consumer price index which includes the NRST.[2]

We should note that we analyzed only law-abiding households, those attempting to comply with the actual tax code. Our conclusions would not remain valid for households engaged in criminal enterprises, or otherwise able to evade their current income taxes.

Our base case economic assumptions include a 3% inflation rate under the status quo (with nominal tax brackets indexed for inflation), incidence of direct taxes entirely on the household, employer payroll taxes incident on workers, corporate income taxes incident on investors, an NRST distributed two-thirds to consumers and one-third to factors of production (divided between workers and investors by their value share in the economy), a 2% increase in economic efficiency (real purchasing power) from lower compliance costs (i.e., significantly less resources used to deal with filing complex income tax forms), a 1% increase in economic efficiency from other economic effects such as lower marginal tax rates, and a minor 0.05% increase in real wage growth under the NRST due to effects such as increased investment.

We tested variations in these base case assumptions to ensure the robustness of our results. We found that perhaps the most significant change in the level of improvement for many families is if the replacement tax rate is changed. Replacing the current income tax with a consumption tax, one might expect at least the modest macro-economic improvements mentioned above at any revenue-neutral tax rate. However, at the time of this analysis there was some uncertainty as to the rate. A lower or higher tax rate would obviously lead to either a better or a more modest improvement (respectively) in most families' real life-time consumption than is calculated at 23%. For low-income families, any differences from the base case results tend to be small, as a proportionately-changed rebate makes up for any change in the NRST tax over the bulk of their expenditures. Differences would be more marked for middle and higher-income families, though the shape of graphs and general conclusions that we present would remain valid over a range of possible rates.

4. Effects on Typical Households

We began our study with an analysis of the finances of a typical middle-class family—the "Cleavers." The Cleavers are a married couple, aged 40. They own their home and are struggling to meet their mortgage payments while raising their two children (ages 10 and 11). Both parents are employed outside of the home. Some key financial information about the Cleavers is shown in Table 1 (below).

---

[1] A tax-inclusive rate is used for easier comparison with the current income tax rates, which are for gross (tax-inclusive) income. A 23% tax rate on gross sales corresponds to a 30% tax rate on net sales. The middle federal income tax bracket in 1996 was 31% of gross income, corresponding to a 45% tax rate on net income.
[2] In figure 2, the solid line represents Cleavers who have chosen never to purchase a home. Only Cleavers with combined average career income above about $40,000 per year are considered homeowners in this graph.

Table 1

The Cleavers' 1998 Household Financial Snapshot (in 1996 dollars)

Budget Item	Amount
Household Gross Wages	$46,439
Taxable Investment Earnings	$615
Visible Income, Employee Payroll, and Property Tax Burden	($10,686)
Mortgage Payments	($8,385)
Charitable Contributions	($471)
Other Household Consumption (excluding Value of Employer-Provided Health Care Plan)	($24,453)
Remaining Income for Savings	$3,060
Value of Employer-Provided Health Care Plan	$4,800
Employer Contribution to Tax-Deferred Retirement Savings Plan	$929

In Figure 2 (below), we find that families with the Cleavers' household profile would be financially better off under the NRST regime. Even over a wide range of incomes from poverty level, about $16,000 per year for the Cleavers' family of four, to the higher income levels families with this profile would be better off than under the current income tax regime.

A combination of factors including lower tax burdens, lower compliance costs, lower marginal tax rates, and increased economic growth and efficiency would allow middle-class families like the Cleavers to enjoy higher real lifetime consumption under the NRST than under the federal income tax.

Effect on Homeowners

One issue of concern to many middle-class households is the effect of the change on the value of their homes. Because the sales tax would apply only to new homes, the market value of owner-occupied homes would increase under the new tax regime (to the point where newly constructed homes would not be disadvantaged from the viewpoint of prospective home buyers). Also, homeowners with fixed-rate mortgages would find it easier to make their mortgage payments under the NRST regime. This is because if enough of the NRST falls on consumers, after-tax consumer prices would rise to some extent. So mortgages could be paid off with less valuable dollars.

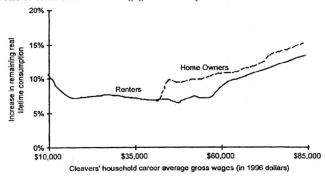

Figure 2. Lifetime Improvement under NRST for the Cleavers*

It is also possible that mortgage interest rates would decline, which would further benefit existing and prospective homeowners (though this effect is not included in our base case analysis). Since many middle-aged families already own their homes and tend to have substantial outstanding fixed-rate mortgages, they would be relatively better off under the NRST regime. Figure 2 (above) illustrates the relative improvement of current homeowners.

Variations with Income

Low-income Households

A critical factor in examining low-income households is the status and amount of government subsidies (including transfer payments) that they receive. These include Supplemental Security Income and food stamps.

The working poor not receiving government subsidies tend to be better off under the NRST regime. This enhancement of their financial condition is due to the rebate system, which effectively exempts the working poor from paying any of the NRST. The repeal of the payroll tax allows this group to take home their entire paycheck and avoid the substantial payroll taxes (less earned income tax credit) that they face under the current federal tax system. They are also relieved of the indirect effects of replaced corporate income and payroll taxes that currently decrease their wages and increase the prices they pay as consumers. Figure 3 (below) illustrates the improvement that would be experienced by low-income families with other characteristics similar to those of the Cleavers.

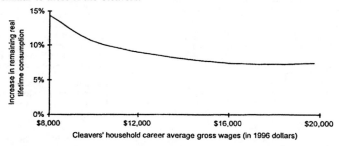

Figure 3. Lifetime Improvement under NRST for Low-Income Cleavers

Currently, most government transfer payments (such as food stamps, Supplementary Security Income, and Medicaid) are indexed for inflation. It is possible that these transfer payments would be indexed to an after-tax consumer price indicator (CPI) that includes the NRST. If so, families would receive both indexed transfer payments and the NRST rebate.

Figure 4 (below) illustrates the improvement under the NRST for the "Lowes," a low-income family with four children. The Lowe household receives enough government subsidies each year to bring them to 100% of poverty line consumption (about $22,000 annually for the Lowe family of six). A combination of rebate and full indexing of benefits would lead to substantial financial improvement for low-income families like the Lowes. In effect, indexing benefits to a CPI that includes the NRST would over-compensate for the change, as the rebate alone already reimburses the entire tax. Even if their subsidies were indexed to a CPI that only partially or not at all included the national retail sales tax, the rebate effectively exempts these families from the NRST, ensuring that they would still be roughly even or financially better off. Under welfare reform that occurred after this study took place, we expect that those families with household gross wages averaging in the lowest range of figure 4 over their entire remaining careers would be unusual cases.

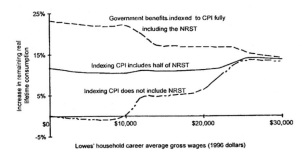

**Figure 4. Lifetime Improvement under NRST for a Low-Income Family
Receiving Government Subsidies**

High-Income Households

Working households with higher incomes would no longer be subject to progressively higher marginal income tax rates, and tend to improve under the NRST regime. The top end of the Cleavers' graph in Figure 2 illustrates their improvement.

6. Variations with Age

We found that age is an important factor in determining the effect of the NRST on households.

Young Households

Younger households, as illustrated by the "Juniors," tend to be financially better off after the change. The Juniors are a married couple, aged 25. They both work, and hope to buy a home and start a family someday. They are just now beginning their careers, and would experience most of their working lives under the new regime.

A combination of factors including lower compliance costs, lower marginal tax rates, and increased economic growth and efficiency would allow younger families like the Juniors to enjoy higher real lifetime consumption under the NRST than under the federal income and payroll tax regime. Figure 5 (below) illustrates the improvement in lifetime consumption for the Juniors over a wide range of income levels.

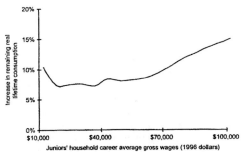

Figure 5. Lifetime Improvement under NRST for a Young Family

Elderly Households

The "Seniors" represent a typical retired couple. We find that the impact of the NRST depends critically on the amount and composition of their savings. Because the sales tax applies only to new homes, the value of the elderly's home equity tends to increase under the new tax regime. Also, portfolios with a higher proportion of their wealth in tax-deferred status (such as in IRAs and "401(k)" plans) and in unrealized capital gains would do relatively better under the NRST, since these holdings would no longer be subject to federal income tax.

376

Some wealthier seniors would tend not to benefit from the redistribution of the tax burden. This is because wealthier seniors have a larger portion of financial assets whose after-tax purchasing power may decline under the new regime.

However, for many seniors the removal of income taxes on asset earnings and retirement account disbursements, and the exclusion of their existing homes from the NRST, along with the repeal of the estate tax more than make up for any initial loss in asset values. Most elderly couples with moderate or limited financial resources would be significantly better off under the NRST (see figure 6). The rebate in place would already cover all taxes on essentials (including some formerly hidden-taxes built-in to today's prices). Provisions to fully index Social Security for any increase in after-tax consumer prices would then more than compensate for any loss on these families' modest savings. And for those households with estates over $1,200,000, the removal of estate taxes could more than make up for any loss of the estate's purchasing power.

Figure 6 shows these effects on the Seniors for a wide range of net worth (including home equity and private pension funds). As a point of reference for this figure, the median family net worth for a household whose head was between 65 and 74 years of age in 1992 was listed as $103,600 (Federal Reserve Bulletin , October 1994). This suggests that the majority of seniors are described in the lower range of wealth in figure 6, and would experience considerable improvement under the NRST.

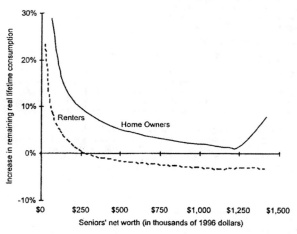

Figure 6. Lifetime Effect of NRST for the Seniors under a Range of Financial Profiles at Retirement

While some wealthier Seniors may experience a reduction in purchasing power, their own financial well-being might not be the only issue they consider in their decision to support a particular tax regime. Factors such as the effect on their grandchildren or on the poor may take precedence in their decision.

7. Effects on Marginal Tax Rates

Under the NRST regime, marginal tax rates on work and savings would be substantially lower for many households, increasing their incentives to work and save. This is primarily due to the replacement of high marginal income tax rates with a low flat rate on consumption.

We measured the incentives to work, computing the additional (after-tax) real goods and services that a household could consume by working additional hours. For example, suppose that the Cleavers are contemplating working an extra hour a year for each year over the course of their remaining careers. And suppose that after all taxes under the existing tax regime, they could purchase a total of 4 pairs of shoes with their additional pay. If, under the NRST, they could instead purchase 5 pairs of shoes for that same extra work, then their marginal incentives will have increased by 25%.

Figure 7 (below) shows that although the marginal incentives may decrease for some low-income households, a broad range of households experience significantly increased incentives. Incentives to work rise by over 20% for many families, depending on their earnings. On an economy-wide level, these improved incentives would lead to higher economic growth and efficiency.

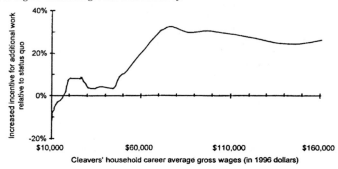

Figure 7. Effect on Cleavers' Marginal Incentives to Work

Figure 7. Effect on Cleavers' Marginal Incentives to Work

8. Regressivity Analysis

There is a common perception that consumption taxes are regressive, which would be supported in a myopic single-year analysis of the tax system.

The argument is that:

In a given year wealthy people save a higher fraction of their income than poor people, so the wealthy would pay a lower fraction of their income in consumption taxes.

However, a lifetime analysis reveals that most or all of the saved income of a household is eventually consumed in retirement or by the heirs, at which time it is subject to the consumption tax. So over a lifetime, a consumption tax—without a rebate—is roughly flat across income categories.

Under the NRST, a consumption tax is combined with a rebate which refunds all taxes up to poverty-level consumption. This clearly makes the NRST a progressive tax.

9. Conclusions

Because the combination of the current tax code and government subsidies is extremely complex, there is probably no change that can guarantee everyone to be better off. But under the National Retail Sales Tax proposed by Americans for Fair Taxation, several factors would allow most families to enjoy higher real lifetime consumption than under the current federal income and payroll tax regime.

These factors include:

• a rebate which would keep the amount of taxes paid by most households similar to or lower than the current income tax regime, and would effectively exempt low-income households from the NRST,

• indexing of Social Security, which would effectively hold recipients harmless against possible after-tax price increases,

• lower compliance costs,

• lower marginal tax rates, and

• increased economic growth and efficiency

Some wealthier seniors would tend not to benefit from the redistribution of the tax burden. However, their own financial well-being might not be the only issue that wealthier seniors consider in their decision to support a particular tax regime. Other factors, such as the effect on their grandchildren or on the poor, may take precedence in their decision.

I would like to again thank the committee for the opportunity to contribute this testimony. Additionally, I should like to recognize a number of individuals that were helpful in this effort. This research has benefited from discussions with William W.

378

Beach, Dale W. Jorgenson, James M. Poterba, and Gary Robbins. David R. Burton and Laura D. Dale have contributed a number of questions and valuable discussions. I am grateful for the dedicated assistance of Roberto Szechtman and Ellynne T. Dec, along with Decisions and Ethics Center research assistants J. Eric Bickel, William F. Carone, Alexis G. Collomb, Jeffrey D. Cornwell, George K. Ferguson, Kenneth B. Malpass, and Marcia F. Tsugawa. Our lifetime model and methodology are an extension of work by Stephen M. Malinak, Frederick V. Giarrusso, and Jeffrey K. Belkora, along with suggested improvements from Paul B. Skov, James M. Knappenberger, Derek D. Ayers, and Michael M. Reeds. Special thanks to Elizabeth C. Brierly for editing large portions of this report. Research guidance was provided by Frederick V. Giarrusso and Center Director Ronald A. Howard. The Decisions and Ethics Center gratefully acknowledges help from those volunteers, and a gift from the National Tax Research Committee that enabled this research effort.
   Sincerely,

Joseph M. Kahn

Statement of Bert Loftman, M.D., Atlanta, GA

Mr. Chairman and Members of the Ways and Means Committee:
   My name is Bert Loftman, and I am a physician based in Atlanta, Georgia. I greatly appreciate the opportunity to present testimony regarding the impact of the FairTax on the US health care delivery system. I am privileged to be the only witness testifying on this subject. I can assure you that I speak for a great many physicians with whom I have discussed the FairTax. I am hopeful that, at some point, there will be formal resolution by the physician groups. Attached to this written testimony is a paper of mine from 1994 titled, "Health Care Reform, An Historic Perspective." This will supplement what I say here.
   During the past few years, Congress has wrestled with the many problems inherent with our current health care system, and for good reason. The costs of health care delivery have escalated exponentially. While it is often argued we have the best heath care in the world, we have a selective system. Too many Americans are without health care.
   What are the root causes of this and how do you, as policymakers, address these causes? I suggest that one of the key causes is our tax system that separates the health care recipient from the real costs of health care. In doing so, we hold health care up as one of the few major U.S. industries that is not responsible to consumers. To turn a phrase, our health care system is in the intensive care unit.
   What are the problems? To begin with, this system has driven up the costs of health care. In 1965,health care was 5 percent of the U.S. economy. Now it has risen to over 15 percent. There are rising numbers of uninsured. These number about 40 million or 15 percent of the population. For them, individual health insurance is very expensive. They must compete with the third party payer systems of employer-based health insurance and Medicare. In the private and governmental sectors, most people have employer-based-insurance. They face the portability problem, where they must change insurance plans when they change jobs. They also face the job lock problem where they remain in unsatisfactory jobs because of the health insurance coverage in their current jobs.
   A few years ago, the third-party payers paid the providers of health care with traditional fee for service or indemnity insurance. Now they pay with a system known as managed care. With this system, the insurance companies make what they consider the appropriate health care choices. The problem is that many patients would rather choose the quality of their own health care and this dissatisfaction has led to political unrest. Many health care reform discussions center about moving away from employer-paid health care.
   One way is a single payer system; but those countries with socialized medicine are experiencing many difficulties. To date, this has not been a popular solution in the US. Another way is to use the income tax codes to offset the employer-based health care exclusion that began during World War II. I refer you to a paper that I wrote a few years back on the history of how this occurred. These tax code changes include tax equity where the income tax exclusion of employer-paid health care are removed or individually paid health care receives the same treatment. Another innovative way is medical savings accounts that Congress legislated with the Kennedy-Kassebaum Bill. These have not proved as popular as the proponents predicted. A major reason was the many restrictions that were placed upon them.
   Enter the FairTax into this debate. It is true that The Fair Tax would greatly impact the U.S. health care system. However, first we should consider what it would

not do. The Fair Tax is designed to be revenue neutral and would make no changes in Medicare or Medicaid. It would leave intact the federal safety net for the elderly and the indigent. Most importantly, I believe, The Fair Tax would remove the income tax exclusion that employer-based health care now enjoys. This would not require employers to drop their benefit of health care coverage. However, the incentive for health care coverage would no longer be exclusively employer-based.

What would the FairTax do? More people would likely begin to choose individually-based health care coverage. They would probably choose non-cancelable policies. This would help bring down the numbers of uninsured as people retained their individually owned health insurance policies, even when they were sick. As people chose individually owned health insurance, the insurance industry would begin to respond with more individually based insurance policies. People would likely begin to look more favorably at low cost non-managed care insurance policies. In other words, they would begin to favor catastrophic insurance policies.

Of course, there is tax-free savings for health care and other wants. When people have savings, they can begin to see the advantages of low cost catastrophic coverage. This would begin to connect people to the cost of their own health care and this would begin to bring the cost of health care down. Thus the Fair Tax would not only move us away from employer-based healthcare with its portability and job-lock problems; the Fair Tax would likely also lower the cost of health care and bring down the number of uninsured. Regarding managed care, individuals would own their own policies and have a choice of whether they had prepaid managed care or catastrophic indemnity insurance coverage.

Congress also wrestles with Medicare and its problem of escalating costs. When Congress legislates to control these costs, it fosters patient and physician unrest. This is because when Medicare makes the choices, it is a form of rationing. Consider that in 1965 when Congress enacted Medicare, many people retired without health care coverage because most was employer-based. They also retired without adequate savings because the income tax is anti-savings. Under the FairTax, people would begin to retire with individually owned catastrophic health care coverage. Perhaps with the Fair Tax, many people would choose not to change their health care coverage when they retire.

The Fair Tax would not solve all the problems of the U.S. healthcare delivery system, and I don't want to leave this impression. Many people would still choose not to obtain health care coverage. However, we must compare the FairTax to the present system and not to an ideal. We must only ask if it helps us get to the idea. In reality, there would likely be less uninsured than the current 40 million people without coverage. Many people would probably still prefer a corporate health care system that manages their care. If so, the Fair Tax does not discourage this.

The FairTax would likely effect the US health care delivery system in a way that would lower costs, decrease the numbers of uninsured, help alleviate the portability problems, give patients choice and defuse the politics of our health care system.

I would make a suggestion regarding professional or trade organization as the American Hospital Association, the American Medical Association, the American Nurses Association, the American Pharmaceutical Organization, etc. These organizations heavily lobby Congress but they have been silent on the impact of taxation on the health care delivery system. Congress should ask them to study this issue and poll their members so they can take a stand on tax reform as health care reform.

A physician's first duty is to do no harm. I believe it is the job of Congress to do the same. Our current US health care system of employer-based health care does great harm. I hope that when you ponder HR 2525 with its Fair Tax and repeal of the 16th Amendment that you consider its favorable impact on the health care delivery system.

Attachment is being retained in the Committee files.

Statement of Daniel J. Mitchell, Heritage Foundation

I wish to thank the committee for the opportunity to testify. The views I express are my own and do not necessarily reflect those of The Heritage Foundation.

Mr. Chairman and members of the committee, the current tax code of the United States is irreversibly broke and should be repealed. The tax laws undermine the country's prosperity by imposing needlessly harsh venalities on work, savings, and investment. Many taxpayers face confiscatory tax rates and often are forced to pay more than one layer of tax on their income, while the politically well-connected can take advantage of special deductions, credits, preferences, shelters, and loopholes to minimize their own tax liability. The result of this double standard is a tax system that not only penalizes productive behavior, but also violates the fundamental constitutional principle of equal treatment under the law.

For both moral and economic reasons, the current code should be replaced by a single-rate, consumption-based tax. The good news is that there are two major plans that meet these criteria: the flat tax and the national retail sales tax. Replacing the current system with either—but not both—of these two taxes immediately would restore the principle of fairness to the tax system because both would treat all taxpayers equally. Both the flat tax and a national sales tax would replace today's discriminatory tax structure with a single low rate. In addition, either plan would eliminate the current tax code's bias against savings and investment and promote the kind of capital formation that America needs to boost workers' incomes and ensure long-term economic growth. In addition, because both tax reform proposals would be simple to administer, the ultimate result would be a dramatic downsizing of the Internal Revenue Service (IRS) bureaucracy and billions of dollars in compliance costs saved each year.

How is it that these different types of taxes could produce such similar results? The answer lies in the fact that the flat taxed and sales tax are almost identical in purpose and principle. Both rest on the fundamentally should principle that all income should be taxes at one low rate and only one time (what is known as a "consumption base"), and that the tax should be collected in the last intrusive way possible. The only significant difference between the two is the collection point. A flat tax is collected up front, imposing a single layer of tax on income when it is earned, and a sales tax imposes one layer of tax when the income is spent. In both cases, income is taxes, but only once and presumably at a very low rate.

WHAT DO THE FLAT TAX AND A NATIONAL SALES TAX HAVE IN COMMON?

Most taxpayers assume that the flat tax and a national sales tax are radically different ways to fund the federal government. Because one tax is collected from the paycheck and the other is collected at the cash register, this assumption is understandable. Yet by almost every standard, the flat tax and a national retail sales tax represent two sides of the same coin. The common features of the flat tax and national sales tax are:

• **A single flat rate.** Under both plans, income is taxed at one low rate. This would ensure that the government treated taxpayers equally and would address the problem of high marginal tax rates. The single low rate would promote faster economic growth by minimizing tax penalities on work, risk-taking, and entrepreneurship.

• **Adoption of the flat tax or a national sales tax also would end the discriminatory treatment caused by a tax code that grants preferences or imposes penalties on certain behaviors and activities. Either reform would change the code so that all taxpayers—and all income—are treated the same under the law.**

WHY THE FLAT TAX IS A CONSUMPTION TAX

• **To many Americans, consumption taxes are those collected as the cash register—such as the state sales tax—or value-added taxes like those they might encounter on a trip to Europe. The national Retail Sales Tax, needless to say, is an example of a consumption-based tax. Yet it also is possible to collect a consumption tax through an income tax structure. This s why economists and public finance experts consider the flat tax a consumption tax. Why? Because, unlike the current tax code, a flat tax does not impose greater penalities on income that is saved and invested that on income that is consumed. A tax code that does not discriminate against savings and investment is considered a consumption-based tax system, regardless of whether taxes are collected at the paycheck or at the cash register. In this respect, the flat tax is a version of a consumption tax.**

WHY DOUBLE TAXATION IS DETRIMENTAL

To understand double taxation, consider a taxpayer who has 410 of disposable after-tax income. That taxpayer has a choice; either to spend the income immediately or to defer consumption by investing it. Consuming the money immediately yields $100 of benefit immediately, but investing it would yield a return that could allow the taxpayer to consumer, say, $115 a year from now. The decision to invest obviously varies according to individual preferences about the value of consumption today compared with consumption in the future, but let us assume a taxpayer would be willing to give up $100 of consumption today in exchange for $100 of consumption one year later. In this example, of course, the taxpayer will choose to invest. In addition to making the taxpayer better off in the future, this decision also has a desirable impact on the economy by increasing capital.

Today's system of multiple taxation, however, undermines capital formation. If the government decides to tax the return earned on the $100 investment, the hypothetical taxpayer in the above example may wind up sacrificing $100 of consumption today to gain only $105 in after-tax consumption one year from now. Fewer individuals under this scenario would choose to invest, opting instead for immediate consumption and thereby depriving the economy of their capital. In addition, under today's system, taxpayers can look forward to paying two additional layers of tax on this $100 investment; capital gains and death taxes. Double taxation, therefore, significantly undermines savings, investment, and future economic growth, and—because every economic theory, even Marxism, acknowledges that capital formation is the key to faster growth and higher wages—is particularly self-destructive.

WHAT ARE THE BENEFITS OF A SINGLE-RATE TAX SYSTEM?

• **Fairness.** The tax code is riddled with discrimination. They are right. The government either imposes tax penalties or grants tax preferences depending on the source, use, or level of income. All of these special provisions violate the principle that all citizens should be treated equally by the law. The flat tax and a sales tax would restore fairness in the system by ensuring that all taxpayers, all income, and all products are treated the same.

• **Economic growth.** Both the flat tax and a sales tax would minimize the tax rate imposed on productive behavior and eliminate the myriad forms of double taxation in the current code. Consequently, either one would boost the economy's potential growth rate and cause permanent increases in economic output. How much the economy would benefit is not easy to predict, but many economists project that, within 10 years, the economy would be 5 percent to 10 percent larger than it would be under the current tax structure.

• **Higher incomes.** A low tax rate increases the incentives to work and the desire to work longer hours. Tax reform also makes workers more productive because companies would be more willing to invest in upgrading their production capabilities, giving their employees better machinery, tools, equipment, and technology. As the attached chart illustrates, this capital-drive increase in productivity is tied closely to higher wages.

• **Job creation.** Tax reform also will make employees more valuable to business, thereby increasing wages for those already working and stimulating the creation of new jobs. The combination of lower taxes and faster growth will make it more profitable to hire certain workers particularly those with low skill levels who previously may have been considered unemployable.

• **Increased wealth.** The value of income-producing assets (everything from stocks and bonds to office buildings and pet stores) is determined by market expectations of future income discounted by inflation, risk, and taxes. Once a lower tax rate is put in place, whether through the flat tax or a national sales tax, and double taxation is eliminated, income-producing assets will become more valuable (that is, there will be an increase in the present value of the future after-tax income stream generated by those assets).

• **Savings and investment.** Tax reform to eliminate these penalties on capital formation would increase the incentives to save and invest. Moreover, a flat tax or sales tax would make the United States a magnet for capital from around the world.

• **Lower interest rates.** Tax reform will reduce interest rates between 25 percent and 35 percent, according to a study published by the Kansas City Federal Reserve Bank.

• **Lower compliance costs.** Because both the flat tax and a national sales tax would eliminate the bewildering complexity of the current system, tax reform would slash the $157 billion annual costs of complying with personal and corporate income taxes.

• **Smaller IRS, more civil liberties.** The current tax code gives the IRS sweeping, virtually unlimited power to monitor people's lives, track their assets, and review their expenditures. Although neither the flat tax nor a national sales tax can be expected to rid the United States of the IRS or eliminate every possible conflict with the government, the dramatic simplification that either reform would bring about would significantly reduce the size, scope, and power of the IRS bureaucracy.

• **Less political corruption.** The tax code today is the result of 97 years of special deals, loopholes, and preferences. Each one of these loopholes benefits a special inters. The flat tax or a national sales tax would remove from the tax system the corrupting process of exchanging loopholes for political support.

• **No social engineering.** One of the most attractive features of both the flat tax and a national sales tax is that politicians no longer would be able to use the tax code for purposes of social engineering. The flat tax would eliminate all the biases and preferences in the income tax, and a sales tax is designed so that all products and services would be taxes at exactly the same rate.

RESPONDING TO THE CRITICS OF TAX REFORM

• **Criticism:** Implementing a national sales tax would create the risk that the United States might end up like Europe, with both income and consumption taxes.

• **Response:** Advocates of a national sales tax properly vow that complete and irreversible elimination of the income tax must occur before such a plan can be enacted. The only certain way to prevent future politicians from pulling a bait-and-switch on a trusting public, however, would be to amend the Constitution by repealing the 16th Amendment, which gives Congress the power to impose an income tax, and expressly forbidding direct taxes or income. This presumably would mean the abolition of Social Security and Medicare payroll taxes as well.

• **Criticism:** Neither the flat tax nor the sales tax will capture the entire underground economy.

• **Response:** This is true but meaningless. A drug dealer is not going to report his income under the flat tax and certainly will not collect taxes on the "products" he sells under a national sales tax system. But the current system does not capture this money either, so this argument hardly serves as a reason to reject ax reform. At the very least, the flat tax and a national sales tax would reduce the level of tax evasion by people who are trying to protect their income from unfair and excessive taxation today.

CONCLUSION

The current U.S. tax system is an unmitigated nature. On both economic and moral grounds, the tax code should be repealed and replaced with a system that treats all taxpayers—and all income—fairly and equally. Both the flat tax and a national sales tax satisfy this standard, and both would improve the economy's performance substantially.

Because plans for the flat tax and a national retail sales tax are so similar, lawmakers have no reason to champion one at the expense of the other. Advocates of tax reform would seek instead to highlight the benefits and similarities of the two plans, and, when the opportunity arises, rally behind the one that has garnered more political and popular support.

Worker Compensation Closely Linked to Investment

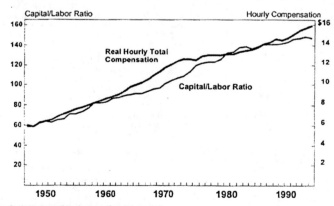

Note: Capital/Labor ratio = Amount of capital per worker.
Source: Aldona and Gary Robbins, "The Truth About Falling Wages," *Economic Scorecard*, Institute for Policy Innovation, TaxAction Analysis, Third Quarter 1995.

Individuals Face Only One Layer of Tax if Income Is Spent Immediately, Up to Five Layers if Invested and Passed on to Heir

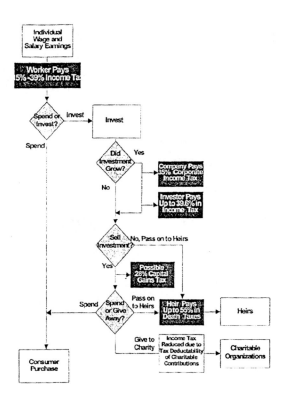

The Flat Tax vs. a National Sales Tax: Individuals Face
One Layer of Tax When Income Is Either Earned or Spent

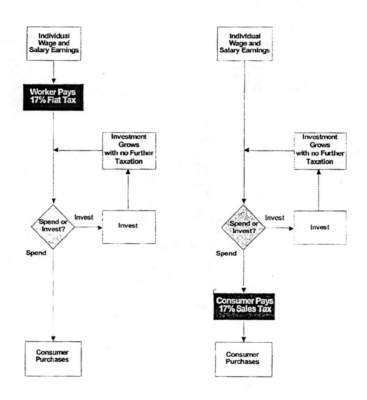

Saving and Investment Can Be Taxed up to Four Times: Message to Taxpayer Is "Spend Now"

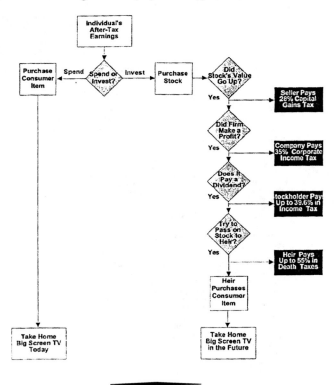

Statement of National Federation of Independent Business

INTRODUCTION

The irony of tax reform is that even as it proponents have grown more insistent, the tax code itself has simply grown. It's larger and more complex today than when Hall and Rabushka first offered their ideas to the world. So while others may argue the relative merits of a flat income tax verses a national sales tax, NFIB has focused its attention at the real problem for America's small business owners—the current IRS Code.

The fact is, the current income tax code is far too complex. The tax code is a quagmire of confusion that forces taxpayers to bear tremendous costs just to comply with it—about $200 billion annually, or $700 for every man, woman, and child in America. Consider this: There are 7 million words in income tax laws and regulations. There are 703 tax forms. There are 101,295 pages of IRS laws and regulations. The IRS sends out about 8 billion pages of forms and instructions each year, the equivalent of paper made from 293,760 trees, according to a 1995 study. The amount of paperwork the IRS receives each year would circle the Earth 28 times. One billion 1099 forms are mailed each year tracking interest and dividend income. The private

386

sector pays $250 billion just to comply with income tax laws. The average cost of compliance for small-and medium-sized corporations is $7,240 for every $1,000 in taxes they pay. Nearly 60 percent of all taxpayers seek assistance to file their tax returns each year, more time than it takes to build every car, truck, and van produced in the United States. When Money magazine asked 46 professional tax preparers to calculate a hypothetical family's tax return in 1997, they responded with 46 different answers. As Albert Einstein once said, "the hardest thing in the world to understand is the income tax."

The fact remains that real tax reform will not occur at the same time the tax code is expanded and complicated even further. We need to abolish the current code first and then replace it with a code that offers lower taxes, encourages work and savings, is fair to all taxpayers, foregoes social engineering, contains no hidden taxes, and is difficult to change.

SMALL BUSINESS AND THE TAX CODE

So why are small businesses leading the charge to scrap the IRS Code? The answer is simple. Small businesses—more than any other segment of our economy—are the favorite target of the IRS Code and the IRS. When tax reformers raise the issue of tax code complexity, they are talking about the burden placed on America's small businesses.

Most taxpayers don't even itemize. They receive their W–2 form, take the standard deduction, and send in their 1040EZ. But all small business owners find themselves buried under the most complex areas of the tax code. An while big corporations have the luxury of accounting offices and high priced tax professionals, many small business owners still file their our returns. Any way you slice it, it's America's small businesses that shoulder the brunt of tax code complexity.

Tax Code Complexity and Small Business

Small businesses historically pay about one-tenth the income taxes collected by the federal government. That was about $60 billion in 1994. But the burden of the tax code on small businesses is much higher.

THe Center for the Study of American Business reported small firms with fewer than 20 employees spent more than $5,000 per employee in 1992 to comply with federal regulations. Paperwork costs alone—mainly comprised of tax-related paperwork—cost these small firms more then $2,000 per employee, or twice as much as the paperwork costs imposed on firms with 500 or more employees.

Why are small businesses disproportionately affected? One reason is that the most complex parts of the tax code are targeted directly at small business owners. Take, for instance, this example:

The individual Alternative Minimum Tax is a remarkably complex and obtuse provision in a tax code not known for its clarity. It literally requires taxpayers to calculate their taxes twice, and then pay the larger amount. Compared to the regular income tax, the MAT imposes lower marginal tax rates on a broader income base. It's sort of a perverse "Flat Tax."

Who did Congress have in mind when it created the AMT? American's small business. Of the AMT's 27 different adjustments and so-called tax preference items—deductions disallowed or reduced—16 are business related. Keep in mind, we're talking about the individual Alternative Minimum Tax. (Corporations have their own ATM.)

How complex is the AMT? Line 8 says, "Enter the difference between regular tax and AMT depreciation." That means small business owners have to recalculate the value of their depreciation allowances using either "the straight line method over 40 years with the same mid-month convention used for the regular tax" or the "straight line method over the property's class life with the same convention used for the regular tax" or the "150 percent declining balance method, switching to the straight line method for the first year it gives a larger tax deduction, over the property's class life." All depending on the type of property involved, of course. And they have to do this calculation for every depreciable asset they own!

Understand? Neither do small business owners. There are 26 other adjustments necessary to calculate AMT taxable income.

Worse yet, the AMT has the side effect of hitting taxpayers when they can least afford the bill. A business suffering from lower-than-expected revenues is more likely to fall into the clutches of the AMT than a thriving business. The AMT literally kicks a small business "when it is down." As your cash flow goes down, you AMT tax bite goes up!

The current tax code is full of "AMTs." Depreciation schedules, death taxes, accounting methods—all fall heaviest on the individual with business-related income.

The only solution America's small business owners have to these problems is to eliminate the 101,295 pages and seven million words of IRS rules and regulations which make up the current IRS code. Scrapping the IRS tax code is one of NFIB's top tax priorities.

WHAT SHOULD THE NEW CODE LOOK LIKE?

Although NFIB is not promoting a specific replacement tax plan, NFIB proposes the following Seven Points of Principle that should be considered when developing a new tax code fair to small business:

- Lower Taxes—to create jobs and opportunities
- Fosters growth—encourages work and savings
- Fair—for all taxpayers
- Simple enough—all taxpayers can understand
- Neutral—no "social engineering"
- Visible—no hidden taxes
- Stable—difficult to change

Some have asked to move beyond these seven principles and outline what sort of tax code small businesses would like to see. Here are some additional guidelines from surveys of our members, and the results from the Small Business Summit NFIB held in June of 1998:

Reduce the Overall Tax Burden

Any discussion of tax reform should only be held within the context of an overall tax cut. Revenue neutrality destroyed whatever benefits may have been derived from the 1986 Tax Reform Act. We should learn our lesson and not be shackled into thinking we have to raise Peter's taxes to cut Pauls. By embracing a tax cut as part of reform, we can minimize the concerns raised about winners and losers.

Moreover, this principle wraps up fairness and complexity all in one. If all income and/or consumption were taxes at the same rate, then much of the perceived unfairness of the current system would be eradicated. Furthermore, distinctions between types of income—earned, unearned—disappear, making the code much less complex.

One important note is to observe that the single rate principle should not exclude two-tiered plans—like Senator Ashcroft's plan—that take payroll tax rates into consideration. While the Ashcroft plan ostensibly includes two rates—10% and 25%—taxpayers only see a single unified (income plus payroll tax rates) of 25% on their income. Taken as a whole, taxpayers still face just one marginal rate.

Tax Income Only Once

When tax reformers talk about "fostering growth" through the tax code, they really mean reducing the current tax on investment and savings. Right now, the tax code is biased against savings and investment because it taxes investment incomes twice or three times.

Here, we have growth and complexity together. Taxing income once means eliminating death taxes. That reform alone would make a dramatic improvement in reducing tax code complexity and riaising economic growth. It also means eliminating the double taxation of interest and dividends. There is overwhelming evidence regarding the negative relationship between taxes on cabins and investment and economic growth. As taxes on savings go up, economic growth does down.

Visible to All Taxpayers

This is an "anti-VAT" principle, pure and simple. The VAT is uniformly hated by small businesses because it is a hidden tax. They've seen the damage the VAT has done in Canada and Europe, and they fear the same results here in America. Back in 1985, we asked our members, "Do you favor or oppose creation of a value-added tax as a replacement for the current income-tax system?" Six out of ten said "No." Our members voted against the VAT because the fear it would be used to supplement, rather than replace, the current income tax code. I believe the case against the VAT has strengthened since then.

Conclusion

"Reckless" and "irresponsible" are the works President Clinton used to describe our plan to abolish the IRS tax code. With all due respect to the President, what is truly irresponsible is a tax code that is anti-work, anti-savings, and anti-family. What's reckless is continuing to live with seven million words that such the life right out of our economy.

President Clinton has indicated that small-business owners want to create "fiscal anarchy" by scrapping the code and then figuring out what to do next. Bust small employers understand that sometimes the old law must be put to rest before a new law can take its place. The time for fundamental tax reform is now!

NFIB thanks the Committee for focusing on this and listening to the views of America's economic engin—small business.

Statement of National Grain Trade Council

The National Grain Trade Council appreciates this opportunity to provide its views on the recent adverse international activities related to Foreign Sales Corporations or FSCs.

The mission of the National Grain Trade Council is to advocate and protect the principles and merits of open and competitive markets for the production and distribution of agricultural commodities. The National Grain Trade Council represents commodity exchanges, boards of trade, national marketing associations and more than 40 individual agribusiness companies.

The Issue

As you know, the World Trade Organization has ruled against the United States use of the Foreign Sales Corporation (after 15 years of use) labeling it an illegal subsidy. The WTO Appellate Body upheld this Panel ruling. The WTO labeling of the United States use of FSCs as a subsidy has resulted in adverse rulings related to the United States Agreement on Agricultural Exports. Under World Trade Organization procedures, the United States is expected to withdraw the illegal subsidy by October 1, 2000.

History

This problem has previously required Congress' attention and time. The United States began using a Domestic International Sales Corporation (DISC) in 1971. The purpose of the DISC was to allow United States exports to be more competitive by adjusting the level of taxes on exports to be more like those of our competitors. As discussed below, the U.S. has to compete with countries that do not tax any economic process beyond their borders (a territorial process) while U.S. corporations are subject to income tax on their worldwide income. Additionally, the countries with a territorial process employee a value added tax (VAT) and charge the VAT on imported goods and services but exempt or rebate the VAT on exported goods and services. This is the root of the unfairness.

In 1972 the European Communities requested dispute settlement consultations regarding the DISC measure, alleging that the DISC constituted an export subsidy. The United States also requested consultations with France, Belgium and the Netherlands contending that if the DISC measure were an export subsidy then the tax exemptions provided by those countries for foreign-source income were also export subsidies. The Panels found that both the DISC measure and the European tax systems had characteristics of an export subsidy prohibited under the General Agreements on Tariffs and Trade (GATT) of 1947. This dispute went on for many years.

In 1984 the United States replaced the DISC provisions with the FSC provisions. The United States enacted the FSC in response to a 1981 decision of the Council of the General Agreement on Tariffs and Trade providing that countries need not tax foreign-source income, including income from export transactions, and the failure to do so does not constitute a prohibited export subsidy. Acceptance of the GATT Council's 1981 decision by the European Community and the United States, as well as other parties to the GATT was instrumental to resolving the more than decade-long dispute between the EC and the United States. However, in 1997 the European Union again challenged, through the WTO, the United States use of FSCs calling them export subsidies.

WTO Ruling

The WTO Appellate Body has ruled against the United States' reliance on the 1981 GATT understanding and instead uses the definition of a subsidy where "government revenue that is otherwise due is foregone or not collected." This in turn has led the Appellate Body to use the "but for" test. That is, would revenue otherwise be due the government "but for" the enacted tax law.

In other words, if a government chooses to write its tax laws such that it has no authority to tax economic processes outside its borders, the foregone revenue is not a subsidy. Whereas if the government writes its tax laws such that it has the right to tax worldwide the economic process but chooses only to tax the economic process that occurs within its borders, the result is a subsidy. This is clearly form over substance and results in an unfair playing field for American exporters.

United States Impact

Without the FSC, American exporters are not able to compete fairly with exporters of other countries. This inability to compete will have a greater adverse impact on agricultural exports than nonagricultural exports. This is due to the very low profit margins related to agricultural commodities and the international buyer's view of purchasing the commodity product, which by its definition is no different than a competitor product, at the lowest price. We expect this would lead to lower US agricultural exports resulting in greater domestic supplies and further depressing US farm prices and the overall US farm economy.

Real Issue

The FSC is not the real issue. We are really talking about a trade issue that is fixed through various tax provisions. We can and perhaps will enact United States tax laws that equalize the international tax playing field and remain WTO compliant. That will require time and thoughtful analysis.

What the WTO Panel and Appellate Body are not recognizing is that there are different economic playing fields in each country and neither is superior to the other. Tax deductions and incentives must be viewed in their entirety. All taxes, both direct and indirect must be accounted for in determining fairness. Substance and not form must be the basis of comparing tax systems

Thank you for your attention to this matter.

Statement of Thurston Bell, National Institute for Taxation Education, Hanover, PA

Mr.Thurston P. Bell submits the following witness testimony. Mr. Bell is the Executive Researcher for the National Institute for Taxation Education. His findings are hereby respectfully submitted to the committee and contain the most unique testimony from one of the most qualified advocates for the people regarding IRS actions and behavior. His appears to be the lone voice calling for reasoned comunication and procedural compliance by the Tax Resistance movement and IRS alike.

Mr. Bell's active investigation and research during the last seven (7) years includes direct correspondence with the IRS and intervention on the behalf of individuals whose cases have previously been the most protracted and belligerent exchanges between citizens and their government.

He is at the forefront in assisting the growing numbers of people who have lost all faith in the IRS and the current means of collecting revenue. This makes him the most moderate and realistic voice in this arena of Law and Public Policy.

His research and reform efforts have aided the IRS in identifing and correcting areas wherein complete breakdowns in procedure had occurred in some IRS districts. He is creidited with helping the service in some districts achieve renewed compliance with statutory, regulatory, and published procedures contained within the agency's Internal Revenue Manual.

Mr. Bell's past efforts and continuing work demonstrate his good faith intent in providing testimony before the committee. Furthermore, he is commited to resolving the growing resentment of "The People" for their IRS. This "Us vs. Them" mindset has been exaserbated by decades of IRS activity in complete disregard of some 25 to 27 clearly delineated procedural requirments and the agency's denial of the people's administrative due process rights.

The following expose of the foundations of the problems and questions that this committee seeks to resolve, must be considered if the congress wants to truly address and fix the tax problem, achieve the chairman's goals, and take decisive action to restore public trust and the appearance of legitimacy in the taxation activites of the U.S. Treasury Department.

Chairman Archer, and the Honorable Members of this Committee:

Thank you for your time in consideration of my testimony. My name is Thurston P. Bell. I am the Executive Researcher with the National Institute for Taxation Education.

Upon my discovery of this Hearing and its notice to the Public that all interested parties provided written testimony for consideration and entry into the Committee's records, I decided to afford myself of this unique opportunity to communicate with a body which could affect change regarding a subject which has absorbed the past 7 years of my life.

I sincerely hope that by sharing my unique experience with, and exposure to, rarely seen or discussed historical documents, I will capture the attention of this vigilant Committee and spark thoughtful consideration of, as well as further inquiry into, the foundations of taxation and the history behind the reasoning of the prior Congresses as you debate future taxation schemes like the National Sales Tax.

It is also my hope that this testimony will further increase the progressive communication between the U.S. Congress and a growing dissatisfied and distrusting sector of the Public that has been denied due process of law by the Executive Branch's and its revenue collection activities.

The IRS' abusive behavior alone caused the overwhelming growth in the tax resistance community and a national mindset of "tax avoidance" appears to be spurring the decision to reconvene these hearings. Therefore, it is time for the two governing parties (we, the People, and our representatives in Congress) to come together and consider our separate positions in order to mediate a reasonable and survivable remedy for individuals as well as the Public.

Unfortunately, over 30 years of IRS abuse has made the disenfranchised and disaffected citizenry notably belligerent. Since animosity is so pervasive in the growing Tax Resistance sub-culture of our society, a mindset fed by the convoluted and seemingly endless conspiracy theories proffered by assumed leaders within this "movement," the voice of these individuals and their "leaders" must be precluded from these reasonable and civil hearings. Subsequently, the other side in this issue, as embodied in this Committee, is doomed to continue to grope for some way to reduce tensions and preserve the Public Peace without coming to a full understanding of the root cause of the tensions inflamed in the populace.

Therefore, in an effort to move this Committee forward to some resolution of action that will be meaningful to all Americans, I am providing this testimony to span this communication chasm between the two sides.

As I understand, this Committee hopes to draft a law that would create a new means of economic stabilization, without adversely effecting the fiscal engines of the States, permanently remove the IRS from the lives of the individuals that make up the United States of America and, finally, the income tax would be removed the at the root—so that it never grows back.

This appears to be a reasonable set of goals for fixing this problem, yet, to understand how to fix a system that has a problem, or has become a problem, the system must be understood and seen for what it is, how it functions, and the purpose for which it was created.

Economic Stabilization

In 1947, Mr. Beardsly Ruml, who was at that time the Governor of the New York Federal Reserve Bank, explained our current system of income taxation before the American Bar Association. He was also the man who created the system of wage withholdings from the pay of those receiving wages as the means of painlessly collecting the income tax.

In Mr. Ruml's speech, he explained that the main function of the income tax was for the purposes of economic stabilization, and that none of the money collected as income tax goes to the operation of government. This full text of his speech can be read at:

In 1973, as shown in an internal IRS Memorandum of the Western Regional Offices, the IRS clearly admits, in its upper echelons of operation, that it understands that the IRS is the administrative arm of the economic stabilization program. (see:www.nite.org/docs/croasmun—report.pdf)

There is little doubt that anything has changed the substantive nature and purpose of the income tax over the past 27 years, as nothing had previously changed in the 26 years between Mr. Ruml's public admissions and the IRS' 1973 internal scheming of a plan to avert economic disaster. The looming disaster began when tens of thousands of people began to claim "exemption" from the withholding of income taxes from their "wages." This action on the part of the people threatened to derail the stabilization program created by Mr. Ruml.

The first point that this Committee must understand, as it considers any new taxation proposals, is that the income tax is all about "stabilization" of a paper currency that is inflated by both the spending practices of the U.S. Congress (in support of a seemingly ever expanding and reaching Federal Government) and the Banking practice known as Fractional Reserve Banking.

In short, tampering with the primary means of economic stabilization system risks the possible extended interruptions of the currency removal stream. Such an event would adversely effect the Power of the U.S. Congress, the ability of the Federal Government to operate and provide for the benefits granted to American Society, and, finally, the benefits enjoyed by those controlling and operating the banking sector of our society.

Considering the function and purposes of the income tax, there is a very good reason for the Chairman's claim that the Code is still "...too complicated and confusinga..." Such is the natural result of a system devised: 1) to hide the existence and exclusive attributes of Blind Trusts; 2) to complicate the operation of Corporations—the primary income tax shelter—so that the average individual can not incorporate and thereby eliminate his exposure to tax liabilities, and 3) to have a taxation regime that favors special interest groups and corporations over individuals.

Still, the vital nature of this taxing scheme—economic stabilization—appears to be the prime reason why the Honorable Chairman might spend the remainder of his illustrious career in the U.S. Congress searching for, and yet never discovering, a solution to the problem of the income tax. He will not be alone, as Mr. Ruml in his 1947 speech was looking for a way to eliminate the corporate income tax. He never was able to do this or claim that it was possible given the realities of paper money and private benefits received by those in control of the fractional reserve banking system.

If my recollection of the reports of the 1997 committee hearings are accurate, then many Economists respected by you, Mr. Chairman, publicly explained therein the potentially disastrous effects of a National Sales Tax (NST). The consensus was that a NST would have to be increased sharply within months of its implementation in order to keep the economy from disintegrating, or at least experiencing hyper-inflation. It appears certain that as long as this nation and the Congress embrace paper money, or a non-intrinsic valued currency, there will have to be an income tax.

State Fiscal Engines

It has been communicated that the proposals before this Committee are to be considered in light of how they will effect the fiscal engines of the State Income Taxes. This is very important given that many States, like New York and California, depend upon their Individual and Personal Income Tax systems as great fiscal engines to operate their local system of Government. Most of the states' income tax laws are dependent on the construction and continued survival of the present Federal Internal Revenue Code.

The income taxes imposed within the several states are completely dependent upon the Federal Definition of "Gross Income" as found in 26 USC § 61 (the Internal Revenue Code), and without that statutory definition all of the state income taxation regimes would fail immediately.

This Committee must therefore take notice that any taxation regime which might replace and/or do away with the Federal Definition of "Gross Income," and its active and enforceable nature and subjugation to the Federal Judiciary, will destroy, if not greatly hamper the operation of this great fiscal engine as used by the States.

This leaves any taxation options outside of an income tax to be untenable at this time.

Intrusion upon the Individual

This present situation is antithetical to the statement of the Honorable Chairman, that his goal is to end the intrusion of the Federal government (IRS) into the lives of individuals. Again, in order to do this, those who deal with the IRS and work with taxpayers on a daily basis cannot ignore the history of the systems intrusion, and this committee cannot maintain any hope of discovering and enacting a viable replacement without knowing this history.

So far, history shows us that the earliest known instance of any realization of this intrusion of the Federal Government into the lives of the individual is found in the Page 37 interview of Mr. W.D. Williamson in the New York Times November 29, 1936 issue.

Mr. Williamson worked with the Social Security Board in the creation of the Social Security Program. His comments are very revealing:

"the biggest value of **the tax,** he added, **would be to introduce the majority** of the 26, 000,000 workers **to** the "privilege" of **contributing directly** and consciously **to the cost of government.**

"It will treat them as adult citizens. Able to bear the thought of contributing to their government, instead of treating them as children and collecting from them in hidden taxation." He said.

He added that **the plan extends Federal income taxes** "in a democratic fashion" **to the lower-income brackets,** the government at the same time agreeing to undertake the new function of paying old-age benefits to the taxpayers." (emphasis added)

This article and the transcript of its content are posted at: *www.nite.org/ref/ny—times.pdf* and *www.nite.org/ref/ny—times.htm*

This comment was made in regards to the first income tax to be placed upon the people, the Social Security Tax, and you see the government reaching into the lives of every individual, including those in the lower income brackets.

It is clear from the above noted article that in order for the Honorable Chairman to reach his worthy goal—getting the IRS out of the lives of individuals—he is going to have to end the direct federal taxation of the people—the root cause of government's intrusion into the citizen's life.

For now, since the income tax is one of the two foundational pillars supporting the present monetary system, and thus our economy, the current tax system's reach into our lives is necessary for the continued operation and health of the economy that fuels our society and international markets.

Given the realities of the dependency of state taxation regimes and the stabilization of the currency—both dependent upon the current taxation of gross income—there appears to be no end in sight to the intrusion of the IRS in the lives of ordinary Americans. Therefore, the National Institute for Taxation Education (NITE) seeks to encourage this Committee to support, in the strongest terms, the reinstitution of proper operation of the Treasury Department and the IRS, in the enforcement of tax laws.

Enforcing the agency's compliance with the laws as written by Congress will ensure citizens receive the rights and remedies contained within the Statutes, regulations, Internal Revenue Manual, and Publications governing the IRS Administration. If Congress will do this, then the long process of rehabilitating the agency's reputation with the enraged citizenry can begin. Such action on the part of the Congress will deter the agency from continuing its errant intrusions and allow for the proper and lawful administration of the current tax system until such time as a viable taxation alternative is discovered.

This is the area in which the NITE is presently working. The previous actions of the Congress and Senator Roth's Senate Task Force indicate that there may be a possibility of cooperation within government and the IRS. Yet the immense efforts on the part of individuals have netted very small reforms within the agency's stilted "culture," as noted by Former Treasury Secretary Rubin. Therefore, Congress must take an active role in properly educating its Staff personnel who handle IRS matters before the People can have any glimmer of hope that the service will one day soon comply with the law in every instance involving a taxpayer controversy.

Since replacement of the current system appears to be an impossibility at this time (and given the parameters of this Hearing as well as the fact that the IRS and the Congress are both in need of a rebuilding of the people's confidence on the matter of taxation) I would encourage this Committee to examine pervasive culture or mindset noted by former Sect. Rubin, and endorse the IRS adjusting its operations by making a concerted effort to reform and comply with the laws and procedures. NITE, and most of its members, believe that this is the most reasonable and constructive activity in the interim.

Proper implementation and notification of the public as to the procedures enacted into law, and as set forth by the Secretary, will reduce building public tensions and re-establish legitimacy of the official behavior of the IRS, and the Congress, in the hearts and minds of the people.

If the People quietly accept that they cannot expect the laws enacted to be enforced, then the legitimacy of government will ultimately fail and the economy will soon thereafter follow. The People are beginning to recognize that there is a dual issue in the subject of taxation—the stability of Economy and the Legitimacy of Government.

Even if an alternative "workable" tax scheme is instituted, there is still going to be the matter of Justice and proper implementation of the law by the IRS. There is a serious question of whether or not the IRS will be able to properly enforce and comply with the requirements of a new laws in the future when it fails so miserably at complying with the currently enacted laws today.

We must face the fact that the Office of Personnel Management will most likely recruit its personnel for the new Revenue Agency from the cadre that worked within the IRS before its dismantling. Thus the old "mind-set and culture," noted by former Secretary Rubin a couple of years ago, will be re-established within the new agency by the re-hiring of the old IRS employees.

If this mindset and culture transfers to any new taxation agency, the result may well be a rose being called by any other name, or in this case a whip. Justice is not endemic to change, and cannot be assumed to be so.

The Root of Income Taxation

The beginning of reduction in tensions between the people and the government, without radical change, can only be found in operating the income tax that we presently do have, within the present day laws and procedures as written. This is something that the IRS has failed for decades in doing. However, the enactment of 1998 Internal Revenue Service Reform and Restructuring Act opens the door to laws that appear to force the IRS to follow proper administration. This would not have come about but for the people and reformers being supported by the Congress today.

The institution of Justice by present means is as immediate justice as the law will allow, short of the tax laws complying with the original precepts of income taxation. Any changes in the income tax laws should from now on be examined under the original precepts and criteria of income taxation:
A. The receipt of Benefits; and;
B. The Ability to Pay.

Anything short of these criteria has been deemed, from the time of the first English Income Taxation Program over North America, as instituted by George the III, as immoral and unjust.

Removal and eradication of the Income Tax

It is well understood, and hard to argue against the Chairman's desire to "...rip the current tax code out by the roots so that it can never grow back." Yet, the notion of this gives rise to the realization that the Committee has a very difficult task before it, as the Congress would have to initiate the repealing of the 16th Amendment, as well as the Income Tax, to assure that the Income Tax is never placed upon the people again.

Only in this circumstance would the people be safe from income taxation, as the subject to income taxation would return to the rule of the U.S. Supreme Court in the *Pollock* case.

Such an action to secure an assurance that the tax would not return would require a two-thirds vote of both houses and the States to achieve. There is therefore great doubt that such could be done. When this difficulty is examined under the fact that the elimination of the 16th Amendment would also remove the present day authority of the Social Security Tax in 26 USC §3101, which is an income tax, any will of the Congress to repeal the 16th Amendment should vaporize. The subsequent political backlash would probably mean that nobody in the Congress and Senate would be re-elected.

In some ways the difficulty of taking action on this matter is a good thing. It provides an assurance to the American People, as it keeps the Congress from doing something brash or impulsive that would send the economy into shock.

The "something brash" I refer to would be best described as the enactment of a National Sales Tax. Such a tax would have to grow very quickly to control inflation and our economy would end up suffering the effects of under-consumption. Or, in the alternative, if the tax rate were too little, then hyperinflation would ensue. Historically, National Sales Taxes cause governments to go into greater debt to their centralized banks to cover deficits. This is an important point in light of the private ownership of the Federal Reserve Bank.

In regards to the National Sales Tax, throughout the current debate I have yet to see any discussion of the fact that in 1922 congress also considered a national sales tax. The Honorable Committee might wish to read the reasons leading to the rejection of this tax. Such a scheme was turned down apparently due to the severe failure of the French National Sales Tax that plunged the nation into 4 Billion Francs of debt to the banks. There is also the fact that the Treasury Secretary and his friends (the Banking Class Elite who had the ability to pay) were not paying their income taxes as the Secretary cried for some tax to be instituted to cover shortfalls.

It is my understanding that the 67th Congress 3rd Session, that Congressman James Frear of Wisconsin stated the following in response to Treasury Secretary Andrew Mellon's urging for the imposition of a National Sales Tax:

'...both houses presumably felt that the sales tax urged by you [Andrew Mellon, Secretary of the Treasury and President of Gulf Oil] was a vicious tax placed upon what both rich and poor ate, wore, and used, not exempted, and that it was an unjust, heavy burden to place on the backs of those who grub to make ends meet, and who were thus asked to bear the rich man's burden of excess profits you had successfully urged for repeal. I refer to the vast army you sought to tax, and who have no income tax to pay, but are glad to eke out a bare existence. All of these would help disproportionately to pay your proposed sales tax, whereas if you [Mellon] contribute the income tax you are properly supposed to pay, as one of the richest men of the world you would pay into the treasury according to Kline's estimates on 300 Million dollars of wealth, an annual tax running well into the seven or eight figures. If any evidence of a sales tax failure, due to enforce under-consumption is desired, then the present French National Deficit of 4 Billion Francs is a warning.

'I do not believe in 'soaking the rich' because they are rich, but in common with the overwhelming majority who make up the country a belief exists that taxes should be laid according to ability to pay, and this is the teaching of every recognized authority in the history of every prosperous people. Your sales tax proposal would pinch the poor by taxing their necessities, and was believed to be unjust and vicious in principle and was defeated in Committee by a vote of 19 to 5.'"

What has changed in 88 years since to cause us to return to considering the siren song of the National Sales Tax? Why does this Committee, or at least the Honorable Chairman, continue to posture politically by acting as though there is a solution to the tax problem short of complete monetary reform?

These proceedings appear to smack of political grandstanding by both parties for the appeasement of the evermore-distrusting masses, which are continuing to grow. This may be a noble and necessary effort in order to keep the Public Peace, but nothing will replace good faith efforts of this governmentally omnipotent Congress to assure JUSTICE in the enforcement of the standing law, and provision of meaningful administrative due process of law, as set forth by the U.S. Supreme Court.

Remedial Congressional Actions

There appears to be no immediate solution to the problem of the Income Tax at this time as there is no "national will" to reform our monetary system or reduce the size of Centralized Government. Yet these were the fundamental reasons for the imposition of the income tax and the creation of the IRS—the most powerful and foreboding agency of the U.S. Government.

In all fairness to the Establishment, I find myself concurring with the words of Federal Reserve Chairman Alan Greenspan on the subject of taxation and monetary stability. In 1999, he provided the Congress with two options on what to do with the opportunities afforded it by the Budget Surplus.

Chairman Greenspan's advice that elimination of the marginal tax rates, and thus taxation upon the poorest Americans was one of the most reasonable statements on taxation and justice that I have seen. I was shocked to see the Fed. Chairman, an official who I used to see as an adversary, encourage the U.S. Congress to embrace the opportunity to bring this Nations Income Tax law into line with one of the two original tenants of income taxation; The Ability to Pay. To eliminate the Marginal Tax Rates does not eliminate the income tax, but then again Mr. Chairman, for 5 years you have been unable to eliminate the Income Tax. Also, remember, that as long as there is paper currency, the Congress cannot and will not eliminate the income tax that is so desperately needed to keep this monetary system afloat.

What such an action does do, is move the taxation regime to be directly in line with the original tenants of income taxation by releasing the poorest of Americans from subjugation to the complexity of the so far obfuscated IRS Administrative process. Such an action is in the interest of Justice, which originally governed income taxation. I say this is, just as the poor are most often lacking in the educational stature to be able to adequately defend themselves from IRS Administrative claims, nor are they able to afford professional and competent assistance to guide and aid them in prevailing against IRS claims.

Just the dollar amounts alone, in the face of the cost of a professional to aid the uneducated person in the defense of their money creates an appearance that making a defense is a waste of time and money. This makes for a situation which is neither fair nor justifiable, and a situation for which nobody has any will or idea as to how to fix. The elimination of marginal tax rates is an action would be in line also with the Chairman's goal of getting the "...IRS out of the lives if the American taxpayers." It might not free all Americans, but it will be a start. And who knows, perhaps the savings to the lower tax rates will trickle up to the middle class in the form of lower child care costs. It is hoped that this Honorable Committee finds agreement with the first option given by Chairman Greenspan, and begins moving towards justice, so that we will one day reach it. If we do not have justice in this Society, debts and government programs will soon mean nothing.

A Just tax system is what is best for America. In light of the 25 procedural and rights violations discovered in the great majority of tax cases examined by the National Institute for Taxation Education, the injustice is clear. Nevertheless, NITE can only wonder as to what reasoning will be used to support the issuance of new powers to the Treasury Department for a new tax, when it is so clearly not complying with the laws that the Congress has already enacted. The greatest fear and trepidation surrounding this issue of a new tax is that fact that no tax, once enacted, has ever been repealed.

History will show that those who realized the income tax would be with us for the foreseeable future also predicted that the most likely event is that the people will be saddled with yet another tax on top of the income and sales taxes that already burden them. At this time, Congress is unwilling to provide any guarantee to the contrary and unable to muster the political will to do abolish the income tax, as this would also require the elimination of Social Security.

Chairman Archer and the Members of this Honorable Committee, thank you for hearing me and placing my words into the record.

THURSTON BELL,
Executive Researcher

Statement of John Berthoud, National Taxpayers Union, Alexandria, VA

The 300,000-member National Taxpayers Union commends the Committee for holding additional hearings on fundamental tax reform.

We have long favored replacement of the current income tax system with a simple tax that would clear away many of the tax obstacles to economic growth. Congress can and should consider many approaches for replacing the current tax law in favor of a better system.

We understand that the hearings scheduled for this week will focus on "tax reform proposals that have been introduced since the last set of hearings in 1997," including "H.R. 134 by Rep. Phil English (R–PA) and H.R. 2525 by Rep. John Linder (R–GA) and Rep. Collin Peterson (D–MN)."

For many years our Board of Directors has been on record that fundamental tax reform can be accomplished by several different approaches. We have already endorsed the flat tax introduced by Rep. Dick Armey and the national sales tax proposal by Rep. Billy Tauzin. In this spirit, we are pleased to announce our support for H.R. 2525, the FairTax.

We commend Rep. English for introducing H.R. 134. Clearly a great deal of thought has been put into this proposal, and it contains many attractive features. We are still studying this proposal.

The FairTax proposes to replace the entire income tax system with a simple federal sales tax on new goods and services sold to consumers. The FairTax would repeal all federal personal income, payroll, corporate income, self-employment, capital gain, estate, death, and gift taxes.

The FairTax meets a number of basic requirements of NTU policy for support of a sales tax, including that the tax would:

• be applied only once and would be visible at the point of final purchase for consumption;

• completely replace all income, death, and gift taxes;

• free individuals from filing tax returns or income reports with the federal government; and,

• ensure fair treatment of low-income taxpayers.

As you know, the imposition of federal personal income taxes in 1913 has led to a number of economically, politically, and socially destructive outcomes. Government's obsession with trapping and extracting revenue from every earned dollar has spawned high rates that penalize productivity, multiple layers that punish saving and investing, and hideous complexity that burdens the economy with over $200 billion in compliance costs alone.

In the meantime, federal receipts have grown an astonishing 175,000 percent over the past 85 years, making the current tax system the biggest boon to bloated government in our nationÕs history. The Tax Code itself has become a political trading vehicle for rent-seeking special interests, while more American citizens fear the Internal Revenue Service as a threat to their civil liberties than any other federal agency.

If America is to remain prosperous and free in the next century, the current system of taxation must be scrapped in favor of an alternative that is simpler, fairer, more visible, more economically efficient, and less burdensome. The FairTax proposal would fulfill all of these requirements. Most Americans would no longer face the anxiety of income tax filing seasons, as federal taxes would simply be collected from purchases.

The FairTax offers several unique advantages not offered by other tax reform proposals.

Taxpayers would get to keep their entire paycheck, pension, or Social Security benefits without any tax withholdings. Since the income tax would be replaced by a consumption tax, this feature would let citizens save money much faster for those important family needs such as a new home, college education, or retirement nest egg.

Since the income tax would be eliminated, we could abolish the IRS along with all individual tax filings. Individuals would never again have to fear an audit or seizure.

Today's tax system also has enormous hidden taxes, as documented in a recent study by Bryan Riley for National Taxpayers Union Foundation. These hidden taxes add as much as 20% to 25% of the price of everything we buy in the stores today.

The FairTax makes the cost of government fully visible to all taxpayers. No taxes are hidden in the form of payroll taxes or corporate taxes. By being aware of the true burden of taxes, Americans can once again rationally debate the size of government without having to take politicians at their word.

Another advantage of the FairTax is that it would completely untax the poor and those who rely on just Social Security. The FairTax includes a monthly tax rebate to ensure that all Americans can afford to buy their necessities tax-free.

That's a stark contrast to the existing tax system that collects hundreds of billions of dollars in taxes buried in the cost of things we purchase. Under current tax laws, even minimum-wage workers pay over 15% from their paychecks for payroll taxes when you count both the employee and employer share of the tax.

Another important advantage of the FairTax is that this reform should be easier to keep intact should it become law. As you know, in 1986 Congress and the President adopted a tax reform plan that lowered the top income tax rate to 28%, but it lasted less than five years, and the top rate today is over 40%.

Since the FairTax would scrap the entire income tax apparatus, including the IRS, it would be much more difficult to reimpose an income tax. We also believe that once people get used to keeping their entire paycheck, pension and Social Security benefits, they will never want to go back to the old system.

Congress can and should consider many approaches toward repealing the current tax law in favor of a better system. Other proposals for a flat tax or consumption tax would address many of the problems weÕve outlined, and NTU has endorsed several such plans. We look forward to debate and concerted action on the FairTax and other tax system alternatives in the near future.

Statement of John B. O'Donnell, Chula Vista, CA

I am pleased the Congress is finally recognizing the destructive nature of the present personal income tax. There is the common misconception that the sixteenth amendment authorized the income tax but as is evidenced by the Supreme Court ruling in *Stanton v. Baltic Mining Co., 240 US 103 (1916)* the sixteenth amendment—

"... conferred no new power of taxation but simply prohibited the ... power of income taxation from being taken out of the category of indirect taxation to which it inherently belonged..."

Unfortunately, court rulings on the tax system have become so befuddled that courts find in some districts the tax is a direct tax authorized by the sixteenth amendment while in others it is an indirect tax that applies only to the exercise of licensed privileges. Such confusion within the courts should of itself be sufficient to declare the statutes in violation of due process for persons of only reasonable intelligence, without the law expertise one can expect of jurists.

However, because others will undoubtedly present better arguments on the problems of the present system, I will address only the issue of economic performance that is affected by this and other forms of transaction taxes.

The current assumption that some form of consumption tax is the only alternative to an income tax is disheartening. I have posted on the internet an analysis entitled *Three Steps to Economic Freedom* at: http://www.geocities.com/CapitolHill/1067/c00r4.html that demonstrates some of the more egregious fallacies of generally accepted economic premises.

In this pamphlet I describe a "Monopoly Tax" that could also be called a "Limited Liability License Fee" that would provide all needed government finance while imposing no burden on American citizens. Further, the method actually causes optimum growth in capital. The details of why this is true are a bit complex to present in this brief, but the essential feature of this system is that it effectively changes taxes collected by government that resolve to "variable" costs of production into costs that resolve to "fixed" costs of production.

Although economists usually recognize taxes that resolve to fixed costs of production are superior to transaction taxes that effectively create a "wedge" between prices paid by purchasers and the price received by sellers, they seem somehow forgetful when it comes to applying this obvious principle to their tax proposals.

The rationale behind the impost and a demonstration of the economic effect of its causing growth when properly constructed is presented in the on line pamphlet. As a brief introduction of the tax/fee, it is based on the capital value of limited liability license holders [corporations] with the amounts of the fee adjusted to maximize the growth rates of their value.

I have calculated an approximation of the tax receipts using the FY 2000 budget as if it were funded by the Monopoly Tax. Some obvious compromises must be used since there has not been the accumulation of empirical evidence that would be developed as described in the article. However, the scale of things can be derived from existing data.

First comes an estimate of the asset value that would be subject to the tax. Using the Wilshire 5000 equity value of approximately $14.0 trillion and a guess that debt supported by those equities is $6.0 trillion gives a total subject to the tax of $20.0 trillion. Although it would be nice to apply the progressive rates as described in my proposed system, that will have to wait for the empirical data from actual application.

Lacking that data, consider a uniform [or average] tax rate of 0.8% per month. While 0.8% per month may appear large to some, consider that:

1. It is not unusual for the market value of these equities to increase by more than 1% *DAILY*.

2. It is also not much different than the charge states and/or localities charge people for the "privilege" of owning a home.

3. And, if that is not enough to dissuade those who find the amount excessive, consider that most, or even all, of the amount to be collected by this tax [Or limited liability license fee.] would have been paid as income and payroll taxes "in the name of their employees" but, because those taxes are eliminated it becomes just a change in accounting these taxes that had been called "wages" but were never seen by the so-called wage earner. [There would, of course, need to be enough time for contracts to adjust nominal wage rates to reflect the new system.]

For the uninitiated, most personal income taxes and other payroll taxes are collected by corporations that would instead pay the monopoly tax while nominal wages [Not after tax wages which likely will actually increase.] are reduced. In further note of this consequence, it may be necessary to remind some that wage rates are not set in a vacuum and the elimination of those liabilities called taxes on wages would substantially affect negotiated nominal wage rates.

Initially, other taxes paid by these corporations would also be eliminated changing only the form [From "variable" to "fixed" costs.] and not the actual amount of taxes paid by or through these corporations. Subsequent amounts would be determined [as demonstrated in "Three Steps, etc."] by maximizing the growth rates of corporate value and the overall economy.

The yearly amount that would be collected by such a tax would then be $0.16 trillions per month times 12 months, or $1.76 trillions per annum. This is only $6 billion less than the $1.766 trillion budget for FY 2000. Not a bad approximation for such a crude estimate.

A significant consequence would be the replacement of a very complex system of government revenue raising that imposes a myriad of forms, rules and other burdens on many millions of people and wastes untold hours of effort to comply with these burdens that could better be applied to useful production with a system that is simple for both the companies affected and the bureaucrats tasked with enforcement. [There are about 7,–8,000 companies in the current Wilshire 5000 index. This could expand to perhaps 10 times as many as some of the larger companies choose to decompose themselves into several smaller units to reduce their tax liability.]

Although a rigid proof of the above is a bit more complicated than this simple example, it is also true that ALL the present taxes collected hinder economic activity and differ only in the way that hindrance occurs, while the above method is recognized by economists as at least neutral or "non-distortionary" in its effect on an economy and, by those willing to examine the arguments presented in the more complete pamphlet, actually can be optimized to cause the greatest rate of capital formation given all other conditions existing.

I hope when it comes time to examine substitute methods for the failing income tax system that this process will be considered.

Thank you,

John B. O'Donnell

Statement of Robert P. Hodous, Payne & Hodous, Charlottesville, VA

The Hon. Bill Archer, Chairman, and Hon. Members of the Committee:

I appreciate the opportunity to provide these comments for your record regarding the need to replace the current Internal Revenue Code with an uncomplicated rational new code. The starting point for this effort should be the proposal for a flat tax. The three basic concepts of the flat tax as applied to individuals are one tax rate, no deductions and large exemptions to eliminate taxes on those least capable of paying them.

A variation of the income tax is preferable to a sales tax, which is considered to be one of the most regressive forms of tax. Implementation of a high-rate national sales tax could be a substantial shock to the economic system. Aspects of the fair tax proposal are intended to minimize this impact and the regressive nature of the tax. However, in minimizing the regressive impact and shock of implementation of a high-rate national sales tax, we again begin to build complications into a new system. In addition, sales taxes can end up with many exemptions and variations which lead to significant complications for merchants trying to apply such taxes. Minimizing these difficulties by harmonizing the system with the various state sales tax provisions would be a nightmare. In short, while a national sales tax or fair tax may seem simple at first blush, it has many pitfalls and complications which will be hard to overcome.

Applying the three flat-tax principles mentioned above should be just the beginning. To do nothing more than flatten and simplify individual rates, exemptions and deductions leaves most of the complicated provisions of the current Internal Revenue Code still in place. For business entities we would still have varying tax treatment for different types of entities. Such varying treatment leaves in place the increasingly complicated series of choices for formation of business entities. The basic choices still remain sole proprietorship, general partnership and corporation. Efforts over time to obtain more favorable tax treatment have lead first to the S corporation, then the limited partnership with an S corporation general partner. Now we have added limited liability companies, single member limited liability companies, registered limited liability general partnerships and registered limited liability limited partnerships. Development of these entities is driven solely by taxes. The drive for new types of entities can be eliminated by treating all entities the same.

Only implementing the three flat tax principles would still leave us with the estate and gift taxes with all of their related complications. We would still have charitable lead trusts, charitable remainder trusts, estate freezes, generation-skipping transfers and differences in basis depending upon whether property is received by gift or inheritance. Adding to the problems are the nightmare of dealing with various types of tax-favored deferred benefit plans and the tax dodge presented by different income and estate and gift tax treatment afforded life insurance in an irrevocable trust.

There are many other complications created by the current code which can easily be eliminated using the flat tax as a starting point. The current code is a hodgepodge of social programs, complicated administrative and bureaucratic procedures and special tax breaks, all of which should be eliminated or minimized in drafting a new code. There must be a commitment to true simplification.

There are seven basic guidelines which should be used in creating a new code. The tax law should be understandable. It should be economically neutral and not encourage one economic decision over another. Administrative requirements should be minimized. The burden of taxation and supporting our government should be reasonably allocated. The focus should be on raising money for the functioning of government, and various provisions encouraging different types of social efforts or actions should be eliminated. Taxes should be paid directly by individuals whenever possible. Finally, all income should be taxed in the same manner.

I undertook to write a new tax code using these guidelines to see how uncomplicated the tax law could be. I have been successful. The code I have written starts with the flat tax and then goes on to eliminate some provisions and simplify others as the principles are applied to the whole tax law. In addition to taxing all income in the same manner, this code:

• Eliminates the distinctions between types of business entities

- Eliminates the marriage penalty
- Provides one type of retirement account with greater individual freedom
- Eliminates special accounting provisions
- Eliminates estate and gift taxes
- Replaces excise taxes and special funds with a low-rate comprehensive sales tax
- Eliminates special litigation procedures
- Eliminates the need for regulations and rulings

All of this is done while still eliminating or at least lowering the tax bills of the persons who can least afford to pay taxes. I have included this code in a book in which I also address problems in the current tax code and deal with objections to the suggested changes. The tax code is just 30 sections, and the whole book, including the code, is only 180 pages. The book is *Let's REALLY Change Taxes*. I would be happy to provide a complimentary copy of the book to any member who would like one. My business address is Payne & Hodous, 412 East Jefferson Street, Charlottesville, Virginia 22902, and my business phone number is 804–977–4507.

I would encourage you to stay with an income tax system as the basic means of raising the money for the functioning of government. I also encourage you to use the concept of the flat tax as the beginning of a truly rational and uncomplicated tax system.

Again, thank you for the opportunity to provide these comments.

Robert P. Hodous

Statement of Glendale O. Herbert, Pembrok Equity, New York, NY

Mr. Chairman and members of the committee, I am grateful for the opportunity to testify today. I am the owner of Pembrok Equity, a New York real estate brokerage firm. Many myths surround the current debate over tax reform alternatives, perhaps more myths than truths.

Many opponents of a national sales tax have stated that it would be bad for homeownership, since the rental of an apartment or the purchase of a home would be taxed but the mortgage interest deduction would be eliminated. This is a myth. If such myths prevail, they will constitute a triumph of rhetoric over reason. In fact the FairTax, introduced on a bipartisan basis by Reps. John Linder and Collin Peterson as H.R. 2525, would have a positive impact on the real estate industry and help make the American dream of owning real estate a reality for many Americans sooner. As a realtor, I am pleased to submit this testimony outlining the positive effects of the FairTax on real estate.

Point 1: Mortgage Interest Will be Paid for Out of Pre-Income and Pre-Payroll Tax Dollars, Which is Much More Advantageous than Today

Yes, the sales tax eliminates the mortgage interest deduction, but when we hear this comment, we should ask ourselves this question: what becomes of the deduction? These deductions would not "disappear" in a negative sense. Rather, they could not exist in the sales tax world since there would be no income tax against which the deduction could be applied.

More importantly, however, they reappear in a different and stronger form: the non-taxation of mortgage interest. Under an income tax, the mortgage interest deduction serves the purpose of ensuring interest payments are made against pre-income tax dollars. Unless one does not have the income to offset or does not itemize, the mortgage interest deduction accomplishes well the purpose of offsetting income taxes paid on the mortgage interest. In fact, in 1996, there were 29.4 million taxpayers who took the mortgage interest deduction, for a total itemized deduction amount of $220.2 billion.[1] The tax expenditure associated with this deduction in fiscal year 1999 is estimated to be $53 billion.[2]

However, it is important to note that as large as it is, the deduction is seriously limited today for lower wage earners (read first time homebuyers trying to latch on to the American dream) in the respect that it only serves to negate the income tax. Today, mortgage interest payments must be made from after payroll tax dollars, which comprises a significant segment of the taxes Americans pay. As a national aggregate, in fiscal year 1997 individual income taxes were $737.5 billion, and payroll taxes were $539.4 billion, or 42 percent of the combined total. Many taxpayers,

---

[1] SOI Bulletin, Winter 1998–1999.
[2] U.S. Budget for Fiscal Year 2000, Analytical Perspectives.

especially lower income individuals, who are purchasing their first home pay a greater portion of their tax liability in payroll taxes than income taxes.

Let us again see the world through the eyes of our fairly average homebuyer. Recall the median family money income in 1997 was $44,568. Recall further that if that income were all wage income, then that couple would have paid $6,819 in combined payroll taxes on those wages (employer and employee share). Even if that couple did not itemize (which they certainly would because of the mortgage interest deduction), the income taxes that they would pay if they filed married filing jointly would be $4,856, or 29 percent less than the payroll taxes. In other words, the couple would have paid more payroll taxes than income taxes. When the couple takes a mortgage interest deduction, the couple cannot take that deduction against the most significant form of taxes that apply to them—payroll taxes.

Now let us consider what happens under the Fair Tax. Under the Fair Tax plan, mortgage interest is simply not taxed—not at all. Therefore, like current law, homebuyers would pay mortgage interest out of pre-income-tax dollars. But more to the point, since the Fair Tax repeals both the payroll taxes and the income taxes, the effect of not taxing their interest payments is to ensure that the payments are made with both pre-income and pre-payroll tax dollars. This will significantly advantage home buyers relative to current law by reducing the costs of their loan. Since the interest must be paid with after payroll tax dollars, a taxpayer today must earn $108.28 to pay $100 in mortgage interest today if only the "employee" share of the payroll taxes are considered. If the employer payroll taxes are considered [3] (or if the taxpayer had a sole-proprietorship), he or she must earn $118.06. Under the Fair Tax, that taxpayer would only need to earn $100 to pay $100 in mortgage interest.

Let us examine the relative advantage of not taxing interest payments vs. the mortgage deduction against income in more detail. We again will use the median purchase price of a previously occupied home, $146,000. But we add the fact that mortgage interest rates are about 7–3/4 percent and that the median term of all loans was about 27 years.

If we were to model our typical married couple above, with a typical home purchase, with a typical interest rate, with a typical term of years in a simple graph, we could compare how much today's mortgage interest deduction benefits the home buyer to relative to the full non-taxation of interest on mortgages under the Fair Tax. Over the course of the 27 year term, an interest rate of 7.75 percent would add $202,834 to the required payoff of the loan. To completely pay off their loan, our couple will have to earn $407,103 once employee payroll taxes and income taxes (at the lowest 15 percent rate) are taken into account. Considering the impact of employer payroll taxes would make the figure higher. Under the Fair Tax, in contrast, the couple would only need to earn $392,444 or four percent less.

This is not the end of the advantages, however. Our family's disposable income will probably go up by the 7.65 percent employer payroll tax and interest rates, and since interest is no longer taxable, interest rates will come down by about one quarter as they settle toward the municipal bond rates. These two factors would save our couple over $142,764, which consists of $92,055 in additional wages and $50,709 in reduced interest costs. If we were just to consider the interest rate reduction, the cost of homeownership would be $341,735 or 16 percent less that under current law.

In short, homeownership under the Fair Tax is vastly more affordable.

Point 2: Mortgage Interest Will Fall

Home mortgage interest rates will fall by 25 to 30 percent (i.e., about two points on a 30 year conventional mortgage). A legitimate question is "why?"

The answer is that current mortgage interest rates include a tax premium, which is the amount lenders pay in taxes on the income received. The magnitude of the wedge can be seen by comparing the interest rates on taxable bonds to tax-exempt municipal bonds of comparable risk and term. The impact of elimination of the tax wedge or tax premium on interest is evidenced each day in the Wall Street Journal. Tax-exempt municipal bonds tend to yield about 30 percent less than taxable corporate bonds of similar term and risk. The decline in interest rates will occur entirely because of the elimination of the tax wedge or premium on interest and will happen independently of the impact of the sales tax on savings and investment.[4]

---

[3] Most economists believe that the employer-employee split is really a fiction; that employees really do bear the full 15.3 percent. However, I make this adverse assumption in order to arrive at a conservative estimate of the advantages of the Fair Tax.

[4] For an more detailed discussion of the impact on a national sales tax on interest rates, see John E. Gobb, *Economic Review*, Federal Reserve Bank of Kansas City, "How Would Tax Reform Affect Financial Markets?," Fourth Quarter, 1995. He estimates a 25–35 percent drop (p. 27).Jorgenson.

Investors will simply no longer need to charge a tax premium to achieve a particular after-tax rate of return.

Moreover, interest rates will probably fall further because the supply of capital for borrowing will increase.[5] That is because a national sales tax is neutral toward savings. Because the attractiveness of savings relative to consumption will increase, investors will choose to save and invest more of their money rather than use it to consume immediately. The after-tax return on their investment makes deferring consumption worthwhile. In contrast, the current income tax is biased against savings and investment. The income tax double, triple and often quadruple taxes savings.

Economic studies show that savings are responsive to changes in tax treatment and that savings rates are closely correlated to the return on savings.

Point 3: Lower Marginal Rates Will Reduce the Costs of Principal Payments to Home Buyers

Sometimes the rhetoric surrounding tax reform loses site of the fact that home principal payments are taxed today. As one editorial put it *"if you bought a $150,000 house, you'd have to pay $22,500 more in taxes."* More in taxes? We forget that taxpayers today must pay for the principal in homes with after income tax and after payroll tax dollars. The interest is deductible but the principal is not.

Under the FairTax, existing homes would never be subject to the sales tax. Similarly, homes built after the FairTax was put in place would only be taxed once when first sold and would never be subject to sales tax again. In other words, used homes are not subject to sales tax, only newly constructed homes are. With respect to new homes, under the Fair Tax as with current law, principal payments would be taxed but under the FairTax the income earned to pay for that principal would not be taxed by the income tax or the payroll tax. Moreover, since the Fair Tax lowers marginal rates new home buyers would face lower after tax costs of their principal payments.

Given the fact that a consumption tax taxes purchases, but the income tax takes the money before we purchase, how can we compare the two as they affect the homebuyer? The only proper comparison is to ask ourselves this question: how much money would a purchaser have to make to earn to pay for the principal in the home? As noted, today, a purchaser of a home must make principal payments with after tax dollars. A taxpayer who is in a 28 percent bracket, and pays a 15.3 percent payroll tax, would have to earn $176,000 to purchase a home of $100,000 devoid of the interest charge. They would have to make $265,000 to pay cash for a new home of $150,000. Under the FairTax, a $100,000 existing home would cost $100,000 after-tax since no sales tax would be imposed. A $150,000 existing home would cost $150,000. At a marginal rate of 23 percent, a $100,000 new home would cost $130,000 after tax and a $150,000 new home, $195,000. So, the cost of making equity payments decreases as well under the Fair Tax compared to current law.

---

[5] "Probably" because their will also be an increased demand for that savings for investment purposes that will have a countervailing effect.

Cost of Purchasing $150,000 House

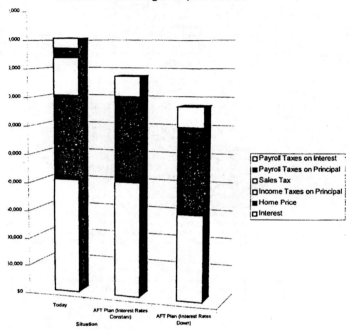

Point 4: Individuals Will be Able to Save for the Purchase of a Home Much Faster, Which Will Increase and Accelerate the Volume of Home Sales

Since the Fair Tax does not tax savings and investment and makes the payment of the tax largely elective, it will enable new home buyers, second home buyers or buyers stepping up, to save for their purchase faster. Buyers will be able to qualify for a mortgage faster and existing owners will be able to sell their homes faster.

Why can individuals save so much faster? First, the Fair Tax removes the enormous disadvantage to savings and investment under our income tax system. Today, savings and investment income is greatly disadvantaged. Wage and salary income is included in the income tax base when it is earned originally. If that income is consumed, the benefits of consumption go untaxed. However, if what is left of the wages and salaries is saved (for example, for a new home), the earnings are taxed as the income from that investment is generated. Then, if the income-producing asset, such as a stock or bond, equipment or real property interest is sold for more than it was purchased, the benefit of the capital investment—the capital gain—is taxed a third time. Corporate income (including capital gains) is taxed at the corporate level and again when it is paid to shareholders as dividends. Inter-corporate dividends are also subject to tax, creating yet another level of taxation.

A principal advantage the Fair Tax has over an income tax, therefore, is that the downpayment can be saved without fighting against the cascading taxes on savings.

To illustrate the effects of the current taxes on savings and investment, let's construct a typical fact pattern and then analyze the effects. Let's take a married couple who wants to purchase a new home of $146,000, which was the 1997 median new home price (the FairTax would tax the sale only of newly constructed homes).[6]

---

[6] Statistical Abstract of the United States, 1998, Table 1203. The median price of a previously owned home was $124,100. See Table 1204.

Let us further assume that that couple will need to save $14,600 (10 percent) for the downpayment. Since the median family money income 1997 was $44,568 [7] , let's further assume that that is the amount our couple earns. Today, the personal savings rate nationwide, as a percentage of disposable personal income, is about 2.1 percent.[8]

Our income tax system attacks their ability to save at the very beginning, when our prospective buyer earns their income. Our family will be taxed on their earnings at the 15 percent rate under the income tax plus payroll taxes. To save $14,600 after-tax that family must earn, at the margin, an additional $18,875 (looking only at the employee share of payroll taxes and income taxes). They would have had to earn $22,688 if they were in the 28 percent tax bracket, a more typical bracket for homeowners.

If the $44,568 of our family's income was all wage income, then that couple would have paid $3,409 in employee payroll taxes on those wages. Note also that their wages were also about $3,409 lower because of the employer payroll tax. Economists generally believe that the employer share of the payroll tax is borne by the employee in the form of lower wages. After the standard deduction and two personal exemptions, the couple would pay income taxes of $4,856. Hence, using a standard deduction, the couple would have paid $8,265 in taxes on $44,568 leaving our family $36,303 after taxes. 2.1 percent of that disposable income is $762.

Today, assuming they earn 8 percent on their savings, they are in the 15 percent bracket and save $762 each year at the beginning of the year, they would be able to save their down payment by early in the 13th year.

Under the AFT plan, their disposable income will increase to $47,977 because of the repeal of all payroll and income taxes. Assuming they continue to save 2.1 percent of this amount, they would save $1,008 each year. Assuming they would earn a lower 6 percent on this amount, then they would be able to save a $14,600 downpayment in the 11th year. Note, however, that the acceleration effect is much more pronounced if they were in the 28 percent tax bracket. Even if we add 23 percent to this amount, they would be able to save $18,961 in the 13th year. This, however, is unrealistically pessimistic since the repeal of all income and payroll taxes will reduce producer prices. Harvard's Dale Jorgenson estimates that construction prices will fall by 25 percent.[9]

What does this mean in national aggregates? It means that we would accelerate the purchase of homes, increasing the velocity of those sales. It also means that realtors would make more money faster since there would be many more home sales crunched into a smaller period of time. More sales mean more commissions.

Point 5: The Fair Tax Makes Housing More Affordable by Repealing Upstream Taxes

Housing today is taxed much more heavily than most people realize. Like other firms, homebuilders pay corporate taxes and payroll taxes, not only on their own accord, but in the form of taxes embedded in the goods they purchase to build homes. These upstream costs would disappear.

Research by Harvard economist Dale Jorgenson shows that producer prices in the construction industry will fall 25 percent under the Fair Tax plan since the income tax and payroll tax is embedded in the price of everything we buy. In this case, new housing prices will be approximately the same price including the sales tax as they are today and the relative price of new and used housing will remain roughly comparable to what they are today. If Jorgenson is wrong and the sales tax causes prices to rise, then existing home prices will rise immediately to reflect the fact that they are not subject to tax. Although this would result in a one-time, quick windfall gain to owners of existing houses, the relative price of new and old homes will be comparable.

Conclusion:

The combination of these factors means that the Fair Tax would be highly beneficial to real estate. The Fair Tax would:
- reduce the tax burden on interest;
- lower interest rates and make homes more affordable;
- lessen the pre-tax earnings a buyer must earn to pay for a home;
- quicken the pace of saving for a downpayment and the pace of home sales;

---

[7] See Economic Report of the President, February 1999, Table B–33.

[8] U.S. Bureau of Economic Analysis, reported in Economic Report of the President, February 1999, Table B–32.

[9] See, The Economic Impact of the National Retail Sales Tax, Dale W.

• make homes more affordable by eliminating the taxes embedded in upstream producer prices.

As you review competing tax reform plans, let us keep in mind one factor. The income tax is not the perfect system for real estate and those that say that real estate might be hurt simply because the mortgage interest deduction is removed are performing a very shallow analysis. It takes a little more effort to see the truth. I am pleased to support the FairTax as a means of assisting more Americans in achieving the American Dream of owning real estate.

Statement of David R. Burton, Prosperity Institute, Alexandria, VA

I am David R. Burton, President of the Prosperity Institute. I am pleased to submit this testimony on behalf of the Prosperity Institute. We would like to take this opportunity to present our analysis of the impact of the leading national sales tax plan on senior citizens. This plan is called the FairTax.

Senior citizens are becoming a larger portion of the overall population. In 1970, those over 65 years of age were 9.8 percent of the population. By 1999, seniors were 12.7 percent of the population. In 2015, seniors will account for 14.7 percent of the population and in 2020, they will account for 16.6 percent.[1]

Under the FairTax, senior citizens, like others, will receive a cash rebate effectively exempting consumption up to the poverty level from tax. The sales tax rebate is equal to the sales tax that would be paid on expenditures up to the federal poverty level. Because the federal poverty level for two persons is not twice the level for one persons, the FairTax provides that married couples would receive an extra rebate amount to prevent any marriage penalty. The rebate is paid monthly in advance. Thus, poor seniors will pay no sales tax. A household spending twice the federal poverty level (or more in the case of a married couple) would pay an effective tax rate of 11–½ percent.

Because income and payroll taxes are embedded in the price of everything we purchase, it is not clear that prices, even including the sales tax, will increase by very much.[2] They may not increase at all because pre-sales-tax prices may fall once the income and payroll taxes are repealed. Nevertheless, the FairTax makes sure that the Social Security benefits indexing formula would be adjusted so that benefits will increase to the extent, if any, that the sales tax results in higher tax inclusive prices. The income tax imposed on Social Security benefits will be repealed.

The income tax imposed on investment income and pension benefits or IRA withdrawals will be repealed. Pensions funds, IRAs and 401(k) plans have assets of well over $11 trillion.[3] An income tax deduction was taken for contributions to most of these plans and the earnings on these plans have accrued free of any income tax. All beneficiaries and owners of these plans expected to pay income tax on them upon withdraw and would not be required to do so since the income tax would be repealed by the FairTax.

Repeal of the corporate and individual income tax and the estate and gift tax will have a substantial positive impact on the stock market.[4] Those seniors that own stocks either directly or through mutual funds, Individual Retirement Accounts, 401(k) plans or otherwise will experience significant gains. More seniors own stocks, mutual funds or have IRAs than other age groups.[5] In addition, unrealized capital gains that would have been subject to the income tax when realized will no longer be taxed.

The FairTax imposes a sales tax on newly constructed homes but exempts existing homes and other used property from any sales tax. Currently, equity payments

[1] Middle Series, U.S. Bureau of the Census, Statistical Abstract of the United States, 1996, Tables 814 and 17, pp. 15 and 17.
[2] Dale W. Jorgenson, Economic Impact of the National Retail Sales Tax, National Tax Research Committee, generally showing that producer prices will fall 20 to 30 percent because of the repeal of income and payroll taxes.
[3] Statistical Abstract of the United States, 1998, Tables 845–847, pp. 533–534. In 1997, private pensions had assets of $4,846 billion and state and local pension funds had assets of $2,100. In 1996, Individual Retirement Accounts had assets of $1,347 billion. In 1997 section 401(k) and other defined contribution plans had assets of $1,730 billion.
[4] In short, by repealing the corporate tax, the tax on dividends and the tax on capital gains, the net of income tax future income stream of corporations will increase and the capitalized value of the that future income stream will increase as well.
[5] U.S. Bureau Labor Statistics, Statistical Abstract of the United States, 1998, Table 798, p. 514.

on homes must be paid from after-income tax earnings (i.e. principal payments are not deductible). The purchase of existing housing is thus subject to the income tax. Owners of existing homes may experience large gains due to the repeal of the income tax and implementation of the FairTax. Seniors and those nearing retirement age have dramatically higher homeownership rates than other age groups. (80 percent compared to 66 percent on average).[6] Homes are often a family's largest asset.

Under the FairTax, the estate and gift tax would be repealed. The need for small businesses and farmers to engage in expensive estate planning, involving attorneys, complex estate freeze transactions and expensive life insurance plans in anticipation of future estate and gift tax liability would disappear. Heirs would no longer need to sell the business or farm out of the family or borrow heavily, putting the business at risk, to pay the estate tax.

Replacing the current tax system with a national sales tax would make the economy much more dynamic and prosperous.[7] Budget pressure on entitlement spending, already significant, will become much more pronounced once the baby boom starts retiring. The economic growth a sales tax would cause would make it substantially less likely that federal budget pressures will result in Medicare or Social Security benefits reductions.

According to work by Stanford University economist Joseph Kahn, those seniors with a net worth over $400 thousand (nearly four times the median) may see a reduction in their purchasing power. The largest decline in purchasing power, about 3.5 percent, is for those with net worth above about $700 thousand. The primary reason for this effect is that wealth spent for consumption purposes that is held in non-tax deferred accounts like IRAs will be taxed when spent under a sales tax and would not be taxed further under an income tax.[8] Kahn assumes, contrary to Jorgenson, that prices will rise.

Most seniors will be better off were the FairTax to replace the current system.

Statement of Redefining Progress, San Francisco, CA

ENVIRONMENTAL TAX REFORM: AN IDEA WHOSE TIME HAS COME

[This testimony is largely excerpted from the monograph, Tax Waste, Not Work: How Changing What We Tax Can Lead to a Stronger Economy and a Cleaner Environment, by M. Jeff Hamond, published by Redefining Progress (RP). For more information about RP's work on tax shifting or to order a copy of the monograph, call (800) 896–2100.]

Despite the sustained overall strong performance of the American economy—such as a high rate of job creation, declining deficits, and low inflation and unemployment—the nation is still struggling with several important long-term problems.

Among the most serious of these are the payroll tax and the exploding growth of entitlement programs; the emergence of global climate change as a significant environmental and economic threat; the lack of economic opportunity in our inner cities; and the dislocation and hardship that are being caused by major economic transformations (such as the rapid growth of information technologies) even as they provide exciting new opportunities. Each of these problems has caused many scholars and activists to look for solutions, but so far few good ideas have moved from theory to actual policy.

A Fresh Approach to Some Old Questions

A new approach to fiscal and environmental policy—a resource-based tax shift—holds the potential for improving many of the country's problems simultaneously,

---

[6] Statistical Abstract of the United States, 1999, Table 1215, p. 726.

[7] "The Economic Impact of Replacing Federal Income Taxes with a Sales Tax," Laurence J. Kotlikoff, April 15, 1993, Cato Institute Policy Analysis; Dale W. Jorgenson, Economic Impact of the National Retail Sales Tax, National Tax Research Committee. See also, "The Economic Impact of Fundamental Taxing Consumption," Dale W. Jorgenson, Testimony before the House Ways and Means Committee, March 27, 1996 and "The Economic Impact of Fundamental Tax Reform," Dale W. Jorgenson, Testimony before the House Ways and Means Committee, June 6, 1995; "Looking Back to Move Forward: What Tax Policy Costs Americans and the Economy," Gary Robbins and Aldona Robbins, Policy Report No. 127, September 1994, published by the Institute for Policy Innovation; "Replacing the Federal Income Tax with a Consumption-Based Tax System," prepared by Nathan Associates for the National Retail Institute (1996).

[8] "Examining a Change to a National Retail Sales Tax Regime: Impact on Households," November 1996.

while attracting support across the political spectrum. This approach would reduce current taxes on labor, innovation, and capital formation and replace the revenue with new levies on pollution and waste. Total federal revenue would be unchanged and the current distribution of the tax burden across income groups would be preserved.

A revenue-neutral tax shift of this type could be accomplished through the use of new taxes or tradable emission permits, but the basic idea—that the new revenue should be used to reduce existing taxes—would be the same under either mechanism. Many of the potential benefits of this policy idea are dependent upon this "revenue recycling." Because other taxes are being reduced, this proposal is not a new revenue source to buttress government expenditures. It would simply replace a portion of federal revenues—perhaps 5 to 10 percent—with revenues from environmental taxes or permits.

The proposed new tax system is designed to be revenue-and distributionally-neutral because the way in which a free society decides to distribute the burden or spend public tax dollars should be a separate issue from that of the method used to raise the revenue. This distinction is not meant to be an endorsement of the current tax distribution or size of government. Rather, it is meant to emphasize the fact that the tax shift is neither a tool to increase government (in fact, it could do just the opposite), nor to shift the tax burden to the rich or the middle class.

This new approach to public policy could create a powerful alliance among those concerned with problems such as high taxes on capital formation or on the average family; the need for additional investments in human capital and research and development (R&D); the threats to the global environment; the costly regulatory burden on private industry; fiscal irresponsibility; the complexity of international tax rules; and job creation in inner cities. It would provide a rare opportunity to enact tax cuts on both labor and investment income. By so doing, it would attract support from both ends of the political spectrum and potentially create incentives for more investment in both human and physical capital—an economic stimulus package with no revenue cost. Given the mounting interest in fundamental tax reform, the weaknesses of the tax reform plans that have been offered, and the growing international momentum for addressing the threat of climate change, such a proposal could not come at a better time.

The Tax Shift Concept

The current tax system sends the wrong signals to virtually everyone. It discourages work, enterprise, and capital formation while it encourages sprawl, pollution, waste, and the inefficient use of resources. There is almost unanimous agreement that the tax system needs reform.

There are really two sides to the tax reform debate—and they aren't "liberal" versus "conservative." Rather, they are what should be taxed and what should be untaxed—and the next attempt at major tax reform should focus on both. Look at it this way: When the government wants to promote a social goal, what does it do? It reduces income taxes—via credits, preferences, and deductions—on particular activities that the government thinks will help accomplish that objective. Retired Sen. Bill Bradley (D–NJ) calls this practice "government by tax break," and it helps explain why the tax system is the part of government that people hate the most. But what if the government can accomplish social goals both through what it taxes as well as what it untaxes?

Common sense dictates that you get less of what you tax and more of what you don't. Since higher rates of saving and investment can drive faster economic growth, many recent tax proposals focus on reducing taxes on capital income in the hopes of creating more saving and investment. Yet in an effort to keep total revenue relatively stable, some of these proposals would increase taxes on labor in order to untax capital. This action would have the perverse result of raising taxes on modest and average income people—and if common sense applies, this in turn would result in less labor.

The argument works the other way as well: Higher taxes on capital holders should not be used to finance tax cuts for working people, because these tax increases penalize the investment and entrepreneurism that creates new jobs and opportunities. Such a policy untaxes labor in order to tax capital. In an economy that needs more of both human and physical capital, considering only these two options presents a false choice.

Make no mistake: A tax code is primarily a means of raising revenue. But it also sends powerful messages through what it does, and does not, tax. In this light, why not develop a socially useful tax system that would tax those things the country needs less of, and untax those things of which society wants more? This idea is being tried around the world, and even the British news magazine *The Economist* has endorsed such an approach. *Tax Waste,* Not Work suggests bringing this concept, commonly called environmental or resource-based tax shifting, to the United States.

This type of tax reform could lead to a cleaner environment at the same time that incentives are provided for more work and investment. Just as importantly, it could be designed without a regressive shift of the tax burden if regressive taxes like the payroll tax are reduced to offset the new levies. Revenues could be gained from taxing carbon dioxide emissions, air and water pollution, or consumption of virgin materials. Emission permits could be auctioned to firms, which would also raise substantial revenue; similarly, fees could be charged for the use of certain assets held in common by the public. On the tax reduction side, payroll, individual, and corporate tax rates could all be reduced—without increasing the deficit or forcing huge cuts in government services.

While such a shift from taxing "goods"—the creation of wealth through labor and investment—to "bads"—the depletion of wealth through pollution and environmental degradation—cannot be a magic bullet for every economic and environmental ill, it does offer a promising chance for promoting work and investment while concurrently moving toward the types of market-based policies that would be an improvement over the current regulatory structure.

Deflecting Past Critiques

The idea of using market-based policies such as taxes or emission permits to deal with environmental problems has been a staple of the academic literature for decades. But these policy tools have been widely criticized in the United States for a number of reasons—all of which a tax shift would address:

• Environmental taxes and permits have often been pushed as tax increases, rather than as a lever for reducing other taxes. A tax shift, however, would substitute higher taxes on some things with lower taxes on others, with the objective of leaving most individuals paying roughly the same amount in total. Only recently has this idea for "revenue recycling" been receiving attention from academics and public policy groups. For example, the World Resources Institute's Green Fees report and Ernst Ulrich von Weizsacker's book, Ecological Tax Reform (both published in 1992), broke new ground in this area; an interesting body of literature has followed these front runners, discussing the potential benefits of such "recycling."

• The business community has lobbied against these so-called "green taxes" in the past, fearing that they would cost jobs, reduce economic growth, or detract from U.S. competitiveness. But a tax shift, by reducing other taxes with high distortionary costs, should greatly reduce or eliminate these concerns.

• Environmental taxes and permits have been criticized for their regressive nature—that is, for affecting the poor and middle classes relatively more than the well-off, since lower income families spend a larger percentage of their income on energy. Yet under a tax shift, other regressive taxes could be reduced to maintain the current distribution of the tax burden.

• Past critics could point to the potential risk of being the first industrialized country to advance these proposals in a major way. But now there are models to look to, as several countries have adopted "green taxes"; and others, including Denmark, Great Britain, and Costa Rica, have passed mild tax shifts.

The Rationales for Change

Philosophic Rationales

A tax shift policy sends a powerful message from the perspective of restoring legitimacy to public finance: Individuals should be able to keep more of the fruit of their toil, but should pay for the costs that they impose on others. This change would restore both a coherent rationale and a sense of values to the nation's tax system. Tax shifting also offers the potential to draw public revenue from resources already owned in common (e.g., public lands, the broadcast spectrum), thereby enabling all citizens to receive dividends from the use of common assets.

To the extent that it replaces the current tax structure, a shift to resource taxes would also restore the notion that the costs of today's actions should not be borne by future generations. This would bring a sense of "honest accounting" back to government. In other words, rather than paying taxes based upon their work or saving, people should increasingly pay taxes based upon the resources they consume and the pollution they cause. Thus, society "pays" for the problems it passes on to its children, rather than passing on the burden.

Finally, by providing incentives for people and businesses to invest in energy efficient vehicles, homes, and equipment, a tax shift empowers people to reduce their own tax bills in a way that the current system does not.

Economic and Fiscal Rationales

While tax shifting is a relatively new idea, the economic rationales for pursuing it are numerous and rest on several long-standing pillars of mainstream thought.

• The current tax system imposes significant efficiency costs and therefore retards economic growth. Replacing a portion of these economically inefficient taxes with "corrective" taxes (which have lower efficiency costs, or "deadweight losses") could reduce the overall economic cost of the tax system. It could also yield several important economic benefits, ranging from more job creation and/or higher wages to new investments in energy efficiency and higher economic growth. Redefining Progress has sponsored research that concludes that, depending on incidence assumptions and revenue recycling choice, approximately three-fourths of industry and workers stand to gain from environmental tax reform, in terms of reduced tax burden and increased competitiveness.

• Current market prices for many goods do not take the social and environmental costs of production or energy consumption into account. Adding the costs of these externalities into the price system, via the tax code or emission permits, would make the economy more efficient. Despite disagreement about how (and by how much) energy prices ought to be raised, most economists would agree that energy prices ought to be higher—and that higher prices would not be as costly to the economy as some critics claim.

• The academic literature has shown that the most efficient use of any revenues from environmental levies would be to reduce other taxes. While there is disagreement over whether tax cuts on work or investment are more likely to yield economic gains, it is this potential for lowering current taxes that is likely to be the most appealing part of this proposal for many individuals, private firms, and elected officials.

Environmental Rationales

Another motivating force for a tax shift is that it would provide a least-cost approach to reducing pollution, waste, and the long-term threat of climate change. In the summer of 1995, the Intergovernmental Panel on Climate Change (IPCC)—a group of more than 2,200 scientists and economists from nearly 60 nations—declared that "the balance of evidence suggests that there is a discernible human influence on global climate," signaling the growing scientific consensus on the issue. In 1998, over 2500 economists, including eight Nobel laureates, signed a statement that global climate change carries with it significant environmental, economic, social, and geopolitical risks, and that market-based policies offer the most efficient solution for slowing the effects of climate change.

The view that climate change is not an economic problem is changing as the staggering costs of dealing with its effects become more apparent. Despite greater energy efficiency in the United States, global emissions of carbon dioxide are projected to grow by 54 percent over the next 20 years. In response, the U.S. government has begun to shift its view of the climate change problem. In July 1996, the Clinton Administration announced its support for the adoption of binding yet flexible targets to reduce global carbon emissions. In 1997, the United States negotiated the Kyoto Protocol, along with 160 other countries, under which it agreed to reduce its greenhouse gas emissions by 7 percent between 2008 and 2012. A tradable emission permit system will be instrumental in achieving these goals.

Industry leaders, policy makers, academic economists, and many members of the environmental community have also shown growing support for market-based approaches to environmental policy. The Clinton administration, presidential candidate George W. Bush, and many members of Congress have all stated that climate change is a problem. Various business sectors—most notably insurance and finance—are increasingly viewing climate change as a threat to economic performance, public health, and geopolitical stability. The focus of these interests has not only been on the climate change issue, but also on pollution, congestion, and solid waste. The possibility of addressing these problems with less regulation creates the potential for new alliances between business, environmentalists, labor unions, tax reformers, and elected officials at all points along the political spectrum.

Tax Shift Efforts at the State Level

Broader acceptance of environmental tax shifting as a concept has gained momentum at the state level. Environmental and tax reform groups in California, Florida, Maine, Massachusetts, Minnesota, New Hampshire, Oregon, Pennsylvania, Texas, Vermont, Washington, and Wisconsin are working on moving specific reforms in their respective states. Proposed bases for increased taxes include land use, vehicle miles traveled, large livestock property, water pollution, and energy emissions, with proposed decreases in payroll, income, sales, and corporate taxes.

Although legislators remain wary of tax shifting, perhaps because of reflexive suspicion of any tax measure, all U.S. states have at least some environmental tax provisions, and several have recently considered or are considering new measures to shift taxes toward environmentally harmful activities. In Minnesota, the legislature introduced the Economic Efficiency and Pollution Reduction Act (EEPRA) in 1997, which would have combined a carbon tax with an offsetting reduction in property and payroll taxes. The House Environment Committee debated the bill, but it was withdrawn without a vote. Environmental tax reform has been suggested as an instrumental base for education finance reform in New Hampshire. A court order mandating increased aid to education, combined with enduring reluctance to introduce a sales or income tax, has made pollution taxes a politically viable alternative to increased property taxes. In neighboring Vermont, a proposed legislative tax shift study lost by one vote in the House in 1999.

It should also be noted that environmental taxes are much more widely accepted in Europe than in the United States. Consider these examples:

• In Denmark, green taxes are being used to reduce income taxes and employers' social security contributions.
• In Finland, lower taxes on income and labor are being offset, in part, by green taxes, such as a landfill tax, and increased energy taxes.
• In the Netherlands, part of the regulatory tax on energy is being allocated to a reduction in employers' social security contributions.
• In Sweden, a 1991 tax reform resulted in higher environment-related taxes and lower marginal income tax rates.
• In the United Kingdom, revenue from a new landfill tax is being used to reduce employers' social security contributions by 0.2 percentage points.

The Potential Benefits of Change

The following are the most important potential benefits of this fresh approach to fiscal policy, each of which is examined in *Tax Waste, Not Work*.

1. Job creation could be spurred, take-home pay increased, and/or incentives to enter the workforce enhanced as a result of lower payroll taxes.

2. Reducing taxes that carry large efficiency losses could enhance economic efficiency, thus improving the economy's overall capacity to create jobs and wealth.

3. The collective threats of climate change (i.e., economic, health, environmental, and political) could be addressed through a proactive solution.

4. Environmental benefits such as less pollution and waste could be realized through market-based solutions, with less reliance on heavy-handed government regulation such as vehicle emission standards.

5. Businesses and individuals would have a greater incentive to make new investments in technological innovations or energy efficiency, thus exerting a new measure of control over their own tax burdens.

6. The taxation of capital and business income could be greatly simplified or reduced without shifting the tax burden down the income scale.

7. New incentives would be created for investment in R&D and the development of the businesses and technologies of the future, helping U.S. companies gain competitive advantage in new markets.

8. Inner cities could become more attractive business locations because of their abundant labor and available scrap materials.

9. Changes in energy prices could reduce congestion and make mass transit investment more viable for private investors, possibly reducing the need for public subsidies.

10. If there is a general consensus that taxing waste, and not work, is reasonable, public trust in government—and compliance with the tax system—will increase.

***

Statement of Barry Cargill, Small Business Association of Michigan

Mr. Chairman and Members of the Ways and Means Committee of the United States House of Representatives:

My name is Barry Cargill; I am Vice President for Government Relations of the Small Business Association of Michigan. We are sometimes recognized by our acronym SBAM. We are a state based small business trade association representing 8,000 small businesses in Michigan. We represent all types of small business, from manufacturing businesses to retailers.

The FairTax is an issue that was heatedly debated by our members and Board of Directors. In the end, our Board of Directors unanimously approved the FairTax as the best alternative to replace the current system. Education is key to understanding benefits of the FairTax. In fact, the more that our members learn about the FairTax, the more enthusiastically they support it.

Todd McCracken of NSBU is scheduled to testify in support of the National Sales Tax proposed by Citizens for Fair Taxation (The Fair Tax Plan) and we would like to associate SBAM with his comments.

SBAM shares the position of NSBU and supports the FairTax as the best alternative for comprehensive national tax reform. The debate over spending our projected federal budget surpluses masks the fact that small businesses struggle under the burden of a troubled federal tax system. The Fair Tax abolishes the current system by replacing all federal income, payroll, death and capital gains taxes. In place of the abolished taxes, the Fair Tax proposes to institute a 23 percent tax-inclusive sales tax on all end-use goods and services.

One of the key reasons we support the plan is that it will reduce compliance costs unlike any other tax alternative. Small businesses must use complex tax accounting rules to keep track of income, inventories, types of expenses, depreciation, various employee benefit regulations, payroll taxes (including Social Security, Medicare, and unemployment taxes) and file the necessary accounting and information returns. This takes precious time away from trying to grow the business and become more profitable.

Apart from the level of compliance costs, there is something fundamentally different in the effect of these compliance costs on small firms. First, small firms pay higher compliance costs as a percentage of revenues. In many cases, compliance costs such as those associated with pension plans, payroll taxes, software, accounting system are fixed costs with regressive effects on small companies. In most cases, small firms must endure the same panoply of laws and regulations as larger firms, the same recordkeeping and system requirements. However, small firms have less revenue against which these costs can be spread. Secondly, small firms do not have the same capabilities to push these costs forward on consumers or customers. When a large firm has associated revenue costs, they often simply push these costs forward in the prices of goods and services. When small firms incur such costs, they result in lower wages, lower returns on investment and fewer opportunities for entrepreneurs. Under the Fair Tax, only one question is relevant to small businesspersons. How much did I sell to customers? By reducing overhead to answering that single question, the FairTax would reduce compliance costs by about 90 percent, freeing capital and entrepreneurial energy.

Another reason we support the FairTax is that it shifts the emphasis of taxation away from saving and investment and productive activity.

Payroll taxes constitute more than one-third of all federal revenue collections. Since 1970, business received nine social security (FICA) tax increases totaling 133 percent, and 19 FICA base increases totaling 677 percent. Additionally, payroll taxes are a tax on employment and thus discourage hiring employees. Employees are the winners when the tax system encourages rather than discourages employment.

The death tax presents families with the problem of liquidating the family business in order to pay for the taxes on inheritance or to drain valuable resources from the business to establish costly and confusing trusts. Only 40 percent of all small businesses make it to the second generation and only 10 percent to the third.

Capital gains incentives have traditionally, and inaccurately, been seen as a tool only of venture capitalists and wealthy investors. However, we must remember the vast networks of informal investors in the small business community. Research conducted by the Small Business Administration (SBA) shows that informal equity investors in small firms are a much larger financing factor than venture capital. Eliminating capital gains taxes would lead to a boon in small business investment.

We would note that Members of this Committee will likely read some testimony by large retailers that believe the FairTax would hurt retail sales. Their statement appears to suggest that there will be a sticker shock to a national sales tax. We disagree with this assessment from several perspectives and wanted an opportunity to advance these points.

First, like other firms, retailers will enjoy a zero corporate tax rate and their shareholders will not be taxed on dividends received from the retailer or capital gains on their investment in the retailer. Like other firms, they will enjoy much lower compliance costs. Instead of having to comply with the complexities of the income tax, payroll tax, and various excise tax, there will be one sales tax on all goods and service. The firm will simply need to calculate on a monthly basis its total retail sales. Retailers will receive an administration fee for complying with the sales tax. There will be no more uniform inventory capitalization requirements. There will be no more complex rules government employee benefits and retirement plans that serve as a barrier to providing employees with retirement plans. There will be no more tax depreciation schedules. Do large retailers really want to continue these onerous laws?

Second, consumers will see their paychecks increase by over $1.1 trillion. Finally consumers will have more money to spend. Since the plan is revenue neutral, the repeal of the income tax will provide consumers with the money necessary to pay for the sales tax. Sales taxes were originally installed at the state level in the 1930's because in times of economic fluctuation, consumption is a more stable source of revenue collection.

Third, retailers will make more money in a prosperous, growing economy. All respected economic projections predict a much healthier economy. People are willing and able to purchase more goods and services in a healthy economy. Typical estimates are that they economy will be 10 to 14 percent larger within 10 years and consumption will grow very substantially. Some studies show the potential gains to be much higher. Real wages will increase.

We would note that in a study prepared by Nathan Associates (March, 1996) for the National Retail Institute, which by its own admission made every conceivable adverse assumption, the economy will grow three percent more in ten years than it would have under the income tax. The increase in consumption will be 1.15 percent less in the first year relative to what it would have been under the income tax. Consumption will be higher in the fourth year and every year thereafter than it would have been under the income tax. The study assumed that every dollar in new U.S. investment must come from the U.S. rather than foreign investors and assumes a very low effects of higher investment on productivity. It assumes no gain in productivity from lower compliance costs.

As this Committee reviews the FairTax proposal, keep in mind that consumption purchases must be made from after-income-tax dollars today. The primary difference between a sales tax and an income tax is that the income tax doubly or triply taxes savings. How much tax on savings is too much? How much of a tax on investment is too much? What is wrong with developing a tax system that fully eliminates the tax on savings and investment and gives consumers the choice to either spend or invest the fruit of their labor?

There are other factors. For one, consumer interest rates will fall dramatically, probably by about 25 percent, and consumer's ability to finance consumption will be higher. In the case of interest that is presently deductible, the fall in interest rates and the lack of deductibility is just about a wash for most people. Since consumer interest is not deductible under present law, this effect will be strong with respect to credit card or consumer loan financed purchases. Finally, the committee should not dwell on the rate. The FairTax does not raise more money than our current system ,it just makes the taxes we pay visible. The relative purchasing power of the dollar will remain the same; in fact, estimates are that real wages would increase. We should not be opposed to truth in advertising the cost of the Federal government.

The FairTax is a refreshing alternative to the current quagmire of taxes and regulations. It would reduce complexity and allow Americans to understand the tax system to which they are subject. It will lower compliance costs. It will make the taxes we pay visible. It will help our international competitiveness. It will help America's entrepreneurs become more prosperous, more vibrant and an even greater job generator. This will help consumption as well as wages. And when the economy does better, we will see even more surpluses so the tax rate can be lowered.

Thank you for the opportunity to present the views of Michigan small business. We encourage this committee to hold additional hearings on the FairTax. We are confident that the more that is learned about the proposal, the better it will sound to you and the American public.

Statement of Raymond J. Keating, Small Business Survival Committee

On behalf of the Small Business Survival Committee (SBSC) and its more than 50,000 members across the nation, I appreciate this opportunity to spell out SBSC's position on the "Fair Tax Act."

SBSC is a non-partisan, non-profit advocate for small business owners across the nation. On a wide array of policy issues impacting the small business community and the economy in general—including taxes, regulations, trade, and government spending—SBSC consistently argues from a principled, free-market perspective.

412

As you know, the "Fair Tax Act" would eliminate all income, payroll, estate and gift taxes, and replace them with a national retail sales tax of 23 percent. The general revenue rate would equal 14.91 percent, with the remaining 8.09 percent going for Social Security and Medicare hospital insurance. No tax would be paid on products or services purchased for business, investment or export purposes. And except for some isolated exceptions, the tax would be collected and remitted (monthly) by the seller. In states that already levy a sales tax, the state would administer the federal sales tax, keeping .0025 percent of the amount collected for administrative costs. In states that do not impose sales taxes, the federal government would administer the tax.

A "family consumption allowance" would be rebated each month to each family/individual in the amount equal to the product of the sales tax rate and the monthly poverty level. The Social Security Administration would mail the monthly rebate, or provide rebates through smart cards.

SBSC supports throwing out the current messy, complicated, unfair and anti-growth tax system that entrepreneurs, businesses and individuals currently labor under in favor of a national retail sales tax. On several occasions, we have outlined the key principles that should buttress any serious effort at tax reform:

• **Low Flat Tax Rate to Promote Economic Growth.** The lower and more proportional, or flatter, the tax rate system the better. Obviously, a low tax rate boosts incentives for working and risk taking.

• **No Taxation of Capital.** Taxing returns on investment and savings makes absolutely no economic sense. First, taxing returns on capital is an example of double, triple or more layers of taxation. Second, since investment and entrepreneurship are the primary engines of economic growth, taxing the returns on such activities is counterproductive. Along these same lines, it must be remembered that labor is powerless without capital, and therefore, taxing capital hurts labor.

• **Inflation Factor.** The detrimental effects of inflation should be factored into any tax system's design. No additional incentive for the monetary authority to inflate should be provided by the tax system, and taxpayers should not be penalized due to inflation. Therefore, tax brackets should be indexed for inflation.

• **Clarity.** The best tax system makes clear how much is owed, who pays, and when the tax is being paid.

• **Simplicity.** Tax payments should be made as easy and as simple as possible for the taxpayer without any loss of clarity.

• **Limited Bureaucracy and Intrusiveness.** The fewer tax collectors and the more limited their powers the better.

• **Minimize Incentives for Tax Avoidance.** Taxes should be low enough so as not to provide significant incentives for avoidance.

• **No Additional Boost to Government Spending.** A tax system's design should not make it any easier for government to increase expenditures.

How does a national retail sales tax—or the Fair Tax—score according to these fundamental principles?

• **Low Flat Tax Rate to Promote Economic Growth.** Obviously, income would not be taxed under this plan and consumption would be taxed at the final retail level at a flat rate of 23 percent. By not taxing work, saving, investing, and risk taking at all, pro-growth incentives and the economy would receive major boosts.

For critics saying that such a tax would be regressive, in fact a small amount of progressivity would be introduced into the system through the family allowance rebate. SBSC's only concern is to lower the proposed 23 percent tax rate.

• **No Taxation of Capital.** The Fair Tax would do away with cases of double, triple or more layers of taxation by not taxing returns on investment and savings at all. Incentives for saving, investment, and risk taking would skyrocket, with entrepreneurship, economic growth, and job creation receiving a significant boost.

• **Inflation Factor.** The inflation question may seem somewhat murky regarding the Fair Tax, but in the end, a retail sales tax provides little incentive for the government to inflate. One need only remember that inflation is a monetary phenomenon, caused by money supply outpacing money demand.

• **Clarity.** It remains difficult to imagine a clearer tax system than the Fair Tax. Whenever one buys something, the tax owed becomes immediately clear and is paid at that moment.

• **Simplicity.** The Fair Tax would be far simpler than an income tax system for individuals and many businesses. However, some questions remain for retail businesses as to whether a national retail sales tax eases or adds to their tax compliance burdens. However, since most states already levy a sales tax, additional compliance costs would be minimal, well worth the elimination of federal income and death taxes.

• **Limited Bureaucracy and Intrusiveness.** The Fair Tax would allow the IRS to be disbanded and replaced with a much smaller, less intrusive bureaucracy to collect sales taxes in the very few states that do not impose sales levies.

• **Minimize Incentives for Tax Avoidance.** One of the most serious questions regarding the Fair Tax relates to tax evasion. A national sales tax rate of 23 percent, especially when combined with state and local sales taxes, and a seemingly easy ability to avoid sales levies, creates a very real and significant temptation for tax avoidance. Obviously, the best way to deal with this issue is to cut the size of government and lower the tax rate.

• **No Additional Boost to Government Spending.** Indeed, regarding its effect on government spending, the Fair Tax actually should act as a restraint on the growth of government. Every time a purchase is made at the retail level, the cost of government becomes clear with the fair tax. Indeed, little evidence exists that retail sales taxes are a major impetus to the growth of government. In contrast, the current income-and asset-based federal tax system fuels the growth of government and hides the total cost of government from most taxpayers.

As you can see, throwing out our current tax code in favor of the Fair Tax would be a major pro-growth, pro-entrepreneur reform. However, the biggest danger regarding the move from our current income-and asset-based tax system to a retail sales tax like the Fair Tax is the looming threat that in the end U.S. taxpayers could be saddled with both a sales tax and an income tax. Therefore, before a national retail sales tax is implemented, the 16th Amendment to the U.S. Constitution, which allows for the imposition of an income tax, must be repealed. Without repealing the 16th Amendment, the chances that politicians—who seemingly always seek to expand the power and resources of government—would eventually impose both a sales tax and an income tax are too great.

If the 16th Amendment were repealed, from an pro-economic growth viewpoint, a retail sales tax is far preferable to any kind of income tax.

Again, I appreciate this opportunity to address the "Fair Tax Act." Feel free to contact me at SBSC with any questions or comments.

Statement of Lori Klein, Taxpayer Protection Alliance, Phoenix, AZ

Mr. Chairman, Honorable Members of Congress, Ladies and Gentlemen:

Fundamental tax reform is an issue that is now sweeping the nation. In a recent poll taken by the Tax Education Association (TEA) 81.7 percent of the electorate now feel that tax reform must be given high priority in the upcoming elections. The study showed that although the IRS has attempted to create a new image for itself, the public consensus is that the agency is still as unpopular as ever. According to the poll, 75% feel the IRS has too much power and 88.6% want to see the agency further reformed or eliminated altogether. It also showed that only 16.2% believe that our current income tax system is fair.

The Taxpayer Protection Alliance is a group of citizens from Arizona who are dedicated to achieving fundamental tax reform, which is non-other than the total elimination of both our state personal and corporate income tax over the course of four years. Currently, we have a petition initiative calling for the abolition of our state income tax coupled with a voter referendum, which does not allow politicians to raise our taxes without voter approval. The ballot measure also calls for all federally elected officials from Arizona to pledge in writing to vote to abolish the federal income tax and replace it with a national retail sales tax on consumption and have it duly noted by their name on the ballot as "Accepts IRS elimination pledge."

As many testifying here today have noted, removal of the federal income tax system to be replaced with a national sales tax has a myriad of benefits to our economy and personal freedom. I would like to address today however, the benefit of the states adopting similar measures throughout the nation to coincide with the elimination of the current progressive income tax on the federal level.

THE ARIZONA ECONOMY

While Arizona's employment rate is low and the economy is strong, things could be much better. Many people who have jobs have low-paying service sector jobs. Arizona ranks near the bottom of the states in annual per capita income. About half of all jobs held by Arizonans are in the bottom third of industries ranked by average annual pay, according to economist Debra Roubik of VisionEcon. 16% of all high-paying jobs in Arizona are high-tech manufacturing jobs, and 14% are in high-tech services (ATTACHMENT 1). These are the jobs being created by the "new economy."

These are the jobs in the sector of the economy with the greatest promise for the future.

THE IMPACT OF ELIMINATING INCOME TAXES ON THE STATE ECONOMY

A study for the Arizona Association of Industries by Deborah Roubik of VisionEcon, published in January 2000, and cited in the Arizona Business Gazette and other publications, verified findings suggested by the classic work of Timothy Bartik in 1991 regarding the effect of state taxes on local economy. She found that for every 1 percent decrease in the state corporate income tax rate there is a 0.3 percent increase in new job creation, compounded annually. Furthermore, she found an inverse correlation between the marginal personal state income tax and high-tech service jobs as a percentage of jobs in the state. That is, the lower the income tax rate, the greater the percentage of high-tech service jobs, and vice versa (ATTACHMENT 2).

The marginal state corporate income tax for a multi-state corporation in Arizona is 3.5%.

Elimination of the state corporate income tax can be expected to generate an increase in job creation of approximately 1.2% per year, compounded annually, and increase the number of high-paying, high-tech manufacturing jobs, according to economist Debra Roubik.

Elimination of the personal income tax will assure that a significantly greater proportion of those additional jobs that are created will be in the high-paying high-tech service fields.

Arizonans are losing out to residents of other states when it comes to growth in earnings and higher paying jobs. Arizona's residents are losing out to states like Nevada, Texas, Washington, and Florida, where the absence of income taxes create jobs with substantive earning potential—jobs with a future. Although Arizona has a low unemployment rate, far too many Arizonans are just barely "getting by" in low-end jobs without much of a future.

ELIMINATING THE ARIZONA PERSONAL AND CORPORATE INCOME TAXES IS THE MOST EFFECTIVE AND EFFICIENT SOCIAL WELFARE PROGRAM OUR STATE CAN EVER PUT INTO PLACE.

SALES TAXES AS A REPLACEMENT FOR THE STATE INCOME TAX

A recent economic study by *VisionEcon,* using Arizona Department of Revenue Annual Reports, demonstrates that, using historical trends, the projected annual increase in sales tax revenue generated by the typical growth patterns in the Arizona tax base (Arizona employment is projected to continue growing by almost 2% more than the national average), could be used to painlessly reduce income tax collections every year. The result would be a "revenue neutral" elimination of the income tax in just seven years. This does not include any dynamic analysis. That means it does not take into account the added revenues we would get from the boom in economic activity and job-creation coming about from reducing or eliminating the income tax. It also does not take into account revenues from luxury tax and estate and property tax revenues (ATTACHMENT 3).

Thus using dynamic scoring, it is plain to see how easily the state's revenue stream can accommodate elimination of the personal and corporate income tax.

Furthermore, in an Arizona Republic news article dated April 2, 2000 it was reported that approximately $4.2 billion in sales tax revenue goes uncollected each year as a result of over 600 exemptions in the state sales tax, most of which were enacted after intense lobbying from special interest groups.

This revelation came as news to most Arizona residents in the private as well as the public sector. Few were aware that these exemptions were ever passed into law. And these exemptions are almost double the revenues currently collected from the state income tax. Some of these special interests who benefit from these exemptions, need them to offset the effects of the income tax—that's the tradeoff. Special interests are holding the average Arizona citizen and businesses hostage to the income tax. IS THIS TAXATION WITH REPRESENTATION?

Governor Hull, in the same Republic article pointed out that it is politically extremely difficult to overcome the will of those special interests. But, if the Taxpayer Protection Act was in effect, since many of those exemptions may have had to get voter approval in order to go into effect, they may have required an increase in some other tax to offset the exemption. The special interests would have thus been cut out of the loop—instead, today we see the voters cut out of the loop. Furthermore, many special interest groups would not find it necessary to seek exemptions if they didn't have to pay personal and corporate income taxes.

WE WOULD BE BETTER OFF AS A NATION WITHOUT THE INCOME TAX

415

The income tax is based on a fundamentally flawed and immoral idea that the
state has a prior claim on the fruits of another person's labor or property. A person's
labor or idea's are his/her property and the state has no right to seize those assets,
according to the precepts of our Founders. Thomas Jefferson's view of government
as the servant and the citizen as the master has been turned upside down in large
part due to the income tax. The income tax inevitably places the citizen on the defensive and takes away his very freedom and privacy. His legal rights are further
jeopardized, when, if found in error on a tax form, he/her is now guilty until proven
innocent.

Furthermore, the laws and constitution have been so weakened in our country,
that it is perfectly acceptable for the government to extort billions and trillions in
income tax dollars and redistribute the wealth with no accountability to those that
they've robbed. If your neighbor came to your house and took half of your property,
he would go to jail. However, if the government does the same and gives it to the
neighbor down the street who chooses not to live a productive life—it's justified.
What kind of lunacy have we become accustomed too. This kind of unfair tax system
corrupts the very soul of the nation. Not only does it, by its very nature, corrupt
the political process, it corrupts the integrity of its citizenry, by creating an environment whereby they feel unfairly assaulted and violated by their government. They
then try to avoid the tax as we've seen with the highest non-compliance to date.
The income tax does not respect the boundaries of a free society and has no place
in a free society. It is frankly Un-American. We can rename the House Ways and
Means Committee, the House Committee on Un-American Activities. (Just kidding)

The Taxpayer Protection Alliance calls for the complete abolition of the income
tax, the Sixteenth Amendment, and the IRS. We would hope that this committee
would adopt legislation introduced by Rep. John Linder (R–GA) and Rep. Petersen
(D–MN). Then we can rest assured that we might usher in a new Millennium of
freedom and prosperity for all Americans. We could do away with taxation without
representation. We could then claim we are the nation that believes in "life, liberty
and the pursuit of happiness." Our Founders would accept nothing less, why should
we?

(Testimony written by Taxpayer Protection Alliance Treasurer, Jeffrey A. Singer
and Executive Director, Lori Klein, 3431 W. Thunderbird Avenue, Suite 302–PMB,
Phoenix, AZ, 85053, (602) 866–2394)

[Attachments are being retained in the Committee files.]

Statement of UWC-Strategic Services on Unemployment and Workers'
Compensation

*Comprehensive Tax Reform Must be Sensitive to Sound Unemployment Insurance
Policy*

UWC-Strategic Services on Unemployment and Workers' Compensation, the only
business organization specializing exclusively in public policy advocacy on national
unemployment insurance (UI) and workers' compensation issues, urges Congress to
Address UI payroll tax issues, including repeal of the 0.2% Federal Unemployment
Tax Act (FUTA) surtax and UI administrative financing reform, when considering
any fundamental federal tax reform proposal. UWC supports a strong UI program
through which employers provide fair and affordable insurance benefits for a temporary period of time to workers with a strong attachment to work and who are
temporarily and involuntarily jobless when suitable work is not longer available.

Several proposals have been introduced in the 106th Congress to significantly
change the current federal tax system. Many of these proposals will repeal sunset
the Internal Revenue Code (IRC) including the FUTA. Rather than dissolving the
federal/sale, we urge Congress to repeal the unnecessary 0.2% FUTA surtax and
enact UI reform as contained in H.R. 3174, The Employment Security Financing Act
of 1999, introduced by Representative Jim McCrery (R–LA). H.R. 3147 is supported
by 36 co-sponsors, as well as a broad based coalition of 32 states and more than
100 business organizations. These measures would ease the tax burden on employers by 25% while providing critically important UI administrative financing reform.

The Dangers of Sunsetting FUTA

The FUTA was enacted in 1935 and made part of the IRC. The FUTA is the basic
controlling federal law for UI, The FUTA provides the basic framework for the state
UI system, as well as the revenue for the state agencies which administer the UI

program and provide a public labor exchange. The FUTA also permits states to receive loans if their UI trust funds are depleted, and it provides and extension of UI benefit duration during periods of high and rising unemployment.

We seriously doubt that a new, equally simple, equally enforceable and similarly equitable system for UI/ES could be re-created and enacted in place of the FUTA.

Completely repealing the FUTA will jeopardize the safety net for workers and employers. Important financial and legal protections for workers will be at risk, and employers will face added payroll taxes. Both workers and employers will be hurt by repealing the federal protection against "raid" on state UI benefit trust fund reserves.

Not one of the proposals being considered at this hearing address these issues. Thus, until a viable solution is debated, proposals to "scrap the Code" should not include provisions that would eliminate FUTA.

Repeal the 0.2% FUTA surtax

Under current law, employers pay the FUTA tax at the rate of 0.8% of taxable payroll ($7,000). This tax rate is 25% too high as a result of a 0.2% "temporary" surtax which is no longer needed. The tax is being collected only because inclusion of FUTA surpluses in the unified federal budget allows the federal government to meet budget targets for unrelated spending programs. The practice of counting FUTA dollars for spending on other programs, leaving only an IOU behind, is contrary to the very reason Congress placed these funds in the Unemployment *Trust Fund.*

Congress originally imposed the surtax in 1976 to pay for a temporary federal program of supplemental UI benefits. This program expired long ago. The deficit created by this program was retired in 1987, but the surtax has been extended until 2007. The FUTA accounts within the trust fund all exceed their maximums, making this surtax unnecessary. The revenue form the surtax is not needed for the UI/ES program. Only 50 cents out of every FUTA dollar is being spent as intended for the administration of the UI/ES, program and no additional funds are necessary to fund the 50% FUTA share of extended benefits.

The FUTA surtax adversely affects nearly every employer. The money collected from employers for this surtax inhibits hiring low wage workers and siphons away dollars that would be better spent on jobs in rural areas, and facility and equipment enhancements to provide a better work environment and increase productivity and competitiveness.

24 years of a "temporary" tax is too long! Congress should act quickly to repeal the 0.2% FUTA surtax by (1) including it as part of the business tax incentives in the minimum wage bill currently in conference and (2) enacting H.R. 3174 (discussed below).

Enact UI Administrative Financing Reform (H.R. 3174)

Although complete FUTA repeal is not desirable, FUTA reform is overdue. The present UI/ES program is not working effectively. Workers are under-served, employers are overtaxed and state UI/ES agencies and under-funded. Under the current system, the federal government collects 100% of the FUTA receipts but returns only 50% to the states. Shortchanging the funding to administer UI has led to workers collecting more weeks of unemployment benefits *during the tightest labor market in recent history*, and states are forced to reach into general revenues and employer pockets (*through add-on payroll taxes*) to make up for the shortfall.

H.R. 3174 is specifically designed to solve this problem. It will restore integrity to the UI trust funds. Not only is the0.2% FUTA surtax repealed, but he remaining trust fund dollars will be returned to the states—in full! This will allow states to provide the necessary resources to better serve UI claimants, job seekers, veterans and employers. H.R. 3174 will combat UI fraud and abuse by providing states with adequate funding.

H.R. 3174 is consistent with the concepts of tax simplification being presented at this hearing. Unnecessary paperwork will be eliminated as employers will only have to complete and submit a single UI tax form rather than two separate federal and state UI tax forms. Equally important, state legislatures—rather than Washington bureaucrats—will be responsible for determining how much is necessary to run their own state UI programs. This will provide added flexibility and accountability—without taking away any protections from jobless workers.

UWC urges swift enactment of H.R. 3174. It is a win for workers, employers and states and is the right direction for UI reform. For more information, please contact Vince Sampson at (202) 682–1515.

Statement Robert L. Schulz, We the People Foundation for Constitutional Education, Inc., Queensbury, NY

Mr. Chairman:

Mr. Chairman, I would like to thank you for the opportunity to submit these remarks for the record of the hearing on fundamental tax reform. I am Robert Schulz, and I am Chairman of the We The People organization from northern New York State. I have been very actively pursuing the cause of good government for 20 years—at the local, state, and federal level. The organizations I chair are devoted to educating citizens about problems of governmental wrongdoing, especially when government behaves in violation of the state or federal constitutions or in violation of the law. I also chair a group called the All-County Taxpayers Association in New York State.

For more than a year now, we have been focusing in particular on issues of illegal operations of the federal income tax system. We have been learning from many sources about numerous aspects of those illegal operations. And for over a year, we, in turn, have been informing millions of people across the country about what we have learned—reaching as many citizens as we can by using various media: radio, newspapers, the internet, newsletters, and even television. I am a talk-radio host on a national radio network and also on a regional talk-radio show in Albany, NY. You may be aware that last July, we held a symposium at the National Press Club here in Washington to examine issues of illegal operations of the federal income tax system. The symposium was broadcast live by C-Span and rerun several times over the next few days. We held another conference at the National Press Club last November to further discuss the income tax issues and what to do about them. Although we asked the leaders of our three branches of government to send knowledgeable representatives to our meetings at the NPC to refute allegations and arguments being presented, they did not respond and did not even acknowledge our requests. That has led us back here to Washington this week for a third time, to deliver a Remonstrance to the leaders of our three branches enumerating the people's grievances over the illegal operations of the federal income tax system. We have provided each of you a copy of the Remonstrance. Thousands of copies of the video tapes of the July symposium and the November conference have gone out and are now circulating all across the country—many in public lending libraries for all to borrow. A number of other individuals have been broadcasting and publishing for years about the problems I am going to tell about, and now millions of citizens are aware of them.

Well, what ARE those issues; what ARE those grievances; and what are the remedies? I will summarize as succinctly as I can.

Congressional hearings for years have been the forum for horror stories by citizens who have suffered all kinds of abuse at the hands of the IRS. Our grievances include those outrageous and arrogant behaviors by the IRS perpetrated by its agents, policies, and procedures. We are particularly distressed at the utter lack of respect for due process and the denial of due process in IRS procedures, including the unwillingness of the IRS to provide information about our due process rights, the denial of our rights to see the evidence against us, to confront and cross-examine those who have testified against us, and denial of our rights against illegal seizure of our property by the IRS because of an unconstitutional anti-injunction law, 26 USC Section 7421.

But as bad as these behaviors are, they are only a small part of it; the problems are much deeper and they started early in the 20th century. Our grievances largely deal with issues of hoax, fraud, and deliberate deception.

It has been well established since 1985, and unrefuted, that the 16th amendment, the so-called income tax amendment, did not even come close to being legally ratified in 1913. It was, indeed, fraudulently declared to be ratified by a lame-duck Secretary of State, Philander Knox, and just a few days before he left office to make way for the Wilson administration. Knox's motive is easy to see. He had for many years been attorney for Carnegie, Rockefeller, Morgan, and the Vanderbilts, and had put together the largest of their cartels. He was paving the way for the Federal Reserve Act that was passed later in 1913. The central bank would want a more reliable flow of revenue to assure payment on the debt that the government would be incurring. Knox had already had practice in this method by his role in taking over the tax collection systems in Honduras and Nicaragua to assure payment of loans to those governments. Senator Nelson Aldrich, spokesman for Rockefeller and Morgan, had pushed the income tax amendment through the Senate in 1909, and, as a result of a meeting he convened at his vacation "cottage" among several of the nation's most powerful bankers representing Rockefeller, Morgan, and the Rothschilds, he designed the Federal Reserve legislation that passed in 1913, under the guise of banking reform.

The research that conclusively revealed the fraudulent ratification of the 16th amendment was done by Mr. Bill Benson, a former investigator for the Illinois Department of Revenue who spent a whole year among the archives of all 48 states and the federal government. Here are some of his findings. [See "Examples of States That Failed to Ratify the 16th Amendment" on page 5.]

What has been the government's response to Benson's work? Well, one senator, until recently a presidential candidate, tried to pay Mr. Benson—offered to make him a millionaire if he would only not publish the results of his work, turn over all 17,000 certified documents he had obtained from the archives, and agree never to talk about his research again. However, to Mr. Benson, our republic is not for sale. He published, and every member of Congress received a personal copy of his two-volume report. I am sure he would be happy to provide a copy to any member of this committee. It is not out-of-date. It is history.

Other responses by Congress have been produced by the Congressional Research Service in the form of a report written in 1985 by Thomas Ripy about the 16th amendment issue and in a 1996 report by John Luckey titled "Frequently Asked Questions Concerning the Federal Income Tax." Neither report mentions or addresses the key issue of fraudulent ratification of the 16th amendment. They are, therefore, non-responses.

The courts have refused to address the fraud issue, calling it a political question for Congress, even though fraud is clearly a matter for the courts and is not subject to the normal statute of limitations. Congress has said that it is a matter for the courts. We say it is an issue for both Congress and the courts, and it must be addressed. The government must not stonewall on this issue any longer.

The IRS has addressed the 16th amendment question in it's publication titled "Why Do I Have to Pay Taxes?" This is sort of a mini-version of the Luckey Report, and can be found on the Internet. Its answer to the argument that the 16th amendment was not properly ratified is to state that the 16th amendment was ratified on February 3, 1913, and then to quote the words of the amendment. This, of course, is a non-response to the question and means nothing. It is pathetic and insulting (and the date is wrong; it was February 25).

Another major issue and grievance is that the IRS operates in such a way as to collect income taxes from almost all citizens even though no law or regulation requires most citizens to file and pay income taxes nor to have those taxes withheld from the money they earn. The IRC and its regulations make liable for the income tax only "foreigners here and citizens abroad," but not most of us, unless we have income earned abroad. This has been demonstrated of late by those, especially employers, who have carefully studied and exercised the rules as written and have succeeded in making the IRS abide by them.

The standard response of the IRS to the liability argument is to quote 26 USC Sections 1,6001,6011,or 6012, which the IRS uses as the all-encompassing filing requirements. Section 1 imposes the tax on "taxable income;" Section 6001 says, "Every person liable for any tax imposed under this title...shall keep such records... make such returns...and comply with such rules and regulations as the Secretary may prescribe;" Section 6011 says, "When required by regulations...any person made liable by any tax imposed by this title shall make a return;" Section 6012 says, "Returns... shall be made by...[e]very individual having...gross income which exceeds the exemption amount..."

These, again, are non-responses that merely beg the original question of just who is liable. The crucial question becomes: What is "gross income?" And when we follow the disjointed, disconnected, and deceptive trail through the code and its regulations, we find in CFR 1.861–8(f)(1) that gross income is income derived from foreign sources, i.e., foreigners here and citizens abroad. When we follow the trail of withholding law to find out what kind of income is subject to withholding, it takes us to the same place and the same conclusion: foreigners here and citizens abroad. The same is true regarding liability for the Social Security tax, derived from the International Labor Agreement of the 1930s. All three trails lead to the same result.

Congressional response to the question of just who is liable is exemplified in a 1989 letter from Senator Inouye to a tax consultant constituent who asked about the precise provisions of the IRC that render an individual liable for income taxes. The letter says: "Based on research performed by the Congressional Research Service, there is no provision which...requires an individual to pay income taxes." The letter goes on to say that Article I Section 8 of the U.S. Constitution gives Congress the power to lay and collect taxes, and then makes the astonishing assertion that,

"Accordingly, the IRC need not specifically state that individuals shall be liable for income taxes because it is inferred from the Congress' authority to so levy and collect." This letter would have us believe that there is no need to bother with the inconvenience of actually writing laws or regulations or anything like that! Further, the letter then points out that Section 7201 et al. sets forth penalties for failure to pay taxes owed. The key word is "owed," but the letter does not explain how it is determined what taxes are actually owed or by whom. Once again, we are given a non-response that simply begs the question, along with a heavy-handed threat of prosecution. The letter tries to give us the impression we can be prosecuted for not doing something that no law or regulation requires us to do.

It is significant that employers are learning of the scam, as they are key to the whole system, along with the denial of due process rights for individual citizens. The IRS uses the false statements from employers (W–2s and 1099s) as prima facie proof that employees have earned gross income that is taxable. The IRS then makes it impossible in their procedures for an employee to challenge the incorrect testimony of the employer by refusing to issue summons so the employee can confront and cross-examine the employer. Tax law 26 USC Section 3402 does not protect employers from submitting false information. But the IRS has bullied and coerced employers since the 1930s to do so. Employees are then coerced into filing tax returns based on false information submitted by employers and to "voluntarily" and unknowingly waive their 5th amendment rights when they sign their 1040 forms, in order to get some small portion of their money refunded.

What are the remedies? First, a national sales tax is not the remedy, and we would not like to see the abuses by the illegal operations of the IRS used as an excuse for imposing such a tax. Excise taxes are most appropriate when used as luxury, sin, or amusement taxes, not when used to tax the necessities. Moreover, a national sales tax will be avoided by those who can use vertical integration strategies, and the people who can least afford it will end up paying a disproportionate share.

The issue of the fraudulent ratification of the 16th amendment must be addressed, not evaded, by Congress and by the courts. Besides that, Congress must act to remove the obstructions that prevent citizens from invoking the protections of their constitutional rights when dealing with the IRS in both administrative and judicial proceedings. The due process issues and abuses must be resolved. The remedy is to make the IRS and its agents obey the tax code and regulations and respect citizens' constitutional rights to due process, especially in administrative procedures. Denial of due process is the main factor in the abuses by the IRS, because it prevents people from defending themselves against those abuses. Three changes to the code can go far towards accomplishing this goal. All are in Chapter F (Administration): Sections 6326, 6404(b), and 7421. Sections 6326 and 6404(b) effectively enable errors or abuse by IRS employees to go uncorrected and obstruct the IRS Commissioner from properly controlling employees. Section 7421, as already mentioned, prevents judicial intervention and review of illegal seizures of property by the IRS in violation of our constitutional rights. No statute can overrule the Constitution. Many of the horror stories and abuses you hear about might be averted if it were not for the obstructions to correcting erroneous or malicious actions of subordinates by those above them or by the courts.

EXAMPLES OF STATES THAT FAILED TO RATIFY THE 16TH AMENDMENT

Philander Knox had received responses from 42 states when he declared the 16th amendment ratified in February, 1913. It was required that 36 of the 48 states at that time approve it. Of the 42, Knox acknowledged that four had rejected the amendment, bringing the number down to 38 that he said approved it.

In Kentucky, the legislature acted on the amendment without even having received it from the governor. (The amendment was sent to the governor of each state in 1909 for transmittal to their state legislatures.) The version of the amendment that the Kentucky legislature made up and acted upon deleted the words "on income" from the text of the amendment, so they were not even voting on an income tax! When they straightened that out, the Kentucky senate rejected the amendment. Yet Philander, inexplicably, counted Kentucky as approving it.

In Oklahoma, the legislature changed the wording of the amendment so that its meaning was the opposite of what was intended by Congress, and this was the version they approved and sent back to Knox. Yet Knox counted Oklahoma as approving the amendment, despite a memo from his chief legal counsel, Reuben Clark, that states were not allowed to change the amendment in any way.

Attorneys who have studied the subject have published that if any state could be shown to have violated its own state constitution or laws in its process of approving the 16th amendment, then that state's approval would have to be thrown out. With that in mind, let's look at some other states.

The state constitution of Tennessee prohibited the Tennessee legislature from acting upon any proposed amendment to the U.S. Constitution received from Congress until after the next election of state legislators. The intent, of course, is to give the proposed amendment a chance to become an issue in the state legislative elections so that the people can have a chance to influence the outcome. It also provides a cooling off period to reduce the tendency to approve ideas just because they're trendy. You can probably guess that I am about to tell you that the Tennessee legislature did not hold off on voting for the 16th amendment until after the next election, and you would be right—they didn't. That means they violated their own state constitution; their approval is and was invalid, and it brings the number of approving states down to 35, one less than required for ratification.

Texas and Louisiana violated provisions in their state constitutions prohibiting the legislatures from empowering the federal government with any additional taxing authority. Now our number is down to 33.

Thirteen states, including Tennessee again, violated provisions in their constitutions requiring that a bill be read three times over a period of at least three days before voting on it. This is not a trivial requirement. So we must subtract a dozen more states, bringing our number down to 21.

Several states returned unsigned, uncertified, or unsealed documents back to Knox, and did not rectify their negligence even after being notified and warned by him. The most egregious offenders, were Minnesota, Ohio, California, Arkansas, and Mississippi. Minnesota did not send any copy at all, only a note from the governor's secretary, so Knox could not have known at all what they voted on. Four of these five states were already disqualified above, leaving California to be subtracted, which brings our number down to 20, which is 16 fewer that the number required. These last five states, along with Kentucky and Oklahoma, have particularly strong implications with regard to the charge of fraud against Knox, in that he absolutely knew they should not be counted.

We could go on, but with the number down to 20, this is a suitable place to rest. Benson's findings show beyond doubt that the 16th amendment was not legally ratified and that Secretary of State Philander Knox did not just commit an error, but committed fraud, when he declared it ratified in February 1913.

Very truly yours,

Robert L. Schulz

Statement of Harold Apolinsky, Esq., Sirote and Permutt, and Dan R. Mastromarco, The Argus Group

Mr. Chairman and Members of the Ways and Means Committee:

We are pleased to submit this testimony which analyzes the impact of the leading national sales tax plan, the FairTax on nonprofit organizations. We believe that a shift to a consumption approach would in fact be extremely beneficial in several respects. It will improve economic growth—the primary determinant of charitable giving. It would remove the bias against non-itemizers. It would enhance the resources both itemizers and non-itemizers have by ensuring that they can make their contributions with pre-payroll tax dollars. This paper presents these arguments.

Background Discussion:

Some 150 years ago, Alexis de Tocqueville marveled at Americans' propensity to "found seminaries, build churches, distribute books... [He]... often admired the extreme skill they show in proposing a common object for the exertions of many and inducing them voluntarily to pursue it." If he would visit America for a third time, he would find that charitable, nonprofit organizations continue to play a vital role in meeting needs unmet by the private sector or by governmental agencies. From centers of learning, to health care facilities, to poverty relief organizations, to public policy research institutions, these institutions are an indispensable part of the American economic and social landscape—and thankfully so. Last year Americans donated more than $100 billion to charities, churches, foundations and other humanitarian causes.

When it comes to evaluating various tax reform proposals, it is right to consider its effect on charities. When considering the effects of shifting to a consumption tax system on the economy, on businesses and on individual taxpayers, we must be careful to ensure the continuing ability of charities to perform their essential role of facilitating charitable acts. We must ensure that, under any tax system, the good works of charities are not diminished.

However, some recent observers of American history incorrectly assume a vast change. They believe that if charitable donations are not deductible then charitable organizations could not exist; indeed, charity itself might cease to exist. The reason they always give is that the level of charitable giving in this country has a one-to-one elasticity tied to the tax code and tax deductions so the steeper the rate of tax, the more pain one feels, the more inclined they are inclined to be "charitable." Their conclusions are axiomatic as a syllogism:

1. steep marginal income tax rates and very high death taxes improve the volume of gifts by reducing the relative cost of giving versus consuming.

2. Reducing those rates will concomitantly reduce giving.

3. A consumption tax must reduce charitable giving since it renders irrelevant a deduction against income, thereby eliminating any advantage to giving.

While this is the crux of the main argument, other arguments are advanced. The relative cost of capital for nonprofits will increase, since a consumption tax may irradiate the distinction between tax-exempts and for-profits on income from passive or related sources.

These arguments have acquired a choristic-like following. The Independent Sector, along with the Council on Foundations, released a report on April 28, 1997 entitled "The Impact of Tax Restructuring on Tax Exempt Organizations," which was intended to criticize consumption tax proposals. The report concluded that under a sales tax contributions to tax exempt groups would decline by at least $33 billion or 35%. They estimated that proposals which eliminate the charitable deduction would lower annual contributions on the order of 10 percent to 20 percent.

The First Misconception: A Deduction is Necessary

Large and small donors are not ignorant of the tax ramifications of their actions, but neither are they primarily influenced by them when doing charitable deeds. Individuals give to charities not for tax deductions, but because they believe in the charitable works they support. There is, of course, much anecdotal data. In the early 1900's, before any death tax and with very low income taxes, the Vanderbilts endowed Vanderbilt University, the Stanfords endowed Stanford University and the Dukes endowed Trinity College in Durham, North Carolina.

The empirical data also suggest that there is, in fact, little linkage between the tax deduction and nonprofit giving.

Giving actually increased after marginal rates were significantly reduced in 1981 and again in 1986 and after the elimination of the charitable deduction for non-itemizers in 1986. Total giving increased (in inflation adjusted dollars) every year between 1983 and 1989.

The linkage assumed by researchers is not tempered by the importance of economic growth in charitable giving. A tax of 90 percent on income, for example, will lead to enormous growth in charitable giving as would an extraordinarily high death tax rate. Apparently, the higher the rate, the higher the marginal incentive to give and the lower the cost of giving. At a 90 percent tax rate, giving—as opposed to consuming—would only cost 10 cents on the dollar. Hence to benefit charities, we need to have a tax policy that makes holding onto the proceeds of our labor is as painful as holding on to a hot pan.

If such a linkage were mandatory for charitable acts, legitimate questions should be raised as to whether or not one's donation truly constitutes a charitable act. Let's take a taxpayer who is in a 40 percent income tax bracket. Assuming the taxpayer is not subject to other restrictions governing charitable donations, and assuming the taxpayer itemizes, if the taxpayer gives "x" dollars to charities, his taxes will be lowered by "x" times 40%. However, this simply means that other taxpayers' taxes would have to be increased to make up the difference of the taxes foregone. Thus, by saying the taxpayer is inclined to be "charitable" because his taxes would be reduced by "x" times 40%, we are saying that the taxpayer is inclined to be charitable only since he can, in part, be charitable with other taxpayers' money. If taxes escalate by income bracket, then we are saying something more. We are saying that the economic votes cast by higher wage-earners are more important than those cast by non-itemizers or lower wage-earners. The government might as well develop a matching program, where the wealthier you are, the greater the government values your opinion on where to spend your eleemosynary resources and the greater your matching resources from the pool of unwitting and unrecognized accomplices. Or alternatively, the wealthier you are the more other taxpayers need to subsidize your generosity in order to prompt it.

Thankfully, this is not the case. Acts of giving are often spontaneous, compassionate impulses. Moreover, the data suggest correlations of greater significance than a deduction. Active civic participation is more important to a healthy nonprofit sector than the presence of any tax credit or deduction. Benefactors are far more influenced by the desire to contribute to charitable causes. Most importantly, perhaps, income growth has more to do with boosting charitable contributions than tax incentives.

How much does economic growth influence charitable giving? It has been said by researchers that as the fortunes of the country go, so goes the contributions to philanthropic causes. In fact, after years of analysis, we can be a whole lot more specific: as the Gross Domestic Product changes, so goes approximately 2% of the total value of the goods and services to philanthropic causes. Total philanthropy as a percentage of GDP has held steady at around 2% for at least two decades.[1] Although the tax code has changed frequently and dramatically over the past 23 years, giving as a share of personal income has hovered around 1.83 percent. This measure reached as high as 1.95 percent (in 1989) and as low as 1.71 percent (in 1985, the year before non-itemizers ability to deduct charitable contributions was permitted). The narrow range has persisted even through the top marginal rate has fluctuated in that period between 28 and 70 percent.

Because of the importance of the relationship between giving and income, slight shifts in GDP represent considerable dollars in charitable giving. For example, one quarter of 1 percent of GDP at $8.8 trillion (the estimated 1999 level) equals $22 billion.[2] As GDP goes, so eventually does voluntary support.

So at least the data—as opposed to theory—suggest that to properly consider the effect of tax reform on charities, we must consider the effect of tax reform on economic growth. Giving is more dependent on how much donors have to give than how much the government will match their contributions with the taxes of middle income taxpayers.

Contrary to the assertions of the anti-consumption tax choral group, one of the most constructive steps that can be taken to improve the rate of economic growth would be to replace the current tax system with a consumption tax. It is the nearly universal opinion of economist that a consumption tax, like the FairTax, for example, would reduce the tax bias against work, savings and investment, improve the productivity and competitiveness of U.S. firms and improve the real wages of American workers. Replacing the income tax with the Fair Tax will dramatically improve the standard of living of the American people.[3]

Economic studies have been done on this as well. Work by Harvard economist Dale Jorgenson shows a quick 9 to 13 percent increase in the GDP after passage of the Fair Tax[4]; similarly, Boston University economist Laurence Kotlikoff predicts a 7 to 14 percent increase.[5] These gains are in addition to the increases that would have been achieved under current income tax law. Most of these gains come in the first decade. Work by economist Gary Robbins shows that replacing the current tax system with a flat tax system that taxed capital and labor income equally—such as the sales tax or the flat tax—would increase the GDP 36.3 percent and increase private output by 48.4 percent over the long run.[6] Even a study by Nathan Associates funded by the National Retail Institute, shows that the economy would be one to five percent larger under a sales tax than in the absence of reform.

---

[1] Giving USA, 1997. AAFRC Trust for Philanthropy, 1997. See, http://www.cae.org/Trends/sk03.htm.

[2] Voluntary Support of Education 1996, Council for Aid to Education. See, *"http://www/cae.org/Trends/sk14.htm*. Other indicators include the stock market. The trough in giving between 1971 and 1984 coincided with a poorly performing stock market during the 1974–1982 period and two recessions. The dips and rises of the stock market are said to be mirrored by charitable support within a year

[3] A quote attributable to Maimonides [Moses ben Maimon[(c. 1170) seems particularly apt. "Anticipate charity by preventing poverty; assist the reduced fellowman, either by a considerable gift or sum of money, or by teaching him a trade, or by putting him in the way of business so that he may earn an honest livelihood, and not be forced to the dreadful alternative of holding out his hand for charity. This is the highest step and the summit of charity's golden ladder."

[4] Jorgenson, National Tax Research Committee. See also, "The Economic Impact of Fundamental Taxing Consumption," Dale W. Jorgenson, Testimony before the House Ways and Means Committee, March 27, 1996 and "The Economic Impact of Fundamental Tax Reform," Dale W. Jorgenson, Testimony before the House Ways and Means Committee, June 6, 1995.

[5] Kotlikoff, National Tax Research Committee. See also, "The Economic Impact of Replacing Federal Income Taxes with a Sales Tax," Laurence J. Kotlikoff, April 15, 1993, Cato Institute Policy Analysis.

[6] Robbins, currently a principal in Fiscal Associates, is former Chief of Applied Econometrics at the U.S. Treasury Department, "Looking Back to Move Forward: What Tax Policy Costs Americans and the Economy," Gary Robbins and Aldona Robbins, Policy Report No. 127, September 1994, published by the Institute for Policy Innovation, p. 31, p. 47.

Those that state that charitable contributions would go down after a consumption based tax approach may still choose to make their arguments. However, to be valid they must succeed in explaining why, after eligibility for itemized deductions was constricted, charitable contributions historically rose.[7] They must also address the issue of economic growth since virtually every economist who opines that deductions are needed for charitable contributions, also makes the case that a consumption tax would improve economic prosperity.. Either there is no linkage between economic growth and contributions or a consumption based approach will not improve the economy—both of which are against the prevailing economic wisdom.

Moreover, it is not enough to point out only that the cost of giving goes down because of the charitable deduction. If the cost of giving is a determinant, they must also address why their enthusiasm for the current income tax system's tax benefits is not dampened by the fact the FairTax lowers the costs of contributions. It does so in two respects.

To begin with, even if we assume that taxpayers are encouraged to give only because of the charitable contribution, the vast majority of contributors today do not receive any tax advantage for their donations. The charitable contribution is limited to those who happen to itemize (typically those who are affluent enough to own real estate). According to the IRS, Statistics of Income, there were only 30,587,000 itemizers in 1996 out of 111,694,000 taxpayers.

Federal Tax Itemizers vs. Non-itemizers

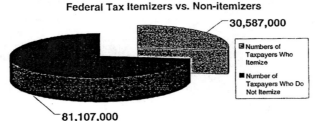

30,587,000

■ Numbers of Taxpayers Who Itemize

■ Number of Taxpayers Who Do Not Itemize

81,107,000

Since only itemizers may take the charitable contribution, only about 27%, or one-quarter of all taxpayers, are even eligible to take the charitable deduction. The relative ratio of itemizers to non-itemizers has remained relatively stable over the near term.

The most important question with respect to the charitable constitution is not how the tax code treats a contribution, but rather *how much a taxpayer has at his or her disposal to contribute*. In other words, what must a taxpayer earn in order to make that contribution? This is where the income tax system severely restricts the ability of a non-itemizer to make a charitable contribution. The graph below simply depicts the effect of the income tax and the payroll tax on the earnings of a taxpayer who does not itemize, but who is in the 28 percent tax bracket. The combined effect of the 15.3 percent payroll tax (assuming the employee bears it) and the 28 percent marginal tax bracket means that the taxpayer must earn $176 to make a $100 contribution to charity. In other words, the government effectively imposes a $76 excise tax on the taxpayer's gift to the charitable organization.

---

[7] Steve Moore, Director of Fiscal Policy Studies at the Cato Institute, points out in a Washington Times article (June 18, 1997) that "the last time the [Independent Sector] tried to measure the impact of tax code changes on charities, it predicted that the 1986 Tax Reform Act would trigger an $8 billion decline in charitable contributors in 1987. Instead charitable giving rose by $6.4 billion, or 7.6 percent after the top rate fell from 50 percent to 28 percent."

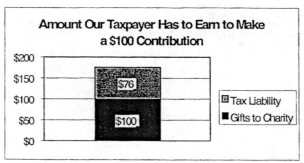

Of taxpayers who are eligible to itemize, an interaction of complex additional restrictions apply to further erode the benefit of the deduction. For example, if a donor contributes appreciated property that is considered "ordinary income-type property,"[8] as opposed to long term capital gain, the donor must reduce the gift by the amount of ordinary income that would have been recognized if the property were sold. Hence, gifts of inventory, art works, letters and other similar property created by or for the taxpayer, are generally severely limited to exclude appreciation. Corporations are limited when making contributions of inventory or depreciable real property to one-half of the ordinary gain that would have been realized if sold.[9] Moreover, the value of gifts of tangible personal property and gifts to certain private foundations, must be reduced by the "total amount of the gain that would have been long-term capital gains if the property were sold for its then fair market value on the date it was contributed."[10] Furthermore, individuals are subject to a deduction ceiling based on the type of property contributed and the type of charity to which the contribution is made—a ceiling that can be as low as 20 percent of the individual's adjusted gross income. These are just a few of the restrictions.

Even if a charitable contribution is allowed, it of course only entitles the donor to make the gift after payroll taxes. The U.S. Office of Management and Budget estimates the total tax revenues lost from charitable contributions[11] (known in tax jargon as tax expenditures) to be $2.7 billion for education, $2.4 billion for health, and $17.1 billion for other purposes, for a total of about $22 billion. However, it is important to note that as large as this tax expenditure is, the charitable contribution is limited in one other significant respect: it only serves to negate the income tax. Under the current system, even if a taxpayer itemizes and even if he can qualify to take the deduction, the charitable deduction only off-sets one type of tax that he pays among the taxpayer's total tax liability—the income tax.

These payroll taxes, be they employer-and employee-combined payroll taxes or self-employment taxes paid by our nation's more than 17 million entrepreneurs, comprise a significant segment of the taxes Americans pay today. As a national aggregate, in 1997 individual income taxes were $737.5 billion. Payroll taxes were $539.4 billion, or 42 percent of the combined total. Many taxpayers, especially lower income individuals, pay a greater portion of their tax liability in payroll taxes as opposed to income taxes.

To graphically illustrate what benefit is provided by the charitable deduction today, let us see the world through the eyes of a fairly average couple. In 1995, the median family income of a married couple was $47,129. If that income were all wage income, then that couple would have paid $7,210 in combined payroll taxes on those wages (employer and employee share). Even if that couple did not itemize (which they certainly would because of the mortgage interest deduction), the maximum income taxes that they would pay if they filed married filing jointly would be $6,433, or 10 percent less than the payroll taxes.[12] In other words, the couple would have paid more payroll taxes than income taxes. Even if that couple itemizes, and the

---

[8] This provision is defined in Internal Revenue Code section 170(a) and the regulations thereunder.

[9] This complex provision is contained in IRC section 170(e)(3).

[10] IRC section 170(e)(1).

[11] See, Budget of the U.S. Government, Fiscal Year 1999.

[12] $47,129—$7,100 (standard deduction for married filing jointly) = $40,109. The income tax on taxable income of $40,109 = $6,433.

couple takes a charitable contribution deduction, the couple cannot take that deduction against the most significant form of taxes that apply to them—payroll taxes.

The graph below depicts what an itemizing taxpayer must earn today to donate $100 to charity.

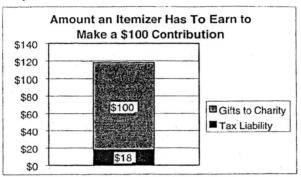

Now let us consider what happens under the FairTax consumption tax. Under the Fair Tax, charitable contributions are not taxed—not at all. They are neither taxed to current itemizers nor to non-itemizers. Therefore, like current law, donors would donate earnings out of pre-income-tax dollars. More to the point, since the Fair Tax repeals both the payroll taxes and the income taxes, the effect of not taxing their contributions is to ensure that the payments are made with both pre-income and pre-payroll tax dollars.

Even for those who believe the deduction is important, this should significantly advantage charities relative to current law by reducing the costs of contributions. A taxpayer today must earn at least $108.28 to contribute $100 if only the "employee" share of the payroll taxes is considered. If the employer payroll taxes are considered [13] (or if the taxpayer had a sole-proprietorship), he or she must earn $118.06. Under the Fair Tax, that taxpayer would only need to earn $100 to contribute $100.

The relative advantage of allowing a deduction against income vs. not taxing income or wages is depicted in the graph below. In this graph, we see that the cost of charitable giving will actually go down considerably under the Fair Tax. Hence, even if taxpayers are wholly motivated to give due to tax treatment, the Fair Tax lowers the cost of charitable giving and increases the resources available for donations. In other words, the cost of charitable giving relative to alternative uses of the funds will go down.

---

[13] Most economists believe that the employer-employee split is really fiction and that employees really do bear the full 15.3 percent. However, we make this adverse assumption in order to arrive at a conservative estimate of the advantages of the Fair Tax.

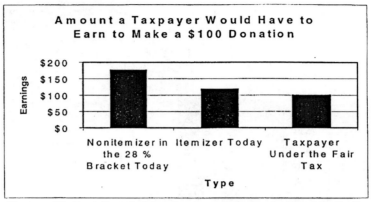

Amount a Taxpayer Would Have to Earn to Make a $100 Donation

However, this is not the end of the advantages. With the adoption of the FairTax corporations may become major contributors to charity. Under the current system, total charitable contributions for corporations may not exceed 10 percent of taxable income. Repealing this limitation will free up corporations to give more.

Second Misconception: The Relative Cost of Capital Will Rise

Charitable giving represents a significant and thankfully growing outlay. Total charitable giving in 1997 was estimated to be $143.5 billion in 1997, which represents the second consecutive year of growth and the largest growth spurt since 1989. However, it is important to bear in mind that individual charitable contributions, while certainly important, are only a portion—and not a major portion—of the resources that fund eleemosynary organizations today.[14]

The major source of nonprofit income is not contributions at all, but an item called "program service revenue," which includes commercial activities. Tax-exempt organizations constitute a significant portion of the Gross Domestic Product (GDP), more than 10 percent of GDP today, and their growth rate has outstripped the GDP and the private sector. Moreover, all tax-exempt nonprofits, particularly 501(c)(3) nonprofits,[15] are increasingly reliant on commercially oriented as opposed to donative oriented sources of income. This activity is concentrated in the largest nonprofits. When nonprofits rely on commercial sources of revenue, they derive that revenue primarily from the service industries. On this income, little tax is paid either because the nonprofits declare the income as substantially related to their exempt function or because they are able to successfully allocate deductions to the unrelated income.

To place this in perspective, in 1994, the latest year for which IRS statistics are available, the total revenue for 501(c)(3)'s was $589 billion. These nonprofits had $993 billion in combined assets in 1994. As a percentage of total receipt contributions, gifts and grants of all types (including from governmental entities) comprised only 18% of the total resources. Direct contributions were only about $50 billion, or 8.4 percent of the total. Program service revenue was $422 billion, or about 72 percent of the total resources of nonprofits.

In fact, organizations with assets of $50 million and above rely on contributions, gifts and grants for only 11 percent or their income in 1991. This figure held steady in 1994, according to the IRS.[16] This can be contrasted with organizations with under $100,000 in assets, which relied on gifts, grants and other contributions for 52 percent of their revenue. The $50 million asset group derived 76 percent of their

---

[14] The Internal Revenue Service, SOI indicates that while the total contributions, gifts and grants received by nonprofits was about $110 billion in 1994, this was divided between contributions directly from individuals and corporations ($49.2 billion), from affiliated organizations ($8.7 billion) and from government grants ($52 billion).

[15] There are a total of 28 different nonprofit exemptions. 501(c)(3)'s are religious, educational, charitable, scientific or literary organizations, testing for public safety organizations, etc. When we refer to "nonprofits" as opposed to other tax-exempt, we generally refer to these 501(c)(3)'s.

[16] Summary of 1998, SOI Bulleting, Report by Cecelia Hilgert.

income from "program service revenue" as opposed to 33 percent of the $100,000 asset class organizations. There is a steady increase in reliance on "program service revenue" as the size of the nonprofit, measured by asset holding or gross income, increases.

Additionally, commercial type activity is concentrated in 501(c)3's. Gross profits from sales and service is the largest source of income for 501(c)3's. If income is "substantially related" to the exempt purpose, it is not considered unrelated business income activity and is wholly exempted from taxation. While the tax paid by nonprofits have increased over the last decade, the increase has not kept pace with the growth of nonprofit's commercial sources of revenue.

The Fair Tax consumption tax does nothing to alter the non-contribution resource base of nonprofit organizations. If the nonprofit earns income that is program service revenue, it is not taxable. It should also be pointed out that if the nonprofit earns unrelated business income—income that is not substantially related to its exempt purpose—that income would also be tax free to the nonprofit under the Fair Tax.

Conclusion

We maintain that the Fair Tax would have extremely beneficial effects on charities and philanthropic giving. The Fair Tax will improve the primary determinants of charitable giving—economic growth and real income. The Fair Tax would remove the bias against taxpayers who want to contribute today by enabling every taxpayer to make donations with tax free dollars. The Fair Tax would enhance the resources both itemizers and non-itemizers have to give by ensuring that they can make their contributions with pre-payroll tax dollars.

○

CPSIA information can be obtained at www.ICGtesting.com
Printed in the USA
BVOW02s1059010714

357887BV00010B/648/P